INDIAN AFFAIRS ANNUAL 2008

INDIAN AFFAIRS ANNUAL 2008

(In 9 Vols.)

Vol. 6

Chronology of Events

(29-10-2007 to 30-11-2007)

Shailendra Sengar

KALPAZ PUBLICATIONS

KALPAZ PUBLICATIONS

DELHI - 110052

Indian Affairs Annual 2008

Rs. 6300 (Set)

ISBN: 81-7835-693-7 (Set)
ISBN: 81-7835-699-6 (Vol. 6)

Published in 2008 in India by
Kalpaz Publications
C-30, Satyawati Nagar,
Delhi-110052
E-mail: kalpaz@hotmail.com
Phone : 9212729499

Laser Type Setting by: Quick Media, Delhi
Printed at : Singhal Print Media, Delhi

INDIAN AFFAIRS ANNUAL 2008

Chronology of Events

(29-10-2007 to 30-11-2007)

3923. (29-10-2007) NEW DELHI : The aim of this expedition is to encourage the adventurous spirit of Air Warriors and spreading the message of peace, harmony and Brotherhood to the people. "INDIAN AIR FORCE FOR THE PEOPLE, DURING PEACE AND WAR". After covering a distance of 3,600 Kms expedition teams were flagged in at the India Gate on 30 Oct. 07 by Air Mshl PS Ahluwalia PVSM AVSM & Bar VM VSM & ADC Air Officer Commanding-in-Chief, Western Air Command. The expedition team consisted of 20 members of various units of Western Air Command converging at India Gate from four different directions from Udhampur, Wagah Border, Gandhi Nagar and Allahabad. The event was conducted jointly with M/S Hero Hønda, who are also conducting M/Cycle expedition to celebrate reaching 20 million landmark. This is the fifth expedition conducted by Indian air Force with requisite support from M/S Hero Honda.

3924. (29-10-2007) NEW DELHI : Shri Kamal Nath, Union Minister for Commerce and Industry, has called for increasing bilateral cooperation between the companies from Utah (USA) and India, in view of tremendous opportunities for cooperation especially in the SME sector that exists. The objective of the mission is to look for business opportunities available in India for Utah companies that have been identified as global partners for the Utah economy, the Governor of the State of Utah (USA), Mr. Jon Huntsman Jr., informed during his meeting with Shri Kamal Nath. The mission led by Mr. Jon Huntsman is focused on infrastructure and financial services, information and communication technology, aviation industry and life sciences for potential commercial tie-ups in India. These areas have been identified by the high-powered Indo-US CEO Forum for priority economic engagements. The mission would be in Delhi on October 29-30 and in Mumbai on October 31-November 1, 2007.

3925. (29-10-2007) NEW DELHI : The Bharat Electronics Limited has paid its highest ever dividend of 180 percent to the government. Chairman and Managing

Director Shri VVR Sastry presented a cheque of 84.96 crore rupees to the Defence Minister Shri AK Antony here today towards 140 percent final dividend. The Secretary (Defence Production) Shri K P Singh was also present on the occasion. With this the Navratna Defence PSU has paid a total dividend of 180 per cent amounting to 109.24 crores for the year 2006-07. This marks a 34 percent leap over the 146 percent dividend in 2005-06 declared by the defence PSU major. The BEL, granted Navratna status earlier this year, has been consistently improving its performance over the years. The company declared 100 percent dividend in 2003-04 for the first time, 112 percent in 2004-05 and has been steadily improving its balance sheet. The BEL also achieved its highest ever turnover of Rs. 3,953 crore during 2006-07 with Profit After Tax (PAT) of Rs. 718.16 crore as against a turnover of Rs. 3,536 crore during 2005-06 with PAT of Rs. 583 crore. The BEL, which manufactures a range of hi-tech products like radars, sonars, wireless and electronic warfare systems for the armed forces, has made tremendous efforts towards indigenization with over 80 percent of the 2006-07 turnover accruing from indigenously designed and developed products. The company's nine units spend nearly five percent of the turnover on R&D. The BEL, set up in 1954, also provides turnkey system solutions.

3926. (29-10-2007) NEW DELHI : The Chairman National Statistics Commission, Dr. S.D. Tendulkar today raised concern about canvassing of long and time-consuming questionnaires such as the one used in consumer expenditure surveys, in view of the Respondent's and Investigator's fatigue. The need to address the issue of condensation of the detailed schedules was highlighted. Inaugurating the National Seminar on the results of NSS 61st round survey on Household Consumer Expenditure and Employment and Unemployment, he said the divergence between the household aggregate consumer expenditure from the NSS and the directly estimated private final consumption expenditure of the National Accounts Statistics (NAS) was a matter of concern. He said a group of officers in National Accounts Division and National Sample Survey Organization are working on the issue. He mentioned about the importance of the selection of suitable reference period for collecting the data on consumer expenditure. This issue became prominent in academic debates after the 55th round of NSS which for the first time, experimented with a 7 days recall period for certain frequently purchased food items of expenditure. Since the poverty estimates released by Planning Commission also determined the eligibility of poverty related benefits, a firm choice of reference period was felt necessary. The Chairman had requested the officers of NSSO and experts from the Indian Statistical Institute, Kolkata to undertake more detailed analysis of the data already collected with different reference periods. He hoped that these studies will throw some light on the appropriateness of the present methodology followed in the consumer expenditure surveys. The NSSO has introduced a series of national seminars based on NSS Survey results right from the year 2000-01 when it organized a year long Golden Jubilee Celebration of NSSO. Till date, six seminars have been conducted discussing the results of NSS 55th round 56th round, 57th round, 58th round, 59th round and 60th rounds. The present national seminar is 7th in the series. It is intended to discuss the results of the Survey. The purpose not only contributes to a better understanding of our economy, but also to policy making national statistical system about the limitations of the data, which is essential for future refinement of data collection methodologies. During the Seminar, three technical sessions and 26 technical papers were presented. In the beginning, there will be a presentation on the results of 61st round. A large number of papers listed for discussion the three technical sessions are written by Officers of various divisions of NSSO covering not only analysis of survey reports and data but also data collection and processing issues leading to well documentation for improvement in future surveys.

3927. (29-10-2007) NEW DELHI : The Congress said here today that the Karnataka soap opera continues unabated. It is a sorry saga of corruption, horse-trading, mismanagement, political opportunism, hypocrisy and unholy alliances which has held the common man of Karnataka hostage to unprincipled and selfish, personalized politics. First, the BJP. They found JD(S) doubtful, distrustful and dishonest only a few days ago. Mr. Yashwant Sinha referred to the great and unprincipled betrayal of no less than a former PM, Mr. Deve Gowda. They ranted and raved against the JD(S). Within a few days their selective memories has erased all the abuses and the JD(S) become paragons of virtues. Unprecedently and unknown in global parliamentary history, a sitting cabinet Minister accused his own sitting CM of no less than a murder charge! Today, the loaves and fishes of office and BJP's lust for power makes Yashvant Sinha eat his own words. This is political opportunism and hypocrisy at its worst. Second, the less said about the JD(S) the better. The (S) in the name is the biggest insult to secularism ever invented by mankind. They know neither the spirit nor the form, nor the spelling of secularism. First, the son hijacks part of the JD(S) in 2004. The father, the former PM Deve Gowda makes a charade of allegations against his son and sheds crocodile tears for secularism. Thereafter, the father and the son, supposedly bury their differences and loot the state for three years through mismanagement and corruption. When the time for power sharing comes, JD(S) develops amnesia and suddenly both father and the son start remembering secularism. Thereafter, the former PM Mr. Deve Gowda, a few days ago, specifically writes the President of India with copies to the Prime Minister and to the Governor, graphically detaching the grave apprehensions of horse trading, supporting election as the only way out of the impasse and ruling out any combination as possessing a workable majority. This letter was acknowledged by the Governor who noted thereon that action would be taken on Mr. Deve Gowda's suggestions. Within a few days, Mr. Deve Gowda and Mr. Kumaraswamy do a volte face yet again. 39 of the JD(S) MLAs are already facing serious anti- defection charges in a petition pending before the speaker and in which the High Court has directed expeditious disposal. Yet, father, son and the JD(S) wax and wane like the tides and the moon. Their views, their stands change every hour. They forget that they had spent crores of rupees to take out full page advertisement abusing the BJP and pointing out how cool they were. The BJP had repaid the complements by even larger advertisements. One can imagine the level of governance –or its absence –in the midst of this soap opera. The only victims are the poor and non-empowered of Karnataka. Amazingly, Mr. Deve Gowda says in the same breath that they want to maintain equidistance from BJP and Congress and yet want to win a coalition government with the BJP. Whether it is BJP or JD(S), whether it is Deve Gowda or Yeshvant Sinha or Kumaraswamy, their only consistency is in their continued inconsistency. The Congress is concerned about the huge and irreversible prejudicial impact of all these unholy antics upon the state. One of India's most prosperous states has been afflicted by paralysis. It has become a den of murky deals and self-centred squandering of state resources. Perhaps, the recent raids involving the serious white collar offences in relation to the Bellary mines may have something to do with the politics of the BJP and the JD(S). In view of the common stand of all parties –including Congress, JD(S) and BJP–that only an election could lead to a workable governmental majority, the central government entitled to dissolve the assembly and called for election immediately. But the Government in deference more to the spirit of Bomamai and the Bihar Judgment than to their letter, did not dissolve the assembly and put it in suspended animation. The Congress calls upon the central government and the Governor to dissolve the assembly forthwith and allow the state to proceed to election to prevent imminent horse trading, as admitted by Mr. Deve Gowda him self. It is ironical that those who are relying on horse trading to avoid elections are accusing us of horse trading. Why are the BJP and the JD(S) afraid of facing the electorate? Is it because they know in advance of the thumping rejection awaiting them? And therefore they are trying to camouflage this real fear in the shroud of principle? The people of Karnataka and of India deserve an answer to all these questions and also deserve to be rid of the incompetent, unholy and opportunistic alliance. To a question citing the Bommai and Bihar jugements Shri Singhvi said, that the Bommai, Bihar and other judgements make it clear that the decision ultimately has to be the exercise of discretion by the man on the spot, the Governor, not you, not me nor the Press and no other entity. The Bommai stage might have been a stage earlier. We are now talking of a stage when it has been found by all parties and affirmed in writing by the JD(S) itself, stated several times orally by the BJP, that the only option is elections. Thereafter the process of dissolution is not something which Bommai has opined on and the process and mechanics and mechanism of dissolution is not something to which Bommai applies. Today in the face of a stage having been passed where all parties have come to the conclusion that there is no alternative except elections merely because the same two unholy alliance partners now have a rethink and want to make that majority through horse trading that cannot become the basis of the negation of the spirit of Bommai.

3928. (29-10-2007) NEW DELHI : The President of India, Smt Pratibha Devisingh Patil appeals to work out arrangements of "Twinning Lakes". Inaugurating the 12th World Lakes Conference TAAL 2007 in Jaipur today she said great efforts have gone into the rehabilitation of some lakes all over the world and improving their water quality. In this context a partnership can be formed between a lake in a developed country with a lake in developed country. The developed country involved in this partnership while sharing its experiences, should commit to make available finances and technology for the conservation of the lake in the developing country. The President said India has a large number and huge variance of lakes. Many of them are unique ecosystems and valuable from historical, cultural, biological and functional point of view. It is a matter of great concern that in the wake of urbanization and industrialization, water bodies have degraded to a great extent. Smt Patil expressed need for effective legal protection to save lakes. In India, we are conscious of these problems and have initiated remedial measures, she added. Welcoming all the guests and participants Sh Namo Narain Meena, Minister of State for Environment and Forests said that the government of India is fully conscious of deterioration of lakes and two major projects for the conservation, management and restoration of lake sand Wetlands have started in India. 94 nationally important wetlands have been identified out of which 25 have been declared as internationally important under the Ramsar Convention. The national lake conservation Plan focuses on pollution abatement and water quality improvement in urban and semi-urban lakes. This programme supports activities around 48 lakes and semi-urban lakes. Sh Meena said that this biennial conference is being organized for the first time in South Asia. Selecting Jaipur for this conference Sh Meena said that Jaipur has an age old tradition of rain-water harvesting and constructing lakes and water bodies which makes it apt place to organize this conference in Jaipur. Sh.Meena said that lakes are not only significant source of water besides, they provide habitat to a variety of flora and fauna.Lakes influence the microclimate and add to aesthetic beauty of landscape. Showing concern about the drastic change in the quality and quantity of water reaching lakes, he stated the causes are rapid population growth and expansion of these urban centres in past few decades. This human slaughtering has affected biodiversity in and around lakes. Even the rural areas have not remained unaffected. The Director General,International Lakes Environment Committee Foundation (ILEC) Sh Hironori Hamanaka informed that this body was initiated in 1984 in Japan and was established as an international NGO with UNEP in 1986. Mr. Hamanaka said that our motto is to promote scientific approach to conserve, develop and maintain lakes all over the world with the help of local participation as well as governments. He said hallmark of this conference is diverse range of participants come together-citizens and government officials for a common cause.

3929. (29-10-2007) NEW DELHI : Gen Sir Richard Dannatt, Chief of General Staff, UK is undertaking an official visit to India from 29 Oct. to 03 Nov 07. This visit by the UK CGS comes at a time when our defence cooperation with British Army has been at an all time high. The joint activities that the two Armies encompass visits, joint exercises, training exchange and participation in Seminars and Conferences etc. Infact, the first ever Joint Exercise between our two Armies has recently been successfully completed at Leh, wherein the UK Royal Marines exercised with the elite Paratroopers of the Indian Army. During his visit, the British Army Chief will interact with senior military and civilian defence hierarchy, discuss defence related issues and prospects for future cooperation between our two Armies. In addition, visits to Indian Army Field Formations in Jaipur, Srinagar and Agra and prestigious Army establishments have also been planned. The visit reconfirms the mutual trust and friendship between the two Armies and will provide the necessary fillip to our on-going Army-to-Army Cooperation.

3930. (29-10-2007) NEW DELHI : Certain reports have been appearing in a section of the press regarding opposition to setting up of a Special Economic Zone (SEZ) at Nandigram in West Bengal. It is to clarify that no SEZ is being set up at Nandigram. Also, there is no application proposing to set up SEZ at Nandigram.

3931. (30-10-2007) NEW DELHI : The Union Minister of Railways Shri Lalu Prasad has launched E-learning portal for Company Secretaries (CS) Foundation Programme at the Institute of Company Secretaries of India (ICSI) Foundation Day function here today. Delivering the Foundation Day Lecture on "Excellence Through Strategic Turnaround", Shri Lalu Prasad said that the basic principles of turnaround of Railways were the honesty, strong will and vision for Railways' reforms with human face. He said the Indian Railways have achieved an excellent performance during the last two years but in order to sustain the momentum several initiatives like construction of Dedicated Freight Corridor, modernization of Railway Stations, opening of outlets for farmers etc. have been formulated. The Minister further said that the Indian economy has been consistently doing well and Indian companies are making footprints on the global economy and doing multinational. He said that the time is opportune for the professionals to show their mite and to realize their strengths in the corporate world. While doing so, the Minister said that Company Secretaries should also keep in mind the interests and the needs of the poor people and should work for the over all development of the downtrodden people of the country. As a first step to this direction, the E-learning portal of ICSI would be imparted to the students of the CS Foundation Programme. In the second phase, the training would be imparted to the students of Executives and Professional Programmes. E-learning is a cost effective training format, where the students can undergo coaching from the comfort of their homes. All they need is an internet connection as per the specifications given in the aforesaid portal. Under the system, the students would be imparted coaching through web based training. A nominal annual of Rs. 250/- only would be charged from the Foundation Programme students for availing the services at the E-learning portal.

3932. (30-10-2007) NEW DELHI : Major General SG Chatterji has taken over as the new Director General Resettlement (DGR). He assumed office on Monday, October 29, 2007 following the retirement of Major General Harwant Krishan. Major General Chatterji, Vishisht Sewa Medal, is an alumni of National Defence Academy, Khadakwasla, Pune and was awarded President's Gold Medal for being first in order of merit. He was awarded the Sword of Honour for being the best all round cadet on commissioning from the Indian Military Academy, Dehradun. Major General Chatterji was commissioned in the Regiment of Artillary on November 14, 1971. During his 35 years of illustrious service, Major General Chatterji has held various important Instructional, Staff and Command appointments. He is a Post-Graduate from the Defence Services Staff College, Wellington and the National Defence College, New Delhi. He has commanded an Artillery Regiment in Siachen. He also served as the Defence Attache in Indian Embassy at Rome (Italy) with concurrent accredition to Spain and Portugal. The General Officer has commanded an Artillery Brigade in a RAPID Division in Operation Parakram and a Mountain Brigade in active counter-insurgency Operations in the North East for which he was awarded Vishisht Sewa Medal. Before his appointment as DGR, Major General Chatterji was serving as the General Officer Commanding of the 14 Rapid (Strike) Division.

3933. (30-10-2007) NEW DELHI : The Minister of Social Justice and Empowerment, Smt. Meira Kumar conferred Vayoshreshtha Samman on the eminent senior Citizens in New Delhi today. Speaking on the occasion, she said that the Vayoshreshtha Samman was just a modest recognition of their compassion., determination creativity and devotion to the cause of humanity and to honour their relentless and remarkable service to the society and nation. She further said that the Ministry of Social Justice & Empowerment has already launched National Policy on Older Persons (NPOP) to ensure active and productive ageing by involving a framework for providing financial, medical, social and emotional support. The Ministry has also formulated a law 'Care and Maintenance of Older People' which is being considered by Parliamentary Committee. In the proposed Bill, the basic thrust to maintenance, care and protection and setting up of Tribunals for every district, which will take care of claiming payments of maintenance from the grand children, she added. The Awardees were presented with shawls, citations and mementoes in the function. To create wider awareness about the issues a 'Meghdoot Postcard' with picture and slogan was also released by Smt. Meira Kumar. The Secretary of Ministry of Social Justice & Empowerment, Dr. Veena Chhotray was also present on the occasion. This year Vayoshreshtha Samman for Institution of Knowledge was given to Alzheimer's and Related Disorders Society of India from Kerala, while Chikmagalur Rotary and Inner Wheel Trust, Jeevan Sandhya was given the Award for Institution of Service. Shri J.L.Dalal from Haryana was conferred the Vayoshreshtha Samman for Centenarian this year. Smt. Mdhobi Mukherjee, a renowned actress from Calcutta got the Samman for creative art and nonagenarian. Prof. Turaga Somasundaram from Hyderabad was given Vayoshreshtha Samman for lifetime achievement. Shri H. Ramegowda, a 75 year Athlete from Karnataka and 83 years old Football Player Shri Shailen Manna from Kolkatta awards in the category for Sport person. For Economic Leadership category the Vayoshreshtha Samman was bestowed upon Shri T.V. Narayana Shastry. Earlier in the Day, a seminar " Addressing the Challenges and Opportunities of Aging: Empowering Older Persons', was organized by the National Institute of Social Defence and the Ministry of Social Justice and Empowerment.

3934. (30-10-2007) NEW DELHI : Defence Minister Shri AK Antony has emphasized promoting a sense of adventure amongst the youth of the country by promoting adventure sports. Addressing the General Body Meeting of Nehru Institute of Mountaineering (NIM) at Uttarkashi in Uttarakhand today, Shri Antony said that NIM has played a major role in disaster management and relief. Commending the Institute for conducting specialized courses in search and rescue operations for persons not only from Defence, Paramilitary and Police Forces but individuals from all walks of life, he said its role in promoting adventure activities deserves all praise from one and all. He called upon the staff and instructors of the Institute to make it a World Class Mountaineering institute. The Minister also inaugurated the new office complex 'Dunagiri' of the Institute. Col MM Masur, Principal of NIM, in his welcome address gave a brief presentation on the activities of the Institute. He said the Institute during its 43 years of existence has trained 18,324 nationals and 448 international mountaineers. Earlier, on his arrival at Uttarkashi helipad, the Chief Minister of Uttarakhand Maj Gen (Retd) BC Khanduri received the Defence Minister.

3935. (30-10-2007) NEW DELHI : Some warship technology products developed by Naval Science and Technological Laboratory (NSTL), Vishakapatnam will be handed over to Indian Navy in Vishakapatnam tomorrow. Dr. A Sivathanu Pillai, Chief Controller (R&D), DRDO will hand over the products to Vice Admiral DSP Varma, Chief of Materials, Naval Headquarters. NSTL is involved in development of warship technologies useful for evading detection by enemy, ships / submarines. These technologies are aimed for use in modern warships under design and construction. NSTL has nurtured these technologies in the recent past and is progressing strongly towards self reliance in this critical arena. Warship technology is a multidisciplinary field covering different aspect such as acoustics and electro-magnetics covering a wide band of frequencies. Hence an inter disciplinary and holistic approach has been adopted in developing these products. A number of products were developed by NSTL to avert damages to naval ships in enemy attacks. Some of the products developed are acoustics enclosures, acoustic silencers, double stage vibration isolation system, Radar transparent ladder, stanchions, camouflage screens, helo net frames and composite blowers among many others. All these products were subjected to extensive laboratory and shipboard evaluations. After successful evaluations, these products were accepted for induction into Indian Navy.

3936. (30-10-2007) NEW DELHI : A surrender ceremony was conducted at Laipuli under the aegis of Dah Division for the 14 cadres of various outfits including Self Styled Private Toor Moni Borgohain wife of Self Styled Lieutenant Prajjal Saikia. A Company Commander 28 Battalion ULFA. On behalf of Major General NC Marwah, General Officer Commanding 2 Mountain Division. Brig

PK Saini, Deputy General Officer Commanding, 2 Mountain Division accepted the surrender. Police and civilian dignitaries including close relatives of the cadres were present at the occasion. The units of 181 Mountain Brigade based in Tinsukia and Dibrugarh districts, Dah Division Artillery Brigade based in Sibsagar district, 25 Sector Assam Rifles based in Arunachal Pradesh and Army Intelligence Units were directly responsible for facilitating the surrender of these hardcore terrorists. This hallmark achievement is part of the overall strategy of "FIGHTING INSURGENCY AND NOT THE INSURGENTS" enunciated by General BS Jaswal, General Officer Gajraj Corps. Based on this strategy intense military operations in concert with initiatives have been launched with renewed vigour by the Army. Dah Division has taken the psychological to make an appeal to ULFA cadres to shun violence and join the mainstream. In this initiative a large number of parents and family members of ULFA cadres including those of some senior and important leaders of 28 Battalion have made an emotional appeal through interaction with media personnel in the three districts of Upper Assam. The latest of such meeting was organized at Sibsagar on 15 Oct. 2007 where parents of over 30 ULFA cadres gathered to convey their feelings with outburst of emotions in the presence of number of civil and military dignitaries. Similar meeting was held at Dibrugarh on 08 September 07 which led to surrender of seven terrorists at Laipuli (Tinsukia) on 01 Oct. 07. This psychological initiative of Dah Division has begun to pay dividends and surrender of Self Styled Lieutenant Pranjal Saikia on 18 Oct. 07 and fourteen cadres is a true testimony to the genuineness and sincerity of the Army to contribute towards bringing about peace to the State of Assam. In order to encourage the cadres to surrender self employment schemes and rehabilitation packages are being worked out by the State Government. At the initiative of General Officer Commanding Gajraj Corps, the Army is also proposing to centrally conduct training for the surrenderees, under the umbrella of Op SADBHAVANA, Dah Division has undertaken numerous development projects and self employment schemes to bring succour to the people in the remote regions of our area of responsibility. In tune with the clarion call given by General Officer Commanding Gajraj Corps, to the misguided youth to return to the mainstream, the Dah Division once again conveys our sincere appeal to ULFA cadres to shun the path of violence and enjoy the fruits of freedom and bliss of living with their families without fear. Dah Division announces that it will facilitate their rehabilitation and extend all possible help to them and their families in his regard.

3937. (30-10-2007) NEW DELHI : The Parliament Standing Committee on Labour has invited suggestions/views/comments of individuals/institutions/ organisations on the Unorganized Sector Workers' Social Security Bill, 2007. The said Bill, introduced in Rajya Sabha on 10 September, 2007, has been referred to the Standing Committee on Labour under the Chairmanship of Shri Suravaram Sudhakar Reddy, MP for examination and report to the Parliament. The text of the Bill as introduced in Rajya Sabha is available on the website http://www.parliamentofindia.nic.in and the Gazette of India, Extraordinary, Part-II, Section 2, dated 10 September, 2007. A copy of the Bill may also be obtained on requisition from the Standing Committee on Labour Branch, Room No. 615, Parliament House Annexe, New Delhi-110001. The Unorganized Sector Workers' Social Security Bill, 2007 inter-alia provides for the social security and welfare of unorganized sector workers' and for matters connected therewith or incidental thereto. The bill also inter-alia provides for setting up of a National Social Security Advisory Board by the Central Government to recommend suitable welfare schemes for different sections of unorganized sector workers' constitution of State Social Security Advisory Board by the State Governments to recommend suitable welfare schemes for different sections of unorganized sector workers' in the States. All those who are interested in submitted written memoranda/suggestions may send two copies thereof either in English or in Hindi to Shri R. K. Bajaj, Director, Lok Sabha Secretariat, Room No. 158, Parliament House Annexe, New Delhi-110001, Tel NO. 23034362, Fax No. 23018010, E.Mail: bajaj.rk@sansad.nic.in within 15 days. The memoranda/suggestions submitted to the Committee would form part of the records of the Committee and would be treated as strictly confidential and not circulated to anyone, as such an act would constitute a breach of privilege of the Committee.

3938. (30-10-2007) NEW DELHI : Shri Kamal Nath, Union Minister of Commerce and Industry, has invited the German businessmen to invest in India. During the Business Luncheon Meeting here today with Dr. Angela Merkel, Chancellor, Federal Republic of Germany, Shri Kamal Nath said: "As India continues its steady march towards becoming an industrialized nation over the next two or three decades, I invite German businesses to participate in this exciting growth story". Given Germany's prowess in the manufacturing sector and India's own engineering eco-system, German investments in India have traditionally been in the manufacturing sector, the Minister added. "The major sectors that have attracted investments from Germany since liberalization are electrical equipment, transportation industry and metallurgical industries. Together, these sectors make up more than 40 per cent of overall German investment in India. In fact, this momentum is being sustained and is even growing; since 2007, there have been more than 200 technical collaborations between Indian and German firms for industrial machinery alone", Shri Kamal Nath said. He further emphasised that today more than 240 Indian firms are already engaged in a business in Germany and the number is constantly growing. While two third of these firms belong to the IT-sector, the rest is spread across the textile industry, engineering industry, pharmaceuticals and automotive components. The Minister underlined that the bilateral trade between India and Germany crossed 10 billion euros in 2006, which was a target that was supposed to have been met in 2010. He said that Germany figures among the top ten FDI destinations in India today, yet it accounts for 3.6 per cent of the total flows that have come into the country so far. FDI inflows have more than doubled from US$7.7 billion in 2005 to a record US $ 19.4 billion in 2006. With strengthening FDI inflows, India has the potential to become a critical part of Asia's elaborate production network.

3939. (30-10-2007) NEW DELHI : Adventure cell of Western Air Command has conducted a motor cycle expedition to celebrate its Platinum Jubilee. The aim of this expedition is to encourage the adventurous spirit of Air Warriors and spreading the message of peace, harmony and Brotherhood to the people. "INDIAN AIR FORCE FOR THE PEOPLE, DURING PEACE AND WAR". After covering a distance of 3,600 Kms expedition teams were flagged in at the India Gate on 30 Oct. 07 by Air Mshl PS Ahluwalia PVSM AVSM & Bar VM VSM & ADC Air Officer Commanding-in-Chief, Western Air Command. The expedition team consisted of 20 members of various units of Western Air Command converging at India Gate from four different directions from Udhampur, Wagah Border, Gandhi Nagar and Allahabad. The event was conducted jointly with M/S Hero Honda, who are also conducting M/Cycle expedition to celebrate reaching 20 million landmark. This is the fifth expedition conducted by Indian air Force with requisite support from M/S Hero Honda.

3940. (30-10-2007) NEW DELHI : The President of India, Smt. Pratibha Devisingh Patil, hosted a reception at Rashtrapati Bhavan for the Indian Men's Hockey team that won the Asia Cup recently and the Indian Cricket team who won the Twenty20 World Cup. The Indian Men's Football team could not be present as they were involved in a World Cup qualifier in Goa. However the Football team was represented by the President of the All India Football Federation, Shri Priya Ranjan Das Munshi. Addressing both teams the President said, "It is heartening to note what a successful year this has been for India in the field of sports! Our teams and sportspersons have delighted the nation with spectacular performances and victories that have made us all proud. This year we have three laurels to our credit, namely, The Nehru Cup in Football, The Asia Cup in Hockey and the maiden Twenty20 Cricket World Cup and in an individual sports the regaining of the World Title in Chess. Unfortunately our Football team is not here this afternoon, as they are playing a match in Goa today, after the originally scheduled match in Chennai yesterday had to be postponed due to rain. I congratulate the victorious teams for their hard work, motivation and dedication. India has a long tradition of sports and athletic activities and the many indigenous games of our country are testament to the fact that we have always encouraged the friendly yet competitive spirit of sports. The importance of sports for a nation goes far beyond victories in the playing field, since the spirit of sportsmanship imbues several values which are essential for a well-groomed citizen of the country. Loyalty, courage, perseverance, teamwork and dedication are but a few of the many qualities which one may learn from sports and these qualities not only enable them to become good sportspersons but also better human beings. It is this socially constructive aspect of sports which is of paramount importance to a nation and in the light of the recent victories of our players, we can be certain that India remains committed in its encouragement of sports. It is also encouraging to note that our achievements in sports are multi-disciplinary and I hope that this will encourage us to promote all sports and not just a select few. As a sports loving nation we must learn to appreciate the unique qualities of each sport and ensure that valiant sportsmanship does not go unappreciated, be it from any sport. The enthusiasm and participation of people is fundamental in the process of creating a culture of professional sports in this country."

3941. (30-10-2007) NEW DELHI : The Codex Committee on Food Hygiene (CCFH) is responsible for drafting basic provisions on food hygiene applicable to all food as well as for considering amendments if necessary pertaining to the provisions on hygiene contained in Codex Commodity Standard. Most of the countries of the world, developed or developing are the members of Codex Alimentarius Commission. The technical meetings of the CCFH is held every year. So far it has had 38 sessions. The Codex Commission while discussing the Strategic Framework and the Action Plan emphasised the need to encourage developing countries to convene Codex Committee meetings periodically. CCFH is one of the important committees whose deliberations have impact on Indian exports. It is considered useful that various segments of Trade and Industry be exposed to its deliberations. In view of this, the Ministry of Health & Family Welfare has organised the 39th Session of the Codex Committee on Food Hygiene from 30th October-4th November 2007. Nearly 200 delegates from all over the world, both developing and developed countries are participating in the session. Inaugurating the 39th Session of the CCFH in New Delhi today, the Minister of State for Health & Family Welfare, Smt. Panabaka Lakshmi emphasised that food safety legislation alone is not enough to maintain a high quality of food hygiene. It must be complemented by efforts to improve the overall standard of education among consumers. This is a fundamental area where progress could easily be made by teaching basic food hygiene in schools and through the media. The function was attended by Shri Naresh Dayal, Secretary, Ministry of Health & Family Welfare, Shri Debasish Panda, Joint Secretary, Ministry of Health & Family Welfare and Co-chairperson, Codex Committee on Food Hygiene, senior officials from the Ministry of Health & Family Welfare and representatives of WHO and FAO.

3942. (30-10-2007) NEW DELHI : The Union Minister of Shipping, Road Transport and Highways, Thiru T.R. Baalu has approved a sum of Rs.1101.06 lakh for High Level Bridge across river Vena in the state of Bihar. Thiru Baalu approved the proposal for the construction of a 12 mt wide high level bridge across river Vena at km. 155 of Bhagalpur-Mirzachouki section of NH-80. The existing screw pile bridge across river Vena was constructed in the year 1965 with a carriageway of 6.75 mt. The bridge is not capable to withstand the present day volume of NH traffic. Therefore, it is proposed to construct a new bridge. The proposal also includes improvement of immediate approaches in a length of 455 m.

3943. (30-10-2007) NEW DELHI : Central Board of Direct Taxes (CBDT) has clarified that the date for obtaining tax audit report under section 44AB of the Income Tax Act has also been extended to 31st December 2007 in the state of Bihar. CBDT has already extended the last date of filing of income tax returns due by 31st October 2007 to 31st December 2007 in the state of Bihar in view of the disruption caused by floods in the state.

3944. (30-10-2007) NEW DELHI : The Prime Minister, Dr. Manmohan Singh, flagged off an exhibition train "Science Express" in the presence of the Chancellor of Germany, Dr. Angela Merkel, here today. The Science Express will travel through fifty seven cities across the country for over seven months and will display important challenges in science, the future of research and reach different target groups especially students and young researchers. Lauding the scientists for conceiving and executing the novel idea of mounting an exhibition of a variety of interesting facets of modern science and its applications, the Prime Minister hoped that it will take the wonders of modern science to remote corners of our vast country and contribute to the propagation of the scientific temper among our youth. Following is the text of the Prime Minister's speech on the occasion: "It gives me great pleasure to be present here today in the company of Her Excellency Dr. Angela Merkel to launch this Science Express. I am particularly happy that this project is being launched by Dr. Merkel. She is not only a world leader of outstanding international repute but also herself is an accomplished scientist. Our collaboration with Germany in science and technology goes back several decades. We recall our partnership with Germany in setting up the Rourkela Steel Plant and Indian Institute of Technology at Chennai. As part of this progressively strengthening tradition, our scientists have now conceived and executed a novel idea of mounting an exhibition of a variety of interesting facets of modern science and its applications. Germany's achievements in the area of science, technology and research and development have made it an economic superpower in the world. As the world moves towards a knowledge economy, German organization, precision and innovation will help it in maintaining its economic leadership. When the Science Express leaves this station it will travel the length and breadth of India during the next several months. It will bring the wonders of modern science to remote corners of our vast country. The Science Express should contribute to the propagation of the scientific temper among our youth, which was a cherished dream of Jawaharlal Nehru, the first Prime Minister of our country. The Science Express will build new bridges of understanding and goodwill between India and Germany. It will symbolize the exciting partnership between our scientists that befits the 21st century. It will symbolize and showcase our cooperation in the popularization of science and its importance to our relationship. I would like to take this opportunity to congratulate and thank the Max Planck Society in Germany, the German Federal Ministry of Education and Research, Indian Railways and the Department of Science and Technology for making this project possible. In conclusion, I wish to reaffirm the importance we attach to our partnership with

Germany. It is my sincere and fondest hope that we will see further such projects between India and Germany in the years to come."

3945. (30-10-2007) NEW DELHI : Chitranjan Locomotive Works (CLW) produced 79 electric locomotives against the target of 76 electronic locomotives and Diesel Locomotive Works (DLW) produced 118 diesel locomotives against the target of 109 diesel locomotives during first half of the fiscal 2007-08 (April-September 2007). Rail Coach Factory (RCF) produced 647 coaches against the target of 645 coaches where as Integral Coach Factory (ICF) produced 550 coaches against the targets of 552 coaches during the same period. Rail Wheel Factory (RWF) produced 62672 wheels and 20335 axles during the same period against the target of 60947 wheels and 20092 axles during April-September 2007. During the month of September 2007, CLW, DLW, ICF, RCF and RWF have produced 18 electric locomotives, 20 diesel locomotive, 118 coaches, 125 coaches, 12210 wheels and 1570 axles respectively against the target of 16 electric locomotives, 18 diesel locomotive, 120 coaches, 1125 coaches, 10850 wheels and 1340 axels. Except ICF, all other units have exceeded the target. The punctuality percentage of mail/ express trains was 92.0 per cent in Broad Gauge and 99.1 per cent in Metre Gauge during the month of September 2007 compared to 92.0 per cent and 97.6 per cent respectively during the same period last year. Railways have realized an amount of Rs. 16 crore approximately during the month of September 2007 through ticket checking, which was 9.84 per cent higher than the amount realized during the same period last year.

3946. (30-10-2007) NEW DELHI : "Science Express", a special exhibition mounted on a train as the result of a partnership in science and technology between India and Germany was flagged off today by the Prime Minister, Dr. Manmohan Singh and Dr. Angela Merkel, Chancellor Federal Republic of Germany at Safdarjung Railway Station in New Delhi. The exhibition on wheels explains how scientists have uncovered some fundamental understanding of nature. Speaking on the occasion Dr. Manmohan Singh was lavish with his compliments for the design teams, Department of Science & Technology and the Indian Railways for planning such a science exhibition that would reach people in 57 places. He expressed hope that the students would make best use of this opportunity to understand what drives a scientist to devote his time, energy, and ideas for finding solutions to new problems. He looked forward to similar outreach activities between the two countries. Felicitating the scientists and engineers involved in the project, Dr. Merkel, herself a researcher, expressed her confidence that this train will create a strong movement in the talented youth of India towards research in science. After visiting some of the coaches, both the Chancellor and the PM waved green flags and the Science Express rolled off a gaily-decorated station to the cheering of the invites. The function began earlier as Shri Kapil Sibal, Union Minister for Science & Technology and Earth Sciences welcomed the dignitaries and traced the developments of this project over the past few months that resulted in Max Planck Society, Germany designing a state of art exhibition for mounting in AC Coaches. He said that as it was not possible to get the famous Science Tunnel in time, the alternative strategy for an exhibition on a train is definitely more effective. Many organizations from Germany and India are associated with this, he added, which would be available for counselling and guidance of interested youth at each halt. The Science Express is a special train that will have three days of exhibition in 57 places over the next nine months. It has large screen displays for audio-visual experience, interactive computers and many other attractions in each of the coaches. The exhibition seeks to address issues from micro-cosmos to macro-cosmos through twelve stories. The Kids' Lab of BASF will be an attraction at each station. It answers how scientists have uncovered our understanding of the Universe, its beginning, its current size, and many other questions. It also raises issues of sustainable development and how scientists are concerned about finding practical solutions for protecting our planet.

3947. (30-10-2007) NEW DELHI : Rural tourism is one of the few activities which can provide solution to problems like falling income levels and lesser job opportunities. The 10th Five Year Plan has identified tourism as one of the major sources of generating sustainable livelihood and employment in India. Rural Tourism is showcasing arts and crafts in its life and traditional setting and providing a platform for tourists to experience rural ambience. Concept of homestays with food, clean water & toilets being promoted among host community. Capacity building for sensitisation community in preparing and serving traditional cuisine & interacting with visitors. Improvement in cleanliness and hygiene in the village and environmental awareness. Guide training among local youths for helping tourists in understanding and appreciating the unique aspects of villages. Ministry of Tourism is implementing Rural Tourism Scheme to promote Village Tourism as primary tourism product to spread tourism and its socio-economic benefits to rural and its new geographic regions in India. The local community has been trained to manage the tourism site, all by its own for sustainability. The community has been equipped through goal setting exercises in the maintenance of the site. For sustainable marketing and operation by the local community, all segments of the tourism industry, media and State Tourism Departments, play a major role. Effective documentation of site through brochures, cards, upgradation of websites etc. www.exploreruralindia.org depicting site attractions. MOT supported rural tourism festival at Delhi Haat in 2006 and is doing the same at Delhi Haat from 3rd to 5th November 2007 and IITF from 14th to 27th November 2007 and a campaign on Rural Tourism in print &Electronic media. Wider and proper publicity of rural tourism sites leading to more awareness amongst tourists leading to regular tourist inflow at the sites. There has been 8% to 10% increase in the arrival of tourists to the village sites after launch of Rural Tourism Scheme. Efforts have been made to integrate the site with other major tourist destinations nearby. Action is being taken to link up with convergent initiative at the project sites through specialized national organizations like Deputy Commissioner Handicraft, Deputy

Commissioner Handloom, National Institute of Design, Ahmedabad, CII, FICCI. Ministry of Tourism considers work plans from all States and Union Territories for funding the hardware activities up to a total of Rs.50.00 lakh and software activities up to a total of Rs.20.00 lakh per site in potential rural tourism locations.

3948. (31-10-2007) NEW DELHI : Shri Kapil Sibal, Union Minister for Science & Technology and Earth Sciences and Dr. Annette Schavan, Federal Minister for Education & Research, Germany had bilateral discussions today on the sidelines of the German Chancellor's visit to India. Both ministers discussed matters of bilateral interests in the areas of Science & Technology. It was mentioned that both India and Germany have agreed to set-up Indo-German S&T Centre in Delhi with the two sides committing 10 million euros each for over a period of next 5 years. The Centre will be a model for Public Private Partnership for Scientific and Industrial research. The MoU for establishing the Indo-German Centre would be concluded later today in presence of the heads of the governments of the two countries and would be signed by their science ministers. MoUs pertaining to cooperation in the fields of S&T were signed during the meeting between the two ministers. These are between 1. DST and DAAD for exchange of senior and young researchers. 2. IIT Delhi and TU Darmstadt for implementing joint research project on Lean manufacturing processes. 3. Anna University and Helmoltz Association on energy research 4. JNU-ICMR-Helmoltz Association on Medical research. Both ministers further agreed to enhance the scope of the on-going S&T activities.

3949. (31-10-2007) NEW DELHI : The Union Rural Development Minister Dr. Raghuvansh Prasad Singh has expressed the hope that by 2012 India will be free of defecation in open and will also be able to meet the international commitments in this regard. Addressing the World Toilet Summit 2007 here today, he said his ministry is leading one of the much appreciated programmes like Total Sanitation Campaign (TSC), for promoting rural sanitation in the country. This programme has been developed after much deliberation and inputs from experts, officials and community to make it community-oriented and demand-driven. So far TSC has been very successful in accelerating the sanitation coverage from 22 percent in 2001 to 48 percent in 2007. Referring to the Nirmal Gram Puraskar (NGP), an incentive scheme to add vigour to the sanitation drive and is given to Gram Panchayats, Blocks and Districts, he said this award has motivated the Panchayati Raj Institutions (PRI) and communities tremendously in the last three years. Moreover, the Government of India is committed to sustain this momentum by increasing its reach and fund allocation. Accordingly, the central plan outlay for rural sanitation has also been increased from Rs.740 crore in 2006-07 to Rs.1060 crore in the current year marking an increase of 43% over the previous year. Today, the programme has crossed Rs. 12,000 crore mark in its total outlay making it one of the largest sanitation progrmmes in the world, the Minister added. Dr. Singh said new components like Solid and Liquid Waste Management have also been added and 10 percent of the total fund of TSC has been earmarked for it, which is important for environmental cleanliness. Also waste is a form of resource and its proper use should be promoted. In addition, efforts are being intensified to focus on school sanitation, aganwadi and community sanitation. Schools particularly are being targeted for providing them with water and sanitation facilities by next year. The Minister also emphasized to focus on the poor and downtrodden people of the country, so far excluded from the mainstream, for making our environment safe and habitable. India is complex and diverse country with 28 States, 600 districts, more than 5000 blocks, and approx. 6 lakh villages. To implement any development programme aimed at the personal level, it is, therefore, necessary that approach and strategy should take into account these facts. Our strategy should be inclusive of these groups to realize the fruits of development. Water and sanitation is the core of this development process, which must reach to all, especially those who traditionally have not had access to it, the Minister added. Later Dr. Singh had a meeting with William-Alexander Nicholas George Ferdinand, Prince of Orange, Netherlands to share his interest and experiences about his visit to a village in Haryana regarding the implementation of TSC programme. The Prince also expressed his interest in India achieving the Milennium Development Goal. Currently, the Prince of Orange is in the Chair of UN Secretary General's Advisory Board on Water and Sanitation. This Board was set up in 2004 by Kofi Annan, former UN Secretary General.

3950. (31-10-2007) NEW DELHI : The Prime Minister, Dr. Manmohan Singh addressed the 22nd Indira Gandhi national integration award function here today. The following is the text of the Prime Minister's address on the occasion "Each year we meet here to pay tribute to the memory of our great beloved leader, Indiraji, the greatest daughter of India and honour men and women made in her mould. The Indira Gandhi Award for National Integration is a fitting tribute to the memory of our beloved Indiraji. Indiraji was a living embodiment of the values that define our nation and our Republic. Through her martyrdom, she helped embed those values deep in our hearts and minds. Her supreme sacrifice was in the cause of national integration. On this solemn occasion, we gratefully recall her legacy of nation building and respectfully pay our homage to her. For Indiraji, national integration was not merely an emotional issue. Nor did she worry only about communal harmony. Indiraji had a holistic view of national integration. She viewed national integration as a process of bridging the many divides in our nation and in our society. This is the essence of the Indian view of national integration. I am delighted that today, two personalities serving the cause of communal harmony have been selected for this prestigious Award. I congratulate Dr. J.S. Bandukwalla and Professor Ram Puniyani. Both of them have dedicated their lives to promote solidarity and understanding among different faiths. They have done so by fighting communalism and communal forces. They have taken steps to improve the social and economic conditions of minorities. What they have done reflect the values and vision of Indiraji. Communal harmony and the co-existence of all the great religions of the world are the building blocks of our civilization. Indiraji strengthened these building blocks by nourishing them. She also understood the importance of equity and social justice in cementing national integration. "The persistence of inequality" she once observed, "posed serious danger to national integration". She therefore worked tirelessly to bridge the many divides in our society and to meet the aspirations of all sections of our nation.

3951. (31-10-2007) NEW DELHI : The Central Board of Direct taxes have extended the last date of filing of income tax /fringe benefit tax returns due by 31st October 2007 as follows:-For electronic returns (companies, and firms requiring tax audit u/s 44AB) to 15th November 2007; and For paper returns (other than those required to file electronic returns) to 2nd November 2007. It is further clarified that the dates for obtaining tax audit report under section 44AB of the Income Tax Act have also been extended accordingly.

3952. (31-10-2007) NEW DELHI : The President, Smt. Pratibha Devisingh Patil, has proceeded on a three-day visit to Kerala and Tamil Nadu today afternoon. She will address the Public Reception Programme at Central Stadium in Thiruvanthapuram on November 1, the Foundation Day of Kerala, and release the document on Clean Kerala Mission and Logo on Kerala State Total Physical Fitness programme and inaugurate the distribution of Scholarships for Higher Education to students. On 2nd November, the President will deliver the 17th Convocation Address of Mother Teresa Women's University in Chennai and return to Delhi on the same day evening.

3953. (31-10-2007) NEW DELHI : The first meeting of Inter Ministerial Group (IMG) constituted to monitor and coordinate issues concerning major steel investments in the country was held under the Chairmanship of Secretary (Steel) yesterday. The meeting was attended by Chief Secretary, Secretary (Steel & Mines) and other Secretaries from Government of Orissa, Secretary (Industry), Government of Karnataka and Resident Commissioners of Jharkhand and Chhattisgarh. The Central Ministries/Departments were represented by respective Joint Secretaries or equivalent officers from Mines, Environment & Forest, Railways, Road Transport & Highways, Coal, Shipping and Petroleum & Natural Gas. The IMG took note of the present production, consumption, export/import and demand growth and the likely scenario during the next 5 years and beyond. Based on the detailed discussion with 15 major steel investors of the country by the Ministry of Steel on 17.8.2007, the 'most likely scenario' of steel production in the country has been estimated at 124.06 million tonnes in the year 2011-12. This translates into an annual compounded growth rate of nearly 16% over the present crude steel production capacity of 56.84 million tonnes. The Group was unanimous in its view that in order to convert this potential into a reality, a huge task lies ahead in creating a conducive investment atmosphere combined with right policy shift and building up of associated infrastructure particularly in railways, roads and port sectors. The issues concerning all major steel projects being set up by SAIL, RINL, Tata Steel,

Essar, JSPL, JSW, POSCO, Arcellor-Mittal, Ispat, Bhushan Steel, Bhushan Power & Steel, Monnet Steel, Uttam Galva etc. were discussed by the IMG and their status appraised. Government of Orissa stated that there has been substantial progress with regard to land acquisition and rehabilitation in respect of major projects such as Tata, POSCO, JSPL, Bhushan Steel etc. The State Government will also hear all the applications for allocation of iron ore mines and likely to send its recommendation to the Ministry of Mines in December 2007. Other State Governments have also achieved substantial progress on land and mining matters. On the issue of raw materials, the IMG considered it necessary to rationalize its allocation and renewal linked to the production milestone of the projects including cancellation of dormant mining leases in accordance with the MM(DR) Act. The Group also decided that a time frame regarding allocation of raw material resources as well as land is vital. A fixed time line, with regard to each major project will be formulated and monitored by the IMG in its subsequent meetings. It was discussed that a more optimum utilization of the reserves with emphasis on higher utilization of fines and up-gradation of mining technology need to be emphasized. On the issue of resettlement and rehabilitation, IMG decided in favour of further augmentation and strengthening the existing land transfer and rehabilitation machinery with more man manpower and better logistics.

3954. (31-10-2007) NEW DELHI : Shri Abhijit Sengupta, IAS (Karnataka, 72) has taken over as Secretary, Ministry of Culture. He replaces Shri Badal K. Das who retired on superannuation today. Earlier, Shri Abhijit Sengupta was working as Principal Adviser, Planning Commission.

3955. (31-10-2007) NEW DELHI : The Union Minister of Social Justice and Empowerment Smt. Meira Kumar leaves for Mauritius tomorrow for signing an MoU for cooperation in the field of Welfare of Older Persons, Persons with Disabilities, Drug Abuse Prevention and Community Development. The MoU addresses the issues of overall development of the marginalized sections of society through mutual cooperation for training, research and documentation. India also offers to provide scholarship for Mauritian participants for training in National Institute of Social Defence and Six National Institutes of Disabilities. During her visit, Smt. Kumar will also call on Rt. Hon. Sir Anerood Jugnauth, President of the republic of Mauritius, Dr. Navinchandra Ramgoolam, the Prime Minister, the Minister of Foreign Affairs, the Minister of Social Securities. Smt. Kumar will also attend the function at Aapravasi Ghat to commemorate the 173rd anniversary of the arrival of the first batch of indentured labourers in Mauritius. It was in the year 1834 that Indian labourers landed on this beautiful island and on this date. Although at Aapravasi Ghat the historical structures have crumbled over time, the '14 Steps' that saw first group of Indians putting their foot on the island in the Indian Ocean have been preserved as the historic testimony to centuries old linkages between the two countries. The Minister will also visit the Samadhi of Sir S. Ramgoolam at the SSR Botanical Garden, Pamplemousses and various other institutions including Chesire Home and Orphanages. The delegation comprises top officials of the Ministry including Joint Secretary, Dr. Arbind Prasad, and Director, National Institute of Social Defeance, Shri Satyendra Prakash.

3956. (31-10-2007) NEW DELHI : The Army Aviation Corps turns Twenty Two on Wednesday. The First Army Aviation Reunion is being held at Combat Army Aviation Training School at Nasik to commemorate the same. The fact that Army has its own aviation assets is not widely known to the uninitiated. Making a humble beginning with four light weight unarmed AUSTER aircrafts in 1947, the erstwhile Air OP made stellar contributions in the Indo-Pak conflicts. On 01 Nov 1986, Government of India formally approved the creation of 'ARMY AVIATION CORPS'. This elite arm, today is wholly manned, maintained and flown by select personnel of the Indian Army. The 'SOLDIERS IN THE SKY' with their versatile helicopters are a lifeline of brave Indian troops deployed in far flung inhospitable terrain. Nothing describes the omnipotence of Army Aviation's reach and presence better than its 24 x 7 application, be it in peace, war or natural calamities. Whether it is a landslide in Sikkim, a Snow storm in J&K, floods in the East, earthquakes or the devastating tsunami, these 'Olive Green Wings' have been the front runners in close support flying operations. The history of Army Aviation corps is replete with many gallantry awards. When it comes to being true 'FORCE MULTIPLIERS', few can claim to exercise so great an impact, in such stark contrast to their small numbers. Presently the Corps is headed by Maj Gen AH Gadre, an army pilot with extensive flying experience. Lt Gen KS Jamwal, General Officer Commanding-in-Chief Eastern Command is the Colonel Commandant of this elite Corps.

3957. (31-10-2007) NEW DELHI : In 2016 India's on road vehicle population will reach 372 million from the present level of 55 million vehicles with a similar increase in fuel consumption. India will enjoy its eminent position of being the largest tractor and three wheeler manufacturer in the world, second largest two wheeler manufacturer and would emerge as the seventh largest car producer and retain its forth position in the truck manufacturing industry. This was stated by Dr. R.C. Panda, Secretary, Ministry of Heavy Industries and Public Enterprises in a presentation at the seminar on "Technology Trends for Fuel Efficiency & Emission Control in Transport Sector" here today. He said, it was, therefore, important to ensure that the vehicles during the next few decades should be 'gas sippers' rather than "gas guzzlers". Dr. Panda said it was pertinent to ensure greener and fuel efficient vehicles through policy intervention by the Government and voluntary measures by the auto industry. He said Government of India was taking a number of steps to face the challenges in automotive technology and emission control technology like tougher regulations, financial incentives, continued research and development, consumer education and marketing. Charting the future path in this direction, he suggested that to achieve the goal we have to have alternate fuel, fuel-efficient vehicles, set emission standards, technology R&D and fiscal incentives and disincentives. Dr. Panda also quoted Rudolf Diesel to drive home the point of the importance of having green fuel. Even in the beginning of this century, this great inventor had said "the Diesel engine can be fed with vegetable oils and would help considerably in the development of agriculture of the countries which use it." The day-long seminar was organised by the Petroleum Conservation Research Association (PCRA) in association with PHD Chamber of Commerce & Industry and Society of Indian Automobile Manufactures (SIAM). Shri S. Sundareshan, Additional Secretary, Ministry of Petroleum & Natural Gas, Shri Ravi Capoor, Joint Secretary, Ministry of Petroleum & Natural Gas and Executive Director of PCRA, Shri Krishan Kalra, Secretary General, PHD Chamber, Shri Sanjay Bhatia, President, PHD Chamber and Shri Dilip Chenoy, Director General, SIAM also spoke on this occasion. The three technical sessions-'Challenges in Automotive Technology', 'Fuel Efficiency Trends' and 'Emission Control Technologies'-were addressed by experts in respective fields. The valedictory address was delivered by Dr. Surajit Mitra, Joint Secretary, Ministry of Heavy Industries & Public Enterprises.

3958. (31-10-2007) NEW DELHI : The Union Minister of Micro, Small & Medium Enterprises Shri Mahabir Prasad has said that among the several policy initiatives that India has undertaken in the last decade of the last century, Cluster Development appears to be an attractive and efficacious one. "After a certain amount of experimentation on the degree and type of intervention that government could undertake or encourage, we veered towards certain successful models", the Minister said. Shri Prasad was speaking at the Asia-Europe Ministerial Meeting (ASEM) on Small & Medium Enterprises in Beijing today. Shri Prasad said the model of Cluster Development that "we have undertaken entails a whole range of schemes, which means that those Ministries, Departments or Agencies that are well versed in a particular subject will be assisting those SME clusters that operate in their domain." Giving specific examples he said clusters of handmade textiles would be looked after by the specialized agency meant for such textile enterprises; clusters of food units would be serviced by the Ministry of Food Processing Industries and so on. In all, the government identified more than 3000 SME clusters of artisan-specific, village and small enterprises in India and took up 1150 such clusters for intervention and improvement, he added. Shri Prasad also informed that India had undertaken a programme for 'Twinning' of Indian SME clusters with similar SME clusters in Italy. India also had a record of disseminating technology amongst certain developing countries in Africa and Asia and this new programme of cluster development could also be included by in such efforts. He further stated that India would also like to learn from other Asian and European countries about their experience in cluster development so that "we may improve our methods and imbibe the best practices in the world." Pointing out that Micro, Small & Medium Enterprises sector has been an integral part of the industrial resurgence of India, Shri Prasad said that the credit policy helped in linking the Indian MSMEs with almost 55000 bank branches and have given loan (outstanding) of over US$ 55 billion. In 2006-07, advances to MSMEs from the public sector banks in India have registered a record growth of over 27 per cent. He further informed that the number of SMEs in India is estimated to be around 13 million while the estimated employment provided by this sector is over 31 million. The export from the SME sector is estimated at US $ 50 billion in 2005-06. Further, the SME sector accounts for about 45 per cent of the manufacturing output and over 40 per cent of the national exports of the country. Accounting for more than 95% of all enterprises in most of Asia-Europe Meeting (ASEM) countries, SMEs act as a main driving force of technological innovation, expanding employment and boosting economic growth. ASEM members pay great attention to SMEs development. In the Hanoi Declaration on closer ASEM Economic Partnership adopted at Fifth ASEM Summit, ASEM members have strong political will to promote SMEs cooperation under the ASEM framework. Against this background, China hosted the ASEM SMEs Ministerial Meeting, which aims at deepening dialogue among governmental agencies of ASEM members in charge of SMEs, discussing policies and measures for better adapting to globalisation, creating sound SMEs social service policy and supporting system, improving SMEs capacity of innovation and competitiveness, enhancing cooperation among SMEs in ASEM members, strengthening regional cooperation of industrial clusters, and expanding mutual investment areas.

3959. (31-10-2007) NEW DELHI : The National Health Policy of India envisages the use of the Ayurvedic, Yoga & Naturopathy, Unani, Siddha and Homoeopathy (AYUSH) systems of medicine in the provision of adequate health care under the overarching umbrella of the national health framework. The AYUSH systems have inherent advantages such as natural plant-based products, low cost, absence of drug toxicity, etc. The holistic nature of these systems is another major advantage. In order to highlight the strengths of AYUSH systems, the Department of AYUSH, Ministry of Health & Family Welfare, Government of India, has decided to launch a number of national campaigns with a view to focus on strengths of each system in specific disease conditions. The national campaign on Homoeopathy for Mother and Child Care is one of these campaigns. There is limited awareness among policy makers, professionals of other systems of medicine and the common man about the potential of homoeopathy in improving the health status of women and children. During pregnancy, many allopathic medicines are contra-indicated whereas homoeopathic medicine can be safely used for the common problems such as morning sickness, heartburn, muscular cramps, breast pain, etc. Such medicines can also alleviate fears and anxieties during pregnancy and labour. Homoeopathic medicines are safe for infants in conditions like diarrhea, colic, ear infections, teething troubles, etc. Sweet pills are palatable to the children and therefore there is better treatment compliance with homoeopathy. These are some areas where homoeopathy has an edge over other systems of medicine, specially in mother and child care. The proposed national campaign aims at sensitising policy makers, medical professionals of other systems and the common man about the strengths of homoeopathy in mother and child health care. There are a large number of

Homoeopathic Medical Colleges and institutionally qualified Homoeopathic Physicians in the country whose services are currently underutilized in various National Health Programmes in general and for mother and child health care in particular. The national campaign will help in mobilising these homoeopathic practitioners and institutions for improving the health standards of women and children. The campaign would provide a platform for the exchange of knowledge and information and establish linkage between medical practitioners of different systems of medicine and further create avenues for coordination amongst medical practitioners so as to promote integrated health care for women and children. The campaign would be flagged off at the National Workshop to be held at India Islamic Cultural Centre, Delhi on 5th and 6th November 2007. The two-day workshop is expected to have participation of policy makers, physicians of all the streams, representatives of homoeopathic pharmaceutical industry and non-governmental organisations (NGOs) working in health sector, etc. This national workshop would be followed by State and district level workshops. The awareness generated during this campaign will lay the foundation for a long-term relationship among the homoeopathic physicians and teachers, allopathic physicians, NGOs and administrators of AYUSH systems in the Central as well as State Governments that could generate new collaboration and coordination on public health issues. It is expected that the campaign would generate increased awareness of the potential role of homoeopathy in the management of Mother and Child Health among practitioners of all the systems of medicine, taking further cause of integrated approach to health care. The activities of the National Campaign are being coordinated by the Central Council for Research in Homoeopathy, an autonomous organization of the Department of AYUSH, Ministry of Health & Family Welfare, Government of India.

3960. (31-10-2007) NEW DELHI : Bharatiya Janata Party delegation has demanded the centre an early and favourable decision of minimum support price of Rs. 1000 to paddy on par with wheat. The delegation led by Shri LK Advani consisted of Shri Rajnath Singh, President, BJP, Shri M Venkaiah Naidu, Shri Anant Kumar, Shri Yediyurappa, leader of the party in Karnataka Assembly and 15 Members of Parliament of the party from Karnataka, met the Prime Minister, Shri Manmohan Singh, here today. The delegation made fervent appeal to the PM to address the concerns of the paddy growers in the country and suggested that MSP of paddy should be raised to Rs. 1000. They pointed out that the production cost of the crop has gone up considerably in the recent years and farmers are not getting remunerative price to their crop. They also brought to the notice of the Prime Minister that the country has been experiencing series of farmers' suicides in various states and large-scale migrations to non-agricultural sectors, which is not in the interest of the country. If the same trend is continued, they told PM, the country would face shortage of paddy also as in the case of wheat. The Prime Minister opined that it is not proper to draw comparisons between wheat and paddy. And also said that the government has to keep the interests of consumers while raising the MSP of paddy, in view. If the government raises the MSP of a crop that would result in further price rise, he said. At this point, Shri M. Venkaiah Naidu intervened to appraise the Prime Minister, about the sufferings of the farmers and also distress among the paddy growers. And said, it is the responsibility of the government to take the issue of price rise in the interest of vulnerable sections of its effect. But, at the same time, the government also has the responsibility of protection of the farmers from precarious situation, he said. He reminded the PM, that in around 11 states the farmers are agitating demanding rise of MSP to paddy, and said it is a reasonable demand from paddy growers. Shri Naidu brought the wide spread discontent among the paddy farmers across the country and urged the PM to take an early favourable decision on MSP to paddy. The Prime Minister informed the delegation that even minimum support price for wheat for the ensuing season is also in consideration and would keep the paddy issue too in mind. Shri LK Advani, Leader of Opposition in the Lok Sabha, has already wrote a detailed letter to the Prime Minister, on 20th of this month, about the agitation of farmers and the demand for enhancement of MSP to Paddy.

3961. (31-10-2007) NEW DELHI : The Trade Marks (Amendment) Bill, 2007, introduced in the Lok Sabha on the 23rd August, 2007 and pending therein, has been referred to the Department-related parliamentary Standing Committee on Commerce, with Dr. Murli Manohar Joshi, Member, Rajya Sabha, as its Chairman, for examination and report. The Bill seeks to amend the Trade Marks Act, 1999 (hereinafter referred to as Trade Marks Act) with a view, inter-alia to:-(i) prescribe a period of 18 months for the registration of trade marks under Section 23 of the Trade Marks Act, in line with the provisions of the Madrid Protocol; (ii) incorporate a new Chapter IVA in the Trade Marks Act containing enabling provisions for accession to Madrid Protocol, including empowering the Registrar of Trade Marks to deal with international applications originating from India as well as those received from the International Bureau (single application with one fee and in one language) and maintain record of international registrations; (iii) reduce the time-period of filing a notice of opposition of published applications, from four months to three months, for speedy disposal of proceedings; (iv) simplify the law relating to transfer of ownership of trade marks by assignment or transmission and to bring the law generally in tune with international practice and modern business needs; (v) omit chapter X of the Trade Marks Act, dealing with special provisions for textile goods, as it has become redundant. The Committee has decided to invite memoranda containing views of the individuals/organisations, etc. interested in the subject matter of the Bill and also to hear oral evidence on the subject. Those desirous of submitting memoranda to the Committee may send two copies (either in English or Hindi) thereof to Shri Surinder Kumar Watts, Director, Rajya Sabha Secretariat, Room No. 240, Second Floor, Parliament House Annexe, New Delhi (Tel: 23034240, Tele fax: 23013158, E-mail: watts@sansad.nic.in) within fifteen days, indicating whether they would also be interested in giving oral evidence before the Committee. The memorandum submitted to the Committee would form part of the records of the Committee and would be treated as confidential and would not be circulated to anyone, as any act contrary thereto would constitute a breach of privilege of the Committee. The Bill was published in the Gazette in India, Extraordinary, Part II, Section 2, dated the 23rd August, 2007. Its copies can be had on written request to the above-mentioned Officer or can be downloaded from the official website of the Lok Sabha (http://loksabha.nic.in), under the caption "Bills with the Committee".

3962. (31-10-2007) NEW DELHI : To address the critical issues of how to reduce emissions of climate changing greenhouse gases (GHG) and how to reduce dependence on finite supplies of petroleum in our country, Petroleum Conservation Research Association (PCRA) in association with PHD Chamber of Commerce and SIAM organized a Seminar on "Technology Trends for Fuel Efficiency & Emission Control in Transport Sector" here today. Inaugurating the Seminar, Dr. RC Panda, Secretary, Ministry of Heavy Industries and Public Enterprises, cautioned that India should take precautions to ward off the green house emissions on account of the dieselization as country is set to become an automobile manufacturing hub of the world. He pointed out that the annual growth rate of automobiles in India is 16 per cent just below the China's growth rate at 18 per cent. Equally significant is the fact that the Asian countries would consume 45 percent of the fuel by 2025. He called for innovative strategies for fuel conservation and abating the emissions besides energy efficient policies that should be pursued at all levels. Referring to the need for Efficient Mass Transport systems, he said that we should reinvent the pattern of mobility. People would be encouraged to use public transport rather than using the personalized vehicles, which choke the roads and add to pollution. He also called upon the Original Equipment Manufacturers (OEMs) to launch vehicles, which are Euro 4 compliant and could run on bio-fuels. Dr. panda underlined the pressing need for enhancing outlays on R&D to evolve technologies that can considerably reduce the emission of carbon dioxide. Fiscal incentives also should be considered for green vehicles and disincentives for those which do not conform to it. He was strongly in favour of standard for fuel efficiency for the automotive sector in the country. Addressing the Seminar, Mr. S Sundareshan, Additional Secretary, Ministry of Petroleum and Natural Gas, hinted at the major initiative that the Government would take for promoting fuel efficiency in all sectors of economy. PCRA, he said, would play an active role in the promotional campaign to bring in an attitudinal change in the minds of consumers across the country. Mr. Sundareshan said that his Ministry would also launch a sensitization campaign for fuel efficiency and petroleum conservation using all available media such as print, electronic etc. to convey the message of fuel efficiency and conservation. Mentioning about the huge burden of the higher global oil prices, Mr. Sundareshan said that the crude oil prices at US$ 90 per barrel would lead to deficit, in other words under-recoveries of Rs.104,000 crore on annualized basis. He announced that the spot price of the fuel has come down by a notch at US$89 per barrel today from US$93 per barrel a few days ago. "This hugeoutflow of foreign exchange can be moderated by enhancing the fuel efficiency and conservation that can have direct bearing on the fiscal deficit of the economy," he added. Mr. Ravi Capoor, Executive Director, PCRA, while delivering his welcome address mentioned that the answer to the problem of rising oil prices and the global warming contributed by fuel emissions lies essentially into two futuristic solutions: (1) Energy from renewables and (2) Energy from efficiency. He informed that while end-use energy demand from road transportation globally will grow @ 2.2% per annum upto 2020, China grows @ 6.3%, Middle East grows @ 4.6%, US & Europe grow @ 1.5%. He noted that growth of Japan will remain flat because of its obsession with efficiency. Mr. Capoor added that with concerted effort for energy efficiency, the global incremental demand of 2.2% can be brought down to less than 1%, almost 60% of global incremental energy requirement can be met through a single source called "Efficiency". In his welcome address Mr. Sanjay Bhatia, President, PHD Chamber emphasized that matching the best possible fuel efficiency standards by Indian automobile manufacturers would greatly help the consumers, the economy and in the long run definitely the industry. Mr. Bhatia said that according to BRIC Report, India has the potential to show the fastest growth in the next 30 years. All this means substantially higher demand for transport and the scarce energy. In the context of the transport sector, the Integrated Energy Policy 2006 announced by the Planning Commission has clearly pointed out that if the energy efficiency of all motorized transport vehicles is increased, our oil requirement could reduce substantially.

3963. (1-11-2007) NEW DELHI : The President of India said, I am delighted to be here with you all at this function on the Foundation Day of Kerala and would like to congratulate the State and the people on the impressive achievements made since 1956. I am deeply touched by the warmth accorded to me at this civic reception and take this opportunity to convey my good wishes for the prosperity and progress of all the people of Kerala. I am also glad that on this occasion, imaginative programmes relating to Clean Kerala Mission, Total Physical Fitness and Scholarships for Higher Education are being launched. In the last five decades, Kerala has progressed a great deal and today, it proudly stands at the forefront for its achievements in human development particularly in the fields of education, health and empowerment of women. The people of Kerala enjoy a quality of life that compares favourably with many developed countries in the world. This remarkable advancement has been possible due to the combined efforts of the Government, various political and social organizations and, more importantly because of the hard work, the spirit of openness and enterprise of the people of Kerala. Social development has contributed to the emergence of a progressive society. Achievements in the social sectors should be matched by sustainable economic growth and enhanced productivity. Kerala has great potential. It should harness its resources and focus on development of major sunrise industries like tourism, knowledge industry, health, exports etc. Kerala is a land of exceptional natural beauty and is one of India's top tourist destinations. Its tropical forests, its fascinating backwaters, misty hill stations, its many rivers, its beautiful lakes and its characteristic coconut trees have created "God's own country". The growth of tourism in Kerala is commendable and its further development could help in generating additional revenues and employment. Apart from good and reliable infrastructure, tourism hinges on a clean and green environment. Hence efforts should be to keep the environment unpolluted, the waters pristine and the air clean by adopting eco-friendly practices. An environment friendly Kerala would ensure that tourists continue to look forward to their travel to Kerala. I am glad that the Action Plan for Clean Kerala Mission is being launched for environmental cleanliness, maintenance of public hygiene and prevention of diseases.

3964. (1-11-2007) NEW DELHI : 66 ULFA cadre and 2 NDFB cadre surrendered with arms and ammunitions before the Assam Police. The surrender was taken jointly by General Officer Commanding 4 Corps and Director General of Police, Assam in presence of other senior Police and Army Official at Guahawati. The surrender led by Ujjawal Gohain, the finance secretary of 28 Bn ULFA. He is among the senior most ULFA leader and had been operating in upper Assam. With this the total number of surrendered ULFA cadre are over 135 in last two weeks

3965. (1-11-2007) NEW DELHI : The Ministry of New and Renewable Energy aims to reduce the consumption of conventional power and to supplement energy supply through renewable energy, particularly in urban areas. After signing of Memorandum of understanding between the Ministry of New and Renewable Energy and The Energy & Resources Institute (TERI) on National Rating System for Green Buildings, Shri Vilas Muttemwar, Minister of State for New and Renewable Energy he further said that among other measures and interventions, the Ministry has been promoting solar passive architecture by providing support for the preparation of project reports and, on a limited scale, for construction of demonstration solar buildings. Support is also being provided for training, documentation and awareness creation activities. Several publications including manuals, guidelines, case studies etc. have been brought out. A set of CDs containing a Knowledge Bank and data base on existing solar buildings has been prepared. More recently, a Handbook on Energy Conscious Buildings has been prepared. The Bureau of Indian Standards (BIS) and Bureau of Energy Efficiency (BEE) have also made efforts to incorporate energy efficiency measures in the National Building Code and the Energy Conservation Building Code. The introduction of solar passive architecture is fairly complex given the involvement of a large number of stakeholders, such as municipal bodies, utilities, architects, engineers, builders, housing finance agencies, equipment manufacturers and the users themselves. An appropriate policy framework and focused approach is, therefore, necessary. Financial incentives and regulations, amendments in building codes and municipal laws may be necessary, together with sustained awareness campaigns, apart from efforts at mainstreaming solar energy into architectural practice and in the construction industry. Stressing on need to use Solar Energy, Shri Muttemwar said the concept of Solar Passive architecture is useful for energy savings. Few states like Himachal Pradesh, Punjab and Haryana have made it mandatory to do construction on this concept. Other states are also following the system.

3966. (1-11-2007) NEW DELHI : Wildlife conservation has a long history in India. In the past, flagship species specific projects have been successfully undertaken and recovery programmes for species like Crocodiles/Ghariyals, tigers, elephants, etc., were initiated in project mode and have shown positive results, both for the conservation of species as well as of their habitats. However, conservation of these mega species could not encompass certain other species, which are not directly linked with the tiger or elephant habitat, but require specific habitat. With mounting demographic pressures, there are today a number of species which are gravely endangered whose long term survival can only be ensured if a determined effort is undertaken to initiate specific recovery plans. The National Wildlife Action Plan (2002-2016) adopted during the XXI meeting of the Indian Board for Wildlife held on 21st January 2002 entails that the isolation of animal species due to fragmentation of habitats reduces relict populations to unviable levels, leading to local extinctions. Some of the important species exist as isolated populations in the country. These species include, the Wild Buffalo, Malabar Civet, Hangul, Uriyal, Pigmy Hog, Gangetic Dolphins, Nicobar Megapode, Andaman Teal, White Winged Wood Duck, Greater Adjutant Stork, Jerdons' Courser. Further, the National Forest Commission Report-2006 has also identified many species, including the species mentioned above, for which a recovery programme could be initiated. The approach could be twin fold. Firstly, a landscape approach in the same fashion of Project Tiger and Project Elephant could be taken up for species like Snow Leopard, Asiatic Lions, Hangul, Great Indian Bustard (inclusive of all the Bustard species) and Gangetic Dolphins, etc., while for the other species, there could be specific detailed recovery programme with a time schedule. The National Board for Wild life was apprised today about endangered Indian Wildlife Species.

3967. (1-11-2007) NEW DELHI : Of the total geographical area of Himachal Pradesh, 51% is above 3000 meters altitude. Many of Himachal's Wildlife Sanctuaries and national Parks are wholly or partly situated above this altitude. Under the present system of release of Centrally Sponsored Scheme funds (which is made in two instalments), the earliest the first instalment is received is June and by the time this instalment is made available to State Wildlife Wing in terms of State budgetary allocation, it is July or August. Thereafter, the monsoon commences and goes on till September. In October, altitudes above 3000 meters become frigid and most works cannot be carried out. For release of the 2nd instalment the Wildlife Wing is expected to spend over 60-80% of the first instalment by that time. By the time 2nd instalment gets released, it is already winter and many of the areas are under snow. It is therefore, only reasonable to release funds under the Centrally Sponsored Schemes either by April and also the entire amount sanctioned in one instalment. This would greatly help in timely planning and execution of works in mountain areas. Under such an arrangement, the proposals from the states can be received and processed in the Ministry during January to March of the preceding financial year. The National Board of Wildlife was apprised and requested for consideration for timely planning and execution of works in Mountain areas.

3968. (1-11-2007) NEW DELHI : Project Tiger, now the National Tiger Conservation Authority (NTCA) has been in the process of refining the All India tiger estimation since 2002. A pilot project was undertaken in the Satpura landscape of Madhya Pradesh, and the estimation protocol was jointly finalized as collaborative initiative with the State Government and the Wildlife Institute of India. The process was totally funded, implemented and monitored by the NTCA, in collaboration with Wildlife Institute of India and all the 17 tiger States. To complement the process, assessment of tiger habitat status in the country was done at Taluka level in the Geographical Information System (GIS) domain, in collaboration with the Wildlife Institute of India. Further, a comparative appraisal of forest cover status in and around tiger reserves (up to a radial distance of 10 kms), in collaboration with the Forest Survey of India for evolving reserve specific restorative strategies involving local people in the peripheral / buffer areas, was undertaken.

3969. (1-11-2007) NEW DELHI : India has around 8, 000 kms of coastline with two island systems, viz, the Andaman & Nicobar and Lakshadweep, and 2, 305, 143 Sq. Kms of Exclusive Economic Zone (EEZ). The marine and coastal environment of India harbours a host of resident and migratory wildlife. The important species found in the Indian waters include, Dugongs, Whales, Dolphins, Olive Ridley Turtles, a variety of fishes including the Whale Sharks & other sharks, Giant Groupers, Sea cucumbers, horseshoe crabs, sea shells, soft & hard corals, etc. At present there are 5 designated Marine Protected Areas in the country, viz, Gulf of Mannar National Park, Tamil Nadu, Gulf of Kutch Marine National Park & Gulf of Kutch Marine Sanctuary, Gujarat, Mahatma Gandhi Marine National Park, Andaman & Nicobar Islands and Gahirmatha Sanctuary, Orissa. Many of the marine species are facing grave threat due to habitat destruction, over exploitation, commercial fishing, etc. One of the major threats is also due to the by-catches during commercial fishing operations, which causes depletion of marine resources. In order to reduce the extent of by-catches during such commercial fishing, it would require improvement in advanced technology, viz, Turtle Exclusion Devise (TED), education & awareness amongst the fishermen folks. However, the information on the exact population status, biology and behaviour etc. of many of the marine species is not adequately known. India is a signatory to the Convention on Migratory Species (CMS), the International Whaling Commission (IWC) and has the responsibility to develop appropriate conservation, research and management action plans for its marine bio-diversity. In the recent past, India has also signed a Memorandum of Understanding with the CMS for Conservation of Marine Turtles and their habitat through out their range.

3970. (1-11-2007) NEW DELHI : With the release of the first instalment of funds for the current year, ground preparations are going on in a big way to implement the National Food Security Mission from the coming Rabi season. The Executive Committee of the Mission met in October to approve Annual Action Plans of the concerned States. Following it, ground level activities have been started for the winter cropping season. Agriculture Minister, Shri Sharad Pawar briefed the members of the Parliamentary Consultative Committee of his ministry here today about the progress made by the Mission so far. The Rs. 4882.5 crore XI-Plan scheme was launched recently following a resolution passed to this effect at the National Development Council's special meeting on agriculture held on 29 May, 2007. The Mission has been launched in 305 districts of 16 States, viz. Andhra Pradesh, Assam, Bihar, Chattisgarh, Guujarat, Haryana, Karnataka, Madhya Pradesh, Maharashtra, Orissa, Punjab, Tamil Nadu, Uttar Pradesh, West Bengal, Jharkhand and Rajasthan. Those districts have been selected that have potential for high rise in productivity. NFSM aims at increasing the production of rice, wheat and pulses by 10, 8 and 2 million tonnes respectively in the next four years. Shri Pawar stated that the strategy of NFSM is to bridge yield gaps in potential areas by introducing modern technologies and improved agronomic practices. This is the only way to meet the projected additional requirement of about 19 million tonnes of foodgrains by 2011-12, he said. Emphasising that NFSM takes an integrated approach to farm production by involving stakeholders at District, State and national level and the panchayati raj instutions, the Minister expressed the hope that selected districts will take local initiatives to make the scheme a success.

3971. (1-11-2007) NEW DELHI : The Bharatiya Janata Party condemns the UPA government for denying justice to paddy growers by not granting MSP of Rs. 1000/- per quintal. This is not only a betrayal of the paddy growers but also is a shortsighted decision, which will ultimately hurt the food security of the nation in future. The government is denying the rise in MSP for paddy on the ground that it will fuel price rise. The government's argument is far from the truth and also full of fallacies. Price is a function of demand and supply. Today, the market price of rice is proportionately much more than wheat, though paddy's MSP is less than wheat. This is primarily because the demand supply position has become precarious as far as rice availability in the market is concerned. The production of the rice is not increasing in tandem with its demand because the farmer is not getting his due through the MSP mechanism. If the country produces more paddy, the prices will not only stabilize but will also come down in the market. This is the economic reality, which will guarantee higher incomes to farmer and reasonable prices to the consumers. The Government is overlooking this vital aspect. Today, there is no policy to narrow down the gap between what the producer gets and what the consumer pays. The 11th Five Year Plan has targeted 10 million tonnes of additional production of rice. This cannot be achieved unless the farmer is ensured a good MSP and new technology is imbibed in the cultivation process. It is pertinent to note that the government has tacitly accepted the recommendation of Dr. M.S. Swaminathan to fix MSP for wheat by adding 50% to the cost of production as calculated by the Commission of Agricultural Costs and Prices. The BJP demands same justice for paddy growers. This is justified, as the costs calculated by the commission are not transparent and always undervalued. Further, the BJP believes that of late in a growing economy, MSP should become an effective tool of ensuring remunerative prices and not just a protection against distress.

3972. (1-11-2007) NEW DELHI : With the release of the first instalment of funds for the current year, ground preparations are going on in a big way to implement the National Food Security Mission from the coming Rabi season. The Executive Committee of the Mission met in October to approve Annual Action Plans of the concerned States. Following it, ground level activities have been started for the winter cropping season. Agriculture Minister, Shri Sharad Pawar briefed the members of the Parliamentary Consultative Committee of his ministry here today about the progress made by the Mission so far. The Rs. 4882.5 crore XI-Plan scheme was launched recently following a resolution passed to this effect at the National Development Council's special meeting on agriculture held on 29 May, 2007. The Mission has been launched in 305 districts of 16 States, viz. Andhra Pradesh, Assam, Bihar, Chattisgarh, Guujarat, Haryana, Karnataka, Madhya Pradesh, Maharashtra, Orissa, Punjab, Tamil Nadu, Uttar Pradesh, West Bengal, Jharkhand and Rajasthan. Those districts have been selected that have potential for high rise in productivity. NFSM aims at increasing the production of rice, wheat and pulses by 10, 8 and 2 million tonnes respectively in the next four years. Shri Pawar stated that the strategy of NFSM is to bridge yield gaps in potential areas by introducing modern technologies and improved agronomic practices. This is the only way to meet the projected additional requirement of about 19 million tonnes of foodgrains by 2011-12, he said. Emphasising that NFSM takes an integrated approach to farm production by involving stakeholders at District, State and national level and the panchayati raj institutions, the Minister expressed the hope that selected districts will take local initiatives to make the scheme a success. Each selected district has been allowed up to Rs. 2 crore for taking local initiatives, and awards have been planned at different levels to encourage better performance among the implementing agencies. The Minister informed that operational guidelines of the mission have been circulated to States and implementing agencies, preparedness of States has been reviewed at State Agriculture Ministers' meeting last month, and about 40% of the approved outlay for the current year has already been disbursed to the designated State Agencies.

3973. (1-11-2007) NEW DELHI : Sixty four persons have appeared before the Committee of Eminent Persons on Sethu Samudram Shipping Channel Project Committee so far. A number of issues have been raised including economic viability and environmental, navigational, security, historical, religious, social and developmental factors. The persons who have submitted their objections/suggestions upto 1700 hrs. on 31st October, 2007 may appear before the Committee upto 1700 hrs. on 3rd November, 2007. However, the Petitioners in the court cases, mentioned in the Order dated 5th October, 2007 of Cabinet Secretariat, may appear before the Committee for oral submissions upto 1700 hrs. on 6th November, 2007.

3974. (1-11-2007) NEW DELHI : Rashtriya Ispat Nigam Limited (RINL), a Public Sector Undertaking under the Ministry of Steel, has received a Commendation Certificate for significant achievement in 2006-07. The certificate was conferred by the confederation of Indian Industry (CII) and the EXIM Bank in Bangalore today. The Chairman and Managing Director of RINL Shri P.K. Bishnoi received the certificate. RINL had also won a Commendation Certificate last year for 'Strong Commitment to Excel'. The CII-EXIM Bank Award for Business Excellence was established jointly by the Confederation of Indian Industry (CII) and Export-Import (EXIM) Bank of India in 1994 to enhance competitiveness of Indian Business Enterprises. The CII-EXIM Bank Award for Business Excellence encourages organizations to strengthen their management systems, practices and capabilities to enhance and sustain their competitiveness to become World class organizations. The award is administered by CII.

3975. (1-11-2007) NEW DELHI : Shri Kapil Sibal, Union Minister for Science and Technology and Earth Sciences and Mrs. Valerie Pecresse, Minister for Higher Education and Research, France, who is visiting India from 1st-3rd November 2007 met today in New Delhi during the 20th anniversary celebrations of the Indo-French Centre for the Promotion of Advanced Research (IFCPAR). Speaking on the occasion, Ms. Pecresse said that her first visit, away from Europe, to India, is in order to underline the importance the French government attaches to the development of Indo-French relations particularly to university and scientific cooperation between the two countries. Addressing the gathering Shri Kapil Sibal paid rich compliments to the Indo-French cooperation in the field of science. He expressed confidence that the two countries will take it forward to bring solutions to the world confronted with huge issues such as environment, water management and health which are global in nature.

3976. (1-11-2007) NEW DELHI : A four day meeting of the representatives of 80 Manuscript Resource Centres and Manuscript Conservation Centres concluded here today at the Indira Gandhi National Centre for Arts, in Delhi. The representatives came from Museums, Universities, Government and private libraries, Oriental Research Foundations and Indological Institutes, and Monasteries from a cross section of diverse disciplines, learning lineages and denominational persuasions.

Discussion was focused on manuscripts in Tibetan, Bodhi, Buddhist, Arabic, Urdu, Persian, Turkish as well as in various regional languages, and on numerous scripts, used in the manuscripts, including Tigalari, Sarada, Pabuch, Gauri, Mori, Kaithi, Takri, Tulu. The discussion ranged across the diversity and complexity of knowledge systems, evolved in India to articulate overarching identities and regional variations. The diversity of languages and scripts, materials and techniques, used for inscribing texts, including materials like palm leaf, birch birk, hand made paper, stone, cloth, wool, terracotta, ivory, tortoise shell, leather, wood and the diversity of agro climatic regimes in the country provided a backdrop to a very lively debate on the need for tailoring conservation methodology to local needs. The discussion moved on to the spiritual, philosophical and theological dimensions of the regional textual traditions, to the vast body of contextual and oral tradition of narration, chanting, recitation, singing, dramatization, visual and performing arts, iconography and iconology that backed up such traditions, and, to the artistic expression of this tradition in murals in palaces and havelis, temples and maths, in miniature paintings and sculpture.

3977. (1-11-2007) NEW DELHI : Second Meeting of the Empowered Committee of the NCR Planning Board was held under the Chairmanship of Shri M. Ramachandran, Secretary, Ministry of Urban Development, recently to discuss, deliberate and decide the inter-state issues and progress in the implementation of development plans in NCR. The meeting was attended by the Chief Secretary of Haryana, Principal Secretary (Transport) and Principal Secretary (Power), Govt. of Haryana, Principal Secretary (PWD), GNCT of Delhi, Principal Secretary (Housing), Govt. of U.P, Spl. Secretary, Deptt. of Transport, Govt. of U.P., Spl. Commissioner (Transport), GNCT-Delhi, Resident Commissioner, Rajasthan besides senior officers from the MoUD, Ministry of Petroleum & Natural Gas, DMRC, DDA, GAIL, IGL, Govt. of U.P., Rajasthan, Haryana and GNCT of Delhi. The issues like free movement of vehicles within NCR; expediting the signing of bilateral agreements among NCR constituent states specially between Delhi-U.P., U.P.-Haryana and Delhi-Haryana which have expired; draft Reciprocal Common Transport Agreement among NCR States for unrestricted movement of vehicles within NCR; disparity in taxes related to transportation in all the States; unified checkpost could be provided to facilitate the movement of vehicles at inter-State borders and reduce the congestion on roads; issues related to Development along Delhi-Mumbai Industrial Corridor; connectivity of metro rail to the NCR, availability of CNG in NCR, etc. Governments of Haryana, U.P. & Delhi were requested to expedite the signing of bilateral agreement between Delhi-U.P., U.P.-Haryana and Delhi-Haryana. The draft Reciprocal Common Transport Agreement among NCR States as finalized by the Committee of Transport Commissioners/ Secretaries of the Constituent States of NCR was discussed and agreed. This would facilitate the unrestricted inter-state movement of vehicles after signing of the Common Agreement.

3978. (1-11-2007) NEW DELHI : Delhi Postal Circle has made special arrangements for disposal of Diwali Greeting Mails. 34 Post Offices and 2 RMS Offices at Railway Stations as detailed below have been identified as collections centres from 05.11.2007 to 12.11.2007. Separate reception counters are being set up at these Post Offices. Members of public can post their Diwali Greetings mail at these collection centres.

3979. (1-11-2007) NEW DELHI : The Ministry of Textiles announced today the continuation of the Technology Upgradation Fund Scheme (TUFS) for the entire period of the Eleventh Five Year plan (2007-12). The decision of the Government places special thrust on garmenting, technical textiles and processing segments of the textiles industry in view of their potential for value-addition and employment generation. This decision is expected to help the textile sector to achieve the targeted growth rate of 16% and make an investment of Rs. 150, 600 crore in the Plan period.

3980. (1-11-2007) NEW DELHI : The Ministry of Petroleum and Natural Gas, FICCI and UNCTAD are jointly organizing a two-day India-Africa Hydrocarbon Conference and Exhibition on November 6-7, 2007 in the capital. The primary objective of this initiative is to provide a platform for exploring mutually beneficial partnership opportunities between Africa & India in the hydrocarbon sector. The two-day event will be inaugurated by the Minister of External Affairs Shri Pranab Mukherjee on November 6, 2007 and the Minister of Petroleum & Natural Gas Shri Murli Deora will deliver a special address during the inaugural session. The Exhibition will be inaugurated by the Minister of State for Petroleum & Natural Gas Shri Dinsha Patel in the afternoon same day. Details regarding the Conference & Exhibition were announced at a curtain raiser Press Conference by Shri Murli Deora here last evening which was also attended by Petroleum Secretary Shri M.S. Srinivasan and FICCI Secretary General Dr. Amit Mitra. With its rich reserves and new finds, Africa is fast emerging as a hotspot in the world energy map. The improving socio-economic conditions of the African countries, substantial onshore/offshore hydrocarbon discoveries, commissioning of numerous fields, initiatives of various African countries in promoting foreign investment in the energy sector have together earned Africa a strategic position in the world energy map. India, one of the leading consumer of hydrocarbons has also established its expertise in providing consultancy services, undertaking turnkey projects, exporting supplies like equipments, plastics, chemicals, pipeline materials etc. required at different stages in upstream, midstream and downstream operations in the sector. Indian hydrocarbon sector, today, has become a hub of opportunities spread across all business segments. A high level of economic growth is driving the country's demand for energy, promising a ready market for energy sources on long-term basis. India is one of the leading importers of oil & gas. It also has tremendous potential for exports of almost all kinds of products and services required in the exploration, operation & maintenance, transportation and refining processes. In this direction, India and Africa could be easily identified as natural allies and have reasons to be interdependent. Against this backdrop, MOPNG, FICCI and UNCTAD have jointly come together for this initiative to forge an 'India-Africa Partnership in Hydrocarbons. India's increased presence and role in the hydrocarbon-rich and strategically significant Africa has important implications.

3981. (1-11-2007) NEW DELHI : India's exports during September, 2007 were valued at US $ 12796.61 million which was 19.26 % higher than the level of US $ 10730.34 million during September, 2006. In rupee terms, exports touched Rs.51621.52 crore, which was 4.31% higher than the value of exports during September, 2006. Cumulative value of exports for the period April-September, 2007 was US$ 72280.60 million (Rs.295233.05 Crore) as against US$ 60985.84 million (Rs.280275.27 Crore) registering a growth of 18.52% in Dollar terms and 5.34% in Rupee terms during the same period last year. India's imports during September, 2007 were valued at US $ 17217.65 million representing an increase of 2.31 % over the level of imports valued at US $ 16828.82 million in September, 2006. In Rupee terms, imports declined by 10.51%. Cumulative value of imports for the period April-September, 2007 was US$ 109204.43 million (Rs.446420.86 Crore) as against US$ 87010.23 million (Rs.399815.04 Crore) registering a growth of 25.51% in Dollar terms and 11.66% in Rupee terms during the same period last year.

3982. (1-11-2007) NEW DELHI : Following is the text of the inaugural address by the Vice President of India Mohd. Hamid Ansari at the Conference on "Vision 2025-A Sustainable Roadmap for India" organised by The Energy and Resources Institute (TERI) here today : "It is my privilege to address this important gathering on the issue of sustainable development. It is heartening that such distinguished personalities from India and abroad have converged here to discuss policy initiatives necessary for establishing a pattern of sustainable development in India and submit a policy document based on the deliberations here to governments and other stakeholders.

3983. (1-11-2007) NEW DELHI : The Ministry of New and Renewable Energy is organising a review meeting with banks and Financial Institutions (FIs) on Solar Water Heating Systems tomorrow. 28 banks, including nationalised banks, public sector banks, scheduled cooperative banks and other financial institutes who are participating in Ministry's Interest Subsidy Scheme on Solar Water Heating System are meeting here for the review. At the inception of the scheme 7 banks joined this scheme. In two years time, there are 28 banks implementing this scheme. The Ministry is providing interest subsidy through various branches of Public Sector Banks and other Financial Institutions to encourage users of different categories to go in for installation of Solar Water Heating Systems. Loans to the users are available at 2% of rate of interest for domestic system, 3% for institutional and 5% for commercial and industrial system. To facilitate banks and FIs in smooth functioning of the programme, a uniform landing rate has been fixed which has been enhanced from 10.75% to 12.5% for the current year Interest Subsidy is continued to be paid on upfront basis to Indian Renewable Energy Development Agency (IREDA) calculated at a discount rate of 6.5%. Solar Water Heating is a full mature technology today. About 150 million sq. meters of collector area has been installed world wide. In India about 2million sq.meter collector area has been installed so far. Of this nearly one million sq. meter has been added during last two and a half years under an accelerated Programme initiated during 2005-06. This review meeting has been organised on behalf of the Ministry of New and Renewable Energy by IREDA. Few more Financial Institutions have been also invited in this meeting to introduce this scheme to expand the network of Solar Water Heating System.

3984. (1-11-2007) NEW DELHI : With the increase in per capita income, insurance is now being seen not only as an instrument for risk coverage but also for savings and investments and this trend is clearly visible. This was stated by the Finance Minister, Shri P. Chidambaram while addressing the Parliamentary Consultative Committee attached to his Ministry, here yesterday. He said that the insurance penetration, which is a reflection of the gross premium as a percentage of the GDP, has gone up from 2.3 in the year 2000 to 4.8 in 2006. Similarly, insurance density which measures the gross premium per capita in USD has gone up from 9.90 in the year 2000 to 38.40 in the year 2006. These figures, though, are comparatively less than the figures of some of the countries in the developed world; it is expected that in the years to come there will be further improvement in the insurance penetration and density, he added. The Finance Minister stated that now people are becoming more cautious about their health and are opting for health insurance schemes which have shown an upward trend. He said that the Government has announced a health insurance scheme on 1st October, 2007 to cover unorganized sector workers belonging to BPL categories and their family members in the country over a period of 5 years beginning 1st April, 2008. In response to Members' suggestion of according a wider insurance cover to agriculture sector, the Finance Minister stated that the National Agriculture Insurance Scheme (NAIS) which was introduced in 1999-2000 season is still continuing. It covers all farmers who take loans from commercial banks, cooperative banks as well as rural banks. The scheme operates on the basis of area approach. He said that for wheat and paddy crops, the premium rates are 1.5% and 2% of the sum assured respectively. This is a subsidised scheme and the amount of subsidy is shared on 50-50 basis by the Central and State Governments. The Finance Minister said that as agriculture loans increase, more and more farmers would be covered under this scheme.

3985. (2-11-2007) NEW DELHI : India's exports during September, 2007 were valued at US $ 12796.61 million which was 19.26 % higher than the level of US $ 10730.34 million during September, 2006. In rupee terms, exports touched Rs.51621.52 crore, which was 4.31% higher than the value of exports during September, 2006. Cumulative value of exports for the period April-September,

2007 was US$ 72280.60 million (Rs.295233.05 Crore) as against US$ 60985.84 million (Rs.280275.27 Crore) registering a growth of 18.52% in Dollar terms and 5.34% in Rupee terms during the same period last year. India's imports during September, 2007 were valued at US $ 17217.65 million representing an increase of 2.31 % over the level of imports valued at US $ 16828.82 million in September, 2006. In Rupee terms, imports declined by 10.51%. Cumulative value of imports for the period April-September, 2007 was US$ 109204.43 million (Rs.446420.86 Crore) as against US$ 87010.23 million (Rs.399815.04 Crore) registering a growth of 25.51% in Dollar terms and 11.66% in Rupee terms during the same period last year.

3986. (2-11-2007) NEW DELHI : The year 2007 is being celebrated as the "India-China Year of Friendship Through Tourism". As a part of the Action Plan drawn up between the two countries to celebrate the year, India is participating as, `Guest of Honour Country' at the China International Travel Mart 2007 being held in Kunming city China from 1st to 4th November 2007. An Incredible India Pavilion has been set up at the travel mart in an area of 225 sq. mtrs, to To showcase the varied tourism products of the country. The main entrance gate of the India Pavilion is a replica of `Sanchi Stupa Gate'. The Indian delegation at the mart is being led by Additional Director General (Tourism) Shri Sanjay Kothari. A total of 17 tour operators from India are participating as co-exhibitors in the pavilion to promote packages to India. Other activities in the pavilion include cultural performances by a group of Chhau dancers from India. India Pavilion has been decorated very tastefully. The other attractions at the India Pavilion are mehndiwalis and churiwalis which are attracting large number of visitors at the mart. An India Evening is also being organized today at the mart to show case India's progress and vibrancy to travel stakeholders and media representatives from China. On this occasion, a presentation on Indian tourism and its growth will be made. A cultural show by Chhau dancers will also be performed. During the four day event, outdoor advertising at different locations and on the buses running in Kuming City is also being done.

3987. (2-11-2007) NEW DELHI : Indian Renewable Energy Development Agency organized an Interaction Meet with banks and financial institutions on behalf of the Ministry of New & Renewable Energy here today. The Meet was organized to discuss the progress made by them on interest subsidy scheme on solar water heating systems being implemented by the banks and chalk out the action plan for the future. Speaking at the occasion Shri V. Subramanian, Secretary of the Ministry asked the banks and the financial institutions to gear up their branches to enhance the business on solar water heating keeping in view of the winters approaching ahead. The meeting was attended by around 50 officials from 16 banks/ financial institutions, a few state nodal agencies and the industry. In India about 2 million square meter collector area has been installed so far. Of this nearly 1 million square meter has been added during the last two and a half years under an Accelerated Programme initiated during 2005-06. The Ministry has set a goal of adding 5 million square meter collector area during the 11th Plan period up to 2012 which includes 6 lakh sq. m. during current year. .To encourage the users of different categories to go in for installation of solar water heating systems, the Ministry is providing interest subsidy through various branches of public sector banks and other financial institutions. 28 banks/FIs are presently participating in implementing the programme. Loans to the users are available at 2% rate of interest for domestic systems, 3% for institutional and 5% for commercial and industrial systems. It was noted in the meeting that the volume of business which is being done by Bank/FIs under the interest subsidy scheme of the Ministry is somewhat low when compared to the total business being done in this sector which reached Rs.400 crore during 2006-07. In order to generate greater lending to this sector, the banks were suggested to take various measures which included easy availability of loans to the users at effective interest rate of 2%, 3% and 5%, loan procedures to be made simpler, tie ups to be made with manufactures/suppliers for easy availability of loans, organize adequate publicity and training at branch level etc. The banks & the financial institutions assured that they will take all these measures and put their best efforts to achieve the goals set by the Ministry during current year as well as during the 11th Plan Period.

3988. (2-11-2007) NEW DELHI : Indian Renewable Energy Development Agency organized an Interaction Meet with banks and financial institutions on behalf of the Ministry of New & Renewable Energy here today. The Meet was organized to discuss the progress made by them on interest subsidy scheme on solar water heating systems being implemented by the banks and chalk out the action plan for the future. Speaking at the occasion Shri V. Subramanian, Secretary of the Ministry asked the banks and the financial institutions to gear up their branches to enhance the business on solar water heating keeping in view of the winters approaching ahead. The meeting was attended by around 50 officials from 16 banks/ financial institutions, a few state nodal agencies and the industry. In India about 2 million square meter collector area has been installed so far. Of this nearly 1 million square meter has been added during the last two and a half years under an Accelerated Programme initiated during 2005-06. The Ministry has set a goal of adding 5 million square meter collector area during the 11th Plan period up to 2012 which includes 6 lakh sq. m. during current year. .To encourage the users of different categories to go in for installation of solar water heating systems, the Ministry is providing interest subsidy through various branches of public sector banks and other financial institutions. 28 banks/FIs are presently participating in implementing the programme. Loans to the users are available at 2% rate of interest for domestic systems, 3% for institutional and 5% for commercial and industrial systems.

3989. (2-11-2007) NEW DELHI : The outstanding balances of 6.75 per cent Loan, 2007 is repayable at par on November 22, 2007 and no interest will accrue theron from the said date. In the event of a holiday being declared on November 22, 2007 by any State Government under the Negotiable Instruments Act, 1881, the Loan will be repaid by the paying offices in that State on the previous working day. To facilitate repayment of the Loan on the due date, holders may tender the securities, duty discharged, at the Public Debt Offices, Treasuries/sub-Treasuries and branches of State Bank of India and its Associate Banks (at which they are enfaced/registered for payment of Interest) 20 days in advance of the due date for repayment. Dull details of the procedure for receiving the discharge value may be obtained from any of the aforesaid paying offices. Department of Economic Affairs, Ministry of Finance New Delhi.

3990. (2-11-2007) NEW DELHI : As per early reports collected by the Agriculture Ministry wheat has been sown in the current Rabi season in 1.84 lakh ha as compared to 1.17 lakh ha during the corresponding period last year. Sowing is reported to be progressing fast in Karnataka, Madhya Pradesh, Punjab and Maharashtra. Winter rice sowing has also started in some southern States in Andhra Pradesh and Karnataka. 18, 000 ha area has come under rice plantation so far. As per early reports received from States the area coverage under jowar is 30.62 lakh ha against 33.41 lakh ha during last year, barley 0.06 lakh ha against 0.20 lakh ha last year, maize 1.20 lakh ha against 1.32 lakh ha last year and total coarse cereals 32.27 lakh ha against 35.50 lakh ha during the corresponding period of last year.

3991. (2-11-2007) NEW DELHI : Government of India have announced the sale (re-issue) of “8.20 per cent Government Stock, 2022 for a notified amount of Rs. 5, 000 crore (nominal) through a priced based auction using multiple price method. Government of India have also announced the sale (re-issue) of “8.33 per cent Government Stock, 2036” for a notified amount of Rs. 3, 000 crore (nominal) through a price based auction using multiple price method. The auctions will be conducted by the Reserve Bank of India, Mumbai Office, Fort, Mumbai on November 8, 2007 (Thursday). Up to 5% of the notified amount of the sale of both the stocks will be allotted to eligible individuals and Institutions as per the Scheme for Non-Competitive Bidding Facility in the Auction of Government Securities. Bids in the prescribed form obtainable from the Regional Director, Reserve Bank of India, Mumbai Office (Public Debt Office), Fort, Mumbai-400 001 and RBI website www.rbi.org.in should be submitted to that Office on November 8, 2007. The NDS members should submit competitive as well as non-competitive bids in electronic format using Primary Market Operation (PMO) module of NDS. All bids should be submitted by 12.30 P.M. The result of the auctions will be announced on November 8, 2007 and payment by successful bidders will be during banking hours on November 12, 2007 (Monday). Both the Stocks will be eligible for “When Issued” trading in accordance with the guidelines on ‘When Issued transactions in Central Government Securities’ issued by the Reserve Bank of India vide circular No.RBI/2006-07/178 dated November 16, 2006.

3992. (2-11-2007) NEW DELHI : The Union Cabinet today gave its approval in principle to the project for taking up river management, flood control, anti-erosion works, drainage development, flood proofing, flood prone area development programme, restoration of damaged flood management works, etc. in the entire country. The national Common Minimum Programme (NCMP) mentions that pending flood control and, drainage schemes in North Bihar and West Bengal, including prevention of erosion in Ganga-Padma and Bhagirathi, would be completed expeditiously. NCMP also states that the Central Government would fully support flood control works in inter-state and international Rivers. An Empowered Committee of Secretaries headed by the Finance Secretary was constituted to select projects under the scheme in the Ganga Basin, Brahmputra and Barak basins and other areas on the basis of Detailed Project Report. The Scheme will be implemented through State Government and monitored by Ganga Flood Board and Central Water Commission. Their progress will be evaluated through remote sensing techniques and through independent agency.

3993. (2-11-2007) NEW DELHI : A search and seizure operation was conducted by the Income Tax department on 24th October on a business group engaged in real estate and infrastructure development. In all 24 premises were covered in the search operation spread over Delhi, Ghaziabad, Gurgaon, Meerut, Saharanpur, Pantnagar and Jaipur. The search action was taken on the basis of information that the group was engaged in procuring bogus bills from its suppliers thereby inflating its expenses and reporting reduced profits leading to tax evasion. The main suppliers of bogus bills were operating from Ghaziabad and through their agents in Delhi. Some specific information in this regard was also received from the Directorate General of Central Excise Intelligence, Delhi. As a result of the search, large number of incriminating documents were found giving credence to the allegations against the group. All such incriminating documents and computers were seized and are being examined. These documents indicate bogus purchases, unaccounted cash transactions in real estate projects, and unaccounted transactions by its associates and suppliers. It was also found that the group has made large-scale investments in real estate, land purchase and other transactions and unaccounted money has been channelised in these transactions. In addition, the group was found to have floated a large number of subsidiary and front companies for cross holdings and transactions to facilitate introduction of unaccounted money. Cash amounting to Rs.1.75 crore was seized in the course of search. Based on the incriminating documents seized and investigation conducted subsequently, the group admitted undisclosed income of Rs.53 crore.

3994. (2-11-2007) NEW DELHI : Two Indian teams from Vishakhapatnam Steel Plant have won gold medals at the International Convention on Quality Control Circles (ICQCC) 2007 at Beijing. SAMRUDDHI from Steel Melting Shop department (SMS) and TRISHAKTI from Light and Medium Merchant Mill Department (LMMM) consisting of 14 members bagged the medals for presentation of their case studies. They presented quality control case studies on 'Elimination of Ladle Opening Problem in Chromium Bottom Addition Heats'and Conversion of unused piling roller table into "Connecting roller table between the line 1 and line 2 in Bar Mill". The convention was organized by China International Conference Centre for Science and Technology (CICCST) at Beijing, China from 24th to 27th October 2007. Teams from Japan, Malaysia, China, Singapore, Korea were among 212 teams from 13 countries that participated.

3995. (2-11-2007) NEW DELHI : The 12th World Lake Conference, TAAL 2007 calls upon governments and organizations to adopt appropriate research methodologies to apply and prepare data banks to facilitate execution of management and Action Plans to preserve lakes and wetlands .Over 600 delegates who took part in the five day deliberations, adopted the "Draft Jaipur Declaration" which acknowledges the importance of lakes and wetlands for domestic, agricultural and recreational uses and improve habitats for conserving biodiversity. On the concluding day of the five day 12th World Lake Conference, TAAL 2007's valedictory function today at Jaipur, Dr. Brij Gopal, NIE presented the recommendations which are called DRAFT JAIPUR DECLARATION, were adopted .Sh Namo Narain Meena, the Minister of State for Environment and Forests, Government of India said that the government has taken due note of these recommendations. He appealed all the participants to make efforts to implement the recommendations. Sh Meena said civil societies, students, academicians, and non-government organizations should work in harmony for promoting awareness. The minister said that unless all of us share a common vision-mission approach, we can not succeed in our noble intentions. Informing about inventories of lakes in the country, Sh Meena said Space Application Centre, Ahmedabad has been given a project to map to prepare state-wise atlases and create digital data-base of lakes. He also said that all the state governments have been asked to constitute lake and wetland conservation authority. Sh Wang Yuquig, Minister, Environment Protection Administration, Chinaextended invitation to hold the next 13th World Lake Conference at Wuhan which is the 3rd biggest scientific and educational cities among major Chinese cities. It is a home to 52 universities. It is called a city of 100 lakes .Sh Yuqing said that Chinese government has intensified the protection dynamics for the lakes. With the support from ILEC and the scientific and technical work for lake research from the different countries, we will be able to hold a successful World Lake Conference and show the world the efforts and results made by China in the field of water environment protection.

3996. (2-11-2007) NEW DELHI : Three World Bank loan/credit agreements amounting to US$ 944 million were signed here today in the presence of visiting World Bank President Mr. Robert B. Zoellick and the Finance Minister Shri P. Chidambaram. Commerce & Industry Minister Shri Kamal Nath & Labour Minister Shri Oscar Fernandes were also present on this occasion. The agreements were signed by Shri Madhusudan Prasad, Joint Secretary, Ministry of Finance, on behalf of Government of India, and Ms. Isabel Guerrero, Country Director, India for the World Bank. The loan/credit agreements are for Strengthening Rural Credit Cooperatives Project for US$ 600 million loan and credit; India Vocational Education Training Project for US$ 280 million credit; and additional financing for the Karnataka Community Based Tank Management Project for US$ 64 million loan and credit. Extending a very warm welcome to Mr. Zoellick on his first visit to India as the President of World Bank, Shri Chidambaram said "The agreements are being signed today for about 950 million dollar of World Bank assistance in three critical areas-rural finance, vocational training and restoration of water bodies. It gives me personally a great satisfaction to see the culmination of project preparation process, as all these three relate to announcements that I have made in my Budget Speech in the Parliament. A well functioning system of finance is essential for sustaining agricultural growth and alleviating rural poverty. Our rural credit cooperatives have been a key pillar in the system of rural finance and the World Bank assistance will help in revitalizing these institutions and provide credit to farmers with significantly enhanced access to formal finance. The World Bank project envisages assistance of $ 600 million, which is, I understand, the largest single project funded by the World Bank in India. NABARD would be helping in implementing this project. The second project addresses the issues of improving the quality of vocational training, in keeping with the Government's keenness to ensure greater competitiveness of the labour force. Under the World Bank project, Industrial Training Institutions will be strengthened to enable our workers to upgrade their skills and contribute to the country's growth process. With $ 280 million of IDA assistance envisaged in this project, 400 ITIs will be upgraded over a period of 4 years.

3997. (2-11-2007) NEW DELHI : The National Seeds Corporation (NSC) achieved an all time record turnover of Rs. 158.86 crore during 2006-07 recording a growth of more than 45% over the previous year. The profit after tax is 13.05 crore marking a 200% increase over 2005-06. Considering the impressive financial results, NSC has declared a dividend of 5% for the year 2006-07. The dividend cheque amounting to Rs. 103 lakh was presented to Shri Sharad Pawar, Minister of Agriculture, Consumer Affairs, Food and Public Distribution by Shri B.B. Pattanaik, Chairman cum Managing Director, NSC here today. Dr. P.K. Mishra, Secretary, Department of Agriculture and Cooperation was also present. NSC has taken several initiatives for brining improvement in its performance, which include forging Strategic Business Alliances for production, processing and marketing of seeds through Public-Public-Partnership with various State Governments, State Seed Corporations and leading seed companies in the private sector. During 2006-07, NSC entered into marketing of planting material of horticultural crop, bio-fertilisers, Bt Cotton seeds, etc. through tie up arrangements and introduced several new/improved varieties and hybrids of seeds. NSC is set to achieve a turnover of Rs. 175 crore during the current financial year.

3998. (2-11-2007) NEW DELHI : The Government is aware of the problems being faced by the garment exporters in the wake of the appreciation of the rupee. The Ministry of Textiles has taken up the matter with the Ministries of Commerce and Finance. This was stated by the Minister of Textiles, Shri Shankersinh Vaghela while addressing the meeting of the Consultative Committee of Ministry of Textiles, here today. Keeping in view the difficulties faced by the garment exporters, the Minister informed the members that the Government has revised the Duty Drawback and DEPB rates which will benefit the textile sector. In addition, premium on export credit guarantee have been reduced by 10%, rates of Duty Drawback enhanced by 10 to 40 % of the existing rates and the rate of interest on pre-shipment and post-shipment credit have been reduced by 2%. The Government has also released about Rs. 600 crores to clear all arrears of terminal excise duties and Central Sales Tax reimbursement, the Minister added. Regarding the Modified Rehabilitation Scheme of the NTC mills, the Minister informed the members that a schedule of implementation has been drawn up to modernize its 22 mills at the cost of approximately Rs. 540 crores. He hoped that 13 mills of NTC will be completely modernized by March next year and the remaining by March 2009. After the modernization, the NTC is projected to produce 600 lakh kilogram of yarn and 250 lakh metre of cloth annually with a turnover of more than Rs.931 crore in the year 2009-10. In addition, BIFR has also approved the modernization of 18 NTC mills through joint ventures. Out of these 18 mills, 2 mills at Coimbatore are likely to be dropped from the joint venture list due to improved performance and will be modernized by NTC itself. The Minister further informed that at present NTC is in the process of inviting proposals for joint ventures with private entrepreneurs to modernize and run some of these mills. He further stated that efforts of the Government to move NTC towards profitability has started bearing fruit and the dependence of the company on the Government has come down to Rs.60 crore from Rs. 300 crore annually. During the discussions, the Members raised several issues concerning modernization of NTC mills and problems faced by the garment exporters in the wake of rupee appreciation vis-à-vis US dollar. The Meeting was attended, among others, by the Minister of State for Textiles, Shri E.V.K.S. Elangovan, S/Shri D. Vittal Rao, Dhanuskodi Athithan, Mahesh Kumar Kanodia, Jai Prakash, Mohan Rawale, Member of Parliaments from Lok Sabha and Shri S. Anbalagan, Member of Parliament from Rajya Sabha.

3999. (2-11-2007) NEW DELHI : The Union Cabinet today gave its approval to pursue the National Jute Board Bill, 2006 in Parliament and to move official amendments in the said Bill at the time of consideration and passing in Lok Sabha. The decision was on the basis of recommendations made by the Parliamentary Standing Committee on Labour and relate to the expansion of functions and membership of the Jute Board and the definition of jute. The establishment of a National Jute Board as envisaged in the Government's National Jute Policy, 2005.

4000. (2-11-2007) NEW DELHI : The Union Cabinet today gave its approval to pursue the National Jute Board Bill, 2006 in Parliament and to move official amendments in the said Bill at the time of consideration and passing in Lok Sabha. The decision was on the basis of recommendations made by the Parliamentary Standing Committee on Labour and relate to the expansion of functions and membership of the Jute Board and the definition of jute.

4001. (2-11-2007) NEW DELHI : Central Water Commission (CWC) under Ministry of Water Resources is monitoring storage position of 81 important reservoirs spread all over the country, of which as many as 36 reservoirs have significant hydro-power benefits with installed capacity of more than 60 MW each. The combined live storage in these 81 reservoirs at the beginning of monsoon *i.e.* 1st June, 2007was 25 per cent of their designed capacity and stood at 79 per cent of the designed capacity as on 26th October 2007. The present storage is 94 per cent of the last year's storage and 119 per cent of last 10 years average storage during the same period. Out of these 81 reservoirs there are presently 9 reservoirs where this year's storage is 80 per cent or less than the average of previous 10 years and in the remaining 72 reservoirs the storage is more than 80 per cent of the average of previous 10 years. In order to derive the best possible benefits from the available water, Central Water Commission is keeping in touch with the Department of Agriculture and Cooperation and providing information of the weekly storage position to the Crop Weather Watch Group for evolving suitable crop strategies and also apprising the situation to various Departments and Ministries involved in Water Resources Planning.

4002. (2-11-2007) NEW DELHI : The Union Minister of Shipping, Road Transport and Highways, Thiru T.R. Baalu has approved a sum of Rs.702.49 lakh for road improvement works on NH-210 in the state of Tamil Nadu. National Highway-210 from Trichy to Ramanathapuram via Pudukkottai, Karaikkudi and Devakottai is an important National Highway in Tamil Nadu. This road connects the important marketing places, towns and leads to Rameswaram a renowned pilgrim centre.

4003. (2-11-2007) NEW DELHI : Farm commodity prices monitored by the Department of Consumer Affairs have generally remained steady or shown mixed trend over the week ending October 29, 2007. Prices of wheat at retail level remained steady at majority of the monitoring centres. The price declined at Jaipur and increased at Lucknow. Retail price of sugar remained steady over the week across most of the centres, but increased at Lucknow and Bhubaneshwar. Prices of gram dal have generally remained steady across majority of the monitoring centres. Prices increased at Delhi and Chennai. Prices of tur dal increased at Lucknow, Jaipur, Bhubaneshwar, Kolkata and Shillong. Over 6.44 lakh tonne of imported pulses have arrived at Indian ports out of 12.18 lakh tonne contracted by STC (3, 15, 000 T), Nafed (2, 60, 000 T), PEC (3, 87, 300 T) and MMTC (2, 56, 250 T). At Delhi, as on 29.10.07, prices of rice, tur dal, groundnut oil, mustard oil, vanaspati, milk and onion were holding steady for one week; those of wheat and salt for one month and price of loose tea was steady for 6 months.

4004. (3-11-2007) NEW DELHI : BJP National President Shri Rajnath Singh today questioned the intention of the communist parties in context of the recent claim of the CPM General Secretary Shri Prakash Karat that the strategic alliance between India and the United States was a move to "counter-balance" and "encircle" China. Shri Rajnath Singh said that such outdated remarks and discourses can only appeal to the intellect of Marxist theoreticians. Shri Rajnath Singh highlighted the fact that implicit in such preposterous claims are the indications of a self created illusionary mindset where the communists appear to believe that China's interests are being impacted. On the one hand, the communists publicly express their concerns for China, but on the other hand, maintain a deafening silence on critical national issues such as the continuing massacres and saga of violence being propagated by the Naxalites and Maoists across an increasing red corridor within the country, or the ruthless crushing of peasants who are fighting to protect their rights and honour in Nandigram. The BJP President questioned the CPM and other left parties for their stand on various issues. China has developed a deep naval base from Pakistan's Gwader to the Coco Island in Burma and right through Bangladesh and Sri Lanka has established posts to monitor the movement of Indian Navy. The Left Party never looked at it as encircling of India by China. They should also clarify their stand on other series of issues like China making ridiculous claims over Tawang and other parts of Indian territory. What was the stand of the left parties when China refused granting a visa to IAS officers from Arunachal Pradesh a few months ago? Why the communists opposed our Pohkran tests in 1998 when they had previously welcomed the Chinese nuclear tests in 1964? How do the communists explain their supporting the murder of democracy through the imposition of Emergency in 1975? Why did the communist parties refrain from calling China an aggressor in the 1962 war? Can the communists explain their support for partition of India in 1947? Or even their taking the side of the British imperialism during the Quit India Movement in 1942? The nation knows the truth about the historical dual character of the communists, whose postulations have always been diametrically opposed to the national ethos and mainstream, he added. Shri Rajnath Singh said the so called protectors of the masses, even after 30 years of textbook Marxist rule, which should have converted West Bengal into a "Marxist Paradise", have miserably converted it into a land of gross poverty and even unprecedented food riots. The comparison of one decade of BJP rule in Gujarat alone juxtaposed against the 30 years of Communist misrule in West Bengal singularly exposes the gap between tall claims and ground reality. The BJP President demanded a clarification from the government about today's news reports that the Central Government had actually issued a circular to prevent Cabinet ministers from attending a felicitation ceremony for the Dalai Lama. Has this circular also been issued under the pressure of the left parties and their concerns towards China, he wondered? The BJP President said that the nation is totally fatigued by the unending drama of the leftists whether they will permit the UPA government to complete its full term or withdraw support earlier. The Left Party position on this issue is like the shifting sands in a barren desert, a tactical strategy to confuse the nation by constantly changing positions on virtually a daily basis, he said. Shri Rajnath Singh finally wanted to know whether the entire opposition of the communist parties towards the Indo-US nuclear deal was inspired by Chinese concerns or an echo of the BJP's nationalist concerns about our strategic sovereignty, the right to develop credible nuclear deterrent and our entire nuclear weapons programme.

4005. (3-11-2007) NEW DELHI : Over 130 (one hundred and thirty) persons appeared before the Committee upto November 3, 2007. The views expressed cover wide range of issues varying from economic viability to environmental, navigational, security, historical, religious, social and developmental factors. Considering the large volume of work, the Committee, which was required to submit its report within one month from the day it starts functioning, has sought an extension for this time period from the Government. The Committee has decided to meet again at Chennai, after completion of personal hearings, on 14th and 15th November, 2007 Committee of Eminent Persons on Sethu Samudram Shipping Channel Project, Malligai, No 30/95, P.S. Kumarasamy Raja (Greenways) Road, Chennai-600 028.

4006. (4-11-2007) NEW DELHI : The Fourth International Conference on Federalism begins here tomorrow. It will be inaugurated by the Prime Minister, Dr. Manmohan Singh. The President, Smt. Pratibha Patil will deliver the valedictory address on Wednesday. The three-day conference is being organized in partnership between the Government of India and the Forum of Federations, a Canada-based international forum of federal countries. The earlier conferences were held in Canada 1999, Switzerland 2002 and Belgium 2005. The aim of the conference is to promote dialogue on the renewal and development of federalism and greater cooperation among practitioners in pursuit of good governance. The Conference will be unique in several respects. The principal actors will be practitioners of federal democracy at all levels including those heading Federal Governments to those heading constituent units and also those representing federal practice at the grassroots. There will also be scholars, experts, administrators and social activists dedicated to federalism. All participants will collectively engage in the process of sharing ideas, experiences and drawing inspiration from one another. They will all be treated equal and provided an environment conducive to a free and frank dialogue. There will be no occasions for 'official' statements of Government positions. The conference will be practitice oriented. It will provide a forum for the sharing of federalism best practices that ultimately contribute to better governance. About 1000 delegates are likely to attend the conference. They include President of Comoros, Mr. Ahmed Abdallah Mohamed Sambi, Prime Minister of Ethiopia, Mr. Meles Zenawi, President of Switzerland, Ms. Micheline

Calmy-Rey and Vice President of Nigeria, Mr. Jonathan Goodluck. Nearly 40 cabinet level Ministers and Provincial heads are expected to lead the delegations of their countries. International invites include Cabinet level Ministers, Provincial Heads, State level Ministers, Diplomats, Administrators, members of Judiciary, former Ministers, Civil Servants and representatives of International Organizations, etc. National Invites include Vice President, Speaker Lok Sabha, Central Cabinet Ministers, Secretaries to Govt of India, Governors, Chief Ministers, Leaders of national political parties, Chief Secretaries and Principal Secretaries of Departments concerned in the States, etc.

4007. (4-11-2007) NEW DELHI : The developments of the past 24 hours in Pakistan have become a matter for international concern. The concern in India is greater since Pakistan is our immediate neighbour. The Bharatiya Janata Party has always believed that the struggle for democracy in Pakistan is inseparable from the struggle against terrorism, which is backed by religious terrorism. The Party conveys its deep solidarity with the people of Pakistan in this hour of struggle in restoration of democracy and the rule of law. For the people of India, particularly for those either born or grew up after 1975, the developments of the past 24 hours in Pakistan is a replica of what India had gone through during the Internal Emergency. It is ironical that the developments were taking place in Pakistan on a day when the President of the AICC, which was responsible for the tyranny of Emergency in 1975, was accusing the BJP of being heartless and lacking concern for the people. The world has repeatedly witnessed democratic constitutions being subverted in the name of proclamation of emergency in order to institutionalize personal power through totalitarianism. Highlighting the threat of extremism, dangers of destabilization, and even encroachment by the judiciary into the Executive domain have been favourite slogans used by the dictators as an alibi for proclamation of emergency. Adolf Hitler used the fire in Richstag as a ground for proclaiming emergency in Germany. Mrs. Indira Gandhi used attempts at destabilizing the country as an alibi. It is not surprising that General Pervez Musharraf has used terrorism and judicial encroachment into the Executive domain to highlight the threat of destabilization. The common thread in the tale of these three emergencies is that there is an inbuilt desire in the proclaimer of the emergency to perpetuate personal power, usurp absolute power, eliminate all possibilities of losing that power and intolerance towards any form of criticism. The constitutional formulation is almost a straight jacket one. Firstly, proclaim a state of emergency on unsustainable grounds; secondly, eliminate the possibility of it being challenged by either terrorizing the judiciary or even replacing it with the pliable judges. Thirdly, eliminating any form of dissent by imposing fetters on the media in the form of censorship, denial of connectivity, arrest of editors, fourthly; suspension of civil liberties by providing for detention without trial and prohibiting judicial review against illegal detentions. Fifthly, arresting and detaining all political opponents. This is further accompanied by generation of atmosphere of personal sycophancy by proclaiming the dictator a saviour of the nation in the hour of crisis. Some proclaimers of emergency go a step further as in India they used the fear psychosis created by emergency to institutionalize and make acceptable a dynasty as an alternative to democracy. It is not uncommon for such proclaimers to then claim that it is ultimately the interest of the poor people that they have at heart whom the emergency will seek to support through faster economic growth. Adolf Hitler announced a 25 point economic programme; Mrs. Gandhi announced the 20-Point Economic programme and we still wait for such an announcement in Pakistan. The Bharatiya Janata Party is stating this so that a very large part of Indian population born after the mid-1970s may remind itself as to what the country had faced during the period of Internal Emergency in 1975-77. The Indian Nation displayed a great resilience in fighting the emergency. We hope for a similar success of our Pakistani counterparts.

4008. (5-11-2007) NEW DELHI : The President has summoned the Rajya Sabha to meet on Thursday, the 15th November, 2007 at New Delhi. Subject to exigencies of business, the Session is scheduled to conclude on Friday the 7th December, 2007 Rajya Sabha Secretariat, Parliament of India PIB, New Delhi.

4009. (5-11-2007) NEW DELHI : The Minister of Petroleum & Natural Gas Shri Murli Deora today held bilateral talks with his counterparts from Chad, Ethiopia and Comoros to accelerate and expand cooperation in various activities in the hydrocarbon sector. In a separate meeting with Mr. Emmanuel Nadingar, Ministre du Petrole from Chad here today, the two leaders discussed possibilities of India's assistance to chalk out exploration acreages and other technical services in the E&P sector. Training of petroleum sector personnel in upstream and down stream was also discussed during the meeting. The Indian side elaborated investment potential by oil PSUs in the overseas ventures which could support development of hydrocarbon industry in Chad. In the meeting with Mr. Alemayehu Tegenu, Minister of Mines and Energy of Ethiopia, the two leaders explored possibilities of cooperation in the oil and gas sector. Indian side suggested to rope in Engineers India Limited (EIL) in the engineering and other services. Similar assistance was also offered in largely unexplored E&P sector of Ethiopia along with utilizing Indian expertise in setting up refinery in the country. The Indian side offered its assistance in developing pipeline network along with building infrastructure for transportation of LNG in smaller quantities to the places which are not connected by pipelines. Ethiopian Minister showed keen interest in India's ethanol blended petrol programme and enquired about the progress in bio diesel production in the country. In his meeting with the Minister of Energy, Mine, Industry and Handicraft of Comoros Mr. Houmadi Abdallah, Shri Deora explained the Indian capabilities and the potential areas of cooperation between the enterprises of two countries. He pointed out that India is keen to take forward cooperation in the hydrocarbon sector between two countries. It was explained that EIL has capabilities in engineering and technical consultancy services in the refinery operations, turn around maintenance, de-bottlenecking studies, etc. The bilateral meeting with Ghana which was held at official level, focused on possibilities of developing CNG facilities in Ghana by GAIL. It was informed that the refinery expansion project planned by Ghana offers another area of cooperation in which EIL could assist in engineering and technical consultancy services. The refinery presently has a capacity of about 2 million tones per annum (MMTPA) which Ghana intends to raise to 5 MMTPA. Ghana also conveyed its interest in importing finished petroleum products from India as India has surplus refining capacity.

4010. (5-11-2007) NEW DELHI : The Defence Minister Shri AK Antony today said the Government is making all efforts to modernize the Indian Armed Forces in the earliest possible time to make it a strong fighting force by equipping it with the latest weapons and platforms but it will not be at the cost of transparency. Addressing the Parliamentary Consultative Committee, attached to his Ministry here today, Shri Antony said every reference from any responsible quarter on issues of corruption will be taken cognizance of and necessary probe will be carried out by the Ministry or the organizations under it. He said in the past there have been controversies relating to deals with some companies 'under cloud' and we will not proceed unless those doubts are cleared. "We will not tolerate corruption", he said. Shri Antony said India's Defence Cooperation with other countries has undergone a sea-change after the end of the Cold War era. India now sources its equipment and platforms from many countries including Russia, UK, France, Germany, Israel and of late, the United States. However, 'India's relationship with Russia is a time-tested one and will continue. We will not abandon old friends for improving relations with new ones', he said. Shri Antony described his recent visit to Russia as 'successful'. The Defence Ministers of the two countries signed an Inter-Governmental Agreement for the Joint Development and Production of the Fifth Generation Fighter Aircraft during Shri Antony's visit to Moscow, last month. He admitted that there was some delay in the delivery schedule of the Aircraft Carrier Admiral Gorshkov but said that the two countries are trying to find a solution to the issues involved.

4011. (5-11-2007) NEW DELHI : The 4th International Conference on Federalism began here this morning. Inaugurating the Conference, the Prime Minister said that in a world of multi-ethnic, multi-cultural plural societies, federal political systems face new political challenges. Managing tensions between centralization in certain spheres of governance and decentralization in others is a challenge for federalism. Dr. Manmohan Singh said that federalism has come to stay, because it has successfully mediated between the opposing pulls and pressures of individual identity and the needs of a national identity. Referring to the working of federalism in India, the Prime Minister mentioned some difficulties in eliminating fiscal barriers to inter-state movement of goods and in the utilization of national resources. Inter-regional disparities in the level of development constitutes a major challenge for the country's federal polity. River water sharing has posed another challenge to the management of federalism. The Prime Minister asked the Conference to reflect on certain issues including whether a single party state has any advantages in managing centre-state relations smoothly as opposed to a multiparty system and whether a multiparty model at the national level is capable of providing the unity of purpose that nation states have to often demonstrate. In his address, the Home Minister, Shri Shivraj Patil said that if used in a wise and imaginative manner, variety can add to the strength of the federal structure. He said that individuals and non-governmental organizations have to be recognized and allowed to work with the units and the federal structure to be able to utilize all the capabilities available in the society. The resources available with the units have to be used in a manner that the units separately and the federal structure in a united form benefit. Addressing the Conference, the Swiss President Ms. Micheline Calmy Rey, the Comoros President, Mr. Ahmed A M Ambi, the Nigerian Vice President, Dr. Goodluck Jonathan and the Ethiopian Prime Minister, Mr. Meles Zenawi dwelt on the benefits of federalism. The Chairman of the Forum of Federations, Dr. Arnold Koller said that the aim of the Conference is not to produce resolutions like an international, intergovernmental conference, but to exchange federal experiences and new ideas to learn from each other.

4012. (5-11-2007) NEW DELHI : India has received "Best Participating Award" and "Excellent Advertising Award" at the recently concluded China International Travel Mart 2007 in Kunming City. India was invited as a 'Guest of Honour Country' in the mart, which was attended by 96 countries. An Incredible India Pavilion was set up at the travel mart in an area of 225 sq.mtrs. to showcase the varied tourism products of the country. The main entrance gate of the India Pavilion was a replica of 'Sanchi Stupa Gate'. The Indian delegation at the mart was led by Additional Director General (Tourism), Shri, Sanjay Kothari. A total of 17 tour operators from India participated as co-exhibitors in the pavilion to promote packages to India. During the four day event, outdoor advertising at different locations and on the buses running in Kuming City was also done to showcase India's progress and vibrancy.

4013. (5-11-2007) NEW DELHI : In exercise of the powers conferred by clause (1) of article 224 of the Constitution of India, the President is pleased to appoint (i) Shri K. K. Sasidharan, (ii) Shri M. Venugopal and (III) Shri V. Periya Karuppiah to be Additional Judges of the Madras High Court, in that order of seniority, for a period of two years with effect from the dates they assume charge of their respective offices.

4014. (5-11-2007) NEW DELHI : The Bharatiya Janata Party takes a strong exception to Tamil Nadu Chief Minister M. Karunanidhi paying a poetic tribute to the slain LTTE insurgent Tamilselvan recently killed in a Sri Lankan Airforce attack. The country has earlier painfully witnessed the disdainful and blasphemous remarks against Lord Rama, followed by the recent lament of the slain LTTE activist by the Chief Minister of Tamil Nadu eulogising a dreaded extremist group.

This is dangerous and deserves the severest condemnation. The elated tribute by the DMK leader about a functionary of a banned outfit that has been officially declared a separatist and terrorist organization, is matter of grave concern. The DMK is an important ally of the UPA government and has Ministers in the Union Cabinet. The deafening silence of the Congress led UPA on Mr. Karunanidhi singing praises for the slain activist belonging to the dreaded extremist group is both disturbing and shocking. Apparently the lust of the Congress Party to cling to power at all costs at the Centre has obviously prompted them to turn a blind eye to such obeisance being paid by their leading alliance partner. That too in the backdrop where this particular banned outfit has been directly involved in the assassination of Rajiv Gandhi in 1991. The nation is already aware about helplessness of the Prime Minister. The fact that those associated with the assassination of Rajiv Gandhi are being eulogized by an important UPA ally and Mrs. Sonia Gandhji being silent about it is also a clear reflection of the Congress president's helplessness. The UP is an unholy alliance of mere convenience. Added to it is the complete debasement of the Congress Party in its quest for power which is even willing to ignore the tributes being paid to those who were directly responsible for the assassination of Rajiv Gandhi. The Bharatiya Janata Party demands that the Congress led UPA government must categorically clear their stand as to their allies sympathising with banned outfits.

4015. (5-11-2007) NEW DELHI : India has a major role in the future of global food business as it has a strong base in agriculture and provides a large and varied raw material base for Food Processing industry. It is a country of over 1.10 billion consumers and there is a largely untapped domestic market of 1000 million consumers in the food processing sector and two hundred million more consumers are expected to shift to processed food by 2010.

4016. (5-11-2007) NEW DELHI : Ministry of New and Renewable Energy will promote technologies to promote productive utilization of biomass for production of energy in Food and Fruit Processing industries in the country. Inaugurating a regional awareness workshop on Energy recovery and cogeneration Projects in Food and Fruit Processing industries today Sh. V. Subramanian, secretary, Ministry of New and Renewable Energy said that the ministry has decided to apply special focus to urban industrial wastes. Sh. Subramanian informed that three main technologies are being promoted by the ministry for productive utilization of biomass are bagasse-based cogeneration in sugar mills, bio-mass power generation and bio-mass gasification for thermal and electrical applications. Now the ministry will focus on food and fruit processing industries The technology is same, the efficiency will vary, hence each industry will have to implant to get maximum benefits. Referring to solar heating system used for drier in chilly, papad and even condoms industries, he said that this renewable energy is doable, profitable and environment friendly. The potential for cogeneration projects is estimated at 3500 MW of additional power generation from existing wastes from industries. He assured that the ministry is ready to give all technical support and interest subsidy. There is tremendous scope for captive power generation in the industries like dairies, starch, poultry, slaughter houses, oil extraction, breweries etc. This workshop was organized by Cogeneration Association of India and was sponsored by the Ministry of New and Renewable Energy.

4017. (5-11-2007) NEW DELHI : Following is the text of the convocation address of the Vice President of India Mohd. Hamid Ansari at the Indian Law Institute here today: "Ladies and Gentlemen, to one not formally lettered in the discipline of law, it is indeed a rare privilege to be invited to deliver the Convocation Address of the Indian Law Institute. Some familiarity with political science, supplemented by decades in the profession of diplomacy did, however, familiarize me with aspects of law and helped me in some measure to fulfil Blackstone's requirement that public duty cannot be discharged 'without some degree of knowledge in the laws'. This is a joyful occasion and I am happy to be a participant in it. A new group of young people is stepping out to join a profession whose relevance remains undiminished. A law school does not undertake to teach success. Its aim, said Judge Oliver Wendell Holmes of the American Supreme Court, is 'not to make men smart, but to make them wise in their calling' and to make them learn 'how to make facts live'. Law, remarked the jurist Carl Friedrich, is 'frozen history'. Record shows that the formulations of law have borne the imprint of human experience; this experience demonstrates a simple thesis: that humankind is a social creature whose existence in society is predicated on norms of behaviour. Thus Sir Paul Vinogradoff defined law as 'a set of rules imposed and enforced by a society with regard to the attribution and exercise of power over persons and things'. These rules are strengthened through recognition and thereby carry the element of consent based on a society's sense of equity and justice. Whenever the latter is perceived to be lacking an appeal is made, as Vinogradoff put it, 'from Caesar to a better informed Caesar' thought to be capable of delivering justice. Having decided upon the unavoidability of rules, every society in history addressed the question of the rule-giver and the law-enforcer. Here, the answer provided by Aristotle still holds good: ' When men are alike and equal, it is neither expedient nor just that one man should be the lord of all, whether there are laws, or whether there are no laws, but he himself is in the place of law'. From this arose, in terms of desirability and legitimacy, the idea of participatory governance or democracy. A condition of this legitimacy is the exclusion of arbitrary governance and the commitment of the State, firstly to its own laws and, secondly, to their uniform application.

4018. (5-11-2007) NEW DELHI : The Union Minister of Shipping, Road Transport and Highways, Thiru T.R. Baalu has approved a sum of Rs. 3122.22 lakh for road improvement work in the State of Uttar Pradesh. An amount of Rs. 1028.32 lakh has been approved for the work of widening and strengthening of existing single-lane carriageway to two-lane carriageway at Km 145.0 to km 158.040 of NH-

76. An amount of Rs. 994.05 lakh has also been approved at km. 89.600 to km. 102.0 of the same highway. NH-76 is an important Highway which connects tourist places of international importance such as Khajuraho, Chitrakoot and Allahabad. The stretches have developed undulations due to heavy loaded traffic and inadequate crust thickness. Therefore, the proposal for improvement of these stretches has been approved. Thiru Baalu has also approved an amount of Rs. 778.65 lakh for the work of improvement of Riding Quality from km 51.0 to 74.0 of NH-86. This highway starts from industrial town of Kanpur in UP and terminates at Sagar in Madhya Pradesh passing through Hamirpur, Mahoba and Chhatarpur. Further, an amount of Rs. 321.20 lakh has been sanctioned for the work of strengthening the road at km 477.0 to 484.0 of NH-76E. This important highway connects holy place of Vindhyachal Sidhpeeth to the major cities of UP such as Lucknow, Kanpur, Varanasi and Allahabad. The present condition of the road is not satisfactory and causing inconvenience to the road users, Therefore, the proposal to improve the NH stretch has been approved.

4019. (5-11-2007) NEW DELHI : Finance Minister Shri P. Chidambaram has personally appreciated the achievement of Shri F.D. Engineer, who is about 100 years old, for filing his Income-tax return on 31st July, 2007 along with payment of due taxes. He congratulated the tax payer and conveyed his best wishes. Shri Chidambaram asked the Income Tax Deptt. to process the Income-tax return of Shri Engineer, resident of Secunderabad, Andhra Pradesh, on 11th October, 07 and the same was done the next day.

4020. (5-11-2007) NEW DELHI : Direct tax collections maintained a growth of over 40 percent up to the period ended October 2007. Net tax collections stood at Rs.1, 28, 864 crore, up from Rs.90, 180 crore during the same period last fiscal registering a growth of 43.15 percent. Corporate tax recorded a growth of 45.71 percent at Rs.78, 785 crore, up from Rs.50, 072 crore during the previous fiscal. Personal income tax (including FBT, STT and BCTT) grew by 39.39 percent at Rs.49, 890 crore, up from Rs.35, 805 crore. Growth in Securities Transaction Tax (STT) was 57.61 percent (Rs.3, 783 crore against Rs.2, 400 crore) and Fringe Benefit Tax (FBT) was 29.94 percent (Rs.2, 755 crore against Rs.2, 120 crore). Banking Cash Transaction Tax (BCTT) grew by a modest 15.79 percent, indicating decreasing incidence of large cash withdrawals. In terms of payment types, advance tax increased by 28.44 percent and tax deducted at source (TDS) by 49.13 percent indicating all-round buoyancy in taxes. Self-assessment tax grew by 77.64 percent, indicating better tax compliance levels. Refund payouts in personal income tax (PIT) category were ahead by 47.16 percent (Rs.6, 135 crore against Rs.4, 169 crore), with over 30 lakh refunds having been issued during the period. The Refund Banker Scheme-launched in Delhi and Patna towards the end of last fiscal and extended subsequently to Kolkata, Chennai, Bangalore and Mumbai-has helped increase the pace of refunds. It will now be extended to the entire country for the PIT category of taxpayers. Continued buoyancy in direct tax collections indicates healthy growth in the economy, better tax administration and improving tax compliance levels.

4021. (5-11-2007) NEW DELHI : Inaugurating the National Workshop on Homoeopathy for Healthy Mother and Happy Child today, the Minister of State for Health & Family Welfare, Smt. Panabaaka Lakshmi said that with the mounting price rise of the modern drugs and increasing incidence of adverse drug reactions more and more people are now using Homoeopathy and the Homoeopathic institutions for the treatment of their ailments. Besides the Secretary and the Joint Secretary for the Department of AYUSH, Dr. Diwan Harish Chand, President, Scientific Advisory Committee, CCRH, Dr. Chaturbhuj Nayak, Director, CCRH, experts and practitioners from the field of Modern Medicine, Homoeopathy and other AYUSH streams were also present at the function. The Minister said that the objective of providing Homoeopathic treatments for mother and child health care can be achieved only when adequate Homoeopathic health care facilities are available throughout the country. In the 11th Plan, the outlay for the Department of AYUSH has been increased tremendously. There is a proposal to upgrade the National Institute of Homoeopathy, Kolkata as a Centre of Excellence in Homoeopathy. The Government is also proposing to establish a North Eastern Institute of Ayurveda and Homoeopathy at Shillong. The Government has already notified the GMP for Homoeopathic drug units. We have already strengthened the Homoeopathic Pharmacopoeia Laboratory. Financial assistance has been given to establish model colleges in Kerala, Andhra Pradesh, West Bengal, Orissa and Madhya Pradesh. With all these steps, the Homoeopathic system is going to expand enormously.

4022. (5-11-2007) NEW DELHI : The Prime Minister, Dr. Manmohan Singh, addressed the inaugural session of the 4th International Conference on Federalism here today. Speaking on the occasion the Prime Minister said that reducing inter-regional disparities is essential for the success of a federal structure. Dr. Manmohan Singh stated that in a world of multi-ethnic, multi-cultural plural societies, federal political systems face new political challenges. We need creative thinking and redesign of institutions to allow the federal concept to adjust to emerging and changing realities, the Prime Minister added.

4023. (5-11-2007) NEW DELHI : The Congress party said here that, the entire nation has witnessed the unscrupulous and opportunistic political drama that has been unfolding in Karnataka over the last few days. The BJP and JD(S) have totally destroyed the concept of constitutional governance by trying to cynically manipulate and distort the fractured mandate given by the people of Karnataka, in a manner that will further their own lust for power. The situation in Karnataka is unprecedented in Indian democracy, or in any democracy. Having formed an opportunistic alliance, to begin with, the glue of power fell apart very quickly. Following upon Mr. H. D. Kumaraswamy refusing to hand over power to the BJP, the entire structure of governance has collapsed. Thereafter began the worst perversion of democracy, ever witnessed in Indian history. BJP leaders, denounced the JD(S) in the strongest possible terms. Mr. Deva Gowda wrote to the Prime Minister and demanded the dissolution of the Assembly. The Chief Minister refused to support the BJP, and declared that communal forces would prevail in Karnataka if the BJP came to power. Full page advertisements appeared in Karnataka newspapers, explaining why the JD(S) could not support the BJP. Thereafter in a sudden volte face, Mr. Kumaraswamy announced that he would support the BJP, but on a conditional basis. A large section of the JD(S) publicly opposed this. The BJP proceeded to flout all norms and principles, and totally went back on its own stand, by staking a claim to form the Government with the support of the JD(S), which had been publicly denounced by the BJP only days earlier. The BJP went on a dharna asking the Governor to call on the BJP, to form the government, but the dharna was neither joined nor supported by the JD(S) or by Mr. Kumaraswamy, who continued to say that he would extend only conditional support. Mr. Deva Gowda's demand for dissolution still stands as also the opposition to forming a Government along with the BJP from senior JD(S) leaders. It is crystal clear that the mandate of the people of Karnataka stands completely destroyed by this opportunistic and unprincipled manipulation of MLAs by the BJP. Any attempt whatsoever to attempt to form a Government on such an immoral and unstable foundation would be unconstitutional and unsustainable. It would also constitute major injustice to the people of Karnataka, and make a mockery of the legislative process and the Constitution of India. The proposal by the BJP to unnaturally cobble together a Government on support which is not only inherently unstable, but also fundamentally inimical to the BJP will destroy and subvert our democratic process. This should not be allowed, and the Constitution of India should be upheld at all cost. The only moral, ethical and democratic way forward out of this ugly imbroglio, would be to dissolve the Karnataka Assembly, and for all political parties to seek a fresh mandate from the people. To a question that if the Governor recommends revoking President's rule in Karnataka and allows them to stake claim to form a government would it be unconstitutional Smt. Jayanti said I am not commenting on what the Governor has said as I have no knowledge of it but in our view the stand taken publicly by the JD(S) and the BJP are fundamentally inimical, hostile to each other. Shri Deve Gowda's letter seeking dissolution of the Assembly still stands and even in his last meeting with the Governor Shri Kumaraswamy has said that he could offer only conditional support. Earlier he had said, in order to prevent communal forces it is important not to let the BJP form the government. It is only yesterday again that he has changed his mind and said publicly, not to the Governor, that now they are willing to offer unconditional support. Therefore, it is our assertion that this is inherently unstable and unnatural alliance which is basically a complete perversion and subversion of the Constitution process.

4024. (5-11-2007) NEW DELHI : The Chairperson of National Commission for Protection of Child Rights (NCPCR), Government of India has directed all District Magistrates to make the children aware of their rights. In a letter addressed to

District Magistrates she has asked to launch a campaign and have direct interaction with children in schools, hostels, orphanages, juvenile observation homes, children's homes and shelter homes and all other public institutions meant for children on the occasion of Bal Divas, on 14th November to make them aware of their rights.

4025. (6-11-2007) NEW DELHI : There has been a hundred percent increase in international flights to and from the state of Kerala including Calicut in the last three years. During the recent visit of the Minister for Civil Aviation Shri Praful Patel to Calicut, the Minister had announced that operation of foreign airlines to and from Calicut would be started from the first quarter of 2008. In the interest of more reliable connectivity to the state of Kerala, Air India will soon provide stand by aircraft for its Kerala operation.

4026. (6-11-2007) NEW DELHI : A Committee is being constituted in DoT to recommend the revision of present "Spectrum Allocation Criterion" to Licensed operators based on the subscriber figures etc. in a scientific and practicable manner. The Committee will have outside experts also. Cellular Operators Association of India and Association of Unified Service Providers of India will also be associated with the Committee. Government had accepted in principle the technical report of Telecom Engineering Centre on Spectral Efficiency on 31st October 2007. The Committee will give its report within three weeks for finalization of spectrum allocation criterion for licensed operators. Further allocation of spectrum to any category shall be determined on the basis of recommendations of committee and directions of TDSAT, if any. Pending applications for grant of new Unified Access Services licenses will be processed as per the existing policy.

4027. (6-11-2007) NEW DELHI : Speaking at the Valedictory Session of the National Campaign on Homoeopathy-Workshop for Healthy Mother and Happy Child, the Union Minister for Health & Family Welfare, Dr. Anbumani Ramadoss said today, that these national campaigns being launched by the Department of AYUSH will be serving a very useful purpose of focusing attention on the urgent need to integrate the Indian Systems of Medicine and Homoeopathy with mainstream health care in the country. The integration of AYUSH services with mainstream health care has long been the stated policy of the Government, but practical integration has not really taken place in most parts of the country. By focusing on specific AYUSH interventions for common health and disease conditions, these national campaigns will, I hope, generate more enthusiasm among health administrators for integrating Indian Systems of Medicine and Homeopathy with mainstream health care in the country. The two-day Workshop was organized by the Central Council for Research in Homoeopathy (CCRH), Department of AYUSH as a part of the National Campaign on Homoeopathy for Mother and Child Care. Besides Dr. V.K. Gupta (former Principal, Nehru Homoeopathic Medical College and Hospital, Delhi), the function was also attended by Smt. Anita Das, Secretary (AYUSH), Dr. N.K. Ganguly, DG, ICMR, Shri Verghese Samuel, Joint Secretary

(AYUSH), Dr. S.P. Singh, Adviser, (Homoeo), (AYUSH), Prof. C. Nayak, Director, CCRH and other senior officials from the Ministry.

4028. (6-11-2007) NEW DELHI : Deliberations by eminent dignitaries continued on the second day of the 4th International Conference on Federalism here today. Addressing the conference, the former President, Dr. A.P.J. Abdul Kalam advocated a region-oriented approach to development in a federal set-up. He said that developmental schemes and solutions to problems need to be region-based, because our resources, climate and terrain are region-based with unique cultures of regions. The states should work to their core competence and complement one another. Overall planning at the central level should focus on regional development. In his address, the Minister for Power, Shri Shushil Kumar Shinde said that the country as vast as ours could not have progressed as well as it did without a federal structure. Discussions in theme sessions also got underway today. The Conference is based on four broad themes and twelve sub-themes. The topics for theme sessions include Building on and Accommodating Diversities, Emerging Issues in Fiscal Federalism, Interaction in a Federal system and, Local Government and Federal Systems. For the first time, local government has been chosen as the topic of a theme session. Addressing the Conference yesterday evening, the External Affairs Minister, Shri Pranab Mukherjee called for hastening the process of devolution of power at the grass-roots level. He said that without a sense of participation in governance, there can be no credible empowerment. In his address, the Minister for Panchayati Raj, Youth Affairs & Sports and Development of North Eastern Region, Shri Mani Shankar Aiyar said that the only way to achieve inclusive growth is by strengthening Panchayats, the third tier of democracy. Addressing the Conference, the Lok Sabha Speaker, Shri Somnath Chatterjee said that democratic governments are better equipped to maintain a cohesive policy amidst diverse interests and priorities. He stressed the need to amicably resolve all fiscal issues without jeopardizing national unity and integrity. The three-day conference is being organized by the Inter State Council Secretariat of the Government of India in partnership with the Forum of Federations, a Canada based international forum of federal countries. The earlier conferences were held in Canada in 1999, Switzerland in 2002 and Belgium in 2005.

4029. (6-11-2007) NEW DELHI : The Union Rural Development Minister, Dr. Raghuvansh Prasad Singh has asked the State/UT Secretaries in-charge of Rural Drinking Water and Sanitation Programmes to visit the rural areas of their respective states on random selection basis so that the implementation of Centrally sponsored schemes meant for rural development, specially related with the Total Sanitation Campaign (TSC) and drinking water supply could gain further momentum. Addressing a two-day review meeting of State/UT Secretaries in-charge of Rural Drinking Water and Sanitation Programmes here today Dr. Singh emphasised the need of tightening and sensitizing the machinery at local level. He also asked to employ voluntary organisations in this process wherever needed. Keeping in mind that the United Nations is has declared the year 2008 as the International Year of Sanitation, it is the need of hour that concerted efforts for millenium goal target under TSC be made in perfection, the minister added. Taking stock of the implementation status of Total Sanitation Campaign in all the participating states/ UTs except the north-eastern states the minister wanted to know the up to date information of works taken up at the village and panchayat level, specially in the schools and Aanganwadi centres as well as at individual household level and the initiation of process for the next Nirmal Gram Puraskars (NGP). The minister further asked the states to furnish the implementation report on monthly basis Referring to recently added Solid and Liquid Waste Management scheme for processing it into manure, the Dr. Singh also pressed for the spread of mass awareness and the inherent as well as coherent benefits of TSC among the rural beneficiaries. The other issues taken up in the meeting were related with the implementation of Accelerated Rural Water Supply Scheme (ARWSP) during the 11th Plan and Online Data Entry and Updation of Integrated Management Information System (IMIS), Progress and review of Sub-Mission Projects to avoid surrender of funds, revision of targets for tackling of quality affected habitations and NRDWQM&S programmes, the Swajaldhara Programme and the Bharat Nirman. Besides the State and UT Secretaries, the Minister of State for Rural Development Shri Chandra Sekhar Sahu, Shri Gouri Shankar Ghosh, Chairman of High powered Technical Expert Group (TEG), Shri Atul Chaturvedi, Additional Secretary, Drinking Water Supply and Shri A. Bhattacharya, Joint Secretary Drinking Water Supply were also present in the meeting. The two-day meet will conclude tomorrow.

4030. (6-11-2007) NEW DELHI : The External Affairs Minister, Mr. Pranab Mukherjee has reiterated India's high resolve at attaining energy security as a matter of national importance for which prospects are being relentlessly explored for sourcing energy from India's neighbourhood and beyond. He said that the newly created Energy Security Unit in the MEA would maintain close coordination with other ministries concerned as well as public and private corporate entities to support their international engagement through appropriate diplomatic intervention. Inaugurating the India-Africa Hydrocarbon Conference, orgainsed jointly by the Ministry of Petroleum and Natural Gas and FICCI with the support of UNCTAD, Mr. Mukherjee said, here today that India would need to expand its current primary energy supply levels by three to four times and electricity generation by five to six times in the next two and half decades to sustain the high growth levels required to attain the developmental goals and eradicate poverty. He underlined that the task of investing in overseas energy assets has therefore become an important aspect of our economic diplomacy. In addition, the Minister said, "the possibility of bilateral cooperation in the downstream sectors, petrochemicals, non-conventional energy and joint ventures are constantly being explored with various resource-rich countries." The first ever India-Africa Hydrocarbon Conference & Exhibition will conclude tomorrow .India, he said, was increasingly looking at taking forward its partnership with Africa as the country was a natural market for Africa's rich hydrocarbon resources. Prospects for cooperation with African nations have received a boost with a surge in investments by Indian companies in countries such as Libya, Sudan, Nigeria, Egypt and Gabon over the past few years, he said. Mr. Mukherjee said: "India stands ready to share its experience with its African partners in the hydrocarbon sector, from exploration to distribution through refining, storage and transportation. It is crucial that over a period of time, investment in this sector should directly assist in the building up of a trained and skilled workforce capable of efficiently running the assets." Mr. Murli Deora, Union Minister for Petroleum and Natural Gas, expressed India's keen desire to partner with African nations by offering its expertise in the upstream and downstream sectors through technology, training, investments, research and development. He called for institutionalizing cooperation between India and African countries at the government-to-government level to address the macro policy issues; at the company and trade body level for joint cooperation in the development of upstream and downstream assets; and at the research institution level to facilitate the setting up of laboratories, carrying out research and technology transfer.

4031. (6-11-2007) NEW DELHI : The President, after consultation with the Chief Justice of India, is pleased to transfer Shri Justice Ananda Prakash Subba, Judge of the Guwahati High Court as a Judge of the Sikkim High Court and the direct him to assume charge of his office in the Sikkim High Court on or before 10th November, 2007.

4032. (6-11-2007) NEW DELHI : In exercise of the powers conferred by clause (1) of article 224 of the Constitution of India, the President is pleased to appoint (i) Shri Biswanath Mahapatra, (ii) Shri Bhabani Prasad Ray, and (iii) Shri Subhash Chandra Parija, to be Additional Judges of the Orissa High Court, in that order of seniority for a period of two years, with effect from the dates they assume charge of their respective offices. The President is also pleased to appoint (i) Shri Justice Amar Nath Jindal and (ii) Shri Justice Mohinder Mohan Singh Bedi, Additional Judges of the Punjab & Haryana High Court, to be Judges of the Punjab & Haryana High Court, in that order of seniority, with effect from the dates they assume charge of their respective offices.

4033. (6-11-2007) NEW DELHI : The National Commission for Enterprises in the Unorganised Sector (NCEUS), under the Ministry of Micro, Small and Medium Enterprises presented two reports to the Prime Minister, Dr. Manmohan Singh on 5th November, 2007. The two reports are on the 'Financing of Enterprises in the Unorganised Sector' and on 'Creation of a National Fund for the Unorganised Sector' (NAFUS). The recommendation on the creation of a National Fund follows from the first report. Addressing a Press Conference here today, Dr. Arjun Sengupta, Chairman, NCEUS said that the report on 'Financing of Enterprises in the Unorganised Sector' deals with financing of the enterprises in the non-farm unorganised sector. It examines in depth the status of financing of the sector and deals with deficiencies in institutional infrastructure and constraints in financing this sector. The Report, besides giving its recommendation on financing has also made a recommendation for the creation of NAFUS. The second Report submitted to the Prime Minister deals in details with the recommendation of creation of NAFUS. The Report on NAFUS gives the rationale, organizational model, functions and sources of financing of the Fund. The mandate for the creation of this Fund derives from the National Common Minimum Programme of the UPA Government. Giving the details of the proposed Fund, Dr. Sengupta said, the National Fund proposed by the Commission is envisaged as a statutory body funded by the Central Government and Financial Institutions that will primarily focus on non-farm micro enterprises with investment of less than Rs. Five lakh. The Commission's report reveals that this segment constitutes 94 per cent of all small enterprises estimated at 58 million in 2007 with a total employment of 104 million. Dr. Sengaupta further said that this Fund would be created on the pattern of NABARD and exclusively meant for meeting the financing and promotional assistance gaps in the development of the Non Farm Unorganised Sector. Being a statutory body it would leverage funds from the market and national and international institutions to meet its objectives, he added.

4034. (6-11-2007) NEW DELHI : Shri Barry Todd, Hon'ble Deputy Minister, Department of Agriculture, Food and Rural initiatives, Province of Manitoba, Canada along with a delegation called on Shri Kantilal Bhuria, Minister of State for Agriculture, CA, Food and Public Distribution here today and held discussions on the proposed MOU between the two countries. Welcoming the delegation, Shri Bhuria said India is deeply interested in promoting bilateral relations with Canada. Substantial progress has been made in the discussions on the proposed MOU between the two countries. Subsequent to the proposal initiated by Canada, Ministry of Agriculture has identified Knowledge Exchange in Agriculture, Sanitary and Phyto-Sanitary issues and post Harvest technologies and grain handling as potential areas for fruitful cooperation, he added. The Minister recalled his visit to Canada in June 2007 and said he was inspired by the potential for collaboration in the field of agricultural research specially production technology in winter wheat and pulse for increasing productivity, research in fruit sector specially apple production in branchless trees, packaging technologies to increase shelf life of vegetables such as tomatoes and these could be potential areas of our interest. Impressed with the grain storage programme at Manitoba University and since India is concerned about maintaining the quality of the stored grains, Shri Bhuria informed that a suitable provision has been proposed in the MOU.

4035. (6-11-2007) NEW DELHI : India will provide expertise to the small defence forces of the Central African Republic of Gabon in disaster management, training and healthcare. This was agreed during talks between the visiting Senior Minister for National Defence of Gabon, Mr. Ali Bongo Ondimba and the Defence

Minister Shri AK Antony in New Delhi last night. Shri Sanjeeva Kumar, Joint Secretary in the Defence Ministry, later gave a presentation on the potential for cooperation during the delegation level talks. Ties between the two countries have been expanding since the visit of a high-level Ministerial delegation led by the Gabonese President Mr. El Hadj Omar Bongo Ondimba to India in May last year. India offered a $14.5 million Line of Credit to Gabon for a housing project during the visit of Gabonese Deputy Minister of Housing Development in July, this year. However, there have been no high-level visits to Gabon from the Indian side. Gabon, which is slightly bigger than Uttar Pradesh in size, has a very small military of about 10, 000 personnel, divided into army, navy, air force and national police. Besides, France, who ruled Gabon for 75 years till 1960, maintain a battalion of 750 marines in the African nation located on the Atlantic Coast. Gabon, whose oil sector accounts for nearly half its GDP, quit the Organisation of Petroleum Exporting Countries (OPEC) in 1995.

4036. (6-11-2007) NEW DELHI : Railways have added another mile stone by signing a joint venture agreement here today, with National Thermal Power Corporation Ltd. (NTPC) to set up a 1000 MW power plant-Bhartiya Rail Bijlee Company Limited at Nabinagar in Bihar. Speaking on the occasion, the Minister for Railways, Shri Lalu Prasad said that nearly 18, 000 route kilometer, out of more than 63, 000 route kilometres of Indian Railways network, has already been electrified which constitutes 28 per cent of the total rail network carrying nearly 63 per cent of freight and 47.8 per cent of passenger traffic. The Minister said that Railways are spending about Rs. 5700 crore per annum for consumption on more than 13000 million units of electricity towards electric energy for traction and non-traction purposes. In order to derive full benefits of the ongoing reforms in power sector, the Minister said that, a decision has been taken by the Ministry of Railways in consultation with the Ministry of Power to set up power projects in joint venture with National Thermal Power Corporation Ltd. The Minister further observed that this is also the need of the hour especially in view of the demands of a globalising economy and mega projects of the Railways such as the planned Dedicated Freight Corridors across the country. The Nabinagar power plant, to be built at a cost of Rs. 5352 crore, will be of 1000 MW capacity and 10 per cent of power from this plant is earmarked to other users. The equity portions of NTPC and Indian Railways will be 74 per cent (Rs. 1188 crore) and 26 per cent (Rs. 417 crore) respectively. Indian Railways is thereby expected to save approximately Rs. 600 crore per annum. The electricity from this plant will be utilized by Indian Railways for running electric trains in Bihar, Jharkhand, West Bengal, Chhattisgarh, Maharashtra, Gujarat and Madhya Pradesh in the eastern and western regions of the country. The Minster said that setting up of such joint venture power project plants will benefit the nation as it would mean net addition to the generation capacity. The Union Power Minister Shri Shushilkumar Shinde complimented the Minister for Railways for the spectacular growth of Railways in the recent past in general and for the proactive initiative for the setting up of this power plant at Nabinagar in Bihar in particular. He added that this joint venture will be mutually beneficial for both the Ministries of Railways and Power in view of the ever rising demand for power in the country. He further added that such cooperation would help pave the way for achieving the target of providing power to each household by the end of the 11th Plan period.

4037. (6-11-2007) NEW DELHI : The Union Minister of Shipping, Road Transport and Highways, Thiru T.R. Baalu has approved a sum of Rs.635.10 lakh for road improvement works on NH-208 in the state of Tamil Nadu. NH-208 is an important National Highway of interstate connectivity connecting Kerala and Tamil Nadu from Kollam to Thirumangalam. This road also connects the important towns like Shencottah, Tenkasi, Rajapalayam to important tourist centres like Sabarimala, Courtallam and Madurai .

4038. (6-11-2007) NEW DELHI : The 2nd Asian Ministerial Conference on Disaster Risk Reduction begins here tomorrow. The two-day event will be inaugurated by the Prime Minister, Dr. Manmohan Singh. 52 countries from the Asia and Pacific Region have confirmed participation in the Conference. 33 country delegations will be led by their Ministers. The total country delegates will be about 150. In addition, more than 100 experts and 50 NGOs will also be participating. The World Conference on Disaster Risk Reduction was held in 2005 at Hyogo, Kobe, Japan in which Hyogo Framework of Action 2005-15 was adopted for building the resilience of nations and communities to natural disasters. The first Asian Ministerial Conference on Disaster Risk Reduction was held in September 2005 in Beijing in which Action for Disaster Risk Reduction in Asia was adopted. The objectives of this conference are to review the action taken by the various national Governments on the Hyogo Framework of Action, review the implementation of the Beijing Action for Disaster Risk Reduction in Asia, take stock of initiatives taken in various sub-regions of Asia for promoting cooperation within and outside the Governments, share best practices on Disaster Risk Reduction, discuss new international initiatives such as global platform and global facility for Disaster Risk Reduction and develop a vision and road map for Disaster Risk Reduction in Asia. The Conference will have an inter-governmental segment to deliberate on four themes namely, mainstreaming disaster risk reduction in national policies and programmes, enhancing public-private partnership in Disaster Risk Reduction, integrating disaster reduction into rehabilitation and reconstruction activities and promoting regional cooperation in Disaster Risk Reduction. Two technical groups will deliberate on the theme of application of science and technology in Disaster Risk Reduction and on integrating Disaster Risk Reduction in development. An exhibition on disaster management is also being organized in which various national and international organisations will be participating.

4039. (6-11-2007) NEW DELHI : The President of India, Smt. Pratibha Devisingh Patil has condoled the passing away of the President of Ramakrishna Mission,

Swami Gahanananda. In her condolence message, the President has said that the Swami was dedicated to the welfare of the poor and needy throughout his life.

4040. (6-11-2007) NEW DELHI : Minister for Petroleum & Natural Gas, Shri Murli Deora, said today, it is indeed an honour for us to receive all the dignitaries from various African Countries. I thank all of you for taking time out from your busy schedules and for reinforcing our commitment to further deepen the cooperation between India and Africa in the vital energy sector. India, as we all know, is experiencing accelerated economic growth. Annual growth rates of between 8% & 9% are driving the nation's increasing demand for energy. Like many other countries, it is natural that India too should be concerned about existing and potential sources of supply for meeting its requirements on a sustained basis. India faces formidable challenges in meeting its energy needs. According to the Integrated Energy Policy document of the Government of India, the country would need to expand its current primary energy supply levels by 3-4 times and electricity generation by 5-6 times in the next 25 years in order to sustain the high growth levels required to attain our developmental goals and to eradicate poverty. Owing to the limited availability of oil and gas within our own country, 70% of our energy requirements are dependent on hydrocarbon imports. What is of particular concern to us is that this import dependence is only going to accentuate further in the coming years. This realization has pushed all of us to adopting proactive approaches for ensuring our energy security, particularly with reference to hydrocarbons, which account for nearly half of India's total energy needs. The task of investing in overseas energy assets for the country has, therefore, become an important aspect of our economic diplomacy. Indian oil companies have concluded arrangements, including investment agreements, with many countries for the supply of oil and its derivatives to India and in most of the cases, delivery has begun. In addition, the possibility of bilateral cooperation in the downstream sectors, petrochemicals, non-conventional energy and joint ventures are also being constantly explored with various resource-rich countries.

4041. (7-11-2007) NEW DELHI : India today outlined an 8-point Cooperation Framework in the hydrocarbon sector at different levels between India and African nations at India-Africa Conference & Exhibition on Hydrocarbons which concluded on a high note here today. The 8-point agenda, mooted by Mr. Murli Deora, Union Minister for Petroleum and Natural Gas, while addressing the Valedictory Session of the conference, envisages forging of Hydrocarbon cooperation agreements between India and the various African countries covering E&P and Downstream policy issues; Cooperation between business entities covering joint development of E&P and Refining businesses through MoUs; Increased oil trade between Indian oil refineries and African oil and gas producing nations on a mutually beneficial basis; Establishing Joint Working Groups for focused discussions where none exist now; Exchange of visits on an increasing scale between businesses and government delegations on a periodic basis to ensure time-bound progress; Cooperation in the area of Research & Development and Technology Transfer;

Cooperation in Retail Marketing of petro products and lubricants by Indian companies in the African markets; Training of technical and managerial personnel of the African oil industry in India. Referring to the successful hosting of the Conference, Mr. Deora pointed out that the range of activities and discussions held during the last two days provided ample evidence of the eagerness with which India and the African countries wish to cement their relationship in the hydrocarbon sector. "This fruitful beginning should be utilized for even more activities and ventures between us so that our citizens are the ultimate beneficiaries in terms of increased economic activity, " the Minister added. In his address, Mr. Anand Sharma, Minister of State for External Affairs, stated that in today's era of globalization, the problems of one region are not confined to it alone. In fact, the effect is cascading and wide-ranging. "The scourge of hunger, disease and the imperative need to build food security make it incumbent upon us to share our strengths and technologies in the hydrocarbon sector for the benefit of the people of Africa and India, " Mr. Sharma said, adding that it was important to access available resources optimally and develop new and renewable energy sources. Mr. Sharma said the African nations were rich in hydrocarbon resources and India's special engagement with Africa, in a partnership mode, gives us the confidence to cooperate by accessing hydrocarbons resources and sharing our technical expertise with Africa. The Minister said over 15, 000 students from Africa were pursuing various courses of study in India, and more than 2, 000 amongst them were getting specialized training. He mentioned the possibility of training of African people in India's institutions and offered to augment the programmes to take in more students from Africa.

4042. (7-11-2007) NEW DELHI : The President, Smt. Pratibha Devisingh Patil addressed the valedictory session of the 4th International Conference on Federalism here today. Following is the text of her speech on the occasion: "I consider it as an honour to participate at the Valedictory function of the Fourth International Conference on Federalism, organized by the Inter-State Council in collaboration with the Forum of Federations. I am happy to note that the Conference is being attended by a large number of practitioners-elected representatives, civil servants, civil society representatives and young professionals from every continent. The theme and issues on which you have deliberated during the last three days-"Unity in Diversity: Learning from Each Other"-has a special relevance in our contemporary world. For us in India, federalism and the preservation of the underlying unity in our diversity are of great importance. We are particularly pleased that we are hosting this Conference just as we have completed the 60th year of our independence. We are proud that in these years we have not only reaffirmed but also strengthened our commitment to democracy, federalism and respect for diversity. India is a country with an enormous plurality in language, religion, culture and ethnicity. India is a country of more than one billion people. One out of every six human beings in the world lives in India. 22 Indian languages are listed in our Constitution and more than 1, 600 dialects are spoken in India. Every religion has its followers in India. From the mountains of Kashmir to the waters of Kanyakumari and from the deserts of Rajasthan to the forests of the North-East, Indians celebrate their varied cultures, festivals and religions and they effortlessly unite to make India a great nation. When India attained its Independence in 1947, the process of nation building began. The Founding Fathers of our Constitution were acutely aware that a country as large in size and as diverse as India demanded a system in which local initiative and central administration were blended. Hence, in the Constitution of India adopted in 1950, the political structure was organized into a Union, States and the elected bodies of local self-government. The working of the Constitution has demonstrated the inherent strength and resilience of the Indian federal structure in withstanding the stresses and strains of diverse aspirations of the people. The Indian Constitution is a living document and has also been amended from time to time reflecting its resilience and dynamism. A significant Constitutional step was taken in 1993 to make "every village a republic". The concepts of democracy and federalism were maximized when people at the grassroots were empowered to elect their own representatives and to plan and implement programmes for their own economic development. As a consequence of the historic amendments to the Constitution, which the late Prime Minister Rajiv Gandhi initiated, we now have a huge network of institutions of local self-government, to which we have elected some 3.2 million representatives, about 1.2 million of whom are women. This is by far the largest number of elected representatives ever in history, or anywhere in the contemporary world. Women, particularly, were given an opportunity through a system of reservation in the local bodies. We, in India, have understood that Unity in Diversity is the real strength of our country. By looking after the interests of each section of our diverse population, we strengthen our unity. It is, therefore, not surprising that India is today counted among federal democracies that have been successful in adopting an inclusive polity.

4043. (7-11-2007) NEW DELHI : In the context of meeting the growing demand for coal from the fast growing national economy underground coal production emerges as an opportunity. This was stated by the Ministry of State for Coal Dr. Dasari Narayana Rao while addressing the first ever Parliamentary Consultative Committee meeting on "Underground Coal Mining-Challenges and Opportunities" at Hyderabad today. He said that the demand for coal in the country will increase to above 2000 million tones per year 2031-32 from that of 463.5 million tones in 2006-07. There is a need to make concerted efforts to ensure the energy security of the country. The Government has already started taking necessary initiatives in this regard he said. Regarding decrease of share of underground coal production to 13 per cent in the total production during 2006-07, from 76 per cent of total production, the Minister said that this was on account of the need to increase production to meet the growing demand from power sector through the easy option of opencast mining. The other factors are difficult underground mining conditions, reserves not being amenable to adoption of underground mass production technology, low mechanization of underground mines, high cost of production etc.

He said that broad strategies to be followed to increase underground coal production including planning new underground mines with mass production systems like continuous miners and long wall technology wherever feasible, entering into risk or gain sharing agreements with equipment suppliers for guaranteed level of production and maintenance of equipment, training of manpower, creation of infrastructural facilities for ventilation, coal evacuation and transportation etc. The Minister stated that following the measures taken by the Government to ensure timely production of coal from coal blocks, it is estimated that a production of 104 Mt. of coal outside the domain of Coal India Limited (CIL) and Singareni Collaries Company Limited (SCCL) during 2011-12, as against only 17 Mt. during 2006-07 will be made. The Government is taking all possible steps to increase the production of coal and reducing the losses, he added. The meeting was attended by Shri Chandrasekhar Dubey, Shri Bagun Sumbrui, Sri Guharam Ajgalle, Smt. Ingrid Mcleod, Shri Chandradev Prasad Rajbhar, Sri Maniksingh, Sri Ghuran Ram, Sri Furkan Ansari and Sri Bhubneshwar Prasad Mehta from Lok Sabha and Sri V. Hanumantha Rao, Sri Surendra Lath, Sri Sudarshan Akarapu and Sri Motiur Rahman from Rajya Sabha, Sri H.C. Gupta, Secy., Department of Coal, Chairman & Managing Directors of CIL, SCCL, Neyveli Lignite Corporation, Subsidiaries of CIL and Senior officials of the Ministry of Coal.

4044. (7-11-2007) NEW DELHI : The President, Smt. Pratibha Patil has said that democracy and federalism should be the guiding principles for a new world order. She was delivering the valedictory address at the 4th International Conference on Federalism here this evening. The President said that the mankind today is facing numerous challenges and expectations from federalism are very high. She expressed hope that the delegates of the conference would depart with a renewed commitment to enhance the federal system of governance and use it as a strategic tool for the fight against inequality and for building an equitable global order. Earlier addressing the conference, the Defence Minister, Shri A.K.Antony said that while fiscal tensions between the Centre and the States would exist, the need of the hour is to attain a harmonious balance between the powers being enjoyed by the Centre and the States and to prevent their misuse and abuse. He also called for carrying out a re-evaluation of the latest developments in relations between the Governments at the Centre and in the States and devise effective strategies to correct or remove the imbalances that might have crept into the system. Over one thousand delegates from different parts of the world attended the conference, held in Asia for the first time. It was organized by the Inter State Council Secretariat of the Government of India in partnership with the Forum of Federations, a Canada based international forum of federal countries. The next conference will be held in Ethiopia.

4045. (7-11-2007) NEW DELHI : Shri Kapil Sibal, Union Minister for Science and Technology and Earth Sciences today inaugurated the Proteomics Facility and also laid down the foundation stone for the Student's Hostel building at the

National Institute of Plant Genome Research (NIPGR), New Delhi. Speaking on the occasion Shri Sibal stressed the need for world-class structures with environment conducive for scientific research to attract more students. He said Biotechnology is important in many ways to find solutions to problems related to environment, food and health. The minister also emphasized that it is equally important that these solutions reach the common man. Earlier, Dr. Rajagopala Chidambaram, Principal Scientific Adviser to the Govt. of India, New Delhi and DAE-Homi Bhabha Professor, Bhabha Atomic Research Centre, Mumbai presented a lecture on Innovation Strategies and Directed Basic Research. He stressed the need for Coherent Synergy within the Science and Technology establishments to make India a global leader in Innovation. The audience included scholars from Universities, Research Institutions, Govt. Departments, media etc. besides NIPGR Community. The Proteomics Facility inaugurated today is a state of art facility to unveil biological process in plants. It is for profiling and isolation of proteins to understand gene expression in plants by using high resolution two dimensional and mass spectrometry fragmentation technique. Post-genomic era has witnessed a quantum leap in the biological research, both in cellular as well as in organismal, level. In this context, NIPGR is uniquely placed for its sole thrust on research in plant genomics. Through its infrastructural base for academic-industry interactions and knowledge cum material resources, NIPGR is poised to contribute towards understanding of plant cell differentiation, development, morphogenesis, growth and regeneration, photosynthesis, plant microbe interaction, plant breeding and genetic engineering.

4046. (7-11-2007) NEW DELHI : India is presently emerging as one of the predominant producers and consumers of steel in the world as our growth rate in the steel sector has increased significantly. India has recently risen to the position of the fifth largest producer of crude steel globally, from its earlier position of seventh in the year 2006. This was stated by Shri Ram Vilas Paswan, Union Minister of Steel and Chemicals & Fertilizers while addressing a press conference followed by the Parliamentary Consultative Committee meeting to review the Steel sector held in Chandigarh today. Underlining the role of Public Sector Undertakings in the rapid expansion of Steel, Shri Paswan said the Steel Authority of India Ltd. (SAIL) and Rashtriya Ispat Nigam Ltd. (RINL) are undertaking ambitious expansion programmes. He said that SAIL's ongoing expansion programme which aims to increase production capacity from the present level of 14.6 million tones of hot metal per annum to around 26 million tones per annum by the year 2010 at an estimated cost of Rs. 53000 crores. SAIL is also planning to further expand its capacity to 60 million tones by the year 2020, he added. Highlighting the progress in Fertilizers Sector the Minister said that Central Government is providing adequate fertilizers to the states of Punjab and Haryana as per their demands. He said that in Punjab against the requirement of 4.2 lakh tonnes of DAP, 2.27 lakh tonnes has already been met by the Ministry of Chemicals and Fertilizers and remaining will be fulfilled upto the end of this month. Similarly, in Haryana 1.45 lakh tonnes fertilizers has been provided as against the requirement of 3.51 lakh tonnes in October 2007, balance 1.13 lakh tonnes requirement will be fulfilled by the end of November 2007. He advised the states to analyse the requirement in a proper way so that Central Government could provide adequate quantity of fertilizers. Speaking on the issue of price control of medicines, Shri Paswan said that a Pharmaceutical Policy is being formulated to check the rising prices of medicines. He said that there is a proposal to bring 354 medicines particularly life saving drugs under the category of subsidized rates. He also said that government is taking a serious action against the manufacturers and the sellers of spurious drugs. The Minister also disclosed that Central Government is providing health insurance to 1.25 crore Below Poverty Line (BPL) families this year on the basis of 75:25 sharing ratio between Central and the State Government. He also stated that free medicines to the tune of Rs. 30, 000/- and other consultation charges with the doctor will be included in the scheme.

4047. (7-11-2007) NEW DELHI : The Patna High Court has quashed the complaint filed against Smt. Kanti Singh, Minister of State for Heavy Industries and Public Enterprises in a child marriage case. The complainant had made allegations that the Minister was patronizing a child marriage in Bhojpur district of Bihar.

4048. (7-11-2007) NEW DELHI : Over the last few days several persons including Mr. Henry Kissinger, the U.S. Ambassador Mr. David Mulford, Mr. M.K. Narayanan, National Security Adviser and Dr. Anil Kakodkar have called on the three of us to discuss various aspects of the Nuclear Deal. The B.J.P's position was put across and is briefly reiterated here: 1. The B.J.P. has been and continues to be of the view that the UPA Government has made a significant strategic blunder by turning this deal into a kind of an icon of India's relations with the U.S. 2. The BJP has consistently stood for close Indo-U.S. cooperation and strategic partnership as between two equal sovereigns. 3. We stand opposed to the deal because in our view it compromises long term strategic programmes of India, vital for country's security, neither will it help meet our energy needs of future. 4. Therefore, the BJP strongly recommends that this deal must be renegotiated and not hustled through as the UPA Government is attempting to.

4049. (7-11-2007) NEW DELHI : Shri P.R.Kyndiah, Minister for Tribal Affairs today inaugurated "AADISHILP"-Third National Tribal Craft Expo in Delhi Hat. Organized by Tribal Cooperative Marketing Development Federation of India Ltd. (TRIFED)-an organization under the Ministry of Tribal Affairs the exhibition showcase rich and ethnic art and craft of tribal artists. Inaugurating the expo, Shri Kyndiah said that the idea behind organizing such Expo is to provide a platform for tribal artisans from all over the country. The Minister said that this Expo is an effort not only to promote the tribal products but also to provide opportunities to tribal artisans to interact with the discerning urban customers to understand their preferences, tastes etc. and adapt their products accordingly. He said that it is a very thrilling, enlightening and educative experience to watch the deft fingers at work and live creation of the exquisite articles. .The Aadishilp is an attempt of TRIFED to present a holistic picture of tribal culture and heritage in all its vibrance and colour. .Tribal artisan from all over the country bring their beautiful creations in Metal, Terracotta, Textile, Bamboo, Jewellery, Forest products etc. It is not only showcasing tribal crafts but also presenting tribal dances. The tribal dances of Jharkhand, Nagaland, Manipur and Banzara Dance of Andhra Pradesh will be performed during ADISHILP. In the recent past, TRIFED has taken a number of initiatives to promote tribal products. From a single sales outlet of TRIBES India in 1999 at Delhi now TRIFED has established 41 outlets across India out of which 21 are its own and 20 outlets have been started on consignment basis in association with the State Level Organizations. In addition, TRIFED promotes tribal products by participating and organizing a number of exhibitions at various places of cities. TRIFED has also initiated a new concept of organizing Tribal Artisan Melas to identify new artisans and products from different regions/States.

4050. (7-11-2007) NEW DELHI : The Ministry of Information & Broadcasting has examined the applicability of new guidelines to the existing Community Radio Operators and it has been decided that the provisions of the new policy guidelines, 2006 shall be applicable to the existing Community Radio Stations/Operators also. All the existing Community Radio Operators wishing to migrate to the new policy guidelines will be required to sign a revised Grant of Permission Agreement (GOPA) with the Ministry for which they may apply separately in prescribed format with necessary documents. Only applications complete in all respects will be accepted. As per the new guidelines, the permission will be for a period of 5 years instead of 3 years allowed under the old policy. In addition, limited advertising and announcements relating to local events, local businesses and services and employment opportunities shall be allowed. The maximum duration of such limited advertising will be restricted to 5 (Five) minutes per hour of broadcast. The detailed Guidelines and proforma for application are available on this Ministry's website www.mib.nic.in .Government of India, in December 2006, had liberalized the Policy on Community Radio by bringing in 'Non-profit' organisations like civil society and voluntary organizations, State Agriculture Universities (SAUs), ICAR institutions, Krishi Vigyan Kendras, etc. also under its ambit in addition to educational institutions with a view to allow greater participation by the civil society on issues of development and social changes.

4051. (7-11-2007) NEW DELHI : Even as the country enters the festive season this month, children can look forward to a time of fun and frolic as Gajju, The Golden Elephant, comes visiting for the fifteenth time with a wide variety of films in the largest children's festival of its kind in this part of the world. A total of just over 40 films including several highly acclaimed productions will compete for the top award in the International Competition while another twenty will vie for the awards in the Asian Panorama sections of the International Children's Film

Festival, THE GOLDEN ELEPHANT-15, in Hyderabad. This was stated by CFSI Chairperson, Mr. Nafisa Ali at a press conference today. The Festival will commence on "Children's Day", which also marks the 119th birth anniversary of the country's first Prime Minister Jawaharlal Nehru, on 14 November and conclude with the Awards Ceremony of the Golden Elephant on 20 November. Held every alternate year, this internationally acclaimed Festival is organised by the Children's Film Society, India, a media unit of the Information and Broadcasting Ministry, in collaboration with the State Government of Andhra Pradesh.Over 300 entries were received from about 40 countries, and a Selection Committee of experts from film and allied fields then short-listed the entries for competition. An international jury chaired by renowned short filmmaker Mike Pandey will judge the films in the International competition. The international jury also includes veteran filmmaker V G Samant, New Zealand producer Mathew Horrocks, Andi Spark of Griffith Film School in Brisbane (Australia), veteran journalist and National award winner Vasiraju Prakasam, and writer and social worker Dr. K. V. Krishna Kumari. The Asian Panorama jury is chaired by Bulgaria's animator and filmmaker Ms Tsvetomira Niikolova, and other members are Poland's Izabela Wierzbinska who heads an International Animation Film Festival, actresses Mrinal Kulkarni and S. Rojaramani, and eminent filmmaker Relangi Narasimha Rao. In addition, a children's jury will be set up to judge the films from the perspective of the young. The jury comprises five children: singer Ms Bhavya Pandit, child prodigy in mathematics Master Nischal Narayana, and child artistes Master T. Saikumar, Master Vishu Teja and Ms Sruthakirthy.

4052. (7-11-2007) NEW DELHI : Dr. Navinchandra Ramgoolam, Prime Minister of Mauritius will be the Chief Guest of Pravasi Bharatiya Divas-2008. This was announced by the Minister for Overseas Indian Affairs, Shri Vayalar Rav, in a press conference here today. He stated that the theme of the 6th edition of PBD is 'Engaging the Diaspora: the way forward' with the objective to encourage Overseas Indians to be part of the socio-economic development of India. Announcing the dates and venue, the Minister said that the 6th Pravasi Bharatiya Divas will be held in Vigyan Bhawan, New Delhi from 7th to 9th January, 2008. The main focus during the event will be on social areas and issues with special emphasis on women including Rural Women. The forthcoming PBD includes a two-day convention featuring diverse themes with eminent speakers; trade and Industry exhibition, business networking and cultural evenings, he added. Shri Ravi further said that the Prime Minister of India will inaugurate the Pravasi Bharatiya Divas on 8 January 2008 and it will culminate with valedictory address and conferment of Pravasi Bharatiya Samman Award by Rashtrapatiji on 9 January 2007. He said Education, Healthcare, Women Empowerment and Leadership, Rural Women, Knowledge Economy, Culture, Trade and Business Opportunities will be the focus areas in the convention and the Marketplace by OIFC, Helpline for the Overseas Indian workers, Additional Benefits for OCI card holders, Functional Overseas Indian Centres at Dubai, Kuala Lumpur and Washington will be the highlights of the PBD-2008. The Minister described that the union governments and state governments will be fully involved in the sessions so that participants can directly interact with government representatives and address their concerns and have exposure to the government' programmes for the common man and how they could be involved in these. There will also be parallel sessions of different region, which have significant number of overseas Indians. The second day of the convention would be dedicated to interaction with Indian states represented by various Chief Ministries. He further said that the session would give impetus to greater interaction between the Diaspora and major Indian states as important investment destinations. The session will consist of experts both from Indian and overseas as well as representatives from central and state governments. Opportunities will be given for longer interactive sessions with the delegates. It will also be a platform where issues of social concerns of regional Diaspora groups would be discussed in detail. The objective of PBD 2008 is to provide a platform for the Socio-Economic Development of India and recognize the contributions made by the Overseas Indians. He also informed that at present 38 delegates have already registered from 10 countries. Three states Bihar, UP and Punjab and one Union Territory Daman & Diu have confirmed their participation in PBD 2008. The Pravasi Bharatiya Divas is the annual flagship event of the Ministry of Overseas Indian Affairs. The event aims to connect more than 25 million overseas Indians and to bring the expertise and knowledge of the Indian overseas community to India and integrating it into India's development process. The forthcoming PBD is being organized with the institutional partnership of the Confederation of Indian Industry (CII).

4053. (7-11-2007) NEW DELHI : Deepavali, the victory of good over evil is celebrated by bursting crackers well past midnight. All our festival seasons coincide with an increase in air, water and sound pollution levels. Over the years, loud speakers and fire-crackers have become a part of our life, whether it is a marriage reception or any festive occasion. Noise levels have been a matter of concern as they are harmful to health and welfare of all.

4054. (7-11-2007) NEW DELHI : Mauritius has invited leading downstream oil PSUs, Indian Oil Corporation Ltd.(IOC) to develop and engage itself in the LPG marketing and distribution in the island country. This emerged at a meeting here today between Shri Murli Deora, Minister of Petroleum & Natural Gas and Mr. Rajeshwar Jeetah, Minister of Industry, Small & Medium Enterprises, Commerce & Cooperatives of Mauritius. The meeting was held on the occasion of the first ever India African Hydrocarbon Conference & Exhibition organized by Ministry of Petroleum & Natural Gas, Government of India and FICCI with the support of UNCTAD. Mr. Jeetah informed that Mauritius is planning to increase its LPG consumption from about 60, 000 tonnes at present to about 1, 00, 000 tonnes. Shri Deora pointed out that the cooperation between India and Mauritius is making a satisfactory progress in various areas of hydrocarbon sector. He referred to a subsidiary of Indian Oil namely, IndianOil Mauritius Limited (IOML) which was set up in October, 2001 and has already established a storage terminal of 24000 Metric Tonne at Mer Rouge. The company is involved in marketing of petrol, diesel, ATF Fuel oil & lubricants, retail, bunker and industrial customers with 9 retail outlets already operational and 5 more to be commissioned by December, 2007. Indian side informed that IOML plans to play a pipeline of 50-60 km. length from its terminal to SSR International Airport to cater to the growing aviation business. They sought early expeditious approvals for laying the pipeline which Mr. Jeetah assured to examine on his return. IOML in consortium with M/s Shell, Total, Caltex-Chevron, has commissioned a terminal of 19800 Kilo litre at SSR International Airport this year with the investment US$ 16 million. During his meeting with Mr. Chimunthu Banda, Minister of Energy & Mines of Malawi, Shri Deora expressed keen interest of India for cooperation with Malawi in the Hydrocarbon sector. India has nearly 100 years experience in hydrocarbon sector which could be utilized in the process of development of Malawi's hydrocarbon industry jointly by India and Malawi. Mr. Banda sought Indian corporates' participation in opening up E&P sector of Malawi and pointed out that Malawi has gathered data in that respect. Responding to the proposal, Indian side suggested that the geological data could be made available to the Indian companies for study and evaluation for possibilities of formulating a specific projects of cooperation in the area. Mr. Banda also sought participation of Indian companies in exploring the potential of coal bed methane (CBM) gas in the areas bordering Mozambique. He explained that on the other side of the border Mozambique is producing coal along the border line which suggests a possibility of CBM gas resources in the coal seams in the coal resources which could possibly be lying on Malawi's side of the border. Indian side showed keen interest in the proposal and requested making available data to the Indian companies for early evaluation for fructifying projects of cooperation.

4055. (7-11-2007) NEW DELHI : The total geographic area of the country is 328.7 million ha. out of which the recorded forest cover is 76.50 million ha. The Forest cover thus, constitute 23.4% of the total geographic area of the nation. As per the latest state of forests report of the Forest Survey of India (FSI 1997), the actual forest cover exists only over 19.27% of the geographic area (63.3 million ha) out of which only 38 million ha of forests are well stocked (crown density >40%). The forests of India are endowed with rich fauna and flora. The plant wealth of India is about 45, 000 species (12% of the global plant wealth). The standing timber stock in the country is estimated at 4740 million m3, and the annual increment of the forests is estimated to 87.62 million m3. This resource has to meet the demand of a population of 950 million people and around 450 million cattle. As such, country has to meet the needs of 16% of the world's population from 1% of the world forest resources. The same forest has also to cater for the 19% of the world cattle population. The forests of the country are, therefore, under tremendous pressure. On the one hand the poor are heavily dependent on the forests for their subsistence needs, on the other, the growing liberalisation, industrialisation and fast spreading economic activities at the national and regional levels are putting pressure on the resource base. Over the years country's forests have suffered serious depletion due to unrelenting pressure from increased demand for fuelwood, fodder, timber, inadequacy of protection and diversion of forest lands to agriculture and pastoral uses etc.

4056. (7-11-2007) NEW DELHI : The Union Minister for Rural Development, Dr. Raghuvansh Prasad Singh has called for implementation of safe drinking water supply to all by the year 2009 and total sanitation throughout the country by 2012. Dr. Singh was addressing the Members of the Consultative Committee attached to his Ministry in New Delhi today. The subject for discussion in the Consultative Committee was 'Rural Water Supply and Sanitation'. A video presentation was given to the Members to show the progress of the various programmes for rural water supply, which is a component of Bharat Nirman programme. The Minister said that a clean village would lead to a healthy village, which will lead to a healthy India. He emphasized on the need of close monitoring of various programmes so that the Accelerated Rural Water Supply Programme and Total Sanitation Programme become a complete success within a specified period. He told the Members that the Ministry is laying special emphasis on sustainability of rural water supply sources. He said that the Department of Drinking Water Supply under the Ministry of Rural Development has accorded highest priority to supply of drinking water sources and system to prevent the slippages. He said that bringing sustainability to drinking water system in rural India is the topmost priority of the Department. He urged the States to undertake rainwater harvesting and water conservation with cost effective technology, which will help in creating more drinking water souces. Low cost technologies are to be promoted not only for meeting drinking water requirements but also for recharging of the water bodies. He urged the Members to closely monitor these schemes in their respective constituencies and inform the Department immediately if they find any shortcomings in implementation. The Minister also emphasized on the need of total sanitation campaign, which has now covered 48% of the country. He said that every village has to become a NIRMAL GRAM by 2012. He also told the Members that the scheme of providing sanitation facilities in school is progressing well and it is estimated that by 2009 every school in the rural areas will have a toilet facility. The Members of Parliament from various States raised the issue of more toilets in rural areas and the problems of contamination of water by arsenic, fluoride, iron and other substances. They urged the Ministry to tackle water quality problems particularly to control fluoride and arsenic in the areas affected by this contamination. The Minister assured the Members that his Ministry is taking full care of this problem and it is getting the topmost priority as it badly affects the health of the people. The Members also brought to the notice of the Minister that more effective monitoring and surveillance of the programme is required at all levels to achieve the implementation within prescribed time limit. The demand of quality water to all sections of the society is to be met to ensure better health and faster socio-economic development of the country, which is very necessary for sustained economic growth, the Members of Parliament urged.

4057. (7-11-2007) BANGALORE : World Travel Awards-2007 Asia, Australiasia and Indian Ocean Ceremony was organized at Bangalore recently. India received the award for the leading destination in Asia and leading Govt. Tourist and Convention Bureau in Asia. For these awards, travel agents from 190 countries selected the winners through Ballet. The winners of the regional categories will now compete for the world category awards, which would be announced in December this year. The above awards are the result of the focused, sustained and successful "Incredible India" Campaigns in the international market coupled with sustained efforts in improving the infrastructure of key heritage and tourist destinations of the country. Further, the popularity of Incredible India website, the promptness/proactiveness of the Ministry and its India Tourism Offices has contributed in India getting the Asia's Leading Govt. Tourist & Convention Bureau Award.

4058. (7-11-2007) NEW DELHI : The Prime Minister has stressed the need for more bilateral and regional cooperation in the Asian region to make effective use of available capabilities to respond to disasters. He was inaugurating the 2nd Asian Ministerial Conference on Disaster Risk Reduction here today. Delegates from over 50 countries, experts and NGOs are attending the two-day event. Dr. Manmohan Singh said that while national capabilities have to be developed to handle disasters, this alone will not be enough. He expressed the hope that the regional effort in creating the Tsunami Early Warning System would be replicated in other areas of disaster management. He also stressed the need for modern societies to come together to deal with health disasters and man made disasters including industrial disasters and disasters, caused by terror attacks. In his address, the Home Minister Shri Shivraj Patil informed the delegates about the legal and institutional frame-work, set up in India for disaster management. He said that several other countries are discussing the law made by India for disaster management so that they can put in place laws suitable to their countries. The Home Minister also stressed the need for intensive training to personnel, collection of modern equipment, research and training, improved communication and proper contingency plans to deal with disasters. In their addresses, the UPA Chairperson, Smt. Sonia Gandhi and the Vice Chairman of the National Disaster Management Authority, Gen. (Retd.) N.C. Vij pointed out that Asia is prone to a number of natural hazards and cooperation among the nations of the region is absolutely essential to prevent these hazards from turning into disasters. The World Conference on Disaster Risk Reduction was held in 2005 at Hyogo, Kobe, Japan in which the Hyogo Framework of Action 2005-15 was adopted for building the resilience of nations and communities to natural disasters. The first Asian Ministerial Conference on Disaster Risk Reduction was held in September 2005 in Beijing in which Action for Disaster Risk Reduction in Asia was adopted.

4059. (7-11-2007) NEW DELHI : Retail prices of majority of essential commodities monitored by the Department of Consumer Affairs have generally remained steady over the week ending November 5, 2007. Prices of wheat at retail level remained steady at all the monitoring centres. Retail price of sugar remained steady over the week across all the centres, except Lucknow where it increased marginally. Prices of gram dal have generally remained steady across majority of the monitoring centres. Prices increased at Chennai, Bangalore and Lucknow. Prices of tur dal declined at Delhi, and increased at Lucknow, Kolkata and Bangalore. At Delhi, as on 5.11.2007, prices of gram dal, groundnut oil and milk were holding steady for one week; those of rice, wheat, mustard oil, vanaspati, potato, salt and tea loose were steady for one month and price of sugar for 6 months. Price of atta was holding steady for over one year.

4060. (7-11-2007) NEW DELHI : The Prime Minister, Dr. Manmohan Singh today inaugurated the 2nd Asian Ministerial Conference on Disaster Risk Reduction here today. Following is the text of the Prime Minister's speech: "I am delighted to have this opportunity to be here at this very important conference, which is deliberating on a subject of immense relevance to the entire Asian region. I also hope that this conference will be yet another milestone in strengthening collaborative, cooperative relations among the nations of Asia. Disasters know no political boundaries and we are all equally vulnerable to them. I firmly believe that this is one area where nations can-and indeed must-cooperate to find collective, cooperative solutions to the challenges that face them. After all, it is in difficult times that we need the best of relations. As a wise old saying goes-a friend in need, is a friend indeed. It is, therefore, heartening to note that in recent years, countries of Asia have come together to help one another during times of natural disasters. We have had joint efforts to provide rescue and relief to those in distress-in the aftermath of the tsunami of 2004, after the recent earthquakes in our regions, including in Jammu & Kashmir. This conference is taking place at a time when we can all feel hopeful that we have the sagacity to cooperate during times of natural disasters. The Asian Ministerial Conference is a natural platform to discuss disaster risk reduction. What is done-or not done-in one country, can have repercussions in another. This conference, therefore, can be a common platform for us to learn to work together in the best interests of all our peoples. Earthquakes, cyclones, floods and tsunami have contributed to disasters across Asia in the recent past. In handling all these disasters, what is important is to have coherent national strategies and national capabilities to handle these disasters. This would be in the realm of both disaster prevention and disaster management. I believe that it is incumbent on each one of us to develop the necessary national capabilities. There can be no substitute for effective national efforts. At the same time, each of the past episodes has shown us that a national response alone is not adequate. While we have the necessary wherewithal in Asia to respond to disasters, we need more bilateral and regional cooperation to make effective use of our capabilities.

4061. (8-11-2007) NEW DELHI : The 2nd Asian Ministerial Conference on Disaster Risk Reduction (DRR) concluded here this evening after adopting the Delhi Declaration on DRR that contains 26 action points. The Declaration calls upon national governments and other stakeholders to take specific measures for reducing risks on disasters in Asia and its different sub regions. It also calls for taking actions along the following themes-Hyogo Framework for Action, Mainstreaming DRR, Early Warning & Preparedness, Climate Change, Integration of DRR into recovery & reconstruction, Partnerships and Regional Mechanisms. The Declaration affirms that the biennial Asian Ministerial Conference on Disaster Risk Reduction which had started in Beijing in 2005 will be expanded as the Regional Platform for Disaster Risk Reduction, with participation of the national government, regional and sub-regional organizations, the UN agencies, International Financial Institutions and other stakeholders including the civil society, scientific and technical organizations, the private sector and the media. The Asian Ministerial Conference on Disaster Risk Reduction will be held once in two years by rotation in different Asian countries to—review the action taken by the national governments and other stakeholders for the implementation of the Hyogo Framework for Action; take stock of initiatives taken in various sub-regions of Asia for promoting and enhancing cooperation among the nations within and outside the governments for disaster risk reduction; share and exchange best practices and lessons learned from disaster risk reduction in various fields including application of science and technology, community based disaster preparedness, public-private partnership etc. and further enhance regional cooperation for disaster risk reduction. In his valedictory address, the Union Home Minister Shri Shivraj Patil highlighted the need for mainstreaming of disaster management initiatives into developmental planning to significantly minimize the losses due to devastating impact of disasters. He informed that during the formulation of the strategy for the 11th Five Year Plan for special efforts have been made to lay greater emphasis on structural and non-structural mitigation efforts, in addition to strengthening the emergency response capabilities in the country. Shri Patil also reaffirmed Government of India's commitment to participate actively in the Regional & Global initiatives for the goal of Disaster Risk Reduction. The Valedictory Session was also addressed by Gen (Retd) N.C.Vij, Vice-Chairperson, National Disaster Management Authority and Shri Madhukar Gupta, Union Home Secretary. Delegates from 50 countries, experts and NGOs attended the two-day Conference. 33 country delegations were led by Ministers. The next Conference will be held in Kuala Lumpur, Malaysia next year.

4062. (8-11-2007) NEW DELHI : Indian Film 'MAHEK' has won the Best Feature Film Award at Arpa International Film Festival 2007, Hollywood .The children's feature film in Hindi has been produced by the Children's Film Society Of India and directed by K Kanade. The cast of the film include Shreya Sharma, Anuya Bhagwat, Madan Deodhar, Anuja Borkar, Dheeresh Joshi, Madhavi Gadgil and Lalan Sarang. 'MAHEK' looks at the world through the imaginative eyes of children and examines their rights. What children miss most is respect-respect for them and respect for their imagination. For a child, as important as food, shelter and clothing, is a flower. In every child there is a revolution. 'MAHEK' is a little girl's journey towards self-realization. The film reflects the changes India is going through-from gradual economic freedom towards a renewed intellectual identity Short Synopsis: 11-yr old MAHEK wants to be the best in everything, but she doesn't know what she's best at. To complicate things further, an old, magic-less Modern Fairy walks into her life. Will MAHEK ever realize her true strength? Short Biography of the director of MAHEK: K. Kanade has done his Film Direction from FTII and Producers Program from UCLA. His thesis film 'Chaitra' won Three National Film Awards and two National Awards at MIFF. It was included in a special DVD release: Master Strokes-20 First Films from 45 yr history of FTII. He is drawn towards themes that deal with the world of children, their imagination and the respect they deserve. 'MAHEK' is his first feature film.

4063. (8-11-2007) NEW DELHI : Shri Kamal Nath, Union Minister of Commerce and Industry, has called for greater Canadian investments into India. Stating that India is having a huge work force with an increasing manufacturing base offering vertical linkages, the Minister stressed that it offers an ideal platform to establish business-to-business contacts with progressive Indian SMEs. This he indicated when Hon. Rona Ambrose, Minister of Intergovernmental Affairs, Minister of Western Economic Diversification and President of the Privy Council of Canada met him here last evening. During the meeting, both sides agreed to step up their bilateral and investment cooperation. Referring to the proposal for Free Trade Agreement made earlier this year, Shri Kamal Nath informed that the same is currently under examination by the CEO's Council. He further informed that the Bilateral Investment Promotion Agreement between India and Canada is expected to be signed soon. Both sides agreed that there is substantial cooperation needed in the area of science and technology. Shri Kamal Nath also raised the issue of business visas for the representatives of Indian companies to participate in trade shows being organised in Canada. India's exports to Canada during 2006-07 was US $ 1110.40 million while imports from Canada was US $ 1777.41. Major commodities of exports to Canada include RMG cotton including accessories, drugs, pharmaceuticals & fine chemicals, manufactures of metals, machinery and instruments and gems & jewellery while the major commodities of imports from Canada are transport equipments, pulses, Metalifers ores & metal scrap, fertilisers manufactured and newsprint.

4064. (8-11-2007) NEW DELHI : The Income Tax department has already issued over 30 lakh refunds in the first 7 months of this fiscal involving a total amount of Rs.18, 448 crore. Refund payouts in non-corporate personal income tax (PIT) category are ahead by 47.16 percent (Rs.6, 135 crore against Rs.4, 169 crore) as compared to the first 7 months of last fiscal. During this year, over 11 lakh electronic returns have already been received. More such returns are expected by

15th November 2007, up to which the last date for filing of mandatory electronic returns stands extended. During fiscal 2006-07, 3, 44, 343 electronic returns were filed by various categories of taxpayers. Out of these, 2, 38, 204 electronic returns have already been processed by the department and refunds amounting Rs.7, 816.89 crore in such cases have already been issued up to 7th November 2007. The remaining 1, 06, 139 electronic returns will be processed by 30th November 2007. Refunds of over Rs.14, 000 crore pertaining to large corporate cases have also been processed. Out of these, refunds of over Rs.5, 400 crores have been issued and the remaining refunds will also be issued by 30th November 2007. The Refund Banker Scheme-launched in Delhi and Patna towards the end of last fiscal and extended subsequently to Kolkata, Chennai, Bangalore and Mumbai-has helped increase the pace of refunds. It will now be extended to the entire country for the non-corporate PIT category of taxpayers in order to facilitate quick and correct issue of refunds. Taxpayers are advised to furnish their bank details and ECS number in their tax returns so that their refunds can be credited to their bank account electronically. With the Refund Banker scheme in place all over the country shortly, the Income Tax department envisages no difficulty in processing refund cases. Tax returns have been made annexure-less to facilitate electronic processing of the same.

4065. (8-11-2007) NEW DELHI : The Officers of Central Excise, Delhi-I have unearthed a huge evasion of central excise duty running into Rs.21.31 Crores by M/s M.R. Tobacco Pvt. Ltd., engaged in the manufacture of Gutkha. The party was defrauding the revenue department by clandestine manufacture of goods out of the unaccounted raw material procured without payment of duty. Since Gutkha is a sensitive commodity attracting high rate of duty @67.98%, Central Board of Excise and Customs had issued directive to the Gutkha manufacturers on 9.7.2007 to declare number of pouch packing machines, number of shifts and speed of pouch packing machines etc. The party had also mis-declared the number of shifts and speed of pouch packing machines with the malafide intention of concealing its earlier as well as ongoing clandestine manufacture and clearance of goods without payment of duty. The Director of the Company was arrested by the Central Excise Officers on 6th November, 2007 and produced before the Hon'ble Additional Chief Metropolitan Magistrate who has remanded the accused to judicial custody for 14 days. Further investigations in the case are in progress. This is the second major case of detection of Central Excise duty evasion booked against a Gutkha manufacturer in Delhi Central Excise Zone, which has jurisdiction over Delhi and Haryana.

4066. (8-11-2007) NEW DELHI : BJP National Spokesperson Mr. Ravi Shanker Prasad today said that the unending saga of cold blooded murder and mayhem being perpetrated in Nandigram once and for all conclusively exposes the true and ugly face of the left front government and its party cadres. Mr. Prasad said that it has become a matter of serious concern for the entire nation to witness the blatant and partisan manner in which the Left Front Government in West Bengal was refraining from conducting its responsibilities towards the citizens of the state and in reality actually encouraging its party cadre to continue with their atrocities against innocent farmers by forcibly intimidating them through violence. The BJP Spokesperson went on to add that the BJP had on numerous occasions sought to expose the role of the CPM party and its cadre in Nandigram. Mr. Prasad recalled the recent statement by BJP National President Shri Rajnath Singh who on 3rd November 2007 said that *"On the one hand, the communists publicly express their concerns for China, but on the other hand, maintain a deafening silence on critical national issues such as the continuing massacres and saga of violence being propagated by the Naxalites and Maoists across an increasing red corridor within the country, or the ruthless crushing of peasants who are fighting to protect their rights and honour in Nandigram."* Mr. Prasad said that the events in Nandigram only confirmed the widely held view of the general public across the nation that the democratic and administrative process in West Bengal had been overwhelmingly subverted by the lower level functionaries of the left parties to the extent that they had now become the final authority in deciding even the administrative course of action at the ground level. He said it was indeed unfortunate that the views of the Home Secretary of the State were being challenged by lower level party functionaries of the CPM and other parties. The perpetration of violence by partisan party cadres and the total breakdown of administrative and efficacy marks the nadir of the administrative democratic functioning and freedom. The BJP Spokesperson highlighted the fact that now news reports were emanating that the Maoists had entered the fray and were trying to organize the villagers in Nandigram under "free peoples zones". This new development exemplifies a stark irony where the left parties on the one hand have always been sympathetic towards China and the Maoist ideology of the various violent groups within the country and on the other hand now need to evolve a strategy to protect the people of the state from being influenced by them. Mr. Prasad criticized Mr. Prakash Karat's latest comments on the US and calling Pakistan a "supplicant" state at a function where he said that *"look at what's happening to General Pervez Musharraf...if you compromise with national sovereignty, this will be the result."* Mr. Prasad said that neither citizens of the country nor any political party require such extreme insights about foreign policy and also how our national sovereignty needs to be protected. The BJP Spokesperson further added that it was indeed ironical that Mr. Karat had chosen to make these remarks while speaking at a function to mark the 90th anniversary of the October Revolution, while failing to emphasize that even the concept of Soviet Union and economy could not withstand the tests of time and had been completed rejected by the very people who propagated it's applicability for much of the 20th century.

4067. (8-11-2007) NEW DELHI : The Finance Act, 2007 had inserted a deeming provision to define concession in the matter of rent for the purpose of determining the perquisite value. It has also reduced the rate of valuation of perquisite in the nature of concessional rent accommodation and leased accommodation with retrospective effect from 1st day of April, 2006, that is with effect from assessment year 2006-2007. This has necessitated similar reduction of rates in case of both rent-free and concessional rent accommodations and leased accommodation in Table I of rule 3 with retrospective effect from 1st day of April, 2006, that is in relation to assessment year 2006-2007 and subsequent years. Further, the Finance Act, 2005 had inserted a new Chapter XII-H in the Act, relating to levy of Fringe Benefit Tax (FBT) on the employer with effect from 1st April 2006, *i.e.* applicable for assessment year 2006-07 and subsequent years. Accordingly, rule 3 was amended vide notification number S.O. 265(E) dated the 28th February, 2005, to avoid double taxation on certain items. Since, Chapter XII-H relating to FBT is not applicable to the employer being an individual or a Hindu undivided family or any fund or trust or institution eligible for exemption under clause (23C) of section 10 or registered under section 12AA, rule 3 is required to be amended so as to include valuation of perquisite in case of benefits provided by such employers to its employees. Accordingly, sub-rules 2, 6, 7 (ii), (iii), (iv), (v) and (vi) have been inserted to provide for such valuation. Sub-rule 7(ix) has been inserted to provide for valuation of any other benefit or amenity, etc., in residual cases relating to any employer. These sub-rules will take effect from the 1st April, 2008 and will, accordingly, apply in relation to the assessment year 2008-2009 and subsequent years. The Income Tax Rules have been amended accordingly and notified by the CBDT on 7th November 2007 vide SO No.1896(E) (Notification No.271 /2007/F.No.142/15/2007-TPL). The Notification is available on the official web-site www.incometaxindia.gov.in

4068. (8-11-2007) NEW DELHI : The first Large Taxpayer Unit (LTU) in Bangalore has completed a year of successful functioning on 3rd October, 2007. Finance Minister in his Budget Speech 2005-06 announced the proposal to set up LTUs to act as a single window facilitation centre for large entities paying excise duty, service tax and corporate tax/income tax. The LTU began with 28 large taxpayers, which during the year itself grew to 45, comprising 350 central excise/service tax registrants and 509 TANs (Tax Deduction and Collection Account Number). The Client Executive model adopted by the LTU has facilitated a proactive approach in resolving all issues faced by large taxpayers. The Client Executive is assigned by the Chief Commissioner, and is the single point interface with the large taxpayer for any assistance, clarification, and grievance redressal. This has also accelerated the disposal in key areas of work. Out of 4911 refund claims filed, 4883 claims were settled within 30 days of filing of the claim. All provisional assessments pending over one year have been finalised. Brand rate fixation of drawback was completed within 45 days. All Show Cause Notices pending beyond 3 months have been adjudicated. Cases in appeal were also decided within three months. All applications seeking approvals or permissions, filed electronically by the taxpayers, were granted within two days. Regular interactive sessions held by the Chief Commissioners and other senior officers with the large taxpayers have improved their compliance levels. 100% Excise Returns (ER 1) were filed electronically, which were scrutinised within one month, leading to detection and recovery of Rs. 32 crore of duty/tax. Over 90% of the taxes have been paid through the electronic mode. Indirect tax collections of the Bangalore LTU have shown a healthy growth. During the first half of current financial year, the central excise collections of LTU grew by 45% and service tax collections grew by 21%. The service delivery standards set by the LTU Bangalore has resulted in reduction of the compliance costs of the large taxpayers, and addressed their tax related concerns in a fair and transparent manner. The Government has decided to operationalise the next LTU in Chennai in December 2007, and thereafter in a phased manner in other metro cities. For Chennai LTU, already 36 potential large taxpayers have expressed their willingness to join it.

4069. (8-11-2007) NEW DELHI : The Prime Minister, Dr. Manmohan Singh presided over the full Planning Commission meeting here today. Following is the text of the Prime Minister's opening remarks on the occasion: "I welcome you all to this very important meeting of the Planning Commission which is to discuss the draft 11th Five Year Plan. This is an important occasion as we are going to leave our collective stamp on the development approach that is going to guide our national efforts in the next five years. The last three years under the UPA government have seen a large number of new initiatives focusing on agriculture, rural development, infrastructure and the social sectors. Most of these initiatives are path-breaking in their own way, commit large resources to individual programmes and have brought the concerns and needs of the poor to the centre of our economic and social agenda. They are all, in many ways, steps towards our larger goal of rapid and inclusive growth. The Eleventh Plan has given us a chance to weave all these individual sectoral initiatives into a coherent whole, focusing on rapid economic growth reaching out to every nook and corner of our vast country. We are certainly entering the Eleventh Plan in a strong position as far as growth is concerned. Growth in the first four years of our government will be close to 9%. We have never had such a consistently good growth performance in the past. It is important to emphasize the importance of growth for our economy. It provides the basis for expanding our resource base and consequently, our expenditures. It is the remarkable growth that we have seen in the last three years and the efforts put in by the Finance Ministry to gather more revenues that have enabled the huge expansion in outlays on rural employment, Bharat Nirman, agriculture, health and education that we have seen during this period. We must continue to create an environment where the growth processes continue to be vigorous and there is simultaneously full scope for individual initiative, creativity and enterprise. Of course, the growth cannot be restricted to isolated pockets or to certain sections of society. We need it to be far more broad based. The Plan, therefore, rightly emphasizes a strategy of inclusive growth. We must certainly do what is necessary to achieve the target of 9-10% growth during the 11th Plan period. We must build on the strengths already evident to achieve this growth outcome. Simultaneously, we must ensure that delivery services of programmes for the empowerment of the poorer sections of our society are effective and free of leakages suggestive of wasteful use of scarce resources.

4070. (8-11-2007) NEW DELHI : Lt Gen Susheel Gupta, Deputy Chief of Army Staff (IS&T) addressed a Special Sainik Sammelan of Second Battalion, the DOGRA Regiment in New Delhi today. The unit is scheduled to be inducted for peacekeeping operations as part of United Nations Mission in Ethiopia-Eritrea (UNMEE) between the third week of November, Addressing the troops on the occasion, Lt Gen Susheel Gupta complimented the battalion for its excellent track record. He expressed his faith that the unit would continue to perform upto the high expectations in the impending tenure. 2 DOGRA has the unique privilege of being awarded the 22 Battle Honours, one Theatre Honour and one Chief of Army Staff Unit Citation, a recognition of outstanding performance in operations. Post independence the battalion got the honour of being awarded one Param Vishist Seva Medal, three Maha Vir Chakra, six Vir Chakra, one bar to Vir Chakra, one Ashok Chakra class III, seven Shaurya Chakra, four Yudh Seva Medals, 25 Sena Medals, two Vishist Seva Medals, 27 Mention in Despatches, 30 COAS Commendation Cards, 30 GOC-in-C Commendation Cards, Battle Honour Uri (J&K) 1947-48, Theatre Honour (J&K) 1947-48, Battle Honour Op HILL (J&K) 1965 and Unit Citation (Op RAKSHAK PUNJAB) 1992. The Deputy Chief of Army Staff (IS&T) also congratulated 8 Mechanized Infantry, EME, Signals, AMC, AD Corps. AOC, AEC, APS &CEC of 18 Field Company whose complements are part of 2 DOGRA Battalion Group.

4071. (8-11-2007) NEW DELHI : The Prime Minister, Dr. Manmohan Singh, reviewed the status of implementation of the programme of affirmative action for the minorities, along with the progress made in the implementation of flagship programmes of the UPA Government On October 26, 2007. Apart from other decisions, Prime Minister had directed that the Principal Secretary to the Prime Minister, Shri T.K.A.Nair, should hold a monthly review of the progress made in the implementation of the Prime Minister's new 15-Point Programme for the Welfare of Minorities and the follow-up action, approved by government, in response to the recommendations of the Sachar Committee. In pursuance of the directions given by the Prime Minister, Principal Secretary to PM reviewed the progress made in the implementation of the Prime Minister's New 15-Point Programme for the Welfare of Minorities and the follow-up action on the recommendation of the Sachar Committee with the Secretaries of the concerned Ministries/Departments. The Secretaries to the Ministries/Departments of Home Affairs, Department of Personnel & Training, Rural Development, Human Resource Development, Financial Services, Planning Commission, Statistics & Programme Implementation, Labour & Employment, Housing & Urban Poverty Alleviation, Women & Child Development and Minority Affairs attended the review meetings. In the Course of the review, it emerged that while progress in some areas relating to the schemes and programmes included in the Prime Minister's New 15-Point Programme for the Welfare of Minorities was encouraging, in some other areas more efforts were required. Some encouraging results were also noted in the trend of the representation of minorities in government, especially, in the para-military forces. As far as the follow-up of the recommendations of the Sachcar Committee was concerned, it was noted that a number of steps had been taken to implement the decisions. However, it was felt that the pace of implementation, especially, of decisions taken in the areas of education and extension of credit facilities needed to be stepped up. Principal Secretary to Prime Minister gave specific suggestions for speeding up the pace of implementation and the need for producing tangible results quickly. In particular, plans were finalized for development of a number of artisan clusters in Muslim dominated areas in an integrated and focused manner.

4072. (8-11-2007) NEW DELHI : The Union Cabinet today gave its approval for setting up of an Special Purpose Vehicle (SPV) empowered with the autonomy and freedom currently accorded to Navratna companies without formal Navratna status, with an initial authorized capital upto Rs.10, 000 crore and an initial equity capital upto Rs.3500 crore to be contributed by the members progressively based on investment opportunities comprising the following equity participants from the public sector-SAIL (Rs.1000 crore), RINL (Rs.500 crore), CIL (Rs1000 crore), NTPC (Rs.500 crore) and NMDC (Rs.500 crore) with eventual provision for inducting private sector partners also as and when warranted. The Cabinet also gave its approval for formation of a Committee of Secretaries comprising Secretaries of the Ministries of Steel, Mines, Power, Finance, Coal, External Affairs, Law & Justice and Department of Public Enterprises to approve overseas investment proposals of this SPV for acquiring metallurgical coking coal assets exceeding Rs.1500 crore in each instance with the proviso that the recommendation of this Committee in each case will be brought before the Cabinet for approval.

4073. (8-11-2007) NEW DELHI : The Institute for Defence Studies and Analyses (IDSA) will celebrate its 42nd Foundation Day on Nov 10, 2007. The highlights will be an address by Vice President Shri Hamid Ansari on the subject, "Emerging Foreign Policy and Security Challenges for India." External Affairs Minister Shri Pranab Mukherjee, who is also the President of IDSA, will preside over the meeting. Guest of Honour Defence Minister Shri AK Antony will also address the gathering. This year's function assumes significance as the IDSA will be conferring the 1st K Subrahmanyam Award on Smt. Sudha Mahalingam, an Energy Specialist and a distinguished scholar of International Affairs. The award carries a cash prize of Rs. 50, 000/- . The Award has been instituted in recognition of the services of Shri K Subrahmanyam, one of the country's foremost Strategic Expert and former Director of IDSA. Selected writings of Smt Mahalingam and a special issue of IDSA's journal 'Strategic Analysis on Energy' will be distributed during the function. A new journal called the Journal of Defence Studies, the Asian

Strategic Review 2007 and a new journal on Chemical and Biological Warfare will also be launched.

4074. (8-11-2007) NEW DELHI: The Bharatiya Janata Party (BJP) here on Wednesday made it clear that it was against the India-United States nuclear deal being "hustled through" as it would like the deal to be "re-negotiated." The political signal from the party was that it would not come to the aid of the United Progressive Alliance (UPA) during the coming winter session of Parliament when the deal is debated and an attempt made to get a sense of the House with or without a vote on it. Top leaders of the party—including party president Rajnath Singh, the Leader of Opposition L.K. Advani, former External Affairs Ministers Jaswant Singh and Yashwant Sinha—met here for over 90 minutes to discuss the deal again in the light of recent meetings between senior party leaders and former Secretary of State Henry Kissinger, U.S. Ambassador to India David Mulford, National Security Adviser M.K. Narayanan and Chairman of the Atomic Energy Commission Anil Kakodkar.

4075. (8-11-2007) CHENNAI: The State Cabinet on Wednesday approved the Rs.9,757-crore metro rail project at the policy-level and the two routes prepared by the Delhi Metro Rail Corporation (DMRC) in its Detailed Project Report (DPR). The first route will be from Washermanpet to Meenambakkam via Egmore and Teynampet. The second route will be from Anna Nagar to St. Thomas Mount via Vadapalani, Ashok Nagar and Alandur. The total distance covered by both the routes is 46.5 km. About 20 km will be underground and the remaining, on the surface. The Cabinet decided to approach the Centre for financial assistance and loans for the project. A release issued after the Cabinet meeting said that Japan's Bank for International Cooperation would also render financial assistance. It was also decided to implement the project through the 'Chennai Metro Rail Limited,' a company that would be set up with contributions from both the Central and State governments. The government took up the mass rapid transit project to reduce traffic congestion in Chennai. It shelved the monorail scheme, proposed by the previous government, and opted for the metro rail because it could carry more passengers at a lower cost.

4076. (8-11-2007) NEW DELHI: Prime Minister Manmohan Singh on Wednesday called upon modern societies to come together to deal with manmade disasters–be they industrial or those caused by terror attacks. "The threat of terrorism looms large in our region and could trigger disasters across borders," he said inaugurating the second Asian Ministerial Conference on Disaster Risk Reduction here. Noting that earthquakes, cyclones, floods and tsunami caused havoc across Asia in the recent past, Dr. Singh said the important aspect was to have "coherent national strategies and national capabilities to handle disasters."

4077. (8-11-2007) NEW DELHI : India and China held a high level official meeting to enhance cooperation between the two Railway systems for mutual benefits. The meeting took place in Beijing during recent visit to China by a high level delegation of Indian Railways led by Shri K.C.Jena, Chairman, Railway Board from 29th October to 1st November 2007. The delegation included Financial Commissioner, Railway Board, Smt Sudha Chobe and other senior officials of Indian Railways. The Indian delegation held discussions with the Chinese Railway Minister Mr. Liu Zhijun and Chinese officials. China has expressed its willingness to cooperate with the Indian Railways on any area of interest to Indian Railways. The visit exposed the Indian Railways team to various types of developments that have taken place in Chinese Railway such as world class stations, double stack container operation, heavy haul operations etc., which will be of immense help in formulating plans of development of Indian Railways. The delegation visited Nanjing and Shanghai South and had an on board experience of the high speed EMU train running between Shangai and Nanjing. The delegation also visited container operation areas with ISO containers of eight and half and nine and half feet and also visited a multi modal logistics park near Shanghai. Further, the team visited a freight station on the Datong-Qinhuangdao heavy haul line for coal traffic where trains upto 20, 000 tonnes are being hauled using twin-bo-bo electric locomotives of 12, 000 HP. The team also saw the automatic train examination systems installed at this station where the defects in a freight train are detected automatically by machines installed on the track and noted in the computerized control centre for attention by engineers.

4078. (8-11-2007) NEW DELHI : The Prime Minister, Dr. Manmohan Singh greeted the nation on the joyous occasion of Deepavali. In a message the Prime Minister said: “The festival of lights, Diwali or Deepavali, is a festival which is a harbinger of joy, happiness and prosperity”. It celebrates the victory of good over evil, of knowledge over ignorance and of light over darkness. It is a national festival in which all communities rejoice and contribute to promoting brotherhood and camaraderie. May this Diwali bring peace and prosperity to the people of our nation, to our neighbours and the world at large”.

4079. (8-11-2007) NEW DELHI : As long-term measures to meet the shortage of pilots, the Cabinet today gave its approval for management contract agreement of the Indira Gandhi Rashtriya Uran Akademy (IGRUA) with M/s. CAE Inc., Canada. The management contract agreement will now be signed at the earliest. This will enable the taking over of management of IGRUA by M/s. CAE Inc. Canada for better management of the Academy in a more professional manner in order to produce 100 pilots per year The Government has also approved the formation of the subsidiary company of the AAI for establishing a flying and aviation training institute at Gondia in Maharashtra as a joint venture enterprise with M/s. CAE Inc. Canada. The company will now be registered very soon. This company will establish a flying and training institute, which will help in meeting the growing requirements of pilots and technical manpower relating to the aviation industry.

4080. (8-11-2007) NEW DELHI : The Cabinet Committee on Economic Affairs today gave its approval for Development of Offshore Container Terminal on Build, Operate and Transfer basis at Mumbai Port, under Licence Agreement to be entered into by Mumbai Port Trust (MbPT) with the BOT operator namely, aConsortium of M/s. Gammon India Limited, M/s. Gammon Infrastructure Limited and M/s. Dragados SPL, Spain.

4081. (8-11-2007) NEW DELHI : The Cabinet Committee on Economic Affairs today gave its approval to the proposal mooted by the Union Ministry of Social Justice & Empowerment for revision of the Centrally Sponsored Scheme of Hostels for SC Girls & Boys. The primary objective of the revised scheme is to attract the implementing agencies for undertaking hostel construction programme, especially for SC girls towards the broader vision of containment and reduction of their drop out rate. According to the revised scheme, focus would be given for construction of hostels for middle and higher secondary levels of education. However, hostels can also be constructed for college and University levels of education. The hostels shall be completed within a period of two years from the date of sanction of the project. The Government of India would meet the entire cost of construction for SC girls' hostels as central assistance. However, in the case of boys' hostels, the prevailing pattern of funding would continue, which is 50% for States, 100% for UT Administration, 90% for Central Universities and 45% for other Universities etc. Further, as hitherto, central assistance for NGOs would be eligible only for expansion of their existing hostel buildings. In addition to meting the cost of construction in the form of central assistance as mentioned above, the Government of India would also provide one-time grant of Rs.2500/- per student for making provisions of a cot, a table and a chair for each hosteller. Another important provision included in the revised scheme is involvement of Panchayati Raj Institutions in the matter of selection of hostel site and overseeing the functioning of the hostels. Further, it has also been provided in the scheme that priority in allotment of hostel accommodation would be given to SC students whose parent are either "Safai Karamcharis" or engaged in unclean occupations.

4082. (8-11-2007) NEW DELHI : The Union Cabinet today gave its approval in principle for setting up a Foundation named 'Babu Jagjivan Ram National Foundation" as a society under the Ministry of Social Justice & Empowerment at the cost of Rs. 54 crores. Babu Jagjivan Ram National Foundation will facilitate implementation of various schemes for the social, educational and economic empowerment of the disadvantaged sections of the society. This will also help these sections to join the mainstream society and face the emerging challenges of the modern world.

4083. (8-11-2007) NEW DELHI : The Union Cabinet today gave its approval for management contract agreement of Indira Gandhi Rashtriya Uran Akademi with M/s. CAE Inc., Canada and also gave its approval for formation of a subsidiary company of Airports Authority of India for establishing a flying and aviation training institute at Gondia in Maharashtra as a Joint Venture Enterprise with M/s. CAE, Canada. The management for taking of IGRUA would be taken over by M/s. CAE Inc., Canada for better management of the Akademi in a more professional manner in order to produce 100 pilots per year. The subsidiary company of AAI will establish a flying and aviation training institute which will help in meeting the growing requirements of pilots and technical manpower relating to the aviation industry.

4084. (8-11-2007) NEW DELHI : The Union Cabinet today gave its approval for introduction of the Block Grant Scheme of funding on the lines of IITs, IIMs, etc., for NIFT. This will provide further functional / financial autonomy to the institute and will encourage it to generate more internal resources, promote innovation and result in an overall improvement in the standard of education and research. The base year for the Block Grant Scheme shall be 2006-07 and the scheme will come into effect from 2007-08.

4085. (8-11-2007) NEW DELHI : The Union Cabinet today gave its approval for setting up of a Centre of NIFT at Rae Bareli as a full-fledged Centre like seven other NIFT Centres already functioning in the country. The infrastructure and other facilities at the full-fledged Centre of NIFT, Rae Bareli would ease pressure on existing Delhi NIFT Centre and minimize the regional mismatch between the number of seats available and the number of applicants based on present locations of NIFT Centres. It would also meet the requirement of additional seats on account of implementation of OBC reservation as and when it is implemented. NIFT, Rae Bareli Centre would be first Centre to be set up in any backward areas of the country.

4086. (8-11-2007) NEW DELHI : The Union Cabinet today gave its approval for enhancement of the authorized share capital of the National Minorities Development & Finance Corporation from Rs. 650 crores to Rs. 750 crores. The main objective of the Corporation is to promote the economic development of the 'backward sections' amongst the minorities. The target group comprises those persons among the minorities who are below double the poverty line. The enhanced share capital to the National Minorities Development & Finance Corporation will enable it to be more effective in helping the target groups.

4087. (8-11-2007) NEW DELHI : The most common hazard in forests is forests fire. Forests fires are as old as the forests themselves. They pose a threat not only to the forest wealth but also to the entire regime to fauna and flora seriously disturbing the bio-diversity and the ecology and environment of a region. During summer, when there is no rain for months, the forests become littered with dry senescent leaves and twinges, which could burst into flames ignited by the slightest spark. The Himalayan forests, particularly, Garhwal Himalayas have been burning regularly during the last few summers, with colossal loss of vegetation cover of that region.

4088. (8-11-2007) NEW DELHI : The Vice President of India Mohd. Hamid Ansari has greeted the people of our country on the joyous occasion of Deepawali, the festival of lights. In his greetings, the Vice President said that the Deepawali is truly a national festival symbolizing the sing of celebration and hope for mankind by providing an opportunity to reaffirm our faith in all that is good, noble and virtuous. While celebrating the festival, there is a great need to inculcate these time-tested values in our lives. The Vice President said that we celebrate this festival in its true spirit with care and concern and this festival foster peace, prosperity and happiness and unite us all in joyful celebrations.

4089. (8-11-2007) NEW DELHI : The normal fire season in India is from the month of February to mid June. India witnessed the most severe forest fires in the recent time during the summer of 1995 in the hills of Uttar Pradesh & Himachal Pradesh. The fires were very severe and attracted the attention of whole nation. An area of 677, 700 ha was affected by fires. The quantifiable timber loss was around Rs. 17.50 crores (US$ 43 million; Rs. 1 crore = 10 million rupees). The loss to timber increment, loss of soil fertility, soil erosion, loss of employment, drying up of water sources and loss to bio-diversity were not calculated by the Committee appointed by the Government to enquire into the causes of fires, as these losses are immeasurable but very significant from the point of view of both economy as well as ecology. The fires in the hills resulted in smoke in the area for quite a few days. The smoke haze, however, vanished after the onset of rains. These fires caused changes in the micro-climate of the area in the form of soil moisture balance and increased evaporation. Lack of adequate manpower, communication and, water availability in the hills helped this fire spread rapidly reaching the crown level. The thick smoke spread over the sky affecting visibility up to 14, 000 feet.

4090. (8-11-2007) NEW DELHI : The President, Smt. Pratibha Devisingh Patil has sent her greetings to her fellow citizen of the country on the occasion of Diwali. In her message, the President has said, "On the joyous occasion of Diwali, I convey my warm greetings and good wishes to the nation. Diwali, the festival of lights is a time for celebration when family and friends come together. Let this festival of lights inspire us to help those as yet untouched by the light of education, heath and prosperity. May this Diwali bring happiness and joy to everyone".

4091. (9-11-2007) NEW DELHI : Thousands of people visited Rashtrapati Bhavan today to greet the President of India, Smt. Pratibha Devisingh Patil on the occasion of Diwali. The visitors included people from all walks of life, women, the elderly, school children, tiny tots and senior citizens. A number of persons from rural areas also were amongst the visitors to Rashtrapati Bhavan.

4092. (10-11-2007) NEW DELHI : Government of India has been keeping a watch on the situation in Nandigram area in West Bengal and has also been in touch with the State Government, calling upon them to take urgent steps to restore normalcy in the area. The Home Minister has also spoken to the Chief Minister of West Bengal, and urged him that the State Government should take immediate steps to ensure that persons who have been displaced from their homes in the ongoing tension should be helped to return to their villages, and an environment of peace and security be created. The State Government has asked for deployment of central forces in the State to help them to do this. Considering the overall situation in the State, the Central Government has decided to make available one battalion of CRPF to the State Government, while urging them to optimally use the State security forces, who are familiar with the language and terrain, etc., to achieve the desired objective of restoring peace and normalcy in the area.

4093. (10-11-2007) NEW DELHI : According to the Constitution of India, the central and state governments in the country are enabled to legislate on forestry issues. The implementation part of the forest policy/programmes lies with the state government. Thus, fire prevention, detection, and suppression activities are the responsibility of the state governments' forestry departments. The policy, planning, and financing are the primary responsibility of the Central Government. There is generally no separate department for carrying out forest fire management in the states. The regular staff of the forest departments in the states carries out various activities of forest fire management. During forest fire seasons in some of the divisions, fire watchers are recruited by the state governments as a special provision. At the central level, the Ministry of Environment and Forests is the ministry responsible for forest conservation and protection. Forest fire management is administered by the "Forest Protection Division" of the Ministry, which is headed by a Deputy Inspector General of Forests. The Ministry is implementing a plan called "Modern Forest Fire Control Methods" in India under which state governments are provided financial assistance for fire prevention and control. This assistance is being used by the state governments for procuring hand tools, fire resistant clothes, firefighting tools, radios, fire watch towers, fire finders, creation of fire lines, research, training, and publicity on firefighting. This project is carried out in fourteen states and covers more than 70 percent of the forest area of the country.

4094. (10-11-2007) NEW DELHI : The Prime Minister, Dr. Manmohan Singh, the Congress President, Smt. Sonia Gandhi and the External Affairs Minister, Shri Pranab Mukherjee had a meeting with Left Leaders, Shri Prakash Karat and Shri A. B. Bardhan here today. It was agreed that the statement made by the Prime Minister on the 123 agreement during the last session of Parliament should be taken up for discussion at the beginning of the forthcoming winter session of Parliament. The next meeting of the UPA-Left Committee on the nuclear issue, which was to be held on 16th November, 2007 will be convened as soon as possible.

4095. (10-11-2007) NEW DELHI : Following is the full text of Defence Minister Shri AK Antony's address at 42nd Foundation Day Celebrations of Institute for Defence Studies and Analyses held in New Delhi today:-"I am happy to be present amidst you at the 42nd Foundation Day of the Institute. At the very outset, I wish to congratulate the Institute for successfully completing over four decades of service to the nation. IDSA was set up to provide inputs on security-related and strategic issues of national and international importance. Till now, it has performed its task admirably. Today, India has firmly established itself on the centre-stage of international politics. In such a scenario, the responsibility on you will no doubt increase manifold. Technology is changing at an unbelievable speed. As a result, the transmission of information takes place at light speed. The challenge therefore, to keep pace with these technological changes is more pronounced than ever before. The choice before us is clear-to either let the events shape us, or enhance our ability to shape the events. Our collective endeavour must be to shape the events-to the maximum possible extent. With our growing stature, the need of the hour is to develop stronger defence capabilities to safeguard our interests. As a prominent regional player, we will be called upon to play an increasingly significant role in ensuring peace and stability in our immediate as well as extended neighbourhood and in the Asian region. We have to ensure that our security apparatus is well-equipped to deal with various challenges effectively. Our security forces face several challenges. Though traditional threats do exist, there are little chances of a conventional war breaking out. However, there may be scattered incidents of localized skirmishes, border incursions, civil strife, maritime or other potential threats. Besides traditional threats, there are the unconventional threats. Terrorism with its global networks, financing and support from various quarters is one such challenge. Increasingly, terrorism is being outsourced to local criminals and miscreants to hide the real source of its origin. Insurgents supported by external forces, propagating extremist ideologies result in irregular, but long-drawn out warfare.

4096. (11-11-2007) NEW DELHI : The Prime Minister, Dr. Manmohan Singh, is in touch with the Union Home Minister on the situation in Nandigram, West Bengal. The Central Government will be sending Central Reserve Police Force units to Nandigram. The Prime Minister is monitoring the situation and has also spoken to the Chief Minister of West Bengal.

4097. (11-11-2007) NEW DELHI : India is a member of the Asia-Pacific Partnership on Clean Development and Climate (APPCDC), launched in January 2006. The partnership aims at developing, deploying and transferring cleaner and more efficient energy technologies in accordance with the national priorities of APPCDC member countries. The other member countries of APPCDC are Australia, China, Japan, South Korea and the USA. Canada has also joined the partnership during the recently held Ministerial meeting on 15 October 2007 at New Delhi. There are in all 8 specific Task Forces. Ministry of New and Renewable Energy is the national focal point to promote cooperation in renewable energy and distributed generation under the Renewable Energy and Distributed Generation Task Force (REDGTF). India has been actively participating in the task force meeting. India has joined in about 20 projects under Renewable Energy and Distributed Generation Task Force (REDGTF) under the aegis of Asia-Pacific Partnership on Clean Development & Climate (APPCDC) out of the total of about 30 projects initiated by other partner countries.

4098. (11-11-2007) NEW DELHI : The Ministry of New and Renewable Energy is hosting the 4th Renewable Energy and Distributed Generation Task Force (REDGTF) meeting of Asia Pacific Partnership on Clean Development on Climate (APPCDC) from tomorrow at Bangalore. During these five day meeting, field visits to the premises of Indian Institute of Science and TATA BP Solar also will be organized. India's hosting of this event reflects its keen interest to foster active cooperation with the other member countries in new and renewable energy technologies. The partnership holds a great promise for developing futuristic energy technologies which will not only address the energy security issue but also the environmental concerns due to greenhouse gas emissions. Representatives from the member countries namely India, Australia, China, Japan, South Korea, the USA and Canada will take part in it. Canada has joined the partnership during the recently held Ministerial meeting in last October at New Delhi. Besides them, academicians, representatives from finance, research and industry will participate in this meeting.

4099. (11-11-2007) NEW DELHI : Forests constitute a large part of earth's renewable natural resources. Besides serving as an important source of food, fuel wood, fodder, timber etc.; it also plays a pivotal role in maintaining a near ideal environmental condition for life sustenance. Of the total geographical area in India, (328.87 mha) recorded forest area constitutes about 77.4mha of which the actual forest cover is 67.8 mha & of this forest cover, good forest cover (*i.e.* density is 40% & above) is around 39 mha. India is endowed with a variety of agro climatic zones & this is reflected in the different forest types of country. There are 16 types & 220 sub types of forests. Forest fires are a world wide phenomena & forests of India are no exception to this. Fire depending on where, when and why it occurs, can be either an essential factor or other wise, in ecological cycle of the forested landscape and the survival of associated plants and animals it is merely a destructive unnatural threat. In tropical deciduous forests, fire is a recurrent phenomenon due to higher levels of water stress during summer. Traditional land use practices and changes in the weather pattern have affected the incidence of fire. Fire being a good servant and a poor master, has been responsible for causing immense damage to both forest flora and fauna, including the soil inhabitants. Every year, a large extent of forest area is affected by fires. There is very little knowledge of the precise cause of these fires though it is assumed that vast majority of fires in India toady are human caused.

4100. (11-11-2007) NEW DELHI : Forest fires have attracted global attention because of s their ecological and social significance. In India, a combination of factors such as the large areas of dry deciduous forest, prevalent land management practices and dependence of a large population on forest resources render about half of India's forests prone to annual fires. Besides the loss of precious flora and fauna, forest fires affect regeneration, soil moisture regime, nutrient balance, and render trees prone to insect and fungal attack. Advances in satellite remote sensing have enhance the ability to provide information for near real time detection of forest fires, fire progression, burnt area assessment and inputs from ecological damage assessment. In this context, the Indian Forest Fire Response and Assessment System (INFFRAS) has been established under the Decision Support Centre, (DSC), under Disaster Manage Support Programme, to facilitate forest fire management. INFFRAS integrates multi sensor satellite data with Geo Informatics System (GIS) data bases to address forest fire management relevant to pre, during and post fire scenarios.

4101. (11-11-2007) NEW DELHI : BJP National President Shri Rajnath Singh today announced that a high level party delegation comprising Shri S S Ahluwalia, Smt Karuna Shukla, Shri Balbir Punj and Shri Ashok Pradhan would be visiting Nandigram over the next couple of days to make an on-the-spot assessment about the ground situation there. Expressing concern over the explosive situation in Nandigram, Shri Rajnath Singh said that both the West Bengal Government and the Central Government had miserably failed in addressing the grievances of common people who had been left at the mercy of violent Marxist sympathizers. "My gravest concern is over the warlike situation which has cropped up in Nandigram. Hundreds of people have been driven out of their homes in the face of the unabated violence being unleashed by the CPI (M) cadres", he said. Lambasting the State Government in West Bengal, the BJP President said that the Marxian way of establishing a SEZ through unprecedented violence is unacceptable for any civilized society. "The violence in Nandigram has exposed the real face of the Left parties whose concern for the Aam Aadmi has given way to their gross insensitivity towards humanity. It has reaffirmed that the State of West Bengal is sitting on a virtual tinderbox. The people in West Bengal are already witnessing the worst kind of food riots in the history of Independent India. The overall situation in the state clearly reflects the complete breakdown of law and order and also the glaring incompetence of the Government in ensuring adequate food to the deprived and needy sections of society" he added. Shri Rajnath Singh said that "the situation in Nandigram has completely gone out of the administration's control. Many innocent people have already lost their lives and there is a widespread fear that this situation may turn even worse leading to unprecedented bloodshed in Nandigram". He added that the BJP strongly expresses its solidarity with the farmers and villagers who are fighting against the injustice being meted out to them by the State Government. The BJP National President demanded that all those men, women and children driven out of Nandigram and its surrounding areas by the armed goons must be safely restored to their homes and the current state of mayhem must immediately come to a stop. "The siege of Nandigram must be lifted at once and the centre should intervene to restore normalcy. The elements responsible for the killings must be brought to book and the injured and the dead be suitably compensated', he added.

4102. (11-11-2007) NEW DELHI : Following is the text of the Prime Minister, Dr. Manmohan Singh's Statement on his departure for Russia here today: "I am visiting Russia for the next annual bilateral Summit with President Putin. Ever since President Putin's first visit to India in 2000, the practice of holding annual summits has led to the progressive consolidation of our relations and maintained the momentum of our very close high level contacts. The India-Russia Strategic Partnership is an enduring bond of friendship, which has strong historical roots. Our relations with Russia have traditionally been a factor of peace and stability in the region and beyond. I am convinced that the strong fundamentals of mutual trust and a shared world view on regional and global issues would continue to bring our two countries closer together in a dynamic international environment. Our multifaceted bilateral cooperation with Russia is based on long-term interests. The year 2007 is the 60th year of the establishment of India-Russia diplomatic relations. As we rejoice in our joint accomplishments during the six decades of unbroken friendship, we also stand committed to further deepen our partnership in the fields of trade and investment, defence, energy security, science and technology, space and other areas of mutual benefit. I look forward to continuing my discussions with President Putin to further strengthen India's relations with Russia. I will convey to him the high priority that India attaches to its partnership with Russia, and the benefits that this partnership has brought to our two peoples. I am confident that my visit will lead to a reaffirmation of our joint endeavour towards creating greater economic prosperity and a secure, stable and peaceful world order."

4103. (11-11-2007) NEW DELHI : Press Information Bureau is organizing a three-day Annual Economic Editors' Conference in the National Media Centre, Shastri Bhawan, New Delhi which will be inaugurated by the Finance Minister Shri P. Chidambaram at 3 p.m. tomorrow *i.e.* November 12, 2007. There will be separate sessions with the Ministers and senior officers of the key economic and infrastructure ministries participating in the Conference. The Conference will enable economic editors and journalists, invited from all over the country to interact with them and get a detailed background of the government's policies and programmes. The mediapersons will get a comprehensive view of the overall economic scenario in the country and the latest initiatives and thrust areas of the Government. The Conference will also provide an opportunity to the Government to get feedback from the economic editors. Ministries participating in the Conference include, Commerce & Industry, Agriculture, Consumer Affairs, Food & Public Distribution, Petroleum & Natural Gas, Civil Aviation, Steel, Chemical & Fertilizers and Labour apart from the Finance Ministry. About 300 editors and financial writers are likely to attend the 3-day Conference.

4104. (12-11-2007) NEW DELHI : Following is the text of the remarks by the Prime Minister, Dr. Manmohan Singh, at the meeting of Indian and Russian Businessmen in Moscow today: “It gives me immense pleasure to meet you all in Moscow. I attach great importance to interaction with entrepreneurs and businessmen of Russia and India. You represent the business and industry of two of the most rapidly growing emerging economies of the world. In the post-1991 period, the content and format of the economic relations between India and Russia have been redefined. The rapid growth of our markets and economic reforms have created trillion dollar economies in both our countries. The Indian economy is today witnessing an annual GDP growth rate of about 9%. Never before has such a growth rate been sustained year after year. Our target is to attain a growth rate of 10% in the 11th Plan period. We have strong macroeconomic fundamentals. Our growth process is largely based on growing domestic consumption. Our foreign exchange reserves have crossed US$ 250 billion. We expect to receive Foreign Direct Investment of about US$ 30 billion this year. Our savings and investment rates are close to 35% of our GDP. We have a highly favourable demographic profile and a robust educational system. We have plans to establish 6000 model schools in the country, open 30 new Central Universities, 370 new colleges, and undertake a huge expansion of Institutes of Technology, Management and Science. I have announced a major expansion in our vocational educational and skill development programme. Infrastructure development is today a high priority in India. Our infrastructure needs are estimated at over 450 billion dollars over the next five years. Mechanisms have been institutionalized to sustain high levels of investment through public-private partnerships, systematic bidding systems and innovative financing mechanisms. There are thus enormous opportunities that are opening up in India and government is playing the role of a facilitator. But there is only so much governments can do. There is no substitute for a vigorous two-way engagement between the business communities of India and Russia. I regard today’s meeting as a vital step in that direction. Trade and investment relations between India and Russia have lagged far behind our excellent political understanding and our joint commitment to strategic partnership. President Putin and I have therefore identified this aspect as having a high priority. We wish to see our economic engagement expand to become a major pillar of the Indo-Russian strategic partnership.

4105. (12-11-2007) NEW DELHI : The Government has also issued guidelines for Broadband Wireless Access (BWA) services. With this the level of broadband penetration in the country, especially in rural areas, will be addressed. Introduction of Broadband Wireless Access (BWA) services will enhance the penetration as well as growth in broadband subscribers.

4106. (12-11-2007) NEW DELHI : Keeping in view the interest of consumers, the Department has decided to introduce mobile number portability in the four metro cities *i.e.* Delhi, Mumbai, Kolkatta and Chennai in the initial phase. This will provide the customer the facility to retain the same number while switching over from one operator to another within the same service area.

4107. (12-11-2007) NEW DELHI : The Congress views the events at Nandigram with the gravest concern. It is evident that issues of safety, security and governance for the ordinary man have been jeopardized. The Congress deplores, with all the strength at its command, the cult of violence which has been spawned in and around Nandigram. We deplore the political culture that empowers party cadres over the law enforcement machinery or the rights of the common man. The primary and fundamental responsibility of any state administration is to do and to be seen to be doing its utmost to maintain law and order. The entire country needs a clear commitment and assurance that this is, indeed, the case as far as the state government machinery in WB is concerned .No abdication of statutory duty or state responsibility can be countenanced in a democracy governed by rule of law. The CRPF and other forces have been fully provided. The state government has to ensure that they are allowed to discharge their duties fully and comprehensively. The human aspect of the problem cannot be ignored or underemphasized. Immediate healing touch for the common man is the need of the hour. To a question that since the Constitutional machinery in West Bengal has broken down completely, why is the Central government not taking a tough stance Shri Singhvi said, let us be very clear that 356 or 355 are not remedies or panaceas, they are not a magical wand for all ills. Where the primary responsibility is to do something on the state government we have to first see that that role is fulfilled. There is no question of any passing of the buck by any one to the Central government. The first and foremost question is, is the state government fulfilling it's role. Obviously that question has to be answered by the state government and we should not divert attention by larger issues at the moment. We are still hopeful that the state government will take note of the situation from all reports around it and will act fast to improve the situation. To a question that Smt. Mamata Bannerjee has asked Congress President Smt. Sonia Gandhi to visit Nandigram, what is the response of the Party Shri Singhvi said, there is no response from the Party at the moment, these are inputs which we receive and we will consider them. The point is that we do not want to make any diversion of the focus of the administration or of the police forces. For us is not related to any gimmickry or politics. For us the concrete hard work has to be done. To a question whether PCC members would visit Nandigram Shri Singhvi said, not at the moment but we have all the Congress cadres in West Bengal who are fully active in and around the area. It is not only the PCC but right down to the block level and they are our eyes and ears for daily, hourly, minute information. To a question whether the Congress is scared to rap CPM, that they might retaliate Shri Singhvi said, we do not hesitate to speak our mind. When we see a human problem, a law and order problem, a Constitutional problem form this podium or any other for a you have had our stand loud and clear. Whether it has this political implication or that political implication is not what we are concerned about. We are concerned about a human healing touch for a very, very live human problem.

4108. (12-11-2007) NEW DELHI : The Government has released the guidelines for 3G services today. With the introduction of 3G services in the country, additional value added services will be available to the public.

4109. (12-11-2007) NEW DELHI : The Ministry of Women and Child Development is organizing weeklong celebrations for children at Pragati Maidan, New Delhi from Bal Divas, 14th November onwards. The celebrations will begin with National Children Awards to 34 children for exceptional achievements. These will be followed with cultural programmes and film shows for children at Shakuntalam Theatre, Pragati Maidan. The National Child Awards for exceptional achievements to 36 children will be presented for the year 2006 which include one gold medal at the national level and 35 silver medals at the State level. On the occasion, Smt. Renuka Chowdhury, Minister of State for Women and Child Development will also inaugurate the pavilion of the Ministry of Women and Child Development in Hall no. 16 in the India International Trade Fare which will have about 90 stalls of Swayamsidha Women Self Help Groups from all States and Union Territories. Products of these Self Help Groups will include various household articles, decorative items, traditional and modern handicrafts and handloom articles, etc. The Pavilion will also provide stage performances by State Cultural Troops, which will include traditional dance, music, magic & puppet shows.

4110. (12-11-2007) NEW DELHI : Following is the text of the Opening Remarks by the Prime Minister, Dr. Manmohan Singh, at the Joint Press Interaction with President Putin in Moscow today: "This is the eighth annual summit between India and Russia and my fourth visit to Russia as Prime Minister. I am truly delighted to be back in your beautiful country. Let me thank you, Mr. President, for the warm reception and hospitality accorded to me and my delegation. I am extremely satisfied with my discussions with President Putin. They were characterized by warmth, cordiality and unanimity on all issues of mutual interest. There has been substantial forward movement on many of the issues that we had discussed at our last Summit in January. We held wide-ranging discussions and identified areas for further cooperation between our two countries. I also had a useful and productive exchange of views with Prime Minister Zubkov. We discussed ways to substantially upgrade our economic ties, which should form the bedrock of our strategic partnership. We agreed that there are enormous opportunities for collaboration. We discussed the recommendations made by the Joint Study Group and the establishment of a Joint Task Force to implement them. I am happy that we have been able to satisfactorily resolve the long pending issue of the utilization of the rupee debt fund. We also agreed to redouble our efforts to achieve a bilateral trade target of 10 billion US dollars by 2010. I will be meeting the captains of Russian industry and a high-level Indian business delegation later in the evening. I will urge them to invest more in this relationship. High technology is an area of great promise. Our cooperation is symbolized by the agreement on Chandrayan II, which will include a joint mission to the Moon involving an orbiter, a lander and a rover to carry out scientific studies. We continued our dialogue on energy. I thanked the President for Russia's steadfast support in supplementing our nuclear energy programme, and its assistance in lifting international restrictions on nuclear cooperation with India that are still in place. Defence cooperation is one of the pillars of our strategic partnership. Our decision on the co-development and co-production of the Fifth Generation Fighter and the Multi-role Transport Aircraft are major steps forward. We had a constructive discussion on regional and global issues. There is a mutuality and convergence in our interests. We highly value Russia's role in international affairs and its global leadership on key issues. Our two countries are preparing enthusiastically for the "Year of Russia in India" in 2008 and "Year of India in Russia" in 2009. We wish to showcase the new Russia in India and the new India in Russia. I have invited both the President Putin and the Prime Minister Zubkov to India. Ours is a strategic partnership that has stood the test of time. Through our discussions today we have consolidated and strengthened our engagement in different areas. I am very satisfied with the results of my visit."

4111. (12-11-2007) NEW DELHI : The Armed forces pavilion at the prestigious India International Trade Fair (IITF), 2007 will focus on their role in bringing the remote North-Eastern region to the national mainstream. This was stated by the Vice Chief of Army Staff Lt. General Milan Lalitkumar Naidu at a media presentation on the Defence pavilion here today. The theme of the Defence pavilion at the fortnight long annual extravaganza has been aptly titled "Defenders of the Dawn". General Naidu also released a brochure "An Eastern Odyssey, which unveils the vast tourist potential of the virgin region. Speaking on the occasion General Naidu said a mind boggling over 27, 000 kms road has been laid in the difficult muddy northeastern Himalayan hilly terrain by the Border Roads Organization (BRO), ushering development in the landlocked, mainly tribal region. Besides, the BRO has constructed nearly 12 kms. of bridges and another 2.3 kms of bridges would be laid by March next year. General Naidu said the armed forces have been integral to the development of the seven northeastern states, linked to the mainland by a slender 30 kms wide corridor at Siliguri. Most of these states have been suffering under the scourge of terrorism sometimes or the other during the six decades of our independence. The Defence pavilion will also showcase, for the first time, the Counter Insurgency and Jungle Warfare School (CIJWS), Vairengte in Mizoram, a premier institute in low intensity warfare which has, despite its low profile, trained soldiers from more than 42 countries including the United States. The role of the armed forces is not limited to fighting insurgency alone. Under Operation Sadbhavana the army has been reaching out to the common man, providing medical aid, education, relief and infrastructure development. The three wings of the armed forces Wives Welfare Association have also shouldered equal responsibilities with the valiant soldiers in ushering development in the region. Viewers to the Defence pavilion can also have a glimpse of the glory of the Assam Rifles and the Territorial Army in defending the nation's borders and their contribution to nation building. A sound and light show "The Saga of Brahmaputra" at Hamsdhwani Theater on 16-17th November at 07.00 PM will also delight the visitors. For the first time the audience can also chat with soldiers on the remote. northeastern frontiers through live video conferencing.

4112. (12-11-2007) NEW DELHI : Corruption complaints in respect of all the Central Universities, Indian Institutes of Technology, Indian Institutes of Information Technology, National Institutes of Technology, Central Board of Secondary Education (CBSE), University Grants Commission (UGC), All India Council of Technical Education (AICTE), National Council for Teacher Education (NCTE), National Council of Educational Research & Training (NCERT), Kendriya Vidyalaya Sangthan (KVS), Navodaya Vidyalaya Samiti (NVS) and other Central Educational Institutions can be made to their respective Central Vigilance Officers (CVOs) and also to Chief Vigilance Officer, Ministry of Human Resource Development, Room No. 215 'C' Wing, Shastri Bhavan, New Delhi, or on Telephone No. 23382298, Fax No. 23070036 or Under Secretary (Vigilance), Room No. 106, C Wing, Shastri Bhavan, New Delhi or on Telephone No. 23386317.

4113. (12-11-2007) NEW DELHI : Dr. Samir K. Brahmachari, FNA, FASc, FNASc and Director, Institute of Genomics & Integrative Biology (IGIB), Delhi, today took charge as Secretary, Department of Scientific and Industrial Research (DSIR) and Director General, Council of Scientific & Industrial Research (CSIR), from Dr. T Ramasami, Secretary, Department of Science & Technology (DST), who was holding the additional charge as Director General, CSIR and Secretary, DSIR. Dr. Brahmachari, a Ph.D in Molecular Biophysics from Indian Institute of Science, Bangalore was earlier a Professor of Molecular Biophysics and Genetic Engineering at the Indian Institute of Science, Bangalore, before joining as Director, IGIB. He has pioneered functional genomics initiative in India and is successfully led the Indian genome Variation Consortium project and presently coordinating a national network project in 'In Silico Biology' for drug target development. He and his coworkers have demonstrated association of two genes to Schizophrenia and Bipolar Disorder and identified several SNP's and other markers associated to various neurological disorders. He is the first to discover how human miRNA can target HIV genes and control virus replication, thus opening up a new vista of antiviral therapeutics. Dr. Brahmachari got several awards and distinctions. To name a few, INSA Young Scientists Award in 1979; Kani Medal (National Cancer Research Centre, Japan), 1981; Shanti Swarup Bhatnagar Award (CSIR) 1990; FICCI Award, 1999; Millennium Medal (Indian Science Congress) 2000; Ranbaxy Award 2001; Prof. B.R. Ambedkar Centenary Award for Excellence in Biomedical Research (ICMR) 2005; J.C. Bose Medal (INSA) 2007; and H. K. Firodia Awards

For Excellence In Science and Technology (2007). Dr. Brahmachari is an elected member of the Human Genome Organization, 1991 and is also an elected member of the HUGO Council, 2004. He has been elected to the fellowship of all the three National Academies. He has also been a member of various Task Forces and Committees, Govt. of India; member, expert group on Human Rights and Biotechnology, United Nations; Council Member, FAOBMB, since 1997; and member Indo-European Commission S&T Steering Committee. He has been included in the Advisory Committee of the X-Prize in Genomics which consists of leading Genomics Scientists of the world. Dr. Brahmachari has also been involved in the issues related to genomics research and human rights. As an advisor to Human Rights High Commission, he has also addressed issues of unethical exploitation of genetic resources of the Third World and has championed the concept of rights of patients in benefit sharing in the development of genomic medicines. He has contributed significantly in promoting industry-academia interactions through novel programme of knowledge partnership. Dr. Brahmachari has over 130 publications in leading international journals and has 5 patents and 10 software copyrights to his credit.

4114. (12-11-2007) NEW DELHI : The 27th India International Trade Fair 2007 is being organized by the India Trade Promotion Organisation (ITPO) at Pragati Maidan, from November 14-27, 2007. The Fair is a mega celebration of the new India that is fast taking shape. The theme of the Fair 'Processed Food and Agro-Industries" figures prominently in the display scheme of the pavilions of the States and Union Territories besides the stand-alone pavilions. India is the 10th most industrialized country and fourth largest economy in terms of purchasing power parity with its GDP projected to grow at nearly 8% in 2006-07. The country also happens to be the most richly endowed agricultural nation in Asia having 169 million hectares of arable land, accounting for one-tenth of the world's arable land and a fifth of the world's irrigated land at 56 million hectares with a coastline extending to 8000 km and vast marine wealth.

4115. (12-11-2007) NEW DELHI : Five weeks after the Indian Air Force (IAF) brought curtains down on its platinum jubilee celebrations on October 8, landmarks in IAF continue to be reached. Two Hawk Mk 132 advanced jet trainer (AJT) aircraft that departed BAE Systems', Warton airfield in UK on November 8, reached their intended destination, Air Force Station (AFS), Bidar in north Karnataka, today. The Hawk trainers will impart stage-III training to the newly commissioned fighter pilots of the IAF at Bidar from June, next. The Hawk pair flown by a mix crew of BAE Systems and IAF pilots, Wing Commander Pankaj Jain and Squadron Leader Tarun Hindwani, first landed in India at the Jamnagar airbase while ferrying from Muscat, their previous stopover, on their way to Bidar. Air Commodore RK Sharma, Air Officer Commanding (AOC), Jamnagar and air warriors of the airbase gave the aircrew an enthusiastic welcome on their maiden touchdown on Indian soil, also more significantly, at the first IAF airbase on arrival. Post the brief stopover for refueling, turn-around-servicing and a brief ceremony to mark the arrival; the Hawk pair took off for Bidar. The Hawk's arrival at AFS Bidar, their designated main operating base, was however marked with even greater an excitement and enthusiasm. The AJT pair was escorted into Bidar airspace by the Suryakirans streaming national colours. They landed in pairs and taxied-in into the designated apron area amidst a rousing welcome by the air warriors of the airbase and their families. Air Marshal GS Chaudhry, Air Officer Commanding-in-Chief, Training Command and Air Commodore Ramesh Rai, AOC, AFS Bidar, oversaw the first arrival of the aircraft. It was a simple but well orchestrated ceremony. Briefly after getting off their new gleaming jets amidst a rapturous applause, the pilots briskly walked over and handed the aircraft documents to Air Marshal Chaudhry, signifying the official aspect of the Hawk Mk 132 aircraft being received into the IAF inventory. The brief ceremony heralded yet another saga towards meeting the training requirements of the IAF pilots. Air Marshal GS Chaudhry seemed visibly pleased to have finally inducted the long awaited AJT into Training Command. He stated that the AJTs inclusion into the training curriculum of the fighter pilots should improve the training and flight safety standards of the IAF. The two jets that arrived today are among the first of the 66 Hawk Mk 132 aircraft to be delivered to the IAF by BAE Systems, UK. By this year-end, four more Hawks will be ferried-in, and by mid-February, six more are scheduled to arrive in a phased manner. Of the 66 aircraft being purchased, 24 are being developed, built and supplied by BAE Systems, UK while Hindustan Aeronautics Limited (HAL), Bangalore will manufacture the remaining 42 aircraft under licence in India. The completion of the delivery schedule will see all the 66 aircraft operational by 2010-11. Meanwhile AFS Bidar that has recently been refurbished to house the latest acquisition is abuzz with anticipation. Apart from the fact that the runway has been extended to 9, 000 feet, technical facilities have also been readied to accommodate the fleet in its entirety. "Framing of the flying and operating procedures in the local flying area will take top priority, " informed Air Commodore Rai, adding that the instructor's conversion will also begin in right earnest after some preliminary formalities, within the next few days.

4116. (12-11-2007) NEW DELHI : Fire is a common feature in the Indian forests every year, causing incalculable damage to the forest wealth and ecosystem. High proportions of these fires are attributed to man-made reasons either deliberately or accidentally. Also the components of fires are very localised and the people who live in the locality know the local conditions best. Therefore, efforts are on to involve communities in fire prevention and control. This necessitates better understanding of the conditions under which community would participate. India, with a forest cover of 76.4 million hectares, contains a variety of climate zones, including the tropical south, northwestern deserts, Himalayan mountains, and the wet north-east. Forests are widely distributed in the country. India's forests are endowed with a variety of biomass and biological communities. The forest vegetation in the country varies from tropical evergreen forests in the West Coast and in the

North-East to Alpine forests in the Himalayas in the North. In between the two extremes, there are semi-evergreen forests, deciduous forests, sub-tropical broad-leaved hill forests, sub-tropical pine forests and sub-tropical temperate forests. With increasing population pressure, the forest cover of the country is deteriorating at an alarming rate. Along with various factors, forest fires are a major cause of degradation of Indian forests. According to a Forest Survey of India Report, about 50 percent of forest areas in the country are fire prone (ranging from 50 percent in some states to 90 percent in the others). About 6 percent of the forests are prone to severe fire damage.

4117. (12-11-2007) NEW DELHI : Finance Minister, Mr. P. Chidambaram, said today, I have always viewed the Annual Economic Editors' Conference as an important platform for interface between the Government and the Fourth Estate on the salient aspects of the economy, the current economic situation, the challenges and the policy responses of the Government. I understand that the participants of this Conference form a highly diverse cross section of informed economic editors from the length and breadth of the country. I extend a hearty welcome to all the participants and wish that over the next two days there will be meaningful discussions on the current state of the Indian economy and the Government's economic policies. Such discussion will generate useful feedback to the Government. The United Progressive Alliance (UPA) Government assumed office in May 2004. It is with a high sense of achievement-and pardonable pride—that we recapitulate the three and half years of the management of the economy. There has been a marked change in the way the Indian economy is viewed both within the country and in other countries of the world. This is largely due to the sustained, well-directed efforts of the Government that have resulted in globally acclaimed rates of economic growth, increased global competitiveness of Indian businesses, strong macro fundamentals, and above all, a highly favourable economic outlook.

4118. (12-11-2007) NEW DELHI: The CPI(M) Polit Bureau began its two-day meeting in the Capital on Sunday to discuss the draft political resolution for the 19th party congress scheduled for March next year in Coimbatore. With the violence in Nandigram hogging the headlines, the situation in the area and West Bengal Governor Gopalkrishna Gandhi's press release calling for "effective action" is on the agenda. Twice in the past week, the Polit Bureau had issued statements on Nandigram. In a statement on Wednesday, the Polit Bureau had attributed the recurrence of violence in the area to the use of Maoists from outside by "the alliance of political forces" which have occupied the area. And, on Saturday, the Polit Bureau, while stating that the Governor was well within his constitutional role to communicate his views to the State and Central governments, had described as "uncalled for" his decision to go public with his views. Because of his preoccupation with Nandigram, West Bengal Chief Minister Buddhadeb Bhattacharjee did not attend the deliberations on the first day. Besides, the Polit Bureau is scheduled to discuss the coming Assembly polls in Gujarat and Himachal Pradesh. Also on the cards are discussions on the India-U.S. nuclear deal. As for the draft political resolution for the party congress, it is likely to be 'finalised' for further dissemination to the branches. These branches of the CPI (M) across the country will discuss it at their local levels and send it back to the party headquarters with suggestions for inclusion in the final resolution that will be adopted at the party congress.

4119. (12-11-2007) NEW DELHI : In exercise of the powers conferred by clause (2) of article 124 of the Constitution of India, the President is pleased to appoint (i) Shri Justice Ganpat Singh Singhvi, Chief Justice, Andhra Pradesh High Court, (ii) Shri Justice Aftab Alam, Judge, Jammu & Kashmir High Court, and (III) Shri Justice Jagdish Madhurlal Panchal, Chief Justice, Rajasthan High Court to be, the Judges of the Supreme Court of India, in that order of seniority, with effect from the dates they assume charge of their respective offices.

4120. (12-11-2007) NEW DELHI : The Ministry of Home Affairs had introduced the facility, 'FCRA-online' on 29th September, 2006 to facilitate associations to file online their applications for registration and submit the statutory annual returns regarding receipt and utilization of foreign contribution under the Foreign Contribution (Regulation) Act, 1976 on the Ministry's website: www.mha.nic.in. The facility of online status enquiry is also available through this website. Taking forward the process, a new feature has been introduced in the "FCRA-Online Service" with effect from today enabling online filing of applications seeking prior permission to receive foreign contribution (Form FC-1A) by associations. This facility aims at providing efficient, transparent and accountable service delivery to stakeholders.

4121. (12-11-2007) NEW DELHI : The following agreements were signed between India and Russia during Prime Minister's visit to Moscow: (i) Agreement between the Indian Space Research Organization and the Federal Space Agency of the Russian Federation in the Field of Joint Moon Exploration within the Framework of the Agreement between the Government of the Republic of India and the Government of the Russian Federation on Cooperation in the Field of Exploration and Use of Outer Space for Peaceful Purposes; (ii) Agreement between the Government of the Republic of India and the Government of the Russian Federation on Cooperation in Development and Production of Multi-Role Transport Aircraft; (iii) General Letters of Exchange (on utilization of Rupee debt funds for Russian investments in India); (iv) Agreement between the Government of the Republic of India and the Government of the Russian Federation on Cooperation to Combat Illicit Trafficking in Narcotics, Psychotropic Substances and their Precursors.

4122. (12-11-2007) NEW DELHI : The Ministry of Environment and Forests is organising a two-day National Workshop on forest fires in New Delhi from tomorrow. Sh. S. Regupathy, Minister of State for Environment and Forests, will inaugurate it at 10.00 a m tomorrow *i.e.* November 13, 2007. There will be sessions on Prevention, detection and monitoring of forest fires, fire suppression and management, ecological effects of forest fires, fire management in protected areas and fire monitoring proforma and data base development. Various papers will be presented during these sessions. The Centrally Sponsored Schemes will be evaluated under Management of Forest Fires through the Involvement of Local Communities. This will also highlight non-availability of funds at beat level. The workshop will enable participants invited from all over the country and government officials to interact with each other and get a detailed picture of the problems, non-availability of funds, different traditional and local managements to improve water retention, effect of fire on forest dynamics, fire identification using satellite imagery, application of Moderate Resolution Imaging Spectroradiometer (MODIS), ecological disastrous effects of forest fires besides other aspects. Principal Chief Conservators of Wild life and Chief Wildlife Wardens from states, organisations like Indian Council of Forestry, Research and Education (ICFRE), Dehradun, Forest Research Institute (FRI), Dehradun, Forest Survey of India (FSI), Dehradun, Ashoka Trust for Research in Ecology and the Environment (ATREE), World Wildlife Fund (WWF), National Remote Sensing Agency (NRSA) and officers from the ministry are participating in this workshop. About 120 experts from the field of forest, environment, department of space are likely to attend this two-day workshop.

4123. (12-11-2007) NEW DELHI : Shri V.L. Chopra, Member, Planning Commission, today inaugurated the 16th Scientific Seminar in Hindi organized by the Ministry of Earth Sciences. Speaking on the occasion Shri Chopra lauded the efforts of the Ministry to popularise the Rashtrabhasha by organizing such a seminar every year. He expressed hope that rich contribution made by several speakers would help people understand the important issues related to Global Warming. 16 Scientists/Professors of various scientific and research organizations from various parts of the country participated in the Seminar and presented their papers in Hindi during the Seminar. The best three presentations were also awarded with cash prize. Addressing the gathering Shri B.C.Mandal, Director (Official Language), Ministry of Home Affairs, emphasized the need for propagating the use of Hindi by Ministries/Departments/Officers of the Union Government. He appreciated the efforts of the Ministry of Earth Sciences for making the Seminar an annual event and also the publication of the proceedings in the form of a book. "Antarctic Abhiyaan (Rajat Jayanti)" the book containing the proceedings of last year's seminar held on 22 November, 2006 is now available. Earlier, Dr. P.S. Goel, Secretary, Ministry of Earth Sciences, in his welcome address congratulated the winners of Prithvi Vigyan Mantralaya Maulik Pustak Lekhan Yojana, 2007. The first prize of Rs.50, 000/- was given jointly to Shri Shyam Sunder Sharma and Dr. Rajiv Nigam for their book "Hamari Aarthik Samridhi Ki Aadhar-Monsoon"; Second prize of Rs.40, 000/- was given to Dr. C.L. Garg for his book "Prakratik Aapdayain Aur Vigyan" and the Third prize of Rs. 30, 000/- was given to Dr. DD Ojha, for "Akshay Nidhi (Prithvi Aur Sagar)". Dr. Goel said that these books will be available on the website of the Ministry.

4124. (12-11-2007) NEW DELHI : Under the National Common Minimum Programme (NCMP) of 2004, healthcare is one of the identified thrust areas for special focus. The NCMP specifically states that the government intends to raise public spending on health to at least 2-3% of GDP over the next five years with focus on primary healthcare, introduce a national scheme for health insurance for poor families and step up public investments in programmes to control communicable diseases and also provide leadership to the national AIDS control efforts. The Tenth Plan witnessed a transition in health care policies and strategies at the primary and secondary and also set in motion a process to develop and promote a regional balance in the availability of tertiary healthcare facilities. Health indicators at the national level have registered a significant improvement over the past decade. Life expectancy has increased from 59.7 in 1991 to 63.7 years for males and from 60.9 to 66.9 years for females during the same period. Crude birth and death rates have also registered a decline during this period and available data for IMR, MMR and TFR has shown a positive trend. The main plank for achieving accessible and affordable rural healthcare at the primary and secondary levels is through National Rural Health Mission launched in April 2005. Focused strategy on other communicable and non-communicable diseases and tertiary healthcare will be complementary to the strengthening of the healthcare delivery system under the Mission.

4125. (13-11-2007) NEW DELHI : Shri Kamal Nath, Union Minister of Commerce and Industry, has welcomed the keen interest of German small & medium sized companies for seeking investment opportunities in India. While welcoming Mr. Peter Harry Carstensen, Chief Minister of the German Federal State of Schleswig-Holstein, who called on him here today, the Commerce Minister appreciated the keen interest of the delegation to enhance bilateral relations with his State and India with a particular emphasis on trade and economic cooperation. "The present visit of business delegation mainly from German Mitelstand (SMEs) led by Mr. Peter Harry Carstensen, is very timely as this is one area in which interaction between the two countries needs to be intensified and SME links should be strengthened", the Minister observed. Senior officials from the Ministry of Commerce and members of business delegation from the German State of Schleswig-Holstein were present at the meeting. Shri Kamal Nath hoped that the State of Schleswig-Holstein would take advantage of India's investor-friendly climate and German companies would show greater engagement with India especially in the sectors of infrastructure, information technology, bio-technology and automobile industry etc. The bilateral trade with Germany has been increasing over the past 3 years. During 2004-05 the bilateral trade was US $ 6841 while during 2005-06 it reached a level of US $ 9610 million. During 2006-07, the trade resulted in a significant jump to touch US $ 16654 million. The main exports to Germany are machinery & instruments, drugs, pharmaceuticals, electronic goods and leather footwear while the imports from Germany include transport equipments, electronic goods, iron & steel, organic chemicals and machine tools etc. In the comparative list of countries for FDI approvals, Germany ranks 5th during the year 1991-92 to April-March 2007 with an investment of US $ 2.79 billion.

4126. (13-11-2007) NEW DELHI : The Minister of Petroleum & Natural Gas Shri Murli Deora has informed that Government is likely to offer 60 exploration blocks under VIIth round of New Exploration Licensing Policy (NELP-VII). Speaking at the annual Economic Editors' Conference organized by Press Information Bureau, here today, he said that NELP-VII is proposed to be launched shortly by December 07-Jan. 08. The blocks would comprise 30 onshore, 15 shallow water and 15 deep water & ultra deep water in both east and west coast offshore area. He also added that work relating to launch of CBM IV has started in consultation with the Ministry of Coal. Out of 26 CBM exploration blocks under operation, 6 thousand cubic feet(TCF) reserves have been established in 4 CBM blocks. First commercial production of CBM has commenced from July 2007.

4127. (13-11-2007) NEW DELHI : The National Biotechnology Development Strategy has been approved by the Government of India. The strategy is an outcome of a two-year-long nationwide consultation process with multiple stakeholders including concerned ministries, universities, research institutes, private sector, civil society, consumer groups, non-government and voluntary organizations and international bodies. The draft strategy, which was posted on the web, received over 300 comments from all sections of the society. The strategy has been finalized after careful scrutiny of these. Announcing this at a Press Conference today the Union Minister for Science & Technology and Earth Sciences, Shri. Kapil Sibal said that recognizing that biotechnology is a sunrise sector which requires focused attention, the Government has accorded approval for the broad framework of this strategy and the sectors proposed therein. The strategy, while enabling the full utilization of currently available opportunities in manufacturing and services, will lay a strong foundation for discovery and innovation, effectively utilizing novel technology platforms with potential to contribute to long term benefits in agriculture, animal productivity, human health, environmental security and sustainable industrial growth.

4128. (13-11-2007) NEW DELHI : Inaugurating the Ninth Conference of the Central Council of Health & Family Welfare today, the Union Minister for Health & Family Welfare, Dr. Anbumani Ramadoss said that a quick review of the National Rural Health Mission (NRHM) programmes during the last two years indicates that the focus of our healthcare system has shifted from a disease centric approach to a patient centric approach. NRHM launched in 2005 has provided a strong platform for community health actions at all levels. Besides Health Ministers and Secretaries from States, the function was attended by senior officials from the Ministry.

4129. (13-11-2007) NEW DELHI : Following are the extracts from the Address of the Finance Minister, Shri P. Chidambaram delivered at the 28th Annual Convocation of Tamil Nadu Agricultural University in Coimbatore, Tamil Nadu today: "I am very pleased to be here on the occasion of the twenty eighth annual convocation of the Tamil Nadu Agricultural University. This is the centenary year of the Agricultural College and Research Institute, Coimbatore, and I greet the Institute-and the University-on this memorable occasion and wish the Institute another hundred years and more of service to the society and, in particular, the farming community. I am grateful to the Chancellor, His Excellency the Governor of Tamil Nadu, the Vice Chancellor, Dr. C. Ramasamy, and the authorities of the University for the opportunity and the honour to deliver the convocation address. Agriculture is the main source of livelihood for more than 50 per cent of the population of Tamil Nadu. For the whole country, nearly 60 per cent of the population is dependent on agriculture. The share of agriculture in the Gross Domestic Product (GDP) has declined for reasons that are obvious. The agriculture sector usually grows at a moderate pace; it is the industry and services sectors that are capable of recording high rates of growth, including double digit growth. While the size of the total pie has increased, and the size of the agricultural economy in that pie has also increased, the share of agriculture has declined. I am afraid, given international experience and India's record, that share will decline further. Nevertheless, agriculture remains important for a number of reasons. Firstly, in terms of contribution to the GDP originating in rural areas, more than one-half of such contribution is accounted for by agriculture. Secondly, according to estimates made in 2004-05, one-half of the total number of persons employed was employed in agriculture. Thirdly, the agriculture sector contributes one-fifth of total exports. Fourthly, the sector provides raw materials to several crucial industries such as cotton textiles, jute, sugar and paper. The most important aspect of agriculture in India is that no country with a population as large as India's can depend on imports to feed its people. There is no alternative to becoming nearly self-sufficient in the production of food grains, pulses and oil seeds. Thirty years ago, India imported food grains to feed 600 million people; today, we are nearly self-sufficient in producing food for a billion plus people. That, I wish to emphasize, is the only alternative open to India. Hence, the paramount importance of agriculture.

4130. (13-11-2007) NEW DELHI : Jawaharlal Nehru was a great Indian of the last century, next only to Mahatma Gandhi, the Father of the Nation. As Independent India's first Prime Minister for seventeen long formative and eventful years, he has left a lasting impression on the country and the world. He was respectfully called 'Panditji'. Nehru believed in a strong, united, industrialized and modern India. Panditji's vision of free India had been formed clearly during the hard and tumultuous years of the freedom movement. At the age of 15 he went to England for higher education. After completing his education he started legal practice at Allahabad. However, he soon gave it up and joined the Freedom Movement. Nehru was impressed by Gandhiji's Champaran (Bihar) and Kaira (Gujarat) movements. Panditji in his Autobiography says "I was thrown, almost without any will of my own, into contact with the peasantry". But this contact subsequently, influenced his mental outlook greatly. Describing the kisans of Pratapgarh he says, "Looking at them and their misery and overflowing gratitude, I was filled with shame and sorrow, shame at my easy-going and comfortable life and our petty politics of the city which ignored this vast multitude of semi-naked sons and daughters of India, sorrow at the degradation and overwhelming poverty of India. A new picture of India seemed to rise before me, naked, starving, crushed and utterly miserable. And their faith in us, casual visitors from the distant city, embarrassed me and filled me with a new responsibility that frightened me". When India became free, Nehruji pledged to build the nation, eradicate poverty and ignorance, disease and inequality of opportunity and work for the good of the people. He initiated several measures to improve the lot of Indian farmers. The Zamindari System was abolished and land reforms were effected. For all round development of the country democratic planning was started in 1951 and Community Development Programmes in 1952. The policies and development programmes initiated by Pandit Nehru were successful and the country marched steadily on the path of progress. In 1963 in an article Pandit Nehru himself described the measures taken by him and their success: "It is no sign of complacency to recognize that these policies have met with an encouraging measure of success. India remains the largest functioning democracy in the world. Without deviating from democratic principles and procedures, She has launched upon extensive programmes of modernization which are already bearing fruit. Far-reaching land reforms have taken place and our economy, still predominantly agricultural, is being steadily transformed by the spread of industrialization and the completion of vast new projects in the field of power, transport and irrigation. Our community development schemes represent a rural reconstruction programme which promises to transform the country-side and the vast population that lives there".

4131. (13-11-2007) NEW DELHI : The World Travel Market in London is one of the largest tourism trade fairs in the world. The 2007 edition of this fair is being held at the ExCel convention centre from 12th November to 15th November. Over 5500 exhibitors from 202 countries and regions of the world are participating in this fair which will be attended by over 45000 travel trade professionals. Over the past 13 years, the World Travel Market has become an established business platform hosting debates, presentations, seminars, workshops and networking events for development and promotion of responsible tourism. India is one of the largest participants at WTM with over 750 square meters of space at a prime location. The Indian travel industry under the aegis of the Ministry of Tourism, Government of India is well represented. Over 91 travel trade organizations including various state governments/ union territories, hotel chains, tour operators, airlines and specialist companies are participating in the Incredible India pavilion. More than 300 professionals comprising of the crème de la crème of the travel and tourism industry of India are promoting their specific destinations and products. Apart from this around 24 other organizations are exhibiting independently covering an additional area of around 500 sq. meter. The Incredible India pavilion sports a different look this year with the theme being the world heritage site of Ajanta. The traditional wooden pillars give the stand the look and feel of an ancient temple. The huge cloth banners depicting the Ajanta paintings are a definite attraction for the visitors. Coming inside the pavilion the visitors can meet with the travel trade from India at their individual booths and discuss business opportunities. The Incredible India pavilion was inaugurated by Shri Shilabhadra Banerjee, Secretary to the Government of India, Ministry of Tourism in the presence of Shri Kamalesh Sharma, High Commission of India to the UK with the cutting of the ribbon and lighting the lamp. The tourism ministers of the states of Kerala, Jammu & Kashmir, Meghalaya, Pondicherry, Mrs Leena Nandan, Joint Secretary (Tourism), Government of India as well as other dignitaries were also present. This was followed by the formal release of the Incredible India fact finder published by Indiatourism London. Traditional Indian sweets and savouries were distributed to all present.

4132. (13-11-2007) NEW DELHI : Labour & Employment Minister of India said, at the outset, let me convey my gratitude to PIB for offering me an opportunity to participate in this Economic Editors' Conference and share my thoughts with the enlightened members of the Media present here. India stands at a crucial juncture as she is poised to touch double digit growth rate. The 11th Five Year Plan seeks to achieve not only a faster but also inclusive growth. This is possible only with effective contribution of all stakeholders. This also forms the basic credo of the Ministry of Labour & Employment. Labour is both a contributor to and beneficiary of economic development. How to ensure its benign involvement in the development process is our biggest challenge. Our background material, has already been circulated. Let me, however, elaborate on some of the important issues. Vocational Training with a view to creating a world-class skilled labour force is being given maximum importance. Hon'ble Prime Minister in his last independence day address to the Nation had stated, "We will soon launch a Mission on Vocational Education and Skill Development, through which we will open 1600 new industrial training institutes (ITIs) and polytechnics, 10, 000 new vocational schools and 50, 000 new Skill Development Centres. We will ensure that annually, over 100 lakh students get vocational training-which is a four-fold increase from today's level. We will seek the active help of the private sector in this initiative so that they not only assist in the training but also lend a hand in providing employment opportunities".

4133. (13-11-2007) NEW DELHI : The Vice President of India Mohd. Hamid Ansari released the 10 volumes of the books titled "Maheep Singh Rachnavali" at a function here today. These volumes contain the various writings of noted writer Dr. Maheep Singh and have been edited by Mr. Anil Kumar. Addressing on the occasion, the Vice President said that he himself is very fond of the books and knows the intricacies of writing a book. A writer explains his point of view for the common masses by sharing his emotions and experiences and Dr. Maheep Singh has expressed his inner feelings and emotions in his writings in a very thoughtful way. The Vice President congratulated Dr. Maheep Singh for his valuable writings. A number of dignitaries and authors were present on the occasion.

4134. (13-11-2007) NEW DELHI : Following is the text of the Speech of the Finance Minister, Shri P. Chidambaram delivered on Growth Prospects in South Asia: Challenges and Opportunities delivered at the Lakshman Kadirgamar Institute of International Relations and Strategic Studies in Colombo, Sri Lanka on 11th November, 2007: "I am deeply grateful to the Lakshman Kadirgamar Institute of International Relations and Strategic Studies for inviting me to deliver this lecture. In particular, I thank Mrs. Kadirgamar who prevailed upon me to find a date for this lecture amidst my rather chaotic schedule. Her persuasion, persistence and patience, I am told, are well known. I am sure that many of you who know her better will agree with me when I say that her qualities can move mountains. As a fitting tribute to Mr. Lakshman Kadirgamar, the Sri Lanka Institute of Strategic Studies was re-christened in August 2006 as the Lakshman Kadirgamar Institute of International Relations and Strategic Studies and given a broader mandate. The objectives of the Institute encompass the vision of Mr. Kadirgamar, the most important feature of which is that Sri Lanka should regain its historic internal harmony by embracing its multi-cultural and multi-ethnic character. Mr. Kadirgamar himself was a product of Sri Lanka's unique character. He was a Tamil; he was born in the Jaffna region; he was a Christian; he celebrated Vesak, the full moon day on which Lord Buddha was born; he read literature at Oxford; he was called to the Bar from the Inner Temple in the United Kingdom; and he practised law at the Judicial Committee of the Privy Council. From international civil servant to foreign minister, he held many offices with great distinction. India regarded Mr. Kadirgamar as a statesman who devoted many years of his life-especially his years as foreign minister-to bring peace to this tortured nation. Under the most adverse conditions, he carried out his duties as a public servant in the manner that he played cricket. And how did he play cricket? To recall his words, "I played without helmet and thigh guards, on matting wickets that were full of holes and stones, and I had my share of broken bones to show for it." None could break his spirit as a cricketer and none could break his spirit as a public servant imbued with the high ideals of a statesman. It is a little over two years since Mr. Kadirgamar was assassinated. I pay my tribute to this great Tamil and great son of Sri Lanka, and I am honoured to deliver this lecture instituted in his memory.

4135. (13-11-2007) NEW DELHI : Shri Kamal Nath, Commerce & Industry Minister, has expressed the hope that the 5th Session of Indo-Greek Joint Economic Committee held today would pave the way for enhancing bilateral trade relations between the two countries. He also called for working towards doubling of the trade between the two countries to reach and exceed 1 billion Euro by 2010. While welcoming Mr. Petros Doukas, Deputy Foreign Minister of Greece who called on him here today, Shri Kamal Nath observed that the bilateral trade between the two countries has shown a robust growth during the last two years. Senior officials from the Government of Greece along with members of business community were also present at the meeting. Shri Kamal Nath while inviting the Greek entrepreneurs to invest in the development of India's infrastructure sectors over the next decade to build and develop various projects in energy, railways, highways and shipping, hoped that once the renegotiations of double-taxation avoidance agreement (DTAA) and the implementation of Bilateral Investment Promotion and Protection Agreement (BIPA) are complete, it would encourage investments in both the countries. He also informed the visiting members of the delegation about India being an established global service provider in the field of IT and software and expressed hope for Indo-Greek cooperation in this sector. The Indian exports to Greece were US $ 564.09 million in the year 2005-06 and rose to US $ 672.03 million in the year 2006-07 achieving an increase of 20%. The main exports to Greece from India include petroleum (crude & products), transport equipments, marine products and cotton yarn etc. while the main imports consist of Metalifers ores and metal scraps.

4136. (13-11-2007) NEW DELHI : Agriculture Minister, Shri Sharad Pawar today re-affirmed government's determination to sustain the growth trend of 4% in agriculture, not only in the short-term, but also with a medium to long-term perspective. Addressing the Economic Editors' Conference here, he informed that the average growth rate of farm sector during the last two years has been more than 4%. "Investment in agriculture has also shown a rising trend in these two years. Market reforms have started providing a better opportunity for the farmers to realise higher prices. The extension which had not been satisfactory seems to be reaching to the farmers. Credit availability has more than doubled in the last three years and irrigation expansion programmes have been taken up in a more focused manner, " he said. "Despite several odds, a revival in the sector in the past two years is quite evident, " Shri Pawar said and highlighted some landmarks that have been reached during 2006-07: "The record production of 216 million tonnes of food grains, 22.7 million bales of cotton and 345 million tonnes of sugarcane restores our confidence that we have the potential to meet the challenges. The encouraging response to the initiatives under the National Horticulture Mission, including that in the north-eastern region, micro irrigation, market reforms and extension reaffirms our commitment towards a more remunerative and efficient agriculture." Stating that the issues facing Indian agriculture necessitated a policy re-orientation, the Minister added that the strategy for rejuvenating agriculture aimed at 4% annual growth, contributing to a more inclusive growth is reflected in the 11th Five Year Plan document. Referring to the initiatives taken for food security, the Minister gave details of the National Food Security Mission (NFSM). This nearly Rs. 5000 crore scheme aims at producing additional 10 million tonnes of rice, 8 million tonnes of wheat and 2 million tonnes of pulses by the end of the 11th plan. Besides, a Rastriya Krishi Vikas Yojna with Central allocation of Rs.25, 000 crores, has been launched to incentivise the States to invest more in the agriculture sector. Recent initiatives to promote fisheries, the Minister said, would result in about 6-7% growth of this sector in the 11th Plan. Speaking on the availability of food commodities for the public distribution system and controlling price rise the Minister emphasized that though the international prices of wheat and edible oils went up 80% or more in the last one year, domestic prices have been maintained at reasonable levels. Though prices of essential commodities were under pressure because of shortfall in domestic supplies, diversion of foodgrain to bio-fuel and animal feed and hardening international prices, timely steps taken by the Government helped in checking rise in price of these commodities. The steps included reducing or abolishing import duty of wheat and pulses, ban on export of pulses import of pulses, by State Agencies, raising the minimum export price of onion and distribution of onion by NAFED.

4137. (13-11-2007) NEW DELHI : The World Travel Market in London is one of the largest tourism trade fairs in the world. The 2007 edition of this fair is being held at the Excel convention centre from 12th November to 15th November. Over 5500 exhibitors from 202 countries and regions of the world are participating in this fair which will be attended by over 45000 travel trade professionals. Over the past 13 years, the World Travel Market has become an established business platform hosting debates, presentations, seminars, workshops and networking events for development and promotion of responsible tourism. India is one of the largest participants at WTM with over 750 square meters of space at a prime location. The Indian travel industry under the aegis of the Ministry of Tourism, Government of India is well represented. Over 91 travel trade organizations including various state governments/ union territories, hotel chains, tour operators, airlines and specialist companies are participating in the Incredible India pavilion. More than 300 professionals comprising of the crème de la crème of the travel and tourism industry of India are promoting their specific destinations and products. Apart from this around 24 other organizations are exhibiting independently covering an additional area of around 500 sq. meter. The Incredible India pavilion sports a different look this year with the theme being the world heritage site of Ajanta. The traditional wooden pillars give the stand the look and feel of an ancient temple. The huge cloth banners depicting the Ajanta paintings are a definite attraction for the visitors. Coming inside the pavilion the visitors can meet with the travel trade from India at their individual booths and discuss business opportunities. The Incredible India pavilion was inaugurated by Shri Shilabhadra Banerjee, Secretary to the Government of India, Ministry of Tourism in the presence of Shri Kamalesh Sharma, High Commission of India to the UK with the cutting of the ribbon and lighting the lamp. The tourism ministers of the states of Kerala, Jammu & Kashmir, Meghalaya, Pondicherry, Mrs Leena Nandan, Joint Secretary (Tourism), Government of India as well as other dignitaries were also present. This was followed by the formal release of the Incredible India fact finder published by Indiatourism London. Traditional Indian sweets and savouries were distributed to all present.

4138. (13-11-2007) NEW DELHI : The 27th India International Trade Fair 2007 is being organized by the India Trade Promotion Organisation (ITPO) at Pragati Maidan, from November 14-27, 2007. The Fair is a mega celebration of the new India that is fast taking shape. The theme of the Fair 'Processed Food and Agro-Industries" figures prominently in the display scheme of the pavilions of the States and Union Territories besides the stand-alone pavilions numbering 7 A, B & C. India is the 10th most industrialized country and fourth largest economy in terms of purchasing power parity with its GDP projected to grow at nearly 8% in 2006-07. The country also happens to be the most richly endowed agricultural nation in Asia having 169 million hectares of arable land, accounting for one-tenth of the world's arable land and a fifth of the world's irrigated land at 56 million hectares with a coastline extending to 8000 km and vast marine wealth. While India is one of the largest food producers of the world with the organized sector accounting for food output worth US$ 34827 million, only a small percentage of its farm produce is processed into value-added products. Although the country is the second largest producer of fruits and vegetables, hardly two per cent of the production is processed. This underlines the enormous scope for investing in the processed food sector in the areas of infrastructure, packaging and machinery. India, in fact, needs US $ 28 billion of investment to raise its food processing levels by 8-10 %. A number of areas have been identified for attracting investment in the processed foods sector. These are: Mega Food Parks; Agri Infrastructure, supply chain aggregation; Logistics and Cold Chain Infrastructure and Machinery/ Packaging The overall potential embodied by the food processing sector, coupled with the policy initiatives of the Government, has facilitated the entry of leading global players with sizeable investments into this sector. Considering the demand, growth, policy initiative and investment parameters in appropriate perspective, a Vision 2015 approach adopted by the Ministry of Food Processing Industries foresees a healthy prognosis for the processed foods sector.

4139. (13-11-2007) NEW DELHI : The National Biotechnology Development Strategy has been approved by the Government of India. The strategy is an outcome of a two-year-long nationwide consultation process with multiple stakeholders including concerned ministries, universities, research institutes, private sector, civil society, consumer groups, non-government and voluntary organizations and international bodies. The draft strategy, which was posted on the web, received over 300 comments from all sections of the society. The strategy has been finalized after careful scrutiny of these. Announcing this at a Press Conference today the Union Minister for Science & Technology and Earth Sciences, Shri. Kapil Sibal said that recognizing that biotechnology is a sunrise sector which requires focused attention, the Government has accorded approval for the broad framework of this strategy and the sectors proposed therein. The strategy, while enabling the full utilization of currently available opportunities in manufacturing and services, will lay a strong foundation for discovery and innovation, effectively utilizing novel technology platforms with potential to contribute to long term benefits in agriculture, animal productivity, human health, environmental security and sustainable industrial growth.

4140. (13-11-2007) NEW DELHI : The technology for the production of Bollcure- a promising botanical biopesticide for cotton bollworm developed by The Energy and Resources Institute (TERI) was transferred today by Biotech Consortium India

Limited (BCIL) to Sri Biotech Laboratories India Pvt. Ltd., a Hyderabad based biopesticide and biofertilizer manufacturing company. The technology transfer ceremony was presided over by Shri. Kapil Sibal, Union Minister for Science and Technology and Earth Sciences. Bollcure is a novel botanical biopesticide to restrict the growth of cotton bollworm, an insect pest which causes extensive damage to the cotton crops. The formulation developed at The Energy and Resources Institute (TERI), New Delhi with support from the Department of Biotechnology, Govt of India, restricts the growth of the insect larvae (juvenile insect) in early stages of development thereby resulting in the death of the larvae thus preventing crop damage. A team of scientists led by Dr. Nutan Kaushik, Fellow and Area Convenor, Plant Biotechnology Division, TERI has put in years of efforts to bring out the Bollcure formulation, which is a Eucalyptus plant extract based biopesticide not only effective against cotton bollworm Helicoverpa armigera, a major insect pest of cotton but also other harmful insect pests of other economically important crops like pigeon pea, chick pea, tobacco, tomato, sunflower etc. for which the laboratory trials are underway. Sri Biotech, an ISO 9001:2000 certified company, is one of the leading agribiotechnology companies in India specialized in product-oriented research, development and manufacturing of organic and biological agricultural inputs. The company has successfully developed products and processes for disease and pest management based on indigenous R & D and has recently won the Department of Scientific and Industrial Research (DSIR) award for its outstanding contributions in the field of agricultural biotechnology. The present technology is developed at TERI which is a premier research organization working towards technology innovations that are environment-friendly, natural resource conserving, and people-oriented. BCIL that has facilitated this technology transfer, is a company promoted by Department of Biotechnology (DBT), Government of India and set up by all India financial institutions including IDBI, ICICI, IFCI, etc. BCIL has been engaged in facilitating accelerated commercialization of biotechnology based products for more than a decade by establishing linkages among the various stake holders which includes industry, R & D institutions, Government, financial institutions and international agencies. Also, the company provides access to technologies, creating awareness about business opportunities, IPR protection, regulatory and biosafety requirements; drafting feasibility and detailed project reports; arranging financial support and manpower training and placement.

4141. (13-11-2007) NEW DELHI : The Minister of State for Defence Production, Rao Inderjit Singh has asked private industry to seize business opportunity in defence industry as India gallops towards a developed economy and the armed forces transform into a lean and mean fighting machine. Addressing an international seminar on Armoured Fighting Vehicles (AFVs) here today, the first of its kind in the country, Rao Inderjit cited success stories in private-public partnership in developing weapon systems, notably Light Combat Aircraft 'Tejas', Prithvi and Brahmos missiles and Multi-Barrel Rocket Launchers (MBRLs). All this has been made possible since the government threw open defence production to private sector in 2001, he added. Rao Inderjit further said the government encourages the DRDO and public-private industry to harness synergies and meet the huge potential for the armed forces' needs. In an RFP (Request for Proposal) for 126 Multi-Role Combat Aircraft (MRCA) issued a few months ago, the Defence Ministry has hiked the Offset value of the contract amount worth thousands of crores from the stipulated 30 to 50 percent for building indigenous capabilities and percolating the benefits to domestic industry. In his address, the Chief of Army Staff, General Deepak Kapoor hoped scientists and engineers, based on their experience in designing the Main Battle Tank 'Arjun', would be able to develop a more versatile AFV for the army's future needs. He said the Arjun tank took a longer time to build as this was the first attempt at indigenously developing an integrated and highly sophisticated mobile weapons platform. Earlier, Lt. General KDS Shekhawat, DG (Mechanised Forces), in his theme-address, emphasized on the need for a compressed timeframe if the vast resources pumped into developing war machines are to retain cutting edge technology. A large number of Indian and foreign companies are participating in the two-day seminar hosted jointly by the Directorate General of Mechanised Forces and the Confederation of Indian Industry (CII). Mahindra Defence Systems, a subsidiary of leading automobile maker Mahindra and Mahindra, unveiled their Light Specialist Vehicle 'Axe' on the sidelines of the seminar. A Company spokesman said the all-terrain vehicle, which can accommodate six/nine soldiers, will undergo field user trials by the army in Uttarakhand next month. Designed prior to the army's RFP, the Axe can be shielded against 7.62 mm armoured piercing. Besides Mahindra, Ford Motors has also showcased its Armoured and Special Purpose Vehicles while TS Kisan and Co. is displaying spares and accessories for T-72 and T-90 tanks and BMP-II. Among others, INTEL Design Systems has also put up an array of chips with defence applications.

4142. (13-11-2007) NEW DELHI : The National Buildings Construction Corporation Ltd (NBCC) has grown to become the big Public Sector Company having a recorded turnover of Rs. 1514 crore for the financial year 2006-07. This was stated by Shri S.Jaipal Reddy, Urban Development Minister at a meeting of the Parliamentary Consultative Committee attached to his Ministry here today. The subject of discussion was NBCC. Shri Reddy said that while improving its performance consistently, NBCC has paid back maiden dividend to the Government. NBCC has also been awarded: The top ten PSU Award for 2004-05 and 2005-06 and the best turn around company Award by the Prime Minister of India. NBCC has made efforts to shoulder social responsibilities as a part of its corporate social mission and has been able to respond very quickly in case of disasters like cyclones, tsunami and earthquakes and participation in the rehabilitation schemes of the Ministry. NBCC also has been actively involved in developing of the North-Eastern States over the last 4/5 years to the great satisfaction of the Ministry as well as the concerned States. Shri Reddy informed the Members. NBCC today has an order book of more than 5, 000 crores against a meager 300 crores five years ago and is now looking forward to achieving a turn over of 4, 500 crores by the year 2010-11 as per their new corporate plan. NBCC has also embarked upon schemes like affordable housing, low cost housing technology, and diversified into Real Estates and Power Projects etc., the Minister said.

4143. (13-11-2007) NEW DELHI : National Small Industries Corporation Ltd. (NSIC), under the Ministry of Micro, Small & Medium Enterprises is organizing "Techmart India 2007", the 15th International Technology Fair from tomorrow at Pragati Maidan, New Delhi coinciding with India International Trade Fair 2007. This annual event will be a centre stage for keeping abreast with latest technology development in the Indian Micro, Small & Medium Enterprises Sector(MSME). The event will assist MSME Sector in marketing their products and services and also help large companies and buyers in identifying MSMEs which can become their ancillaries, partners in joint ventures and sub-contracting. This information was given by Shri H.P. Kumar, CMD, NSIC at a press conference here today. He said, this year a new dimension of sectoral approach has been added to the display profile of the exhibition and emphasis is laid on sector specific products and technologies like low cost building material, auto components, information technology, light engineering and machines tools, textiles, coir etc. A new initiative has been taken by NSIC by providing special enclosure of "Working Techmart" where stand-alone technologies for entrepreneurs will be on display besides live cluster demonstration of units from North Eastern States. During Techmart India 2007, a seminar on NSIC support services for Micro, Small & Medium Enterprises will also be organised. In reply to a question Shri Kumar said developing and Latin American countries consider India a role model in MSME sector. About 35 Foreign delegations from South Africa, Sri Lanka, Kenya, Uganda, Mozambique etc. are expected to visit Techmart India, 2007. More than 200 Micro and Small units will be displaying their technologies/products during the exhibition.

4144. (13-11-2007) NEW DELHI : The Union Public Service Commission (UPSC) will conduct the Civil Services (Main), Exam 2007 papers on the subjects- (i) Political Science & International Relations and (ii) Public Administration-on November 23, 2007. These papers were earlier scheduled for October 31, 2007 but had been postponed by UPSC. The venues, the centre of examination and timings of the papers would remains the same as earlier notified in the individual Admission Certificates except for Jaipur centre. The venue of examination in Jaipur centre earlier scheduled at Examination Hall, Yojana Bhawan, Block-B, Tilak Marg, Jaipur has now been changed to Tagore Public School, Shastri Nagar Road, Jaipur-302016.

4145. (13-11-2007) NEW DELHI : November 13, 2007 The Tourism and Culture Minister Smt. Ambika Soni has stressed the need to promote India as the new emerging Medical Value Travel destination abroad. She was speaking at the 4th

India Health Summit here today. Smt. Soni said the way medial tourism has developed in recent times is largely linked to economics and technology and India is positioning itself as the primary medical destination for the most complex medical procedures in the world. She said we need to work out a strategy to retain our pre-eminence in this area. The Minister said, her Ministry in collaboration with the Ministry of Health and the Industry is committed to making this happen. The market is growing, the revenue generated was approximately $ 333 million in 2004 is expected to increase @ 20% and is estimated to touch $ 2.2 billion by 2012. Smt. Soni said the private and public hospitals need to synergies their efforts and promote India as the Healthcare destination worldwide and should strategize to bring international medical conferences to India in various specializations such as urology, cardiology etc. Listing the efforts of the Tourism Ministry in promoting medical tourism, the Minister said her Ministry in close consultation with Home Ministry has been able to bring out a special type of visa known as M Visa for foreign patients visiting India for treatment. It would be valid for one year duration and can be extended further on arrival in India. She said it also makes provision for a patient to be accompanied by the companion. She said Tourism Ministry is already working on low budget hotels and Bed and Breakfast Schemes to provide accommodation to the tourists. She said the medical fraternity should integrate these developments into its strategy. Smt. Soni said to promote medical tourism, we need to address the medical infrastructure and the hygiene issues. Developing countries, especially and South and South East Asia are feared to be infested with infectious diseases .We should convert our medical centres sanitation zones with zero tolerance for uncleanness. At the same time, our tourist destinations should acquire a clean environment ambience. She said the tour operators, guides and travel agencies should work on inculcating this sense amongst the citizens at the local level. The Ministry of Tourism's 'Athithi Devo Bhava' campaign has a message for all citizens of the country to come together against graffiti and the need for maintaining clean environment. Smt. Soni said every stakeholder including the Doctors, hospitals, medical professional, travel agency and all other agencies must work towards achieving the objective of cleanliness. A patient should leave India spiritually enhanced and physically rejuvenated at the end of his/ her stay. The two-day conference is being attended by top health experts, doctors and captains of industry.

4146. (13-11-2007) NEW DELHI : The Petroleum Minister said here that, Friends from the Media, my colleague Shri Dinsha Patel, Secretary Shri Srinivasan, other officials of the Ministry of Petroleum and Natural Gas and the representatives of the oil and gas sector. The importance of energy security can not be over emphasized. In my Ministry, we are working towards sourcing both indigenous and external sources of oil and gas. At the same time, in order to protect the vulnerable sections of population, despite very high levels of international prices of crude oil, prices of kerosene meant for public distribution system and price of domestic LPG have not been revised.

4147. (13-11-2007) NEW DELHI : Billiards sports person Rupesh Ashwinbhai Shah of Indian Railways has become new World Champion. The World Billiards Championships 2007 organised by International Billiards & Snooker Federation was held in Singapore from 5th to 14th September 2007. Both the finalists of this Championship, *i.e.* Rupesh Ashwinbhai Shah and Ashok Harishankar Sandilaya were from Indian Railways and Rupesh Shah emerged as the new World Champion. Fourteen countries participated in this Championship. Shri K.C. Jena, Chairman, Railway Board has announced a Cash Award of Rs. Two lakhs to Rupesh Ashwinbhai Shah for his outstanding sports achievement and for becoming new World Champion.

4148. (13-11-2007) NEW DELHI: Communist Party of India (Marxist) general secretary Prakash Karat on Monday accused the Trinamool Congress-led alliance of taking the help of Maoist cadres to establish their hold over the Nandigram area in West Bengal where sporadic violence has gone on for the past 11 months. "Since October-November, Maoists have built bunkers in Nandigram area, set up training camps and started expanding. It is now that people who have legitimate right to cultivate their land and live in that area have started returning to their homes. Normal life will be resumed soon and the State government will be able to take up all developmental work in the area. The process has begun to restore normality in the area," Mr. Karat said. He was addressing a press conference at the party headquarters after a two-day meeting of the party's Polit Bureau here. Answering questions relating to the disturbances in the Nandigram area, he said National Security Advisor M.K. Narayanan had also confirmed the presence and active involvement of the Maoist cadres in fanning trouble in Nandigram. Mr. Karat said that even Prime Minister Manmohan Singh said the Maoists were the single biggest threat to the country's internal security. "The Maoists have entrenched themselves in the area and are running a parallel raj there, not even allowing the local administration, police and the State government to function. It is clear that people are not with the Maoists ... rule of gun cannot be allowed," he said. Mr. Karat said the Trinamool Congress and its allies had tried unsuccessfully to dislodge the Left Front democratically in successive elections in the past and were taking the help of Maoists in the Nandigram area to dislodge Left Front's elected representatives. "We are not going to allow them to dislodge our elected panchayat members and MLAs physically by using Maoists," he asserted. He said there was no question of land acquisition or setting up of a chemical hub in the Nandigram area for which the State government has selected another place and wondered what was the entire struggle about.

4149. (13-11-2007) NEW DELHI : Twenty five soldiers from the Maldives National Defence Forces (MNDF) have arrived at the Indian Army's elite Counter Insurgency and Jungle Warfare School (CIJWS) Vairengte, Mizoram being commanded by Brig RM Painuly, to undergo an intense four week course in Counter Insurgency and Counter Terrorist Operations. As the Commandant says, "Low Intensity Conflict are becoming global in scope. It is widely believed that terrorism is becoming less territorially defined, global in reach and more decentralized. Indeed, terrorism has now truly become a global phenomenon. They are not longer bound by limits of geography. Modern militancy has become a complex phenomenon. The globalised world is now matched by a globalised militant ideology. We need to tackle the menace of terrorism globally and hence joint training is a step in global war on terrorism". The Maldives National Defence Forces (MNDF) are keen to learn from Indian Army's experience in combating insurgency for the last 50 years. And one can't think of a better staging ground for this exchange of expertise between the two forces than the Indian Army's unique Counter Insurgency and Jungle Warfare (CIJW) School, located in Mizoram. The motto of the School is 'Fight the Guerrilla Like a Guerrilla'. The School has been recognized as a "Centre of Excellence for Counter Insurgency". The School trains all ranks of the Indian Armed Forces, Indian Air Force, Indian Navy, Para Military Forces and Central Police Organisations. Going global, the School is providing training to Officers and Personnel Below Officers Rank (PBOR) of various friendly countries including Afghanistan, Bhutan, Botswana, Bangladesh, Nepal, Ghana, Iraq, Kenya, Mauritius, Singapore, Seychelles, Sri Lanka, South Africa, Myanmar, Kyzgystan, Mongolia, Uzbekistan and Nigeria. Training facilities provided by the School are greatly appreciated by the subscribing countries. Many other countries have elicited interest in the training being imparted here and the demand is on the increase.

4150. (13-11-2007) NEW DELHI : The Directorate General for Civil Aviation has issued the following guidelines for low visibility conditions at IGI Airport: The Low Visibility Procedures (LVP) prepared for the operation of aircraft upto CAT IIIB visibility conditions at IGI Airport Delhi and notified through AIP Supplement No. 33 of 2006, shall be strictly followed by all the agencies at the airport including the security agencies. With the deteriorating trend of visibility detected, Duty Officer MET, IGI airport, shall inform the WSO as the RVR becomes less than 1200 meters and also when the visibility forecasted indicates deterioration of visibility to 800 meters or less. This information shall also be passed by MET at IGI airport to the Airlines and other agencies whenever enquiries about visibility conditions are received from Airlines to plan their flight scheduling. The Airlines on the basis of the above information shall plan their departures and arrival at IGI airport and simultaneously commence necessary facilitation processes to avoid inconvenience to their passengers. The Met Department should draw a contingency plan to include the continuous serviceability of Met equipments and positioning of senior officials. Airport Terminal Managers of DIAL at all the three terminals at IGI Airport shall also monitor such information and in coordination with the Airlines take necessary steps to facilitate passengers as drawn up in their fog contingency plan. The Low Visibility Procedures shall start from the moment the RVR value drops to 800 M and less. The MET Department at the airport shall continuously monitor the trend of RVR which shall be broadcasted and updated from time to time. All airlines shall monitor this trend through telephone or the ATIS broadcast for their planning of flight departures and passenger facilitation. WSO on receipt of visibility reports shall at the appropriate time ensure broadcasting on ATIS, whenever CAT II and CAT III-A/B conditions are in vogue. Once the LVP commences, all the agencies at the IGI airport shall start taking respective action contained in the Low Visibility Procedure. Proper and strict RT discipline shall be maintained by all the pilots, ATC and Apron Control during LVP operations. Airlines shall ensure that only those pilots who are adequately trained and certificated for Low Take-off Minima are rostered for operating flights during low visibility conditions from/to Delhi to ensure aircraft operation during low visibility conditions especially during CAT II and CAT III-A/B conditions.

4151. (13-11-2007) NEW DELHI : Shri S. Regupathy, Minister of State for Environment and Forests said that today climate change is no more a future threat but we are already in it. Inaugurating a two-day National Workshop on Forest Fires, he further said in the emerging scenario forests will be critical to the issue of climate security. Forests are not only impacted by the climate change but also are natural resources that impact the climate. Any destruction/deforestation of forest areas will contribute to enhancing the rate of climate change. Forest fires, not only contribute significantly to Green Houses Gases (GHG) emission but loss of resource renders the area more vulnerable to climate change. Therefore, it is imperative that we must make efforts to protect forest wealth which is the best cover for climate security. Shri Regupathy said that forests fires are an area of concern as every year large extent of forest areas are affected by forest fires. In India, forest fires are annual feature. Consequences of uncontrolled forest fires are serious degradation of forests, ecological changes as well as deterioration of social and economic conditions. The main ecological damage occurs in form of destruction of biodiversity extinction of plants and animals, deterioration of soil ecosystem resulting in erosion and loss of soil fertility, loss of wildlife habitat and depletion of wildlife, degradation of watershed zone resulting in loss of water as well destruction of natural regeneration leading to forest reduction. Ecological and social losses due to fire destruction include losses of valuable timber resources, NTFP fuel wood and fodder. The factors like high biotic pressures, large areas of dry, deciduous forests, hot and dry climate etc. render the precious wealth of forests prone to the current fires. In such circumstances along with conventional approach for fire prevention, reduction and control need to be planned properly. Besides this we must look newer and effective methods of fire detection modeling and control. Effective and fast response tools like remote sensing and GIS based assessments in conjunction with ground data can play a significant role.

4152. (13-11-2007) NEW DELHI : The annual-SARAS-2007, India International Trade Fair (IITF), organized jointly by the Ministry of Rural Development and Council for Advancement of People's Action and Rural Technology (CAPART) commences from tomorrow. The fortnight long Saras Mela will be inaugurated by Dr. Raghuvansh Prasad Singh, Minister for Rural Development at 3 pm in Hall No. 7, Pragati Maidan, New Delhi. Dr. Singh will also inaugurate the Rural Development Pavilion, in Hall No. 17 at 5 pm simultaneously. The theme of Saras Mela this year is the 'Sari'. The Ministry organizes this Fair every year for facilitating the Special Swarnajayanti Gram Swarozgar Yojna (SGSY) beneficiaries, rural artisans, craftsmen, self help groups (SHGs) and NGOs to exhibit and sell their products, and to provide them the opportunity for additional income and exposure on a large scale. This exhibition-cum-sale fair under the brand name of SARAS will display a wide range of products manufactured by the rural artisans, craftsmen and beneficiaries of SHGs across the country. The mela also aims at creating a unique platform for developing linkages with customers and providing an opportunity to artisans to interact with the buyers directly. Saras 2007 is exhibiting over 350 stalls of DRDAs and NGOs from 21 States displaying a variety of products prepared by rural artisans across the country. As per the theme of this year, Craftsmen are displaying an array of 'saris' from different cultural regions of the country. Other attractive products on sale include bamboo artifacts, traditional and ayurvedic medicines, metalwork, woodwork, Madhubani paintings, terracotta, shawls, carpets, food products etc. Lively cultural programmes by artists from different States will be another major attraction of this mega event.

4153. (13-11-2007) NEW DELHI : Following is the text of the speech of Finance Minister, Shri P. Chidambaram delivered at the inauguration of the Economic Editors' Conference, 2007, here yesterday: "I have always viewed the Annual Economic Editors' Conference as an important platform for interface between the Government and the Fourth Estate on the salient aspects of the economy, the current economic situation, the challenges and the policy responses of the Government. I understand that the participants of this Conference form a highly diverse cross section of informed economic editors from the length and breadth of the country. I extend a hearty welcome to all the participants and wish that over the next two days there will be meaningful discussions on the current state of the Indian economy and the Government's economic policies. Such discussion will generate useful feedback to the Government. The United Progressive Alliance (UPA) Government assumed office in May 2004. It is with a high sense of achievement-and pardonable pride—that we recapitulate the three and half years of the management of the economy. There has been a marked change in the way the Indian economy is viewed both within the country and in other countries of the world. This is largely due to the sustained, well-directed efforts of the Government that have resulted in globally acclaimed rates of economic growth, increased global competitiveness of Indian businesses, strong macro fundamentals, and above all, a highly favourable economic outlook.

44154. (13-11-2007) NEW DELHI: Communist Party of India (Marxist) general secretary Prakash Karat on Monday said there was a possibility that something would come out of the meeting of the United Progressive Alliance-Left committee on the nuclear deal with the United States. He was briefing reporters after a two-day meeting of the party's Polit Bureau. The 15-member committee was to meet on November 16 but it was postponed. A fresh date is expected to be announced soon. The Left parties have reiterated that the committee's findings should be considered before the government operationalised the deal. "The government did not go to the International Atomic Energy Agency (IAEA) for negotiations in September-October as demanded by us. We are also trying not to be adamant. Neither the government nor we are adamant. Both sides have their respective stand on the nuclear agreement," Mr. Karat said. He, however, appeared confident that the issue would be "sorted out" and the UPA-Left dialogue would continue to see how it could be sorted out. "We are keen on a discussion in Parliament. I hope all parties for and against the deal will express their views." The Polit Bureau reiterated the Left parties' stand that the government should not go ahead with operationalising the deal. "There has to be a discussion on the deal in the coming session of Parliament," it noted. Among other issues that came up for discussion at the Polit Bureau meeting were price rise, support price of Rs. 1,000 a quintal for paddy, oil price hike, delay in notification of Tribal Forest Act, women's reservation and the 19th party congress to be held in Coimbatore from March 29 to April 2. Mr. Karat said an outline of the draft political resolution was discussed. Based on this a draft would be prepared and placed at the next meeting of the Central Committee in December. On Emergency in Pakistan, the Polit Bureau reaffirmed its solidarity and support to the people of Pakistan, who were struggling for restoration of democracy.

4155. (14-11-2007) NEW DELHI : Shri Arjun Singh, Minister for Human Resource Development will inaugurate Chindren's Assembly and Integration Camp (November 14-20, 2007) on Children's Day. Thereafter he will release the Bal Bhavan publications-"Voice of Youth on Sustainable Development"-a book in Hindi and English reflecting children's thoughts on Sustainable Development. A poster on the theme of the assembly (Education for Sustainable Development) will also be released. Thereafter a colorful cultural programme will be presented by the participating children comprising of a vocal music, a ballet, classical dances on the theme of the assembly and presentations by International teams. The theme of this year's International Children's Assembly is "Education for Sustainable Development". This theme has been chosen with a view to sensitize children the significance of Sustainable Development since the world is going deeper into ecological debt and global warming and concrete steps needs to be taken against this biggest threat facing humanity. Apart from Indian Children, Children from Mauritius, Norway, Kyrghyztan and China would also participate in this year's assembly. Children who have been honoured for their creativity with the Bal Shree Honour from 1995-2005 and have been invited for a reunion camp would also be participating in the inaugural programme of this year's assembly. This being children's day a special creativity fair will be organized during which children will take part in various activities and fun games. Children would also enjoy Puppet Show, Magic Show, Joy Rides, Games and Jumping Castle.On 14th

November, a cultural fiesta will be organised in which children of National Bal Bhavan and children of other friendly countries would make presentations on the theme. The presentation would include fushion dance in Kathak and Bharatnatyam style, classical song and drama. Throughout the assembly special programmes are being organized for children wherein children would get an opportunity to meet and interact with some of the renowned personalities who have made difference in our lives directly or indirectly. On 15th November the participating children and the Bal Shree Awardees of the Creative Arts stream will make beautiful collage on large boards. On 16th November children would take part in Yoga and Creative Sports Activities. A play 'Shabri', directed by Mrs. Sushma Seth an eminent theatre and film personality would be put up at 6:00 p.m. Mrs. Seth would also interact with the children. On 17th November children would make presentations on difference aspects of Sustainable Development viz Biodiversity, energy etc. In the evening valedictory function will be organized for the Bal Shree Awardees. On 18th November children will visit Rural Bal Bhavan, Mandi indulge themselves in varied creative and science related activities. In the evening their would be screening of Ex-US Vice-President Al Gore's Oscar winning documentary on climate change-"An Inconvenient Truth". On 19th November there would be programmes to make the birth anniversary of Smt. Indira Gandhi. On the same day there will be a declamation contest in which children participating in the International Children's Assembly and children of various schools of Delhi will speak on the theme of the assembly *i.e.* "Education for Sustainable Development". On the concluding day of the assembly *i.e.* on 20th November valedictory programme would be organized wherein participants of International Children's Assembly will be felicitated and mementoes and certificates will be given to the children.

4156. (14-11-2007) NEW DELHI : The President of India, Smt. Pratibha Devisingh Patil, met and interacted with thousands of children from various parts of the country today at Rashtrapati Bhavan on the occasion of Children's Day. The following is her message for the children of India: "My Dear Children, today is a very special day for all of us and particularly for you, the children of India. On this day, every year, the birthday of our first Prime Minister, Pandit Jawaharlal Nehru is celebrated as Children's Day. Panditji visualised the nurturing and welfare of children as a national priority. Children are the future of India. By studying hard and imbibing good values they can contribute to building India as a strong and prosperous nation in which all sections of society enjoy the benefits of economic and social advancements. Today, India stands at the threshold of a new era of progress. India is rapidly progressing and is emerging as a global power. The world is watching India's growth with admiration. This progress has been possible because of the dedicated work and commitment of the people of India. The children of today, when they grow up, must continue to work hard as they will have the responsibility for ensuring a glorious future of India. I would like the children of India not only to work for the economic progress of the nation but also to contribute to a caring society that provides the benefits of growth to all, particularly the weak and the disadvantaged. I would like all of you to be sensitive to the fact that many children are not fortunate to have the opportunity of getting a good education. You can be sensitive to your surroundings by helping at least one disadvantaged child. By doing so, you become a child who cares for others. I would like to see every child, boy and girl in the country to be touched by the light of modern education. Empowerment of women is particularly important, as I believe this leads to the empowerment of the nation. I have a special message for the girl child, who will grow up to be equal partners to shape the destiny of this country. You must not give up your education at any cost-as the education of the girl child is critical for our progress both economic and social. When we educate a girl child, we have not only educated an individual but also a family. With these words, I wish all the children of India, a very happy Children's Day."

4157. (14-11-2007) NEW DELHI : South Africa has evinced keen interest in enhancing cooperation in the Micro, Small and Medium Enterprises (MSME) Sector. A South African delegation led by Deputy Minister of Trade & Industry H.E Ms. Eizabeht Thabethe called on Shri Mahabir Prasad, Union Minister for MSME here today. Ms. Eizabeht Thabethe said that her country look forward to draw inspiration from the specialized and focused endeavour of India in the MSME sector. She said, "Gandhiji came to our country as a lawyer and went back as a great leader." Earlier, welcoming the South African Minister Shri Mahabir Prasad said, India share a common history, culture and economy with South Africa and unemployment scenario in both the countries are somewhat similar. India will be too glad to offer help to South Africa in the MSME sector. Both the countries could explore the possibilities of identifying the specific areas of cooperation, Shri Prasad added. Shri Prasad invited the South African delegation to visit the pavilions under the Ministry of MSME at the on going India International Trade Fair, 2007.

4158. (14-11-2007) NEW DELHI : The Palme D' OR winner of Cannes 2007-titled 4 months, 3 weeks & 2 day would be the opening film at International Film Festival of India-2007 (IFFI-2007), which will be inaugurated on November 23, 2007 in Goa. This was stated by Director, DFF, Smt. Neelam Kapur while addressing a press conference here today. The opening ceremony would be simple and elegant and keeping with international standards she added. Noted film actor Shahrukh Khan will be the Chief Guest at the inaugural ceremony which will be attended by Minister of Information & Broadcasting and Parliamentary Affairs, Shri P. R. Dasmunsi and Chief Minister of Goa, Shri Digambar Kamat besides several important film personalities. The inaugural lamp will be lit with the assistance of Priyamani, the rising star of southern cinema. The Director of the opening film Mr. Cristian Mungiu and the main actress, Anamaria Marinca would be present at the inaugural ceremony. Besides, there would be other foreign delegates representing various international film festivals from Netherlands, China, Poland and Mexico. A major delegation from Poland and China will also be present. Smt. Kapur said, Indian Panorama at IFFI-2007 would present a bouquet of 36 films, 21 features and 15 non-feature films. The package is a mixed bag with stalwarts like Budhadeb Dasgupta and Adoor Gopalakrishnan presenting two films each. The section would have Ami Iyasin Aar Amaar Madhubala (The Voueurs-Feature) and Naushad Ali-the Melody continues (Non Feature) by Budhadeb Dasgupta and Naalu Penunungal (Four Women-Feature) and The Dance of the Enchantress (Non Feature) by Adoor Gopalakrishnan. The debut directors like Sameer Hanchante, Samir Chanda, and Bhavna Talwar would present their films Gafla (Scam), Ek Nadir Galpo (Tale of a river), and Dharm respectively at the festival. The Festival Director said, a specialized competition for feature films by Asian, African and Latin American Directors is being organized. Films produced after First September 2006 are eligible for the entry. Fourteen films have been selected from 13 countries for the competition. Competition Jury is headed by the eminent award winning film maker from Hungary Ms Marta Mazaros, who has directed more than 60 films in her film career and has won awards in Cannes/ Berlin/Venice and San Sebastian Intl Film Festivals. Other members of the Jury are, Ms Meltem Cumbul a young leading actress from Turkey; Mr. Shaji N Karun, Cinematographer, Film Director and Script writer from Kerala; a noted Argentinian film director Mr. Pablo Cesar, who has won awards in the Montreal Intl Film Festival and National awards in Argentina and Mr. Robert Sarkies, a young film maker from New Zealand. The Director said a special section celebrating 60 years of India's independence, India @ 60, would showcase seven patriotic films including three feature and four documentaries.

4159. (14-11-2007) NEW DELHI: A crucial meeting of the United Progressive Alliance-Left committee on the India-U.S. civilian nuclear deal will be held on November 16 as originally scheduled. A day after Communist Party of India (Marxist) general secretary Prakash Karat said there was a possibility that something would come out of the UPA-Left committee meeting, the government appeared to have taken the signal from Left quarters to indicate a slight softening of their stance against operationalising the 123 agreement with the U.S. "The meeting of UPA-Left committee has been reconvened on November 16," Pranab Mukherjee, External Affairs Minister and convener of the 15-member panel, told journalists on Tuesday. "We hope a way out will be found at the meeting." Earlier, the meeting stood postponed, with the government promising to announce a fresh date soon. "Let us wait for the November 16 meeting," said Mr. Karat. While briefing reporters on the Polit Bureau meeting of the CPI(M) on Monday, Mr. Karat appeared confident that the nuclear issue would be "sorted out" and the UPA-Left dialogue would focus on how it could be sorted out. The joint committee, constituted to go into the apprehensions over the nuclear deal, has covered a lot of ground in its five meetings held over the past two-and-a-half months. The Communist Party of India general secretary, A.B. Bardhan, indicated on Monday that the Left might consider allowing the government to discuss with the International Atomic

Energy Agency an India-specific safeguards agreement needed for operationalising the nuclear deal but without initialling it. Informed sources in the Left parties suggested that one way out could be allowing the government to bring the India-specific safeguards draft for consideration before the UPA-Left committee. "If the committee approves it, it is fine, otherwise the draft stands rejected," these sources said. However, All-India Forward Bloc general secretary Debabrata Biswas told Hindu The that Parliament itself could discuss the 123 agreement with the U.S. in totality and come to a view. He contended that it would be in keeping with the spirit of the Constitution. Parliament's winter session begins on November 15. The main opposition Bharatiya Janata Party on Tuesday alleged that the "climbdown" by the Left on the Indo-U.S. nuclear deal was the result of a "trade off" between the government and the CPI(M) over Nandigram. "The moment they got into political difficulties because of Nandigram," senior BJP leader Yashwant Sinha asserted, "they have come forward to compromise with the government on the deal and offered concessions."

4160. (14-11-2007) NEW DELHI : The Union Minister for Science & Technology and Earth Sciences, Shri Kapil Sibal has said that if the long-term goals are to be attained and growth and problem solving are to become indigenous and sustainable, developing countries need to develop their own capabilities in science, technology and innovation. Delivering the inaugural address at the 13th Technology Summit and Technology Platform in New Delhi today, he stressed the need to endeavour to democratize technology development and use and also to make it more participative and more inclusive. With globalization taking unprecedented progress, increased diffusion should lead to abatement of technological divide amongst nations. Setting the agenda for the Summit, Shri Sibal called for "Building Partnerships for Development" and "In cooperation with the private sector, making available the benefits of new technologies, especially information and communications". The Minister observed that the engine of economic progress in any country rides on four wheels, namely, Human Resources (Education, knowledge, skill, discipline, motivation etc.), Natural Resources (Land, minerals, fuel, environmental quality etc.), Capital Formation (Machines, factories, roads etc.) and Technology (Science, engineering, management, entrepreneurship etc.). Sharing with the audience the different views of technology the Minister emphasized the need to tame it. Terming Science & Technology as the first level of interaction between alien countries, Shri Sibal said that India's partnerships with different countries and organizations are progressing well. He also termed the long-standing relationship of India with Russia as another good example in this respect. The Summit is being attended by a large number of delegates both from India and abroad. Technology Summit & Technology Platform is one of the major initiatives of Department of Science and Technology & CII to showcase premier technology knowledge of India & participating countries. The Summit provides a platform for symbiotic partnership in the technology arena for promotion of joint ventures, technology tie-ups and investment opportunities to & from partner/participating countries. In the past editions of the summit have resulted in technology collaborations, bilateral linkages and capacity building benefiting India and the Partner Countries.

4161. (14-11-2007) NEW DELHI : Food is the basic necessity of life. On one side the world is facing the problem of under-nutrition while on the other side Diet Related Chronic Non-Communicable Disorders which were considered earlier the problem of the affluent, are also increasing in developing nations. The most important diet related chronic disorders which are prevalent in the country are cardiovascular diseases, hypertension, obesity, diabetes, etc., Thus, the challenges are immense. It is a matter of concern that not only the rich but also the poor are getting increasingly affected due to sedentary life styles and bad food habits. The number of juvenile diabetes is also on the rise. The word diabetes is derived from a Greek word meaning "to siphon; to pass through" and mellitus comes from a Latin word "honey". Thus the two characteristic symptoms copious urination and glucose in urine gives the name to the disease. Diabetes doesn't happen overnight. It usually takes years to develop. It is know that genetic factors predispose certain people to diabetes but all of the data suggest that lifestyle factors, particularly diet and exercise can determine whether those genetic factors actually manifest in the disease. Heredity is a major factor in the development of the disease. But it is important to note that heredity is like a cannon and obesity pulls the trigger. According to a common saying that it is not work but worry that kills. Grief, worry and anxiety also have a brief influence on the metabolism and may aggravate the symptoms in a diabetic individual. Diet and diabetes have always been intimately connected. Since what one eats has a major impact on the blood sugar and insulin, food is a prime player in triggering, exacerbating and controlling diabetes. Worldwide the number of cases of diabetes have been currently estimated around 150 million. This number is predicted to be double by 2025 with greatest number of cases being expected in India and China. Increases in both the prevalence and incidence of type 2 diabetes have occurred globally. But the increases have been specially dramatic in societies in economic transition in much of the newly industrialized world and developing countries. Type 2 diabetes results from an interaction between genetic and environmental factors. The rapidly changing incidence rates, however suggest a particularly important role for the latter as well as potential for stemming the tide of the global epidemic of the disease. Noticeable increases are occurring in societies in which there have been major changes in the type of diet consumed, reductions in physical activity, and increases in overweight and obesity. The diets concerned are typically high in fats like butter, ghee, vanaspati (saturated fats), low in fruits and vegetables, and with a higher consumption of junk foods.

4162. (14-11-2007) NEW DELHI : The President has constituted the Thirteenth Finance Commission under Article 280 (1) of the Constitution. Dr. Vijay L. Kelkar, former Union Finance Secretary and Adviser to the Finance Minister has been appointed as Chairman of the Commission. Shri B.K Chaturvedi, Member, Planning Commission will be the part-time Member, and Dr. Indira Rajaraman, Emeritus Professor, National Institute of Public Finance and Policy, Dr. Abusaleh Shariff, Chief Economist, National Council of Applied Economic Research, Prof. Atul Sarma, Former Vice-Chancellor, Rajiv Gandhi University (formerly Arunachal University) shall be the full time Members of the Commission. Shri Sumit Bose will be the Secretary to the Commission. The Finance Commission is a Constitutional body set up every five years to make recommendations relating to the distribution of the net proceeds of taxes between the Union and the States, the principles which should govern the grants-in-aid of the revenues of the States out of the Consolidated Fund of India and the measures needed to augment the Consolidated Fund of a State to supplement the resources of the Panchayats and the Municipalities. In addition, any other matter may be referred to the Commission by the President in the interests of sound finance. Apart from the terms of reference specifically laid down in the Constitution, the Thirteenth Finance Commission will review the state of finances of the Union and the States keeping in view the operation of the States' Debt Consolidation & Relief Facility 2005-2010(DCRF) and suggest measures for maintaining a stable and sustainable fiscal environment consistent with equitable growth. The Thirteenth Finance Commission will also review the present arrangements as regards financing of Disaster Management with reference to the National Calamity Contingency Fund and the Calamity Relief Fund and the funds envisaged in the Disaster Management Act, 2005. As in the case of the previous Finance Commissions, the 13th Finance Commission will also take into consideration various aspects while making its recommendations. These relate to assessment of the resources of the Centre and the State for the five year period, taxation efforts and the potential of additional revenue mobilization, demands on the resources of the Central Government, the requirement of States to meet the non-salary component of maintenance expenditure on capital assets and plan schemes, the objective of not only balancing receipts and expenditure but also generating surpluses, and the need to ensure commercial viability of irrigation and power projects, departmental undertakings and public sector enterprises through various means including levy of user charges and adoption of measures to promote efficiency.

4163. (14-11-2007) NEW DELHI : There is need to raise awareness and sensitize various constituencies to the roles and impacts of fire, both detrimental (*e.g.* as in case of unplanned, uncontrolled burns) and beneficial (*e.g.* as in the case of burns managed to facilitate the collection of certain forest products or prescribed burns to pre and the occurrence of intense fires or as a tool and wild life habitat management). This is one of the recommendation made today on the concluding day of two-day National Workshop on Forest Fires. The Workshop has also recommended to observe Forest Fire Week and it was informed that Ministry of Environment and Forests is also in the process to prepare a mascot for this. The

Experts suggested to prepare vulnerability mappings, public panchayat partnership and capacity building at State level. They also felt that in the present scenario of changing climate to reduce carbon secretion in atmosphere, which damaging atmosphere. We must control forest fire. There is a need to create a National level as well as State level data base on forest fires which should be freely accessible based on information generated from both field level fire monitoring and reporting, and satellite based fire monitoring. The Workshop further recommended a need for pilot initiative to link on-going field monitoring and fire reporting to a National level data base. The Workshop also agreed on involvement of local communities and civil society in fire prevention, detection and management in accordance with existing policies and guidelines. Existing methods of fire prevention, as practiced by the Forest Department which include cutting and maintenance of fire lines as well as controlled burning be strengthened, including the timely and adequate resources being made available for this. It was also recommended that in conjunction with field level fire monitoring and reporting, and on the ground verification of satellite information provided by Forest Survey of India (FSI) and National Remote Sensing Agency (NRSA) should be operationalised in the States using standard methods and involving all possible stakeholders. There is also need for in depth research on the ecological consequences of fire in different bio-geographic zones and eco-system types and in depth research and monitoring of socio-economic drivers of wild land fire

4164. (14-11-2007) NEW DELHI : The Ministry of Labour and Employment has launched today a fortnight long nationwide 'Enforcement Drive against Child Labour' in order to step up enforcement of the Child Labour (Prohibition & Regulation) Act. The Union Labour and Employment Minister Shri Oscar Fernandes has already written letters to all the State Chief Ministers in this regard. The Union Labour Secretary is also in constant touch with all the State Chief Secretaries for follow up action on this issue. During this drive, enforcement activities would be stepped up, awareness generation campaigns would be launched and sensitization workshops, etc. would be organized for various sections of the society against evil of the child labour across the country. The States have been asked to draw up a plan for intensifying the enforcement drive and for launching an awareness generation campaign against child labour during this fortnight. Funds for this purpose have also been allocated to the States. During this period, the State Labour Departments would be conducting inspections, raids and rescue operations as well as intensive awareness generation campaigns through newspapers, electronic media, hoardings, etc. Although the Government has been taking steps for rehabilitating child labour through the National Child Labour Project (NCLP) Scheme, yet it was felt equally important that stringent enforcement measures are taken as deterrent against this evil. For spreading awareness across the level, a multi media campaign has been launched and the Ministry has already released advertisements in prominent national and regional dailies for enhancing awareness against the evil of child labour. TV spots on Doordarshan National Network and other major channels will also be telecast during this period. At the conclusion of the drive, the Union Labour Minister would review the action taken by the States in this regard in the national level consultations.

4165. (14-11-2007) NEW DELHI : On the occasion of Bal Divas, Smt. Renuka Chowdhury, Minister of State for Women and Child Development presented the National Child Awards to 36 children for exceptional achievements in a function at Pragati Maidan today. These Awards are given every year by the Ministry of Women and Child Development to the children in the age group of 4 to 15 years to recognize their exceptional achievements in the fields like art, culture, sports, academics etc. The awards carry a medal, certificate and a cash prize of Rs. 20, 000/- for gold medal and Rs. 10, 000/- for silver medal. The gold medal at the national level was awarded to Master Fenil Chetan Shah of Gujarat for winning several national and international chess tournaments. Silver medals were awarded to 35 children for their exceptional achievements at the State level. These children include Budding scientist, mathematician, painter, folk singer, classical dancer, international skates player and child with exceptional photographic memory. The awardees also include four children with physical disabilities. National awards for child welfare were also presented to five institutes and three individuals for their work in the area of child welfare. These awards carry a cash prize of rupees three lakh and a certificate to each institution and rupees one lakh and a certificate in the case of individual. The Minister also presented Rajiv Gandhi Manav Seva Award to Shri Ahanthem Tolen Singh for child welfare, Smt. Shobhana Ranade, Maharashtra for child development and Smt. Maha Jabeen, Andhra Pradesh for child protection. Each awardee was presented along with a silver plaque. Congratulating the awardees, Smt. Renuka Chowdhury said the development of children and women is very high priority of the Government. A number of initiatives are being planned and significant increase is being made in the allocation for children related schemes and programmes. She said that achievement of the awardees shows that the country has a very bright future.

4166. (14-11-2007) NEW DELHI : The Union Minister for Health & Family Welfare, Dr. Anbumani Ramadoss, today released the National Disaster Management Guidelines-Medical Preparedness and Mass Casualty Management, drafted by the National Disaster Management Authority (NDMA). The meeting was attended by Gen. N. C. Vij, Vice-Chairman, NDMA, Gen.(Dr.) J. R. Bhardwaj, Member, NDMA, Shri H.S. Brahma, Addl. Secretary, NDMA and other senior Officials from the Defence Research Development Organisation, NDMA and Ministry.

4167. (14-11-2007) NEW DELHI : Retail prices of farm commodities monitored by the Department of Consumer Affairs have generally remained steady or shown mixed trend over the week ending November 12, 2007. Prices of wheat at retail level remained steady at all the monitoring centres except at Thiruvanthapuram. Retail price of sugar remained steady over the week across most of the centres.

Prices increased at Delhi, Patna and Hydeabad. Prices of gram dal have generally remained steady across majority of the monitoring centres. Prices increased at Chennai, and Mumbai and decreased at Ahmedabad, Kolkata, Patna and Bangalore. Prices of tur dal declined at Kolkata and increased at Ahmedabad, Mumbai, Patna, Hyderabad and Thiruvananthapuram. At Delhi, as on 12.11.2007, prices of wheat, gram dal, tur dal, groundnut oil, potato and milk were holding steady for one week; those of mustard oil, vanaspati and salt were steady for one month and price of atta was holding steady for over one year. Prices of onion declined and those of rice and sugar increased over the week.

4168. (14-11-2007) NEW DELHI : The meeting of the Parliamentary Consultative Committee attached to the Ministry of Civil Aviation was held here today. It was chaired by the Minister for Civil Aviation, Shri Praful Patel. A presentation of Pawan Hans Helicopters was made to the Members present which highlighted the performance, initiatives, and business opportunities of the company. It was highlighted that PHHL which currently has 35 helicopters plans to acquire 20 more at a cost of Rs. 496 crores. In the year 2007-08 (ending September 07) the Company has earned a net profit after tax of Rs. 13.45 crores. A number of new initiatives have been taken by the Company including the Helipad concept in India-it plans a Helipad each in Mumbai and Delhi, setting up a maintenance centre in Mumbai, equity participation in the National Flying Training School to be set up in Gondia, promoting religious tourism, air ambulances, highway helipad services, increased off-shore E&P activities etc. Pawan Hans envisages the requirements of at least 100 more helicopters to meet the emerging business opportunities for hub and spoke synergy in India. The Members called for increased focus on the development of helicopter services in India and emphasized that the potential of business growth of Pawan Hans was considerable in the current scenario of high growth in the aviation sector. Members cutting across party lines also called for a re-look at the existing Airport Policy of the Government to allow for multiple airports at metropolitan cities. They stressed that, as is the practice world over, with the growth of civil aviation sector more airports would be required in the country and multiple airports would be necessary to address the existing problems in metropolitan airports. Responding to the concerns expressed by the Members the Chairman of the Committee, the Minister for Civil Aviation, Shri Praful Patel said that the Ministry fully shared the views and the concerns of the members. The issue was raised by the Ministry in the recent meeting on the infrastructure headed by the Prime Minister. A group consisting of the Finance Minister, the Civil Aviation Minister, and the Deputy Chairman of the Planning Commission had been set up to see how to take this process further. He assured the members that a new Policy for Airport would be in place in the first half of 2008. The Members raised concern and criticized the misreporting about near misses by aircraft in the Indian skies as well as other irresponsible reporting about the sector in the media. They were assured that the Ministry would take up steps and bring out campaign to educate the people about the reality and the safety and security being maintained in the Indian skies. Members also protested against the 'night curfew' that is imposed by a number of European nations, which leads to inconvenience for passengers travelling from other countries as well as operational problems of airlines connecting to those countries. The Ministry of Civil Aviation has been asked to take up the issues with concerned authorities. The Members also emphasized that more acquisition of aircraft by national carriers-Air India and Pawan Hans should be done early. The other issues that were discussed in the meeting include more connectivity to different parts of the country on-time and reliability factor of airlines etc. Members of Parliament who were present at the meeting were: S/Shri Rahul Gandhi, Madhu Goud Yashki, Santosh Gangwar, Ratilal K. Verma, Ramswaroop Koli, Deepender Singh Hooda, Santosh Bagrodia, Dr. M.S. Gill, Tarlochan Singh, Abdul Wahab Peevee, Vijay Darda and Rajeev Shukla.

4169. (14-11-2007) NEW DELHI : The Food Processing Industries Minister, Shri Subodh Kant Sahai today said that the growth and development of Food Processing Industries will provide long-term and better economic stability to farmers. Addressing the Economic Editors Conference-2007, he stressed the need for linking agriculture with the industry and to create substantial employment opportunities in rural sector. The Plan allocation for Food Processing Industries has been increased for the seventh time and the Planning Commission has agreed to allocate Rs. 4031 crore in the Eleventh Plan outlay. He added that UPA Government had identified Food Processing Industries as one of the "thrust areas". The Food Processing Sector is among top 10 sectors attracting FDI equity. FDI upto 100% equity is permitted under automatic route in food infrastructure like food park, cold chain etc. The government's concern to protect the interest of small retailers from FDI in food retail and also the farmers from the misuse of contract farming are being examined. The Government has set up a National Institute of Food Technology Entrepreneurship and Management (NIFTEM) at Kondli, Haryana as an apex knowledge centre in the field of latest food technology. Enacted, Food Safety & Standards Act, 2006-an integrated food law and a Regulatory Authority to replace multiplicity and enforcement agency. The Minister said that the Food Processing Sector needs to be accorded equal emphasis as that of agriculture. "To attain inclusive growth" in agriculture as a part of National Food Security Mission, the growth and development of post harvest management, value addition, creation of substantial off-farming, rural employment opportunities and providing long term economic sustainability to farmers need to be addressed on priority. The food processing sector has substantial potential to generate employment opportunities in the medium, small and micro enterprises sector, the employment generation has increased from 38 lakh in 2002-03 to 45 lakh in 2006-07. He also stressed the need for application of Nano-technology in food industry. Developed countries have already tapped this new technology for packaging and enhancement of shelf life.

4170. (14-11-2007) NEW DELHI : That the Indian Navy, the men in Shining gold and whites are a benevolent lot was at display when on the occasion of the Children's Day on 14 November 2007, they showed that they care. The Indian Navy organized a touching event for the not so privileged children-About 50 special and nderprivileged children were taken out for a day of fun and frolic to Appu Ghar. The significance of the event coinciding with Children's day has added meaning to the lives of these children. 15 Children of Four steps school (South ExII) 12 each of NIMH, Model special education centre& Anchal special Education Centre would attend. Also, another 15 Children of Navy's supported SANKALP at Nausenabaug I, Chanakya puri would be a part of the group. INS India, the administrative and logistics base of Indian Navy is conducting the event as a part of activities preceding the navy week celebrations. The president of Naval Wives Welfare Association(NWWA), Mrs Maria Teresa Mehta graced the occasion and spent time with them as they enjoyed the joy rides, enjoy the magic show, Puppet show. To cheer up the little ones gift hampers, refreshments and lunch has also been organized in their favourite Appu Ghar. All these hopefully bring some smiles back in their lives. A similar picnic has been scheduled on 20 Nov 07 for 65 underprivileged children from GyanShakti Vidyala NOIDA, SANKALP (Gurgaon) and ANAFCA NOIDA. To cheer up the National Capital and citizen Band performances at Chesire Home (15th 1100-1200) Central Park, CP (17 th1700-1800) have been organized. Melodies of both the present and past era including tapping, classical and popular filmi tunes is being played by the famous Naval Band, comprising about 30 musicians, composers and Conductors. One of the finest, the band has given international performances at new York, Washington, London and a number of other countries abroad. Medical Camp at MCD School, Shahdra (1000 Hrs onwards) would include free medical check up by specialists, issue of health cards to students, lecture for parent/students and teacher, First aid training to teachers as also a Street Play to improve awareness.

4171. (14-11-2007) NEW DELHI : Dr. Shakeel Ahmad, Minister of State for Communications and Information Technology today released a set of two postage stamps, a miniature, a first day cover and three maxim cards on the occasion of Children's Day. The Department of Posts commemorates Children's Day every year by bringing out stamps designed by children themselves. The stamp designs are selected by holding an all India Stamp Design Competition. The theme for the Stamp Design Competition this year was "The Magic of the Night". The competition elicited great response and the entries revealed beautifully the flight of a child's fantasy. This year's stamps are based on painting made by Kum. Swarali V.Bhakare, Class IV, Annasaheb Raje Bhosale, Primary School, Satara (Maharashtra) and B.Karthick, Class VIII, T.E.L.C, Middle School, Pudukottai (Tamil Nadu) which won the first prizes in Group I and Group II respectively. Miniature sheet is based on the painting made by Master Pradhan Karnik, Class IX, Kendriya Vidyalaya, NAL Campus, Jeevan Bhimanagar, Bangalore (Karnataka) which won the first prize in Group III. The design of the First Day Cover is based on a painting by Raj Ballav Hazarika, Class XII, K.V.Narangi School, Assam APS, which won the second prize in Group III of the competition. The three Maxim Cards are based on paintings by Master Sankar Dinesh Kamath, Class III, Bhavan's Varuna Vidyalaya, Thrikakkara, Ernakulam (Kerala), second prize winner in group I and Jyotirmay Biswas, Class VIII, Jawahar Navodaya Vidyalaya, Kalyani, Nadia (West Bengal), second prize winner in Group II and Riti Sodhi, Class XII, Delhi Public School, Ranipur, Sector-3, BHEL, Ranipur, Hardwar, Uttarakhand, third prize winner in Group III.

4172. (14-11-2007) NEW DELHI : Filaria was identified as one of the diseases to be eliminated globally. Global elimination of this disease by the year 2020 has been envisaged by World Health Organisation (WHO) and the Government of India is also signatory to the World Health Assembly Resolution in 1997 for its Global Elimination. The National Health Policy (2002) has envisaged elimination of lymphatic filariasis in India by 2015. For controlling this disease, Govt. of India launched National Filaria Control Programme (NFCP) in 1955. The strategy for filariasis control in this programme has been vector control measures and treatment of individual patients reporting to the filaria clinics. The recommended dose for treatment of filariasis for interruption of transmission is Diethylcarbamazine citrate (DEC) tablets @ 6mg per kg body weight for 12 days to those persons who are detected as microfilaria positive. NFCP activities are implemented through 206 control units and 199 filaria clinics located in urban areas. This year MDA is scheduled on 15th November and 13 states namely Andhra Pradesh, Assam, Chhattisgarh, Goa, Karnataka, Kerala, Madhya Pradesh, Maharashtra, West Bengal, Andaman & Nicobar Islands, Daman & Diu, Lakshadweep, and Dadra & N Haveli are launching this campaign of Mass Drug Administration (MDA). The remaining states have rescheduled due to local festivals and will be completing MDA before December 2007. On the National Filaria Day, drug distribution is made by door-to-door campaign and some booths are set up at health facilities and town centres, etc. These tablets are supplied free. The drug, DEC, can also be obtained from filaria clinics and primary health centres (PHCs) in endemic States/UTs. Lymphatic Filariasis (LF) is a disabling, disfiguring infection caused by parasitic worms. It is estimated that 100 and 20 million people are infected in around 83 countries throughout the tropics and sub-tropics. LF is major cause of disability, social stigmatization, phsyco-social and economic reductions in life opportunities and a major burden on health and hospital resources, especially on account of cost for surgical intervention. The disease is caused by worms and transmitted by mosquitoes. The infection is acquired in childhood and develops in man and woman of all ages. Its most frequent victims are rural and urban poor. It has been estimated that globally over a billion people are at risk. Although this disease is the most prevalent tropical disease, it is rarely fatal and thus in the developing countries it has been overshadowed by the killer diseases like HIV/AIDS, TB and Malaria.

4173. (14-11-2007) NEW DELHI : Ministry of Water Resources is participating in the 27th Edition of Indian International Trade Fair being organized at ITPO from 14th November to 27th November, 2007 by way of raising a pavilion and display of models on water related issues. The theme of the pavilion is "Water Year-2007". Prof. Saifuddin Soz, the Union Minister for Water Resources will inaugurate the Pavilion. Shri Jai Prakash Narain Yadav, Minister of State for Water Resources, Smt. Gauri Chatterjee, Secretary, Ministry of Water Resources and senior officers of the Ministry will be present on the occasion. The models indicating various aspects of water including its various uses, forms, source etc. will be displayed inside the pavilion. Various organizations under the Ministry viz. Central Water Commission, Central Ground Water Board, Central Soil and Material Research station, Central Water Power Research Station, National Institute of Hydrology, Water and Power Consultancy Services, National Projects Construction Corporation Ltd., National Water Development Agency will also exhibit models and other display material to disseminate information about their activities, achievements and vision. With a view to attract younger generation, especially the children, street play on the theme of Necessity of conservation of water through music and dance show will also be displayed. The modern techniques of communication viz. plasma TV will also be used to inform visitors about various facets of water conservation with emphasis on Rainwater Harvesting and Artificial Recharge.

4174. (14-11-2007) NEW DELHI : The President of India, Smt. Pratibha Devisingh Patil, today inaugurated the 27th India International Trade Fair (IITF) 2007. Speaking at the inaugural ceremony, the President said that IITF has proved to be an effective showcase for Indian trade and industry. "The theme of the IITF 2007 is "Processed Food and Agro Industries and about 44 countries including the SAARC nations are participating in the 14 day event. The Trade Fair should also display innovative technologies available in farm equipment, storage and food processing. In addition to this, the Trade Fair could be a platform for working out partnerships for investment, business and technology sharing in the agro-industry sector", the President further stated. While presiding over the function, Shri Kamal Nath, Union Minister of Commerce and Industry, has said that the Government's growth-friendly policies relating to investment, taxation, external trade, banking and finance, Foreign Direct Investment, capital markets and small scale industries have all evolved towards making our industry and enterprises more efficient, globally competitive and as free from restrictions as possible. "As we move on the trajectory of high rate of growth, we have to remain alive to the needs and concerns of our rural areas, agriculturists, artisans and youth", he added. The Chief Minister of Meghalaya, Shri D.D. Lapang; Shri G.K. Pillai, Commerce Secretary; and Dr. Sheela Bhide, Chairman & Managing Director of ITPO; also spoke on the occasion. The 14-day event (14-27 November 2007) is being organised by the India Trade Promotion Organisation. Observing that exhibitions like IITF are a powerful and highly cost-effective business tool-as well as being significant wealth generator in their own right, Shri Kamal Nath hoped that the participants who have come from different parts of the world will achieve the objectives of their participation. "ITPO has played the role of a catalyst and facilitator in increasing exports as also giving an impetus to intra-country trade through its events in India and abroad. In the process, it has been serving the cause of integrating the Indian economy with the global mainstream", he added.

4175. (14-11-2007) NEW DELHI : Shri Kamal Nath, Union Minister of Commerce & Industry, has stressed on developing new infrastructure for the healthcare sector in view of the tremendous opportunities that are available for public-private partnership. Speaking at the 4th India Health Summit "Healthcare Engagement: Strategies and partnerships" here today, the Minister said: "Large windows of opportunities are opening up. To give just one example, Indian medical tourism was estimated at $350 million in 2006 and this has the potential to grow into a $2 billion industry by 2012". Dr. C. Prathap C. Reddy, Chairman of Apollo Group of Hospitals also addressed on the occasion. The 2-day Summit has been organised jointly by the Confederation of Indian Industry (CII) and Indian Healthcare Federation. Shri Kamal Nath stated that there are five areas for government and organized industry action in the healthcare sector, *i.e.*, to create low-cost, high-quality facilities, with a focus on underserved areas; second is to work towards creating standards for high-quality healthcare; third is to invest in training and developing healthcare manpower; fourth is to work with health insurers to improve coverage; and fifth and most important is to create public-private partnerships in healthcare. According to the joint study by CII and McKinsey on this sector, Shri Kamal Nath informed: "During the 1990s, Indian healthcare grew at a compound annual rate of 16%. Today the total value of the sector is more than $34 billion. This translates to $ 34 per capita, or roughly 6% of GDP. By 2012, India's healthcare sector is projected to grow to nearly $ 40 billion".

4176. (14-11-2007) NEW DELHI : There will be 150 more Bal Bhavans next year, said Shri Arjun Singh here today. Inaugurating the International Children's Assembly and Integration Camp on the occasion of Children's Day, Human Resource Development Minister Shri Arjun Singh said "there are only 74 Bal Bhavans within the country that do not suffice the need of children. Therefore, our aim should be to bring up 150 more Bal Bhavans next year and one Bal Bhavan in each village in the future". He also paid homage to Pt. Jawaharlal Nehru on his birthday. He said that the Bal Bhavan is the realization of his dreams of an out of school activity centre for children where they take part in varied activities in a tension free environment. Shri Arjun Singh released the Bal Bhavan publications- "Voice of Youth on Sustainable Development"-book in Hindi and English reflecting children's thoughts on Sustainable Development. Theme of this year's assembly is "Education for Sustainable Development". A poster on the theme of the asembly was also released by the Minister of State for School Education and Literacy, Shri M.A.A. Fatmi. On this occasion a colourful cultural programme was witnessed.

Apart from Indian children, children from Syrian Arab Republic, Norway, Kyrghyztan and China are also participating in this year's assembly. An activity fair is being organised in the sprawling grounds of Bal Bhavan which include activities like painting, wood work, mask making, story telling, paper making, electronic games, aero modelling preparing models of satellites, acquarium, puppet show, magic show, joy rides, games and jumping Castle. In the evening, a cultural fiesta is being organised in which children of National Bal Bhavan and children of other friendly countries are making presentations on the theme of the assembly. The programme will be graced by the Minister of State, Higher Education Smt. D. Purandeswari. She will also inaugurate an exhibition titled 'Traditional Art and Craft-Treasure for Future Generation' at the National Children's Museum of National Bal Bhavan. The festivities at Camp are on from today to November 20, 2007.

4177. (14-11-2007) NEW DELHI : Shri Mahabir Prasad, Union Minister for Micro, Small & Medium Enterprises will inaugurate 'MSME Expo 2007', Techmart, KVIC & Coir Board Exhibitions at India International Trade Fair here tomorrow. The major attraction of first ever MSME Expo will be 'Hall of Excellence' which will display an array of high quality and sophisticated products manufactured in the MSME sector. During the Expo, more than 100 participants from all over the country will display their products which include Engineering products, Electrical and Electronic goods, Glass and Ceramics, Handicrafts, Imitation Jewellery, Readymade and Embroidered Garments, Cosmetics and Herbals, Carpets and Shawls, Soft toys, Pickles, Spices and Condiments, Leather and Footwears, Hospital Equipment and Medical Rehabilitation Goods, Stainless Kitchenware and Tableware, Bamboo based Toys and Ready-to-eat Foods etc. Many of the participants are National Award Winners and ISO-9000-14000 certificate holders. SC/ST, Women and Minorities entrepreneurs are also displaying their products. National Small Industries Corporation Ltd. (NSIC), under the Ministry of Micro, Small & Medium Enterprises is also organizing "Techmart India 2007", the 15th International Technology Fair coinciding with India International Trade Fair 2007. This annual event will be a centre stage for keeping abreast with latest technology development in the Indian MSME sector. The event will assist MSME Sector in marketing their products and services and also help large companies and buyers in identifying MSMEs, which can become their ancillaries, partners in joint ventures and sub-contracting. This year a new dimension of sectoral approach has been added to the display profile of the exhibition and emphasis is laid on sector specific products and technologies like low cost building material, auto components, information technology, light engineering and machines tools, textiles, coir etc. A new initiative has been taken by NSIC by providing special enclosure of "Working Techmart" where stand-alone technologies for entrepreneurs will be on display besides live cluster demonstration of units from North Eastern States. During Techmart India 2007, a seminar on NSIC support services for Micro, Small & Medium Enterprises will also be organised. About 35 Foreign delegations from

South Africa, Sri Lanka, Kenya, Uganda, Mozambique etc. are expected to visit Techmart India, 2007. Shri Mahabir Prasad will also inaugurate KVIC & Coir Board pavilions tomorrow.

4178. (14-11-2007) NEW DELHI : The children of Anglo-Arabic School, Ajmeri Gate, New Delhi enjoyed the screening of Science Safari in the presence of Union Minister for Science & Technology and Earth Sciences, Shri Kapil Sibal on the occasion of the Children's Day today. Science Safari produced by the Department of Science and Technology in coordination with National Geographic Channel showcases Indian Science and Technology. The 48-minute film is an eclectic mix of scientific achievements across India and presents various innovations made by well known Indian scientists and some unknown inventors in an interesting travelogue format. Science Safari is a celebration of the spirit of innovation that inhabits the cities and towns of India. It showcases the spirit of innovation and discovery in the fields of biotechnology, drugs, medicines, stem cells, agriculture, genetic engineering, education, bio-processing, manufacturing, non-conventional energy and more. Interacting with the children, Shri Sibal stressed the need to understand nature to understand science. His message to the children was to first think science and then think beyond science to use it for the benefit of society and to bring solutions to the problems of day to day life. Expressing their views on the Science Safari the students said that it helped them to understand science and also motivated them to take up science as a career option. The Minister also formally launched the website www.sciencesafari.org on this occasion. Since its launch in September 2006, the film is being screened in several schools across the country to sensitize students to the challenges faced by scientists. In NCR territory it is being screened in 86 schools.

4179. (14-11-2007) NEW DELHI : The newly appointed Norwegian Ambassador to India, Ms. Ann Ollestad called on the Union Minister of Shipping, Road Transport and Highways, Thiru T. R. Baalu, here today. The Ambassador discussed the issues relating to the Maritime cooperation between the two countries especially in context of the proposed visit of an Indian team to Norway next month. The Ambassador also briefed the Minister on the developments relating to the areas of cooperation in the shipping sector. Ms. Ann Ollestad also conveyed the Minister about the interest and readiness of the Norwegian entrepreneurs to make investments in the Indian road and shipping infrastructure endeavours.

4180. (14-11-2007) NEW DELHI : The high powered committee constituted by the Shipping Ministry to look into the problems associated with the container traffic at Kolkata and Haldia has submitted its report to the Minister for Shipping, Road Transportation and Highways, Thiru T. R. Baalu, here today. The committee has suggested both short term and long term recommendations to cope with the likely growth in container traffic at both these ports. The Report was presented by the Chairman of the Committee Capt. P V K Mohan to Thiru Baalu. Kolkata Port being the major gateway port for the entire North Eastern Region, Nepal and the hinterland of West Bengal, Bihar, Jharkhand, Uttar Pradesh and Orissa, has great significance in the growing economy of the country. Concerned about the various impediments, the Ministry constituted a high powered committee under the Chairmanship of Capt. P V K Mohan, the senior most Member of the National Shipping Board The committee has identified areas of improvement on both short and long term basis after arriving at the present working scenario and understanding the deficiencies in the existing systems and bottlenecks and has made several recommendations based on its findings to the Ministry today. As part of the short term recommendations for improvement of Kolkata Dock Complex, the high powered committee has recommended induction of at least four Mobile Harbour Cranes (MHCs) preferably one each per berth, Augmentation of Rubber Tyred Gantry Crane (RTGC), Rail Mounted Gantry Cranes (RMGC) and Trailers, acquisition of modern tugs for efficient ship handling, uniform tariff structure for all container berths for harmonization and reduction of cost to trade. Other recommendations include providing six gates for the Netaji Subhash Dock (NSD) container terminal for speedy evacuation of container traffic, introduction of two shift system for Customs works for avoiding congestion, introducing Information Technology systems for better Yard management, abolishing mandatory 0.3 meters trim for all vessels and introduction of night navigation, nominate additional two berths for containers and use Kidderpore docks. The committee has also recommended creating more yard space by demolishing the Lybian Warehouse and unused residential quarters near NSD gate no. 3. The warehouse at No. 2 and No. 3 NSD are also to be demolished to create more stacking area and facilitate direct delivery. A single window system is to be introduced to enable trade take various permissions from customs, port authorities and CONCOR etc. for speedy clearance of import and export cargoes. As part of the long term strategy the committee has recommended for planning a dedicated alternate route from Kidderpore docks to the second hooghly bridge for evacuation of containers round the clock. The recommendations made by the high powered committee for short term improvements at Haldia Dock Complex included Operations of lock gate to facilitate at least eight movements per tide to reduce waiting periods, and the Haldia port to take up entire container handling on its own to reduce terminal handling charges. Haldia Dock Complex (HDC) is to deploy additional tugs, give priority to container ships to avoid undue delays and earmark atleast two berths for container ships with a minimum length of 300 meters in total. The long term recommendations include a second lock gate for Haldia Dock Complex as an immediate priority and atleast one riverine jetty of 200 meters length dedicated to container traffic and expediting clearance of the long pending capital dredging proposal to improve draft at Haldia.

4181. (14-11-2007) NEW DELHI : Ministry of Tourism, Government of India as a part of its endeavours for promotion of tourism and with a view to simplify procedures for recognition / renewal to Service Providers such as Travel Agents, Tour Operators and other categories of Travel Trade has made certain amendments.

Initial recognition for all categories of Travel Trade viz., Tour Operators, Travel Agents, Tourist Transport Operators, Domestic Tour Operators & Adventure Tour Operators shall now be given at the Headquarters for a period of five years instead of three years as was given earlier, based on the Inspection report / recommendation of a Committee comprising of Regional Director concerned and a member of TAAI / IATO, etc.. Renewals, thereafter, shall be granted for five years after inspection conducted by a Committee comprising of Regional Director concerned and a member of TAAI / IATO, etc., on an application made by the Service Provider of Travel Trade along with the requisite fee / documents to the Regional Director of the concerned region. The renewal shall be granted within a period of two months from the receipt of complete application / documents. Essentially, the revised guidelines, seek to delegate the task of renewal to the Regional Directors of Tourism, a task that is centralized in the Ministry of Tourism, at present. This would do away with the need for such applications to be sent to the Ministry of Tourism, from all over the country for mere renewal, thereby expediting the process.

4182. (14-11-2007) NEW DELHI : The President of India, Smt. Pratibha Devisingh has urged children to develop their personality in such a way so that they are disciplined, have good habits and are responsible citizens. Interacting with about 400 children from Delhi and surrounding areas who visited Rashtrapati Bhavan today on the occasion of Children's Day, the President spoke about the need to persuade the families of the weaker sections to educate their children for a brighter future. Smt. Patil emphasised on the important role that a mother can play in a family to create this awareness. The President also touched on the subject of corruption and urged the youth to discuss amongst themselves as well as create awareness through street plays about this menace. She said that the message should go through children to adults that the younger generation is against corruption. The President urged the children to play their part in spreading literacy, by each one teaching one illiterate person in their neighbourhood. Smt. Patil also spoke about some incidents, which she still remembers from her childhood. The children who visited Rashtrapati Bhavan included orphans from the Central Adoption Resource Authority (CARA), an autonomous body of the Ministry of Women and Child Development, Government of India. Children affected by thalassaemia were also present. They were brought by the organization Foundation against Thalassaemia.

4183. (14-11-2007) NEW DELHI : A group of about 120 children including those affected by HIV met the President of India, Smt. Pratibha Devisingh Patil at Rashtrapati Bhavan on the occasion of Children's day. These children were from the states of Andhra Pradesh, Jammu and Kashmir, Gujarat, West Bengal and Assam. They were accompanied by officials of the Guild of Service (North India). The President commended the children for their bravery and wished them a happy future with prosperity. She asked the children to study hard for their good and for the progress of the nation. She also thanked the organisations which had given these children a new life.

4184. (14-11-2007) NEW DELHI : President of India, Smt. Pratibha Devisingh Patil, said I am very happy to be amidst all of you today on the occasion of the birthday of Pandit Nehru and extend my greetings to the children. I am delighted to be present at the inauguration of the 27th India International Trade Fair (IITF), which is the largest exposition of its kind in Asia. The IITF has proved to be an effective showcase for Indian trade and industry. I am glad to see the impressive turnout by representatives of Indian and foreign business organizations on this occasion. Years ago, India embarked on a course of economic reforms aimed at opening up our economy in a progressive manner; encouraging foreign investments, upgrading technology, augmenting and strengthening infrastructure development, promoting industrial growth and increasing exports. Our economy is now witnessing an accelerated growth rate. Industry is seeing a phase of considerable growth particularly in automobiles, pharmaceuticals, consumer durables, telecommuni cations, electronics, biotechnology and information technology sectors. It should be our endeavour to sustain this growth and ensure that it is socially inclusive, particularly for the disadvantaged and the marginalized sections. We must also ensure that every region participates in and benefits from the process of economic growth that is transforming our nation. I am happy to note that the theme for the India International Trade Fair 2007 is "Processed Food and Agro Industries". The agriculture scenario in the country is gradually looking up. Our agricultural exports increased last year by around 20 percent over the previous year and its contribution to the overall exports of the country is now around 7 percent. Although India is one of the largest food producers in the world, only 2 percent of the total food production is processed, which is a negligible amount. Processing of agricultural goods, significantly adds value to agricultural produce and we look at it as a strong emerging sector in India. The Government has declared the food-processing industry as a priority sector for India. Our strong agricultural base provides a large and varied raw material source for the food processing industry. The food processing industry should be encouraged to set up small and medium scale units closer to agricultural production centres. That would be useful in generating employment in rural areas and would also be beneficial to the food processing industry in terms of ensured availability of good raw materials and savings on transportation costs. This theme, "Processed Food and Agro Industries", is of special relevance globally too, as we are grappling with the formidable task of eradicating hunger and poverty from our planet. Efforts towards sustainable agriculture can be greatly augmented with the help of advances through research in agricultural technology as well as bio-technology and extending the findings of research to the field. We must also make our policies and programmes flexible and conducive to gender considerations in all areas of agricultural research, education and extension; since, nearly 60 percent of farm labour in India is women. The pioneering role played by women in the preservation of topsoil and forests is well recognized. Therefore, we need to catalyze agricultural growth through holistic agricultural development strategies that should include women. Using processed food for the Government's Midday Meal Scheme for children is a possibility. Agricultural produce specific to the area could be utilized, its food value enhanced by adding nutrients and women could be engaged to prepare healthy, hygienic and ready-to-eat meals for children.

4185. (14-11-2007) NEW DELHI : The Minister for Steel, Chemicals and Fertiliser Shri Ram Vilas Paswan today inaugurated the Steel Pavilion at the India International Trade Fair at New Delhi. The Pavilion highlights the 'Innovative Usage of Steel' in everyday life. From highways, flyovers and different modes of transport, the pavilion showcases imaginative and useful tools. The underlying statement of the Pavilion remains Innovation, and the imagination of the human mind. From Metal to Metamorphosis. How Steel has become the mainstay metal of Curved Cable-stayed Bridges, Creek Bridges, Cliff Bridges across waterways. Closer home in High-rise Buildings, Shopping Malls, Cineplexes, Stadia and Multi-level Parking Lots. From safety pins to submarines, the world revolves around this marvel of a metal. Speaking on the occasion Shri Paswan lauded the role of the Ministry of Steel and the Public Sector Undertakings. He said the steel sector is on a high growth trajectory, recording around 12 to 13 per cent growth in production and consumption. He said, the growth in consumption could go up further as the present per capita consumption of steel is low.

4186. (14-11-2007) NEW DELHI : The formal inauguration of these impressive new quarters of the Foreign Service Institute would have been a significant duty for me to perform on any day of the calendar. That it should coincide with the 118th birth anniversary of Pandit Jawahar Lal Nehru marks it as a particularly auspicious beginning. As independent India's first Prime Minister and Minister for External Affairs, Pandit ji not only played a critical role in shaping modern India's foreign policy, but also took a personal interest in the selection and training of Foreign Service officers. With him as the guiding spirit of this institution, I am confident that the Foreign Service Institute is well-equipped to discharge its functions of training the coming generations of India's diplomats and imparting them the knowledge and skills they need to serve the nation in today's world. The world that the alumni of this Institute are training to serve in is characterized by relentless change. The effects of this change are felt more keenly than ever before because the world today is also connected like never before. Interdependence is the defining characteristic of international relations today. The notion of power, critical to understanding international relations at any time in history, has also evolved significantly and the relatively new construct of "soft power" now attracts significant attention in foreign offices across the world. The Indian mind is comfortable with change and connectedness. The enabling environment created since the mid-80s, and especially since 1991, has allowed India's entrepreneurs and professionals to leverage change and create wealth and employment on an unprecedented scale. In the same vein, the challenge before the Indian Foreign

Service in today's interdependent world is to leverage India's unique soft power to sustain the right external environment and enable India to pursue her national goals successfully I am confident that with the efforts of this Institute and with the backing of other significant actors in foreign policy, such as Parliament, media and academia, this is eminently possible. The world today is unfortunately not only about expanding economic and technological horizons. There are dangers and pitfalls such as poverty, environmental degradation, constriction of political freedom and choice, growth of extremism and intolerance, international terrorism, proliferation of weapons of mass destruction and the risk of their falling into the hands of irresponsible actors, pandemics, energy security and climate change. Quite often, the manner of addressing some of these challenges poses a challenge in itself. For a large, diverse, developing democracy located in a region going through many painful transitions, these are not academic concerns, but real, daily issues. We have to respond to them energetically, creatively and in partnership with other actors on the international stage.

4187. (14-11-2007) NEW DELHI : The annual-SARAS-2007 at India International Trade Fair (IITF), Pragati Maidan, New Delhi, took off with a colorful opening today. Inaugurating the fortnight long event Dr. Raghuvansh Prasad Singh, Minister for Rural Development emphasized the need to promote, further and foster the marketing of Rural Products prepared by the Self Help Groups established under the Swarna Jayanti Gram Swarozgar Yojana (SGSY) and spread across the country in a systematic way. It is the need of hour to promote the rural artisan and provide them an equal platform to compete in the era of global economy, Dr. Singh added. The minister also called for providing all possible help for appropriate branding, packaging, financing and training amenities as an effective tool to eradicate poverty prevailing in the rural areas of the country. Till now about 26 lakh SHGs have been established under the SGSY scheme of his ministry and since the inception of the SARAS movement from 2003-04, 67 such fairs have been organized so far and with an expenditire of nearly Rs. 29.04 crore 24, 404 SHGs have been benefited and a sale of more than Rs. 76 crore has been made by these SHGs, the minister added. He also informed that so far 11 states have agreed to provide land for the marketing of rural products in the respective state capitals. Dr. Singh also gave details of the ongoing projects of permanent shops at Pitampura and Jasola in Delhi and informed of the inauguration of Rajiv Gandhi Crafts Bhawan at Baba Kharag Singh Marg, New Delhi tomorrow. Later the Minister also inaugurated the Rural Development Pavilion at Hall No. 17 Pragati Maidan, New Delhi. This Pavilion will ensure the availability of quality rural products under one roof round the year and will work as a catalyst in enhancing the income as well as morale of rural artisan across the country, the minister hoped. Organized jointly by the Ministry of Rural Development and Council for Advancement of People's Action and Rural Technology (CAPART), the fortnight long Saras Mela is a true symphony of colors from the rural India. The theme of Saras Mela this year is the 'Sari'. This Fair is organized by The Ministry every year for facilitating the Special Swarnajayanti Gram Swarozgar Yojna (SGSY) beneficiaries, rural artisans, craftsmen, self help groups (SHGs) and NGOs to exhibit and sell their products, and to provide them the opportunity for additional income and exposure on a large scale. This exhibition-cum-sale fair under the brand name of SARAS will display a wide range of products manufactured by the rural artisans, craftsmen and beneficiaries of SHGs across the country. The mela also aims at creating a unique platform for developing linkages with customers and providing an opportunity to artisans to interact with the buyers directly. Saras 2007 is exhibiting nearly 370 stalls of DRDAs and NGOs from 21 States displaying a variety of products prepared by rural artisans across the country. As per the theme of this year, Craftsmen are displaying an array of 'saris' from different cultural regions of the country. Other attractive products on sale include bamboo artifacts, traditional and ayurvedic medicines, metalwork, woodwork, Madhubani paintings, terracotta, shawls, carpets, food products etc. Lively cultural programmes by artists from different States will be another major attraction of this mega event.

4188. (15-11-2007) NEW DELHI : A two-day search and rescue exercise began in the Bay of Bengal off Port Blair today. Various maritime agencies including the Andaman and Nicobar UT Administration are participating in the Search and Rescue Exercise (SAREX-07), being conducted by the Indian Coast Guard. The exercise will help prepare contingency plans for quick response to tackle natural and manmade disasters like tsunami and oil spill. Increasing cargo, oil tankers and passenger liners in the sea lanes passing through Bay of Bengal and the Indian Ocean have posed a challenge to disaster management agencies. The exercise will fine-tune contingency plans to test the alerting, mobilization and management of resources for search and rescue and the welfare of survivors. It will also help national and local authorities and other emergency services deal with a major maritime search and rescue operations as laid down under International Maritime Organization (IMO) guidelines. Mock missions for mass rescue and evacuation of ship will also be undertaken. The Indian Coast Guard, which has been delegated as the coordinating agency for search and rescue missions the Indian Maritime Zone, has three Maritime Rescue Coordination Centres at Mumbai, Chennai and Port Blair besides 10 sub-centres.

4189. (15-11-2007) NEW DELHI : Central Board of Excise and Customs (CBEC), Department of Revenue issued Notification No. 113/2007-Customs (N.T.) dated 15th November, 2007 notifying tariff values of edible oils and brass scrap (all grades) as shown in the Table below. The tariff values of six palm group oils and crude soyabean oil remain unchanged. However, tariff value of brass scrap (all grades) has been reduced.

4190. (15-11-2007) NEW DELHI : According to the Indian Meteorological Department (IMD) a very severe cyclonic storm "SIDR" has formed in the Bay of Bengal on 13th November. As per the latest message received from the IMD, this system lay centered at 0830 hours IST of today over east central and adjoining west central and north Bay of Bengal about 530 km south of Kolkata. It is likely to intensify further and move in a northerly direction. The system with maximum sustained wind speed of 200 kmph is likely to cross West Bengal-Bangladesh coast east of Sagar Island today around midnight as the system has shown fast movement during last 3 hours. The matter was taken up as an emergency measure in the Cabinet meeting today. The Ministry of Home Affairs has issued advisory to the States/UTs of Andaman & Nicobar, Orissa and West Bengal with information to Tamil Nadu, Puducherry and Andhra Pradesh to keep a close watch and requested them to take appropriate precautionary measures keeping MHA informed about any development. MHA has also contacted Relief Commissioners of the States of West Bengal, Orissa, Andhra Pradesh and Andaman & Nicobar Island informing them about the latest status. MHA has further contacted Commandants of BSF, NDRF Kolkata and CISF Battalion at Mundali (Orissa) for deployment and relief work. Ministry of Railways, Road Transport & Highways, Communication and Power have also been requested to take appropriate action in mobilizing a regional/ local offices. Control Room of MHA is constantly monitoring the situation by keeping in touch with IMD and the concerned States/UTs.

4191. (15-11-2007) NEW DELHI : The Union Cabinet today gave its approval for introduction of an amendment Bill of the Mines and Minerals (Development & regulation) Act, 1957 in the Rajya Sabha to introduce auction through competitive bidding as a selection process for allocation of coal blocks for captive mining for specified / notified end uses. This will make allocation of coal blocks not only objective but also transparent.

4192. (15-11-2007) NEW DELHI : The Union Cabinet today gave its approval for moving a resolution by the Minister of Railways in both the Houses of Parliament for adoption of the recommendations contained in Para No. 54, 55, 56, 57, 58, 59, 60 and 61 of the Railway Convention Committee (2004)'s Sixth Report. This decision would enable the ministry of Railways to implement the said recommendations of the Railway Convention Committee.

4193. (15-11-2007) NEW DELHI : The Union Cabinet today gave its approval for increasing the authorized capital of India Tourism Development Corporation from Rs. 75.00 crore to Rs. 150.00 crore by creation of 7.5 crore equity shares worth Rs. 10/- each. The increase in the authorized capital would enable ITDC to renovate its hotels, so as to make them commercially competitive in this field.

4194. (15-11-2007) NEW DELHI : The Union Cabinet today gave its approval for signing of the Agreement between India and Iceland for Avoidance of Double Taxation and prevention of Fiscal Evasion with respect to Taxes on income. The Agreement will stimulate the flow of capital, technology and personnel from India to Iceland and Vice-versa. It will provide tax stability and reduce any obstacles in providing mutual cooperation.

4195. (15-11-2007) NEW DELHI : The Union Cabinet today gave its approval for ratification of International Tropical Timber Agreement, 2006. As India is a member country of the ITTO, the ITTA, 2006 would help in India's contribution to the international trade in tropical timber and will generate goodwill to the country and enhance the status of India on the world forestry map under the aegis of this UN Organization.

4196. (15-11-2007) NEW DELHI : In exercise of the powers conferred by clause (1) of article 217 of the Constitution of India, the President is pleased to appoint (i) Shri Justice Ajay Kumar Tripathi and (ii) Shri Justice Dharnidhar Jha, Additional Judges of the Patna High Court to be Judges of the Patna High Court, in that order of seniority, with effect from the dates they assume charge of their respective offices.

4197. (15-11-2007) NEW DELHI : Union Minister for Rural Development Dr. Raghuvansh Prasad Singh, today inaugurated a SARAS gallery at Baba Kharag Singh Marg in Cannaught Place, New Delhi. Speaking on the occasion the Minister stressed for providing all necessary support and help the rural craftsmen so as to withstand and compete in the era of global market oriented economy. The minister also called for providing all possible help for appropriate branding, packaging, financing and training amenities as an effective tool to eradicate poverty prevailing in the rural areas of the country. The Commerce Ministry is being approached for having an exclusive export promotion council for the sale of rural goods outside the country, Dr. Singh added. The minister further disclosed that if needed, he will take the matter with Prime Minister's Office also. Dr. Singh also hoped that this gallery will provide unlimited and free of hassle opportunities on permanent basis to rural craftsmen round the year. The SARAS Gallery opened today has been established with a view to assist the Swarna Jayanti Gram Swarozgar Yojana(SGSY) rural artisans/beneficiaries and self help groups(SHGs) to exhibit and sell their products in the city. The gallery, first of its kind intends to create a unique platform for developing linkage with customers and providing a prospect of interaction with the buyers directly. The gallery is spread across 398.89 sq.mtr where 24 stalls have been erected presently. The stalls will be allotted regularly to states on rotation basis, for organising thematic fairs for a period of 15 to 20 days for display and sale of rural products from across the country. Minister of State for Rural Development Shri Chandra Sekar Sahu, Secretary Drinking Water Supply in the Ministry of Rural Development, Mrs. Shantha Sheila Nair, Director General CAPART Mrs. V.S. Rao was also present on the occasion.

4198. (15-11-2007) NEW DELHI : The Indian programming at International Film Festival of India-2007 (IFFI-2007), would be under eight different segments. Besides the section Indian Panorama wherein 21 feature and 15 non-feature films will be screened, the Indian programming would have retrospective of legendary director Tapan Sinha's four films. 'Kabuliwala', 'Sagina Mahato', 'Adalat O Ekti

Meye' and 'Aadmi Aur Aurat' will be screened in this section. Another retrospective 'Eternal Romantic' will be on the legendary director Vijay Anand. Four of his masterpieces-Nau Do Gyarah, Tere Ghar Ke Samne, Guide and Jewel Thief-will be showcased. Under the Homage Section, one film each on legendary actress of Hindi and Marathi cinema Vanamala Devi (film-Shyamchi Aai), renowned music director, O. P. Nayyar (film-Aar Paar) and renowned cinematographer K. K. Mahajan (film-Saara Akash) will be screened. As a tribute to living legend Aribam Syam Sharma, his film Ishanou would be screened. Navya Movement in Kannada language inspired a generation of film makers and marked a turning point in Kannada cinema. A section 'Navya Movement and Kannada Cinema' would showcase three landmark Kannada films. These are, Samskara (1970) directed by Pattabhi Rama Reddy, Chomana Dudi (1975) directed by Late B V Karanth, and Ghatashradha (1977) directed by Girish Kasravalli. The Section 'India @ 60', celebrating India's independence, would showcase three feature films and four documentaries based on the spirit of freedom and patriotism. Curated by Government of Goa, the section presents three prominent features from three different languages. The films are: 'Nam Iruvar' (Tamil), a landmark film by A V Meiyappan, 'Biyallis' (Bengali), a landmark film by Hemen Gupta and the all time favourite by Manoj Kumar, 'Shaheed' (Hindi). The four documentaries of the Films Division to be screened are, 'Call for swaraj and swadeshi' by Prem Vaidya, 'India wins freedom' by N S Thapa, 'Then came Gandhi' by N S Thapa and 'Gandhi-An Emerging Reality' by D Gautaman.

4199. (15-11-2007) NEW DELHI : Khadi has been the mainstay of rural employment generation as also the mantra to uplift the poor masses. This was stated by Shri Mahabir Prasad, Union Minister for Micro, Small & Medium Enterprises, while inaugurating the Khadi & Village Industries Commission (KVIC) pavilion, at the 27th India International Trade Fair here today. Elaborating on the performance of KVIC Shri Prasad said, during the Tenth Plan, 1, 21, 961 units were established under Rural Employment Generation Programme to which margin money assistance of Rs.1452 crore was released by the Government through KVIC to the beneficiaries. An estimated 25.25 lakh additional employment opportunities have been generated during the Tenth Plan. He said, there was an urgent need for substantially enhancing the wages of Spinners and Weavers from the present level. Earlier, Shri Prasad inaugurated National Small Industries Corporation Ltd. (NSIC) pavilion-'Techmart' and MSME pavilion-'MSME Expo-2007' under the Ministry of Micro, Small & Medium Enterprises. The major attraction of first ever MSME Expo is 'Hall of Excellence' which is displaying an array of high quality and sophisticated products manufactured in the MSME sector. More than 100 participants from all over the country are displaying their products in the Expo, which include Engineering products, Electrical and Electronic goods, Glass and Ceramics, Handicrafts, Imitation Jewellery, Readymade and Embroidered Garments, Cosmetics and Herbals, Carpets and Shawls, Soft toys, Pickles, Spices and Condiments, Leather and Footwears, Hospital Equipment and Medical

Rehabilitation Goods, Stainless Kitchenware and Tableware, Bamboo based Toys and Ready-to-eat Foods etc. NSIC is also organizing "Techmart India 2007", the 15th International Technology Fair coinciding with India International Trade Fair 2007. This annual event is a centre stage for keeping abreast with latest technology development in the Indian MSME sector. The event will assist MSME Sector in marketing their products and services and also help large companies and buyers in identifying MSMEs, which can become their ancillaries, partners in joint ventures and sub-contracting. This year a new dimension of sectoral approach has been added to the display profile of the exhibition and emphasis is laid on sector specific products and technologies like low cost building material, auto components, information technology, light engineering and machines tools, textiles, coir etc. A new initiative has been taken by NSIC by providing special enclosure of "Working Techmart" where stand-alone technologies for entrepreneurs are on display besides live cluster demonstration of units from North Eastern States. During Techmart India 2007, a seminar on NSIC support services for Micro, Small & Medium Enterprises will also be organised. A South African delegation visited Techmart today. Shri Mahabir Prasad also inaugurated the Coir Board pavilion and went round various stalls to have a glimpse of innovative coir products.

4200. (15-11-2007) NEW DELHI : Prof. Samir Brahmachari, the newly appointed Secretary, Department of Scientific and Industrial Research (DSIR) and Director General, Council of Scientific and Industrial Research (CSIR) today spelt out a three-fold agenda to give a fillip to in-house R&D in industry and position India's innovation efforts in the international arena. Inaugurating the 21st National Conference on In-House R&D in Industry with the theme "R&D Innovations for Indian Growth Dynamics", organized jointly by DSIR and FICCI, Prof. Brahmachari stressed the need to be aggressive in the pursuit of innovations by earmarking 25% of total private sector and government investment in long-term R&D, not with an eye on the immediate gains but for returns in the future. He said such efforts need to be combined with operational expenses of the private sector and the capital expenditure of the government to connect the vast army of young scientists with national R&D efforts. Earlier, the DSIR National R&D Awards (2007) were given away to nine companies in various spheres of research by Prof. Samir Brahmachari; Dr. T Ramasami, Secretary, DST; and Mr. Y K Modi, Past President, FICCI. The areas of research and the award winning companies are: Chemical and Allied Industries-Laila Impex, Vijayawada (A.P); Agro & Food Processing Industries-Pest control (India) Pvt. Ltd, Bangalore; Pollution Control & Environmental Protection United Phosphorous Ltd, Vapi (Gujarat); Mechanical Engineering Industries-Minda Industries Ltd, Gurgaon; Electrical Industries-Crompton Greaves Ltd, Mumbai; Electronics/Opto Electronics Industries-Ananth Technologies Ltd, Hyderabad; Computer Software-Sasken Communication Technologies Ltd, Bangalore; Technology Absorption of Imported Technologies-Reliance Industries Ltd, Surat; and Successful Commercialization of Technologies acquired from others-Tata Steel Ltd, Jamshedpur. Dr. T. Ramasami, Secretary, DST, in his address emphasized on the importance of R&D and the close relationship between R&D and overall growth. He said that with competition increasing at a rapid pace, it is important that the companies plan the dynamics of growth in a very structured manner. Observing that after a long time we are coming out of the developing country mindset of having limited resources, Dr. Ramasami expressed hope that the speed, scope and scale of innovation in the country would increase over a period. Mr. Y K Modi, Past President, FICCI and Chairman, YKM Holdings, in his welcome address mentioned that today the world is globalising at a rapid pace and this is creating uncertainties for the businesses. He added that in this highly uncertain future, winners would be eventually those who willingly challenge themselves in unprecedented ways to create unique technologies with benefit to the masses.

4201. (15-11-2007) NEW DELHI : Presently the entry fee in the ticketed monuments of Archaeological Survey of India (ASI) for foreigners are US $ 5 per person for World Heritage Sites and US $ 2 per person for other monuments. These rates were fixed when exchange rate of US $ was about Rs.50/- per US $. However, keeping in view the international practices and also to avoid any anomaly on account of falling exchange rates of US $ vis-à-vis Rupee and consequent fall in revenues, the Government has decided to denominate the entry fee for the foreigners for all the monuments in Indian Rupees only *i.e.*, @ Rs.250/- and Rs.100/- per person respectively.

4202. (15-11-2007) NEW DELHI : The Union Minister for Shipping, Road Transport & Highways, Thiru T.R. Baalu has approved the proposal for construction of a new berth at North breakwater at the Tuticorin Port. The construction of the new berth to be known as North Cargo Berth-1, would cost Rs. 40 crore. It will add a capacity of 2.93 Million Tonnes Per Annum (MTPA) to the port and would help the Port to ease the congestion in handling bulk/dusty cargoes in the existing berths. The North Cargo Berth-1, would enable the Port to handle coal vessels of 65, 000 to 75, 000 Dead Weight Tonnage (DWT) with a maximum draft of 12.8 meters. Thiru Baalu has expressed the hope that the new berth will help meet the growing demands for handling bulk cargo in the coming years and would be especially useful for the Cargo meant for the proposed Thermal Power Plant at Tuticorin to be set up by Tamil Nadu Electricity Board and M/s Neyveli Lignite Corporation Ltd. Presently, Tuticorin Port boasts of seven cargo berths, one container terminal, one oil jetty, two coal jetties and two shallow draft beths with a total operating capacity of 20.55 Million Tonnes Per Annum (MTPA).

4203. (15-11-2007) NEW DELHI : The Union Minister for Shipping & Road Transport Thiru T.R. Baalu has approved an amount of Rs. 4, 24, 93, 500/- for grant-in-aid to fifty seven Orgnizations under the scheme "Two days Refresher Training for Heavy Motor Vehicle Drivers in Unorganized Sector" to impart training to about 60, 000 HMV drivers from various States and Union Territories.

Under the scheme among other states, 13000 drivers from Delhi, nearly 12000 from Andhra Pradesh, over 7000 drivers from Tamil Nadu, 3250 drivers from Gujarat, 7500 from Maharashtra and 4000 drivers from Uttar Pradesh will be imparted training in better and safer driving skills. The organizations which have been entrusted the task to conduct refresher training include Institute of Driver Training and Research, Delhi, Central Institute of Road Transport (Pune), and Western India Automobile Association, Mumbai. All these organizations have been recommended by the State Governments which are responsible for satisfying themselves about the availability of adequate infrastructure with these organizations to impart training to the drivers in the Unorganised Sector. Under the scheme, the total grant is released in two installments-50 per cent as the first instalment (in advance) after execution of bond and submission of detailed time bound programme and remaining 50 per cent as second and final instalment after conclusion of the programmes and submission of necessary documentary proof of completion as well as Final Action Taken Report (FATR) from the concerned State Government.

4204. (15-11-2007) NEW DELHI : Minister of Food Processing Industries Shri Subodh Kant Sahai said that the proposed Food Regulatory Authority will be placed by the end of December this year, after which the Prevention of Food Adulteration Act (PFA) will become null and void on matters related to Food Processing. Addressing the Economic Editors Conference-2007 he said that, India has a major role in the future of global food business as it has a strong base in agriculture and provides a large and varied raw material base for Food Processing Industry. He further said that National Wine and Meat Board will be set up in January 2008. Unveiling the future plans of the government in promoting the Food Processing Sector, the Minister explained that the centre will identify SEZs and AEZs for setting up Mega Food Parks. This will help in sourcing food and vegetables from the farmers with lesser transaction cost. The government will also draw up a 10 year plan to tap solar energy for the Food Processing Industry. The Minister stressed that the Food Processing Sector needs to be accorded equal emphasis as that of Agriculture. Shri Sahai said Food Processing Ministry has launched a 'food street' mission for 25 heritage lanes. The government will spend Rs. 5 crore on developing each heritage street and make changes to meet a certain standard. Technology knowledge and management will be the drivers of growth for food industry. The country has seen the era of Information Technology (IT) and Bio Technology (BT) and now the time has come for ushering the era of Food Technology (FT). Addressing the Conference Shri P. I. Suvarathan, Secretary Food Processing Industries said that keeping in mind the poor hygienic conditions of the abattoirs in the country the Government is planning to set up 25 abattoirs shortly. He said that Ministry will spend Rs. 48 crore for upgradation of Paddy Processing Research Centre, Thanjavur.

4205. (15-11-2007) NEW DELHI : Prof. Saifuddin Soz, the Union Minister of Water Resources inaugurated the Ministry of Water Resources pavilion on the theme "Water Year-2007" in the 27th Indian International Trade Fair organized by ITPO here today in Hall No. 7-D at Pragati Madain. He witnessed the various models displayed and encouraged the officers and scientists for their innovative ideas. Shri Jai Prakash Narayan Yadav, the Minister of State for Water Resources, Smt. Gauri Chatterjee, Secretary, Ministry of Water Resources and senior officers of the Ministry and subordinate offices were present on the occasion. A cultural and musical programme on the 'essentiality of Water Conservation' was presented on the occasion. The pavilion showcases many models on water related issues and the models indicating diverse aspects of water including its various uses, forms, sources etc. With a view to creating adequate mass awareness on water related issues, street plays coupled with music and dance shows on water use efficiency, rain water harvesting and the importance of water conservation are being organized throughout the duration of the fair from 14th November to 27th November 2007. Adequate arrangements have been made by the organizations in deputing senior officers to explain the salient features, intricate aspects and the working of the models for proper appreciation and understanding of the people who will be visiting the pavilion in large numbers. For the spread of knowledge and the benefits of people visiting the pavilion the techniques on rain water harvesting, artificial recharge to ground water and the nuances of the Integrated Water Resources Development and Management will be explained in a lucid manner not only for the discrimination of knowledge but also for the motivation of the people in appreciating the utility and necessity of such techniques for the conservation of water for posterity in the years to come. The modern techniques of communication viz. plasma TV is being used to inform visitors about various facets of water conservation with emphasis on Rainwater Harvesting and Artificial Recharge. Various organizations under the Ministry viz. Central Water Commission, Central Ground Water Board, Central Soil and Material Research station, Central Water Power Research Station, National Institute of Hydrology, Water and Power Consultancy Services, National Projects Construction Corporation Ltd., National Water Development Agency are exhibiting models and other display material to disseminate information about their activities, achievements and vision.

4206. (15-11-2007) NEW DELHI : A one-day Seminar on "Planning and Development of Metropolitan Regions in the context of Special Initiatives relating to Infrastructure Development and Provision of Basic Services' will be held here on November 17, 2007. The Association of Municipalities and Development Authorities (AMDA) in collaboration with Ministries of Urban Development and Housing and Urban Poverty Alleviation, Government of India, HUDCO, and Development Authorities of Delhi, Chennai, Hyderabad, Ahmedabad, Mumbai, Punjab, Bangalore and Haryana is organizing the Seminar. Shri S.Jaipal Reddy, Minister for Urban Development, would inaugurate the seminar on November 17, 2007. Kumari Selja, Minister of State (Independent Charge) for Housing and Urban Poverty Alleviation, Government of India will be the Chief Guest at the Validictory Session. The broad objectives of the Seminar are to: Stimulate awareness about the new challenges facing metropolitan regions emerging from investments such as SEZs located nearby, immigration from rural areas, growth of population as well as diversification of activities and how such activities should be spatially integrated in the metropolitan regional planning process; identify the need of strategic infrastructure for managing rapid growth of metropolitan regions; and look into the current planning processes of cities with a view to promoting social inclusion and provision of housing and basic services to the urban poor. The Seminar seeks to address some critical issues relating to the above under the following three Sub-themes: Urbanisation and Metropolitan Regions: The Emerging role of Urban and Regional Planning in the context of SEZs; Sustainable Development in Metropolitan Regions in the context of JNNURM and Mainstreaming Urban Poor and Provision of Urban Basic Services within the Framework of Master Plans. About 75 participants comprising representatives of municipalities and development authorities including members of AMDA across the country, as well as policy makers administrators, academicians and experts from national and international organizations are expected to participate in the Seminar.

4207. (15-11-2007) NEW DELHI : In view of the increased air traffic in the winter holiday season, the Ministry of Civil Aviation has today decide to allow airlines to increase their capacity during this period. To counter the winter rush, all airlines will be allowed to upgrade their aircraft to ANY capacity level on their existing frequencies at all airports in India. This dispensation will be available to the airlines from 1 December, 2007 to 31 January, 2008.

4208. (15-11-2007) NEW DELHI : The Environment and Science and Technology Minister of Nepal Shri Mahanta Thakur called on the Minister for Steel, Chemicals and Fertiliser Shri Ram Vilas Paswan here today and discussed matters of mutual interest. The visiting Minister recalled traditional friendly relations between the two countries. Expressing similar sentiments Shri Paswan said that we have to work together to further deepen existing relations between the two nations. Shri Thakur is also a Central Committee Member and treasurer of the Nepali Congress. He was the Deputy Speaker in the House of Representatives elected in 1991.

4209. (15-11-2007) NEW DELHI : UNESCO Regional Conference on Global Literacy is being organised by the Ministry of Human Resource Development, Department of School Education & Literacy with UNESCO on 29-30th November, 2007 at Vigyan Bhawan, New Delhi. Smt. Sonia Gandhi will be the Chief Guest of the inaugural session whereas Smt. Mahashweta Devi, Jnanapeeth award winner and recipient of Saraswathi Samman, will be the keynote speaker. The Conference at Delhi is a part of a series of regional conferences being organized as a follow up of the White House Conference on Global Literacy held in September 2006 hosted by Laura Bush, first Lady of the United States of America and Honorary Ambassador for the United Nations Literacy Decade (UNLD) Delhi Conference is the fourth in the series of six Regional Conferences being organized covering

Arab States, Asia and the Pacific, Europe and the Latin America and Caribbean as a part of major drive to promote literacy at national and international levels. Other three conferences held earlier were at (1) Doha, Qatar, on 12-14 March, 2007, (2) Beijing, People's Republic of China on 31 July and 1 August 2007, and (3) Bamako, Mali, on 10-12 September, 2007. The First Ladies from 10 countries namely, Afghanistan, Bangladesh, Bhutan, Kazakhstan, Kyrgyz Republic, Maldives, Pakistan, Sri Lanka, Tajikistan, and Uzbekistan have been invited to participate in the conference. As Goodwill Ambassadors, the First Ladies would play a vital role to promote literacy in the entire region. Education and Finance Ministers of the 14 countries of the region namely, Afghanistan, Bangladesh, Bhutan, India, Islamic Republic of Iran, Kazakhstan, Kyrgyz Republic, Maldives, Nepal, Pakistan, Sri Lanka, Tajikistan, Turkmenistan and Uzbekistan are among the other dignitaries expected to grace the occasion. The Conference is, therefore, of utmost importance for UNESCO and its member States and partners in their effort to achieve the goals of Education for All (EFA) and Millennium Development Goals (MDGs) and to fulfil their commitments to the United Nations Literacy Decade (UNLD) and the Decade of Education for Sustainable Development (DESD). The Delhi Conference is important for the Indian sub-continent because 3 highly populated countries among E-9 countries namely, Bangladesh, India and Pakistan continue to face major literacy challenges, including the sheer number of illiterates. In addition to a serious gender gap, there is a high urban-rural disparity. As a key instrument for lifelong learning, indispensable for effective participation in social and economic life and essential for peace, literacy is a crucial issue in the region. The countries of South and South West Asia have the highest number of illiterates in the world, and out of the 388 million adults in this region who cannot read and write 63.5 per cent are women.

4210. (15-11-2007) NEW DELHI : The Prime Minister, Dr. Manmohan Singh called on the former Prime Minister Shri Atal Bihari Vajpayee yesterday to enquire about his health. He conveyed his good wishes to Shri Vajpayee for Deepawali. The Leader of Opposition, Shri L.K. Advani was present on this occasion. In the course of the meeting, they discussed current political issues, including the nuclear deal.

4211. (15-11-2007) NEW DELHI : The Airports Authority of India (AAI) today paid a sum of Rs. 112.00 crore as dividend to the Government. This is its full and final dividend for the financial year 2006-07. Earlier AAI had paid an interim dividend of Rs. 60.00 crore to the Government of India in January 2007. With this, the total dividend payout for the year 2006-07 stands to Rs. 172.00 crore. This is the highest ever dividend paid by AAI to Government of India. The dividend cheque was handed over by Dr. K. Ramalingam, Chairman AAI, to Shri Praful Patel, Minister for Civil Aviation, today. Shri Ashok Chawla, Secretary, Civil Aviation, Board Members of AAI and other senior officials of Ministry of Civil Aviation were also present on the occasion. During the year 2006-07,

Airports Authority of India earned highest ever revenue of Rs. 3726.00 crore and earned profit after tax of Rs. 860.00 crore. During the year 2006-07, AAI incurred highest ever capital expenditure of Rs. 1040.00 crore to modernize the airports and passenger facilities all over the country. AAI is also undertaking development of 35 non-metro airports to meet the growing demand of civil aviation sector.

4212. (16-11-2007) NEW DELHI : Government of India have announced the sale (re-issue) of "7.99 per cent Government Stock, 2017 for a notified amount of Rs. 3, 000 crore (nominal) through a priced based auction using multiple price method. Government of India have also announced the sale (re-issue) of "8.35 per cent Government Stock, 2022" for a notified amount of Rs. 4, 000 crore (nominal) through a price based auction using multiple price method. The auctions will be conducted by the Reserve Bank of India, Mumbai Office, Fort, Mumbai on November 23, 2007 (Friday). Up to 5% of the notified amount of the sale of both the stocks will be allotted to eligible individuals and Institutions as per the Scheme for Non-Competitive Bidding Facility in the Auction of Government Securities. Bids in the prescribed form obtainable from the Regional Director, Reserve Bank of India, Mumbai Office (Public Debt Office), Fort, Mumbai-400 001 and RBI website www.rbi.org.in should be submitted to that Office on November 23, 2007. The NDS members should submit competitive as well as non-competitive bids in electronic format using Primary Market Operation (PMO) module of NDS. All bids should be submitted by 12.30 P.M.

4213. (16-11-2007) NEW DELHI : ISRO has achieved a significant milestone through the successful test of indigenously developed Cryogenic Stage, to be employed as the upper stage of India's Geosynchronous Satellite Launch Vehicle (GSLV). The test was conducted for its full flight duration of 720 seconds today (November 15, 2007) at Liquid Propulsion test facility at Mahendragiri, in Tamil Nadu. With this test, the indigenous Cryogenic Upper Stage has been fully qualified on the ground. The flight stage is getting ready for use in the next mission of GSLV (GSLV-D3) in It may be recalled that a ground test for 480 seconds of the complete stage was conducted on August 4, 2007. The indigenous Cryogenic Upper Stage (CUS) is powered by a regeneratively cooled cryogenic engine, which works on staged combustion cycle developing a thrust of 69.5 kN in vacuum. The other stage systems include insulated propellant tanks, booster pumps, inter-stage structures, fill and drain systems, pressurisation systems, gas bottles, command block, igniters, pyro valves and cold gas orientation and stabilisation system. Liquid Oxygen (LOX) and Liquid Hydrogen (LH2) from the respective tanks are fed by individual booster pumps to the main turbo-pump, which rotates at 39, 000 rpm to ensure a high flow rate of 16.5 kg/sec of propellants into the combustion chamber. The main turbine is driven by the hot gas produced in a pre-burner. Thrust control and mixture ratio control are achieved by two independent regulators. LOX and Gaseous Hydrogen (GH2) are ignited by pyrogen type igniters in the pre-burner as well as in the main and steering engines. Apart from the complexities in the fabrication of stage tanks, structures, engine and its sub-systems and control components, CUS employs special materials like Aluminum, Titanium, Nickel and their alloys, bi-metallic materials and polyimides. Stringent quality control and elaborate safety measures have to be ensured during assembly and integration. Liquid Propulsion Systems Centre (LPSC) is the lead centre for the development of Cryogenic Upper Stage with the involvement of Vikram Sarabhai Space Centre (VSSC) and other ISRO centres as well as several industries, both in public and private sector. The successful ground test of the indigenous Cryogenic Upper Stage for the full flight duration has validated the design robustness and performance adequacy for its use in GSLV.

4214. (16-11-2007) NEW DELHI : As per reports received in the Agriculture Ministry, rabi sowing has started in some states of the country. As on today, wheat has been sown in 34.75 lakh ha as compared to 52.71 lakh ha during the corresponding period last year. Winter rice sowing has also started in some southern States. So far, 35, 000 ha area has come under rice plantation. Coarse cereals have been sown in 44.55 lakh ha as compared to 48.88 lakh ha by this time in 2006. Rabi oilseeds have been sown in 47.24 lakh ha as compared to 68.18 lakh ha in the last rabi. Mustard/rapeseed coverage has reached 35.10 lakh ha (last rabi, up to this time: 52.76 lakh ha). Rabi pulses cover 67.5 lakh ha (last year: 69.85 lakh ha).

4215. (16-11-2007) NEW DELHI : The Cabinet has approved India Tourism Development Corporation Ltd. (ITDC) to increase its authorized capital from Rs. 75 crore to Rs. 150 crore. ITDC has worked out a plan to undertake a major renovation work in Hotel Ashok, New Delhi at a total cost of Rs. 146.35 crore. The proposed renovation plan project of Rs. 146.35 crores for renovating/upgrading the Hotel Ashok is envisaged to be funded @ 50% (*i.e.* Rs. 73 crore) through equity to be provided by Government of India and balance (*i.e.* Rs. 73.35 crore) is to be raised by ITDC through term loans from Banks/ Financial Institutions and internal resources. With this increase in the authorized capital, ITDC will be able to accommodate and operationalize the budgetary support of Rs. 73 crore from Government of India in form of equity to renovate the Hotel Ashok, New Delhi. Through this renovation work, ITDC will be able to maintain décor and upkeep of world class level and to provide modern state of the art facilities in the Hotels which will help them to compete with private players in the hospitality sector.

4216. (16-11-2007) NEW DELHI : Ministry of Tribal Affairs had organized a National level photographic competition 2007, for amateur photographers on the theme of 'joyful tribals', in collaboration with photo division of Minister of Information and Broadcasting. The aim of this competition was to create awareness on the colourful lifestyle of the tribals and collect good quality photographs for the purpose of documentation and exhibitions. The last date of entry was 30th September, 2007. 1949 entries from 322 participants were received. A jury comprising of experts from photo division, the Ministry of Tribal Affairs and a non-official selected the best photographs. The first, second and third prizes have gone to Shri Buddhadeb Saha, Burdwan (WB), Shri Shailesh Nigam, Rewa (MP) and Shri Pranabendu Samajpati, Kolkata (WB) respectively. The remaining ten have been selected for Commendation. The jury did not find any entry suitable for the special talent awards for the best tribal photographer. The first three winners will be invited to New Delhi during the ensuing Tribal Festival, likely to be held in December, 2007 to receive the awards.

4217. (16-11-2007) NEW DELHI : Delhi Postal Circle, New Delhi has entered into an arrangement with Reserve Bank of India for distribution of coins and exchange of soiled notes through selected Post Offices located in New Delhi HO (Gol Dak Khana, New Delhi-110001), Delhi GPO (Kashmere Gate, Delhi110006), Lodi Road HO (Lodi Road, New Delhi-110003), Ramesh Nagar HO(Ramesh Nagar, New Delhi-110015) and Krishna Nagar HO (Krishna Nagar, Delhi-110051). The members of the public may visit these Head Post Offices for their coin requirements. These Head Post Offices will also exchange soiled notes from the public.

4218. (16-11-2007) NEW DELHI : The Committee constituted by the Government to recommend revised subscriber based spectrum allocation criterion for allocation of spectrum in a scientific and practical manner met on 16.11.2007 under the Chairmanship of Shri R.Bandhopadhyay, Additional Secretary (Telecom), Department of Telecommunications. After detailed discussions, the committee decided to invite the stakeholders and experts in this field to give their views before the committee on 26th and 30th November, 2007. For this purpose committee shall be meeting for full day on 26th November, 2007 and 30th November, 2007.

4219. (16-11-2007) NEW DELHI : After 11 years of silence, Manipuri cinema came alive again with the entry of Makhonmani Mongsaba's Manipuri feature film 'Yenning Amadi Likla' into the feature film section of the Indian Panorama of the International Festival of India (IFFI) 2007. The last Manipuri film, which entered in the feature film section of Indian Panorama of IFFI was Shyam Sharma's 'Sanabi' (The Frey mare) in 1996. Makhonmani Mongsaba's 154-minute film is among 21 selected feature films. Aribam Syam Sharma's 58-minute documentary 'Rajarshi Bhagyachandra of Manipur' and Haobam Paban Kumar's 19-minute short fiction film 'Ngaihak Lambida' (Along the way) are among 15 selected non-feature films. Selections were made out of 119 feature films and 149 non-feature films. Yenning Amadi likla is a story of a nature loving child who was neglected by his parents. The film made in 16mm and blown up in 35mm and is produced by six ladies namely Umarani, Saroja, Santibala, Ibemhal, Sunitibala and Victoria. Moirangthem Inao penned the story. 'Ngaihak Lambida' produced by the Satyajit Ray Film and Television Institute, Kolkata was made in 35mm. The film scripted by MK Binodini is about the story of a woman who searches for freedom. Syam Sharma's 35mm film 'Rajyashree Bhagyachandra of Manipur' is made in English and produced by Films Division, Mumbai. The film is scripted by MK Binodini and Syam Sharma. The film is all about the story of Bhagyachandra who was one of the greatest Vaishnava kings of Manipur. A versatile person of immense qualities, he was an expert strategist who wielded his sword to defend his land and people, and yet an artistic genius of divine sensibilities who gave the world the classical dance of Manipuri Ras. A list of 21 feature films and 15 non-feature films have been selected for the Indian Panorama of the International Festival of India 2007 to be held in Goa from November 23 to December 03, 2007. Manipur is basically producing video films. Manipur could not produce any feature films for the last many years. According to the Central Board of Film Certification (CBFC), no Manipuri feature film was produced in the year 2006. in place of it, 62 Manipuri video films were produced during the year as per the record of CBFC.

4220. (16-11-2007) NEW DELHI : Alongside the International Film Festival of India (IFFI) beginning on 23rd November, 2007, the National Film Development Corporation (NFDC) will be organizing the Film Bazaar from 24th to 26th November, 2007. The Film Bazaar is aimed at providing an interactive platform between prospective buyers and sellers of film rights from India and abroad. The international participants, among others, for the Film Bazaar are, Global Film Initiative, Back Up Films, Onoma International, Mauritius Broadcasting Corporation, Shanghai Film Group, China Film Co-production, Arclight Films Malaysian Broadcasting Corporation, Astra and Miriam Arab of Cannes Market. Sales agents and financiers including Fortissimo Films and Paris based Memento Films, and Germany's Pandora are set to attend the three-day event. As part of the Film Bazaar, 15 pre-selected projects drawn from all over India will be presented to the participants. These projects are at different stages of Development. The NFDC is also organizing a Script Development Workshop, Screenwriters Bloc which is scheduled to begin in Goa on Sunday as a run up to the IFFI. The Workshop pairs six mentors with the writers of eight pre-selected screenplays. Danis Tanovic, Bernd Lichtenberg and Olivia Hetreed are among the high-profile writers who will mentor eight students. Tanovic wrote as well as directed No Man's Land, while Lichtenberg's credits as writer include Goodbye Lenin! And Hetreed scripted Girl With A Pearl Earring. The three European writers will join India's Shaji Karun (Nishad), Anjum Rajabali (Legend of Bhagat Singh) and Ashwini Malik (Clever And Lonely) as mentors at the six-day workshop. In addition, writer-director Mani Ratnam (Guru) will participate as a guest mentor and hold a master class. Participating projects include English-language scripts such as Pubali Chaudhuri's Happy Ever After, along with scripts in Hindi and other Indian languages.

4221. (17-11-2007) NEW DELHI : 54th All India Railway Tennis Championship organized by Railway Board Sports Association began here today. The tournament will conclude on 21st November 2007. Shri V.N. Mathur, Member Traffic Railway Board, was the chief guest at the inauguration function today. About 70 players from different zonal railways are participating in the five-day event. The

Championship is having four events namely: Team Championship, Opens Singles, Veterans' Singles and Veterans' Doubles. Speaking on the occasion, Shri V.N. Mathur said that it is a matter of pride that the railways have many a sportsmen of national and international standing who deserve all appreciation for their contribution in promotion of sports in the country. Referring to the Tennis Championship, Shri Mathur said that over the period, Railways have produced a number of illustrious tennis players who brought laurels at the national and international level. Shri Methew John, Secretary, Railway Board, who is also President of Railway Board Sport Association, said that the Championship will prove to be a grand success. He also announced the increase in the prize money for various events. He said that the revised prize money in case of Open Men's Singles is Rs.25, 000/-, in case of Veterans' Singles Rs. 15, 000/- and in case of Veterans' Doubles Rs.5, 000/- each. For the first time the prize money of Rs.50, 000/- has also been announced for the Team C'hampionship. The prizes for the runners up have also been increased in all the categories. On this occasion, a souvenir was also released by Member Traffic Shri V.N.Mathur. Senior officials of Railway Board and office bearers of Railway Board Sports Association were among those who attended the inaugural function.

4222. (17-11-2007) NEW DELHI : The criticism of the BJP at today's AICC session is yet another attempt by the Congress President Smt Sonia Gandhi to divert the attention of the public from their government's and party's pathetic litany of failures. This will neither diminish the truth about the dismal performance of the Congress led UPA alliance at the centre nor distract the common man from reality. Rather than comment on the BJP, the Congress and the UPA would do well to introspect on their own performance and character. The only glue that binds this government and the coalition of opportunism is the patent hatred of the UPA constituents towards the BJP whose impeccable nationalistic credentials are well known. Before speaking about terrorism, the Prime Minister and Congress President should inform the nation about the truth as to why Afzal Guru is yet to be hanged or why no appeal has been filed against Abdul Rashid Madani the prime accused in the Coimbatore serial bomb blasts which killed 58 innocent citizens and injured over 200 others? Terrorists and their patrons are well aware that under the UPA strong initiatives to combat terrorism are tradable for votes. The BJP is all for women's reservation but the vacillation of the Congress is well known. The BJP is the first national party that has already begun the process of reserving one-third posts within the party organization for women. Before speaking about women's reservation, will the Prime Minister and Congress President come on record and let the nation know whether the mass rape of innocent women and the state organised mayhem perpetrated by their allies the CPM and left party cadre in Nandigram bear their stamp of approval? Beyond the semantics and pseudo minority tokenism, what is shocking is the deafening silence of the Prime Minister and Congress President over the atrocities committed against muslims in Nandigram by their allies the CPM and left parties. Does their continued silence indicate that their conscience has been effectively over-shadowed by the compulsions of power and the urge to hold onto it at any cost? The BJP completely dismisses the comments made against it by both the Prime Minister and Smt Sonia Gandhi. The BJP does not require any certification about its performance or credentials from the Prime Minister, Congress Party or it's president. The BJP has successfully led the NDA coalition government at the centre for six years under the able leadership of Shri Atal Bihari Vajpayee. Today the party is in power by itself or in coalition in ten states of the country on the basis of popular support. The BJP is also the principal opposition party in Parliament. The principal leader of the UPA alliance calling the BJP obstructionist clearly reflects the undemocratic mindset of Smt Sonia Gandhi.

4223. (17-11-2007) NEW DELHI : Urban Development Minister Shri S. Jaipal Reddy has said that better integration of regional space through regional planning process will lead to balanced development through integration of urban and hinterland. Shri Reddy was speaking at a one day Seminar on 'Planning and Development of Metropolitan Regions in the context of Special Initiatives relating to Infrastructure Development and Provision of Basic Services' which he inaugurated here today. The Seminar is organized by the Association of Municipalities and Development Authorities. Shri Reddy said that adopting regional planning and complimentary functional plans to augment infrastructure has led to a decline in percentage share of net migrants to NCT Delhi from 45.06 to 39.82. Shri Reddy said that small and medium towns falling within metropolitan regions have an important role to play in the development of rural hinterland as they can absorb rural population and act as links between rural areas and metropolitan cities while the metropolitan engine can continue the role of promoting economic development. The regional plan can thus act as a catalyst providing a vision for the urban centres. He said the regional plan should be the first level of planning based on territorial vision for different levels of plans and management. He said the investment programmes for urban infrastructure need to be defined at the state level by taking into account available financial resources across different urban levels. The innovative part of the JNNURM programme includes reforms with a system of grants to cities to enable them to undertake projects for improving basic infrastructure such as water supply, waste water disposal, bus transport etc. The Government is promoting the public-private partnership model for metro rail transport in mega cities, he added. Earlier Shri P.D. Sudhakar, Chairman AMDA and Member Secretary NCRPB welcomed the gathering. Shri B.N. Singh, Director, AMDA made a theme presentation and presented a vote of thanks. About 75 participants from all over the country participated in the seminar. The broad objectives of the Seminar are to: Stimulate awareness about the new challenges facing metropolitan regions emerging from investments such as SEZs located nearby, immigration from rural areas, growth of population as well as diversification of activities and how such activities should be spatially integrated in the metropolitan regional planning process; identify the need of strategic infrastructure for managing rapid growth of metropolitan regions; and look into the current planning processes of cities with a view to promoting social inclusion and provision of housing and basic services to the urban poor.

4224. (17-11-2007) NEW DELHI : There are around 3, 000 forest villages in the country out of which more than 500 villages have been converted into revenue villages during last four years. Forest villages are those villages, which were set up in remote and inaccessible forest areas during the British period with a view to providing uninterrupted manpower for forestry operations. These villages are well recorded in the records of State Forest Departments. Many of these villages, despite their long existence, are, even today, not revenue villages and the land is recorded as forest land, covered under the Forest (Conservation) Act, 1980.

4225. (18-11-2007) NEW DELHI : The President of India, Smt. Pratibha Devisingh Patil has condoled the loss of lives due to the recent hurricane in Bangladesh. Smt. Patil in her condolence message to the President of Bangladesh, Professor (Dr.) Iajuddin Ahmed, has said she is deeply saddened to learn about the tragic loss of lives and substantial damage to property in the aftermath of the hurricane and has conveyed her deep condolences to the President and the people of Bangladesh. Smt. Patil has also said she is confident that, as always, the people of Bangladesh will face this tragedy with courage and fortitude.

4226. (18-11-2007) NEW DELHI : BJP Vice President Shri Mukhtar Abbas Naqvi today charged the Congress Party for making *"Doordarshan into a Congress Darshan Channel."* In a statement issued today, Shri Naqvi said that yesterday's live coverage of the AICC session in Delhi and in particular the speeches of Smt Sonia Gandhi and Rahul Gandhi on the official state channel Doordarshan, was a clear indication about how the Congress party was willing to go to any extent to misuse the government's electronic media machinery for its own political gains. The BJP Vice President pointed out that it was truly unfortunate that while the election process was already on in both Gujarat and Himachal Pradesh, the Congress Party was misusing the government machinery for its own propaganda purposes. He further pointed out that that the manner in which Doordarshan was being misused by the Congress Party at the AICC session, was clearly indicative about how the official electronic channel would be completely misused over the next few months when elections to many state assemblies and the Lok Sabha would take pace. Shri Naqvi said that the BJP would strongly oppose the political misuse of the state apparatus and ensure that all political parties get a level playing field on the state media network. Shri Naqvi requested the Election Commission to take serious note about the misuse of the Doordarshan network particular since the Model Code of Conduct was in operation in Gujarat and Himachal Pradesh. This was critical since Doordarshan reached the remotest corners of the country and such telecasts could influence the minds of the electorate while the election process was already on in these states.

4227. (18-11-2007) NEW DELHI : The Union Ministry of Culture has decided to involve school students in the campaign against vandalisation of monuments. As a part of this initiative, school children across the country will take an oath on 19th November every year. A symbolic beginning is being made this year itself with school children of Delhi taking the oath at Red Fort, Delhi on 19th November, 2007. World Heritage Week is celebrated from 19th to 25th November every year to create awareness about the rich cultural heritage of the country among the general public, students and children. According to the new plan approved by the Minister of Tourism & Culture Smt. Ambika Soni, schools will be requested to administer the oath to their children. If possible, they should take the children to a monument in their vicinity and administer the oath there. If not, they should administer the oath in the school premises and organize at least one visit of their students to a monument during the World Heritage Week. The Superintending Archaeologists of all the Circles of the Archaeological Survey of India would be instructed to render necessary help to schools in arranging the oath taking/ students visits.

4228. (18-11-2007) NEW DELHI : The Prime Minister, Dr. Manmohan Singh, has conveyed the heartfelt condolences of the Government and people of India to the people of Bangladesh for the loss of lives in Bangladesh caused by the hurricane on November 15, 2007. In a letter to Dr. Fakhruddin Ahmed, Chief Adviser, Government of the Peoples' Republic of Bangladesh, Dr. Singh also expressed his deepest sympathies to the members of the bereaved families. Dr. Singh said India stands ready to assist in whatever way to help in the relief process.

4229. (19-11-2007) NEW DELHI : President Smt. Pratibha Devisingh Patil, has urged the Government and Khadi and Village Industries Commission (KVIC) to pay special attention to see that artisans can get finance easily and through the nearest banks. The requirements of the needy to get proper benefits through loans and grants should also be kept in mind. The President was inaugurating the concluding session of KVIC's Golden Jubilee Celebration function here today. She said, the Khadi and village industries while retaining the intrinsic beauty of their products, will survive in the long run, if they take into account the changes occurring in the world in terms of market, technology and customer preferences. Blending khadi with other fibres such as silk, wool etc. will give it a new image and open further market. Khadi could also be given a new look, where necessary, so as to attract the younger generation. There is now a growing preference for natural products and khadi has an inherent advantage, in that it is eco-friendly and can be marketed as such. There is also a need for paying attention to standardization of khadi and village industries products. Stating that there was a need to set up more employment generation units especially for women the President said, one of the main objectives of promotion of khadi and village industries is to create employment opportunities in rural areas and urban slums for improving the quality of life. The President dedicated to the nation an electronic charkha which will not only produce yarn but also generate power to light a lamp and play a transistor radio in remote villages. The Finance Minister Shri P. Chidambaram, who was the Guest of Honor urged in his speech to set aside a small amount of the budget of every Indian to buy at least a khadi product every month to help not only the poor artisans but also to contribute to the employment generation as well. He also released two Commemorative coins of Rs. 5 and Rs. 50. The Union Micro, Small and Medium Enterprises Minister Shri Mahabir Prasad said in his speech that the total value of production in KVI sector amounted to Rs. 14, 029 crore in 2006-07 and KVIC has helped to generate an estimated additional employment opportunity to 88.92 lakh persons so far. He however said that looking to the mass unemployment scenario, much more efforts have to be taken to double the employment opportunities in the XIth Five Year Plan and we have to gear ourselves for accepting this challenge. The Governor of Maharashtra, Shri S.M. Krishna and the Chairperson of KVIC Ms. Kumud Joshi also spoke on this occasion.

4230. (19-11-2007) NEW DELHI : The Indira Gandhi National Old Age Pension Scheme (IGNOAPS) named after the late Prime Minister Smt. Indira Gandhi on to all those senior citizens who are 65 years of age or above and living below the poverty line (BPL) was today formally launched by the Prime Minister Dr. Manmohan Singh in a function held at G.M.C Balayogi Auditorium in the Parliament Library Complex. A large number of senior citizens had come from different parts of the country to attend the launching ceremony. .Welcoming the Prime Minister The Union Rural Development Minister Dr.Raghuvansh Prasad Singh termed the IGNOAPS as a broad based scheme and urged for a reduction in the present age of 65 years to 60 years and extend it to all needed persons from the BPL families including the widows, destitutes and physically challenged persons of that age group. Reffering to the various shemes of the Rural Development Ministry like the NREGA, SGSY, TSC and the Bharat Nirman the minister expressed the hope that the new scheme will cater all rural poors. Speaking on the occasion the Finance Minister P. Chidambaram said the government wants to double the number of present 87 lakh beneficiaries under this scheme and has asked the states to respond positively. So far 11 states have responded positively towards matching the Central Aid given under this head. States will have to provide Rs.3772 crore as their share.for it. Shri Chidambaram also asked rhe Rural Development Ministry to instruct the states for having a bank account for all the beneficiaries by July 2008 so as to send the pension money directly to the beneficiaries. He expressed the hope that the programme will go unhindered, with out leakage and uninterrupted. Speaking on the occasion the Prime Minister Dr. Manmohan Singh said by providing some sense of security to our vulnerable elderly citizens in 1995 and keeping the rise of living cost in mind revised the assistance being provided by the Central Government from Rs.75 to Rs.200 per month. The State Governments have been asked to match this raise. He complimented those states which have responded positively. Dr. Singh termed the new scheme as a demand driven social security programme not restricted by budget allocations. He hoped that the new criteria will almost double the coverage from about 87 lakhs now to almost 1.6 crores. Calling for the proper dissemination of information and greater awareness regarding the scheme and the entitlement Dr. Singh asked the states to own this scheme as their own and increase their contribution to the benefits and ensure that no one is left out .He said there is merit in including widows and physically challenged persons in the ambit of social assistance. The old age pension scheme needs to be further extended to cover all those above 60 years. We hope to do this in future, he added.

4231. (19-11-2007) NEW DELHI : The President of India, Smt. Pratibha Devisingh Patil has condoled the passing away of the former Chief Justice of India, Shri Justice R.S. Pathak. President in a message to Smt. Asha Pathak, the wife of the former Chief Justice, has said "Justice Pathak was an eminent jurist who rendered several landmark judgments during his career and who also had the distinction of serving on the International Court of Justice. He was known for his interests in social welfare, environment and ecological development."

4232. (19-11-2007) NEW DELHI : Post harvest losses on an average range from 10 to 30 percent in fruits and vegetables and 8-10 percent in respect of pulses. Though post harvest management technology is available in certain sectors, the supply chain inefficiency and inadequate infrastructure are the main causes for such wastages. The Government has launched several schemes which involves component to check wastage as under: (i) For horticulture crops, the Government has launched two Centrally Sponsored Schemes. 'The Technology Mission for Integrated Development of Horticulture in North Eastern States and Sikkim' has been launched during the year 2001-02 which was also extended to the Himalayan States of Jammu & Kashmir, Himachal Pradesh and Uttarakhand during 2003-04. 'The National Horticulture Mission' has been launched during 2005-06 for the remaining States. Both the schemes provide assistance for creating post-harvest infrastructure, including cold storage facilities as back-ended subsidy @ 33.33% of the project cost with a ceiling of Rs. 60 lakh per unit for hilly and tribal areas and @ 25% of the project cost not exceeding Rs. 50 lakh per unit for other states. During 2006-07, a new Component has been introduced under the National Horticulture Mission to facilitate setting up of Modern Terminal Markets in the country, which will have state-of-the-art cold chain and other infrastructure and will help in establishing an efficient supply chain right from the farm gate to the consumer/processor/exporter. (ii) The National Horticulture Board (NHB) is also implementing programmes aimed at reducing the losses of horticulture produce through the schemes 'Capital Investment Subsidy for Construction/Expansion/Modernization of cold storage/storages for Horticulture Produce' having the same norms and 'Development of Commercial Horticulture through Production and Post-Harvest Management' providing back ended subsidy @20% of the total project cost with a maximum limit of Rs. 30 lakh for the North-

Eastern/Hilly/Tribal Areas States and Rs. 25 lakh for other States. (iii) The Ministry of Agriculture is also implementing a Capital Investment Subsidy Scheme, titled 'Gramin Bhandaran Yojana' for Construction/Renovation of Rural Godowns in the country through the Directorate of Marketing & Inspection since 1.4.2001. One of the objectives of the Scheme is to provide scientific storage near the production centres (excluding municipal corporation areas) in order to reduce the losses. (iv) A Central Sector Scheme, titled 'Development/Strengthening of Agricultural Marketing Infrastructure, Grading and Standardization' has also been launched by the Ministry of Agriculture on 20.10.2004 to facilitate development of marketing infrastructure, market user common facilities, infrastructure for direct marketing of agricultural commodities, infrastructure for e-trading, market intelligence etc. and mobile infrastructure for post harvest operations (excluding transport equipment) by providing credit-linked back-ended capital investment subsidy to entrepreneurs and direct assistance to State agencies. This information was given by Shri Kanti Lal Bhuria, Minister of State for Agriculture in written reply to a question in the Lok Sabha today.

4233. (19-11-2007) NEW DELHI : The Government has, in recent years, in consultation with the Reserve Bank of India and NABARD, initiated several measures for providing loans to farmers. Some of the important measures are as follows: 1. Banks have been advised to simplify the procedure for documentation for agricultural loans; 2. Effective from Kharif 2006-07, the Government has lowered the interest rates on crop loans to 7% with an upper limit of Rs. 3 lakhs on the principal amount. It has been decided to continue this policy for the year 2007-08 also; 3. Loans upto Rs. 50, 000/- have been made collateral and margin free; 4 Banks have been advised to provide all eligible farmers with Kisan Credit Cards to enable them to have hassle free access to credit. 5 Under Agri Clinic and Agri Business Centre Scheme, credit linked capital subsidy @25% of the capital cost of the project is funded through banks. The scheme has been envisaged with a view to provide extension and other services to farmers on payment basis. The subsidy would be 33.33% in respect of candidates belonging to SC/ST, women and other disadvantaged sections and those from North Eastern and Hill States. 6. To improve the outreach among the poor and the informal sector, the SHG-Bank linkage programme was intensified, particularly in 13 priority States namely Assam, Bihar, Chhattisgarh, Gujarat, Himachal Pradesh, Jharkhand, Maharashtra, Madhya Pradesh, Orissa, Rajasthan, Uttar Pradesh, Uttranchal and West Bengal with vast majority of the rural poor. Banks have also been advised to finance Joint Liability Groups and Tenant Farmers' Groups; 7. As part of the measures announced by the Reserve Bank of India for financial inclusion, banks have been advised to open "No Frills" accounts and issue simple overdraft facility against such accounts. Banks have also been advised to issue General Credit Cards upto Rs. 25, 000/- without insisting on security and end use of funds; 8. Banks have been advised to undertake, on a pilot basis, 100% financial inclusion in at least one district in each State. Based on the success of the pilot, the State Level

Bankers Committee in the States will draw a time bound plan for achieving 100% financial inclusion in other districts of the State; 9. To improve the financial outreach, detailed guidelines for Banking Correspondent/Banking Facilitator models have been provided to banks; and 10. In order to examine the issue of financial exclusion in greater depth and to suggest measures for promoting financial inclusion, the Government had appointed a Committee on Financial Inclusion under the Chairmanship of Dr. C. Rangarajan. Based on the interim recommendations of the Committee, Government has announced creation of two funds, *i.e.*, Financial Inclusion Fund and Financial Inclusion Technology Fund in the Union Budget for 2007-08. This information was given by Shri Kanti Lal Bhuria, Minister of State for Agriculture in written reply to a question in the Lok Sabha today.

4234. (19-11-2007) NEW DELHI : The Prime Minister, Dr. Manmohan Singh, is leaving New Delhi tomorrow to attend the 6th India-ASEAN Summit and the 3rd East Asia Summit in Singapore. Following is the text of the Prime Minister's statement on the eve of his visit : "I will be visiting Singapore from November 20th to 21st, 2007 to attend the 6th India-ASEAN Summit and the 3rd East Asia Summit. Ever since India became a Sectoral Dialogue Partner of ASEAN, our engagement with the ASEAN has grown manifold. We are actively implementing the ASEAN-India Partnership for Peace, Progress and Shared Prosperity. I will inform ASEAN leaders about the several initiatives that India has taken since the last Summit in Cebu in different areas of our cooperation. Our trade with the ASEAN countries has grown rapidly, and surpassed our expectations. It today stands at US $ 30 billion. I will discuss with the ASEAN leaders new measures to expand the horizons of our cooperation to include not just greater economic integration, but also people-to-people contacts, science and technology, health, transport, human resource development, and information and communication technology. I will also attend the third East Asia Summit later in the afternoon of November 21. This Summit is one of the most ambitious exercises of community building and integration ever attempted in Asia. The East Asia Summit has identified five areas of cooperation-energy, education, finance, avian influenza and national disaster mitigation. India has taken and is ready to take many initiatives in these areas. The Summit is likely to adopt a Declaration on Climate Change, Energy and the Environment. The Summit is also expected to discuss regional and international issues, and future directions for cooperation. East Asia is home to some of the fastest growing economies of the world. The creation of a cooperative framework in East Asia will have a profound impact on the global economy and international relations. India's role in the success of this enterprise is crucial. The project for the revival of the Nalanda University as an international centre of excellence has received the support of East Asian countries. I will attend a reception being hosted by Prime Minister Lee of Singapore on the occasion of a special Exhibition on Nalanda. Many ancient and priceless artefacts have specially been flown in from India for this Exhibition. On the sidelines of both Summit meetings I will have the opportunity to meet leaders from other countries, including

Premier Wen Jiabao of China, Prime Minister Yasuo Fukuda of Japan, Prime Minister Badawi of Malaysia and Prime Minister Thein Sein of Myanmar amongst others. India's 'Look East' policy is now blossoming and showing results on the ground. I consider our participation in the India-ASEAN Summit and EAS to be essential pillars of this policy, and vital for the qualitatively enhanced engagement which India seeks with the region.

4235. (19-11-2007) NEW DELHI : The Government is implementing a Central Sector Scheme, National Project on Organic Farming (NPOF) for production, promotion, certification and market development of organic farming in the country, wherein financial assistance is being provided for the capacity building through service providers, setting up of organic input production units of fruits/vegetables waste compost, bio-fertilizers and Vermiculture hatcheries, promotion of organic farming through training programme, field demonstrations, setting up of model organic farms and market development. Government is also implementing a Centrally Sponsored Scheme on National Horticulture Mission (NHM) in the country from 2005-06 under which promotion of organic farming has been included as one of the components and financial assistance is being provided for organic cultivation of horticultural crops, setting up of vermin compost units and for organic farming certification. In addition, Agricultural & Processed Food Products Export Development Authority (APEDA), Ministry of Commerce & Industry is promoting export of organic products and implementing National Programme for Organic Production (NPOP). Under the Scheme financial assistance is being provided to its registered exporters for Market Development Infrastructure Development, Quality Development, R&D and transport assistance. This information was given by Shri Kanti Lal Bhuria, Minister of State for Agriculture in written reply to a question in the Lok Sabha today.

4236. (19-11-2007) NEW DELHI : Budget allocation is not made language-wise. A statement indicating details of funds allocated to different institutions under the Ministry of Human Resource Development engaged in the development of various Indian languages, alongwith the expenditure incurred for the last three years, is annexed. This information was given by the Minister of State for Human Resource Development, Smt. D. Purandeswari in a written reply to a question by Shri O.T. Lepcha in the Rajya Sabha today.

4237. (19-11-2007) NEW DELHI : The Sarva Shiksha Abhiyan(SSA), which provides for universalisation of elementary education in the country in a time bound manner has inter-alia components relating to school infrastructure, alternative schooling for out of school children, girls education, education of children from disadvantaged sections of society, education for children with special needs, quality of education, teacher recruitment etc. State-wise targets fixed during the last three years and achievements thereof are given in the Annexure. Since 2001-02 a large number of children have been brought into the fold of elementary school education. The number of out of school children which was 320 lakh in 2001-02 has come down to 70 lakh in 2006-07 as per State reports received. This information was given by the Minister of State for Human Resource Development, Smt. D. Purandeswari in a written reply to a question by Shri Smt. N.P. Durga in the Rajya Sabha today.

4238. (19-11-2007) NEW DELHI : Railway Women's Central Organization organized a Women's Day here today. Speaking on the occasion, Shri K.C. Jena, Chairman Railway Board said that RWWCO is one of the fore-runner voluntary organizations in the country today. He said that while the primary concern of the organization is a welfare of Railway employees and their families, it has always risen to the call of the society and the nation by paying particular attention on betterment of women folk of vast Railway family and their children. He congratulated outstanding Railway women employees who were honoured on the occasion for their excellent performance. He also congratulated talented children from Indian Railways, who won prizes in All India drawing and painting competitions and essay competition categories. In all 32 outstanding Railway women employees and 45 talented children were awarded on the occasion. The noted Kathak exponent Shovana Narayan has said that women represents 'Shakti' and are capable of transforming society. She said that the importance of women in the society has been well recognized in the Indian philosophy. Referring to the incidents of female foeticide and discrimination against girl child, Ms. Narayan said women should themselves take lead in protesting against these practices. Appreciating Railways' efforts to promote art and sports, Ms. Narayan pointed out that Railways have produced several sports persons of national and international standing. In 1986, RWWCO decided to organize Women's Day on 19th November every year to commemorate the birthday of late Prime Minister Smt. Indira Gandhi. On this day every year RWWCO honours the services of selected outstanding women employees of Group C and Group D in the Railways. The purpose is to boost up the morale of those women, who show exemplary dedication, integrity and courage in discharge of their duties and who also work quietly in any other field viz. Hospital, School, Sports, Blood Donation, Family Welfare Programme, Scouts & Guide etc.

4239. (19-11-2007) NEW DELHI : Law Commission's report has recommended the setting up of a three-member panel of reputed medical persons, to clear the decision to withdraw Life Support System from the terminally ill and that patients and their relatives should notify a High Court of the decision, so that the doctor is immune from legal action. The Commission has cited several decisions of USA, Britain, Canada and Australia and maintained that withdrawal of Life Support System from terminally ill patients has always been held lawful in all the countries, while euthanasia is and continues to be unlawful. The Government has examined the recommendation and is not in favour of accepting the same. This information was given by Minister of Law and Justice, Shri H. R. Bhardwaj in written reply to a question in Rajya Sabha today.

4240. (19-11-2007) NEW DELHI : The number of vacancies of judges in the Supreme Court is four and in various High Courts in the country, as on the 1st November, 2007 is one hundred. Supreme Court has a strength of 22 judges against the sanctioned strength of 26. The various High Courts in the country have working strength of 589 judges against the sanctioned strength of 689 judges. All High Courts except Guwahati, Himachal Pradesh and Uttaranchal had some shortfall in their strength. Pursuant to the Judgement of the Supreme Court dated October 6, 1993 and their Advisory Opinion dated October 28, 1998, the proposals for appointment of Judges in the Supreme Court are to be initiated by the Chief Justice of India and for High Courts, the proposals are to be initiated by the Chief Justice of the concerned High Court. The Government has, however, been requesting the Chief Justices of the High Courts, from time to time, to initiate proposals for filling up of the present and anticipated vacancies during the next six months. This information was given by Minister of Law and Justice, Shri H. R. Bhardwaj in written reply to a question in Rajya Sabha today.

4241. (19-11-2007) NEW DELHI : State Governments of Kerala, Andhra Pradesh, Maharashtra, Madhya Pradesh and Rajasthan have informed that the imported red wheat allocated under TPDS is not being preferred by TPDS beneficiaries. Complaints about quality of imported red wheat have also been received from State Governments of Maharashtra, Madhya Pradesh and Rajasthan. On receipt of complaints, officers of Department of Food and Public Distribution and Food Corporation of India jointly collected samples of imported red wheat from Andhra Pradesh, Madhya Pradesh, Rajasthan and Maharashtra regions during second fortnight of October 2007 and got them analysed for quality. This analysis has shown all conforming to quality standards prescribed under the Prevention of Food Adulteration Act, 1955. Comparison of results of analysis with quality parameters of indigenous wheat have also revealed that the quality of imported red wheat is comparable to that of indigenous wheat. Before the imported wheat is allowed to be discharged from the ships at Indian ports, quality of the wheat is tested by the authorities competent under the Prevention of Food Adulteration Act and by the Plant Quarantine authorities. Only if the imported wheat is found conforming to all the specifications laid down, it is allowed to be discharged from the ships. Out of ships of imported wheat arrived so far during the current year, the wheat in each of them has been found to be meeting the required quality specifications. The State Governments of Kerala and Andhra Pradesh requested for allocation of imported red wheat together with domestic wheat. As per their request, imported and domestic wheat in the ratio of 50:50 has been issued by FCI depending upon availability. Recently, the State Governments of Maharashtra, Madhya Pradesh and Rajasthan have also requested for allocation of only domestic wheat or imported white wheat under TPDS. However, in view of the limited quantities of indigenous wheat available in the central pool, it is not possible to allocate only indigenous wheat to the States. This information was given in the Lok Sabha today by Shri Sharad Pawar, Minister of Consumer Affairs, Food and Public Distribution and Agriculture in written reply to a question.

4242. (19-11-2007) NEW DELHI : The e-courts project was approved by Government of India in February, 2007 and the first phase is already under implementation. National Informatics Centre (NIC) which is the implementing agency for this project has reported that hitherto, laptops to 12155 judges across the country have been provided and around 13000 laser printers are getting delivered for those laptops. Three months' training on the usage of computers has already begun and so far 8700 judicial officers and around 32000 court staff are getting trained by 1210 faculty members. This training is going on at majority of the District Courts and in some of the Taluka/Tehsil Courts. The High Courts have constituted Project Monitoring Committees to oversee the project activities in the District/Taluka Courts under their jurisdiction. Many High Courts have also constituted Committees for getting site preparation executed with the help of State Public Works Department. For around 13000 judges E-mail/Internet facility is being provided through Bharat Sanchar Nigam Limited. It would inter link all the courts across the country and help the litigants to have access to authorized documents. The entire project is scheduled to be implemented by February, 2009 across the country including in the districts of Orissa. This information was given by Minister of Law and Justice, Shri H. R. Bhardwaj in written reply to a question in Rajya Sabha today.

4243. (19-11-2007) NEW DELHI : There is no proposal with the Government of India to allow foreign solicitors to participate in judicial process. The issue of allowing foreign law firms to establish their offices to give legal advice and assistance on foreign law is being discussed with the stake holders including the Bar Council of India. Views of the Bar Council of India are being awaited. The Government will take a decision after considering the views of Bar Council of India in the best interest of the legal profession. This information was given by Minister of Law and Justice, Shri H. R. Bhardwaj in written reply to a question in Lok Sabha today.

4244. (19-11-2007) NEW DELHI : India receives solar energy equivalent to over 5, 000 trillion kWh per year. The daily average solar energy incident over India varies from 4-7 kWh per square meter depending upon the location. Solar energy can be harnessed through two routes, namely solar photovoltaic (PV) and solar thermal, by direct conversion to electricity and heat energy respectively. The utilization of solar energy in the country is regularly increasing, however, the high initial cost of the solar energy systems is a barrier in its large-scale utilization. The estimated unit cost of electricity from grid connected solar energy plant is estimated to be around Rs. 12-15 per unit, which is very high compared to electricity generated from conventional sources including thermal power and other renewable energy sources such as wind, small hydro and biomass. A total of 33 grid interactive solar photovoltaic power plants have been installed in the country with financial assistance from the Ministry. These plants, with aggregate capacity of 2.125 Megawatt peak are estimated to generate about 2.5 million units of electricity in a year. In view of the high initial cost, at present, solar energy systems are mainly being used for stand-alone applications in lighting, telecommunication, small power requirements, battery charging, water heating and cooking etc. so far around 14 lakh solar photovoltaic systems aggregating to about 110 Megawatt peak solar photovoltaic module capacity have been installed in the country. In addition about 6 lakh solar cookers and about 20 lakh square metre collector area has been installed for solar water heating applications, which is equivalent to about 1400 Megawatt thermal capacity.

4245. (19-11-2007) NEW DELHI : Sardar Sarovar Dam height has been effectively raised to its crest level 121.92 m. All the six units of River Bed Power House (RBPH) (6x200 Megawatts) and five units of Canal Head Power House (CHPH) (5x50 Megawatts) have been commissioned. The Narmada Main Canal has been completed upto 357.196 km (out of total length of 458.318 km up to Gujarat-Rajasthan border) except two major structures falling within km 263.165 to km.357.196. The construction work in NMC from km 357.196 to km 458.318 is in advanced stage by the State Government. The Command Area Development work has been completed in 276562 ha till August 2007. The cumulative expenditure on construction work of Sardar Sarovar Project in Gujarat as reported by the Sardar Sarovara Narmada Nigam Ltd. Till August 2007 after allocation of common expenditure is Rs. 24562.53 crore. Irrigation is a State subject and planning, execution and funding of the projects is within the purview of state Government. On the request of State Government, the project has been included in Accelerated Irrigation Benefit Programme (AIBP) since 1996-97 and so far, Central Assistance amounting to Rs. 4887.7385 crore has been released in favour of the project in the form of loan/grant. On the basis of demand received from State Government of Gujarat and in view of AIBP guidelines in force from time to time, grant amounting to Rs.471.8885 crore has been released to the State during last three years. In addition to above an amount of Rs. 74.77 crore has been released to the State for the project so far under the Command Area Development and Water Management Programme. This information was given by the Minister of State for Water Resources, Shri Jai Prakash Narayan Yadav in response to a question by B.K. Hariprasad in the Rajya Sabha today.

4246. (19-11-2007) NEW DELHI : The demand of Government of Delhi for water from Yamuna is for three Water Treatment Plants (WTPs), viz. Wazirabad, Chandrawal and Haiderpur-II. The total capacity of these three WTPs is 310 Million Gallons per day (MGD), which can be serviced by 625 cusec of raw water. In addition to these three plants, during monsoon period (July to October) Yamuna water is also demanded for Haiderpur-WTP with a capacity of 100 MGD, which can be serviced by 200 cusec of raw water. The capacity of these plants dependent upon Yamuna have remained the same for the last three years and so is the demand of raw water. An MoU on sharing of Yamuna waters was signed on 12th May, 1994 by Uttar Pradesh, Haryana, Rajasthan, Himachal Pradesh and Delhi. As per the MoU, annual allocation of Yamuna waters to Delhi is 0.724 billion cubic meters (BCM). The allocation to Delhi are made by Upper Yamuna River Board as per the MoU of 1994. Further as per the directions of Hon'ble Supreme Court vide order dated 29th February 1996, full pond level is being maintained at Wazirabad and Haiderpur so that there is no shortage of water for Wazirabad, Haiderpur and Chandrawal WTPS. The supplies/releases of Yamuna waters to Delhi are made by Haryana at Tejawala in accordance with MoU of 1994 and the Hon'ble Supreme Court order dated 29th February 1996. There is some increase in demand of water due to increase in population. To meet the major future demand several measure are being taken that is completion of parallel line channel from Munak to Haiderpur WTP and taking up of storage dams including Renuka, Kishau & Lakhwar Vyasi in upper Yamuna basin. This information was given by the Minister of State for Water Resources, Shri Jai Prakash Narayan Yadav in response to a question by Shri Ramdas Athawale in the Lok Sabha today.

4247. (19-11-2007) NEW DELHI : Ministry of Food Processing Industries (MFPI) has submitted a scheme to Planning Commission, which envisages providing financial assistance for setting up of thirty mega Food Parks in the country during 11th Five Year Plan period. The scheme which is project oriented, aims to provide a mechanism to bring together farmers, processors and retailers and link agricultural production to the market so as to ensure maximization of value addition, minimization of wastages and improving farmers' income. Mega Food Park envisages a well-defined agri/horticultural-processing zone containing state of the art processing facilities with support infrastructure and well established supply chain. The primary objective of the scheme is to facilitate establishment of an integrated value chain, with processing at the core and supported by requisite forward and backward linkages. Under the scheme, financial assistance in the form of grant-in-aid upto 50% of the project cost in general areas and upto 75% of the project cost in special category states subject to a maximum of RS. 50.00 crore or the cost of approved facilities, whichever is lower, has been envisaged for all implementing agencies. Under 10th Plan Scheme, MFPI has approved financial assistance of Rs. 208.54 crore for fifty six (56) food parks in the country including four food parks in Rajasthan upto 31st March, 2007. Of this, financial assistance of Rs. 12.51 crore has been approved for four Food Parks at Ranpur (District Kota), Boranda (District Jodhpur), Sri Ganganagar and Alwar in Rajasthan. This information was given by Shri Subodh Kant Sahai, Minister of State for Food Processing in reply to a question raised by Shri Kalraj Mishra and Shri Santosh Bagrodia in Rajya Sabha today.

4248. (19-11-2007) NEW DELHI : Grid-interactive renewable power plants with an aggregate installed capacity of about 10, 985 MW as on 30.9.2007 are located in 31 States/UTs. In small Hydro Power sector, total 2014.66 MW, in Wind Power sector 7660.20 MW, in Bio Power including Bio Mass and Waste Energy 1308 MW and in Solar Power Sector 2.12 MW grid interaction renewable power generation capacity has been installed. Five such plants with an aggregate capacity of 21.25 MW are located in Vidarbha region of Maharashtra. They are located in Amaravati, Gondia and Nagpur Districts. The 11th Plan proposals of the Ministry envisage grid-interactive renewable power capacity addition of 14, 500 MW during the Plan period. This information was given by the Minister of State in the Ministry of New and Renewable Energy Shri Vilas Muttemwar in a written reply to question by Shri Vijay J.Darda in the Rajya Sabha today.

4249. (19-11-2007) NEW DELHI : A National Rating System for rating the performance of Green Buildings has been developed. The broad objective of the Rating System is to catalyze the speedy adoption of building techniques, technologies and procedures that will promote design and construction of energy efficient and sustainable buildings in the country. The National Rating System has been developed through interactions with various stakeholders including private developers, academic and research institutions, practicing architects and Government Ministries and Agencies. It will function under the advice and direction of eminent architects, engineers, builders, experts and officials from concerned Government Departments and Agencie The National Rating System would be applicable to major building typologies across all climatic zones of the country.

4250. (19-11-2007) NEW DELHI : A Programme for providing financial support for electrification of those remote unelectrified census villages and unelectrified hamlets of electrified census villages in various States, where grid extension is either not feasible or not cost effective and which are not taken up under the Rajiv Gandhi Gramin Vidyutikaran Yojna, is being implemented by the Ministry. Such villages are provided basic facilities for lighting / electricity through various renewable energy sources including solar energy. From 2005-06, support is provided for those remote villages / hamlets which are identified by the Rural Electrification Corporation (REC) for coverage through renewable energy sources. Central Financial Assistance of upto 90% of the costs, subject to pre-specified maximum amounts for each technology, is provided for projects approved under the programme. As of October 2007, 3338 remote unelectrified census villages and 830 remote unelectrified hamlets have been covered under the programme. Further, projects are under implementation in 1866 remote unelectrified census villages and 638 remote unelectrified hamlets in various States. This information was given by the Minister of State in the Ministry of New and Renewable Energy Shri Vilas Muttemwar in a written reply to question by Shri O.T.Lepcha in the Rajya Sabha today.

4251. (19-11-2007) NEW DELHI : Periodic evaluation of functioning of Employment Exchanges is carried out by a Monitoring Committee under the

Chairpersonship of Director General of Employment & Training which consists of representatives of concerned Central Ministries & Departments, State Governments and Union Territory Administrations to ensure uniformity in implementing national policies and procedures as laid down in National Employment Service Manual. This information was given by the Minister of State for Labour and Employment Shri Oscar Fernandes (Independent Charge) in a written reply in the Lok Sabha today.

4252. (19-11-2007) NEW DELHI : The Ministry of Health and Family Welfare has a permanent Pavilion at the India International Trade Fair (IITF), Pragati Maidan. During the duration of the Trade Fair every year, the Ministry showcases a particular theme at the Health Pavilion. The duration of the trade fair is from 14th November to 27th November, 2007. Taking into account the emphasis of the Ministry on Healthy Life Style, the theme for this year's IITF is on Healthy Life Style. The focus is on healthy habits, healthy people and healthy India under the banner of NRHM. In the entire Health Pavilion, this theme has been highlighted by focusing on issues such as dietary habits, food habits, exercise habits to keep fit, life style diseases-preventive and curative aspects, and cleanliness and hygiene including importance of hand washing. The ill effects of bad food habits has been emphasized by focusing on avoidance of junk food. In the entire area in the Health Pavilion these themes have been highlighted through messages in the forms of panels, proto types, awareness generation material, pictures, posters, leaflets and other images. The attempt has been to create vibrancy within the complex so that the visitor values the relevance of life style habits in every day life. The Do's and Don'ts of life style diseases has also been focused through themes such as diabetes and heart diseases. The Panels on Nutrition and Diet Charts have also been put up on display. One of the key highlights of the Health Pavilion is the provision of health care services through eminent doctors drawn from leading hospitals in and around Delhi. The services offered during the duration of the trade fair include Routine Health check up, blood group examination, eye check up, counselling for contraceptive choices, family planning methods, NSV at the Pavilion, Gynaecological check up, HIV/AIDS counselling, etc. The services provided at IITF also include free counselling on health issues by Allopathic, Ayurvedic, Unani and Homoeopathic doctors, etc. Last year, the Ministry had organized the exhibition on 'Janani Suraksha Yojana'. The theme was showcased through messages, advocacy tools, print material and above all through a story board which explained the nuances of the programme. As the programme was new, efforts were made to sensitize the visitors through adequate publicity material in the form of posters and pamphlets. The Pavilion was received extremely well and was awarded the First Prize amongst the category of Government Departments. The endeavour this year will be to sensitize the masses on life style related diseases. At the same time, the best practices to ensure a Healthy Life style is being showcased so that an individual is able to absorb the same in day-to-day life.

4253. (19-11-2007) NEW DELHI : The steps initiated by the Government to fulfil the promises made in the National Common Minimum Programme include the following:-a) 2 per cent cess on Central taxes was introduced to fund education in the year 2004-05. An additional 1 per cent cess exclusively earmarked to finance Higher and Secondary education has been introduced from the year 2007-08. With these steps public spending on Education has increased from 3.49 per cent in the year 2003-04, to 3.66 per cent (provisional) in the year 2005-06. b) An action plan has been prepared for implementing the recommendations of a Central Advisory Board of Education (CABE) Committee on measures to enhance the autonomy of higher education institutions and to institutionalize regulatory provisions for promoting autonomy and accountability of higher educational institutions. Powers to enter into MOUs with foreign universities have been restored to all Universities. Government has further established transparency and autonomy in the processes of selection of senior faculty in institutions such as the Indian Council of Philosophical Research, Indian Council of Social Sciences Research, Indian Institute of Historical Research and the Indian Institute of Advanced Study, Shimla. c) The National Curriculum Framework 2005 has been revised to subscribe to the principles of secularism, democracy and equality stated in the Constitution and in the National Policy on Education. d) A Mid-Day Meal Programme was introduced in schools in 2004-05, benefiting 12 crore children studying in classes I-V in Government, Government aided and local body schools, as well as centres run under Education Guarantee Scheme (EGS)/Alternative & Innovative Education (AIE) scheme in all States/UTs. From 2007-08 the scheme will be extended to cover children in upper primary (classes V to VIII) in educationally backward blocks in the country. Universal Elementary Education has not yet been fully achieved; however, the Government implements a number of schemes mainly Sarva Shiksha Abhiyan (SSA) and Mid-Day Meal (MDM) Programme in association with the State/UT Governments to provide free education to children in the 6 to 14 years age group and ensure their universal retention. 3.68 crore children have joined schools since the launch of SSA in 2001 and the number of out-of-school children has reduced from about 3.20 crore in the year 2001-02 to about 70 lakh in the year 2006-07. This information was given by the Minister of State for Human Resource Development, Smt. D. Purandeswari in a written reply to a question by Shri Abu Asim Azmi in the Rajya Sabha today.

4254. (19-11-2007) NEW DELHI : The University Grants Commission (UGC) has a scheme namely 'UGC-Infonet Connectivity Programme' to provide for networking of university campus with state-of-art campus wide networks and recurring costs on Internet bandwidth. UGC also has another scheme namely 'UGC Infonet Digital Library Consortium' to provide for access to more than 5000 electronic journals and three major bibliographic database under this initiative. UGC has provided financial assistance to 3486 colleges so far under the Scheme of Establishment of Network Resource Centre (UGC-NRC) in colleges during X Plan period, which are eligible to receive financial assistance under Section 2 (f)

& 12 B of the UGC Act, 1956. The assistance is provided for the purchase of computers and also for Internet Connectivity for an amount of Rs. 1, 50, 000- towards purchase of Computers and Rs. 10, 000/- per annum for Internet Connectivity, for the second time. This information was given by the Minister of State for Human Resource Development, Smt. D. Purandeswari in a written reply to a question by Shri Manohar Joshi in the Rajya Sabha today.

4255. (19-11-2007) NEW DELHI : Government is discussing various implications of exporting defence systems which are not strategically sensitive. DRDO is examining opportunities for collaborative development and production of tactical defence systems with friendly countries. This information was given by the Defence Minister Shri AK Antony in a written reply to Shri Adhir Chowdhury and Shri Uday Singh in Lok Sabha today.

4256. (19-11-2007) NEW DELHI : The overall progress of repair and re-equipping of the ship, ex-Admiral Gorshkov, in Russia is slow. The Russian side has submitted a revised Master Schedule indicating a delay in the project. The Russian side has attributed the delays to "Growth of Work". In order to supervise the project for repair and re-equipping of the aircraft carrier Vikramaditya (earlier called Admiral Gorshkov), an apex level committee under Defence Secretary and a Steering Committee under a Vice Admiral have been set up. A team has also been stationed at the shipyard where the repair and re-equipping work is going on. From time to time, teams comprising senior officers are also sent to monitor progress of the project. The matters are also taken up between the two countries at appropriate level. This information was given by the Defence Minister Shri AK Antony in a written reply to Shri Uday Singh in Lok Sabha today.

4257. (19-11-2007) NEW DELHI : Direct tax collections recorded a growth of over 42.9 percent for the period 1st April 2007 to 15th November 2007. Net tax collections stood at Rs.1, 40, 373 crore, up from Rs.98, 216 crore during the same period last fiscal. Corporate Tax registered a growth of 45.74 percent at Rs.83, 934 crore, up from Rs.57, 593 crore during the previous fiscal, while Personal Income Tax (including FBT, STT and BCTT) grew by 39.96 percent at Rs.56, 212 crore, up from Rs.40, 453 crore. Growth in Securities Transaction Tax was 69.37 percent (Rs.4, 924 crore against Rs.2, 908 crore) and Fringe Benefit Tax was 27.11 percent (Rs.3, 078 crore against Rs.2, 422 crore). Banking Cash Transaction Tax grew by 16.99 percent. Tax deduction / collection at source increased by over 50 percent, while self-assessment tax (paid voluntarily before submission of tax return) increased by 89.3 percent, indicating continued improvement in tax administration and tax compliance levels. With net collection of Rs.1, 40, 373 crore, over 52 percent of the budgeted direct tax target of Rs.2, 67, 490 crore stands already achieved.

4258. (19-11-2007) NEW DELHI : Requests have been received from the State Governments of Kerala and Gujarat for setting up of satellite campuses of IIT-

Madras and IIT-Bombay respectively in their States. However, the Government has taken a decision that establishment of large satellite campuses with regular Bachelor and Master Programmes amount to setting up of new IITs should be avoided. The Government, however, has no objection to the setting up of small extension centres of existing IITs outside their main campuses, devoted to continuing education, diploma courses, finishing schools, incubation programmes, etc. This information was given by the Minister of State for Human Resource Development, Smt. D. Purandeswari in a written reply to a question by Smt. N.P. Durga in the Rajya Sabha today.

4259. (19-11-2007) NEW DELHI : The Central Advisory Board of Education (CABE) Committee on Financing of Higher and Technical Education has recommended that revenue generation through student fees beyond 20 per cent may seriously affect access to higher education. According to information furnished by the University Grants Commission (UGC), the institutions of higher learning in the country have a variable fee structure which differs from institution to institution. The matter relating to fee structure was, among other things, discussed in the Conference of Vice Chancellors held on October 10-11, 2007 and the UGC proposes to set up an expert committee to look into various aspects of the fee related issue and arrive at a strategy whereby the fee for higher education is neither ridiculously low nor it poses a barrier in equitable access to higher education. This information was given by the Minister of State for Human Resource Development, Smt. D. Purandeswari in a written reply to a question by Shri Datta Meghe in the Rajya Sabha today.

4260. (19-11-2007) NEW DELHI : The Minister further informed that there is no provision under schemes implemented by Govt. to provide any special compensation directly to the artisans engaged in handicrafts & carpet manufacturing sector. However, the Master craft persons are sponsored to participate for display and live demonstration in the international fairs/exhibitions under agreed Cultural Exchange Programme between India & other nations from time to time. In addition, Master crafts persons also participate in the overseas events thorough Central/ State Handicrafts Development Corporations/Export Promotion Councils, etc. Apart from this a health insurance Scheme for the artisans is also implemented. The Minister also informed that the Government has taken steps under 11th Plan which include participation in international exhibitions/fairs, organizing of seminars on Brand Image Promotion of Indian Handicrafts abroad with a view to create awareness/exposure which ultimately helps to enhance share of handicrafts in the global market.

4261. (19-11-2007) NEW DELHI : The actual power generation happens to be less than the installed capacity of power projects as some of the generating units remain out of service due to planned maintenance works, forced outage, etc. The actual power generation from the available generating units also depends on age, design of generating units, operation & maintenance practices adopted, availability of the required quality and quantity of fuel, availability of water in the rivers (for hydro stations) and system conditions. The Plant Load Factor (PLF) of a generating unit is an important indicator of the utilization of generation capacity of thermal and nuclear power stations. On the other hand, the utilization of installed capacity of hydro power station depends on inflow of water in the rivers (which in turn depends on rainfall and snowmelt), irrigation requirements and availability of generating units at the power stations.

4262. (19-11-2007) NEW DELHI : RAJYA SABHA, As per the reassessment studies completed by Central Electricity Authority (CEA) in 1987, the hydroelectric potential of the country, in terms of installed capacity, has been estimated to be about 1, 48, 700 MW out of which a capacity of 30, 873 MW (20.76% of the potential) has already been developed and another 13, 446 MW is under implementation. The Policy on Hydro Power Development was first announced by the Government of India in 1998. It lays emphasis on basin wise development, evolving consensus on inter state issues, mitigation of geological risks, simplified procedure for transfer of clearances, promoting joint venture arrangements etc. It also lays emphasis on increasing private investment in the power sector through Independent Power Producers (IPPs) and joint ventures. The National Electricity Policy announced in February, 2005 also lays emphasis on the expeditious development of feasible hydro potential in the country. The Government has also announced a Mega Power Policy to incentivize development of Mega Power Projects.

4263. (19-11-2007) NEW DELHI : President of India, Smt. Pratibha Devisingh Patil, said, "It is a great pleasure and privilege for me to present the Indira Gandhi Prize for Peace, Disarmament and Development for the year 2006 to Professor Wangari Muta Maathai, who is well known internationally for her contribution to development and for her passionate commitment to the protection of the environment. I extend my heartiest congratulations to her for receiving this prestigious Prize. Professor Maathai is no stranger to India. She was here earlier this year when the Jawaharlal Nehru Award for International Understanding for 2005 was conferred on her. I welcome her as a friend of India. The history of the human race is full of triumphs and achievements made in the quest for knowledge and in the search for a better life. Human history is also replete with the innumerable difficulties and dilemmas faced by mankind. The challenge of how to balance individual need as opposed to collective needs, the needs of the present generation as opposed to those of the future generations, has always confronted us. However, in history there have been human beings of exceptional stature who have done exemplary work in making the world a better place and in promoting a better understanding of the complex fabric of harmony between human beings and nature. Smt. Indira Gandhi, the first and the only woman Prime Minister of India, was one such personality. Throughout her life she worked tirelessly for human dignity, eradication of poverty and harmony in the world. Smt. Indira Gandhi symbolized the link between our freedom struggle and a free India seeking its place in the world. She closely witnessed and participated in the freedom struggle and was aware of the tremendous sacrifices made to gain Independence. She was firm in her resolve to take India forward and was the image of a progressive India seeking to use science and technology for advancing the nation in the areas of health, education and industry while being rooted in the culture and tradition of India. Drawing on the old Indian concept of Vasudhaiva Kutumbakam that is, the world is one family, Indiraji saw all of humanity as one and all the world as one, where living together harmoniously and peacefully was possible. Speaking in 1983, she said and I quote "Our world is small but it has room for all of us to live together in peace and beauty." She strove for building an equitable world and bringing the concerns of the developing countries, in particular eradicating poverty, to the forefront of the global agenda. She also understood the need to look at environmental issues. In 1972, at the First World Summit on Environment, Indiraji, as a visionary statesperson, expressed concern about the environment when global interest on the issue was still nascent. The ideals and the vision of Smt. Indira Gandhi are as much relevant today as they were during her lifetime. She has been the source of inspiration for many women in India and the world over. It is befitting that the Indira Gandhi Peace Prize is being conferred to Professor Wangari Muta Maathai, whose commitment to the cause of development, women's issues and the environment are praiseworthy. Her Green Belt Movement has succeeded in planting 300 million trees across Kenya to prevent soil erosion. She is now spearheading the United Nations Billion Tree Campaign. I am hopeful that India will contribute to increasing the forest cover on the Planet. We will be launching a major afforestation programme called "Green India" for planting trees in 6 million hectares of degraded forest land. This will probably be one of the world's largest afforestation efforts in recent times.

4264. (19-11-2007) NEW DELHI : During last few months no financial incentives have been announced by the Central Government to specifically boost electricity generation capacity. However, fiscal concessions/benefits for generation projects are available to Mega Power Projects, under the Mega Power Policy, which are aimed at reducing the power tariff from large capacity power generating plants. In addition during the 10th Plan, the scheme of Accelerated Generation & Supply Programme was also continued under which a specified level of interest subsidy was made available. During 2006-07, interest subsidy of approximately Rs.457 crore and Rs.30.2 crore respectively was released to Power Finance Corporation and Rural Electrification Corporation which were disbursing the interest subsidy, for making it available to power utilities. This information was given by the Union Power Minister Shri Sushilkumar Shinde in a written reply to a question in the Rajya Sabha.

4265. (19-11-2007) NEW DELHI : As per National Mineral Inventory prepared by India Bureau of Mines, as on 1.4.2005, the total resources of gold ore (primary) and diamond are estimated at 390.29 million tones and 4.58 million carats respectively. This information was given by Shri Dr. T. Subbarami Reddy, Minister of Mines in the Parliament today.

4266. (19-11-2007) NEW DELHI : Apart from the regional exploration for gold and diamond undertaken by Geological Survey of India, since the year 2000, the Central Government has been giving prior approvals for grant of reconnaissance permits for regional exploration of gold and diamond to various applicants, including private companies. These may be converted into mining leases based on the outcome of the exploration, including detailed prospecting. As per available information, since 1.1.2004 till date, prior approval for grant of mining lease for Gold has been conveyed to respective State Governments in favour of M/s. Jindal Saw Limited in Rajasthan, M/s. Ramgad Minerals and Mining Private Limited in Karnataka, M/s. Geo Mysore Services India Private Limited in Andhra Pradesh and M/s. Adi Gold Mining Private Limited in Uttarakhand respectively. The Central Government has not conveyed any prior approval for grant of mining lease for diamond during the last three years.

4267. (19-11-2007) NEW DELHI : The Minister of State for Textiles, Shri E.V.K.S. Elangovan, informed the Lok Sabha today, in a written reply to a question by Shri K.S. Rao that the Government has decided to launch Investment Regions for the Textile Sector to consolidate the phenomenon of agglomeration, visible in textiles to further reduce transaction costs and enhance competitiveness. Concentrated, contiguous investment and production regions with high quality infrastructure and covering the entire value chain can help obviate, to an extent, the burden imposed by multiple levies, high power costs, bottlenecks in shipment and delays in legal clearances. They can become textile hubs with billions of dollars of investment-both domestic and foreign. The investment region is proposed to be developed in a Public Private partnership mode to enable leveraging Government investments in these regions. Accordingly, a Concept Paper on the "Policy Resolution for Textile Infrastructure Development Fund and Textile Territorial Investment & Production Complex" has been drawn up. No further details have been worked out.

4268. (19-11-2007) NEW DELHI : The Minister of State for Textiles, Shri E.V.K.S. Elangovan, informed the Lok Sabha today, in a written reply to a question by Shri Mohan Rawale that the Government have recognized a need for restructuring of labour laws to create a productive and productivity-conducive environment to ensure smooth production. The Working Group has recommended that "while the genuine interests of the labour need to be protected, the policy environment and the implementation machinery should induce confidence among the entrepreneurs. The labour law reform would lead to consolidation and merger of the units to achieve economies of scale and become internationally cost competitive in the globalized scenario". Government held discussions with the stake holders in this regard to reach a consensus. However, no decision could be arrived.

4269. (19-11-2007) NEW DELHI : The Union Minister of Shipping, Road Transport and Highways, Thiru T.R. Baalu has approved road improvement works in various stretches of NHs in the state of Tamil Nadu at a cost of about Rs. 42 crore.

4270. (19-11-2007) NEW DELHI : The Scheme of Conditional Cash Transfer for girl child with insurance cover has been included in the Annual Plan 2007-08 and includes cash transfers to the family of the girl child based on the fulfilment of four important conditionalities viz. birth and registration of the girl child, immunization, retention in school and delaying marriage beyond 18 years of age. The procedural formalities for approval of the above scheme are under process. This was stated by Smt. Renuka Chowdhury, Minister for Women and Child Development in a reply to a question by Shri Mahendra Mohan in Rajya Sabha today. She further stated that as per information received from Haryana under their Ladli Scheme cash incentives are provided to all parent residents of the State whose second girl child is born on or after 2nd August, 2005. 16623 girls have been covered under the scheme up to August, 2007. As per information received from Government of NCT of Delhi under their Girl Child Protection Scheme cash incentives are provided to the permanent residents of Delhi up to two girl children in a family. During the year 2006-07, 1960 girls were given the benefit and during the year 2007-08. 1560 girls have been covered upto 30-10-2007, she added.

4271. (19-11-2007) BANGALORE: With just hours to go for the B.S. Yeddyurappa government to face the all-important floor test at a specially convened session of the Karnataka Legislative Assembly on Monday, the Janata Dal (Secular) leadership has said the "discussions on power sharing have failed" and consequently the party legislators would vote against the motion of confidence. The former Prime Minister and national president of the JD(S), H.D. Deve Gowda, who held several rounds of discussions with senior leaders of his party, including the former Chief Minister, H.D. Kumaraswamy, State president of the JD(S), N. Merajuddin Patel, the former Deputy Chief Minister, M.P. Prakash, and N. Cheluvarayaswamy late on Sunday, told The Hindu that he had directed the JD(S) Legislature Party leader and the State president that the legislators should vote against the motion of confidence and that necessary steps should be taken in this regard. "What else can I do? The national leadership of the BJP has not responded to the JD(S) demand to sign a written understanding which could ensure the smooth running of the government. The conditions were drafted following some bad experiences faced during the Kumaraswamy government and I was particular that this should be complied with."

4272. (19-11-2007) NEW DELHI : The Home Minister, Shri Shivraj Patil administered here today the National Integration Pledge to the officers and staff of the Ministry of Home Affairs in connection with the Quami Ekta Week. The Week is observed every year from the 19th to 25th November to foster the spirit of patriotism, communal harmony and national integration. The National Foundation for Communal Harmony, an autonomous body under the Ministry of Home Affairs is observing the Communal Harmony Week to coincide with the Quami Ekta Week. The National Foundation of communal harmony has been set up to raise funds for the rehabilitation of child victims of communal, caste or ethnic violence and for promotion of communal harmony, national integration and fraternity.

4273. (19-11-2007) NEW DELHI : Having a Social Security Card/Number is not a prerequisite condition for settlement of claims with regard to the P.F. payments. However, the offices of Employees' Provident Fund Organisation have been instructed to collect filled in Social Security Number (SSN) application forms alongwith the claim forms so that SSN could be allotted subsequently for creating a subscribers' database.

4274. (19-11-2007) NEW DELHI: India has offered help to cyclone-ravaged Bangladesh. President Pratibha Patil and Prime Minister Manmohan Singh have expressed their condolences over the deaths and pledged support and relief to the people of that country. In a condolence message to Bangladesh President Iajuddin Ahmed, Ms. Patil said, "I am deeply saddened to learn about the tragic loss of lives and substantial damage to property in the aftermath of the hurricane. I am confident that people of Bangladesh will face this tragedy with courage and fortitude."

4275. (19-11-2007) NEW DELHI : There is no proposal before the Government to increase from three shifts to four shifts in factories. This information was given by the Minister of State for Labour and Employment Shri Oscar Fernandes (Independent Charge) in a written reply in the Lok Sabha today.

4276. (19-11-2007) NEW DELHI : As per the information furnished by the Ministry of Commerce &Industry, Department of Commerce, more than thirty thousand workers were affected due to the closure of 33 gardens as on 1st April, 2007.Out of these 33 gardens, 17 are in West Bengal, 14 in Kerala and 2 in Assam. The Government of India on 29th June, 2007 had announced a rehabilitation package for providing financial relief to the extent of Rs. 38.65 crores for the closed tea gardens. The package provides for restructuring of the outstanding bank dues, provision of fresh working capital with interest subsidy from Government, waiver of outstanding loan dues to Tea Board and settlement of provident fund dues in instalments. It is envisaged that after the account of the gardens are regularized they would become eligible for term loan for replanting under the Special Purpose Tea Fund and upfront subsidy for the machinery items under the Quality Upgradation Scheme of Tea Board. The Government has also constituted a Committee for evaluating the proposals received for change of management of closed tea gardens under the provisions of Tea Act, 1953. Some of the State Governments like Kerala and West Bengal where the number of gardens closed are more, have provided certain relief measures in order to alleviate distress of the jobless workers and their families. Relief measures essentially include ensuring food security and wage employment through various rural development schemes.

As a measure of interim relief the Government of India on 15th October, 2007 approved the payment of lumpsum amount of Rs. 1000/- per ward of the plantation workers of tea gardens which has remained closed as on date. As on date 10 of these 33 closed tea gardens have reopened. 9 of these opened gardens are in Kerala and one is in West Bengal. This information was given by the Minister of State for Labour and Employment Shri Oscar Fernandes (Independent Charge) in a written reply in the Lok Sabha today.

4277. (19-11-2007) NEW DELHI : The Second National Commission on Labour has gone into and made recommendations on various facets of labour viz; review of labour laws, social security, women & child labour, skill development labour administration, unorganised sector etc. Consultations and interactions have been held with the stakeholders in various fora. While carrying out the amendments in labour laws, the recommendations of the Second National Commission on Labour are also taken into account. This information was given by the Minister of State for Labour and Employment Shri Oscar Fernandes (Independent Charge) in a written reply in the Lok Sabha today.

4278. (19-11-2007) NEW DELHI : With a view to providing social security to the unorganised sector workers, the Government has constituted Welfare Funds for Beedi, Cine and certain Non-Coal Mine workers. Under these Welfare Funds, Welfare Schemes providing for health care, housing, education to the children etc. are being implemented. The schemes are being implemented through regional offices of Directorate General of Labour Welfare. The beneficiaries under Labour Welfare Funds are getting direct benefits from these welfare scheme and funds are not released to the State Governments. For providing coverage beyond the existing beneficiaries amongst the unorganised sector workers, the Government has introduced the Unorganised Sector Workers Social Security Bill, 2007 in the Rajya Sabha on 10.09.2007 to provide social security to such workers. This information was given by the Minister of State for Labour and Employment Shri Oscar Fernandes (Independent Charge) in a written reply in the Lok Sabha today.

4279. (19-11-2007) NEW DELHI : As per latest available information, the number of placements made through Employment Exchanges in the country during 2006 was 1.77 lakhs. Under the National e-Governance Plan, a Mission Mode Project (MMP) on computerization of Employment Exchanges has been initiated under which all the Exchanges are proposed to be computersied and connected with a National web portal which will contain information about jobs available in various enterprises and details of persons trained in various trades by industrial training institutes/centres. Employment Exchanges, when interconnected, are expected to provide better and speedy services to job seekers as well as industry. This information was given by the Minister of State for Labour and Employment Shri Oscar Fernandes (Independent Charge) in a written reply in the Lok Sabha today.

4280. (19-11-2007) NEW DELHI : The National Rural Employment Guarantee NREG Act, 2005 provides for the enhancement of livelihood security of the households in rural areas of the country by providing at least one hundred days of guaranteed wage employment in every financial year to every household whose adult members volunteer to do unskilled manual work. Thus, NREG Act makes the Government legally accountable for providing employment to those who ask for it and thereby goes beyond providing a social safety net towards guaranteeing the Right to Employment. However, if a worker who has applied for work under NREG Act is not provided employment within 15 days from the date on which work is requested, an unemployment allowance shall be payable by the State Government at the rate prescribed in the Act. It was implemented in 200 identified districts in the country in its first phase with effect from 2.2.06 and has been extended to 130 more districts in the second phase with effect from 1.4.2007. However, the Government has now decided to extend the National Rural Employment Guarantee Act to the rural areas of all the remaining districts in the country including the Union Territories with effect from 1.4.2008. This information was given by the Minister of State for Labour and Employment Shri Oscar Fernandes (Independent Charge) in a written reply in the Lok Sabha today.

4281. (20-11-2007) NEW DELHI : Following is the text of the address of the Vice President of India Mohd. Hamid Ansari at the 'Ernst & Young's Entrepreneur of the Year Award Programme' here today: "I deem it a privilege to address this distinguished gathering today on the occasion of the presentation of the Entrepreneur of the Year Awards. Entrepreneurship and wealth creation are indeed ancient themes in Indian history. Kautilya wrote in the Arthashastra: "The king shall ever be active and discharge his duties; the root of wealth is activity, and of evil its reverse." Over the years, wealth creation was an act of reverence, an instrument of influence and even considered worthy of worship. Yet, entrepreneurship is also a very recent theme. A young India today sees opportunity all around. Never before in our history have so many entrepreneurs in India become as successful and demonstrated such an extent of wealth creation as in the past decade. We are told that the aggregate net worth of the four richest Indians, all entrepreneurs, stands at US$ 180 billion; the net worth of India's 40 richest stands at US$ 351 billion, more than double their net worth last year. For perspective, this amount is roughly over a third of our GDP at current prices! Ladies and Gentlemen, any economic or social process to be sustainable in the long term has to find broad-based and multiple sources of sustenance in the economy, polity and the society at large; it should represent an aspirational matrix for people and there must be a reasonable consensus that such a phenomenon adds to the public good. Entrepreneurship development and wealth creation are no exception. What then are the core elements that must be taken into account if the tremendous successes of our entrepreneurs of the last decade are to be sustainable? Firstly, a much under-discussed issue of entrepreneurship in India is that of "Social Capital". It has been said that 'social capital is not what you know, but who you know'. In India, existing facts substantiate that social capital plays a crucial role in human capital formation, economic performance of firms and superior performance of some social groups and geographic regions. What are the affiliations that produce bonds and networks of trust and reciprocity that aid in economic performance of firms and individuals?

4282. (20-11-2007) NEW DELHI : The young winners of 'Bal Bharati Essay Competition-2007', were felicitated at the hands of Chief Guest Smt. Asha Swarup, Secretary, Ministry of Information & Broadcasting in a function organised by Publications Division here today. Instituted by the Publications Division's children's magazine Bal Bharati, the awards were presented to 13 school children for their best essays on the given topic 'Azadi ke 60 saal: Hame Garv Hai Bharat ki Upalabdhiyon par, Lekin Abhi Bahut Kuchch Karna Baaki Hai'. Gunjan Dube's essay was adjudged to be the best to win the first prize of Rs. 3000. She is a student of Navyug School, Lodi Road, New Delhi. The second prize of Rs. 2000 went to Kendriya Vidyalaya, Masjid Moth, New Delhi's student Anand Vibhor and the third to Rachna Sharma of Government Higher Sectondary Girls' School No. 1 Najafgarh, Delhi .Ten other children won consolation prizes. They are-Yatin Bhardwaj (Sanjivani Public School, Uttam Nagar, New Delhi), Ankit Kumar (Neo Convent School, Paschim Vihar, New Delhi), Akriti Singh (Holy Child School, Tagore Garden, New Delhi) Abhilash Gupta (Mata Shiv Devi Public School, Tri Nagar, Delhi) Komal Pandey (Government Sarvodaya Girls' School, Dallupura, Delhi) Ushank Shastri (Dev Samaj Modern School, Nehru Nagar, Delhi) Shivam Vishnoi (G S B V, Laxmi Nagar, Delhi), Geeta (Janaki Devi Sarvodaya School, Mayur Vihar, Delhi) Vikranti Singh (NDMC Girls' Sr. Secondary School, Gole Market, New Delhi) and Naman Jain (Green Fields Public School, Dilshad Garden, Delhi). All the children were given a citation along with the prize. An introductory book on human rights for children titled 'My Book of Human Rights' written by Dr. Jayashree Gupta, Chairperson-cum-MD, IDPL, was also released in the function by the guest of honour Shri P C Sharma, Member, National Human Rights Commission. The book through basic information and interactive exercises on human rights, tries to bring out the activists in the young readers and tells how even they can help less privileged children around them. On the occasion the Chief Guest Smt. Asha Swarup said that Bal Bharati has been making good efforts to encourage children to speak up their minds and develop in them the spirit of nationalism.

4283. (20-11-2007) NEW DELHI : In exercise of the powers conferred by clause (1) of article 224 of the Constitution of India, the President is pleased to appoint (i) Shri Kartikeya Madhusudan Thaker, (ii) Shri Zahiruddin Khairuddin Saiyed, (iii) Shri Rajesh Harivadan Shukla, and (iv) Shri Janakray Chandubhai Upadhyaya to be Additional Judges of the Gujarat High Court, in that order of seniority, for a period of two years with effect from the dates they assume charges of their respective offices. In exercise of the powers conferred by clause (1) of article 224 of the Constitution of India, the President is pleased to appoint (i) Shri Jitendra

Kumar Maheshwari, (ii) Shri Brij Mohan Gupta, and (iii) Anil Prakash Shrivastava to be Additional Judges of the Madhya Pradesh High Court, for a period of one year with effect from 25.11.2007. IN exercise of the powers conferred by clause (1) of Section 100-A of the Constitution of Jammu & Kashmir, the President is pleased to appoint Shri Mohammad Yaqoob Mir, to be an Additional Judge of the Jammu & Kashmir High Court for a period of two years with effect from the date he assumes charge of his office. Ministry of Law & Justice, Department of Justice PIB, New Delhi, Dated:Kartika 29, 1929/November 20, 2007

4284. (20-11-2007) NEW DELHI : The Government proposes to broadcast fresh programmes on All India Radio (AIR) and Doordarshan (DD) to cater to the needs of the remote and far-flung inhabitants in the North Eastern Region. Prasar Bharati have informed that Doordarshan has a scheme to commission fresh programmes to cater to the programme needs of all the inhabitants of North East Region. All the Doordarshan Kendra of North East except Sikkim *i.e.* Agartala, Aizwal, Dibrugarh, Guwahati, Imphal, Itanagar, Kohima, Shillong, Silchar, Tura and PPC, Guwahati have been selected for telecasting fresh programmes. The guidelines for the prospective producers have already been notified. Applications have been invited for empanelment of producers for these commissioned programmes. AIR stations are provided with budgetary support for producing In-House programmes at their respective Stations based on the felt needs of the region, in which they are located. In 2003, AIR invited Proposals under the commissioned category for producing radio programmes under the North East Special Package of the Software Plan Scheme. However, no fresh proposals have been invited under this category after 2003. Funds are also provided under North East Special Package for AIR Stations in North Eastern States including Sikkim. This information was given by Shri P.R. Dasmunsi, Minister for Information and Broadcasting & Parliamentary Affairs in a written reply to a question in the Parliament today.

4285. (20-11-2007) NEW DELHI : The Ministry of Information & Broadcasting has permitted 149 news & current affairs TV channels and 106 non-news & current affairs TV channels to uplink from India, as on 15.11.2007. Five (5) TV channels, uplinked from abroad, have also been permitted to downlink in India. In addition to this, 52 TV channels, uplinked from abroad, have been provisionally permitted to downlink in India. The permissions are for operation on an all-India basis and are not State-wise. Out of the total 255 channels permitted to uplink from India, 123 channels have Indian ownership whereas 132 have varying components of foreign equity in the parent company. Out of the total 57 TV channels uplinked from abroad and permitted to downlink in India, 2 TV channels have Indian equity whereas the remaining 55 TV channels have foreign equity. The Ministry is considering the proposed draft of the Broadcasting Services Regulation Bill. The said Bill is still at drafting stage and is under consultation with States/UTs and other stakeholders. No time frame can be given for finalization of the said Bill as consultation is on-going process. This information was given by

Shri P.R. Dasmunsi, Minister for Information and Broadcasting & Parliamentary Affairs in a written reply to a question in the Parliament today.

4286. (20-11-2007) NEW DELHI : The Chairman, Press Council of India, has requested the Government for establishment of a common authority for content regulation of the media and preservation of its freedom by extending the jurisdiction of Press Council over electronic as well as print media and renaming it 'Media Monitoring Commission Of India'. The request was examined but it was not found possible to accede to the proposal. This information was given by Shri P.R. Dasmunsi, Minister for Information and Broadcasting & Parliamentary Affairs in a written reply to a question in the Parliament today.

4287. (20-11-2007) NEW DELHI : The Government is seriously working to finalize the draft of the proposed Broadcasting Service Regulation Bill in close consultation with various stakeholders and State Governments. The Bill, inter alia, seeks to set up a Broadcasting Regulatory Authority of India to deal with content issues, amongst others. However, it is not specifically focused on Sting Operations. The present draft of the Bill is available on the Ministry's website www.mib.nic.in TV channels are autonomous and there is no proposal to curb their autonomy. However, they have to abide by the Cable Television Networks (Regulation) Act 1995 and rules framed there under and any other regulation issued from time to time. This information was given by Shri P.R. Dasmunsi, Minister for Information and Broadcasting & Parliamentary Affairs in a written reply to a question in the Parliament today.

4288. (20-11-2007) NEW DELHI : The Vardhman Mahavir Medical College (VMMC) premises in the Safdarjung Hospital complex was dedicated to the Nation today by his Excellency the Vice President of India, Shri M. Hamid Ansari. Dr. Anbumani Ramadoss, Union Minister for Health & Family Welfare, Shri Naresh Dayal, Secretary (HFW), Dr. R.K. Srivastava, DGHS, Dr. Jagdish Prasad, Principal, VMMC and Medical Superintendent, Safdarjung Hospital, and senior officials from the Ministry were present at the function. The following is the text of the Health Minister's speech: I am very happy to be present here with you all on this important occasion of dedication to the nation of the first Medical College of the new millennium. Imparting medical education is not new to Safdarjung Hospital (SJH). Safdarjang Hospital was a centre for training and teaching of postgraduate students since 1962. In 1973 the University College of Medical Sciences was set up at Safdarjang Hospital. The hospital faculty was responsible for imparting medical education to the students from 1973 till 1989 when the college was shifted to the Guru Teg Bahadur Hospital at Shahdara. The hospital however continues to impart postgraduate and post doctorate training in various specialities. Vardhman Mahavir Medical College opened its portals to the first batch of students in 2002. We are very fortunate to have the college under the aegis of Guru Govind Singh Indraprastha University. I am very pleased to inform you all that the first batch of students will be completing their internship this year.

Also I am happy to inform you that MCI has already given recognition to the college. Further, we are considering introduction of postgraduate seats in pre-clinical, para-clinical and clinical subjects and enhancement of seats in clinical specialities. In addition we are also intending to start postdoctoral courses in super specialty areas. We would like to start these courses under the aegis of I.P. University. The Vice Chancellor of I P University has always been very accommodating to our requirements. One cannot have a medical college or proper training of medical students without patients. Safdarjang hospital cannot be said to be lacking here; being one of the busiest hospitals. Last year, the hospital OPD's received over twenty one-lakh patients or about 7000 patients per working day. More than 800 patients visit the various emergencies daily. The total number of admissions in the past year was 1, 17, 254 with a bed occupancy of 113.5%. The bed occupancy in medicine and its specialities was 129.9% and in obstetrics an astounding 214.5% with 23, 537 deliveries. There are several speciality and super-speciality departments like Cardiology and Cardiothoracic Surgery, Urology, Respiratory and Sleep Medicine, Neurology and Burns & Plastic Surgery departments to name a few who have been providing yeoman service. With such a wide variety of patients there is no dearth of clinical material for learning. Safdarjang hospital also has another very unique problem *i.e.* it receives every day over a hundred cases daily from AIIMS and other hospitals in the city due to 'non availability of beds' there.

4289. (20-11-2007) NEW DELHI : The Government has finalized Integrated Child Protection Scheme and very soon it will be launched in selected blocks in the country. Under the scheme, child protection and welfare cells will be set up at the District level to ensure that rights of the children are protected and children related schemes are implemented on priority basis this was stated by Smt. Renuka Chowdhury, Minister for Women and Child Development while addressing the children on International Child Rights Day. She said that the investment today made in our children would brighten the future of our country hence the Government has given child welfare a very high priority in each and every scheme and programmes of the Government, child related component are on the top of the agenda. Inaugurating the national conference on the occasion being organized by National Child Rights Commission, UPA chairperson, Smt. Sonia Gandhi, said that health, education and welfare of the children would decide the future of the country, hence child should be given all possible opportunity to grow in his or her full potential. She said that children should get the right of education and it is the duty of all the Governments and private sector to help in this endeavour. On the occasion, Chairman, Child Rights Commission, Smt. Shanta Sinha expressed the concern over incidents of child labour, trafficking and violence against children. She said that the Commission would make all efforts to create mass awareness about the rights of the children and to realize the people that children are the asset of the country.

4290. (20-11-2007) NEW DELHI : On the occasion of Child Rights Day today, Smt. Renuka Chowdhury, Minister of State for Women and Child Development and Shri Rahul Gandhi arranged a Special Film show of Chak De India in Shakuntalam Theatre, Pragati Maidan for about 300 underprivileged children. Shri Rahul Gandhi, Member of Parliament was also present on the occasion. The Minister greeted the children on the occasion of Child Rights Day and briefed about various programmes run by the Government for the welfare of the children. Shri Rahul Gandhi also addressed the children and mingled with them. Smt. Renuka Chowdhury and Shri Rahul Gandhi also distributed toys to children. Later the Minister and Rahul Gandhi also visited Vatsalaya, the Pavilion of the Ministry of Women and Child Development in Hall No. 16 in IITF and motivated the women Self Help Group members to come forward and sell their products with confidence and vigour. He was very appreciative of the efforts of the Ministry in providing a platform for selling the SHG products.

4291. (20-11-2007) NEW DELHI : Government of Andhra Pradesh in May 2005 made complaint to the Central Government that construction of Babhali Barrage by Government of Maharashtra within the submergence area of Sri Ram Sagar Reservoir is in violation of GWDT award. Government of Tamil Nadu also made complaint to Central Government regarding the non-implementation of certain aspects of interim order of Cauvery Water Disputes Tribunal such as monthly and weekly quantum of inflows into Mettur Reservoir in Tamil Nadu and area irrigated from Cauvery water in Karnataka. As per Inter-State River Water Disputes Act, 1956, the decision of a Tribunal constituted under the Act after publication in the official Gazette is final and binding on parties to the dispute and is required to be given effect by them. It was amended in year 2002 whereby the decision after publication in official Gazette now has the same force as an order or decree of the Supreme Court. This information was given by the Minister of State for Water Resources, Shri Jai Prakash Narayan Yadav in response to a question by Shri T.T.V Dhinakaran in the Rajya Sabha today.

4292. (20-11-2007) NEW DELHI : In pursuance of Article 21 A of the Constitution, which makes education a Fundamental Right for children in the age group of 6-14 years by providing that "the State shall provide free and compulsory education to all children of the age of six to fourteen years in such manner as the State may, by law, determine", a draft Model Right to Education Bill was formulated and circulated as framework to the States/UTs with a view to seek their comments thereon.

4293. (20-11-2007) NEW DELHI : The proposal addresses the need of vocational education in Madarsas, linking Madarsas with the National Institute of Open Schooling for certification purposes, training teachers of Madarsas for effective delivery of modern subjects like mathematics and science, revising the current norms in respect of teachers and one time assistance for teaching aids as well as books. The proposal is based on inputs received from a Sub-committee of the National Monitoring Committee for Minority Education, which interacted with Madarsas management and Muslims minority communities in several States. The proposed scheme would continue to be voluntary. This information was given by the Minister of State for Human Resource Development, Smt. D. Purandeswari in a written reply to a question by Shri S.K. Kharventhan in Lok Sabha today.

4294. (20-11-2007) NEW DELHI : The Minister of Petroleum and Natural Gas Shri Murli Deora informed the Rajya Sabha in a written reply today that Public Sector Oil Marketing Companies (OMCs) have not reported any shortage of LPG connections in the country. As on 1.10.2007, OMCs are serving 979.8 lakh LPG customers through their 9355 LPG distributorships, out of which 12.12 lakh LPG customers and 120 LPG distributors are in the State of Himachal Pradesh. OMCs have released 27.7 lakhs new LPG domestic connections in the country during April-September, 2007. Shri Deora further told the House that OMCs have reported a waiting list of only 68813 in certain States/Union Territories as on 1.11.2007 for release of new domestic LPG connections with their LPG distributors because of backlog in supplies due to road breaches, floods, natural calamities & strikes which are beyond the control of the OMCs. This waiting list is expected to be liquidates by 15th December, 2007. There is no waiting list for new domestic LPG connections in the State of Himachal Pradesh as on 1.11.2007. He also said that the OMCs have reported that at present, there is no overall shortage of LPG in the country, including the State of Himachal Pradesh and LPG supplies to distributors are being made by the OMCs through indigenous production and imports in accordance with the genuine demand of customers registered with the LPG distributors.

4295. (20-11-2007) NEW DELHI : The Minister of Petroleum and Natural Gas Shri Murli Deora informed the Rajya Sabha in a written reply today that the Production Sharing Contract (PSC) provides for pricing of gas on the basis of sales on arms length principles. The formula or basis on which the prices shall be determined for the purposes of determining the Government take is required to be approved by the Government prior to sale of natural gas to the consumers/ buyers. Accordingly, RIL submitted a proposal on 18.5.07 for approval of gas price formula which was arrived at by following a bidding process. He emphasized that after taking into account the concerns voiced in some quarters regarding pricing of gas from KG Basin Block of RIL, the Government took the action of constituting an Empowered Group of Ministers (EGoM) to consider and decide the issues of gas pricing and commercial utilization of gas under New Exploration Licensing Policy (NELP). EGoM considered the price basis/formula submitted by RIL and decided the issue of pricing of gas under NELP. EGoM has decided that the price basis/formula submitted by M/s RIL-NIKO under Article 21.6.3 of the PSC for valuation of natural gas may be accepted with modifications.

4296. (20-11-2007) NEW DELHI : The Minister of Petroleum and Natural Gas Shri Murli Deora informed the Rajya Sabha in a written reply today that the Central Government has consistently followed a consumer friendly pricing policy. Consequently, the burden of high international oil prices is being shared by the oil PSUs and the Government and not borne by the consumer. He also said that Central Government has reduced taxes from time to time to protect the vulnerable section of the society. Central taxes-both customs duties and excise duties-have been made nil for PDS kerosene and domestic LPG. In addition, domestic LPG has been placed under the category of 'Declared Goods' restricting the ability of the State Governments to levy taxes in excess of 4%. Shri Murli Deora further told the House that customs duties on all petroleum products and crude have come down during the tenure of UPA Government.

4297. (20-11-2007) NEW DELHI : The Minister of State for Petroleum and Natural Gas Shri Dinsha Patel informed the Rajya Sabha in a written reply today that India's reserves are not shrinking. Reserve accretion to oil production ratio (R/P ratio) is more than one indicating that oil reserves are getting accreted every year. He further informed that the position of balance recoverable crude oil reserves in the country has increased to 766.880 Million Metric Tonne(MMT) in 2006-07 from 713.550 MMT in 2003-04.

4298. (20-11-2007) NEW DELHI : The Budget Proposals for the year 2007-08 include the proposal to recapitalize, in a phased programme, the Regional Rural Banks (RRBs) which have a negative networth. RRBs are jointly held by Central Government/State Governments/ Sponsor Banks in the proportion of 50:15:35 respectively. The concurrence of the State Governments concerned and Sponsor Banks for contribution of their respective shares for re-capitalization is required. The matter has been taken up with the State Governments concerned for seeking their concurrence. The State Governments of Assam and Jharkhand have agreed to contribute their share of re-capitalization. The recapitalization will strengthen the RRBs financially. The infused capital would help RRBs to expand their business and become financially stronger. This information was given by Shri Pawan Kumar Bansal, Minister of State for Finance in reply to a question raised by Shrimati Supriya Sule in the Rajya Sabha today.

4299. (20-11-2007) NEW DELHI : The Chief Minister of Assam Shri Tarun Gogoi called on the Union Minister of Shipping, Road Transport and Highways, Thiru T.R. Baalu here today to discuss issues relating to road development in the State of Assam. Thiru Baalu directed NHAI to take up repair work from Khanapura to Jorabat and Jorabat to Nagaon on top priority and requested the Chief Minister to expedite the work relating to the acquisition of land, cutting of trees and shifting of utilities for the progress on East-West corridor. The Chief Minister proposed diversion of about 90 km on the stretches of NH 37, which has to be 4-laned by NHAI to avoid Kaziranga National Park and offered in alternative route on NH-52 between Tejpur and Gohpur. Thiru Baalu assured the Chief Minister that a team of senior officials would be sent to Guwahati to sort this out in consultation with the State Government officials. Thiru Baalu directed the Ministry officials to expedite sanction of the estimate submitted by the State Government regarding Moran-Naharkatia road at 57 km under CRF at a cost of Rs. 50 crore. Shri Gogoi proposed the remaining 10 district headquarters to improve the connectivity by 2-lane roads. He also requested the construction of bridges over river Lohit, Dibong and Dihang alongwith development of NH-52 in Arunachal Pradesh to interconnect NH-37 and NH-52. Thiru Baalu assured to look into the matter. The Chief Minister proposed that a 300 years old bridge at Namdang Silor Shako may be retained and 4-laning of the corresponding stretch of NH-37 may be done by constructing a bypass. He also sought enhancement of funds to Rs. 17.5 crore (against Rs. 5 crore) to repair the flood damages during 2007-08 and Rs. 10 crore for restoration of damages. Thiru Baalu assured that the matter will considered subject to overall availability of funds. Thiru Baalu assured the Chief Minister that the NHAI has been directed to prepare proper design for the development of junction at Jalukbari and assured efficient traffic circulation on all the connecting arms of the roads. The State Government is to acquire land for construction of diversion of Guwahati University and thereafter the project will be considered for sanction.

4300. (20-11-2007) NEW DELHI : According to the latest available information, India's total external debt amounted to US $165.4 billion as at end of June 2007. According to the World Bank's Global Development Finance, 2007, India's position among the indebted developing countries of the world was seventh in 2005. The per capita burden of total foreign debt worked out to US$139.6 (Rs. 6, 086.5) at end-March 2007. This information was given by Minister of State in the Ministry of Finance Shri Pawan Kumar Bansal in reply to a question raised by Shri Jai Parkash Aggarwal in Rajya Sabha today.

4301. (20-11-2007) NEW DELHI : Government had prescribed guidelines on Public Private Partnership in infrastructure project which had set the eligibility criteria, funding, appraisal and approval procedures of PPP projects. Subsequently detailed guidelines on financial support to Public Private Partnership on infrastructure and guidelines on formulation, appraisal and approval of Public Private Partnership projects were prescribed. The guidelines prescribe step by step procedures to obtain Viability Gap Funding and for approval of the projects. They do not prescribe revenue sharing for the private partners. However, the scheme of financial support will apply only in the case of a private sector company in which 51 percent or more of the subscribed and paid up equity is owned and controlled by a private entity. This information was given by Minister of State in the Ministry of Finance Shri Pawan Kumar Bansal in reply to a question raised by Shri Santosh Bagrodia and Shri Mahmood A. Madani in Rajya Sabha today.

4302. (20-11-2007) NEW DELHI : No communication regarding enhancement of prices of wheat and rice for the Mid-Day Meal Scheme has been received from the Department of Food and Public Distribution. As per the existing terms and conditions, the cost of foodgrains is reimbursed at BPL rates. Some complaints about irregularities in the implementation of the Mid Day Meal Scheme have come to the notice of the Government. Details of the action taken is annexed. As and when complaints come to the notice of the Government, State Governments/Union Territory Administrations are asked to conduct suitable enquiry and initiate corrective actions. States/UTs are continuously advised and encouraged to establish systems to avoid recurrence of such incidents and give full attention to the issues of quality and regular supply of food and prevent misuse of resources. States have also been urged to involve the parents, community members, Village Education Committee members and Panchayati Raj Institutions to supervise the cooking and serving of mid day meal to children. This information was given by the Minister of State for Human Resource Development, Shri M.A.A. Fatmi in a written reply to a question by Shri Adhir Chowdhury in Lok Sabha today.

4303. (20-11-2007) NEW DELHI : There has been no interference on the part of the Government, especially the Ministry of Micro, Small & Medium Enterprises in the day to day work of Khadi & Village Industries Commission (KVIC), for that matter any organisation under it, as this will impede the smooth functioning of that organisation. This was stated by Shri Mahabir Prasad, Union Minister for Micro, Small & Medium Enterprises at the closing ceremony of the Golden Jubilee Celebration function of KVIC here today. Shri Prasad said the Government has given priority to addressing infrastructure and basic needs of rural people through creation of sustainable employment opportunities, exploitation of local resources, increasing production and offering opportunities to all for employment in the service of the community. KVIC as a part of its commitment to rural industrialization has been assessing rural resources, augmenting deficient resources and formulating plans, programmes and schemes for the most effective and balanced utilisation of these parameters and determining priorities, the Minister added. Shri Prasad further stated that from a highly centralised urban planning system, the Indian economy is gradually moving towards the rural sector and it is here that the KVIC concerns itself with the building of a long term strategic vision of the future rural strategy and decide on priorities of the rural sector. KVIC has been working out sectoral strategy for providing promotional stimulus to the rural economy to grow in the desired direction. Shri Prasad said, KVIC plays an integrative role in the development of a holistic approach-to the areas of human and economic development in the rural sector. He said, keeping in view its social objectives KVIC has embarked upon convergence programme with various professional agencies like IIT, NID, NIFT, IIP etc. Recalling the mission undertaken by Mahatma Gandhi, Shri Prasad said, "Let us take the mission of Pandit Nehru, Indira Gandhi and Sonia Gandhi to every household of our country". He also urged the people to emulate Khadi in true spirit. Shri Prasad released "Commemorative Postal Inland Letters and Post Cards" at the function. Union Minister of State for Labour & Employment (Independent Charge) Shri Oscar Fernandes and Chairman,

Department Related Parliamentary Standing Committee on Industry, Shri Santosh Bagrodia presented Awards to 34 persons in various categories-Best Spinners, Best Weavers, Best Bankers, Best REGP Units and Science & Technology Innovators. Ms. Kumud Joshi, Chairperson, KVIC also spoke on this occasion.

4304. (20-11-2007) NEW DELHI : LOK SABHA, The Sarva Shiksha Abhiyan (SSA) programme strives to achieve universalisation of elementary education in the country by 2010. Details of children enrolled in States and Union Territories (UTs) as in 2004-05 and funds released by Central Government to States and UTs towards SSA during the last three years and current year are given in Annexure-I. Details of targets and achievements during last three years and current year, States and Union Territories-wise is given in Annexure-II. This information was given by the Minister of State for Human Resource Development, Shri M.A.A. Fatmi in a written reply to a question by Shri Mahavir Bhagora in the Rajya Sabha today.

4305. (20-11-2007) NEW DELHI : Exports of iron ore are guided by the Export-Import policy enunciated by the Department of Commerce. As per information available with the Indian Bureau of Mines, the average ex-mines cost of production of iron ore was Rs. 524 in the year 2005-06, apart from transportation costs and other taxes levied on the ore produced. As per information available with the Department of Commerce the sale price of iron ore is around Rs.3000 per tonne. This information was given by Dr. T. Subbarami Reddy, Minister of State for Mines in a written reply to a question in the Parliament today

4306. (20-11-2007) NEW DELHI : As per information available, in 2007, till 31-10-2007, there have been a total of 1285 naxalite incidents and 571 casualties, as against 1285 incidents and 610 casualties in the corresponding period of 2006. Of this, there have been 983 incidents and 467 casualties in Andhra Pradesh, Chhattisgarh and Jharkhand, till 31-10-2007, as against 1035 incidents and 507 casualties in these States in the corresponding period of 2006. Regarding damage to property, the naxalites have been observed to be targeting certain types of Government buildings and infrastructure pertaining to road and rail transport and, in some cases, power transmission facilities. State Governments undertake necessary action to combat naxalite activities, with the Central Government supplementing their efforts and resources through a range of measures that include deployment of Central paramilitary forces to assist the State police forces, strengthening of the State police and intelligence agencies through the Modernization of State Police Forces scheme, reimbursement of security-related expenditure under the Security Related Expenditure scheme, providing training to State police forces, sharing of intelligence, bringing about inter-State coordination and assistance in development works. This was stated in a written reply to a question in Lok Sabha today by the Minister of State in the Ministry of Home Affairs, Shri Sriprakash Jaiswal.

4307. (20-11-2007) NEW DELHI : India and Qatar today signed an Additional Protocol to the 1985 bilateral Agreement on the Regulation of Employment of Indian Manpower between the two countries. Shri Vayalar Ravi, Minister of Overseas Indian Affairs on behalf of India and H.E Dr. Sultan Bin Hassan Al-Dhabit Al-Dosari, Minister of Labour and Social Affairs on behalf of the Government of the State of Qatar signed the Protocol here today. H.E Dr. Al-Dosari is on a two-day visit to India on the invitation of the Minister of Overseas Indian Affairs. Both sides negotiated the additional protocol to address mutual concerns regarding employment of Indian manpower in Qatar. Speaking on the occasion Shri Vayalar Ravi said that the Protocol enlarges the mandate of the Joint Committee and stipulates that the Joint Committee would meet twice a year alternately in India and Qatar. He said that in case of premature repatriation without any fault of the worker, the Protocol provides for the payment of full wages and other entitlements under the contract and the Labour Laws for the entire un-availed period of the contract. Shri Ravi said that the Protocol also provides for the welfare of Indian workers in the unorganized sector. This assumes significance given the fact that a large number of expatriates work in the informal sector in Qatar and are particularly vulnerable in the absence of the protection of labour laws, the Minister added. The Minister said that the Protocol is based on the principle of benefit to all-the workers, the employers, the sending country and the receiving country. He said that both the countries are equally concerned about malpractices by intermediaries. To address this issue, the Protocol provides for appropriate steps to be taken to curb practices detrimental to the welfare of the workers, he added. Shri Vyalar Ravi said that India and Qatar have been enjoying friendly bilateral relations since the beginning. Both countries share many interests and have common views on major global and regional issues. Giving the background of the Additional Protocol, he stated that a bilateral Agreement on the Regulation of Employment of Indian Manpower between India and Qatar was signed on 11.4.1985, which was one of the first bilateral agreements that India had signed for the protection and welfare of Indian workers abroad. Shri Ravi also congratulated the Qatari Minister of Labour and Social Affairs for having swiftly undertaken necessary labour reforms to support their rapidly growing economy and enacting a new labour law to consolidate the reforms. He thanked Dr. Al-Dosari for looking after the interests of Indian workers due to which the flow of our workers to Qatar has been increasing over the years. Qatar has drawn up huge development plans in view of its rapid economic growth and need for infrastructure development, which will create additional demand for foreign workers. The signing of the Protocol reflects the commitment of both countries to work together for mutual benefit, which will unleash further opportunities for the Qatari employers and the Indian workers. Qatar is a popular overseas destination for the Indian emigrants. There are about 1.5 lakh Indian workers in Qatar. During 2006 alone 76, 324 Indian workers emigrated to Qatar on ECR passport through the Protectors of Emigrants compared to 50, 222 in 2005.

4308. (20-11-2007) NEW DELHI : The provisions of the Companies Act, 1956 regulate a large number of corporate processes. The statutory obligations of a company include filing of annual returns and various other event based filings. The interests of investors are primarily associated with the listed public companies where the compliance rate, including in filing of annual returns and balance sheets etc. is found to be considerably higher than 50%. Prosecutions are filed against the non-compliant companies, when detected on the basis of inspections/ investigations etc., in the courts of competent jurisdiction. Under the provisions of section 621A of the Companies Act, 1956, any offence punishable under this Act (whether committed by a company or any officer thereof), not being an offence punishable with imprisonment only, or with imprisonment and also with fine, may either before or after the institution of any prosecution, be compounded by the Central Government on payment or credit, by the company or the officer, as the case be. In case the option of compounding of offence is not resorted to, the petitions are filed before the Competent Court of Law. This was stated by the Minister of Corporate Affairs, Shri Prem Chand Gupta in written reply to a question in the Rajya Sabha today.

4309. (20-11-2007) NEW DELHI : The Ministry of Home Affairs, The Ministry of Women and Child Development, the National Human Rights Commission and National Commission for Women are working in collaboration to draft an Integrated Plan of Action to Prevent and Combat Human Trafficking with Special Focus on Children and Women. The various steps being taken by the Government to combat trafficking are:-. (i) A Central Advisory Committee (CAC) on implementation of Immoral Traffic (Prevention) Act is functioning at Central level in the Ministry of Women & Child Development, which is represented by States as well as Central Organizations and NGOs etc. The CAC holds quarterly meetings. Immoral Trafficking (Prevention) Act is in the process of being amended to make it more stringent against traffickers. (ii) The Ministry of Home Affairs has set up a Nodal Cell to coordinate, matters relating to trafficking in human beings between the State Governments/Union Territory Administrations and other related Ministries etc. and organize coordination meetings to review and sensitize Police Officers of the States/Union Territories on the subject. (iii) The Bureau of Police Research and Development (BPR&D) has prepared a training manual on "Human Trafficking Handbook for Investigators" for use in the Police Training Institutes. (iv) BPR&D is organizing regional anti-trafficking workshops for sensitizing police personnel towards the safety and security of women. Several workshops have been held in various cities till date. (v) The Ministry of Women & Child Development is also implementing a pilot project to combat trafficking of women and children. This was stated in a written reply to a question in Lok Sabha today by the Minister of State in the Ministry of Home Affairs, Shri Manikrao H. Gavit.

4310. (20-11-2007) NEW DELHI : It has come to the notice of the Ministry of Home affairs that some Government agencies while using the State Emblem of

India on their official stationery, documents, seal etc. often omit the motto 'Satyamev Jayte', which is part of the State Emblem, and only depict the profile of the Lion capital. The Ministry has since issued an advisory to all State Governments/UT Administrations, and Ministries/Departments of the Govt. of India reiterating the position that all Government agencies authorized to use the State Emblem on their stationery, seals, documents etc., should depict the State Emblem together with the motto 'Satyameva Jayate'-written in Devanagari script-below the profile of the Lion Capital. They have also been requested to ensure that the motto 'Satyameve Jayate' is not omitted from the State Emblem. This was stated in a written reply to a question in Lok Sabha today by the Minister of State in the Ministry of Home Affairs, Shri Manikrao H. Gavit.

4311. (20-11-2007) NEW DELHI : The Kasturba Gandhi Balika Vidyalaya Scheme (KGBVS) is helping to improve the educational status o Muslim Minority Girls including in Andhra Pradesh, where 94 KGBVs have been sanctioned during 2004-05 and 169 out-of-school muslim girls are studying in these KGBVs. In the year 2006-07, 25 KGBVs have been sanctioned exclusively for Muslim Minority Girls. A total of 526 Madrasas are supported through the Sarva Shiksha Abhiyan in Andhra Pradesh. Formal education is being proided in madrasas. Training for volunteers and resource teachers is imparted for teaching English, Maths, and Science in Madrasas. Text Books are supplied free of cost to students in Madrasas. Midday meal is also being provided.

4312. (20-11-2007) NEW DELHI : At present, only the All India Council for Technical Education (AICTE) has framed regulations for entry and operation of foreign universities/institutions imparting technical education in India. A legislative proposal for entry and operation of foreign educational institutions in the country is presently under consideration of the Government. This information was given by the Minister of State for Human Resource Development, Smt. D. Purandeswari in a written reply to a question by Shri N.N. Krishnadas in Lok Sabha today.

4313. (20-11-2007) NEW DELHI : The Gross Enrollment Ratio(GER) in higher education in the relevant age groups is at present about 10 per cent. Enhancement of access in higher education is a continuous process through establishment of more universities and colleges, increasing intake of students through expansion of existing institutions and blending of the open and conventional systems of higher education.

4314. (20-11-2007) NEW DELHI : Myanmar is a close and friendly neighbour and developments in that country have a bearing on India. We attach importance to our relations with Myanmar. This was Prime Minister's first meeting with new Prime Minister of Myanmar. Discussions covered bilateral and regional issues. The Myanmarese Prime Minister briefed PM on internal developments in Myanmar and the efforts of his Government at political reform and national reconciliation. PM conveyed India's position that the reform process should be broad based, including Daw Aung San Suu Kyi and the various ethnic nationalities, and that it should be carried forward expeditiously towards a satisfactory conclusion. India supports the efforts of the UN Special Envoy to engage the Government of Myanmar on behalf of the international community to facilitate the process of reconciliation. The two leaders also reviewed the status of various bilateral projects.

4315. (20-11-2007) NEW DELHI : Following is the text of the address of the Vice President of India Mohd. Hamid Ansari at the 'International Conference on Emerging Security Concerns in West Asia' here today: "It is a pleasure to be back on a familiar platform. Familiarity in this case, however, is a disadvantage since I may be in danger of repeating what I may have articulated on previous occasions! Many years back the British philosopher Gilbert Ryle had drawn attention to the dangers of expressions that are 'couched in syntactical form improper to the facts recorded'. This observation is relevant to our subject today since the theme of the conference begs definition and delineation. Unanimity of perception, of course, would have been ideal; since that is lacking, the two operative terms-'emerging' and 'security concerns'-need to be spelt out. Centrality has been the curse of West Asia. It is hardly necessary to remind this audience that external security concerns pertaining to the region have been around for over a century. Writing in 1917, Marriott defined the Eastern Question as 'the problem of filling up the vacuum created by the gradual disappearance of the Turkish Empire from Europe'. In May 1917, Britain and France used the Sykes-Picot Agreement to acquire 'the right of priority in enterprises and local loans' in designated Arab areas of the Ottoman Empire and to deny any facilities to a third Power in the Arabian Peninsula and the Red Sea. In a parallel move, the secret Balfour Declaration of November 1917 carried the commitment for the 'establishment in Palestine of a national home for the Jewish people'. A decade earlier on August 31, 1907, the Anglo-Russian Entente was signed, dividing Iran into three zones only one of which was under Iranian control. 'The Iranians', in Professor Nikkie Keddie's words, 'were neither consulted on the agreement nor informed of the terms'. That exercise, of division and occupation, was repeated during World War II.

4316. (20-11-2007) NEW DELHI : As per information received from the Indian Space Research Organisation (ISRO), under Department of Space, survey of different landscapes to spot out ground water resources has been conducted in 10 States, viz., Andhra Pradesh (part), Chhattisgarh, Karnataka, Kerala, Madhya Pradesh, Rajasthan, Jharkhand, Himachal Pradesh, Orissa and Gujarat. Over two lakh wells have been drilled with a success rate of over 90 percent. This information was given by the Minister of State for Water Resources, Shri Jai Prakash Narayan Yadav in response to a question by Shri Sanjay Raut in the Rajya Sabha today.

4317. (20-11-2007) NEW DELHI : Criteria adopted for sanctioning of financial assistance to State Government for control of floods is as per procedure laid down by the Planning Commission. As per information provided by National Agricultural Bank for Rural Development (NABARD), the State-wise details of total amount sanctioned and financial assistance provided for flood control projects, under Rural Infrastructure Development Fund (RIDF) by NABARD during the year 2006-07.

4318. (20-11-2007) NEW DELHI : Schemes for anti-sea erosion works are planned and implemented by the respective State Governments. Ministry of Water Resources has no scheme for providing central assistance to States for coastal protection. However, realizing the importance of such woks, Central Water Commission requested the State Governments to identify the critical reaches and submit suitable proposal with a view to prepare a scheme namely National Coastal Protection Project (NCPP) for seeking external funding. Proposals from various States including Maharashtra have been received. Government of Maharashtra has submitted a proposal with an estimated cost of Rs.195.50 crore in July 2002 for inclusion in the National Coastal Protection Project (NCPP). The proposal includes construction of 72.36 km of anti erosion works in Mumbai, Mumbai Sburban, Thane, Raigad, Ratnagiri and Sindudurg Districts. The compliances to observations of Central Water Commission on the proposals submitted by the coastal states of Andhra Pradesh, Goa, Karnataka and Union Territory (UT) of Lakshadweep for inclusion in the NCPP have not been received. UT of Andaman & Nicobar Islands has not submitted any proposal. An Approach Paper prepared by Ministry of Water Resources on NCPP had been forwarded by Department of Economic Affairs (DEA) to the Asian Development Bank (ADB) for consideration. ADB approved administering technical assistance to the Government of India for technical study on "Integrated Coastal Management and Related Investment Development". The Project Preparation Technical Assistance team in its report recommended Project Preparatory Technical Assistance (PPTA) to prepare a project/programme in 2007 having key components for (i) institutional strengthening, capacity building and investment support for coastal management; (ii) capacity building and investment support for coastal protection. Based on the recommendation of the PPTA, an ADB Fact Funding Mission visited three States namely Maharashtra, Goa and Karnataka during April-May, 2007. The Mission also recommended to work initially in Karnataka, Goa and Maharashtra. Thereafter, a meeting was held in DEA and these three states have been requested to confirm arrangement regarding mode of implementation of the project as a State sector project and that the fund from the ADB would be passed on the States on a back to back basis as is being done for all externally aided project. The confirmation of Maharashtra Government has been received. This information was given by the Minister of State for Water Resources, Shri Jai Prakash Narayan Yadav in response to a question by Shri Manohar Joshi in the Rajya Sabha today.

4319. (20-11-2007) NEW DELHI : The Ministry of Water Resources (erstwhile Ministry of Irrigation) and Central Water Commission formulated a National Perspective Plan (NPP) for Water Resources Development in 1980. The NPP comprises of two components viz. i) Peninsular Rivers Development and

ii) Himalayan Rivers Development and envisages construction of storages on various river systems along with interlinking canal systems to transfer water from water surplus areas to water deficit regions. National Water Development Agency (NWDA) was set up on 1982 to study the feasibility of Inter-basin water transfer proposals and give a concrete shape to NPP. The Inter-linking proposals under NPP envisages additional benefits of 25 million ha. of irrigation from surface waters, 10 million ha. by increased use of ground waters and generation of 34 million KW of power apart from the incidental benefits of flood moderation, navigation, water supply, salinity & pollution control etc. Based on various studies conducted, NWDA has identified 30 links for preparation of feasibility Reports (FRs). Out of these, FRs of 14 links under Peninsular Component & 2 Links (Indian portion) under Himalayan Component have already been completed. NWDA has taken up the work of Preparation of Detailed Project Report (DPR) for one priority link viz. Ken-Betwa under Peninsular Component. The implementation of inter basin water transfer proposals depends upon the consensus and cooperation of the concerned States and agreements with the neighbouring countries. This information was given by the Minister of State for Water Resources, Shri Jai Prakash Narayan Yadav in response to a question by Shri Rajeev Chandra Sekhar in the Rajya Sabha today.

4320. (20-11-2007) NEW DELHI : Available references indicate that water-logging in Sindhu region was known before the Indus Water Treaty 1960. However they do not provide any unique area of water-logging in Sindhu region and the area that India got. The report of the Irrigation Commission-1972 states that about 10.9 lac hectares of area was affected in the Punjab state as estimated in the year 1958. Further, as per the book "The Indus Basin-History of Irrigation, Drainage and Flood Management" by C.D. Thatte and others, the survey in 1943 indicated that roughly an area of 0.2 million ha. was affected by thur (alkali and saline soils) and sem (waterlogged) whereas the aerial reconnaissance survey got conducted by Government of Pakistan in 1954 indicated that an area of more than 4.45 million ha. in West Pakistan was poorly drained and water-logged.

4321. (21-11-2007) NEW DELHI : This was stated by Goa Chief Minister, Shri Digambar Kamat at a press conference today. Addressing media at the major pre-event conference in Goa, Shri Kamat apprised the media of the arrangements for smooth conduct of IFFI-2007. Shri Kamat said, infrastructure for the Festival has been improved and altogether a seating capacity of around 4000 is available in nine different theatres. The Chief Minister said that so far around 3500 delegates have registered, of which about 1400 are Goa-based. The number is likely to go up, he said. Of the 300 media persons who have registered so far, around 80 are from Goa. With a view to have a properly regulated system, ticketing system for media and delegates has been introduced which is expected to help delegates and media persons plan their choice of film shows in advance and would reduce waiting in Queues. Fifteen ticketing booths have been set up, and one will be exclusively for the media. He allayed media apprehensions about the newly introduced ticketing system and expressed confidence that it would effectively tackle the issue of long waits for entering the cinema hall. Director, DFF, Mrs. Neelam Kapur informed the media that the response from the film industry was enthusiastic. She said French Embassy is also participating in the Festival. She further informed the media of the various segments of the IFFI-2007. The Palme D' OR winner of Cannes 2007-titled 4 months, 3 weeks & 2 day would be the opening film at the Festival which gets underway on November 23. Noted film actor Shahrukh Khan will be the Chief Guest at the inaugural ceremony which will be attended by Minister of Information & Broadcasting and Parliamentary Affairs, Shri P. R. Dasmunsi and Chief Minister of Goa, Shri Digambar Kamat besides several important film personalities. The inaugural lamp will be lit with the assistance of Priyamani, the rising star of southern cinema. Indian Panorama at IFFI-2007 would present a bouquet of 36 films, 21 features and 15 non-feature films. Budhadeb Dasgupta will be the Chief Guest at the closing ceremony. A specialized competition for feature films by Asian, African and Latin American Directors is being organized. Fourteen films have been selected from 13 countries for the competition. Competition Jury is headed by the eminent award winning film maker from Hungary Ms Marta Mazaros. A special section celebrating 60 years of India's independence, India @ 60, would showcase seven patriotic films including three feature and four documentaries.

4322. (21-11-2007) NEW DELHI : The Prime Minister, Dr. Manmohan Singh, is leaving New Delhi tomorrow to attend the Commonwealth Heads of Government Meeting in Kampala, Uganda. Following is the text of the Prime Minister's statement on the eve of his visit : "I am leaving for Kampala to attend the Commonwealth Heads of Government Meeting (CHOGM) that begins tomorrow. CHOGM 2007 has a rich agenda before it. This includes a review of global developments, including Climate Change, the Millennium Development Goals, Human Rights and Terrorism. The special theme of the Meeting is "Transforming Societies to achieve Political, Economic and Human Development". Issues relating to the 32 Small States which are members of the Commonwealth will also be taken up. India is strongly committed to the Commonwealth's role of nurturing a sense of belonging to a shared past and a shared destiny based on common values. The Commonwealth is a forum that is uniquely placed to harness the strength and diversity of its membership in cooperating with each other and addressing the global challenges of trade, sustainable development and social advancement. India has consistently played an active role in the Commonwealth. We have several technical assistance and cooperation programmes in place, particularly for the developing countries in Africa and the Small States, which we will seek to enhance. I look forward to meeting a large number of leaders and having a constructive dialogue with them on both bilateral and international issues. I will use the opportunity to highlight the major socio-economic transformation that is underway in India, and the opportunities this provides for the emergence of a new world order."

4323. (21-11-2007) NEW DELHI : The Union Minister of Social Justice and Empowerment, Smt. Meira Kumar has said that the higher education in the country has become costlier and it is becoming difficult for the children from the disadvantaged sections of the society to go for it. In such a situation, she said, the children from Scheduled Castes and Scheduled Tribes would have to be very alert while looking for the right opportunities. Smt. Kumar was speaking at a function to give away awards to the recipients of Dr. Ambedkar National Scholarship here today. Speaking on the occasion, the Minister said that the available data clearly shows that representation of the students from SC and ST categories gradually keeps on declining in the higher education. Smt. Kumar said that the population of Scheduled Castes in the country is over sixteen per cent and that of Scheduled Tribes eight per cent and thus these two categories constitute one-fourth of the country's total population. She said that if we are not able to take one fourth of the population along with us on the path of development, we cannot claim to have achieved the desired goal of growth and development. The Minister said that we have to ensure that the disadvantaged sections, which were deprived of their basic rights for centuries together, are brought in the mainstream and her Ministry is working with full dedication to achieve this goal. Reminding the students that 'Information is Power', the Minister exhorted them to be on their toes in this age of communication and information revolution and make every effort for their all-round development. She said that education is the only vehicle through which they, along with their families and communities, can join the mainstream and become part of the growth process. Students from Delhi, Tripura, Goa, Andhra Pradesh, H.P. Jharkhand, Haryana, Sikkim, Mizoram, Karnatak and Bihar, and Rashtriya Vidyalaya Pariksha Parishad were presented with meritorious awards. A total cash award of Rs. 57.2 lakh was given away to 189 students. The Minister informed that students from other States would also be invited to Delhi for receiving the meritorious awards in coming months. The Ambedkar National Merit Scholarship is given to three students scoring highest marks in the regular Class X-level-examination conducted by the State Education Board/All India Board. Students securing highest, second highest and third highest marks are given Rs. 60, 000/-, Rs. 50, 000/- and Rs. 40, 000/- respectively. Girl student securing highest marks in case she is not in the above three categories, is given a cash award of Rs. 40, 000/- . The scheme provides for separate provisions both for scheduled castes and scheduled tribes.

4324. (21-11-2007) NEW DELHI : In the country, 53.1 % of the India's forest are prone to fire, and out of this 9% of the area is affected by frequent fires. This has been revealed in the State of Forest Report, 1995 analysis of the record of occurrence of fire within and around the sample plot activity, over a period of two decades. Forest fire management involves prevention, timely detection, control and monitoring. A combination of technologies such as Remote Sensing, Geographic Information System etc. is being used for detection and monitoring of forest fires. Under the Centrally Sponsored-Integrated Forest Protection Scheme, Forest Fire Control and Management is one of the component. Financial assistance is provided to the States/UTs on sharing basis to take up various activities for effective prevention and control of forest fires including use of modern technology. This information was given by the Minister of State in the Ministry of Environment and Forests, Shri S.Regupathy in a written reply to question in the Lok Sabha today.

4325. (21-11-2007) NEW DELHI : Lok Sabha The State Government of Rajasthan has submitted the project proposal "Second phase of Rajasthan Forestry and Bio-diversity Project". The estimated project cost is Rs. 569.53 crores. This project will be completed in the period of 6 years seeking external assistance from the Japan Bank for International Cooperation (JBIC). The proposed Project envisages to cover all 32 districts in Rajasthan. The project proposal has been submitted to the Department of Economic Affairs, Ministry of Finance for further necessary action. This information was given by the Minister of State in the Ministry of Environment and Forests, Shri S.Regupathy in a written reply to question in the Lok Sabha today.

4326. (21-11-2007) NEW DELHI : National Environment Policy (NEP) has recognized the various ecological services provided by wetlands and emphasized on the need for setting up a legally enforceable mechanism for the identified wetlands on the basis of their usage for preventing their degradation and strengthening conservation efforts. A special multi-disciplinary Expert Group constituted for this purpose provided a draft regulatory framework for wetlands to be notified under the provisions of Environment (Protection) Act, 1986. The proposed regulatory structure has provision of Central Regulatory Authority, State Regulatory Authority and District Regulatory Authority. The classification of wetlands is based on their size, threat perceptions and importance at various levels. The Ministry has identified 94 wetlands under National Wetland Conservation Programme. State-wise details are given in the Annexure. The Central Government invites the comments of State Governments and other stakeholders on the draft regulatory framework before the regulatory regime for the wetlands is finally approved and notified.

4327. (21-11-2007) NEW DELHI : The Vice President of India Mohd. Hamid Ansari released the music album 'Sada-e-Sufi' by artiste Ms. Anita Singhvi at a function here today. Brought out by Saregama the album spreads the massage of Sufism-spirituality that transcends religion. Congratulating Ms. Singhvi the Vice President said that the tradition of Sufism is not new in this country and to popularize the songs of Sufism among the masses is a big achievement of her. Ms. Singhvi said that the sole motive of the album is to disseminate the message of love, peace and fraternity and to shed hatred. Noted film maker Muzaffar Ali was the guest of honour. Film personality Farukh Shekh and the Vice Chairman of RPG Group Mr. Sanjiv Goenka and many dignitaries were present.

4328. (21-11-2007) NEW DELHI : Following is the text of the remarks of the Prime Minister, Dr. Manmohan Singh at the Asian Civilisation Museum Exhibition "On the Nalanda Trail: Buddhism in India, China and Southeast Asia" in Singapore today: "I am very pleased to join my distinguished colleague and good friend, the Prime Minister of Singapore, in welcoming you to this extraordinary exhibition on Nalanda. I extend a special welcome to the leaders of the European Union present here. We seek your support in making the initiative on Nalanda a success. The Nalanda University was a part of the intellectual life of Asia for over seven centuries. It was one of the first great Universities in recorded history, and one of the world's first residential universities. The university was an architectural masterpiece, attracting students from China, Japan, Korea, Persia and Turkey. Through the exchange of scholars and the spread of ideas, the University made an invaluable contribution to international understanding. Earlier today, we have discussed our collective efforts to revive the Nalanda University as a centre of cross-cultural understanding and learning. There is much we can learn from each other. We recognize the contribution of the Mentor Group, whose recommendations provide a roadmap to recreating a unique international institution and preserving a common cultural heritage. Nalanda will focus on becoming a centre for excellence for research and teaching with an emphasis on postgraduate studies. It will have departments for philosophy and Buddhist studies, regional history, business and management studies, international relations and peace studies and study of languages. It will be established as an international university through an international treaty. This Exhibition has recreated the spiritual and physical splendour of Nalanda. It comprises 116 of the most precious art objects from four prestigious Museums in India, which have been specially sent to Singapore. The artifacts include rare paintings and bronze and stone sculptures. There are great masterpieces like the Nalanda Copper Plate, depicting the royal patronage to the Nalanda University, and the Sacred Relics of the Buddha himself. The Exhibition covers all the eight important events of Buddha's life, which relate to the eight important Buddhist pilgrimage sites in India. By doing so, it brings to life Buddha's message of compassion, tolerance and contentment. It is a poignant reminder of the rich cultural heritage of our region. The Exhibition truly brings a very memorable day to a most appropriate conclusion. The Third East Asia Summit has emerged as an important forum for dialogue on issues of common interest and concern. The EAS process is an ideal vehicle for promoting peace, stability and economic prosperity in East Asia." The promotion of greater people-to-people contacts and cultural understanding is one of its important objectives. This Exhibition will go a long way in achieving this goal. I would like to convey our sincere gratitude to the Government of Singapore for seeking to recapture the spirit of Nalanda and the Asian Civilisations Museum for making it a reality."

4329. (21-11-2007) NEW DELHI : There is no shortage of soldiers in the Army. However, there is a shortage of 11, 371 officers in the Army which is mainly in the ranks of Lieutenant Colonel and below. Several measures have been taken by the Government to enhance recruitment in the Army. All officers including those in Short Service Commission (SSC) have been made eligible to hold substantive rank of Captain, Major and Lieutenant Colonel and equivalents after 2, 6 and 13 years of reckonable service respectively. The term of SSC Officer has been extended to 14 years. This has made the Army an attractive career option. Besides Army has undertaken sustained image projection publicity campaign to create awareness among the youth. Awareness campaigns, participation in career fairs and exhibitions, advertisements in print and electronic media are also some of the other measures in this direction. This information was given by the Defence Minister Shri AK Antony in a written reply to Shri Amir Alam Khan in Rajya Sabha today.

4330. (21-11-2007) NEW DELHI : Some of the marine species are facing threat due to habitat destruction, over exploitation, commercial fishing, by-catches during commercial fishing etc. The issue of conservation and management of marine species was one of the agenda items for the 4th meeting of the National Board for Wildlife held on 1st November 2007 under the Chairmanship of Prime Minister. The steps taken to provide protection to marine species are as given below: All cetaceans (Whales, Porpoises & Dolphins) and 10 species of elasmobranch (sharks & rays), Holothurians, Corals, 9 species of Molluscs, Sea Horses, Giant Grouper have been included in the Schedule I of the Wild Life (Protection) Act, 1972, thereby affording them highest degree of protection. Hunting of these species is prohibited as per the provisions of the Act. With the amendments in the Wildlife (Protection) Act, 1972, the penalty for poaching of species included in the Schedules of the Act and illegal trade in its parts and products has been enhanced. Financial and technical assistance are provided to the State/UT Governments under the Centrally Sponsored Scheme of 'Development of National Parks & Sanctuaries' for development of protected areas which include marine national parks as well. All developmental activities within the Coastal Regulation Zone area are regulated. India is a signatory to the International Whaling Commission (IWC), Convention on Migratory Species (CMS) and Convention on International Trade in Endangered Species of Wild Fauna and Flora (CITES) for conservation of marine species and its habitats and for control of illegal trade in its parts & products. This information was given by the Minister of State in the Ministry of Environment and Forests, Shri Namo Narayan Meena in a written reply to question in the Lok Sabha today.

4331. (21-11-2007) NEW DELHI : Defence Institute of Psychological Research (DIPR), a laboratory of Defence Research and Development Organisation (DRDO), had conducted two studies. One of the "Psycho-Social aspect of optimizing the operational efficiency of Security Forces to combat insurgency" during September 2000-May 2005 in the North Eastern Region. The major outcomes of the study are: Three main operational stressors, like fear of torture, uncertain environment and domestic stresses are responsible for most of psychological problems in various groups of Armed Forces. Middle rank officers as compared to Jawans and Junior Commissioned Officers (JCO) were found to be more vulnerable and stressed out. Mental disorders in the form of Post Traumatic Stress Disorder (PTSD) have been observed in traumatized troops, which forms the basis for various somatic symptoms. About six to nine months after the detention of captured militants is most appropriate period to change in the attitudes of youth and influence their minds towards national identification. A strong need to inoculate and orient officers by undertaking Combat Stress Management training programmes. Need for immediate therapeutic intervention during post-traumatic stress disorders jointly by unit leaders and professional psychologist. There is a strong need to carry out a appropriate need analysis with repect to demographic variables of a particular region. Another study was carried out in December 2006 on "Suicide and Fratricide among troops deployed in counter insurgency areas" and suggested a number of remedial measures to deal with stress related issues in the Army. Some of the suggestions are: liberalized leave policy, deployment of psychological counsellors in counter insurgency areas, periodical review, monitoring and analysis of stress related incidents, organizations of stress management training programmes and disseminations of reading materials on stress management in appropriate languages, etc. The remedial measures to manage stress have been implemented in entire Army both in field and peace areas. This information was given by the Defence Minister Shri AK Antony in a written reply to Shri Motilal Vora and Shri Satyavrat Chaturvedi in Rajya Sabha today.

4332. (21-11-2007) NEW DELHI : The terms of reference of the Kargil Review Committee was to review the events leading up to the Pakistani aggression in the Kargil District. The Committee among other things emphasized on the necessity of publishing authentic accounts of the Indo-Pak wars of 1965 and 1971 besides the Kargil War of 1999. A Committee to review the publication of War Histories was constituted by the Government. The Committee has given its recommendations which are being considered for arriving at a final decision on this issue. This information was given by the Defence Minister Shri AK Antony in a written reply to Shri Pyarelal Khandelwal in Rajya Sabha today.

4333. (21-11-2007) NEW DELHI : The perceptions of Line of Actual Control (LAC) of both India and China overlaps at many places on India-China border. From time to time, on account of differences in the perception of the LAC, situations have arisen on the ground that could have been avoided if we had a common perception of the LAC. In order to address this issue, the matter has been taken up at appropriate levels in the Government. The two sides have signed the Agreement on the Maintenance of Peace and Tranquility along the line of Actual Control in 1993, Agreement on Confidence Building Measures (CBM) in the Military Field in 1996, Protocol on Modalities for the implementation of CBMs in Military Field along the LAC in the India-China Border Areas, in 2005 and memorandum of Understanding (MoU) in 2006. As a follow up to this MoU, the Annual Defence Dialogue between the two sides was held at Beijing during 12-13 November 2007. Government regularly takes up such perceived violations along the LAC with the Chinese side through established mechanisms set up under these Agreements / Protocol including the Joint Working Group, the Expert Group border personnel meetings, flag meetings and normal diplomatic channels. Mechanism to address instances of intrusions along the LAC and well established. Peace and tranquility has been maintained on the border areas. Government of India keeps a constant watch on all developments having a bearing on India's security and takes all necessary measures to safeguard it. Furthermore, various Government agencies involved in the issue do not have differing perceptions on the issue. This information was given by the Defence Minister Shri AK Antony in a written reply to Ms Mabel Rebello and Shri Santosh Bagrodia in Rajya Sabha today.

4334. (21-11-2007) NEW DELHI : The Environmental Clearance Process has been revised through an Environment Impact Assessment (EIA) Notification issued vide S.O. No. 1533 (E) dated 14th September, 2006 to make the Environmental Clearance Process more transparent efficient and de-centralized with certainty in time frame. The Forest (Conservation) Act, 1980 deals with Forest Clearances in respect of projects involving Forest Land and Environmental Clearances are dealt under the Environment (Protection) Act, 1986. The proposals under each act are considered independently irrespective of the provisions of either act. Hence there is no question of development projects pending for environment clearance under the Forest (Conservation) Act, 1980. The EIA Notification, 2006 provides for Scoping for preparation of quality EIA Report, Structured Public Consultations with stipulated time frame, Decentralization of environmental clearance by constituting State Level Environment Impact Assessment Authorities (SEIAA) and State Level Expert Appraisal Committees (SEAC) and time limits at each stage, thus enabling speedy clearance of projects. This information was given by the Minister of State in the Ministry of Environment and Forests, Shri Namo Narayan Meena in a written reply to question in the Lok Sabha today.

4335. (21-11-2007) NEW DELHI : Lok Sabha The Central Pollution Control Board (CPCB) has formulated 'Draft Guidelines for Environmentally Sound Management of E-Waste' for the State Pollution Control Boards and Pollution Control Committees of the Union Territories and the industries for handling E-waste. These draft Guidelines are available on CPCB's website A Task Force has been constituted by the Ministry of Environment and Forests for finalization of these Guidelines. The Ministry of Environment and Forests have notified the Hazardous Waste (Management & Handling) Rules 1989 as amended in 2000 and 2003 under the Environment (Protection) Act, 1986 which includes e-waste. These Rules regulate collection, storage, treatment, disposal and import of hazardous wastes including E-waste. The residues and wastes generated from the operations in electronics industry are considered as hazardous wastes and are listed at Sl. No. 31 of Schedule 1 of these rules. Further, the export and import of e-waste is regulated under Schedule 3 of these rules as Electrical and Electronic Assemblies covered under Sl. Nos. A 1180 and B 1110 of this Schedule. The import of wastes under this category is only permitted for direct reuse and not for recycling or final disposal. Further, the Department of Information Technology (DIT), Ministry of Communication and Information Technology, has taken steps to promote adoption of cleaner technologies and to motivate the electronics industry to minimize the generation of waste in the electronics industry. A comprehensive technical guide on 'Environmental Management for Information Technology Industry in India' published in 2004, has been circulated widely by the DIT. This information was given by the Minister of State in the Ministry of Environment and Forests, Shri Namo Narayan Meena in a written reply to question in the Lok Sabha today.

4336. (21-11-2007) NEW DELHI : Lok Sabha, The Central Pollution Control Board (CPCB) has formulated 'Draft Guidelines for Environmentally Sound Management of E-Waste' for the State Pollution Control Boards and Pollution Control Committees of the Union Territories and the industries for handling E-waste. These draft Guidelines are available on CPCB's website A Task Force has been constituted by the Ministry of Environment and Forests for finalization of these Guidelines. The Ministry of Environment and Forests have notified the Hazardous Waste (Management & Handling) Rules 1989 as amended in 2000 and 2003 under the Environment (Protection) Act, 1986 which includes e-waste. These Rules regulate collection, storage, treatment, disposal and import of hazardous wastes including E-waste. The residues and wastes generated from the operations in electronics industry are considered as hazardous wastes and are listed at Sl. No. 31 of Schedule 1 of these rules. Further, the export and import of e-waste is regulated under Schedule 3 of these rules as Electrical and Electronic Assemblies covered under Sl. Nos. A 1180 and B 1110 of this Schedule. The import of wastes under this category is only permitted for direct reuse and not for recycling or final disposal. Further, the Department of Information Technology (DIT), Ministry of Communication and Information Technology, has taken steps to promote adoption of cleaner technologies and to motivate the electronics industry to minimize the generation of waste in the electronics industry. A comprehensive technical guide on 'Environmental Management for Information Technology Industry in India' published in 2004, has been circulated widely by the DIT. This information was given by the Minister of State in the Ministry of Environment and Forests, Shri Namo Narayan Meena in a written reply to question in the Lok Sabha today.

4337. (21-11-2007) NEW DELHI : Lok Sabha, The 13th Conference of the Parties to the United Nations Framework Convention on Climate Change (UNFCCC) is scheduled to be held from 3rd to 14th December 2007 at Bali, Indonesia. The Indian position on the Climate Change issue is that our GHG emissions are among the lowest in per capita terms and account for only 4% of the world's emissions. Nonetheless, India attaches great importance to issue of climate change. India is a Party to the UNFCCC and is engaged constructively and productively with the international community to preserve and protect the environment. India is determined that India's per-capita GHG emissions would not exceed those of developed countries even while pursuing policies of development and economic growth. The Human Development Report 2007 of United Nations Development Programme (UNDP) has not been released till date. This information was given by the Minister of State in the Ministry of Environment and Forests, Shri Namo Narayan Meena in a written reply to question in the Lok Sabha today.

4338. (21-11-2007) NEW DELHI : The Government conducts a National Environment Awareness Campaign (NEAC) every year for creating awareness among public towards various environmental issues. This campaign is conducted with active participation and in consultation with NGOs, professional groups, academic institutions etc. various action oriented and awareness activities like Padyatras/Rallies, Street Theatre, Folk Dances, Essay/Debate/Painting competitions, seminars etc. are conducted for diverse target groups including general public, school children etc. The main theme for National Environment Awareness Campaign (NEAC) 2007-08 is "Biodiversity Conservation". The Ministry gives funds to various State Governments and Union Territories for this purpose.

4339. (21-11-2007) NEW DELHI : The Wildlife Institute of India has conducted an assessment of status of tigers in Sariska Tiger Reserve. This was based on the directives from the Ministry. It has been reported that there is no evidence of tigers in the said Tiger Reserve, this has been The Special Investigation Team of the Central Bureau of Investigation has also reported the disappearance of tigers from Sariska, primarily on account of poaching.

4340. (21-11-2007) NEW DELHI : Congress spokesperson Smt. Jayanti Natarajan said that the Congress views with grave concern the further development and spilling over of the agitation and rioting in relation to Nandigram and other issues, even into Kolkata. This is a very serious issue which impacts upon the lives of ordinary citizens, particularly women, children, minorities and the poorest of the poor. Therefore, we believe that this situation has to be brought under control at the earliest possible time. The Hon'ble Prime Minister has already expressed his concern in the matter and the Indian National Congress too would like to extend our condolences to the family of all those who lost their lives and to those who have been rendered harm less. We also express our anguish over the large-scale destruction of properties. In short, we would like to once again reiterate our anguish over this large-scale violence, loss of life and hostility between various sections of our own people. It is the duty of the state govt. to bring the situation under control without further delay and we would like to call upon the Chief Minister of West Bengal and also the government to immediately bring relief to those who have been affected to put a halt to the violence and to ensure that peace and law and order are immediately restored. To a question that despite showing concern, AICC did not send any delegation to Nandigram, Smt. Natarajan said that our concern is not superficial, it is very deep and very conscious. Sending a delegation does not make or enhance the gravity of our concern or detract from it. As and when the Congress President feels it relevant and necessary, she will take whatever action she feels fit. I don't think sending or not sending a delegation has a bearing upon the concern we feel. To a question about the role of the state govt., Smt. Natarajan said at the beginning that our concern has multiplied because the violence has spilt over to Kolkata. We call upon the state govt. to take steps to bring the situation under control immediately. Without any delay. To a question as to what is Congress stand on the situation in Nandigram, Smt. Natarajan said that I think it should be dealt with on the merits of it and the merits will be dealt with by the Home Ministry. To a question that does the Congress believe that there are Maoists in Nandigram, Smt. Natarajan said that Congress believes that innocent people have suffered, there has been loss of life, and the situation in Nandigram with armed hostilities between our own people is something that is very unfortunate. On the issue of the presence of Maoists, we do not have inputs to tell you about them. To a question about the role of the state govt., Smt. Natarajan said that I think the state govt. should take the responsibility for the situation and restore law and order instead of blaming others. To a question that the Central govt. should intervene to control the situation, Smt. Natarajan said that I think the issue about the intervention of the Central govt. is a Constitutional procedure laid down between governor's report and the view taken by the Union Cabinet. I can only say that we call upon the state govt. to restore order immediately. To a question on social fragmentation happening on religious lives, Smt. Natarajan said that I feel that this situation is something which is a dangerous precedent and any hostilities arisesing out of fragmentation of opinion. It is the primary and constitutional responsibility of the govt. of that state to ensure that such hostilities do not occur.

4341. (21-11-2007) NEW DELHI : Retail prices of farm commodities monitored by the Department of Consumer Affairs have generally remained steady or shown mixed trend over the week ending November 19, 2007. Prices of wheat at retail level remained steady at almost all the monitoring centres. Retail price of sugar remained steady over the week across most of the centres. Prices increased at Delhi by 50 paise per kg. Prices of gram dal have generally remained steady across majority of the monitoring centres. Prices increased at Delhi, Shimla and Chennai, and decreased at Ahmedabad and Bangalore. Prices of tur dal declined at Jaipur and increased at Shimla; in other centres prices remained steady.

4342. (21-11-2007) NEW DELHI : AIIMS like institutions are to be set up at six places in different parts of the country. For the construction of medical college and hospital complex, the Design Detailed Project Report (DPR) consultants have been selected for all the six sites. DPR would be available by May-June, 2008.

In so far as construction of housing complex is concerned, the bid process for selecting the turnkey developer was carried out for all sites. However, only 2 bids were received, of which one was found responsive. The work has been awarded to developer (M/s. Rajasthan State Road Development Corporation) for Jodhpur. The work relating to construction of housing complex at Rishikesh and Patna has been entrusted to HLL and for Bhubaneswar and Raipur to HSCC, on nomination basis. For Bhopal site, housing complex work would be awarded alongside with the hospital-medical college work. The state-wise progress regarding construction of AIIMS like institutions can be seen at Annexure.

4343. (21-11-2007) NEW DELHI : Based on the teaching and other infrastructural facilities available at a medical institution/college and the recommendations of Medical Council of India (MCI) thereon, permission is granted by the Central Government for the establishment of new medical college. The State-wise list of medical colleges, which have been permitted by the Central Government for being set up during the last three years, *i.e.* 2005-06, 2006-07 and 2007-08 can be seen at Annexure. As per MCI inspection report on medical colleges there is a shortage of teachers in pre-clinical and para-clinical subjects of Anatomy, Physiology, Biochemistry, Microbiology, Pharmacology, Forensic Medicine and Community Medicine. The State Governments and Medical Colleges are being encouraged to start more postgraduate courses in these disciplines. Permission is also given by the Central Government to applicant institutions to start these courses.

4344. (21-11-2007) NEW DELHI : Shri K.C. Jena, Chairman. Railway Board gave away the prizes to the winners of the 54th All India Railway Tennis Championship, organized by Railway Board Sports Association, here today. The prize money of Rs. 50, 000/- for the team championship was given to the Western Railway whereas South Central Railway was given a cash prize of Rs. 25, 000/ - for Runner-up in this category. The winner in Men's Single, Vishnu Vardhan of South Central Railway has bagged a cash prize of Rs. 25, 000/- and Aditya Medkekar has won cash prize of Rs. 15, 000/ for Runner-up. Winner in the Veteran Singles, Sunil Jain of Western Railway was given a cash prize of Rs. 15, 000/ - and P.Ram Kumar of South Central Railway was given Rs. 10, 000/- for Runner-up. From South Central Railway, the winners K.Purushottam and M.Samuel in the Veteran Doubles final won a cash prize of Rs. 5000/- each and Runner-up Hanumantha Rao and P.Ram Kumar given a cash prize of Rs. 3000/- each. Speaking at the closing ceremony of the Championship, which was held from 17th to 21st November 2007 in New Delhi, Shri K.C.Jena said that championship winners' deep-rooted dedication, sheer hard-work and utmost zeal to be victorious has taken them to the forefront of individual excellence. He said that performances of players in the championship have not only won laurels for the Zonal Railways which they represent but has also added to the pride of Indian Railways.

4345. (21-11-2007) NEW DELHI : Despite clear directions of the High Court of Delhi against any strike restraining employees/doctors of AIIMS from resorting to any strike around 500 meters of AIIMS, the doctors of AIIMS were on strike on a number of occasions during 2006-07 and 2007-08. The details are as under:- i) During 14.5.2006 to 31.5.2006, AIIMS doctors resorted to strike protesting against the policy of the Government for providing reservation to OBC in Central Educational Institutions. AIIMS premises was used as hub of activities during the said period. ii) During 5.7.2006 to 7.7.2006, the AIIMS doctors again resorted to strike mainly against the decision of the Institute Body to curtail the tenure of Director, AIIMS. Services were resorted only on the orders dated 7.7.2006 of High Court of Delhi. iii) During 28.8.2007 to 30.8.2007, the Doctors of AIIMS were on strike which was mainly because of delay in holding of Convocation for issue of degrees. iv) On 8.11.2007, emergency services were stopped due to manhandling of doctors by the relatives of a patient. The Government has advised the Director, AIIMS to ensure that the doctors/other employees of AIIMS do not resort to strike in violation of the orders passed by the High Court/Supreme Court of India, if necessary, with the assistance of Police. The Institute Body at its meeting held on 18.10.2006 also sought the response from Director, AIIMS on the action taken to ensure that the patient care services were not affected during the strike period of 2006. His response is yet to be considered by the Institute Body. This information was given by the Minister for Health & Family Welfare, Dr. Anbumani Ramadoss in a written reply to a question in the Lok Sabha.

4346. (21-11-2007) NEW DELHI : In order to overcome the shortage of Scientists/ Engineers, an exclusive Institute *i.e.* Indian Institute of Space Science and Technology (IIST) has been started by Indian Space Research Organization (ISRO). The education is totally subsidized and the students passing out of the institute with more than 60% of marks will be given guaranteed jobs in ISRO establishment with the condition for serving a minimum period of 5 years. It is estimated that about 150 graduates from IIST would be absorbed into ISRO/DOS annually. This will significantly improve the situation. This information was given by the Minister of State in the Prime Minister's Office, Shri Prithviraj Chavan in the Lok Sabha today.

4347. (21-11-2007) NEW DELHI : Shri Jay Prakash Narain Yadav, the Minister of State for Water Resources has said that the people should not feel inferior while using Hindi language. Presiding over the Hindi Salahakar Samiti Meeting of the M/o Water Resources here today, he said that the use of Hindi language in our day to day life as well as in official capacity should be encouraged by all. He called upon the officials of the Ministry of Water Resources to contribute for the development of Hindi language as Hindi is the beat of the heart of the country and the progress of the country cannot be imagined without Hindi. He however, said that some commonly used English words may be adopted for smooth communication purposes. He asked the Ministry officials to provide official information in Hindi language for their better understanding. Shri Yadav also presented the 'Raj Bhasha Vaijayanti Puraskars' to the three organizations of the

Ministry of Water Resources-WAPCOS; Central Water Commission and CSMRS, for the optimum use of Hindi in official matters. The Members who attended the Meeting included S/Sh Prasana Kumar Patsani, Syed Hamid Ail, Dr. Smt. Sarojini Mahishi, Dr. Premanand Panchal, Smt. B.S. Shanta Bai, Ms. Aradhana Chaudhary, Krishna Das, Narayan Kumar, and Dr. B.S. Roy Chaudhary. Secretary Water Resources Smt. Gauri Chatterjee and senior officials of the Ministry of Water Resources and its subordinate offices attended the Meeting.

4348. (21-11-2007) NEW DELHI : Following is the text of the address of the Vice President of India Mohd. Hamid Ansari at the 'International Conference on Emerging Security Concerns in West Asia' here today: "It is a pleasure to be back on a familiar platform. Familiarity in this case, however, is a disadvantage since I may be in danger of repeating what I may have articulated on previous occasions! Many years back the British philosopher Gilbert Ryle had drawn attention to the dangers of expressions that are 'couched in syntactical form improper to the facts recorded'. This observation is relevant to our subject today since the theme of the conference begs definition and delineation. Unanimity of perception, of course, would have been ideal; since that is lacking, the two operative terms-'emerging' and 'security concerns'-need to be spelt out. Centrality has been the curse of West Asia. It is hardly necessary to remind this audience that external security concerns pertaining to the region have been around for over a century. Writing in 1917, Marriott defined the Eastern Question as 'the problem of filling up the vacuum created by the gradual disappearance of the Turkish Empire from Europe'. In May 1917, Britain and France used the Sykes-Picot Agreement to acquire 'the right of priority in enterprises and local loans' in designated Arab areas of the Ottoman Empire and to deny any facilities to a third Power in the Arabian Peninsula and the Red Sea. In a parallel move, the secret Balfour Declaration of November 1917 carried the commitment for the 'establishment in Palestine of a national home for the Jewish people'. A decade earlier on August 31, 1907, the Anglo-Russian Entente was signed, dividing Iran into three zones only one of which was under Iranian control. 'The Iranians', in Professor Nikkie Keddie's words, 'were neither consulted on the agreement nor informed of the terms'. That exercise, of division and occupation, was repeated during World War II.

4349. (21-11-2007) NEW DELHI : As compared to the month of September, 2007, the All-India Consumer Price Index Numbers for Agricultural Labourers and Rural Labourers (Base: 1986-87=100) for October, 2007 increased by 3 points each to stand at 413 (Four hundred and thirteen) points for both the series. The rise/fall in index varied from State to State. In the case of Agricultural Labourers, 17 States reflected an increase in index ranging between 1 and 7 points; in 1 State the declining index decreased by 2 points while in 2 States the index remained constant. Haryana with 447 points topped the index table whereas Manipur was at the bottom with the index level of 362 points. In the case of Rural Labourers, in 17 States, index reflected an increase ranging between 1 and 7 points; in 1 State the index decreased by 1 point whereas in 2 States the index remained constant. Punjab was at the top of the index table with 447 points whereas Manipur was at the bottom with 363 points. The Consumer Price Index Numbers of Bihar and Himachal Pradesh for Agricultural Labourers and Bihar and Haryana in respect of Rural Labourers registered the highest increase of 7 points each mainly due to increase in the prices of rice, wheat atta, maize, milk, onion, vegetables & fruits, firewood, leather shoes and allopathic medicine. The indices in respect of Uttar Pradesh registered a fall of 2 points and 1 point for Agricultural and Rural Labourers respectively mainly due to decrease in the prices of rice, maize urd dal, mustard oil, fish fresh, vegetables & fruits and gur.1

4350. (21-11-2007) NEW DELHI : The Prime Minister, Dr. Manmohan Singh, met the Prime Minister of Malaysia, Mr. Datuk Seri Abdullah Ahmad Badawi in Singapore today on the sidelines of the 6th ASEAN Summit. The meeting took place in an extremely warm and cordial atmosphere. The Malaysian Prime Minister invited PM to visit Malaysia. Both leaders reviewed the progress of negotiations on the India-ASEAN FTA and agreed to accelerate efforts to conclude them by March 2008. Dr. Manmohan Singh welcomed the participation of Malaysian companies in India particularly in infrastructure development. Both sides agreed to increase bilateral trade and economic cooperation as well as investment in each other's country. It was a useful and productive meeting. The leaders looked forward to meeting once again during the forthcoming CHOGM Summit in Kampala.

4351. (21-11-2007) NEW DELHI : The Government introduced a new kind of visa called 'Medical Visa' to foreign tourists in June, 2005. It is granted to foreigners who have sought preliminary medical advice from their country of origin/residence and have been advised to go for specialised medical treatment. The Indian Missions/Posts abroad scrutinise the medical documents to satisfy themselves about the bona fide purpose for which medical treatment visa is being requested. The initial validity of medical visa is one year or the period of treatment, whichever is less. It can be extended for a further period of one year by the State Governments/Foreigners Regional Registration Offices (FRROs)/Foreigners Registration Offices (FROs) on production of medical certificate from reputable/ recognised/specialised hospitals in India. Further extensions can be granted by the Ministry of Home Affairs on the recommendations of the State Governments/ FRROs/FROs supported by appropriate medical documents. The visa is valid for a maximum of three entries during the year. Foreigners coming to India on medical visa are required to get themselves registered with the concerned FRROs within 14 days from the date of their arrival in India. The objective of such a visa is to help foreigners who wish to utilise specialised medical health care facilities in India and to promote medical tourism. The Medical visa is different from a tourist visa. The purpose of tourist visa is tourism and such a visa cannot be converted into any other type of visa or extended beyond six months *i.e.* the initial period for which it is granted. Foreigners holding tourist visa are not required to register themselves with the concerned FRROs if their continuous stay in the country does not exceed six months. Medical visa is initially granted for one year and can be extended as per the requirements of the medical treatment. Medical visa holders are required to register themselves with the concerned FRROs within 14 days of their arrival in India. The above information was given by the Minister of State in the Ministry of External Affairs, Shri E. Ahmed in written reply to a question in Lok Sabha today.

4352. (21-11-2007) NEW DELHI : Government are in the process of considering a Logistics Support Agreement with the USA as a facilitating framework for mutual logistical support when deploying defence resources in disaster relief operations or joint exercises and without commitment for assistance in situations of armed conflict. The Agreement will not affect the independence of India's foreign policy. The logistical support that will be provided in disaster relief operations abroad will enhance India's ability to assist affected countries efficiently. This was stated by the Minister of External Affairs, Shri Pranab Mukherjee in written reply to a question in Lok Sabha today.

4353. (21-11-2007) NEW DELHI : The Minister of State in the Ministry of External Affairs, Shri E. Ahmed informed the Lok Sabha today in written reply to a question that the Government of India makes arrangements to facilitate the transportation of 110, 000 pilgrims going to Saudi Arabia for Haj 2007 through the Haj Committee of India and facilitates provision of accommodation and other logistical support for them. For efficient management and supervision of Haj arrangements, seasonal local staff, supervisors, data entry operators, drivers and messengers have been appointed by the Consulate General of India, Jeddah. In addition, Doctors, Nurses and other para-medical staff, Coordinators, Assistant Haj Officers, Haj Assistants and Khadimul Hujjaj are sent from India on short-term deputation to Saudi Arabia. A hospital in Makkah and branch offices-cum-dispensaries in Makkah and Madina are set up for Haj pilgrims. Medicines provided at these dispensaries and hospital are supplied from India and also procured locally. Eight additional ambulances for the Haj Mission in Jeddah have been sanctioned which would substantially add to the medical facilities which are provided to the pilgrims. The Government is also making arrangements for providing polio, meningitis and influenza vaccinations for the pilgrims. The Haj Committee of India is providing to the pilgrims information regarding confirmation of their seats, travel documents, transportation, accommodation, release of foreign exchange, embarkation points and departure dates etc. The Government has taken a number of decisions to streamline the functioning of Private Tour Operators so that they provide proper services and facilities for 47000 pilgrims. Varanasi has been introduced as 16th Embarkation Point from this year. The Government would ensure that satisfactory arrangements are made to facilitate the travel of the Haj pilgrims to Saudi Arabia through all the 16 embarkation points in India to Jeddah and Madinah. Both Air India and Saudi Arabian Airlines have rendered service to the pilgrims in this effort. The expenditure incurred by the Government for the Haj 2006-II is estimated as Rs.23, 35, 42, 728/- and subsidy granted (Provisional) is Rs. 348.00 crores.

4354. (21-11-2007) NEW DELHI : The Minister of State in the Ministry of External Affairs, Shri E. Ahmed informed the Lok Sabha today in written reply to a question that the Government of India makes arrangements to facilitate the transportation of 110, 000 pilgrims going to Saudi Arabia for Haj 2007 through the Haj Committee of India and facilitates provision of accommodation and other logistical support for them. For efficient management and supervision of Haj arrangements, seasonal local staff, supervisors, data entry operators, drivers and messengers have been appointed by the Consulate General of India, Jeddah. In addition, Doctors, Nurses and other para-medical staff, Coordinators, Assistant Haj Officers, Haj Assistants and Khadimul Hujjaj are sent from India on short-term deputation to Saudi Arabia. A hospital in Makkah and branch offices-cum-dispensaries in Makkah and Madina are set up for Haj pilgrims. Medicines provided at these dispensaries and hospital are supplied from India and also procured locally. Eight additional ambulances for the Haj Mission in Jeddah have been sanctioned which would substantially add to the medical facilities which are provided to the pilgrims. The Government is also making arrangements for providing polio, meningitis and influenza vaccinations for the pilgrims. The Haj Committee of India is providing to the pilgrims information regarding confirmation of their seats, travel documents, transportation, accommodation, release of foreign exchange, embarkation points and departure dates etc. The Government has taken a number of decisions to streamline the functioning of Private Tour Operators so that they provide proper services and facilities for 47000 pilgrims. Varanasi has been introduced as 16th Embarkation Point from this year. The Government would ensure that satisfactory arrangements are made to facilitate the travel of the Haj pilgrims to Saudi Arabia through all the 16 embarkation points in India to Jeddah and Madinah. Both Air India and Saudi Arabian Airlines have rendered service to the pilgrims in this effort. The expenditure incurred by the Government for the Haj 2006-II is estimated as Rs.23, 35, 42, 728/- and subsidy granted (Provisional) is Rs. 348.00 crores.

4355. (21-11-2007) NEW DELHI : The Minister of State for Textiles, Shri E.V.K.S. Elangovan, informed the Rajya Sabha today, in a written reply to a question by Shri Jai Prakash Aggarwal that apart from China, Indian textile exports is also facing competition from countries like Indonesia, Cambodia, Vietnam and Pakistan.

4356. (21-11-2007) NEW DELHI : The Minister of State for Textiles, Shri E.V.K.S. Elangovan, informed the Rajya Sabha today, in a written reply to a question by Shri B. J. Panda And Ms. Pramila Bohidar that taking into account submissions of textiles and clothing export promotion councils and other associations, that the exports of textiles have been adversely affected due to the appreciation in the value of the Indian rupee vis-a-vis US dollar in the recent months, the Government has provided several relief measures, which include increase in Duty Entitlement Pass Book and Duty Drawback rates, exemption from service tax on select services, reduction in interest rates of pre-shipment and post-shipment credit and faster clearance of arrears of terminal excise duties and Central Sales Tax. These measures are applicable for the entire country including the State of Orissa. The Minister further informed that the target for the current fiscal year for textiles and clothing exports is US$ 25.06 billion. It is hoped that the textiles industry would be making sincere efforts to achieve the export target in the current fiscal year.

4357. (21-11-2007) NEW DELHI : The Railways have generated Rs. 25423.59 crore of revenue earnings from freight traffic during the first seven months (*i.e.* April-October 2007) of the current financial year 2007-08 as compared to Rs. 22894.67 crore during the corresponding period last year, registering an increase of 11.05 per cent. Railways carried 435.71 million tonnes of freight traffic during April-October 2007 as compared to 403.33 million tonnes carried during the corresponding period last year, reflecting an increase of 8.03 per cent. The Net Tonne Kilo Metres (NTKM) went up from 265201 million during the months of April-October 2006 to 279367 million during April-October 2007, with an increase of 5.34 per cent. The earnings from freight traffic during the month of October 2007 was Rs. 3976.29 crore, compared to Rs. 3356.77 crore during the corresponding period last year showing an increase of 18.46 per cent. Railways carried 66.05 million tonnes of freight traffic during the month of October 2007 as compared to 58.76 million tonnes of freight traffic during the corresponding period last year, registering an increase of 12.41 per cent. The Net Tonne Kilo Metres (NTKM) went up from 38690 million during the month of October 2006 to 41804 million during October 2007, showing an increase of 8.05 per cent. Of the total earnings during the month of October 2007, Rs. 1461.51 crore came from transportation of 27.97 million tonnes of coal, followed by Rs. 648.48 crore from 11.92 million tonnes of iron ore, Rs. 367.66 crore from 6.93 million tonnes of cement, Rs. 249.04 crore from 2.97 million tonnes of petroleum oil and lubricant (POL), Rs. 241.39 crore from 2.57 million tonnes of foodgrains, Rs. 255.00 crore from 2.41 million tonnes of iron & finished steel, Rs. 236.60 crore from 3.56 million tonnes of fertilizers, Rs. 64.43 crore from 0.97 million tonnes of raw material for steel plants except iron ore and Rs. 452.18 crore from 8.84 million tonnes of other goods.

4358. (21-11-2007) NEW DELHI : The Economic Ministers of ASEAN and India held an informal consultation on November 20, 2007 at the sidelines of the 13th ASEAN Summit in Singapore. They reviewed the progress of negotiations for the Trade in Goods Agreement of the AIFTA. The Economic Ministers noted with satisfaction the progress made since the last meeting at Cebu. While the main elements of the modalities have been agreed upon, a few issues relating to preferential access for a few products remain. Both sides have agreed to settle these issues by March 2008 with a view to concluding the AIFTA Trade in Goods Agreements by the ASEAN Economic Ministers (AEM) Retreat in May 2008.

4359. (21-11-2007) NEW DELHI : President Smt.Pratibha Devisingh Patil will release a set of four commemorative postage stamps on Renewable Energy tomorrow in New Delhi. The stamps depict the four common applications of renewable energy *i.e.* Solar Energy, Wind Energy, Small Hydropower and Biomass Energy.

4360. (21-11-2007) NEW DELHI : Prof. Saifuddin Soz, the Union Minister for Water Resources has said that the choice of water resources development project is governed by many factors including geographical and geological conditions. Earlier, developments were done at the best possible sites and in future, we have to develop projects at more challenging sites for which we need detailed investigations and adoption of latest techniques and technologies. Addressing the Consultative Committee Meeting of the Ministry of Water Resources on the subject " The Role and Functions of Central Soil and Material Research Station (CSMRS)" here today, the Minister said that CSMRS plays a vital role in research in the area of Geo-technical Engineering, Construction Materials and Material Quality etc. the field investigations backed by analysis of sample in laboratories provide valuable input for planning and design etc. Prof. Soz further said that we are fully aware about the importance of research which provides valuable input in planning any development activity and helps to make it more technically sound, economical and safe. This is all the more so in the case of water resources sector where we face numerous challenges. We have made considerable development in water resources sector and many projects have been developed. However, a lot more remains to be done. Addressing on the occasion Minister of State for Water Resources Shri Jai Prakash Narayan Yadav said that CSMRS is doing commendable in the field of Soil and Material Research and it should expand its activities to all parts of the country.

4361. (21-11-2007) NEW DELHI : Following is the Statement of the Tourism Secretary, Govt. of India, Sh. S. Banerjee on "Climate Change and Tourism". The Statement was delivered at the Ministerial Summit on Tourism and Climate Change held at London on November 13, 2007. "As a developing country, it is important for India to strive to bring to its people a better quality of life and a higher level of human development. In this regard, we are making major efforts to achieve the Millennium Development Goals and other internationally agreed development objectives apart from those we have set ourselves nationally. India is acutely aware of the considerable challenge we face today from climate change. We, like other developing countries, bear an inordinate share of the burden of Climate Change even though this is due to high-level emissions of developed countries. In such circumstances, we must significantly shore up our abilities to cope with and adapt to Climate Change. To be able to do so, we need development, which is also the best form of adaptation. Tourism now plays an extremely important role in the economy of our country and we would like to see this sector deliver on its full potential in assisting us with accelerated economic growth and development. The Indian tourism industry has witnessed an increase of 13.5% in international tourist arrivals in 2006 and this on the rise. We are very conscious of the need to promote sustainable development of tourism. Our efforts are aimed at making India an ecologically and socially sensitive tourism destination. The UN Framework Convention on Climate Change (UNFCCC) has one of the largest number of State Parties of any multilateral instrument. It is, therefore, appropriate that matters relating to climate change are addressed in the UNFCCC. At the UN-WTO we need to try and take stock of the situation as it affects our sector and see what can be done to adapt to the inevitability of further global warming, especially as far as developing countries are concerned. One of the main aims of UNWTO is to pay particular attention to policy measures in the field of tourism and not concern itself with matters relating to negotiations on climate change and what is being addressed in other forums. In this regard, we would like to see the Davos Declaration that we have before us, concentrate on policies and measures in the tourism sector. We have made some suggestions to ensure that the Declaration focuses on our mandate. We note that the Declaration seeks to promote the concept of 'tourist destination carbon footprint'. Such a measure needs to reflect the inherent carbon footprint of the destination and should not be used as non-tariff barriers to the flow of tourism in the world. The UNWTO aims at assisting developing countries in the field of tourism. It should not become an instrument to maintain economic status quo and encourage the use of environmental conditionalities as barriers to international tourism, particularly in developing countries".

4362. (21-11-2007) NEW DELHI : Various Committees such as Malimath Committee, Prof. Madhav Menon Committee and Soli Sorabjee Committee have emphasized the need for investigation and prosecution of crimes having inter-state and international linkages by a central agency. The Ministry of Home Affairs has been considering this issue in consultation with the State Governments. Most of the States, from which comments have been received, have expressed reservations/ apprehensions on this issue, police and public order being subjects in the State list in the Seventh Schedule of the Constitution. This was stated in a written reply to a question in Rajya Sabha today by the Minister of State in the Ministry of Home Affairs, Shri Sriprakash Jaiswal.

4363. (21-11-2007) NEW DELHI : The Government is in the process of amending the Persons with Disability Act, 1995 to make it more effective in the present context. Stating this at a joint workshop of the Ministry and the World Bank, the Minister of Social Justice & Empowerment, Smt. Meira Kumar said that her Ministry is following a consultative process for this purpose where the stakeholders representing Disabled Peoples' Organizatio[illegible] NGOs, experts of various disciplines and members of civil society are participating. Smt. Kumar said that the consultations with regard to proposed changes in the Act were held across the country to ensure that the concerns from different regions are adequately addressed when the Ministry proposes the amendments in the Act. The Minister emphasized that persons with disabilities are always involved in the process of policy and implementation framework through their organizations in Central as well as state coordination committees and also through Central and State Executive Committees, which are the highest policy making and monitoring bodies established under the Act. Even in the management committees of the most of our institutions, the persons with disabilities are always represented, she pointed out and added that the Government is committed to the full empowerment of persons with disabilities. Referring to the UN Convention on the rights of persons with disabilities, the Minister said that it has brought out a number of new concepts like alternative mode of communication, concept of accessibility of Information and Communication Technologies including web access to PWDs and the concept of reasonable accommodation to enable them to be equal participant in all spheres of activities. These concepts would be considered in due course and necessary changes in legislations, rules, policies and programmes of the Government would be made, she said. However, Smt. Kumar reminded the participants that the objective to empower the persons with disabilities would be achieved only if we empower those living in remote, inaccessible and rural areas and give special emphasis to empower women and children with disabilities. "We have to bring them in mainstream and work towards improving their quality of life and ensure that they lead the life of dignity and self-respect", she reiterated.

4364. (21-11-2007) NEW DELHI : India is rushing humanitarian relief supplies of about Rs 4 crores for cyclone affected victims of Bangladesh. The first consignment of about 40 tonnes of material including tents, blankets, made ready-to-eat food packets and medicines will leave tomorrow morning in an IL-76 aircraft of Indian Air Force. A decision to this effect was taken today at a high level meeting held in the Ministry of Defence and was attended by representatives from Ministries of External Affairs and Home. It may be recalled that Bangladesh was hit by a severe cyclone on Nov 15, 2007, which reportedly left more than 3000 people dead, several thousands homeless and severely damaged the infrastructure.

4365. (21-11-2007) NEW DELHI : "In-principle" approval has been accorded by the Government of India for the coastal sites at Kudankulam in Tamil Nadu and Jaitapur in Maharashtra, for setting up of 2 X 1000 MWe nuclear power reactors each. Further, the Site Selection Committee (SSC) constituted by the Government of India has evaluated the potential of coastal sites in Andhra Pradesh, Gujarat, Orissa and West Bengal for setting up of future nuclear power reactors. However, no decision has been taken. The Government has been exploring international cooperation in the civilian nuclear energy sector with all potential partners. This information was given by the Minister of State in the Prime Minister's Office, Shri Prithviraj Chavan in the Lok Sabha today.

4366. (21-11-2007) NEW DELHI : Prime Minister, Dr. Manmohan Singh had a bilateral meeting with Premier Wen Jiabao of the People's Republic of China today in Singapore. This is their second meeting this year. They had earlier met at the Second EAS in Cebu in January. The Two Prime Ministers reiterated their readiness to take the India-China Strategic and Cooperative Partnership for Peace and Prosperity to a new level. Premier Wen conveyed that friendship with India is the strategic and long term objective of China. Prime Minister told Premier Wen that India attaches great importance to our partnership with China, and is resolved to ensuring the comprehensive development of bilateral relations for mutual benefit and on the basis of mutual sensitivity to each others' concerns. They reiterated their readiness to see a fair, reasonable and mutually acceptable solution to the Boundary Question and expressed satisfaction at the progress that is being made by the Special Representatives in this regard. The two Prime Ministers discussed opportunities that exist for furthering cooperation in regional and multilateral forums on global issues such as climate change and energy security. Premier Wen was forthcoming and supportive of international civil nuclear energy cooperation with India. Premier Wen conveyed that the Chinese Government and people were eagerly awaiting the visit of Prime Minister to China. Prime Minister said that he is looking forward to his visit early next year, and expressed his confidence that his visit will further strengthen the friendly relations between the peoples of the two countries.

4367. (21-11-2007) NEW DELHI : The Prime Minister, Dr. Manmohan Singh, made a statement at the 6th India-ASEAN Summit in Singapore today. Following is the text of the speech of the Prime Minister on the occasion: "I thank you for your warm welcome, the friendly atmosphere and your generous hospitality. I am very happy to be here in Singapore, a country that epitomizes the qualities of courage, strength and excellence. It is always a pleasure to be among friends. India is privileged to be part of a process that is contributing to ever widening circles of prosperity. Our relationship with the ASEAN countries is the pillar of our "Look East" policy. Ever since we became Sectoral Dialogue partners of ASEAN 15 years ago, we have taken substantial strides in integrating our economies, societies and institutions. We are determined to take this process forward because we are convinced that it is a win-win formula for both of us. India is now on a new growth trajectory, where sustained economic growth of 9-10% per year seems possible. Our expanding market, human resources and strengths in science and technology and the knowledge economy are what we contribute to the process of economic integration.

4368. (21-11-2007) NEW DELHI : During the current financial year 2007-08, the Ministry of Tourism has released Rs. 294.50 crore for 126 projects (upto

October, 2007) to State Governments and Union Territory Administrations for development and creation of infrastructure at tourist destinations/circuits.

4369. (21-11-2007) NEW DELHI : The Prime Minister, Dr. Manmohan Singh, met the Prime Minister of Japan, Mr. Yasuo Fukuda in Singapore today. Following are the briefing points of the meeting: The Prime Minister had a bilateral meeting with the Prime Minister Yasuo Fukuda of Japan today. This was Prime Minister's first meeting with Prime Minister Fukuda. The meeting was marked by warmth and friendship. The two Prime Ministers reiterated their commitment to Strategic and Global Partnership which has been established between India and Japan and exchanged views on the way to deepen their partnership. They agreed on the importance of maintaining regular high level exchanges and the need to expedite progress on projects that are part of the Special Economic Partnership Initiative. They reviewed the progress in regard to the Dedicated Freight Corridor and the Delhi-Mumbai Industrial Corridor. Both Prime Ministers shared the view that the East Asia Summit is an important building block for the creation of an Asian Economic Community and pledged to work closely to further their objective. They agreed to strengthen their cooperation in regional and multilateral fora on important issues such as UN Security Council Reforms and Climate Change. Prime Minister Fukuda invited Prime Minister to visit Japan next year. Prime Minister has accepted the invitation with pleasure.

4370. (22-11-2007) NEW DELHI : The 38th International Film Festival of India (IFFI-07) takes off tomorrow at Goa. Noted film actor Shahrukh Khan will be the Chief Guest at the inaugural ceremony. The inaugural lamp will be lit with the assistance of Priyamani, the rising star of southern cinema. Inaugural function will be attended by Minister of Information & Broadcasting and Parliamentary Affairs, Shri P. R. Dasmunsi and Chief Minister of Goa, Shri Digambar Kamat besides several important film personalities. The Palme D' OR winner of Cannes 2007-titled 4 months, 3 weeks & 2 day would be the opening film. The Director of the opening film Mr. Cristian Mungiu and the main actress, Anamaria Marinca would be present at the inaugural ceremony. Besides, there would be other foreign delegates representing various international film festivals from Netherlands, China, Poland and Mexico. A major delegation from Poland and China will also be present. Portugal-Spain film 'Fados' directed by Carlos Saura will be the closing film for the Festival. The Cinema of the World Section will feature a choice of year's best international cinema. This section will have 76 films from 42 countries. A specialized competition for feature films by Asian, African and Latin American Directors is being organized. Under this section, fourteen films from 13 countries have been selected for the competition. Competition Jury is headed by the eminent award winning film maker from Hungary Ms Marta Mazaros, who has won awards in Cannes/Berlin/Venice and San Sebastian Intl Film Festivals. Other members of the Jury are, actress Meltem Cumbul (Turkey); Cinematographer Shaji N Karun, Film Director and Script writer from Kerala; noted Argentinian film director Pablo

Cesar and Mr. Robert Sarkies, film maker from New Zealand. Hungary will be in focus under the section 'Country Focus'. Seven films "Black Brush' (Director: Roland Vranik), 'Dealer' (Director: Benedek Fliegauf), 'Eastern Sugar' (Director: Ferenc Torok), 'Hukkle' (Director: Gyorgy Palfi), 'Temptations' (Director: Zoltan Kamondi), 'The Porcelain Doll' (Director: Peter Gardos) and 'Vagabond' (Director: Gyorgy Szomjas). In 'Film India Worldwide' category, three films 'AIDS Jaago' (Mira Nair), 'Amal' (Richie Mehta) and 'The Pool' (Chris Smith). Retrospective of Ingmar Bergman would feature seven of his highly acclaimed films, namely, 'Autumn Sonata', 'Fanny and Alexander', 'The Seventh Seal', 'The Virgin Spring', 'Through a Glass Darkly', 'Shame', and 'Wild Strawberries'. Indian Panorama at IFFI-2007 would present a bouquet of 36 films, 21 features and 15 non-feature films. The package is a mixed bag with stalwarts like Budhadeb Dasgupta and Adoor Gopalakrishnan presenting two films each. The section would have Ami Iyasin Aar Amaar Madhubala (The Voueurs-Feature) and Naushad Ali-the Melody continues (Non Feature) by Budhadeb Dasgupta and Naalu Penunungal (Four Women-Feature) and The Dance of the Enchantress (Non Feature) by Adoor Gopalakrishnan.

4371. (22-11-2007) NEW DELHI : Smt.Pratibha Devisingh Patil, said that today as we aim for a 10% growth rate we must recognise the critical importance of energy security. We will need a new paradigm of energy security to address our development goals which are environmental friendly and leads to sustainable developments. Inaugurating the Silver Jubilee function of the Ministry of New & Renewable Energy, the President further said that today India is among the global leaders in the development and deployment of renewable energy technologies, we need to significantly augment our efforts in front line research and development. Paying tribute to Smt. Indira Gandhi, the then Prime Minister, Smt. Patil said her vision was translated into vigorous action by Shri Rajiv Gandhi to meet the increasing demands for energy. Appreciating the increasing involvement of the private sector in the renewable energy sector, she said we have to concentrate in this sector. She said we have to secure our planet for future generations. Excess to critical and promising clean, new and renewable energy technologies to developing countries should be the keys in the global environment agenda.

4372. (22-11-2007) NEW DELHI : International Film Festival of India (IFFI)-2007 starts in Goa on November 23, 2007 with the Palme D' OR winner of Cannes 2007-titled 4 months, 3 weeks & 2 day as the opening film. The opening ceremony would be simple and elegant and keeping with international standards. Noted film actor Shahrukh Khan will be the Chief Guest at the inaugural ceremony which will be attended by Minister of Information & Broadcasting and Parliamentary Affairs, Shri P. R. Dasmunsi and Chief Minister of Goa, Shri Digambar Kamat besides several important film personalities. The inaugural lamp will be lit with the assistance of Priyamani, the rising star of southern cinema. The Director of the opening film Mr. Cristian Mungiu and the main actress, Anamaria Marinca would be present at the inaugural ceremony. Besides, there would be other foreign delegates representing various international film festivals from Netherlands, China, Poland and Mexico. A major delegation from Poland and China will also be present.

4373. (22-11-2007) NEW DELHI : 17 Cadres of various outfits surrendered today at Laipuli Army Camp in Assam. Police and civilian dignitaries including close relatives of the cadres were also present at the occasion. The protracted and sustained efforts by the units of 181 Mountain Brigade based in Tinsukia and Dibrugarh districts led to the surrender of these militants. The surrender ceremony at Laipuli camp was held in the presence of Brigadier Binoy Poonnen the Commander of 181 Mountain Brigade, Mr. Phukan, ADC Tinsukia, Mr. P Gogoi, ADC Dibrugarh, Mr. Prashant Bhuyan, SP Tinsukia, Commanding Officers of 11 GUARDS, 6 JAMMU and KASHMIR RIFLE, 2 BIHAR, 19 KUMAON and other army officials. Brigadier Poonnen spoke on behalf of Major General NC Marwah, General Officer Commanding, Dah Division and congratulated the surrendered cadres for their bold and wise decision to return to the mainstream of society.

4374. (22-11-2007) NEW DELHI : An IAF IL-76 aircraft carrying relief material for the cyclone-Sidr affected people of Bangladesh departed today from Palam airport at 1110 hrs. The IL-76 carried a part of Indian Government aid for relief of the victims in Bangladesh comprising, Tents, Rations (ready to eat), medicines, water purifying kits and Blankets. The balance of relief material would be dispatched by IL-76 aircraft on 23 and 24 Nov 07. The IAF's IL-76 would be delivering these loads at the Bangladesh Capital city of Dhaka. The IL-76 which carried the load belongs to the Nagpur based 44 Sqn and was captained by Wg Cdr J Narula Speaking the media persons prior to the departure Wg Cdr Narula said "It is a privilege for me and my crew members to be the instruments in providing relief and succor for our brethren in their hour of need". It may be recalled that the Nagpur 44 Sqn had earlier carried the relief aid on behalf of the Indian Government to the Hurricane Katrina victims in US and also to Philippines. The Integrated Defence staff of MoD is coordinating of the task for providing the relief material to Bangladesh, where the estimated death toll and damage due to the cyclone 'Sidr' is substantial. The relief worth one million USD on behalf of the Indian Government is being overall coordinated under the auspices of Ministry of External Affairs.

4375. (22-11-2007) NEW DELHI : The Minister of State for Petroleum and Natural Gas Shri Dinsha Patel informed the Lok Sabha in a written reply today that the second phase of the redevelopment of Mumbai High South has been approved by ONGC Board on October 3, 2007 at an estimated cost of Rs. 5713.07 crore with completion schedule of 31.5 months from the date of approval. The project envisages an incremental gain of 20.7 MMT of oil and 3.32 BCM of gas by the year 2030.

4376. (22-11-2007) NEW DELHI : A team of 12 cyclists from Directorate General of Quality Assurance (DGQA) was seen off from Delhi today by Major General Arun S of DGQA. These cyclists had arrived here from Chandigarh on their way to Pune. The DGQA has organized this 1800 Kms Cycle Rally passing through seven states over a period of 22 days. This rally has been organized as an adventure sports activity to commemorate the Golden Jubilee year of DGQA. Shri V Uma Maheswara Rao, Additional Director General Quality Assurance flagged off the rally on 19th of this month at Chandigarh. The cyclists shall reach Pune, the finish point, by 10 Dec 07. A total of 50 personnel comprising army and civilian employees of different age groups and disciplines from all over the country are participating in the event. The aim of this expedition is to foster the spirit of adventure and develop comradeship and team building amongst participants. During the rally, cyclists shall endure physical and mental challenges. All among the route, they will get an opportunity to experience the pristine beauty of our rich culture and heritage. The bonds of national integration and unity in diversity shall be further strengthened. The Cycle Rally also spreads the message of reducing vehicular pollution and protecting our environment. Every drop of fuel matters and hence save fuel for tomorrow. Through the cycle rally, the emphasis is on under-taking a healthy exercise to remain fit, while on the road, the rising concern for 'Road Safety' and 'Traffic Discipline' shall attract the attention of on lookers.

4377. (22-11-2007) NEW DELHI : The National Environment Policy 2006 of Ministry of Environment & Forests inter alia addresses the issue of global warming. The following comprise essential elements of India's response to climate change: Adherence to the principle of common but differentiated responsibilities and respective capabilities of different countries in respect of both mitigation of green house gases (GHGs), and adaptation measures. Reliance on multilateral approaches, as opposed to bilateral or plurilateral or unilateral measures. Equal per-capita entitlements of global environmental resources to all countries. Over-riding priority of the right to development. Identify key vulnerabilities of India to climate change, in particular impacts on water resources, forests, coastal areas, agriculture, and health. Assess the need for adaptation to future climate change, and the scope for incorporating these in relevant programmes, including watershed management, coastal zone planning and regulation, forestry management, agricultural technologies and practices, and health programmes. Encourage Indian Industry to participate in the Clean Development Mechanism (CDM) through capacity building for identifying and preparing CDM projects, including in the financial sector. Participate in voluntary partnerships with other countries both developed and developing, to address the challenges of sustainable development and climate change, consistent with the provisions of the UN Framework Convention on Climate Change. Further, the Government has also set up "Expert Committee on Impacts of Climate Change" in May 2007 to study the impacts of anthropogenic climate change on India and to identify the measures that we may have to take in the future in relation to addressing vulnerability to anthropogenic climate change impacts. A coordination committee chaired by Hon'ble Prime Minister called "Prime Minister's Council on Climate Change to coordinate national action for assessment, adaptation and mitigation of climate change" was constituted on 6th June 2007. The focus of the Committee would be to: Evolve a coordinated response to issues relating to climate change at the national level; Provide oversight for formulation of action plans in the area of assessment, adaptation and mitigation of climate change; Periodically monitor key policy decisions. This information was given by the Minister of State in the Ministry of Environment and Forests, Shri S. Regupathy in a written reply to question in the Rajya Sabha today.

4378. (22-11-2007) NEW DELHI : The Minister of Tourism and Culture Smt. Ambika Soni has said that ten states namely; Andhra Pradesh, Karnataka, Goa, Kerala, Maharashtra, Himachal Pradesh, Rajasthan, Jammu & Kashmir, Uttar Pradesh and Delhi have deployed tourist police in one form or another In a written reply in the Lok Sabha today she said, safety & security is a State subject and the decision regarding introduction of tourist police has to be taken by the concerned State Governments. The Ministry of Tourism has been advising all State Governments to deploy tourist police for the safety & security of foreign & domestic tourists.

4379. (22-11-2007) NEW DELHI : Five lions in Gir Forests in Gujarat have been killed recently due to electrocution caused by electrified wire fencing put up by the villagers.This information has been received from the State Government of Gujarat. The State Government has investigated the matter. Following the investigation, four persons have been arrested and sent to judicial custody. To ensure non-recurrence of such cases, the State Government has taken the following steps: The peripheral region of Gir and other habitats of lion have been scanned for illegal electric fencing. Patrolling in the peripheral region has been intensified. Paschim Gujarat Vij Supply Company has been requested to guard against such illegal use of power and illegal electrified fencing. Awareness campaign has been intensified in the region to sensitize villagers against wildlife crime. This information was given by the Minister of State in the Ministry of Environment and Forests, Sh. S. Regupathy in a written reply to question in the Rajya Sabha today.

4380. (22-11-2007) NEW DELHI : Bt cotton is the only genetically engineered crop approved by the Genetic Engineering Approval Committee (GEAC) for commercial cultivation in nine cotton growing states. These states are Andhra Pradesh, Gujarat, Haryana, Karnataka, Madhya Pradesh, Maharashtra, Punjab, Rajasthan and Tamil Nadu. The total area under Bt cotton cultivation is approximately 128, 44, 000 acres. The GEAC has also approved the field testing of Bt rice, Bt okra, Bt brinjal, Bt tomato, Bt potato, Bt groundnut and Bt cotton expressing new gene events of which field trials of Bt rice, Bt okra, Bt brinjal and Bt cotton have been initiated. The states where field trials of GM crops have been undertaken include Andhra Pradesh, Bihar, Chhattisgarh, Delhi, Gujarat, Haryana, Jharkhand, Karnataka, Madhya Pradesh, Maharashtra, Punjab, Rajasthan,

Tamil Nadu, Uttar Pradesh and West Bengal. Extensive Rules and guidelines have been framed for evaluating the environmental and health safety aspects of genetically modified crops. The GEAC also takes into consideration the results of the biosafety data, findings of the field trials as well as recommendations of the Monitoring cum Evaluation Committee (MEC) constituted by the Government for evaluating the field trials of GM crops and recommendations of the Indian Council of Agriculture Research (ICAR) before approving the GM crop for commercial cultivation. Only those transgenic crops which are found to be safe for human consumption as well as the environment are approved for commercial release This information was given by the Minister of State in the Ministry of Environment and Forests, Sh. Namo Narain Meena in a written reply to question in the Rajya Sabha today.

4381. (22-11-2007) NEW DELHI : The forest areas does not continuously reduce in the country. A report on the status of forest cover which is brought out by Forest Survey of India though say that about 3000 Km2 has been increased from the year 2001 to 2003. The total area of forests was 675538 KM2 in 2001. The assessment of 2003 shows the forest cover increased to 678333 Km2. For protection of existing forests financial assistance is provided to the states and Union Territories under the integrated forests protection Schemes. The activities carried out under the scheme include forest fire management and control, mobility, survey, demarcation etc. This information was given by the Minister of State in the Ministry of Environment and Forests, Shri S. Regupathy in a written reply to question in the Rajya Sabha today.

4382. (22-11-2007) NEW DELHI : 844 Projects in various sectors of developmental activities are pending for environmental clearance. The Government has revised Environmental Clearance Process through an Environment Impact Assessment (EIA) Notification issued vide S.O. No. 1533 (E) dated 14th September, 2006 superseding the earlier EIA Notification, 1994 to make the Environmental Clearance Process more transparent, efficient and de-centralized with certainty in time frame. The EIA Notification, 2006 provides for Scoping for preparation of quality EIA Reports, Structured Public Consultations with stipulated time frame, Decentralization of environmental clearance by constituting State Level Environment Impact Assessment Authority (SEIAA) and State Level Expert Appraisal Committee (SEAC) and time limits at each stage, thus enabling speedy clearance of projects. This information was given by the Minister of State in the Ministry of Environment and Forests, Shri S. Regupathy in a written reply to question in the Rajya Sabha today.

4383. (22-11-2007) NEW DELHI : Apart from the discharge of effluent into the surplus water course of the river Cauvery, There is no hazardous chemical residue is reported to be mixed in the river Cauvery, but only effluent into the surplus water cores is being discharge as per information provided by Tamil Nadu Pollution Control Board (TNPCB). M/s Chemplast Sanmar Pvt. Ltd. group is operating five units in Mettur area of Tamil Nadu. Four units of the group were generating trade effluent from their processing activities and the same were reported to be discharged in their own land from the initial period onwards. Presently, the treated trade effluent of the three units is being discharged using pipelines after satisfying the standards prescribed by the Board into the surplus water course of the river Cauvery. The effluent of the fourth unit is reported to be treated and reused in the process. The fifth unit is reported to recycle the effluent of their process, hence producing no discharge. The TNPCB has received a representation in respect of the units of M/s Chemplast Sanmar Pvt. Ltd. The State Pollution Control Board has directed two units of the group to achieve zero discharge. Works are under progress in the units to achieve zero discharge. As regards the third unit, the same is reported to have been converted from mercury cell process to membrane cell process, which has been commissioned during August 2007. The Chemplast group has also been directed to carry out the health study in the vicinity of the unit in Mettur and also in the nearby villages. This information was given by the Minister of State in the Ministry of Environment and Forests, Sh. Namo Narain Meena in a written reply to question in the Rajya Sabha today.

4384. (22-11-2007) NEW DELHI : An IAF IL-76 aircraft carrying relief material for the cyclone-Sidr affected people of Bangladesh departed today from Palam airport at 1110 hrs. The IL-76 carried a part of Indian Government aid for relief of the victims in Bangladesh comprising, Tents, Rations (ready to eat), medicines, water purifying kits and Blankets. The balance of relief material would be dispatched by IL-76 aircraft on 23 and 24 Nov 07. The IAF's IL-76 would be delivering these loads at the Bangladesh Capital city of Dhaka. The IL-76 which carried the load belongs to the Nagpur based 44 Sqn and was captained by Wg Cdr J Narula Speaking the media persons prior to the departure Wg Cdr Narula said "It is a privilege for me and my crew members to be the instruments in providing relief and succor for our brethren in their hour of need". It may be recalled that the Nagpur 44 Sqn had earlier carried the relief aid on behalf of the Indian Government to the Hurricane Katrina victims in US and also to Philippines. The Integrated Defence staff of MoD is coordinating of the task for providing the relief material to Bangladesh, where the estimated death toll and damage due to the cyclone 'Sidr' is substantial. The relief worth one million USD on behalf of the Indian Government is being overall coordinated under the auspices of Ministry of External Affairs

4385. (22-11-2007) NEW DELHI : The scheme of plantation of trees is being implemented is 28 states of the country. This includes hill regions also. The Ministry of Environment and Forests is implementing the National Afforestation Programme (NAP) Scheme to regenerate degraded forests and adjoining areas through a two-tier decentralized mechanism of Forest Development Agency (FDA) at Forest Division level and Joint Forest Management Committees (JFMCs) at village level. The members of the JFMCs include farmers in the JFM villages. As on 31.3.2007, 729 FDA projects were approved at a total cost of Rs. 1658.09

crores to cover project area of 9.36 lakh hectares through 24, 215 JFMCs. The benefits from the area regenerated under the scheme are shared with the members of JFMCs as per the JFM resolution of the respective States to directly support the livelihoods of the people. In addition, the scheme supports livelihoods of JFMC members by providing assistance for taking up Entry Point Activities which are decided by the JFMC members themselves. This information was given by the Minister of State in the Ministry of Environment and Forests, Shri S. Regupathy in a written reply to question in the Rajya Sabha today.

4386. (22-11-2007) NEW DELHI : Developed countries who are Party to Kyoto Protocol have emission reduction targets and overall they have to reduce their emissions by 5.2% during 2008-12 from 1990 levels. As per their National Communications to the United Nations Framework Convention on Climate Change (UNFCCC), these Parties claim to be taking actions to achieve their targets. However it is early to judge whether they will be able to achieve their targets. Some non-Parties to Kyoto Protocol, namely, USA and Australia, have also taken some measures for reducing emissions.

4387. (22-11-2007) NEW DELHI : The criteria for establishing the core or critical tiger habitat in tiger reserves has been finalised, and action has been taken for delineating such areas by States based on the assessment made by Project Tiger (now the National Tiger Conservation Authority) and the Wildlife Institute of India. An amount of Rs. 30 cores has been allocated for village relocation to create inviolate areas in identified core or critical tiger habitats in tiger reserves during the current financial year. This information was given by the Minister of State in the Ministry of Environment and Forests, Shri S. Regupathy in a written reply to question in the Rajya Sabha today.

4388. (22-11-2007) NEW DELHI : Mr. Vilas Muttemwar said that Renewable Energy is the ultimate answer to the Climate Change and Global Warming. This carbon free energy is seen as energy of the future whose development and deployment requires all possible encouragement. Addressing a Conference on "Clean Energy & Energy Efficiency" organised by PHD Chamber of Commerce and Industry, Mr. Muttemwar added that the Renewable Energy is now in Global focus. It has come into centre stage in all International Deliberations on the future of the planet in the context of Global Warming. This year's Nobel Peace Prize being conferred to the Inter-Governmental Panel on Climate Change (IPCC) is a testimony to the World-Wide realisation that Global Warming and Climate Change are the stark and the biggest challenge the world has to grapple with. Mr. Muttemwar informed that the Ministry is working for facilitating the implementation of broad spectrum programme covering the entire range of New and Renewable Energy sources. Referring to the Industrial Sector the Minister said there is significant opportunity to produce electricity and thermal energy in the cogeneration mode. There is potential for generation of about 15000 MW through cogeneration in various core industries such as pulp and paper industries, breweries, food and fruit processing industries, caustic soda plants, textile miles, distilleries, fertilizer plants, solvent extraction units, rice miles etc. Mr. Muttemwar said such conferences will provide an effective platform where a big push can be given to Renewable Energy and Energy Conservation. He appealed industries to come forward in this field. The message of the Minister was read by Dr. K.P. Sukumaran, Advisor, and Ministry of New & Renewable Energy. Clarifying certain form the participant Dr. Sukumaran said that the Ministry is supplementing energy need of the country, not replacing the present energy scenario he further added the initial hiccup regarding carbon credit have been cleared. He also informed that turbines have been modified and comprehensive data for wind energy is available.

4389. (22-11-2007) NEW DELHI : Researchers have estimated 3-4 % increase of carbon emissions per annum which is not the fastest globally. The Government of India had submitted its inventory of Green house gases (GHGs) emissions including Carbon-dioxide emissions as of 1994 and United Nations Framework Convention on Climate Change (UNFCCC) in its first National Communication in June 2004.

4390. (22-11-2007) NEW DELHI : Railways have introduced a number of schemes like a slew of Freight Incentive Scheme this year for attracting more rail traffic like: Traditional Empty Flow Direction (30% discount), loading Bagged Consignment in BOXN (40% discount), Long term Special Incentive Scheme (20% concession), Incremental Traffic (15% discount), Lump sum Special Rates and Service Level Agreement, Freight Forwarders, Two Leg Freight Concession (15% in busy season and 20% in lean season). Besides, Ministry of Railways has been considering individual proposal for grant of Freight Concession in Freight Rates to tap traffic. Few proposals are; 30% concession of booking of Iron-ore, 50% concession for rice traffic, 15% concession for timber waste and 13% concession on movement of gunny bale or jute traffic. For passenger traffic, steps taken to increase the earnings are; Generating additional seating capacity in trains by introducing new trains, reduction of fare of Ist AC and 2nd AC, attaching additional coaches to clear wait listed passengers and introduction of up gradation scheme to upgrade full fare paying passenger to next higher class against available accommodation.

4391. (22-11-2007) NEW DELHI : The State Government of Orissa has asked for Rs. 23 crores from Ministry of Environment & Forests to save the coastal areas of the State from losses due to sea tide. As per the information made available by the National Disaster Management Authority, the Government of India has formulated a National Cyclone Risk Mitigation Project (NCRMP) to be implemented with World Bank assistance. One of the investment proposals received under the Project from Government of Orissa is on "Shelterbelt Plantation" in Balasore, Bhadrakh, Jagatsinghpur and Kendrapada Districts at a total cost of about

Rs.23 crore. The Project is yet to be posed to the World Bank for their appraisal and funding. The Government of India has issued a Coastal Regulation Zone Notification in 1991 delineating the coastal areas into different zones and listing out permissible and non permissible activities. The activities which are permissible are appraised by duly constituted expert committee, wherever necessary, and decisions are taken such that environmental balance in the coastal areas are harmonized with activities taking place in that area. This information was given by the Minister of State in the Ministry of Environment and Forests, Shri S. Regupathy in a written reply to question in the Rajya Sabha today.

4392. (22-11-2007) NEW DELHI : The electromagnetic radiations are always present from any antenna emitting radio signals, whether it is a mobile phone tower or a broadcast tower etc. The level of electromagnetic radiations within safety limits is harmless. The latest Fact Sheet of World Health Organisation (WHO) (No. 304 of May, 2006)states that from all evidence accumulated so far, no adverse short or long-term health effects have been shown to occur from the RF signals produced by base stations. Since wireless networks produce generally lower RF signals than base stations, no adverse health effects are expected from exposure to them. Further, a Committee was setup up under the Director General, Indian Council of Medical Research (ICMR), as per the orders of Hon'ble High Court, Mumbai, to study the effects of radiations from mobile phone towers and related aspects. The Committee had studied the effects and concluded that overall there is not enough evidence to show direct health hazards of RF exposures from mobile base stations. This information was given by Dr.Shakeel Ahmad, Minister of State for Ministry of Communications and Information Technology in the Rajya Sabha today in a written reply to a question by Shri Motilal Vora and Shri Satyavrat Chaturvedi.

4393. (22-11-2007) VIENNA: India on Wednesday began the process of negotiating a country-specific safeguards agreement with the International Atomic Energy Agency (IAEA) after the Left parties gave the clearance to the government to go ahead with talks with the agency. Atomic Energy Commission Chairman Anil Kakodkar, arriving here in the morning, held discussions with IAEA Director-General Mohammad ElBaradei. It was decided to initiate consultations on India-specific safeguards, which will pave the way for international civilian nuclear cooperation, the IAEA said in a statement. An Indian team will have meetings this week with the IAEA secretariat to work on a safeguards agreement, it said. After months of standoff over the civilian nuclear deal with the United States, the Left parties last week allowed the government to go ahead with negotiations with the IAEA on the condition that it will not initial any accord but bring back the draft to the United Progressive Alliance-Left committee on the nuclear deal.

4394. (22-11-2007) NEW DELHI : Communications have been sent to Prime Minister on issues related to licencing and allocation of spectrum aspects which includes, among others, licensing procedures, enhancement of subscribers linked spectrum allocation criteria, spectrum charges, use of dual technology by telecom service providers etc. M/s S. Tel Ltd., in their letter, have stated, among others, that "S Tel is of the view that the policy that was evolved when the industry was at its infancy, will not serve the public purpose now, when the industry is among the most advanced. Consistent with its knowledge and understanding of the business of telecom and the high value of spectrum, S Tel comes forward voluntarily to pay additional revenue share to the extent of Rs. 6000 crores to the DOT, over and above the spectrum charges revenue share payable as per the existing policy, over a period of 10 years from the date of the spectrum allotment. This will bring into effect a prioritization model, which will fully subserve the larger public interest." The Government has decided to grant new Unified Access Services (UAS) Licences as per the existing policy. This information was given by Dr.Shakeel Ahmad, Minister of State for Ministry of Communications and Information Technology in the Rajya Sabha today in a written reply to a question by Shri Gireesh Kumar Sanghi and Shri Dharam Pal Sabharwal.

4395. (22-11-2007) NEW DELHI : Government have set a target to achieve 80 million rural subscribers by 2010. Department of Information Technology has embarked upon a programme of setting up 100, 000 Community Service Centres (CSCs) to cater to e-governance requirements of 600, 000 villages in the country in a phased manner. Government have launched a scheme, through Universal Service Obligation Fund (USOF), for provision of support for setting up and managing 631 infrastructure sites spread over 70 districts in North-Eastern states for providing mobile services including other Wireless Access Services (WAS) in the specified rural and remote areas, where there is no existing fixed wireless or mobile coverage. The Government has also approved a scheme for providing support for establishing 100, 000 Broadband, Internet enabled, Common Services Centres (CSCs) in rural areas of the country including that of North-Eastern States. Department of Information Technology will implement the scheme in a public private partnership mode. The support for the North-East for this scheme has been pegged at 75% of the normative value as against national value of 33per cent. This information was given by Dr.Shakeel Ahmad, Minister of State for Ministry of Communications and Information Technology in the Rajya Sabha today in a written reply to a question by Shrimati Shobhana Bhartia and Shrimati Supriya Sule.

4396. (22-11-2007) NEW DELHI : As on 30-9-2007, Government has provided Village Public Telephones (VPTs) to 34, 554 villages including Gram Panchayats. Universal Service Obligation Fund (USOF) has entered into an agreement with Bharat Sanchar Nigam Limited (BSNL) for provision of VPTs in remaining 12, 386 unconnected villages in Rajasthan. This excludes villages having population less than 100, lying in thick forest areas/naxalite infested areas etc. As on 30-9-2007, out of 12, 386 unconnected eligible villages in Rajasthan, 10, 696 villages have been provided with VPT facility and the remaining 1, 690 villages will be provided with VPTs progressively by June, 2008. This information was given by Dr.Shakeel Ahmad, Minister of State for Ministry of Communications and Information Technology in the Rajya Sabha today in a written reply to a question by Shri Harish Rawat.

4397. (22-11-2007) NEW DELHI : On 29th August 2007, Government received the recommendations of Telecom Regulatory Authority of India (TRAI) on "Review of license terms & conditions and capping of number of access providers". TRAI has made recommendations, inter-alia, on number of Access Services telecom operators, spectrum allocation criterion, mergers and acquisitions etc. Government has already taken a decision on TRAI's recommendations on 17.10.2007, inter-alia, accepting that there should be no cap on the number of access services provider in any service area and usages of dual technology (Code Division Multiple Access (CDMA) and Global System for Mobile Communications (GSM) be permitted to existing Unified Access Services (UAS) licensees. TRAI has made above said recommendations after following a consultation process with the stakeholders including GSM operators and their association viz. Cellular Operators Association of India (COAI). However, COAI & some of the GSM Operators have challenged the decision of Government on TRAI's recommendations in Telecom disputes Settlement and Appellate Tribunal (TDSAT) and the matter is sub-judice. This information was given by Dr.Shakeel Ahmad, Minister of State for Ministry of Communications and Information Technology in the Rajya Sabha today in a written reply to a question by Shrimati N.P.Durga.

4398. (22-11-2007) NEW DELHI : The Computers stolen from Defence Materials & Stores Research & Development Establishment (DMSRDE) Kanpur were used for routine work and did not contain any classified or secret data. DMSRDE has filed FIR with the local police station for investigations as per the preliminary report submitted by the enquiry committee. DMSRDE is basically Science & Technology related laboratory working in the areas on non-metallic materials and textiles.

4399. (22-11-2007) NEW DELHI : Various passenger amenities/facilities have been provided at railway stations for the convenience of the passengers. These are augmented on regular basis. During the year 2006-07, Railways spent Rs. 407.9 crore on various passenger amenities works. During the current year budgetary provisions of Rs. 493 crore under Passenger Amenities Head has been made.

4400. (22-11-2007) NEW DELHI : A Memorandum of Understanding (MoU) has been signed between Ministry of Railways and M/S Kirloskar Pneumatic Company Limited (KPCL) on 19.07.2007 for running of Road-Railer (RR) train initially on Delhi-Chennai sector as a pilot project. No agreement has yet been signed for this purpose. However, as per the MoU, Indian Railways will provide line haul service with its locomotives to operate RR Trains. M/S KPCL will operate inter modal freight service with Road-Railer equipment. This would cover freight consolidation/collection of freight on road, long distance line haul between end points on rail and delivery of freight on road. M/S KPCL will provide all necessary equipment including Road-Railer units for the inter modal operation and will be responsible for marketing, freight consolidation, collection and delivery of freight on road, coupling and de-coupling of Road-Railer units at terminal. Indian Railways will be benefited by way of attracting light weight, high value, white goods traffic which generally moves by road, increase in pool of rolling stock with new versatile multimode wagons. Such wagons which move both on rail as well as road are presently not available with Indian Railways. Through this pilot project Indian Railway can judge the efficacy of such wagons. This information was given by the Minister of State for Railways Shri R.Velu in written reply to a question in the Lok Sabha today

4401. (22-11-2007) NEW DELHI : Indian Railways have sanctioned a pilot project namely Satellite Imaging for Rail Navigation (SIMRAN) for Real Time Passenger Information System. This project is being developed by utilizing Global Positioning System (GPS). This project is being carried out jointly by Research Designs & Standard Organization (RDSO), Lucknow and Indian Institute of Technology (IIT), Kanpur. The pilot project is sanctioned for development for hardware and software for providing Real Time Train Running Information to the passengers.

4402. (22-11-2007) NEW DELHI : Most of the new line and gauge conversion projects except a few required on operational considerations are aimed to improve connectivity to backward, tribal, remote and under-developed areas of the country so as to bring about socio-economic development of the region through which the line passes. However, railways have a huge throwforward of projects requiring over Rs. 61, 000 crore for completion. The funds are limited and projects are being progressed as per the availability of resources.

4403. (22-11-2007) NEW DELHI : The State Government of Maharashtra has requested the cooperation of Mumbai Port Trust to jointly work with the Government of Maharashtra so as to work out a land development plan that would benefit the city of Mumbai. It has, therefore, been decided to set up a Standing Committee under the Chairmanship of Chief Secretary, Maharashtra with Chairman, Mumbai Port Trust and other stake-holders as members to sort out various issues of Mumbai Port vis-à-vis development of Mumbai City. This information was given by the Minister of Shipping, Road Transport and Highways, Thiru T. R. Baalu in a written reply in the Rajya Sabha today.

4404. (22-11-2007) NEW DELHI : The Minister of Tourism and Culture Smt. Ambika Soni has said that the Ministry of Tourism extends Central Financial Assistance (CFA) to the State Governments/Union Territories for development of tourism circuits/destinations including Eco-Tourism sites under the Scheme of Product/Infrastructure Development for Destinations and Circuits.

4405. (22-11-2007) NEW DELHI : It is proposed to develop two new national waterways in West Bengal-Orissa and Andhra Pradesh-Tamil Nadu. A proposal to declare Kakinada-Puducherry stretch of canals consisting of Kakinada canal, Eluru canal, Commannur canal, Buckingham canal and Kaluvelly tank along with Bhadrachalam-Rajahmundry stretch of River Godavari and Wazirabad-Viyayawada stretch of River Krishna (1095 kms) as a National Waterway is under consideration of the Govt. This Waterway System is in the States of Andhra Pradesh, and Tamil Nadu and Union Territory of Puducherry. The Bill for enacting Central legislation was introduced on 08.12.2006. It was referred to the Parliamentary Standing Committee on Transport, Tourism and Culture for examination. The Parliamentary Standing Committee has recently submitted its report. Follow up action is being taken. The total estimated cost of the project is Rs 542 cr (at 2002 prices). Similarly, a proposal to declare Geonkhali-Charbatia stretch of East Coast Canal (217 km) along with Charbatia-Dhamra stretch of Matai river (40 km), Talcher-Dhamra stretch of River Brahmani (265 km) and Mangalgadi-Paradip stretch of Mahanadi delta rivers (101 km) in the States of West Bengal and Orissa as a National Waterway is also under consideration of the Government. The bill for enacting Central legislation for this waterway was introduced in the Parliament on 08.12.2006. It was referred to the Parliamentary Standing Committee on Transport, Tourism and Culture for examination. The Parliamentary Standing Committee has recently submitted its report. Follow up action is being taken. The total estimated cost of this project is Rs 1526 cr. (at 2002 prices). This information was given by the Minister of Shipping, Road Transport and Highways, Thiru T.R. Baalu in a written reply in the Rajya Sabha today.

4406. (22-11-2007) NEW DELHI : The Ministry of Information & Broadcasting is examining a draft Optical Disc Law to check piracy in the film sector. This was stated by Secretary, (I&B), Smt. Asha Swarup in her remarks at the "India-The Big Picture Conference 2007", organized by Confederation of Indian Industry (CII) in Goa today. The draft law has been prepared by the members of film sector at the initiative of Government of India. The Government is encouraging digital exhibition as it helps access the market easily, she added. Smt. Swarup said that the Government is attempting to enhance the benefits relating to custom duty also for this sector as digitalization reduces the cost of distribution of films and also helps films in reaching B and C category centres very fast, besides acting as a deterrent to piracy. The Secretary said that the I&B Ministry is actively pursuing the creation of a National Centre for Excellence in Animation, Gaming and Visual Effects with a view to promote this emerging sector. The Ministry of Human Resource Development has been also requested to include these sectors in the curricula, at colleges and ITIs. She said that the Government initiative of setting up an Export Promotion Council for the entertainment sector has been very well received and the Indian film industry under the lead of the Film and Television Producers' Guild of India has come forward to form the Export Promotion Council. She exhorted all industry members to be a part of this initiative. She assured the industry of the continued Government support in helping the film industry grow at a faster pace and participating in foreign film festivals and markets. For a very long time films were also our best known exports. Though the audience have largely been the Indian disapora, we seem to be gradually developing audience among different cultures as well. Signing of co-production agreements with other countries facilitates films production. Film co-production agreements have been signed with Italy, Germany, Brazil and UK. Smt. Swarup said, discussions with the Government of UK for the Annex to the co-production agreement have come to conclusion and we are hopeful of signing this when the Prime Minister bilateral negotiations take place in January next year.

4407. (22-11-2007) NEW DELHI : The Ministry of Youth Affairs and Sports have been encouraging all sports disciplines in the country by giving financial assistance to recognized National Sports Federations. BCCI which is promoting the sports of Cricket however has never applied for financial assistance under the Scheme of the Ministry. Under the Scheme, the Ministry is providing financial assistance for participation in International Tournaments abroad, organizing International Tournaments in India, National Championships in India, Coaching Camps, engagement of foreign coaches, procurement of equipments etc. The financial assistance provided to various recognized National Sports Federations during the last 3 years is at Annexure, which excludes expenditure incurred towards National Coaching Camps and the engagement of foreign coaches, which is implemented through the Sports Authority of India. To encourage various sports and games in the country, financial assistance is given to promising sportspersons for training and training-cum-competitions in India and abroad, purchase of equipment, scientific support in sports disciplines, in Olympics, Asian, Commonwealth, Afro-Asian Games and other international events under the Scheme relating to Talent Search & Training etc.

4408. (22-11-2007) NEW DELHI : Should women be considered for combat roles? Vital issues like this and more concerning mental health, stress and behaviour would be intensely debated at a three-day International Conference in New Delhi on "Psychological Assessment in personnel selection", organized by the Defence Institute of Psychological Research (DIPR), a DRDO laboratory. Billed as the first such event in India on the theme of personnel selection, the conference would be inaugurated by the Defence Minister Shri AK Antony on Friday, November 23, 2007. More than 200 experts from India and abroad would discuss various aspects of personnel selection like development of psychological tests, ethical and gender issues and psychological aspects of job analysis. This includes 27 participants from 11 countries including the US, UK, Canada, Europe, Russia, Nigeria and Thailand. Prof. Robert Hogan (US), Dr. Richard Brady (UK), Prof. JP Das

(Canada), Prof. Chockalingam Viswesvaran (US), Prof. Filip Lievens (Belgium), Dr. Scott Hamilton (US), Mr. Oussama Mansour (Dubai) and Prof. Udai Pareek (India) are among the key speakers. Senior officers of the Army, Navy, Air Force and DRDO would also be joining the deliberations. Twenty nine papers would be presented by the delegates in six sessions. Besides, more than 30 posters depicting research studies by academicians and practioners would be exhibited on the sidelines of the conference. Underling the role of spirituality as a stress buster, the defence institute has intentionally scheduled a valedictory lecture by the Athrva Veda Sankaracharya of Srividya Peetham, Shri Ramakrishananda Saraswathy Swamigal on "The Spritirual Quotient". On Saturday Nov 24, the papers to be presented include 'Perceived stress as a predictor to adjustment in Army personnel', 'Occupational stress among defence personnel' in relation to their mental health', while on Sunday Nov 25, the topical issues include 'Stress coping strategies of Austrian Alpine soldiers' and an interesting poster presentation on 'Emotional competence of Manipuri students studying in Delhi and Manipur'.

4409. (22-11-2007) NEW DELHI : A team of 12 cyclists from Directorate General of Quality Assurance (DGQA) was seen off from Delhi today by Major General Arun S of DGQA. These cyclists had arrived here from Chandigarh on their way to Pune. The DGQA has organized this 1800 Kms Cycle Rally passing through seven states over a period of 22 days. This rally has been organized as an adventure sports activity to commemorate the Golden Jubilee year of DGQA. Shri V Uma Maheswara Rao, Additional Director General Quality Assurance flagged off the rally on 19th of this month at Chandigarh. The cyclists shall reach Pune, the finish point, by 10 Dec 07. A total of 50 personnel comprising army and civilian employees of different age groups and disciplines from all over the country are participating in the event. The aim of this expedition is to foster the spirit of adventure and develop comradeship and team building amongst participants. During the rally, cyclists shall endure physical and mental challenges. All among the route, they will get an opportunity to experience the pristine beauty of our rich culture and heritage. The bonds of national integration and unity in diversity shall be further strengthened. The Cycle Rally also spreads the message of reducing vehicular pollution and protecting our environment. Every drop of fuel matters and hence save fuel for tomorrow. Through the cycle rally, the emphasis is on under-taking a healthy exercise to remain fit, while on the road, the rising concern for 'Road Safety' and 'Traffic Discipline' shall attract the attention of on lookers.

4410. (22-11-2007) NEW DELHI : 33 works costing Rs. 600.00 crores have been completed on NH-7. Three contracts of four-laning of NH-7, one contract each in the States of Andhra Pradesh, Karnataka and Tamil Nadu have been delayed due to problems associated in acquisition of land, shifting of utilities, delay in construction of Road over Bridge (ROB) and poor performance of contractors. However, no request related to pending works has been received from the Government of Andhra Pradesh. The pending works are likely to be completed by June 2008. This information was given by the Minister of State for Shipping, Road Transport and Highways, Shri K.H. Muniyappa in a written reply in the Rajya Sabha today.

4411. (22-11-2007) NEW DELHI : Detection of road accidents on National Highways and to provide medical assistance to road accident victims is basically the responsibility of the State Government. The Ministry of Shipping, Road Transport & Highways has been providing ambulances to States/UTs/NGOs to evacuate accident victims to the nearest medical centre under National Highways Accident Relief Service Scheme. During the period from 2000-01 to 2006-07, 337 ambulances had been given to various States/NGOs under this scheme. In addition, National Highways Authority of India provides an ambulance at an average interval of 50 kms under their Operation and Maintenance Contracts/Build operate Transfer agreements on the completed stretches of National Highways entrusted to them. 96 ambulances have been deployed on National Highways by National Highways Authority of India. In strategic locations of few stretches, cameras were installed by National Highways Authority of India which facilitates quick detection of road accidents. During the IX & Xth Five Year Plan periods, Ministry of Health & Family Welfare were operating a scheme under which financial assistance of up-to Rs.1.50 crores was being provided to the State Government Hospitals located on National Highways for upgradation and strengthening of emergency facilities. Under this scheme, 113 State Government Hospitals were provided financial assistance during IX & Xth Five Year Plan. Ministry of Health & Family Welfare have now formulated a scheme to be implemented during the XIth Five Year Plan under which an integrated Trauma Care Centres Network is proposed to be got established in the State Government Hospital/Medical College located along the Golden Quadrilateral, North-South and East-West Corridors of the National Highways by providing financial assistance. This information was given by the Minister of State for Shipping, Road Transport and Highways, Shri K.H. Muniyappa in a written reply in the Rajya Sabha today.

4412. (22-11-2007) NEW DELHI : The pricing policy for new and expansion projects in urea sector has been notified by the Government in January 2004. There has been no indigenous investments in the Urea sector in last 8 years. The availability of gas, which is the critical feedstock for production of urea, has been one of the major constraint in attracting investments in this sector. In view of the projected improvement in availability of gas in future, the Government is looking into all options for finalisation of a new policy for investments in urea sector, which may attract investments in Urea Sector in all parts of the country. This information was given by the Minister of State for Chemicals & Fertilisers and Parliamentary Affairs Shri B.K. Handique in a written reply in the Lok Sabha today.

4413. (22-11-2007) NEW DELHI : A task force was set up by Ministry of External Affairs to review India's existing positions on disarmament and non-proliferation issues and to make recommendations in the light of India's status as a nuclear-weapon state, India's security interests, present international realities and possible developments. The task force has submitted its Report to Foreign Secretary. The task force was not mandated to deal with the issues related to the 123 Agreement with the United States. This was stated by the Minister of External Affairs, Shri Pranab Mukherjee in written reply to a question in Rajya Sabha today.

4414. (22-11-2007) NEW DELHI : External Affairs Minister, Shri Pranab Mukherjee informed the Rajya Sabha today in written reply to a question that it is correct that China refuses to recognize the Mac Mohan Line as the border between India and China. There is no commonly delineated Line of Actual Control (LAC) between India and China. From time to time, on account of differences in the perception of the LAC, situations have arisen on the ground that could have been avoided if we had a common perception of the LAC. Government regularly take up such perceived violations along the LAC with the Chinese side through established mechanisms including the Joint Working Group, the Expert Group, border personnel meetings, flag meetings and normal diplomatic channels. Both sides have also agreed to an early clarification of the LAC. The Joint Declaration issued during the visit of Chinese President to India in November last year stated, "It was agreed to complete the process of exchanging maps indicating their respective perceptions of the entire alignment of the LAC on the basis of already agreed parameters as soon as possible."

4415. (22-11-2007) NEW DELHI : The Prevention of Cruelty to Animals (PCA) Act, 1960 was enacted by the Central Government to prevent infliction of unnecessary pain or suffering on animals. Prevention of cruelty falls in the Concurrent List of the Constitution and hence the appropriate law enforcement machinery are the State Governments/Local Authorities. Animal Welfare Board of India (AWBI), the statutory body under the Ministry of Environment & Forests addresses all the State Governments to enforce the provisions regarding cruelties to animals and to book the offenders suitably. This information was given by the Minister of State in the Ministry of Environment and Forests, Sh. Namo Narain Meena in a written reply to question in the Rajya Sabha today.

4416. (22-11-2007) NEW DELHI : Prices of most of the anti cancer drugs are quite high. In order to reduce the prices of cancer medicines the Government has recommended to the Department of Revenue for Customs and Excise Duty exemption for all anti cancer drugs. Moreover in the proposed Draft National Pharmaceuticals Policy, 2006 it has been proposed, inter-alia, that Government would completely exempt all anti cancer drugs (bulk and formulations) from all types of Central taxes, excise duty, import duty etc., and effort would be made that the benefit would be passed on to the consumers. Industry and trade would be requested to reduce their margins to the barest minimum level and pass on the benefit to the consumers. A Cancer Medicines Assistance Scheme as a public-private partnership model has also been proposed for providing cheaper medicines to the patients through cancer hospitals. Draft National Pharmaceutical Policy was considered by the Cabinet at its meeting held on 11.1.2007. The Cabinet has referred the Policy to Group of Ministers (GOM). The First meeting of the GOM was held on 10.4.2007 and the Second meeting was held on 12.9.2007. No time frame has been set for finalizing the National Pharmaceuticals Policy.-Hide quoted text-This information was given by the Minister of State for Chemicals & Fertilisers and Parliamentary Affairs Shri B.K. Handique in a written reply in the Lok Sabha today.

4417. (22-11-2007) NEW DELHI : The Delhi Development Authority (DDA) has informed that in Rohini, apart from allotment of alternative plots to the farmers, whose land has been acquired, the allotment of DDA flats under different housing schemes, disposal of the residential plots through open auction and allotment of land to Group Housing Societies were undertaken. A HIG Housing Scheme was also implemented in Rohini by DDA in 2003. This information was given by Shri Ajay Maken, Minister of State for Urban Development in the Rajya Sabha today in a written reply to a question by Shri Rajkumar Dhoot.

4418. (22-11-2007) NEW DELHI : An Expert Committee was set up by this Ministry under the Chairmanship of Dr. P.V. Indiresan, Retd. Director, IIT Chennai to evaluate the Sky Bus System and examine its feasibility and techno-economic aspects. The Committee has submitted its report in August, 2005. The Committee has treated Sky Bus System as a technology development project rather than finished technology. The Committee, recommended extension of this project as technology development project not merely because of its novelty but also because of possibility of incidental technological benefits that may accrue to the nation through the processes developed in designing and producing the system. The Ministry of Railways has appointed a technical advisory group with ten eminent members to evaluate the novel system and guide for further development of further technology. The group has held three meetings so far. Ministry of Railways has also allocated an amount of Rs.25 crore for conducting further trial of sky bus metro leading to certification of technology under the guidance of Technical Advisory Group. This information was given by Shri Ajay Maken, Minister of State for Urban Development in the Rajya Sabha today in a written reply to a question by Shri Abu Asim Azmi.

4419. (22-11-2007) NEW DELHI : Steel Authority of India (SAIL) proposes to modernize and expand capacity of its plants and mines. The expansion plan of SAIL for its steel plants targets to increase production of hot metal from the present level of 14.6 million tonnes per annum (2006-07) to about 26 million tonnes per annum by the year 2010. Apart from augmenting the production capacity at the plants, the plan also envisages removal of technological obsolescence, reduction in energy consumption, improvement in product mix, up-gradation of pollution control measures and augmentation of infrastructure facilities in all the plants to support higher production. To meet the enhanced requirement arising from the expansion plans of the steel plants, SAIL has decided to modernize and expand its existing mines at Kiriburu, Meghahataburu, Gua, Bolani and Barsua and develop new mines at Rowghat, Chiria, Taldih and Thakurani. Rourkela Steel Plant (RSP) proposes to expand its capacity to achieve hot metal production of 4.5 million tonnes per annum at an indicative cost of Rs. 7668 crore. The expansion work of RSP is likely to commence by June'2008. This information was given by the Minister of State for Steel Dr. Akhilesh Das in a written reply in the Lok Sabha today.

4420. (22-11-2007) NEW DELHI : The people of Uttarakhand are still enjoying their traditional rights known as haq haqoob. However, the quantity of these rights have been reduced due to the ban imposed by Supreme court on felling of trees .The Government of India has enacted the Scheduled Tribe and Other Traditional Forest Dwellers (Recognition of Forest rights) Act, 2006 for recognition of the rights of the people living in and around forests This information was given by the Minister of State in the Ministry of Environment and Forests, Sh.S.Regupathy in a written reply to question in the Rajya Sabha today.

4421. (22-11-2007) NEW DELHI : The studies carried out by Department of Science & Technology on Gangotri Glacier have revealed that the Glacier was receding at the rate of 17.15 m/year during 1971-2004 period. Another study estimated a retreat of 12.10 m during the year 2004-05. Compilations of the data on secular movement of glaciers have revealed that the majority of the glaciers of the Himalayan region are passing through a phase of recession, which is a worldwide phenomenon. The causative factors for this variable retreat may be subnormal snowfall, higher temperature during summer, less severe winter or a combination of all of them. It could also be attributed to the phenomenon of rise in temperature, global warming, to some extent. The Government has not undertaken any study to correlate the river discharge, water level changes in sea and ocean and the recession of the glaciers. In addition to the glaciers, seasonal snow cover, groundwater and rainfall contribute to the river discharge. Due to enhanced melting of ice, consequent upon faster recession, the runoff of the Himalayan rivers may increase marginally. The recession of glaciers cannot be prevented on a large scale in view of the nature of Indian Himalayan Glaciers being debris covered, the economic feasibility, the scale of operation and the likelihood of pollution. As the prime responsibility of reducing emissions that enhance global warming lies with the Developed countries, the Government of India has been pressing in international negotiations that these countries should take deeper emission reduction commitments and for a longer period. This information was given by the Minister of State in the Ministry of Environment and Forests, Shri Namo Narayan Meena in a written reply to question in the Rajya Sabha today.

4422. (22-11-2007) NEW DELHI : The Union Minister of Social Justice & Empowerment, Smt. Meira Kumar has written to all the States to strengthen their

Channelising Agencies (SCAs) to meet the requirement of early disbursement of loans to the intended beneficiaries of the schemes of the National Backward Classes Finance and Development Corporation (NBCFDC). Addressing the Meeting of the Parliamentary Consultative Committee attached to her Ministry last evening, Smt. Kumar emphasized that unless the SCAs actively participates in the process of loan disbursement, it would be difficult for the NBCFDC to expand its coverage amongst the artisans and other small entrepreneurs belonging to the backward classes. She informed the Members that with the disbursement of Rs. 1282.82 Crore through SCAs to assist over eight lakh beneficiaries, the NBCFDC has achieved utilization of released funds upto 94% and cumulative repayment from SCAs is about 89% at the end of the financial year 2006-2007. The Minister said that the Corporation (NBCFDC) has streamlined the system of sanction of loan to the State Channelising Agencies and the funds are allocated to the SCAs on the basis of Annual Action Plan submitted by them at the beginning of the financial year. This measure, she said, has decentralized the delivery system and accelerated the pace of implementation of NBCFDC schemes at the grass-root level. Smt. Kumar said that the Corporation has also taken-up the cause of Micro Financing through SCAs and its loans are available to 4% p.a. to the women beneficiaries under Mahila Samirdhi Yojana. A sum of Rs. 108 Crore cumulatively has been disbursed under Micro Finance Scheme of NBCFDC benefiting over three lakh six thousand beneficiaries. The SCAs are also asked to identify best available artisans and handicraft persons and sponsor them to the exhibitions being held at prominent Fairs in Delhi and other Metros and big cities throughout the year. This year, the beneficiaries would be participating in 12 such exhibitions across the country and outside, she said. Participating in the discussion, the Members expressed satisfaction that the recovery rate of 89% on the loans disbursed by the Corporation is very good and this fact also makes the case that the coverage of loans to needy amongst the backwards classes should be enhanced. One Member suggested that a meeting of the concerned Ministers and officials of all the States should be organized to sort out the issues relating to the strengthening of the SCAs to ensure that the coverage of the loans to the needy artisans amongst the backward classes is increased as the present number of eight lakh beneficiaries needs to be enhanced.

4423. (22-11-2007) NEW DELHI : A Technical Group on Estimation of Housing Shortage has estimated Housing Shortage of 24.71 million at the end of the Tenth Five Year Plan in urban areas. Out of this, 99% of the shortage pertains to Economically Weaker Sections and Low Income Groups. This information was given by the Minister of State for Housing & Urban Poverty Alleviation, Kumari Selja in the Rajya Sabha today, in a written reply to a question by Shri Dharam Pal Sabharwal. The Minister further informed that the Government of India has launched the Jawaharlal Nehru National Urban Renewal Mission (JNNURM) to cope with the problem of shortage in housing and infrastructure services in a mission mode for 63 select cities under Basic Services to Urban Poor (BSUP). For remaining cities, a scheme namely Integrated Housing and Slum Development Programme (IHSDP) has also been launched under JNNURM. The component of assistance under the scheme includes upgradation and new construction of houses and infrastructural facilities like water supply and sanitation as part of slum improvement. Both BSUP and IHSDP are demand driven schemes and the fixation of targets as well as quantum of progress depends upon proposals submitted by State Governments/ Local Bodies. The Minister also informed that the Government is concerned about the rise in prices of houses. The Government, with a view of providing interest rate subsidy for housing loans availed by the urban poor including SCs/STs has made a budget provision of Rs.30.00 crore in the financial year 2007-08.

4424. (22-11-2007) NEW DELHI : A task force was constituted to prepare a National Urban Housing and Habitat Policy under the chairmanship of the then Secretary of Ministry of Urban Employment and Poverty Alleviation on 27.1.2005 with representatives from Planning Commission, Ministry of Finance and other Ministries/Departments/State Governments and Financial and other Institutions dealing with Housing Sector. This information was given by the Minister of State for Housing & Urban Poverty Alleviation, Kumari Selja in the Rajya Sabha today, in a written reply to a question by Shri Manohar Joshi. The task force had submitted a formal draft policy to this Ministry based on various inputs in the matter of Legal, Regulatory, Financial and Technological issues. The Minister further informed that Recommendations of the task force as well as inputs received from various State Governments and Central Ministries, non-Government organizations and other stakeholders have been utilized to formulate a draft National Urban Housing & Habitat Policy 2007 which among other issues also envisages measures for augmenting housing stock for Economically Weaker Sections and Low Income Groups.

4425. (23-11-2007) PANJI : The 38th International Film Festival of India (IFFI-07) got off to a flying start today at Goa. Noted film actor Shahrukh Khan inaugurated the Festival in the august presence of Minister of Information & Broadcasting and Parliamentary Affairs, Shri P. R. Dasmunsi and Chief Minister of Goa, Shri Digambar Kamat. The inaugural lamp was lit with the assistance of Priyamani, the rising star of south. In his remarks, Shahrukh Khan said, this premier event is a pride of the nation. Recognizing the contribution of the ordinary man in raising the popularity of cinema, he said 'lets dedicate 38th IFFI to ordinary people.' Mr. Khan said, cinema provides people independence from loneliness and a perceived bond with the celluloid characters. This enlivens the dreams and a course to look up to. He said, through the medium of cinema we try to reach out to others crossing cultural barriers. Shri Dasmunsi in his remarks announced the Government decision to confer life time achievement award on the veteran actor Dilip Kumar. Melody queen, Lata Mangeshkar will be conferred with the life time achievement award for film songs. Shri Dasmunsi said that in the present era of technological innovations, a new vision is needed to ensure its fruition for the benefit of commoners. Affordable cinema for the huge mass of film lovers in the country should be ensured by harnessing new technology. Indian film legends like Raj Kapoor, Amitabh Bachchan and Shahrukh Khan have been the true cultural ambassadors of India commanding worldwide following. He described Shahrukh Khan as a true icon of Indian youth and sports. The Minister said that the committee set up to suggest measures to tackle piracy in the film sector has since submitted its report and the Government is likely to finalize its view on Optical Disc laws for this purpose by December end. Shri Dasmunsi said that improved infrastructure in Goa is necessary to ensure its position as a desired destination. Continuing as a venue for IFFI, Goa should be able to grow up as an ultimate brand, he added. Chief Minister of Goa, Shri Kamat said that with the fourth consecutive IFFI, Goa has proved that it can successfully host events of this magnitude. Each year we have made improvements but for such events do take time to settle down, he said. Shri Kamat felt that brand IFFI would make Goa a sought after destination for foreign as well as Indian film makers. Secretary (I&B), Smt. Asha Swarup, Chief Secretary, Goa, Shri J. P. Singh, Panjim Mayor, Mr. Tony Rodrigues, Festival Director, Smt. Neelam Kapur and prominent film personalities were among those present.

4426. (23-11-2007) NEW DELHI : The Vice President of India, Mohd. Hamid Ansari has strongly condemned the simultaneous blasts that occurred today at Varanasi, Faizabad and Lucknow in Uttar Pradesh, killing and injuring innocent civilians. He expressed his sympathy for the families of those killed and injured in the explosions. He said that such acts of terrorism should be thwarted through our national resolve to maintain peace and harmony and counter all disruptive forces.

4427. (23-11-2007) NEW DELHI : The Ministry of Tribal Affairs has received some complaints, alleging (i) evacuation of the tribals and forest dwellers from the land being cultivated by them prior to 13.12.2005, by the Forest Department of the States of Gujarat, Rajasthan and Madhya Pradesh, (ii) surveys of land in occupation of tribals by the Forest Department in certain districts of Jharkhand with a view to prevent the process of giving pattas on the land to tribals, (iii) removal of tribal people from their dwelling places in the forest areas by the Government Madhya Pradesh despite enactment of the Scheduled Tribes and Other Traditional Forest Dwellers (Recognition of Forest Rights) Act, 2006, and (iv) diversion of forest land in Dhule District for wind power projects by the Government of Maharashtra. As the complaints were against the actions of the State Forest Departments, the same have been forwarded to the Ministry of Environment & Forests for necessary action. This was stated by the Minister of Tribal Affairs, Shri P.R. Kyndiah, Minister of Tribal Affairs in a reply to a question by Shri ABU Ayes Mondal in Lok Sabha today.

4428. (23-11-2007) NEW DELHI : The Prime Minister Dr. Manmohan Singh, has condemned the blasts in Uttar Pradesh. Dr. Manmohan Singh has condoled the loss of lives in the blasts and has expressed concern for the injured. The Prime Minister has announced an ex-gratia relief of Rs. One lakh for the next of the kin of the dead and Rs. Fifty thousand for the seriously injured from the Prime Minister's National Relief Fund

4429. (23-11-2007) NEW DELHI : The legal framework for contract farming under the State Agricultural Produce Marketing (Regulation) Acts will be quite helpful to the small farmers in securing better remuneration for their produce, particularly in backward areas/ districts, as such arrangements would cover the price risk and also the production risk to a great extent. Contract Farming has the potential of combining small farmers' efficiency with economy of scale, utilizing corporate management skills, providing assured markets and reducing transaction costs in the value chain by ensuring vertical integration. Several national and multinational processors or fast food chains are increasingly entering into contract with the farmers to encourage them to cultivate farm products (fruit, vegetables, etc.) of the desired quality by providing them not only seeds and other inputs but also assured procurement of the produce at pre-decided prices. Such tie-ups have special significance for small and marginal farmers, who have small marketed surplus and do not have staying power. They may not individually be capable of investing in technology, but through self help groups or cooperatives, there could emerge a desirable institutional framework, through which farmers can suitably reap the benefits of contract farming arrangements. Contract farming is particularly useful for high value crops because it enables the corporates to associate with the farmers and helps in imparting the latest technological know how to them. The Model Agricultural Produce Marketing (Regulation) Act circulated by the Central Government to the States in 2003 for implementing marketing reforms has provisions for the registration of contract farming sponsors and recording of contract farming agreements with the Agricultural Produce Marketing Committee (APMC) or a prescribed authority under the Act, protection of title or rights of the farmers over the land under such contracts, dispute settlement mechanism and a model draft agreement suggesting various terms and conditions. To help States in the formulation of Rules in this regard, the Ministry of Agriculture has also circulated a set of Model APMC Rules to them for adoption. By now, relevant provisions have been made by several State Governments/ UTs in their respective APMC Acts for providing a legal framework to contract farming. In seven States/ Union Territories there are no APMC Acts, therefore, there is no regulation of contract farming in such States / UTs. The Model Act circulated by the Ministry is suggestive in nature, and, since Agriculture is a State subject, it is for the State Governments to decide on the implementation, intermediation and monitoring of the contract farming arrangements in their State. This information was given by Shri Kanti Lal Bhuria, Minister of State for Agriculture in written reply to a question in the Rajya Sabha today.

4430. (23-11-2007) NEW DELHI : As per data compiled by Agriculture Ministry as on today, sowing is progressing well in the present rabi season. Wheat has been sown in 80 lakh ha as compared to 35 lakh ha at the end of last week. However, it is yet low as compared to the acreage under wheat during the corresponding period last year [104 lakh ha]. Winter rice sowing has just started in some southern States. So far, 90, 000 ha area has come under rice plantation. Coarse cereals have been sown in 49.44 lakh ha as compared to 53.75 lakh ha by this time in 2006. Rabi oilseeds have been sown in 57.32 lakh ha as compared to 75.33 lakh ha in the last rabi. Mustard/rapeseed coverage has reached 42.44 lakh ha (last rabi, up to this time: 57.58 lakh ha). Rabi pulses cover 78.88 lakh ha (last year: 79.07 lakh ha).

4431. (23-11-2007) NEW DELHI : The Union Home Minister, Shri Shivraj Patil has strongly condemned today's blasts in Uttar Pradesh. The following is the text of his statement. "I strongly condemn the blasts which have taken place in three different cities of Uttar Pradesh today. I convey my sympathies to the bereaved families and pray for speedy recovery of the injured. This is yet another attempt by anti-national elements to spread panic. I am confident that peace-loving people of the country will give a fitting reply to such elements. The Government will continue to fight terrorism in a resolute manner. We are in touch with the State Government to see if any assistance is required by them from the Centre".

4432. (23-11-2007) NEW DELHI : Addressing the delegates at the International Conference organized by the Association of Medical Doctors of Asia (AMDA) and Gandhi Ashram Reconstruction Trust (GART) on the theme 'How to Create a Network of Doctors and Support Staff for Crisis Areas due to Natural Calamities' today, the Union Minister for Health & Family Welfare, Dr. Anbumani Ramadoss said that the requirement of rural India to manage peripheral emergencies would be addressed when the National Rural Health Mission (NRHM) would be fully operative. The NRHM has laid down public health standards for medical care and operationalized Community Health Centres to work on 24x7 basis. The urban India's health care problems are being addressed through Urban Missions. Besides Dr. Nirmala Deshpande, President, Gandhi Ashram Reconstruction Trust (GART) and Dr. Shigeru Suganami, President, AMDA other members from GART and AMDA were also present at the function.

4433. (23-11-2007) NEW DELHI : The Reserve Bank of India has informed that printing of small denomination currency notes viz Re. 1/-, Rs. 2/- and Rs. 5/- has been stopped and notes of these denominations have been coinised in view of the lower circulation life of notes. There is no shortage of coins of these denominations Though printing of Re. 1, Rs. 2 and Rs. 5 denomination notes has been stopped, these notes have not been withdrawn from circulation. This information was given by Minister of State in the Ministry of Finance Shri Pawan Kumar Bansal in reply to a question raised by Shri S.K. Kharventhan in Lok Sabha today.

4434. (23-11-2007) NEW DELHI : A draft scheme having various provisions for the relief and rehabilitation of victims of rape is under the consideration of Ministry of Women and Child Development. This was stated by the Minister of State for Women and Child Development, Smt. Renuka Chowdhury in a reply to a question by Shri Adhalrao Patil Shivajirao and Shri Milind Deora in Lok Sabha here today. She further stated that a proposal to amend the legal provisions relating to rape is being processed by the Ministry of Home Affairs.

4435. (23-11-2007) NEW DELHI : There has been significant progress in the implementation of ICDS Scheme during the last three years both, in terms of increase in number of sanctioned projects and Anganwadi Centres (AWCs) and coverage of beneficiaries. During the period of three years from 31.3.2005, the number of sanctioned Projects and AWCs has increased from 5671 and 7.64 lakh to 6284 and 10.53 lakh, respectively, as on 30.6.2007. Similarly, the number of beneficiaries for Supplementary Nutrition have increased from 484.42 lakh to 736.80 lakh (52% increase) and the number of children (3-6 Years) attending Anganwadi Centres for pre-school education has increased from 218.41 lakh to 314.92 lakh during the same period (44 % increase). This was stated by the Minister of State for Women and Child Development, Smt. Renuka Chowdhury in a reply to a question by Shri Mahavir Bhagora in Lok Sabha today.

4436. (23-11-2007) NEW DELHI : The States of Rajasthan, Uttar Pradesh, Maharashtra, Himachal Pradesh, Chhattisgarh, Andhra Pradesh, Tripura, Punjab, Meghalaya, Haryana, Tamil Nadu, Goa and UTs of Andaman & Nicobar and Dadra & Nagar Haveli have provided information. The information from the remaining States/UTs is awaited. This was stated by the Minister of State for Women and Child Development, Smt. Renuka Chowdhury in a reply to a question by Shri Hansraj G. Ahir in Lok Sabha today. She further stated that the Ministry of Women and Child Development has formulated a new centrally sponsored scheme-"Integrated Child Protection Scheme (ICPS)" for implementation during the 11th Plan Period under which there is provision for setting up of 'National Website on Missing Children' for children who have run away or are missing for various reasons, with its headquarters at National Institute of Public Cooperation and Child Development (NIPCCD) with linkages to State Child Protection Units (SCPUs) and District Child Protection Units (DCPUs).

4437. (23-11-2007) NEW DELHI : The leaders of the 10 member Association of South East Asian Nations (ASEAN) met in Singapore from 18th to 22nd of this month to give a further boost to regional integration of their economies. Singapore Prime Minister Mr. Lee Hsien Loong addressing a gathering of business leaders on the eve of the Summit meeting said that ASEAN countries offer a neutral core around which the rest of Asia can build economic ties and a regional framework of cooperation. To sustain this, ASEAN itself has to become more integrated and cohesive and only then can the ASEAN nations keep up with larger and stronger economies like China and India. Mr. Lee added, ASEAN states must show the political will to implement both the charter and economic community blueprint which sets the stage for a single market and production base by 2015. He said, the blueprint and the charter, which marks the first time that the 40 year old bloc will codify its basic principles and organizational rules, would be critical in enhancing ASEAN's credibility and attracting investors. The charter commits ASEAN nations to strengthen democracy, enhance good governance and rule of law and promote and protect human rights and fundamental freedoms. The economic blueprint, which brings forward ASEAN's target date for creation of a free market from 2020 to 2015, will mean greater benefits for companies and more than half a billion people residing in the countries of this regional group. ASEAN was formed on the 8th August 1967 by Indonesia, Malaysia, the Philippines, Singapore and Thailand with the aim of accelerating economic growth and social progress and promoting regional peace. Later, the group expanded with the inclusion of Brunei Darussalam in 1984, Vietnam in 1995, Laos and Myanmar in 1997 and Cambodia in 1999. Since nation building is often vulnerable to foreign intervention, the governing council of the ASEAN right from the beginning wanted to have free hands to conduct their policies in the knowledge that neighbours would refrain from interfering in their domestic affairs. As a result non-interference became the cardinal principle of the organization. Its members while remaining committed to non-use of force, were also often reluctant to institutionalize and legalize regional cooperation. Keeping this history of the organization in mind, it is therefore, significant to note that the member countries this time attempted to make ASEAN a rule based legal entity like the European Union.

4438. (23-11-2007) NEW DELHI : The total number of Project Affected Persons (PAPs) in the land acquired by NTPC Ltd. for Sipat Super Thermal Power Project (STPP) is 3106. However, there are no homestead oustees in the project. Till date, 43 number of PAPs have been provided regular employment at NTPC Ltd.'s Sipat STPP and the recruitment process for further employment continues. During the inauguration of the 765 kV transmission system at NTPC Sipat on 20.01.2007, it was favourably considered to allocate 300 MW of power from Sipat STPP to Chhattisgarh State for a period of one year since the commissioning of the first unit. Chhattisgarh has been allocated 158 MW from the Stage II (2x500 MW) of Sipat STPP based on the Central Formula for allocation. Chhattisgarh has also been allocated additional unallocated power of about 75 MW from the pool of unallocated power of Central Generating Stations in the Western Region with effect from the date of commercial operation of the first unit of Stage II of Sipat STPP, keeping in view the shortage of power in Chhattisgarh as well as that of other States/UTs in the Region. Besides the above, Chhattisgarh has been allocated 313 MW of power from Stage-I (3x660 MW) of Sipat STPP. Chhattisgarh will also get allocation from the unallocated quota of Sipat STPP Stage I. This information was given by the Union Power Minister Shri Sushilkumar Shinde in the Lok Sabha today

4439. (23-11-2007) NEW DELHI : Gen Bruno Cuche, Chief of the French Army, is undertaking an official visit to India from 26-30 Nov 07. The visit will give the necessary impetus to the on-going defence relationship between India and France and broad-base it further into a mutually beneficial partnership. During his visit, the French Army Chief will interact with senior military and civilian defence hierarchy, discuss defence related issues and prospects for future cooperation between our two Armies. With common concern on increased terrorism in the world, discussions on global and regional security situation including enhanced cooperation in combating terrorism are also envisaged. In addition, visits to Indian Army Field Formations and training institutions in Nagrota, Rajauri, Agra and Pune are being organized. India's Army-to-Army cooperation with France is progressing very smoothly and it comprises numerous joint activities viz, visits, observers in joint exercises, training and courses, exchanges between experts and equipment procurement. The activities between our armies in 2007 have shaped very well and the plan for 2008 will be finalized soon, between the Defence Ministries. This visit reconfirms the mutual trust and friendship between the armies of India and France and will provide the necessary fillip to our on-going Army-to-Army cooperation.

4440. (23-11-2007) NEW DELHI : A number of glaciers have been taken up for monitoring studies in the different parts of Indian Himalaya by several Government agencies like Wadia Institute of Himalayan Geology (WIHG), Dehradun, Geological Survey of India (GSI), Snow and Avalanche Study Establishment (SASE), Chandigarh etsc. The research on Himalayan glaciers shows that most of the Himalayan glaciers are receding gradually due to the orographic and climatic variability. A number of weather stations have been set up to collect real time weather observations at different altitudes in the glacier areas of the Himalaya to assess and evaluate the climate change.

4441. (23-11-2007) NEW DELHI: Despite a record rise in the global crude oil price during the last year, the government had not raised domestic fuel prices under the direction of United Progressive Alliance (UPA) chairperson and Congress president Sonia Gandhi, according to Petroleum Minister Murli Deora. Replying to a question on the issue in the Lok Sabha on Thursday, Mr. Deora said: "I have no hesitation in saying that the UPA chairperson had directed us to see that petroleum product prices do not increase and we are trying to do just that." Mr. Deora said despite a marked increase in price of crude oil to nearly $100 per barrel a day from the $40 to $45 last year, the government had not increased prices even by one rupee.

4442. (23-11-2007) NEW DELHI : Based on the revised Index of Industrial Production for the Small Scale Industries (SSIs) sector, with base year 2001-02, the rate of growth of production of SSIs in the country during 2004-05, 2005-06, and 2006-07(projected) have been 10.9%, 12.3% and 12.6% respectively. To assist the States/UTs and supplement their efforts in this regard, the Central

Government implements several schemes/ programmes for promotion and development of SSIs. These, inter alia, include, (i) facilitating availability of credit mainly through public sector banks/institutions, (ii) assistance for (a) technology upgradration, (b) marketing, (c) integrated infrastructural development, (d) comprehensive need-based development of clusters, and (iii) entrepreneurship development. The Government has also enacted the Micro, Small and Medium Enterprises Development (MSMED) Act, 2006 to facilitate the promotion and development of micro, small and medium enterprises and enhancement of their competitiveness. The Act came into effect from 2nd October, 2006. Besides, Government implements the Pradhan Mantri Rozgar Yojana (PMRY) and Rural Employment Generation Programme (REGP) specifically designed for creating self-employment opportunities among unemployed youth. This information was given by the Minister of Micro, Small & Medium Enterprises, Shri Mahabir Prasad in a written reply to a question in Rajya Sabha today.

4443. (23-11-2007) NEW DELHI : LOK SABHA, During the recent visit of German Chancellor to India on 30th October 2007, India and Germany signed a Memorandum of Understanding (MoU) to set-up Indo-German Science Research and Technology Centre (IGSTC) in India, under the umbrella Inter-Governmental Agreement on Cooperation in the Field of Scientific Research and Technological Development signed in 1974.

4444. (23-11-2007) NEW DELHI: The Privileges Committee of the Lok Sabha has recommended that the privilege issue against the Ambassador to the U.S., Ronen Sen, be treated as closed in view of his "unconditional apologies" for his reported comments against the Members of Parliament who were critical of the India-U.S. civilian nuclear deal. The committee's report was tabled in the House on Thursday.

4445. (23-11-2007) NEW DELHI : The annual growth rate of Micro, Small & Medium Enterprises has so far been consistently higher than that of the country's industrial sector as a whole and their share in national exports is about 33% .The number of MSME has grown from 109 lakh in 2002-03 to 128 lakh in 2006-07 and their production has increased from Rs.314850 crore to Rs.587196 crore. To enable MSMEs to sustain themselves in the international market and strengthen their export worthiness, the Government has accorded high priority to this sector in India's export promotion strategy, which includes simplification of procedures, incentives for higher exports, preferential treatment in the market development fund, simplification of duty drawback rules, etc. The supportive measures also include the assistance for participation in international exhibitions/fairs, training programmes on packaging for exports, Marketing Development Assistance Scheme for MSME exports, assistance for obtaining bar-coding, National award for quality products, etc. The Government, with a view to further enhancing competitive edge of MSMEs (both domestically and globally) have put in place several measures, which include assistance for technological upgrdatation, accessing markets, improved infrastructure, better availability of credit, facilities for training and capacity building of entrepreneurs. This information was given by the Minister of Micro, Small & Medium Enterprises, Shri Mahabir Prasad in a written reply to a question in Rajya Sabha today.

4446. (23-11-2007) NEW DELHI : Following is the text of the inaugural address of the Defence Minister Shri A K Antony at the International Conference on Psychological Assessment In Personnel Selection delivered in absentia in Delhi, today:-"It is a pleasure for me to be present at the inauguration of a three-day international conference on psychological assessment in personnel selection. Developed more than five decades ago, the personnel selection system of the Indian Armed Forces is based on firm psychological principles and has, by and large, withstood the test of time. If today, the Indian Armed Forces are considered to be among the most combat-efficient, it is a tribute to the quality of the selection system employed for the screening of the personnel. Nevertheless, no system is immutable and this is equally applicable to the manner in which we select our soldiers, who are after all our nation's most important national security asset. It has been estimated that there are currently, on an average, at least 40 armed conflicts active in the world in any one year, routinely involving destruction of communities, ethnic conflicts and atrocities. This is further complicated by the challenge posed by terrorism, where it is difficult to identify the enemy, the tactics he will use or the place he will strike. Often added to this already complex matrix are inhospitable physical conditions under which soldiers are required to operate efficiently, ranging from sub-arctic conditions of the mountains to the heat of the deserts. The adjustment capabilities demanded of the soldiers can, at best, be described as extreme. Exposure to such life-threatening situations leads to an entire range of emotional, psychological and behavioural stress reactions amongst soldiers and officers-a condition commonly referred to as the Post-Traumatic Stress Disorder (PTSD). This combat stress need not come from enemy actions alone, but can also be generated from within the soldier's own unit, or the mission he is expected to accomplish. Reactions to this include fear, anxiety, frustration and depression leading to fragging and suicide. The importance, therefore, of ensuring that our Armed Forces are not just physically healthy, but also in good psychological health, cannot be understated. This is where psychological techniques of selection and screening are of paramount importance. I wish to emphasise that selection and screening constitute only one side of the coin. It is equally important that these techniques are tailored and refined in such a manner that they not only identify individuals vulnerable to stress during the screening process itself, but also enable combatants to cope with stressful environments and events in the course of their duties. In the Indian context, the break-up of the joint family system has added yet another stress on Armed Forces personnel. Often, unresolved domestic problems in a nuclear family, coupled with a lack of support available in a joint family add to such pressures. You may like to deliberate on finding ways and means to have in place a more efficient and humane man-management system.

4447. (23-11-2007) NEW DELHI : Following is the text of the address of the Vice President of India Mohd. Hamid Ansari at the 'Third International Congress of the Asian Political and International Studies Association' here today: "I confess I did not understand until quite recently the import of the adage 'accept in haste, repent at leisure'. The point was driven home to me when, some weeks after having accepted Professor Chandhoke's invitation, I started thinking about the implications of the commitment and was gripped with trepidation at the prospect of standing before an audience of distinguished political scientists to expose the inadequacy of my thought process on so weighty a subject. Having unburdened my conscience, let me thank the organisers of the 3rd Congress of APISA for conferring on me the privilege of inaugurating your conference. I am happy to do so, confident in the knowledge that your deliberations would clarify and amplify concepts and further understanding on a subject of crucial relevance to social well being. I notice that since its inception, your Association has structured its work on the specific theme of Asia in New Millennium. This makes sense since yours is an ASIAN association and rightly retains the focus on Asia, more so because the misfortunes of Asian history for a few centuries not only subjected it to colonial and neo-colonial domination but also ensured intellectual subordination by making the world Euro-centric. Terms like the Near East, Middle East and Far East entered the political vocabulary and Orientalism became an intellectual industry. The focus on Asia has helped APISA explore specific areas of the Asian experience. The 1st Congress dwelt on development, democracy and security. The 2nd Congress focused on aspects of governance. The theme of this 3rd Congress is Asian concepts of justice. I am, I confess, enthused by the theme and intrigued by it. The concept of justice is integral to social well being; for this reason, it must be reiterated on every possible opportunity. It is also in the category of universal values, rather than location-specific. Talk of an Asian concept may, therefore, convey an impression that there is something specific by way of a value addition or value subtraction. This, presumably, is not intended. The primacy of Asia in terms of religious or ethical traditions is a matter of recorded history. Virtually all the world religions-Hinduism, Judaism, Zoroastrianism, Confucianism, Buddhism, Christianity, Shinto, Jainism, Islam and Sikhism-emanated in Asian lands. Each has an ethical system and thus an approach to the concept of justice. Even if we take Toynbee's categorisation of twenty one societies for his comparative study of civilisations, we find a majority of them emerging from Asia. Let us take a closer look into the subject matter. The human being is a social animal. Living in society necessitates social arrangements that determine the division of responsibilities and ascribe rights and duties. Such an allocation is made on a basis that is broadly acceptable; this is considered the principle of social justice.

4448. (23-11-2007) NEW DELHI : '28' The total number of Project Affected Persons (PAPs) in the land acquired by NTPC Ltd. for Sipat Super Thermal Power Project (STPP) is 3106. However, there are no homestead oustees in the project. Till date, 43 number of PAPs have been provided regular employment at NTPC

Ltd.'s Sipat STPP and the recruitment process for further employment continues. During the inauguration of the 765 kV transmission system at NTPC Sipat on 20.01.2007, it was favourably considered to allocate 300 MW of power from Sipat STPP to Chhattisgarh State for a period of one year since the commissioning of the first unit. Chhattisgarh has been allocated 158 MW from the Stage II (2x500 MW) of Sipat STPP based on the Central Formula for allocation. Chhattisgarh has also been allocated additional unallocated power of about 75 MW from the pool of unallocated power of Central Generating Stations in the Western Region with effect from the date of commercial operation of the first unit of Stage II of Sipat STPP, keeping in view the shortage of power in Chhattisgarh as well as that of other States/UTs in the Region. Besides the above, Chhattisgarh has been allocated 313 MW of power from Stage-I (3x660 MW) of Sipat STPP. Chhattisgarh will also get allocation from the unallocated quota of Sipat STPP Stage I. This information was given by the Union Power Minister Shri Sushilkumar Shinde in the Lok Sabha today.

4449. (23-11-2007) NEW DELHI : The Government received a request for inclusion of The city of Motha, district Amrawati in the list of wind potential sites", which are having a minimum wind power density of 200 Watt/square meter or more at 50 meter elevation. The proposal was examined in detail by the scientists of the Centre for Wind Energy Technology (C-WET), Chennai and Maharashtra Energy Development Agency (MEDA), Pune. Based on this, it was suggested to MEDA that areas in and around Motha, having elevation in excess of 1040 meters above sea level, could be considered suitable for setting up of grid connected wind power projects, based on micro siting report to be prepared by the developer(s). This information was given by the Minister of State in the Ministry of New and Renewable Sources, Sh.Vilas Muttemwar in a written reply to a question in the Lok Sabha today.

4450. (23-11-2007) NEW DELHI : A National Biogas and Manure Management Programme ((NBMMP), which caters to promotion of family type biogas plants, is under implementation in all States and Union Territories in the country. Its objective is to meet cooking fuel requirements and provide pollution-free fuel. As on 31.10.2007, subsidy has been provided for setting up around 39.70 lakh family type biogas plants in the country. A target of setting up of 1, 01, 860 family type biogas plants has been allocated to States and Union Territories for 2007-08. This information was given by the Minister of State in the Ministry of New and Renewable Sources, Sh.Vilas Muttemwar in a written reply to a question in the Lok Sabha today.

4451. (23-11-2007) NEW DELHI : The main objectives of the the Accelerated Programmeon Energy Recovery from Urban Waste are to promote setting up of projects for recovery of energy from urban wastes; creation of conducive conditions and environment including fiscal and financial regime to develop and demonstrate projects for recovery of energy from wastes; and, harnessing of the available potential. Under the Programme, a project for generation of 3 MW power from biogas being produced at three sewage treatment plants has recently been supported for the city of Surat in Gujarat. Projects on energy recovery from urban wastes have earlier been undertaken in other States namely, Andhra Pradesh, Punjab, Tamil Nadu and Uttar Pradesh. No projects have so far been taken up in West Bengal under the Programme. This information was given by the Minister of State in the Ministry of New and Renewable Sources, Sh.Vilas Muttemwar in a written reply to a question in the Lok Sabha today.

4452. (23-11-2007) NEW DELHI : The government has been encouraging private investment in renewable energy sector through a mix of fiscal and financial incentives that include capital/ interest subsidy, accelerated depreciation, nil/ concessional excise and customs duties. Further, as applicable to all new infrastructure projects, profits earned from sale of renewable power are exempt from Income Tax for any 10 years out of the first 15 years of project's operation. This apart, preferential tariff for grid interactive renewable power is being given in most potential States. There is no proposal to set up corpus for the research and development in various new and development technologies at present. However, an amount of Rs.1100 crores has been proposed to support Research and Development on different aspects of new and renewable energy technologies during 11th Plan period. This information was given by the Minister of State in the Ministry of New and Renewable Sources, Sh.Vilas Muttemwar in a written reply to a question in the Lok Sabha today.

4453. (23-11-2007) NEW DELHI : Proposals for grant of central financial assistance under the schemes/ programmes of the Ministry are received on an ongoing basis through State Governments / designated State Nodal Agencies. Complete proposals in line with the schemes/ programmes are considered and approved promptly subject to budget provisions. This information was given by the Minister of State in the Ministry of New and Renewable Sources, Sh.Vilas Muttemwar in a written reply to a question in the Lok Sabha today.

4454. (23-11-2007) NEW DELHI : Under a programme on "Biomass Energy and Co-generation in Industry" partial financial assistance is provided in the form of capital subsidy of Rs. 2.00-2.50 lakh / 100 KW gasifier system for power generation and / or thermal applications to meet their captive energy requirements. A number of biomass gasifiers have been installed in rice mills in different parts of the country. In West Bengal, in particular, 64 rice mills have already installed such systems that are running successfully. This information was given by the Minister of State in the Ministry of New and Renewable Sources, Sh.Vilas Muttemwar in a written reply to a question in the Lok Sabha today.

4455. (23-11-2007) NEW DELHI : No proposal has been received during the current year from West Bengal for wind, solar & hybrid systems in non-electrified villages. However, financial support has been provided in the past for electrification of 1177 non-electrified villages using renewable energy such as wind, solar, biomass, hybrid systems, etc. An amount of around Rs.53 crores has been released to the state towards the Central Financial Assistance for these projects. This information was given by the Minister of State in the Ministry of New and Renewable Sources, Sh.Vilas Muttemwar in a written reply to a question in the Lok Sabha today.

4456. (23-11-2007) NEW DELHI: The Communist Party of India (Marxist) said in the Rajya Sabha on Thursday that the Nandigram issue was being exaggerated by the Opposition to politically demolish the Left parties in their bastion. On the other hand, taking part in the inconclusive seven-hour debate on Nandigram, the Congress largely took a middle-of-the-road approach, the Bharatiya Janata Party (BJP) sought President's rule in West Bengal and other Left Parties wanted the issue judged from the larger perspective of the neo-liberal macroeconomic policies being pursued by the Centre. Initiating a short duration discussion on "the proposal to set up Special Economic Zone (SEZ) in Nandigram and consequent large-scale violence," Sushma Swaraj (BJP) demanded imposition of President's rule in West Bengal as, she claimed, the State government had failed to act on directions of the Centre for restoring law and order, peace and normality in violence-affected Nandigram area. Ms. Swaraj narrated tales of sufferings and hit out at the CPI(M) for labelling Nandigram as a mere law and order problem and trying to prevent a discussion in Parliament on the ground that it was a State subject. She sought to know from the Home Minister if the Maoists had indeed invaded Nandigram and even if the Maoists were there did the Centre approve of the method of unleashing violence by party cadres to recapture the area from them ? Countering the charges of the BJP Deputy Leader of the House, CPI(M) leader Sitaram Yechury said that his party condemned the violence and loss of innocent lives in Nandigram. "Whatever has happened in Nandigram since January 3 should not have happened." Mr. Yechury said no formal notification had been issued to set up a chemical hub in Nandigram. Countering the BJP's demand, he said out of 341 blocks in the State, the demand for imposing President's rule was made only in the area of one-and-a-half block. "You show your concern for internal security but at the same time you are encouraging them [Maoists]. The political objective is destruction of CPI(M)," he said. The CPI(M) leader cautioned against the Maoist violence which amounted to "open declaration of armed action against the Indian state and has nothing to do with the land acquisition issue. We want peace, tranquillity and I assure that no crime in Nandigram will go unpunished. Please do not reduce it to settle petty political scores and do not lose sight of the larger picture."

4457. (23-11-2007) NEW DELHI : India signed a Double Taxation Avoidance Agreement (DTAA) with the Government of Iceland, here today for the avoidance of double taxation and for the prevention of fiscal evasion with respect to taxes on income. The Agreement also aims at promoting economic cooperation between the two countries. The Agreement was signed by Shri P. Chidambaram, Finance Minister on behalf of the Government of India and Mr. Arni Mathiesen, the

Minister of Finance of Iceland on behalf of the Government of Iceland. Welcoming the 45 member business delegation, Shri Chidambaram expressed the confidence that the agreement would result in high degree of comfort level of investors of both the countries. Mr. Arni Mathiesen, in his response, said that the DTAA would facilitate flow of more investment in both the countries and would further enhance mutual economic relationship. The DTAA between India and Iceland which will come into force on a date to be notified in due course, covers in the case of India, income-tax including any surcharge thereon and in the case of Iceland, income-tax to the State and to the municipalities. The DTAA provides for taxation of dividend, interest, royalties and fees for technical services-both in the country of residence as well as the country of source. However, the rate of tax in the country of source shall not exceed ten percent of the gross amount of payment in case the beneficial owner of the payments is a resident of the Contracting State. The DTAA provides that capital gains from alienation of shares of a company shall be taxable in the country where the company is a resident. The incidence of double taxation shall be avoided by one country giving credit for taxes paid by its residents in the other country. There is a provision for exchange of information in cases, which are under investigation in either of the two countries. Both the countries shall assist each other in collection of revenue claims. There is also a provision for limitation of benefits under the DTAA to prevent misuse of the provisions of the DTAA. The Agreement will further stimulate the flow of capital, technology and personnel between the two countries. It will also contribute to the tax stability and facilitate mutual cooperation.

4458. (23-11-2007) NEW DELHI : Smt. Ambika Soni, Minister Tourism and Culture is leaving to Cartegana de Indias (Colombia) on 24.11.2007 on a three day (25th-27th November 2007) visit to attend the 17th Session of General Assembly of UNWTO. During the General Assembly of the UNWTO, Smt. Ambika Soni will attend the ministerial meeting and make a statement in the plenary session. She will also have bilateral meetings with her counterparts of Colombia, China, Turkey Egypt, South Africa and South Asian Countries. Before returning to New Delhi she will have a halt at Miami and interact with tour operators there to promote India as a tourist destination. The World Tourism Organization, a specialized agency of the United Nations, is the leading international organization in the field of tourism. It serves as a global forum for tourism policy issues and practical source of tourism know how. In 2006, the UNWTO's membership comprised of 150 countries, seven territories and more than 300 Affiliate Members representing the private sector, educational institutions, tourism associations and local tourism authorities. With requests received from three more countries (Montenegro, Tajikistan and Brunei Darussalam) the total membership of UNWTO will increase to 153 countries at the end of 17th Session of General Assembly. The Executive Council is WTO's governing board is responsible for ensuring that the Organization carries out its work and adheres to its budget. It meets twice a year and is composed of 30 members elected by the General

Assembly in a ratio of one for every five full Members. As host country of WTO's Head Quarters, Spain has permanent seat on the Executive Council. At present Tunisia is the Chairman of the Executive Council and Argentina and Hungary are the Vice Chairmen. India is a member of the Executive Council. India was elected to the Executive Council in the last session of the General Assembly which was held in Dakar, Senegal in 2005. India has presented its candidature for the post of the Chairmanship of the Executive Council which according to the principle of the geographical rotation between the regions, should be given to a member country from South Asia at the forthcoming session of the General Assembly. The new Chairman of the Executive Council will take over the charge in the 82nd Meeting of the Executive Council which will be held on 29 November 2007 after the session of General Assembly ends.

4459. (23-11-2007) NEW DELHI : The President, Smt. Pratibha Devisingh Patil in her message on the occasion of the martyrdom day of Guru Teg Bahadur, which falls tomorrow, has said, " On the occasion of Guru Teg Bahadur's Shaheedi Divas, let us remember the glory of his sacrifice. The life, teachings and martyrdom of Guru Teg Bahadur form a message of everlasting significance. Guru Teg Bahadur worked for the alleviation of the sufferings of the people. On this day, let all of us resolve to re-dedicate ourselves to his message of love."

4460. (23-11-2007) NEW DELHI : The President, Smt. Pratibha Devisingh Patil, has sent her greetings to her fellow citizens on the occasion of Guru Nanak Jayanti, which is being celebrated tomorrow. In a message, the President has said, "On the auspicious occasion of the birthday of Guru Nanak Devji, I convey my heartiest greetings and good wishes to all my fellow citizens. Guru Nanak Devji's message of equality, peaceful co-existence and universal love is an abiding source of inspiration for all. Let us resolve to deeply understand his noble teachings and rededicate ourselves to the cause of humanity, equality, brotherhood and harmony".

4461. (23-11-2007) NEW DELHI : Steel Authority of India Limited (SAIL) is planning to set up three new greenfield pellet plants. A plant of 0.9 million tonnes per year capacity at Dalli mines in Chhattisgarh and a plant of around 1 million tonnes per year capacity at Gua mines in Jharkhand are being planned. There will no investment by SAIL for setting up these two plants. SAIL will provide iron ore fines to the parties who will set up the pellet plants and the parties will supply pellets to SAIL on 'conversion cost' basis. It has also been planned to set up another plant of 2 million tonnes per year capacity at Taldih mines in Orissa for which the total investment will be made by SAIL. The process for engagement of consultant has been initiated. The cost of setting up the pellet plant would be known after finalisation of the Detailed Project Report. An Inter Ministerial Group (IMG) under the Chairmanship of Secretary (Steel) and comprising Secretaries of the concerned Ministries and the Chief Secretaries of the concerned State Governments has been set up to monitor and coordinate various issues concerning major steel investments in the country. Issues relating to land acquisition and iron ore linkages are key factors to be settled before various investments proposals of new steel projects progress. The Inter Ministerial Group (IMG) will also be addressing some of these key issues confronting fresh steel investment proposals. The Ministry co-ordinates and recommends. Land acquisition is done by the State Government. Government of India has also declared a new National Rehabilitation & Resettlement Policy 2007, which is expected to ease problems relating to the acquisition of land for such plants. This information was given by the Minister of State for Steel Dr. Akhilesh Das in a written reply in the Rajya Sabha today.

4462. (23-11-2007) NEW DELHI : Boom in the entertainment media sector has to be supported by low cost good quality theatres in order to reach to the public at large, says the Union Minister of Information & Broadcasting and parliamentary Affairs, Shri P. R. Dasmunsi. Speaking at the valedictory session of 'India-The Big Picture' Conference 2007, Shri Dasmunsi said that in the long run digitalization has to ensure that technology is made available at affordable cost to sustain the cinema-seeing habits of the common man. He said, of late building up of good theatres is confined only to set up multiplexes which a common film goer cannot afford. Additional investments on creating more single screen theatres are warranted, he added. The Minister said, the core group set up by the Ministry on Internet Protocol Television (IPTV) has made its presentation to the Ministry and a view in this regard would be finalized by this year end. On measures to check piracy in the film sector, Shri Dasmunsi stated that the group set up to look into it has since submitted its report on Optical Disc laws and the Ministry is examining the draft provisions. Commenting on TRP rating system of TV programmes, Shri Dasmunsi said that the present system is faulty and the Ministry is in the process to address this issue.

4463. (23-11-2007) NEW DELHI : The Government had launched two Simplified Exit Schemes (SES) in the years 2003 and 2005 to enable names of defunct companies being struck off expeditiously under Section 560 of the Companies Act, 1956. Pursuant to these Schemes, names of 29069 companies under SES 2003 and 22885 companies in SES 2005 respectively have been struck off. The Government also initiated a review of companies which had not filed their balance sheets and annual returns during the last three years, as of 2005, for action to strike off the names of such companies as were found to be defunct and fit to be struck off. Names of 45, 470 companies have so far been struck off through such action. Orders of striking off the name of a company are passed by the Registrar only on a finding based on the statutory process and in exercise of powers provided under section 560 of the Companies Act, 1956. This was stated by the Minister of Corporate Affairs, Shri Prem Chand Gupta in written reply to a question in the Lok Sabha today.

4464. (23-11-2007) NEW DELHI : The Government proposes to set up the Indian Institute of Corporate Affairs. The institute would provide policy research and knowledge support to the Ministry of Corporate Affairs on an ongoing basis and serve as a think tank and implementation arm of initiatives and programmes under progress in the Ministry. The project has been given an in principle approval by the Planning Commission for the XI Five Year Plan. This was stated by the Minister of Corporate Affairs, Shri Prem Chand Gupta in written reply to a question in the Lok Sabha today.

4465. (23-11-2007) NEW DELHI : India is one of the largest food producers of the world with the organized sector accounting for food output worth US$ 34827 million, only a small percentage of its farm produce is processed into value-added products. The theme of the 27th India International Trade Fair 2007 being held at Pragati Maidan is 'Processed Food and Agro-Industries". The Fair is a mega celebration of the new India that is fast taking shape.

4466. (23-11-2007) NEW DELHI : Since opening up of insurance sector to private sector, the market share of the e private sector insurers has increased to 18.08% for life insurance and 34.72% for non-life insurance in the year 2006-07. The market share of public sector life and non life insurance companies was 81.92% and 65.28% respectively during 2006-07. Although, the market share of public sector insurance companies has declined but they have shown a healthy growth in quantum terms. With respect to life insurance, the business of Life Insurance Corporation (LIC) has grown to Rs.56, 223.56 crore in terms of First Year Premium in 2006-07 as against Rs.9, 700.95 crore in 2000-01. Similarly, in case of the four public sector non-life insurance companies, the gross direct premium underwritten has grown to Rs.16258.90 crore in 2006-07 as against Rs.9799.81 crore in 2000-01.

4467. (23-11-2007) NEW DELHI : In order to attract the foreign tourists, Indian Railways introduced Indrail Pass Scheme in the year 1977 as a tourism promotion meal sure. These passes are issued to the foreign nationals and Non Resident Indians (NRIs) against payments in the US dollars. The pass holder is entitled to travel throughout the Indian Railways' Net work within the period of its validity in a class it is issued for. Further, Indian Railways also run five luxury tourist trains for tourists including foreign tourists *i.e.* Palace on Wheels, Heritage on Wheels in Rajasthan sector, Steam Safari Train-the Fairy Queen on Delhi-Alwar sector, Deccan Odyassey in Maharashtra Sector and Mahaparinirvan Express covering places related to Buddhism. In addition to above, two new luxury tourist trains in Karnataka and Rajasthan may also be launched shortly. One luxury tourist strain in the Punjab sector has also been approved. These luxury tourist train facilities are availed by foreign tourists.

4468. (23-11-2007) NEW DELHI : For providing rail connectivity to Sikkim a survey for new rail line from Sivok to Rangpo has been completed recently. As per survey report, cost of construction of this 62 km. long line has been assessed as Rs. 1329 crore. The survey report is under scrutiny in the Ministry of Railways. Further, a survey for construction of new line from Rangpo to Gangtok has been sanctioned recently. This information was given by the Minister of State for Railways Shri R.Velu in written reply to a question in the Rajya Sabha Sabha today.

4469. (23-11-2007) NEW DELHI : The National AIDS Control Programme Phase III aims at halting and reversing the epidemic by 2012. It was approved with a total outlay of Rs 8023 crore for the five year period 2007-2012. Of this, Rs. 1125 crore (US 250 million dollar) has been obtained from the World Bank. The World Bank loan is proposed for up-scaling targeted interventions among high risk groups and vulnerable population, improving access to safe blood, strengthening services for the treatment of sexually transmitted infections, capacity building, condom promotion and increasing awareness about preventive measures and demand generation for services available. The fund will also be utilized for augmenting the capacity for programme delivery at district, state and national levels and also to strengthen the information management system to improve the effectiveness of data collection and analysis. These activities will be taken up throughout country with a higher focus on 195 districts, which have a higher prevalence of HIV infection in the country.

4470. (23-11-2007) NEW DELHI : As per the World Health Organization estimates, out of total 37 million blind persons (Visual Acuity <3/60) in the world, 6.7 million are in India, which is one-fifth of the total global blind population. As per the Eye Bank Association of India, Hyderabad, there are 500 Eye Banks/ Eye Donation Centres in the country including 148 in Maharashtra. Around 30, 000 donated eyes are collected annually in the country. There are about 6000 Optometrists in India and about 1200 pass out every year. More Optometrists are needed to fulfil patients' requirements for eye care in the country as the Ophthalmologists-para medical personnel ratio should be 1:4. As per the survey conducted during 2006-07, the prevalence of Blindness in the country has come down to 1% as compared to 1.1% during the year 2001-02. The National Programme for Control of Blindness (NPCB) is committed to reduce the burden of avoidable blindness to 0.3% by the year 2020.

4471. (23-11-2007) NEW DELHI : According to an article entitled "G-8 nations must lead efforts to combat global water and sanitation crisis; UN report", published in UN News service Newsletter dated 19.11.2007, each year 1.8 million children die from diarrhoea that could be prevented with access to clean water and a toilet. National Institute of Communicable Disease (NICD) Government of India has initiated an Integrated Disease Surveillance Project (IDSP) in November, 2004, to strengthen surveillance activities and to promote early detection of outbreak and to institute appropriate action for prevention and control of communicable diseases including Acute Diarrrhoeal Diseases (ADD). IDSP is being implemented in phased manner to cover 32 states/UTs, with NICD as the nodal agency for capacity building and supervision of the programme. So far, the Act of 1993 has been adopted by 20 States and all UTs. 5 States Arunachal Pradesh, Manipur, Mizoram, Nagaland and Sikkim have reported that there are no dry latrines or they are scavengers free. 2 States of Rajasthan and Himachal Pradesh have enacted their own Act. The State of Jammu & Kashmir is yet to adopt the Act. The State Government of Jammu and Kashmir have been mpressed upon time and again to adopt the Act. This information was given by the Minister for Health & Family Welfare, Dr. Anbumani Ramadoss in a reply to a question in the Rajya Sabha.

4472. (23-11-2007) NEW DELHI : Ayurvedic herbal mineral and metallic formulations which are prepared according to the standard operative procedure laid down in the formularies and which have been detoxified in terms of the purification processes laid down in the classical texts are safe and are not hazardous to health. Such medicines are widely used in the country and no adverse reports have been received about them. The regulatory authorities in some countries have issued alerts against certain Ayurvedic products on the grounds that they contain heavy metals in higher limits that permissible in food material. These alerts have been issued on the basis of the standards prescribed in those countries for health food supplements. As per the Government orders, it is mandatory to enclose the test report for heavy metal estimation with export consignments of purely herbal Ayurvedic, Siddha or Unani medicine with effect from 1st January, 2006. Exporters have been asked to comply with these orders. The State Drug Licensing Authorities have been directed to ensure full compliance by all ASU drug manufacturers of the provisions of Rule 161 (1) and (2) of the Drug and Cosmetics rules, 1945 relating to displaying on the label of the container or in a leaflet to be inserted in the package of an ASU drugs, the true list of all the ingredients used in the manufacture of the preparations together with the quantity of each of the ingredients incorporated therein. Government has instructed all States under the provision of Rule 154 (2) of the Drugs and Cosmetics Rules, 1945 to constitute Expert Committees for advising the State Licensing Authority before any manufacturing unit is given a license for the manufacture of any patent and proprietary Ayurveda, Siddha and Unani medicine. This information was given by the Minister for Health & Family Welfare, Dr. Anbumani Ramadoss in a written reply to a question in the Rajya Sabha.

4473. (23-11-2007) NEW DELHI : In a significant move to accelerate the growth of railway freight traffic in core sectors like steel and coal, a decision has been taken to set up working groups to chalk out a long term strategy in this regard. The decision was taken at a meeting held by Shri K.C. Jena, Chairman. Railway Board with Shri S.K.Roongta, Chairman, Steel Authority of Indian Limited (SAIL) and Shri P.S.Bhattacharyya, Chairman, Coal India Limited to discuss future prospects of growth of railway freight traffic in both coal and steel sectors. The two working groups separately for each sector comprising of officers from Railway Board, Coal India Limited and SAIL, will prepare long term vision scenario for both the sectors. This is expected to provide a platform for taking proper investment decisions and equipping Railways to meet the growing demands in both sectors. The meeting deliberated on anticipated growth in the 11th Five Year Plan and beyond. During the meeting various important issues like reducing detentions to rolling stock and loading & loading activities, developing new areas for movement of raw materials etc. were also discussed.

4474. (23-11-2007) NEW DELHI : As the Report of the Working Group on Fertilizers on 11th Five Year Plan, the expected demand of all types of fertilizers is likely to be around 559 lakh tonnes. The supply is proposed to be met through indigenous production/imports. In urea sector, in view of the projected improvement in availability of gas in future, the Government is looking into all options for finalisation of a new policy, which may attract investments by incentivising increased production from existing units, revival of closed units and setting up of new fertilizer units. In phosphatic sector, the indigenous resources are meager and are in a position to meet only 10% of the country's requirement. 90% of the country's requirement is being presently met through imports of raw materials, intermediates and finished fertilizers. The potassic requirement is 100% import dependent as currently there are no economically exploitable reserves of potash in the country. The Government is exploring possibilities for setting up Joint Ventures abroad for manufacture/supply of phosphatic and potassic fertilizers. This information was given by the Minister of State for Chemicals & Fertilizers Shri B.K. Handique in a written reply in the Rajya Sabha today.

4475. (23-11-2007) NEW DELHI : Finance Minister, Shri P. Chidambaram has approved 22 Foreign Direct Investment proposals recommended by Foreign Investment Promotion Board (FIPB) in its meeting held on 16th November, 2007. The approval amounts to Rs. 511.4616 crore. The proposals are related to Ministries/ Departments, namely, Commerce, Food Processing Industries, Heavy Industry, Industrial Policy & Promotion, Information & Broadcasting, Shipping, Railways and Economic Affairs. The major investment proposals pertain to the Ministries/ Departments of Heavy Industry, Shipping, Railways and Economic Affairs.

4476. (23-11-2007) NEW DELHI : With a view to ameliorate the conditions of urban poor, and to reduce the urban poverty in the country, Ministry of Housing and Urban Poverty Alleviation is implementing an employment oriented urban poverty alleviation scheme namely, Swarna Jayanti Shahari Rozgar Yojana (SJSRY) on all India basis, since 1.12.1997. This was informed by Minister of State for Housing & Urban Poverty Alleviation, Kumari Selja in the Lok Sabha today, in a written reply to a question by Shri Haribhau Rathod, Shri Rayapati Sambasiva Rao, and Shri M. Appadurai.

4477. (23-11-2007) NEW DELHI : The year 2007 has become memorable for various reasons. The event has become a historic milestone in humanity's quest for global nonviolence with the United Nations declaring Gandhi Jayanti as the International Day of Non-Violence. This event also coincides with the 150th anniversary of the first war of India's Independence, 1857; 60th anniversary of India's Independence; 100th anniversary of Satyagraha and the 60th anniversary of the Martyrdom of Mahatma Gandhi. To mark these historic events, the Gandhi Smriti and Darshan Samiti is organizing "GANDHI KATHA" by Sh. Narayan Bhai Desai, the son of Mahatma Gandhi's personal secretary and close associate Sh. Mahadev Desai from November 25-29, 2007 at Gandhi Smriti, 5 Tees January Marg, New Delhi. Conducted in lyrical Hindi, Sh. Narayan Bhai has held Gandhi Katha programmes in various parts of the country, which include Ahmedabad, Jaipur, Bhimtal, Wardha, Pune. The Gandhi Katha will take place everyday from November 25-29, 2007 from 11.00 am.

4478. (23-11-2007) NEW DELHI : The Prime Minister, Dr. Manmohan Singh, greeted the nation on the auspicious occasion of Guru Nanak's birthday. In his message, Dr. Manmohan Singh said that Guru Nanak's message of fraternity and universalism, acquires a crucial dimension in today's world. The Prime Minister said that Guru Nanak stressed that inner purity could be achieved through detachment. His teachings show the path to spiritual salvation and inspire us to embrace equality compassion and humanism, he added. The Prime Minister hoped that Guru Nanak's life and teachings would continue to guide humanity for all times to come.

4479. (23-11-2007) NEW DELHI : The government will establish food processing and training centres at the village-level in clusters of production of fruits and vegetables all over the country. This will provide solution for sustainable agricultural growth and economic woes of the farmers. Talking to reporters at the Trade Fair in New Delhi today, the Food Processing Minister, Mr. Subodh Kant Sahai said, this will provide massive training-cum-awareness to the entrepreneurs for setting up of food processing units at the village and Panchayat levels. He said, food processing adds value to the farm produce and links farmers to the market directly resulting in huge economic gains to them. Sh. Sahai said food processing industries in India has registered a record 18 per cent growth this fiscal. It witnessed 10 per cent jump during the last four years. Sh. Sahai further said during the 11th five year plan the government will come out with a comprehensive package for this sector to help the farmers to get due price of their produce. The Minister said food processing sector is emerging as the leading sector for economic growth of the country in the Eleventh Plan. He said, the Ministry has put up a large pavilion to create awareness to the millions of visitors regarding food processing and show case the products of large number of units from all over the country in the 'India International Trade Fair 2007'. About 110 units are showcasing their products in this pavilion. The Minister said, the investment in the organized small scale industries in this sector has gone up from 30, 000 crore rupees to 34, 000 crores. The Secretary, Mr. P.I. Suvrathan said, the food processing sector has lot of opportunity of employment and over four lakh people are directly or indirectly getting employment in this sector. He said that the foreign direct investment have gone up from 174 crore rupees to 441 crores. Foof Processing Ministry to take training facilities & capacity building efforts to the doorstep of the farmers and enterprenreneurs The Ministry is launching a massive training cum awareness as well as Entrepreneurshilp Development Programmes exercise right from the village / Panchayats level to the District level all over the country in the Eleventh Plan.

4480. (24-11-2007) NEW DELHI : The digital entertainment tools for children should create Indian brands and be aimed at giving some message for the younger generation. This was stated by Union Minister of Information & broadcasting and Parliamentary Affairs, Shri P. R. Dasmunsi at the Seminar on "Digital Entertainment: Animation, Gaming and Visual Effects", organized by FICCI alongside IFFI-2007 in Goa today. Without blindly copying the foreign icons, brands and characters, the ones from our own culture should be highlighted so as to promote scientific temper, he said. Shri Dasmunsi said that wider transfer of technology and knowledge should keep pace with the advancements in the field of technology. The Minister felt that the use of animation and visual effects would gain further prominence in Indian cinema in the near future. The changing technology is creating new environment and at the same time posing newer challenges on the issues like copy rights and inter-operatability, he observed The Minister said, new advancements in technology help in producing better quality at cheaper rates but still the costs remain considerably high from the viewpoint of the mass of Indian people. The endeavour has to be to develop technology which can be afforded by our common people. If not at one go, this position need to be achieved in a reasonably short phased duration. The Minister said, piracy in the film sector is caused mainly due to non-reach of the benefits of advanced technology right up to the masses. He appreciated the role of FICCI for its effort to check piracy by drafting and suggesting the provisions of Optical Disc Laws which are now under the consideration of the Ministry.

4481. (24-11-2007) NEW DELHI : Minister of Information & Broadcasting and Parliamentary Affairs, Shri P. R. Dasmunsi inaugurated the Exhibition 'Behind the Frames' at IFFI-2007 today. The first of its kind at IFFI, it exhibits antique cameras and other equipments used for making films in the olden era to the latest gadgets. Organized by the Films Division of the I&B Ministry, the Exhibition gives insight into the hard effort that film makers of yester years had to put in towards making of their films. Sanjit Narvekar directed 'Dreaming Movies', an exclusive documentary on the history of Indian cinema after the independence was released on the occasion. This 30-minute film has the celebration of Indian cinema from 1947 till date, as the theme. Chief Minister, Goa, Shri Digambar Kamat, Goa Chief Secretary, Shri J. P. Singh and Chief Producer, Films Division, Shri Kuldeep Sinha were present on the occasion. At the Expo, on display are, cameras as old as those used in the 1920s like Mitchell, Arricord, Eymo to the latest ones. Arri 435, 16 SR3, DVC Pro, old and new recording and editing equipments, lights, lenses, rare photographs and other paraphernalia. All these are precious preserves of Films Division. The Exhibition is intended to take the cinema lovers to a journey down the memory lane from the magic world of film making of the yore to the digital age. Apart from these, props and rare photographs collected from different sources are also exhibited. The rare equipments on display, it is believed, will give an insight into the technical nuances of film making, over the times. Films related to history of Indian cinema, film making and akin subjects will also be screened at the Exhibition venue. The Exhibition will remain open till December 02, 2007.

4482. (24-11-2007) SHIMLA: A grand alliance of forces, ranging from the Trinamool Congress to the Rashtriya Swayamsevak Sangh and from foreign-funded non-governmental organisations to the corporate media, had joined hands against the Communist Party of India (Marxist) in West Bengal. They were trying to compare the Nandigram incidents with the Godhra carnage in a well-planned move to bring down the democratically elected government, senior CPI(M) leader and Polit Bureau member Sitaram Yechury said here on Friday. This was nothing but trivialising the serious issue of state-sponsored genocide in Gujarat, in which more than 2,500 people were killed. Expressing surprise at the comparison, he said the problem in Nandigram was limited to just one- and a-half blocks, of the 341 in the State. Releasing the list of party candidates for the second phase of elections in Himachal Pradesh, he said it was the CPI(M) that had borne the brunt and suffered the maximum casualties in Nandigram. Twenty seven CPI(M) members had been killed there. Mr. Yechury blamed the naxalites, who were being supported by the Trinamool Congress, the Socialist Unity Centre of India and the Bharatiya Janata Party for the situation in West Bengal. The demand by these parties for imposition of President's Rule in the State was ridiculous. Stating that the Gujarat and Himachal Pradesh elections would have an important bearing on national politics, he said the CPI(M)'s priority would be to defeat the communal forces and strengthen the Left forces to influence the policies of any secular government that comes to power. On the shifting of Bangladeshi writer Taslima Nasreen outside West Bengal, Mr. Yechury said it was the prerogative of the Union government to allot or deny visa to any foreign national. It was for the Centre to decide where she should live or work. Earlier, State CPI(M) secretary Rakesh Singha announced the names of seven candidates. The party would fight 15 seats in alliance with the CPI in Himachal Pradesh.

4483. (24-11-2007) NEW DELHI : Indian Panorama at IFFI-2007 was inaugurated by Minister of Information & Broadcasting and Parliamentary Affairs, Shri P. R. Dasmunsi today in the presence of Goa Chief Minister, Shri Digambar Kamat. In his remarks, Shri Dasmunsi said, Indian panorama provides to viewers a comprehensive perspective of Indian Cinema. It gives an insight into the Indian ethos and film industry as a whole. The Minister appreciated the role of juries for Feature and Non-Feature Sections for the nice selection of films to be screened in this category. The members of the two jury were felicitated on the occasion. The jury are headed by renowned film makers, Mr. K S Sethumadhavan (feature films) and Arun Khopkar (non-feature films). Mr. Shyama Prasad, director of the opening Feature Film 'Ore Kadal' (Malayalam), Bisnu Deb Halder, director of the Non-Feature Section opening film, 'Bagher Bachcha' (Bengali) and main cast of the two films were also felicitated. In all, 36 films will be screened in Indian panorama. Of these, 21 are Feature and 15 Non-Feature Films. The selections were made from 119 Feature Films and 149 Non-Feature Film entries.

4484. (24-11-2007) NEW DELHI : The Planning Commission has constituted an Expert Committee called Integrated Energy Policy Report (IEPR) covering all sources of energy including renewable energy sources. This report has highlighted the need to maximally develop domestic supply options and diversify energy sources. It has also projected that renewables may account for 5 to 6 per cent of India's energy mix by 2031-32 and has observed that the distributed nature of renewables can provide many socio-economic benefits for the country, including its rural, tribal and remote areas. The recommendations of the IEPR are yet to be accepted by the Government. Meanwhile, the Ministry has proposed an outlay of Rs.10, 460 crore for the 11th Plan period for development of new and renewable energy in the country. The Ministry has provided assistance for various renewable energy schemes and programmes. Under small hydro power projects, Rs. 135.59 crore have been allotted during 2004-05 to 2006-07. Biomass Power schemes have been provided financial assistance to the tune of Rs. 33crores and Biomass Gasifier Projects nearly Rs. 14 crores. Various schemes to produce energy from wastes received Rs.15 crore as Central Financial Assistance. During the same period Wind Power Projects were given Rs.22.80 crore, Biogas Plants got Rs.101 crore, Small Wind Energy Systems got Rs. 8.5 crores, Solar Photovoltaic Systems Rs. 92 crores, Solar Thermal Projects, Rs. 44 crores and Remote Village Electrification got Rs. 122 crores.

4485. (24-11-2007) NEW DELHI : Following is the Statement made by the Prime Minister, Dr. Manmohan Singh on the selection of Kamalesh Sharma as the Secretary General of the Commonwealth in Kampala, Uganda today: "I am delighted that the Commonwealth Heads of Government have selected Kamalesh Sharma as the next Secretary General of the Commonwealth. His long record of public service in the international community has been capped by this recognition of his capability and his inclusive vision of the Commonwealth. I am confident that he will acquit himself well in his higher responsibilities as the first servant of the entire Commonwealth."

4486. (24-11-2007) NEW DELHI : Following is the text of the address of the President, Smt. Pratibha Devisingh Patil at the International Conference of Jurists on the Rule of Law here today : "I have great pleasure in participating at the International Conference of Jurists on the Rule of Law and am delighted to speak before this august gathering of legal luminaries and jurists. I would also like to congratulate the winners of the National Law Day Awards and the International Jurists' Awards. Differing theories and the current ongoing debates do not permit a clear jurist's definition of what the "Rule of Law" means internationally. However, the concept in simple terms translates itself to mean not only the need to abide by the rulebook but also the need to guarantee that while the rule is being interpreted, the law should not be seen as unjust, inequitable, discriminatory and arbitrary. These principles have guided many democratic nations in their efforts to establish responsible and responsive governing systems. In fact, a democratic form of government must have its foundations on a rule of law that advocates the absence of arbitrary power, equality before law and protection of individual liberties. The Constitution of India provides a powerful framework for the protection and enforcement of basic rights of the individual and rejects the arbitrary use of power; its provisions reflect a commitment to promote the rule of law. Article 14 of the Indian Constitution specifically provides for equality before law and the equal protection of the laws. Parliament and the State Legislatures are democratically elected on the basis of adult suffrage. There is independence of judiciary and the power of judicial review. All these provisions together constitute a firm commitment to the rule of law. We recently celebrated the 60th year of our Independence. It marked a long journey in realizing our constitutional goals and democratic aspirations. We can be sufficiently proud of our unwavering commitment to function on the basis of the rule of law. We, as Indians, are also proud of our achievements in education, science and technology, agriculture, industry and commerce. However, there are still a large number of people living below the poverty line. What does social and economic justice mean to them? As Mahatma Gandhi wished, could we contribute to wiping a tear from every eye or an eye at a time? While, I am fully aware, of the service rendered by the higher judiciary in India in upholding the rule of law, I believe lawyers and jurists can contribute much more to helping the needy who knock on the doors of justice. Clearly, in a country with the size and magnitude of India, there remain many challenges in providing social justice as well as justice to the marginalized sections of our society. High cost of judicial remedy is a cause of concern that needs rectification. Alternative dispute settlement systems need to be encouraged.

4487. (25-11-2007) NEW DELHI : Following is the text of the NCC day lecture delivered by Defence Minister Shri A K Antony in New Delhi today. "I am really delighted to be amidst you all on the 59th Raising Day of the National Cadet Corps (NCC). At the very outset, I extend my greetings and best wishes to everyone involved with the NCC. Unity in diversity is the defining feature of our nation. Through its vast network that covers nearly the entire length and breadth of the country, NCC has indeed been a crucial vehicle of national integration. The training provided by NCC is aimed at instilling character and discipline among the youth. Youth can and must act as powerful agents of social change. Adventure activities and active participation in social causes was introduced to enhance greater self-awareness and sensitivity, so that today's youth grow up into mature and responsible citizens of our nation. The strength of the NCC comprises 4% of the total number of students in the country. You must devise ways and means to further popularise NCC in schools and colleges. The Government is already considering a proposal to enhance the numerical strength of NCC in a phased manner. The world order of today is marked by an inter-dependence of nations. The NCC must continue to evolve, in tune with the changing times. Recent initiatives to start career counselling, personality development and communication skills development will prove beneficial for all of you, particularly those from the rural areas. One of the aims of NCC is to provide the right environment to motivate youth to join the Armed Forces. However, the training provided by NCC and imbibing virtues such as discipline, dedication and commitment would definitely help NCC cadets to excel in other walks of life too. You must make yourselves strong. As Mahatma Gandhi said, "Strength does not come from physical capacity. It comes from an indomitable will." Today, you must re-dedicate yourselves to render selfless service to the nation. Nation-building is a continuous endeavour. You must strive tirelessly to realize your dreams and aspirations. However, rather than setting an example for others, you must be an example to yourself. As Father of the Nation observed, "As human beings, our greatness lies not so much in being able to remake the world-that is the myth of the atomic age-as in being able to remake ourselves."

4488. (25-11-2007) NEW DELHI : The screening of the film 'Emotional Arithmetic' directed by Paolo Barzman stands cancelled due to non-receipt of prints from Paris in the wake of transporters' strike in France. Directorate of Film Festivals is making efforts to get the prints during the course of the Festival. In case prints are received within time, the film will be re-scheduled for screening.

4489. (25-11-2007) NEW DELHI : Retrospective of Tapan Sinha's movies began at IFFI-07 with the screening of highly acclaimed film Kabuliwala. Under the section, four of his acclaimed movies would be screened. The other movies are, 'Sagina Mahato', 'Adalt O Ekti Meye' and 'Aadmi Aur Aurat'. The film Kabuliwallah is based on a story by Rabindranath Tagore of the same name, the film is a touching tale of Rahmat Sheikh, a pathan who came from Afghanistan to Kolkata to make a living. However, he is homesick and seeks the company of children, particularly little girls as they remind him of his own daughter back home. One day he meets Mini, a five-year-old daughter of a writer, and they become great friends. The beautiful friendship that develops is suddenly interrupted by Rahmat's being sent to prison for assaulting his landlord. Years pass, and when Rahmat is released, he goes back to see Mini. Still expecting to meet the charming little girl he had left behind, he is stunned to realize that he has reached on Mini's wedding day and that she no longer recognizes him. He also realizes that his won daughter must also be of a similar age and tears well up in his eyes. Mini's father presents him the money kept for the decoration of the house during the wedding and urges him to return as soon as possible to his house in Afghanistan.

4490. (25-11-2007) NEW DELHI : Film screening under the section 'Flander's Image' (Retrospective) at IFFI-2007 began today with the Belgium films 'Gilles' directed by Jan. Verheyen. The film narrates the story of a young talented soccer player 'Gilles' whose father Bert's passionate support and coaching feed their dream that Gilles will make it to the Red Devils pro team. When Bert's enthusiasm causes a heart attack, a grieving Gilles finds a way to bring his father back to life so that he (but no one else) sees his dad everywhere, especially when playing soccer. But there's a downside to Bert's continuing presence: When Gilles learns that soccer might jeopardize his future, Bert still pushes Gilles to keep playing. Is this Gilles' desire too, or only his father's? While his mother urges him to quit and his friends offer encouragement, in the end Gilles must rule an offside, either as his penalty or his father's trap. Under this section four Belgian films will be screened. The other three films are, 'King of the World' (Director: Guido Henderickx), 'Love belongs to everyone' (Director: Hilde Van Mieghem) and 'The Intruder' (Director: Frank Van Mechelen).

4491. (25-11-2007) NEW DELHI : India is implementing one of the world's largest programmes in renewable energy. The country ranks second in the World in Biogas utilization and fifth in Wind Power and Photovoltaic production. A potential of 45, 000 MWe from around 20mha of wastelands assumed to be yielding 10MT/ha/annum of woody biomass having 4000 k-cal/kg with system efficiency of 30% and 75% PLF has not been taken into account. In order to realize this potential a major inter-Ministerial initiative is required. A Biomass Atlas is under preparation which is expected to more accurately assess state-wise renewable energy potential from agro-residues. Potential based on areas having wind power density (wpd) greater than 200 W/m2 assuming land availability in potential areas @ 1 per cent and requirement of wind farms @ 12 ha/MW, not all of which may be technically feasible and economically viable for grid-interactive wind power. Technically feasible and economically viable hydro potential is generally accepted at 40% of the total estimated potential. Accordingly, the technically feasible and economically viable small hydropower potential could be around 6000MW. With the establishment of new sugar mills and modernization of existing ones, technically feasible potential is assessed at 5000 Mwe. Current technically feasible municipal waste-to-energy potential is assessed at 1700 Mwe.

4492. (25-11-2007) NEW DELHI : The 10th NCB International Seminar on Cement and Building Materials is scheduled to be inaugurated here on 27 November 2007 by Shri Ajay Shankar, Secretary, Department of Industrial Policy & Promotion, Ministry of Commerce and Industry. The 4-day (27-30 November, 2007) Seminar aims at discussing threadbare for converging the joint efforts of the Government, industry and the internationally recognized expertise for bringing excellence in cement manufacturing technologies, quality excellence and energy efficiency in Indian cement industry. The seminar will be participated by the cement plant technologists, machinery manufacturers, construction experts, entrepreneurs, technocrats, consultants and professionals from different parts of the world and discuss new trends and services that have come up on the world arena in the recent times. This seminar and exhibition is being organized as a follow-up of the nine international seminars held earlier on alternate years since 1987 by the National Council for Cement and Building Materials (NCB), an apex scientific and industrial research organization under the Department of Industrial Policy & Promotion, Ministry of Commerce & Industry, Government of India. About 700 delegates from across the world are expected to participate in the Seminar. A Special Publication Sustainable Development of Indian Cement Industry and Infrastructure-Challenges carrying technical articles by experts in their specific areas would be released to mark the occasion. With the specialist topical articles, expert opinions and the messages by dignitaries, the Special Publication would prove to be a collector's delight. A Technical Exhibition, bearing on themes of the Seminar, would showcase the latest in products and services.

4493. (25-11-2007) NEW DELHI : The 10th National Conference on Safety in Mines will be inaugurated by the Minister of State for Labour & Employment (Independent Charge), Shri Oscar Fernandes here tomorrow. The two-day Conference is being organized by the Directorate General of Mines Safety (DGMS), Dhanbad, an apex body of the Ministry of Labour and Employment. The emerging safety issues in mines will be dwelt upon by different stakeholders of the country to identify the thrust areas for improvement in the safety standards in Indian mines. The Conference will review the status of safety in mining and adequacy of existing measures in improving working conditions in mines in a spirit of mutual cooperation. In this changing perspective, important issues like safety of contractor's workers in mines, mechanization in underground coal mines to reduce exposure of manual workers in hazardous areas, measures to reduce accidents due to roof and side fall, occupational health surveillance, implication of ratification of ILO Convention 176, safety issues in oil mines and introduction of safety management system in mines etc. are going to be deliberated in two days. It is expected that after detailed deliberations, the Conference will come out with important recommendations suggesting measures for further improvement in safety, welfare and health of mine workers of the country. This National Conference is the highest tripartite forum at the national level for deliberation on issues connected with safety and health in mines. CEOs of the mining companies as employers' representatives, the leaders of the Central Trade Unions as workers' representatives, representatives of the Central and State Governments, Professional Institutions, Academic and Research Institutes and Members of Parliamentary Standing Committee of the Ministry of Labour and Employment will be participating as Delegates in the Conference. Smt. Sudha Pillai, Secretary, Ministry of Labour & Employment alongwith other senior officials from the Ministry and Shri M.M. Sharma, Director-General of Mines Safety will also be present during the inaugural session of the Conference.

4494. (25-11-2007) SRINAGAR : Following is the text of the address of the Vice President of India Mohd. Hamid Ansari at the '4th Convocation of Sher-e-Kashmir University of Agricultural Sciences and Technology, Srinagar' at Srinagar today:

"Rakht kusha ba-Kashmer, kohe tal-o-daman mee-gar Sabz a jahaan jahaan bibeén, laleh chaman chaman ni-gar I deem it a privilege to be the Chief Guest at the Fourth Convocation of the Sher-e-Kashmir University of Agricultural Sciences and Technology. I am not a stranger to the Jammu and Kashmir, except in my new responsibility. I consider it a good sign that its focus is on the world of learning. The opportunity to meet the youth of the state, who symbolise the Kashmir of tomorrow, is precious and invaluable. Graduation is an important aspect of academic life, for the institution and for the students. A university is a place of learning where the students learn to think, acquire knowledge, polish their thought process and learn a thing or two about how the world functions in the diversity of its activities. When they step out of its precincts, they discover that the real world is more complex, somewhat harsher. The training of the mind, however, helps them understand this better and respond appropriately. This is all the more important in a specialised, technical, institution devoted to the most important area of activity, namely, agriculture.

4495. (25-11-2007) NEW DELHI : The President, Smt. Pratibha Devisingh Patil has congratulated Dola Banerjee for wining the Gold Medal in the women's individual recurve competition at the Archery World Cup. In her message, the President said " By becoming the first Indian to win this title you have boosted the morale of all our archers for the Olympic Games in Beijing next year.

4496. (25-11-2007) NEW DELHI : The President of India, Smt. Pratibha Devisingh Patil has said that generation of social awareness and public education is very important for access to justice for women. The President was speaking while delivering the inaugural address at the National Conference on Access to Justice for Women in New Delhi today. Smt. Patil said the subject of discussions at the Conference were very close to her heart and are also are important for national development. She added that it must not be forgotten that during the Independence struggle women also participated as equal partners under Mahatma Gandhi's leadership. Today, we need to follow the example of Mahatma Gandhi to mobilize the entire nation on issues related to the development of women, she emphasised. The President appreciated the role of NGOs in fighting against various social evils and practices and urged that their organizations can be further strengthened. A movement should be created with the sprit to develop society. The movement should also help in percolating the benefits of development, she said. Smt. Patil emphasised that the sprit of service is very important for large scale mass awakening. Colleges and schools should impart education in such a way that it inspires the younger generation, so that the energy of the youth could be properly mobilized. The President also stressed on the role of women in creating social awareness and hoped that women would come forward to launch a large-scale civil movement. They should come forward to enhance their status and fight against all inequalities and stand for not only promoting national causes but also international causes for sake of global peace and prosperity. Smt. Patil quoted the poem "All the Rivers" in this context. A part of the poem is:-" If all the trees were one tree, what a great tree it would be; If all rivers were one river, what a great river it would be; ..." She said that she has always felt that if all the women in the world speak in one voice, what a great voice it will be, to bring peace, prosperity and happiness in the world.

4497. (25-11-2007) NEW DELHI : The President Smt. Pratibha Devisingh Patil has congratulated India's High Commissioner to the United Kingdom Shri Kamalesh Sharma on his selection by the Commonwealth Heads of Government as the next Secretary-General of the Commonwealth. In her message, the President said, "Your elevation to this post is a recognition of your outstanding abilities, which you have shown during your long diplomatic career. The achievement is even more worthy as you will be the first ever Secretary-General of the Commonwealth from India, thus emphasizing the respect that our country has in this grouping of nations."

4498. (26-11-2007) NEW DELHI : A Programme for providing financial support for electrification of remote unelectrified census villages and unelectrified hamlets of electrified census villages in various States, where grid extension is either not feasible or not cost effective and which are not taken up under the Rajiv Gandhi Gramin Vidyutikaran Yojna, is being implemented by the Ministry. Such villages are provided basic facilities for lighting / electricity through various renewable energy sources including solar energy. State-wise details of villages and hamlets taken up under the Programme through solar light systems are given in the enclosed Table. From 2005-06, support is provided for those remote villages / hamlets which are identified by the Rural Electrification Corporation (REC) for coverage through renewable energy sources. In Maharashtra, 190 tribal and economically backward villages have so far been provided support under the Programme.

4499. (26-11-2007) NEW DELHI : Madhya Pradesh Government has forwarded proposals to the Ministry of New and Renewable Energy for electrification of 185 villages located in inaccessible and forest areas. Out of these, proposals for 116 villages were submitted by 2004-05. The Ministry sanctioned financial support for electrification of 48 of these villages. However, projects in 18 villages were later cancelled by Madhya Pradesh Urja Vikas Nigam Ltd.(MPUVN). From 2005-06 onwards, it was decided to provide financial support under the Remote Village Electrification Programme for only those villages which are identified by the Rural Electrification Corporation (REC) for unfeasibility of electrification through grid connectivity. Proposals complete in all respects for electrification of 150 such REC identified villages, received from MPUVN have been approved by the Ministry for financial support. The work has been taken up on priority basis by MPUVN and so far it has been completed in 70 villages. This information was given by the Minister of State in the Ministry of New and Renewable Sources, Sh.Vilas Muttemwar in a written reply to a question in the Rajya Sabha today.

4500. (26-11-2007) NEW DELHI : There is potential for setting up wind power projects at six locations in Rajasthan. This indication came after wind resource assessment studies were carried out at 38 locations in Rajasthan .They have wind power density of 200 watts per square meter or more. Based on this, a gross wind power potential of 5400 MW has been estimated in the state assuming land availability @ 1% of potential areas and wind farm land requirement @ 12 Hectares per MW. A wind power installed capacity of 494 MW has been set up in the State of Rajasthan upto September, 2007. The Government of India promotes setting up of commercial wind power projects in the country, including in the State of Rajasthan, by providing fiscal incentives such as concessional import duty on certain components of wind electricity generator, excise duty exemption, ten years tax holiday on income generated from wind power projects, benefit of accelerated depreciation and loan from Indian Renewable Energy Development Agency (IREDA). Technical support including detailed wind resource assessment to identify further potential sites is provided by the Centre for Wind Energy Technology (C-WET). This apart, preferential tariff is being provided for wind power in most of the potential States, including Rajasthan. This information was given by the Minister of State in the Ministry of New and Renewable Sources, Sh.Vilas Muttemwar in a written reply to a question in the Rajya Sabha today.

4501. (26-11-2007) CHENNAI: Chennai will become a smoke-free city by 2010 and Tamil Nadu a smoke-free State by 2012. As a first step in this direction, Health and Family Welfare Minister Anbumani Ramadoss launched the Tamil Nadu Tobacco Control Coalition (TTCC) here on Sunday in the presence of Chennai Mayor M. Subramanian and released an audio CD on 'Smoke-Free World.' Delivering the special address at the 'Consultation on Tobacco Control in Tamil Nadu,' organised by the TTCC and Pasumai Thaayagam, Dr. Ramadoss said that he would urge the State Chief Minister to make Tamil Nadu the first smoke-free State in the country. He has been urging the Chief Ministers of Delhi and Maharashtra to make Delhi and Mumbai 'smoke-free' cities. In the next 3-4 months, the Centre would form the Central Tobacco Regulatory Authority to monitor and implement tobacco control laws. It would be a law-implementing agency entrusted with full powers. The Centre would also launch a national programme to bring down the use of tobacco products in public places. The programme would empower police, headmasters, bus drivers and conductors and law enforcers to penalise offenders. "The fine is Rs 200 per offence, whereas we want it raised to Rs 2,000," he added. He urged people to take to the streets to oppose the use of tobacco products in public places. Most people were not aware of the Tobacco Control Act that prohibited smoking in public places.

4502. (26-11-2007) NEW DELHI : The President, Smt. Pratibha Devisingh Patil, is leaving New Delhi on a three-day visit to Maharashtra this evening. Smt. Patil will inaugurate 'PRASADALAYA' of Shri Sai Baba Sansthan Trust at Shirdi on November 27. She will inaugurate the 11th Inter-University Sports Tournament-the 'ASHWAMEDH' at Nashik, the same day. On November 28, She will unveil the plaque of the Institutional Complex of Mumbai Educational Trust at Bhujbal Knowledge City, Adgaon, Nashik. She will also inaugurate Shri Yashwantrao Chavan Planetarium & Science Centre and Nashik Festival to celebrate the Silver Jubilee Year of Nashik Municipal Corporation at Nashik on the same day. The President will return to New Delhi on November 28 late in the evening.

4503. (26-11-2007) NEW DELHI : The Committee, constituted by the Government to recommend revised subscriber based Spectrum allocation criterion for allocation of spectrum in a scientific and practical manner, met on 26.11.2007 for the second meeting under the chairmanship of Shri R. Bandhopadhyay, Additional Secretary (Telecom), Department of Telecommunications. The Committee also has members from COAI, AUSPI and experts from premier technical institutions. Presentations were made by the representatives of the following companies/groups on their views before the committee on the issue of allocation of spectrum.

4504. (26-11-2007) NEW DELHI : Wind Power Projects with an aggregate installed capacity of 7660 MW, comprising of Wind Turbines of 225 kW to 1650 kW unit capacities, have been set up in the country, till 30th September, 2007. State-wise details are given in Annexure-I. 216 potential sites, having annual mean wind power density of 200 Watt/square meter or more at 50 meter elevation, have been identified, which are considered suitable for installation of wind power projects. State-wise information is given in Annexure-II.

4505. (26-11-2007) NEW DELHI : A Working Group on New and Renewable Energy has been established under the India-Japan Energy Dialogue to coordinate cooperation activities in new and renewable energy. The first meeting of the Working Group was held on the 28th June 2007 at New Delhi wherein it was decided that both sides will explore ways and means to further cooperation in the field of new and renewable energy. This information was given by the Minister of State in the Ministry of New and Renewable Sources, Sh.Vilas Muttemwar in a written reply to a question in the Rajya Sabha today.

4506. (26-11-2007) NEW DELHI : The government has been providing several concessions in the form of fiscal and financial incentives to encourage the use of renewable energy sources. These include capital/interest subsidy, accelerated depreciation, nil/ concessional excise and customs duties. Further, as applicable to all new infrastructure projects, profits earned from sale of renewable power are exempt from Income Tax for any 10 years out of the first 15 years of project's operation. This apart, preferential tariff for grid interactive renewable power is being given in most potential States. This information was given by the Minister of State in the Ministry of New and Renewable Sources, Sh.Vilas Muttemwar in a written reply to a question in the Rajya Sabha today.

4507. (26-11-2007) NEW DELHI : The Bharatiya Janata Party has taken a serious note about yesterday's incidents in Malaysia. The Indians peacefully protesting against the injustice meted out to them by the Malaysian government, became victims of police atrocities in Kuala Lumpur. Some of the protestors were brutally beaten and hundreds of them were detained by the police. The BJP expresses its concern over the plight of Indians facing discrimination and marginalization in Malaysia, which has forced them to take to the streets. Ethnic Indians constitute about 7 percent of the population. Although Indians are the third largest ethnic group in Malaysia yet they are apparently living a life of poverty and deprivation in the country. When Malaysia became independent in 1957 there was a ray of hope for people of Indian origin that they would be able to gain some respect and dignity in the country. Their dreams appear to have been shattered. Trepidation and frustration is taking its toll on the Malaysian Indian, given the lack of job opportunities in the government or the private sector. Even their places of worship have not been spared by the Government. A policy of indiscriminate and unlawful demolition of Hindu temples has further hurt the religious sentiments of the Indian people. According to media reports three Hindu temples have been pulled down since February this year. The BJP seeks immediate diplomatic intervention from the UPA Government on this issue. The government should register its protest with the Malaysian envoy in New Delhi and also convey its displeasure on the developments in Malaysia. The BJP expresses its solidarity with the people of Indian origin in Malaysia and hopes that their struggle against the injustice and inequality would reach to a logical conclusion.

4508. (26-11-2007) NEW DELHI : New and renewable energy has been assuming increasing significance in recent times with the growing concern for the country's energy security and environment. Bulk of the energy needs of the common man come from renewable energy, mainly agro and forest residues as well as animal wastes. Already, over 40 lakh family size biogas plants, about 14 lakh solar photovoltaic systems for lighting and other applications and solar thermal systems covering 20 lakh square meters collector area have been installed. Beside, about 11, 000 MW power from renewables has been added to the electricity grids. Ministry of New and Renewable Energy is supporting deployment of renewable energy systems by providing fiscal and financial support to reduce the capital costs of these systems. This information was given by the Minister of State in the Ministry of New and Renewable Sources, Sh.Vilas Muttemwar in a written reply to a question in the Rajya Sabha today.

4509. (26-11-2007) NEW DELHI : In terms of the Government of India notification F.No.4(9)-W&M/2002 dated July 12, 2002, the holders of 6.72 per cent Government Stock 2007/2012 had the discretion to exercise "put option" after giving a notice of two months on or after completion of 5 years tenure from the date of issuance of the Government Stock on any coupon date falling thereafter. Accordingly, put options have been exercised by eleven holders, amounting to Rs.885, 58, 30, 000 and are repayable at par on January 18, 2008. In the event of a holiday being declared on January 18, 2008 by any State Government under the Negotiable

Instruments Act, 1881, the Loan will be repaid by the paying offices in that State on the previous working day.

4510. (26-11-2007) MOSCOW : Shri Murli Deora, Minister of Petroleum and Natural Gas, accompanied by a high level delegation in the hydrocarbon sector, visiting Moscow from 25th to 27th November, 2007 had a meeting with Mr. Victor. A. Zubkov, Prime Minister of the Russian Federation today. The meeting was held in a cordial and friendly atmosphere characteristic of the bilateral relations between the two countries. This meeting was a follow up of the successful summit between Dr. Manmohan Singh, Prime Minister of India and Mr. Vladimir. V. Putin earlier this month in Moscow. Both the sides discussed various avenues of cooperation between the two countries. The emphasis was on the mutually beneficial projects in upstream, mid-stream and down stream sectors in India, Russia and third countries between the companies of the two countries in hydrocarbon sector. It was agreed that the National Oil Companies of the two countries should concretize mutually beneficial projects in the fields of exploration and production, grassroots refineries, modernization of refineries, gas based petrochemical plants, gas processing plants, participation in liquefied natural gas (LNG) and inform the progress to the leadership of the two countries. Both the sides noted that India has emerged as a hub of refining in Asia. Shri Murli Deora underlined that Indian exports of refined petroleum products to some of the world's most sophisticated markets have touched US$ 40 Billion. The growing refining sector in India also offers immense opportunities for the Russian companies to participate. The discussions between the two sides will continue at the second Indo-Russian Forum on Trade and Investment scheduled in February, 2008 at New Delhi when a delegation of leading Russian businessmen will be led by the Russian Prime Minister himself. Earlier on 25th November, 2007 en route to Moscow, The Minister (P&NG) had a brief stopover at Ashgabat, Turkmenistan and held wide ranging discussions with Mr. B. Muradov, Head of State Agency for Hydrocarbons Resources on various issues related to bilateral cooperation in oil and gas sector. Minister (P&NG) was accompanied by Secretary (P&NG), CMD, ONGC, Chairman, IOC and MD, OVL. Indian Ambassador in Turkmenistan was also present in the meeting. The Turkmen side invited the Indian oil companies in upstream, mid-stream and downstream areas to participate in projects of mutual interest in Turkmenistan. It was agreed that a delegation comprising CEOs of IOC, ONGC, GAIL and OVL, led by a senior Ministry representative will visit Turkmenistan shortly for discussions for identification of specific projects for cooperation. An overarching MOU covering cooperation in the entire hydrocarbon value chain between the two Governments and identified projects is expected to be formalized during the ensuing meeting of the Joint Working Group on cooperation in Hydrocarbons scheduled to be held in the first quarter of 2008 at New Delhi.

4511. (26-11-2007) NEW DELHI : As per the report received from the Government of NCT of Delhi, Hon'ble Supreme Court of India has ordered for closure of all industrial units that have come up in residential/non-conforming areas on or after 01.08.1990 and impermissible household industries in Delhi. The State Government of NCT of Delhi has taken the following steps to safeguard the interest of labourers working in the industries: 22749 industries operating in residential/non-conforming areas have been given allotment of alternate industrial plots/flats in conforming areas developed by the Government of Delhi in Bawana, Narela, Badli and Jhilmil industrial areas. Approximately 475 hectares of land is likely to be acquired for development of industrial plots for relocating other eligible industrial units. Under Master Plan for Delhi-2021, clusters of industrial concentration of maximum 4 hectares of contiguous area, having more than 70% plots within cluster under manufacturing and industrial activities, can be considered for redevelopment on the basis of surveys. Notification in respect of 19 such clusters which qualify for redevelopment has been issued. As per Master Plan for Delhi-2021, 51 more items have been added in the list of household industries. The above steps would ensure minimum dislocation of industries and the labourers employed therein. The Government of NCT of Delhi is the appropriate authority in this regard. This information was given by the Minister of State for Labour and Employment Shri Oscar Fernandes (Independent Charge) in a written reply in the Lok Sabha today.

4512. (26-11-2007) NEW DELHI : Transfer of Provident Fund amount of a member is effected in accordance with the provisions of the Employees' Provident Funds Scheme, 1952. On joining a new establishment, a member is required to submit an application to the present employer in prescribed form for transfer of balance of Provident Fund who will submit the same to the Regional Commissioner under whose jurisdiction the previous establishment is situated. In other words, the transfer application form is to be submitted to the present employer for onward transmission to the Commissioner by whom the transfer is to be effected. A Public Grievance Handling Machinery exists at Employees' Provident Fund Organization. On receipt of any grievance, appropriate action is taken for redressal thereof. This information was given by the Minister of State for Labour and Employment Shri Oscar Fernandes (Independent Charge) in a written reply in the Lok Sabha today.

4513. (26-11-2007) NEW DELHI : The Bonded Labour System (Abolition) Act, 1976 does not differentiate between the Adult bondage and child bondage. The Bonded Labourers are identified, released and rehabilitated by the State Governments and the Central Government is providing Grant-in-aid for rehabilitation of Bonded Labouerers at the rate of Rs. 20, 000/- per bonded labour which is shared by the Central and State government concerned on 50:50 basis.

4514. (26-11-2007) NEW DELHI : The Prime Minister Dr. Manmohan Singh has congratulated Ms. Dola Banerjee for winning the Gold Medal in the women's individual recurve competition at the Archery World Cup. In a message, Dr. Singh said that Dola Banerjee has done the Nation proud and has become an inspiration for the upcoming archers. "I wish her the very best in all her future endeavours", the Prime Minister added.

4515. (26-11-2007) NEW DELHI : India is the second largest producer of vegetables in the world. Total production of vegetables is estimated at 108.20 million metric tones from an area of 7.05 million ha during 2005-06. The Centrally Sponsored Schemes being implemented by the Ministry of Agriculture, namely Technology Mission for Integrated Development of Horticulture in North Eastern and Himalayan States (TMNE) and National Horticulture Mission (NHM), aim at increasing the production and productivity of horticultural crops including vegetables. Under these Schemes, assistance is provided to the farmers for quality planting material of elite cultivars, adoption of news technologies, integrated pest and disease management, Integrated nutrient management and farm mechanization. Besides, National Horticulture Board is also implementing schemes which provide assistance for production of vegetables such as tomato, capsicum, etc. The Centrally Sponsored Scheme of Micro-irrigation provides assistance to farmers for efficient use of water. These measures are expected to enhance the productivity of horticultural crops including vegetable crops to reduce their cost of production and increase the supply to meet round the year demand of these food items. This information was given by Shri Kanti Lal Bhuria, Minister of State for Agriculture in written reply to a question in the Lok Sabha today.

4516. (26-11-2007) NEW DELHI : The Congress Party has said here today that, it is ironic that those who have no respect for human rights, those who have shunted Taslima Nasreen from one part of India to another, from Rajasthan to Delhi in particular, the BJP is trying to preach to us and blame us. Let us be clear Taslima Nasreen is in India because of the UPA Government permission. The state governments do not give her permission. The Central Government does. Let us also be clear that this is part of the Central Government tradition in India, followed invariably for decades of giving permission or refuge, subject to certain basic conditions, in all cases, for example that the person concerned will not indulge in political activity, for example that he or she will not affect sovereign relations between nations and so forth. We have also apprised the fact that when the permission was sought to be renewed there were legitimate objections, because anybody has the right to object from the West Bengal government hence the word legitimate is being used, and the Central Government overruled those objections and granted her permission. Who is the BJP to lecture to us? The BJP should come clean to the nation. They should answer a few basic questions. Why did they move heaven and earth to shunt her out from Rajasthan to Delhi? And as if putting somebody in Rajasthan Bhavan in Delhi, is it Rajasthan territory? Who looks after law and order in Delhi? It's a Central Government administered issue as far as law and order is concerned. And why this double-speak of talking in front of cameras or accusing the Congress Party and operating in the back room to try to shunt Taslima from A to B. So this is a classic case of trying to pass on the buck, ulta chor kotwal ko dante. They have done nothing. Here is an example where the devil is trying to quote the scriptures. And we want to ask this question: What is the motive behind the BJP preaching to us on Taslima Nasreen. Their so-called anxiety does not appear to be natural, does not appear to be genuine. Is it because they want to conflagrate the issue, is it because they want to drive a wedge between different segments of a particular community? Who is this BJP lecturing? Look at their track record on minorities in Rajasthan, whether it is Christians or Muslims. It is a very strange case where they want the country to forget their known history on such issues. They should rest assured that the rest of the country will not be lulled into some kind of a trance by a so-called opium party. The Congress-led UPA Government has not only given permission but has been completely unassociated and non-associated with the movements of Taslima Nasreen within India. We have neither moved her nor pushed her nor compelled her nor coerced her. And, like anybody else she is free to go where she wants. At least we are not part of any other movement to stop her movements. But we find it supremely ironic, we find it ridiculous and we find it laughable when we find the BJP attacking us on such an issue. To a question that unlike the Left front and the BJP is the Congress Party for Taslima's stay in Kolkata, Shri Singhvi said, let me make a few things very clear. First, the fact that Taslima Nasreen has been given permission not now but many times in the past and now, is a matter governed by rules, regulations and established precedent of the Congress-led Central government exercised in this case already. Second, it does not mean, should not mean and cannot mean, has never meant that any government which gives permission agrees or disagrees with the content of her views. This is an important point. We are a democracy and we have a right to agree and disagree and you have the same right and the state governments have the same right. But agreement or disagreement with the content of her views has nothing to do with the grant or denial of permission and that is the basic fault and fallacy which people are committing. Third, whatever movements you have seen in the last few days, whatever flurry of activity you have seen, the Central government has been kept completely in the dark. The Central government or the Congress Party has nothing to do with it. If a state government pushes her from A to B and the BJP tries to accuse us, it is the height of hypocrisy and it is the height of double speak and double standards. To a question whether she has the right to stay in this country, Shri Singhvi said, this has nothing to do with the content of her views. This is to do with the practice so long as she observes the conditionality's put upon her, she has the right to stay in this country subject to the permission being there. To a question whether she goes or wait till further orders, Shri Singhvi said, as far as we are concerned we are providing her even now with appropriate security because as you know Delhi is a Centre-administered territory as far as law and order is concerned. To a question as to where she will stay if the state government has right to give security as it is BJP government in Rajasthan, Shri Singhvi said, that in this whole, totally false, fabricated and hypocritical confusion generated by the BJP the impression sought to be given is that she is being kept in Rajasthan merely because she is kept in a place called Rajasthan House. That is the point I am making. This is a joke. Does the BJP think that all of us eat grass? If you have a place in Delhi called Rajasthan House does Rajasthan state government provide security on the territory of Delhi? Under the law it has to be proved the permissive regulation of the Delhi government or the Central government as far as Delhi is concerned. That is the only part I am clarifying. I am not suggesting that we pushed her here or we pushed her from there. The point is that even now the Rajasthan government which is a BJP government is not prepared to keep her and they are giving us lectures about not keeping Taslima Nasreen and giving her affiliate status. That is the hypocrisy I am talking of. She is here, being moved by the Rajasthan government and I am only talking about the security being provided to her in Delhi.

4517. (26-11-2007) NEW DELHI : Setting up of Farm Schools, as per the recommendations of the National Commission on Farmers, has been made an eligible activity in 2007-08 under the Scheme 'Support to State Extension Programmes for Extension Reforms', based on Agricultural Technology Management Agency (ATMA) model. Farm Schools can be set up by the outstanding farmers and the participants would normally be leaders of farmers' groups producing the same agricultural commodities. 'Farmer awards' at block, district and state levels have been added in 2007-08 as an eligible activity under the scheme 'Support to State Extension Programmes for Extension Reforms'. In addition, awards could also be given under this scheme to 'farmers groups' and 'best performing ATMA district'. This information was given by Shri Kanti Lal Bhuria, Minister of State for Agriculture in written reply to a question in the Lok Sabha today.

4518. (26-11-2007) NEW DELHI : The Government fixes Minimum Support Prices (MSPs) for 25 crops namely Paddy, Jowar, Bajra, Maize, Ragi, Arhar (Tur), Moong, Urad, Cotton, Groundnut-in-shell, Sunflower seed, Soyabean, Sesamum, Nigerseed, Wheat, Barley, Gram, Masur (Lentil), Rapeseed/Mustard, Safflower, Toria, Copra, Jute and Tobacco and Statutory Minimum Price (SMP) for Sugarcane. In addition, Government implements Market Intervention Scheme (MIS) on the request of a State/UT Government for procurement of agricultural and horticultural commodities notcovered under the Price Support Scheme. The MIS is implemented in order to protect the growers of these commodities from making distress sale in the event of bumper crop when the prices tend to fall below the economic level/ cost of production. Losses, if any, incurred by the procuring agencies are shared by the Central Government and the concerned State Government on 50:50 basis (75:25 in case of North-Eastern States). However, the amount of loss to be shared between Central Government and the concerned State Government is restricted to 25% of value of procurement. Profit, if any, earned by the procuring agencies is retained by them. Appropriate procurement arrangements are made by the designated agencies to buy agricultural produce at MSP in different States. Further, with the amendment of the Agricultural Produce Marketing Committee (APMC) Act, the farmers now have more options to sell their produce to the prospective buyers. If the market price is more than the MSP fixed by the Government, farmers are free to sell their produce in the open market. This information was given by Shri Kanti Lal Bhuria, Minister of State for Agriculture in written reply to a question in the Lok Sabha today.

4519. (26-11-2007) NEW DELHI : Indian Renewable Energy Developer Agency Limited (IREDA), a public sector enterprise under the Ministry of New and Renewable Energy presented a cheque of Rs 7 crore to the Government for the financial year 2007-07 towards dividend. The dividend cheque was presented by Sh. Debashish Majumdar, Chairman and Managing Director to Sh Vilas Muttemwar, Minister of State for New and Renewable Energy in a function today. During the year IREDA's performance has been rated as very good in terms of MoU signed with the Government of India. It sanctioned additional 33 projects involving loan commitment of Rs 588.51 crore. IREDA also disbursed a sum of 410.87 crore during the year. Cumulatively it has sanctioned 1816 projects involving loan commitment of Rs. 8039.50 crore till March, 2007. The cumulative disbursement stands at Rs 4429.46 crore. A major chunk of the loan amount sanctioned during the financial year was for the establishment of 258.91 MW capacity of power generation and conventional fuel replacement. The cumulative Mega Watt (MW) and conventional fuel replacement till 31st March, 2007 since inception through renewable energy projects sanctioned by IREDA was 2927 MW and 12.91 lakh (MTCR/year) respectively. IREDA has a target of Rs 714 crore and Rs. 550 crore towards loan sanctions and disbursements respectively for the year 2007-08, in terms of MoU signed with the Government.

4520. (26-11-2007) NEW DELHI : A scheme for the relief and rehabilitation of rape victims is under the consideration of the Ministry of women and Child Development. The Ministry has suggested an outlay of Rs. 201 crore for the scheme in the 11th Plan. This was stated by the Ministry of Women and Child Development Minister, Smt. Renuka Chowdhury in a reply to a question by Smt. Supriya Sule in Rajya Sabha today. She further stated that the proposal for approval of the scheme by Expenditure Finance Committee is now under finalization. According to the scheme, a maximum compensation of Rs. 2.00 lakh may be awarded to the victims.

4521. (26-11-2007) NEW DELHI : Integrated Child Development Services (ICDS) Scheme is reviewed regularly by holding periodic meetings with Secretaries of the State Government and Union Territory (UT) Administrations and through fields visits of the Officers of the Ministry from time to time. This was stated by the Minister of Women and child Development, Smt. Renuka Chowdhury in a reply to a question by Shri Jai Parkash Aggarwal in Rajya Sabha today. She said that the Prime Minister in a letter addressed to the Chief Ministers of States/UTs has impressed upon them the need to set up an institutionalized review process at their level after carrying out a detailed assessment of the programme in their States, lay special emphasis on the programme status in areas with concentration of minority communities and preponderance of Scheduled Castes and Tribes, adequately empower Panchayati Raj Institutions (PRIs) and Urban Local Bodies (ULBs) to monitor and supervise the working of these centres; make line officials firmly accountable for their acitons and report on a quarterly basis on further developments in this sector, she added.

4522. (26-11-2007) ASHGABAT : The Minister of Petroleum & Natural Gas Shri Murli Deora had a fruitful meeting with Mr. Baimurat Muradov, Head of State Agency for Hydrocarbon Resources on various issues related to bilateral cooperation in Oil and Gas sector at Ashgabat (Capital of Turkmenistan) yesterday afternoon. The two sides agreed upon a roadmap to take forward cooperation in various activities in the hydrocarbon sector. Accompanied by Secretary-Petroleum, CMD-ONGC, CMD-IOC, CMD-OVL along with senior officials of MoPNG and ONGC, Shri Deora made a brief stop-over at Asghabat enroute to Moscow. The Turkmen dignitary briefed about the Turkmen strategy to fulfil the commitments for gas export and oil production. He referred to OMEL (JV between OVL and Mittal-Arcelor) which has recently acquired a stake of 30% in Block No.11 & 12 in the Turkmen sector of Caspian Sea. He expressed hope for grater participation OMEL and other Indian Oil & Gas companies in Turkmenistan. Mr. Muradov outlined the three directions in which the Indo-Turkmen energy cooperation can proceed. These include Production Sharing Agreement (PSA) in the off-shore Caspian Shelf for Oil and Gas blocks, Service contracts for Indian companies in the on-shore Hydrocarbon facilities as on-shore PSA is not allowed in Turkmenistan and Turkmenistan-Afghanistan-Pakistan-India (TAPI) gas pipeline project on which 10th steering committee meeting will be held in Islamabad by end 2007 He invited the Indian side to participate and work in all these three spheres. He assured of full cooperation in completing the formalities for applying for PSAs in the Caspian sector. Regarding on-shore facilities, he said that the Indian companies should sign service contracts by participating in tenders. He reiterated that Turkmenistan is interested in Indian participation owing to India's known expertise in these sectors. Indian side proposed that India and Turkmenistan should sign Inter-Governmental MOU for cooperation in both upstream and downstream activities where ONGC, IOC and GAIL could work with the Turkmen counterparts. In response, Mr. Muradov proposed to identify the exact areas of cooperation and better understanding of each other before signing the MOU. It was agreed that delegations from Indian companies namely ONGC, GAIL and IOC along with a senior officer of MoPNG would visit Turkmenistan in near future to apprise the Turkmen side about the potential, expertise of Indian side and prospects of cooperation. This would be followed by MOU signing during 2nd JWG meeting on energy in the first quarter of 2008. The two leaders also discussed Turkmenistan-Afghanistan-Pakistan-India(TAPI) gas pipeline project. Indian side mentioned that India would require 250 Million cubic meter of natural gas per day by next year and Turkmenistan can be an ideal partner in this context. Indian side was briefed about the huge reserves of oil and gas under Turkmen possession. The doubts raised on credibility of Turkmen reserves were satisfactorily dispelled Chairman IOC briefed Turkmen side about India's capabilities in up gradation and setting up of new refineries. In the context of a new tender for setting up a refinery in Turkmenistan, he agreed to send a delegation to Turkmenistan and to participate in the tender. Chairman ONGC mentioned about the training that ONGC could offer to Turkmen specialists and it was decided that Turkmenistan will send 8-10 specialists for advanced training to ONGC. Similar offer of IOC was accepted by the Turkmen side. Shri Deora invited Mr. Muradov and Turkmen Oil & Gas Minister to visit India and see the facilities in the Hydrocarbon sector there. Indian Ambassador Shri Mohammed Afzal and Embassy officials also participated in the meeting.

4523. (26-11-2007) NEW DELHI : Shri Kamal Nath, Union Minister of Commerce and Industry, has informed that a proposal is underway for commencing negotiations for an India-Malaysia Comprehensive Economic Cooperation Agreement (CECA) from January 2008. Inaugurating a Seminar on "Malaysia-India Business Opportunities", organized by the Confederation of Indian Industry (CII), the Minister said: "I am confident that this Agreement would take our bilateral relations to newer heights and would contribute to the growth of our economies". To take the trade and investment relations forward, both the countries had set up a Joint Study Group (JSG), and have recently adopted the JSG which recommended the establishment of a CECA, he added. The India-Malaysia Joint Study Group has outlined the huge potential for trade in goods, services and investment between the two countries. Shri Kamal Nath exuberated confidence that the recently concluded Joint Study Group estimate of catapulting the bilateral trade to US $ 16 billion by 2012 would be achievable. During the occasion, Hon. Dato' Seri Rafidah Aziz, Minister of International Trade and Industry, Malaysia, stated that Malaysia and India have continued to deepen the relationship and the scope of cooperation has expanded to cover many areas of trade, investment, education and tourism. The Malaysian Minister further emphasized that today's Seminar is to provide the business communities of the two countries with: (a) an update of trade and investment opportunities in both countries; and (b) explore possibilities for cooperation in trade, investment, services and collaboration in other areas of mutual interest. The business delegation accompanying the Malaysian Minister include, companies in sectors such as manufacturing, trading and services to explore business opportunities. The bilateral trade between India and Malaysia during 2002-03 was to the tune of US $ 2.2 billion and it increased three-fold during 2006-07 to the tune of US $ 6.6 billion. During 2006-07, India's exports to Malaysia stood at US $ 1.3 billion and imports from Malaysia at US $ 5.3 billion.

4524. (26-11-2007) NEW DELHI : Shri Kamal Nath, Union Minister of Commerce and Industry, during his bilateral talks with the visiting Dutch Minister for Foreign Affairs, Mr. Frank Heemskerk, here today has observed that there is great potential for further intensification of trade and investment relations between India and Netherlands. He expressed satisfaction that the bilateral trade between the two countries has increased by 22.3% in 2006 while the total trade between India and the Netherlands in the past five years (2002-2006) has almost doubled (97.79% growth). Exports from India to the Netherlands in these five years have increased by 87.23% while Dutch exports to India increased by 11.16%. "We are happy that the Dutch delegation consists of both Small and Medium Enterprises and has identified focus areas such as biotechnology, agro-industry, medical sector, infrastructure and logistics, R&D etc. The focused approach will help to identify concrete collaborations in the light of vast potential that exists in these areas", Shri Kamal Nath said and added that the Netherlands, today, is among India's top ten trading partners and in terms of investments. On Indo-EU Free Trade Agreement (FTA), both the sides observed that common areas have been identified and further discussions would be held in the 3rd round, which is slated to be in December, 2007. Discussions have also been held in other areas to be covered in the agreement, viz., SPS and TBT measures, intellectual property rights and Geographical Indications, competition policy, government procurement, dispute settlement etc. Senior officials from both India and the Netherlands participated in the meeting. As regards foreign direct investments, Shri Kamal Nath emphasised that there is large scope for Dutch investments in India in the areas like agriculture, infrastructure, automotives, biotechnology, food processing and pharmaceuticals. He informed that Netherlands now ranks 4th in the list of countries in terms of cumulative FDI inflows into India during the period August 2001 to July 2007 with total inflows amounting to about US $ 2.8 billion.

4525. (26-11-2007) NEW DELHI : There is a proposal to develop Advanced Medium Range Surface-to-Air Missile in collaboration with Israel. Procurement/ acquisition of items to meet defence requirements of the armed forces is made from various indigenous as well foreign sources including Israel. This is a continuous process undertaken to keep the armed forces modernized in order to meet any eventuality. Divulging details in this regard would not be in the interest of national security. This information was given by the Defence Minister Shri AK Antony in a written reply to Shri HG Ahir and Shri Naveen Jindal in Lok Sabha today.

4526. (26-11-2007) NEW DELHI : The Government is processing a proposal for procurement of C-130J transport aircraft for the Air Force. No contract has been concluded for the procurement as yet. There is also a proposal for joint development of a Medium Transport Aircraft by India and Russia. This information was given by the Defence Minister Shri AK Antony in a written reply to Shri KV Patel and Shri BK Tripathy in Lok Sabha today.

4527. (26-11-2007) NEW DELHI : Brahmos Supersonic crulse missile has been successfully developed for Indian Navy and Indian Army as joint effort with Russia. Development of air version has also been sanctioned and is progressing for integration with SU-30 MKI for the Indian Air Force. The re-design and development of the air launched version of missile has been completed and missile is ready for testing. Suitable universal launcher for different types of aircraft has also been designed. The tests would be carried out in 2009. This information was given by the Defence Minister Shri AK Antony in a written reply to Shri Raghuveer Singh Koshal in Lok Sabha today.

4528. (26-11-2007) NEW DELHI : The requisite Defence land has not been handed over to Airport Authority of India for development of the Dibrugarh Airport as the process relating to agreement on the terms and conditions of transfer of land with the Airports Authority of India has not been completed. There is also no offer as yet from the State Government of Assam on the alternative land to be exchanged in lieu of the defence land. This information was given by the Defence Minister Shri AK Antony in a written reply to Dr. A K Sarma in Lok Sabha today.

4529. (26-11-2007) NEW DELHI : The Indian Air Force has sought permission for Red Flag exercise with United States. Red Flag Exercise is to be held to Nellis Air force Base, USA in August 2008. In this exercise Air Forces of various countries participate with their aircraft. This exercise would give and opportunity to the Indian Air Force (IAF) to gain knowledge in the area of state-of-art technology, ground handling and logistic support. Besides, this would given an exposure to the IAF to witness some of the best practices followed by other Air Forces in the world. The likely expenditure on participation in this exercise is expected to be around Rs. 80 crores. This information was given by the Defence Minister Shri AK Antony in a written reply to Shri RR Singh and Shri Milind Deora in Lok Sabha today.

4530. (26-11-2007) NEW DELHI : Government have approved induction of 66 Hawk Advanced Jet Trainer (AJT) aircraft from M/s. BAE System of the United Kingdom. Twenty four such aircraft will be supplied by BAE Systems in Flyaway condition and the remaining 42 aircraft will be licensed manufactured in India by Hindustan Aeronautics Limited (HAL). Four aircraft have been delivered by M/s BAE Systems in the United Kingdom. Out of these, two aircraft have reached Air Force Station Bider on 12.11.2007. The twin seater Hawk AJT is a transonic, ground attack/trainer aircraft, powered by a single Rolls Royce Adour MK 871 turbo fan engine. It provides basic, advanced and weapons training. The aircraft is equipped with modern avionics. The induction of Advanced Jet Trainer will help IAF to ensure safe and smooth transition of young trainee pilots to high performance/technology aircraft in front line fighter squadrons. This information was given by the Defence Minister Shri AK Antony in a written reply to Shri Sugrib Singh in Lok Sabha today.

4531. (26-11-2007) NEW DELHI : A laboratory is being created at Gun Carriage Factory, Jabalpur for taking up development of new products, up-gradation of existing products and facilitating easy absorption of technology. Government has recently decided to place a greater focus on R&D work in Ordnance Factories, and the laboratory is being set up for this purpose. Development of new products or upgrades takes considerable time; as such, it may not be possible at this stage to know details of the products that would be developed, or the possibility for increasing production targets. This information was given by Minister of State for Defence Production Rao Inderjit Singh in a written reply to Shri Rakesh Singh in Lok Sabha today.

4532. (26-11-2007) NEW DELHI : Project for construction of three stealth frigates at Mazgaon Dock Limited (MDL) was sanctioned in 1998 with scheduled delivery as December 2005, December 2006 & 2007 for the three ships. However, the schedule was revised both for stealth frigates and missile destroyers. Now, these projects are progressing as per the revised schedule of delivery without slippage. The major reasons for the delays are; Concurrent design and construction of warships, Delay in finalization of system and system interfaces for developmental equipment, Delay in ordering of some weapon systems and Non performance of some of the indigenous vendors. Important steps taken by the Government were having stringent monitoring mechanism on half yearly basis by Apex Steering Committee under Secretary (Defence Production) and quarterly review by Controller of Warship Production and Acquisitions, half yearly review at Inter Governmental level for Russian equipment and delegation of enhanced financial power to MDL. This information was given by Minister of State for Defence Production Rao Inderjit Singh in a written reply to Shri Anandrao V Adsul and Shri AP Shivajirao in Lok Sabha today.

4533. (26-11-2007) NEW DELHI : Contract for limited upgrade of Sea Harrier aircraft was concluded with M/s Hindustan Aeronautics Ltd in March 2005. The limited upgrade is expected to be completed by September 2008. Contract for procurement of MiG 29K and MiG 29 KUB aircraft was concluded with FSUE RAC MiG, Russia in January 2004. The aircraft are expected to be delivered by November 2008. This information was given by the Defence Minister Shri AK Antony in a written reply to Dr. KS Manoj in Lok Sabha today.

4534. (26-11-2007) NEW DELHI : The Border Roads organization (BRO) is planning to construct roads for Mansarovar Yatra. Ghatiabagarh-Lipulekh road (75.54 Km) in Uttarakhand along Mansarovar Yatra route is to be constructed by BRO by 2012. This information was given by Defence Minister Shri AK Antony in a written reply to Shri SK Kharventhan in Lok Sabha today.

4535. (26-11-2007) NEW DELHI : The Union Government proposes to open new Fashion and Textile Technology Institutes during the Eleventh Plan period. New Centres of National Institute of Fashion Technology are being set up subject to the conditions that the State Government is willing to provide land and financial support and fulfilment of feasibility conditions. Decisions about the new centres are taken by NIFT Board, a Statutory body under Ministry of Textiles, as and when the proposals from State governments are received. This information was given by the Minister of State for Textiles, Shri E.V.K.S. Elangovan, in the Lok Sabha today, in a written reply to a question by Shri N.N. Krishnadas and Shri Tathagata Satpathy. The Minister further informed that proposals have been received from Government of Bihar and Government of Kerala for setting up NIFT Centre in their states. No formal proposal has been received from Government of Orissa. He further stated that proposal for setting up of NIFT Centre in Bihar has been approved by NIFT Board and the matter has been taken up with State Government for allotment of land and funding support. Proposal for setting up of NIFT Centre in Kannur, Kerala will be placed for consideration of the Board in its next meeting.

4536. (26-11-2007) NEW DELHI : The Government has chalked out a plan to promote Domestic Technical Textile Sector. This information was given by the Minister of State for Textiles, Shri E.V.K.S. Elangovan, in the Lok Sabha today, in a written reply to a question by Shri Eknath M. Gaikwad & Smt. Nivedita Mane. The Minister further informed that Based on the recommendation of an Expert Committee on Technical Textiles (ECTT), the Government has approved implementation of the "Scheme for Growth and Development of Technical Textiles" (SGDTT) with a budgetary provision of Rs.48.00 crore during the 11th Five Year Plan. The scheme consists of three components: (i) Conduct of Baseline Survey, (ii) Setting up of 4 (four) Centres of Excellence, one each for Agrotech, Buildtech, Geotech and Meditech, and (iii) Conducting Awareness Programme. Regarding the question of increase of more employment opportunities during the 11th Plan period, the Minister informed that employment generation could be assessed only after implementation of the Scheme.

4537. (26-11-2007) NEW DELHI : The National Water Development Agency (NWDA) after carrying out Preliminary Water Balance Studies of Kosi, Sarda (at Poornagiri), Ghagra (at Chisapani) and Gandak (at proposed dam in Nepal) has identified that these rivers flowing from Nepal to Uttar Pradesh and Bihar have surplus water which can be optimally utilized. Under National Perspective Plan(NPP) for water resources development, NWDA has identified five link canal proposals namely (i) Sarda Yamuna, (ii) Ghaghra-Yamuna, (iii) Gandak-Ganga, (iv) Kosi-Ghaghra and (v) Kosi-Mechi for utilization of surplus water of rivers flowing from Nepal to Uttar Pradesh and Bihar. The Feasibility Reports of Sarda-Yamuna & Ghaghra-Yamuna link proposals in India portion have been completed. The implementation of these link proposals depends upon the consensus and cooperation of the concerned states and agreements with the neighbouring countries. This information was given by the Minister of State for Water Resources, Shri Jai Prakash Narayan Yadav in response to a question by Shri Abdul Rashid Shaheen in the Lok Sabha today.

4538. (26-11-2007) NEW DELHI : Irrigation is a State subject and Planning, execution, priority of execution as well as funding of irrigation projects is within the purview of the respective State Governments. Government of India provides Central Assistance under Accelerated Irrigation Benefit Programme (AIBP) to eligible major/medium irrigation projects and surface water minor irrigation schemes on the basis of proposals to avail Central assistance under AIBP received from respective State Governments and in accordance with guidelines of the AIBP in force. As per prevailing guidelines, surface water minor irrigation schemes of special category States and drought prone/tribal area of non special category states are eligible for 90 per cent grant of the project cost included in the AIBP. The major and medium irrigation projects benefiting drought prone/tribal areas are also eligible for grant up to 90 per cent of project cost included in the AIBP. The extent of grant provided is based on the drought prone/tribal areas benefited from the project and such areas included in the AIBP. This information was given by the Minister of State for Water Resources, Shri Jai Prakash Narayan Yadav in response to a question by Shri Harikewal Prasad and Smt. Sangeeta Kumari Singh Deo in the Lok Sabha today.

4539. (26-11-2007) NEW DELHI : Most of the region of the country are technically feasible for provision of telecom facilities on demand. Some of the regions viz. North-East, certain pockets of Tribal and Rural areas are technically non-feasible due to difficult terrain. BSNL has made plans to make all such areas technically feasible by using Wireless in Local Loop (WLL) and Satellite techniques to provide telecom facility in such regions. All Short Distance Charging Areas in BSNL network have been planned to be provided with minimum 3 Base Transceiver Stations of WLL to give umbrella coverage on all India basis in the areas of operation of BSNL. This information was given by Dr. Shakeel Ahmad, Minister of State for Communications and Information Technology in the Lok Sabha today in a written reply to a question by Shri Harisinh Chavda.

4540. (26-11-2007) NEW DELHI : In the XIth Plan the Department of Posts has submitted a proposal to the Planning Commission for computerization of 17598 Departmental Post Offices and 64, 000 Branch Post Offices and network all computerized offices; provide Automatic Mail Processing Centres; Provide Remotely managed Franking Machines and Cash Counting Machines and Provide anywhere anytime banking. Following steps have been taken by the Department to enhance the revenue earning ability of the organization: Business Development and Marketing Directorate has been set up in the Department of Posts. It aims at developing new products and services and aims to make Department of Posts a customer oriented organization with business approach; A number of business products like Speed Post, Express Parcel Post and Business Post have been introduced; Value additions like collection from customer premises, credit facility, volume based discounts, door to door delivery, online track and trace system, pre-mailing services etc. have been introduced; Retail network of the Department of Post has been leveraged for providing new services and generating additional revenue and The department has taken initiatives to work out various business alliances and partnership with public and private corporations for leveraging the postal network in rural as well as urban areas. This information was given by Dr. Shakeel Ahmad, Minister of State for Communications and Information Technology in the Lok Sabha today in a written reply to a question by Shri Kashiram Rana and Shrimati Sangeeta Kumari Singh Deo.

4541. (26-11-2007) NEW DELHI : A Committee has been set up to recommend the revised subscriber based spectrum allocation criteria for allotment of 2G Spectrum. However, the matter is sub-judice in Telecom Disputes Settlement and Appellate Tribunal (TDSAT). The initial spectrum for 2G is allotted to the mobile telecom operators in accordance with the relevant provisions of their Service License Agreement. With growth of service and increased subscriber base, additional spectrum is allotted as per their request and taking into account the subscriber based eligibility criteria and subject to availability of spectrum in a telecom service area. This information was given by Dr. Shakeel Ahmad, Minister of State for Communications and Information Technology in the Lok Sabha today in a written reply to a question by Shri L.Rajagopal.

4542. (26-11-2007) NEW DELHI : Integrated Child Development Services (ICDS) Scheme is reviewed regularly by holding periodic meetings with Secretaries of the State Government and Union Territory (UT) Administrations and through fields visits of the Officers of the Ministry from time to time. This was stated by the Minister of Women and child Development, Smt. Renuka Chowdhury in a reply to a question by Shri Jai Parkash Aggarwal in Rajya Sabha today. She said that the Prime Minister in a letter addressed to the Chief Ministers of States/UTs has impressed upon them the need to set up an institutionalized review process at their level after carrying out a detailed assessment of the programme in their States, lay special emphasis on the programme status in areas with concentration of minority communities and preponderance of Scheduled Castes and Tribes, adequately empower Panchayati Raj Institutions (PRIs) and Urban Local Bodies (ULBs) to monitor and supervise the working of these centres; make line officials firmly accountable for their acitons and report on a quarterly basis on further developments in this sector, she added.

4543. (26-11-2007) NEW DELHI : As per the data available from the Population censuses 1991 and 2001, the gap between the literacy rates of Scheduled Tribes (STs) vis-à-vis all population, at all India level, has reduced over the decade. As per the reports of National Family Health Survey conducted by Ministry of Health & Family Welfare from time to time, gap for certain health indicators like 'Infant Mortality Rate', 'Under Five Child Mortality' and 'Ante Natal Checkup' between STs and General category population has also reduced over the years. This was stated by the Minister of Tribal Affairs, Shri P.R. Kyndiah in a reply to a question by Smt. Brinda Karat in Rajya Sabha today. He further added that although the gap between literacy rates and health indicators for STs vis-à-vis General category is reducing over the years, yet the Government endeavour continues to bridge the gap further by implementing various Plan schemes for STs. While the Ministry of Human Resource and Development is the nodal Ministry for promoting literacy across the country including Tribal Areas, the Ministry of Tribal Affairs has also been implementing a gender specific scheme of Educational Complex in the low literacy pockets for development of women literacy in tribal areas through the Non Government Organizations. Further a National Rural Health Mission (NRHM) has already been formed by the Ministry of Health & Family Welfare. The Minister said that the main objectives of NRHM is to provide accessible, affordable, accountable effective and reliable health care facilities, especially to poor and vulnerable sections of population, in rural areas of entire country with special focus in eighteen states viz. Bihar, Jharkhand, Madhya Pradesh, Chattishgarh, Uttar Pradesh, Uttarakhand, Orissa, Rajasthan, Assam, Meghalaya, Arunachal Pradesh, Manipur, Mizoram, Nagaland, Sikkim, Tripura, Himachal Pradesh and Jammu & Kashmir. Under the strategy of NRHM, the gaps in the existing scenario of rural health care, is to be addressed through 4-5 lakhs Accredited Social Health Activists to assist the Anganwadi worker and Auxiliary Nurse Midwife at village level to make the increased health services accessible to rural people of the country, he said.

4544. (26-11-2007) NEW DELHI : The Film India World Wide (FIWW) Section at the IFFI-2007 started today with the screening of 'The Pool' directed by Chris Smith. This American film has been shot entirely in Panaji, Goa by 36-year-old Chris Smith, and is made in Hindi, a language the director does not know. Its story follows Venkatesh, who works as a hotel house-boy alongside his staunch buddy, Jahangir. The two make extra money selling plastic bags to pedestrians. Venkatesh is mesmerized by the aquamarine glow of a backyard swimming pool, which he gazes from a mango tree. He gets to know the owners, a wealthy man (Nana Patekar) originally from Mumbai and his edgy daughter Ayesha, who take to him in their separate ways. This encounter changes the lives of the two boys, aspiring to better themselves without the benefit of any education or skills. The film's leisured pace and seemingly effortless telling captures the essential spirit of Goan living, from its mansions, its music, its street life and its work-force. Director Smith is known for his searching, introspective documentaries and their natural setting and universality of theme-attributes that he brings with gentle understanding to his film, The Pool. The other movies to be screened in the FIWW Section are: 'AIDS Jaago' comprising of four short films directed by Mira Nair, Santosh Sivan, Vishal Bhardwaj and Farhan Akhtar and 'Amal' directed by Richie Mehta.

4545. (26-11-2007) NEW DELHI : While information on incidents of ragging is not Centrally maintained, the Committee for monitoring the recommendations of the Raghavan Committee on measures for prevention of ragging, also appointed by the Supreme Court, has come across 70 cases of ragging reported in the print media during the current academic year (2007-08). Ragging is reported to be the cause of nine cases of suicide and three cases of serious injuries among these cases. The Central Government has drawn the attention of States and regulatory institutions (like the All India Council for Technical Education (AICTE), University Grants Commission (UGC), Medical Council of India) to the various recommendations contained in the Report of the Committee for Prevention of Ragging for implementation. This Ministry has also launched a media campaign through newspapers. Provisions of the Indian Penal Code, 1860 are attracted in appropriate instances and the directions of the Apex court mandates filling of First Information Reports by institutions with local police authorities, wherever victims are not satisfied with the action taken by the institutional authorities. This information was given by the Minister of State for Human Resource Development, Smt. D. Purandeswari in a written reply to a question by Shri Rajeev Chandrasekhar in Rajya Sabha today.

4546. (26-11-2007) NEW DELHI : To assess progress of States and Union Territories towards the goal of Universalisation of Elementary Education, an Educational Development Index (EDI), has been developed by National University of Educational Planning and Administration (NUEPA). The EDI has been developed on four broad parameters of access, infrastructure, teacher related indicators and elementary education outcomes. State-wise ranking on a composite index for primary and upper primary level of education based on 2005-06 data, is given at Annexure. Educationally Backward States receive priority in allocation of funds under the Sarva Shiksha Abhiyan. In addition, capacity building of these States through trainings and workshops has been undertaken, especially in components in which these States are not performing well. This information was given by the Minister of State for Human Resource Development, Shri M.A.A. Fatmi in a written reply to a question by Dr. Gyan Prakash Pilania in Rajya Sabha today.

4547. (26-11-2007) NEW DELHI : Literacy rate in the country is collected only through the decennial census operations. As per the last Census conducted in 2001, the literacy rate of the country was 64.84 per cent and female literacy was 53.67 per cent in respect of the population aged 7 years and above. The literacy rate of Andhra Pradesh was 60.47 per cent and the female literacy rate was 50.43 per cent. A statement showing the State-wise literacy rates of all persons, males and females as 2001 Census is enclosed. The approach Paper to the XI Plan of the Planning commission has set a target of achieving 8.5 per cent literacy rate by the end of the Plan period. This information was given by the Minister of State for Human Resource Development, Shri M.A.A. Fatma in a written reply to a question by Shri Ravula Chandra Sekar Reddy in Rajya Sabha today.

4548. (26-11-2007) NEW DELHI : At present, only the All India Council for Technical Education (AICTE) has framed regulations for entry and operation of foreign universities/institutions imparting technical education in India. According to information furnished by the AICTE, four institutions have been registered by them for providing technical education in India in collaboration with foreign universities/institutions. A legislative proposal for entry and operation of foreign educational institutions in the country is presently under consideration. This information was given by the Minister of State for Human Resource Development,

Smt. D. Purandeswari in a written reply to a question by Shri Amir Alam Khan in Rajya Sabha today.

4549. (26-11-2007) NEW DELHI : The Directors of Indian Institutes of Management (IIMs) are appointed by the Appointments Committee of the Cabinet (ACC) on the basis of recommendation of a Search-cum-Selection Committee constituted for this purpose. In accordance with this procedure, Prof. Samir Kumar Barua has been appointed to the post of Director, Indian Institute of Management, Ahmedabad w.e.f. 08.11.2007.

4550. (26-11-2007) NEW DELHI : In the Independence Day Speech of the Prime Minister, it was mentioned that adequate numbers of colleges will be set up across the country especially in the districts where enrolment rates are low. Colleges will be set up in 370 districts in the country.

4551. (26-11-2007) NEW DELHI : The 10th National Conference on Safety in Mines was inaugurated by the Minister of State for Labour & Employment (Independent Charge), Shri Oscar Fernandes here today in the presence of Dr. T. Subbarami Reddy, the Minister of State for Mines and Shri M.V. Rajasekharan, Minister of State for Planning. The two-day Conference is being organized by the Directorate General of Mines Safety (DGMS), Dhanbad, an apex body of the Ministry of Labour and Employment. Speaking on the occasion, Shri Fernandes said that Safety is not merely a concept or practice but it also recognizes the dignity of work and therefore all efforts should be made for the protection and safety of workers who are toiling for the prosperity of the nation. Shri Fernandes said that to work towards the objective of achieving 'Zero Accident Potential', serious introspection and analysis is needed for making an impact. He said there is a need for resources-for research, the subsequent development of new processes, equipment and work method and above all for training and establishment of suitable reward system. These actions must accompany the development and implementation of legislation. Shri Fernandes said that the various techniques of risk assessment and risk management contribute greatly towards improvement in the safety of mining operations. It is thus desirable that this technique, though in vogue in piecemeal manner as of now, be given the due impetus and dynamism that it deserves so as to realize its full potential. He said that investment in safety has a direct bearing on the overall performance of the mining company and it is expected that the mining companies will put adequate thrust on the safety budget to reduce accidents in mines and thereby improving the safety scenario of the country. Speaking on the occasion, the Minister of Mines Dr. T. Subbarami Reddy said that mining is very important for the growth of our economy and therefore all efforts should be made to make the mining activity totally safe for the workers. For this, Shri Reddy said, modern technology should be brought in and we should also learn from the countries like South Africa, Australia and Canada in this regard. Shri M.V. Rajasekharan, Minister of Planning also advocated adequate investment in the safety measures and he especially called upon the private sector to be more forthcoming in this regard. He said that all the progress we achieve would be meaningless if we cannot provide adequate security to our workers. The two day Conference will deliberate upon and give recommendations on the following specific issues: (i) Contract workers in Mines-problems and Issues vis-a-vis Safety, Health and Welfare, (ii) Safety issues in Unorganized mining sector, (iii) occupational Health Surveillance & Notified Diseases, (iv) Mechanization with a view to phase out Manual Loading and to improve safety standards, (v) Reduction of Risks from Roof & Side fall in Indian Coal Mines, (vi) below Ground Communication & Tracking system, (vii) safety issues in oil Mines, (viii) "Safety Management systems" :strategies for implementation and Path forward and (ix) implementation of ILO Convention 176 in Mines. The present Conference, being the apex consultative forum in the country for deliberation on issues related to Safety and Health at work place in mines, assumes greater importance in the context of the fast changing work environment in the mining industry due to globalization of workplace and more and more contribution of technology in the production processes.

4552. (26-11-2007) NEW DELHI : Red Fort, Delhi, popularly known as Lal Qila, constructed between A.D. 1639 and 1648 by Mughal emperor Shahjahan, was a part of the Shahjahanabad. Red Fort show-cases the very high level of art form and ornamental work. The art work in the Fort is a synthesis of Persian, European and Indian art which resulted in the development of unique Shahjahani style, which is rich in form, expression and colour. Red Fort, Delhi is one of the important building complexes of India which encapsulates a long period of Indian history and its arts. Its significance has transcended time and space. It is relevant as a symbol of architectural brilliance and power. The fort, located on the west bank of the river Yamuna, is octagonal in plan, with two longer sides on east and west and is provided with four gates viz. Lahori, Delhi, Yamuna and Salimgarh gate. The ramparts, covering a perimeter of 2.41 km. have a moat all along on the outside, which originally was connected with the river Yamuna. On the north, the Red fort is connected with the Salimgarh Fort by a bridge. Lahori gate, a magnificent three-storeyed structure, later screened by a barbican by Aurangzeb, served as the main entrance. Palaces, lying on the eastern side of the Fort, are approached from the Lahori gate through a roofed passage, flanked by double-storeyed arcaded apartments called Chhatta-Chowk and being used as shops. The Delhi gate is flanked on the outside by two elephants, commissioned in 1903 by Lord Curzon in place of the original ones demolished by Aurangzeb. A study of some of the old site plans, paintings and photographs, available at different places, shows that within the fort, a large number of the old enchanting buildings were demolished and replaced with military barracks and other modern constructions by the British after 1857. The British Army had occupied the Red Fort in 1857 and converted it into an army stronghold. They demolished a number of buildings to accommodate construction of barracks for their use. The fortress palace is an important focal point of the medieval city of the Shahjahanabad. The planning and aesthetics of the Red Fort represent the zenith of Mughal creativity which prevailed during the reign of the emperor Shahjahan. The fort has seen many layers of development after its construction by emperor Shahjahan. The significant phases of development were under Aurangzeb and later Mughal rulers. Important physical changes were carried out in the overall settings of the site after the First War of Independence during British Rule in 1857. After independence, the site experience, a few changes in terms of addition/ alteration to the structures. Salimgarh, with its thick rubble-built ramparts and circular bastions, which have undergone considerable repairs, is roughly triangular on plan and stands to the north-east of the Red Fort on the bank of the Yamuna. It is believed to have been built by Islam Shah Sur (1545-54), also known as Salim Shah, son and successor of Sher Shar Sur. The inscription of the Red Fort Complex is also significant for the country since it was from the ramparts of the Red Fort that the country's Independence was declared .The Independence Day Celebrations, every year, are organized at the ramparts of the Red Fort and the Prime Minister unfurls the National Flag.

4553. (26-11-2007) NEW DELHI : President of India Smt. Pratibha Devisingh Patil, said I am happy to be associated with the inauguration of the 9th All India Conference of Urban Cooperative Banks and Credit Societies, especially as I have been associated with the working of NAFCUB. The theme of the Conference "Financial Inclusion Through Urban Cooperative Credit Institutions" is topical and timely. I would like to pay homage to Sawai Singh Sisodia whose statue I just unveiled. He came on the scene when the cooperative movement was suffering a crisis. His passing away is a great loss to the movement. The urban cooperative credit movement in India is a century old. There are over 20 million members of urban cooperative banks in India making it, in terms of membership, the largest cooperative system in the world. It is a vast sector comprising over 1, 850 urban banks and around 40, 000 credit societies. The reserves of urban cooperative banks aggregate to over Rs.1.1 lakh crore. Though the share of the cooperative banking sector in the entire banking system in India is about 5 percent, it is an important segment considering the number of consumers availing of its services. Visualizing the importance of cooperatives in the development process, the first Prime Minister of India, Pandit Nehruji, said that he wanted to "convulse" the nation with cooperatives. He had an abiding faith in the cooperative system, the objective of which was to give small traders, artisans, factory workers and others access to institutional credit, instead of them going to the private moneylender and then often meeting with disastrous consequences. By catering to the credit requirements of people with limited means in the urban and semi-urban centres, the urban cooperatives seek the financial inclusion of people who are economically disadvantaged and this is extremely important for the equitable growth in the country. In a fast globalizing world order and growing competition, the challenge is to has a strategy for the urban cooperative banks who have the resilience to adapt to new requirements. A small number of cooperatives have grown to be big entities and are in a position to meet competition, but a number of others need support for their survival. The strength of the cooperative movement is in its collectivity. Cooperative institutions, particularly small urban cooperative banks and credit societies find it difficult to face competition from bigger players in the field, as the latter have at their command resources, technology and managerial competence, far greater than what cooperative banks have. For the individual banks and societies to be competitive, the sector as a whole must be strong and each unit should be backed by collective strength. The urban banks ought to seriously consider ways of networking amongst themselves and aggregating their resources as well as their requirements so that they have the advantage of size while approaching the financial markets and dealing with larger entities. Such systems and structures exist in many countries, where a single strong apex body is providing the expertise and resources for the grassroots level banks to operate. The possibility of this could be examined in the Indian context. It is equally important to make use of new management systems and technological advancements to modernize the urban cooperative sector. They may also consider mobile banking to reach out to their clientele. The unprecedented growth of our economy, year on year for the last few years, is also bringing about huge demographical changes. Rapid urbanization through migration is now resulting in a significantly large section of the population in urban areas being financially excluded. To bring them under the institutional fold for their financial and banking requirements is a challenge but it is also a tremendous opportunity for the urban cooperative banks and credit societies. Organizational strengths such as committed leadership, efficient use of resources, transparency in operations and involvement of members are, however, pre-requisites for the cooperatives to be able to take advantage of the opportunities. Improvement in overall governance should strengthen cooperatives and equip them to become premier vehicles of financial inclusion.

4554. (26-11-2007) NEW DELHI : Following is the text of the Speech of the Prime Minister, Dr. Manmohan Singh at the felicitation to Dr. R.K. Pachauri and scientists of IPCC: "I am delighted to welcome this distinguished group of scientists led by Dr. Pachauri in our midst and felicitate them for the distinction conferred on the Inter-Governmental Panel on Climate Change (IPCC). We were all delighted to hear the news of the Nobel Committee's decision. The award of the Nobel Peace Prize to IPCC is the latest feather in the much acclaimed cap of India's scientific community! I commend Dr. Pachauri for his outstanding leadership of the IPCC and for his contribution to bringing India in the forefront of the international discourse on this very important subject. Dr. Pachauri's election to the chairmanship of the IPCC was itself a unique honour. It was both a recognition of India's balanced approach to the issue, and an overdue recognition of the good work being done at TERI. We are all proud of TERI's good work. I have had the opportunity to learn from Dr. Pachauri's work for a long time. I believe he and his colleagues at TERI have given a new direction to the thinking on global warming and climate change. I commend them for their vision and their commitment. TERI has also been at the forefront in research on energy security. I appreciate its forward-looking approach to questions of energy security. I do believe research institutions and think tanks have an obligation not just to the present, the society we live in, but also to the future, to generations unborn. Far too much of our policy discourse and public debate is focused on the issues of the day. Not enough is invested in thinking about the future. I therefore, attach particular value to the work being done by scholars and analysts like Dr. Pachauri. I have also admired the fact that Dr. Pachauri has tried to bridge the gap between experts and the general public. Considerable energy has been invested in reaching out to policy makers and to opinion makers. It is important that intellectuals and experts should shape public discourse on matters of national and public interest. Even good quality research is of little use if its results remain confined to ivory towers. By making knowledge available to the lay public we empower them and give meaning to our democracy. This is all the more necessary on issues like climate change and global warming. It is important for every citizen of the world to understand what our obligations are to nature and to humanity. We are all tenants and travellers on this Planet. Here today, gone tomorrow. But life on this Planet will go on, must go on. We owe it to posterity that we give more than what we have received. We owe to nature that we renew it constantly so that the future is not imperilled by the present. The Nobel Committee has wisely chosen to give the Peace Prize this year to persons engaged in protecting our environment. Protection of life on our Planet for all time to come is the true peace that mankind seeks. We in India are committed to doing what is required to discharge our due in this regard.

4555. (26-11-2007) NEW DELHI : The Union Cabinet today gave its approval for constitution of National Disaster Response Fund (NDRF) under the administrative control of the Ministry of Home Affairs. An amount of Rs. 100 crore would be provide in the National Disaster Response Fund. The proposal will meet the statutory requirements of the provisions of the DM Act, 2005 duly enacted by Parliament and notified by Government of India. It will enable the National Executive Committee (NEC) under the chairmanship of Home Secretary / Secretary, in-charge of Disaster Management to meet the expenses for emergency response, relief and rehabilitation in the wake of disasters.

4556. (26-11-2007) NEW DELHI : The Union Cabinet today gave its approval for accession of the Cape Town Convention / Protocol by India. The Cape Town Convention and the Protocol provide an international legal and institutional framework for creation, prioritization and enforcement of international interests in aircraft, which greatly facilitate cross-border financing and leasing of aircraft. Accession of the Cape Town Convention / Protocol by India would provide greater confidence to the intending creditors reduction of risk applicable to asset-based financing and leasing transactions. The risk reduction will not only result in the availability of aviation credit at a cheaper cost, but will also broaden the spectrum of financing alternatives available to the aircraft operators. This will be of immense help to the Indian aviation industry. It will also help the passengers and other end users by pass-through price reductions and increased levels of service.

4557. (27-11-2007) NEW DELHI : St. John's College of the University of Cambridge announced the 'Dr. Manmohan Singh Scholarships' here today. The Scholarship programme has been set up exclusively for Indian students to study M.Phil. and Ph.D degrees in areas such as science, technology and social sciences. Following is the text of the remarks of the Prime Minister, Dr. Manmohan Singh on the occasion: "This is a rather special and indeed a sentimental moment for me. I am deeply touched by the initiative that has been taken by the Master and Fellow of St. John's College, Cambridge to institute these scholarships in my name. It is a rare privilege and a warm gesture. I am truly grateful to all those who have done me this unique honour. I must, however, offer my deepest and abiding gratitude to those teachers and tutors at Cambridge who accepted me as a student more than half-a-century ago. I must mention the names of R.F. Kahn, Lord Nicholas Kaldor, Ms. Joan Robinson, Prof. Maurice Dobb, Prof. R.C.O. Mathews and Sir F.H. Hinsley who was my tutor. I must also thank my colleagues and superiors at the University of Punjab who made it possible for me to take a scholarship and go to Cambridge. As I said at St. John's last year, "Cambridge made me". The values, the ideas and the discipline instilled in me at Cambridge have lasted through my life. The University of Cambridge has a special place in the hearts and minds of our people. Jawaharlal Nehru studied there and so did Rajiv Gandhi. Sarojini Naidu studied there and so did Prof. P.C. Mahalanobis. J.C. Bose studied there and so did Homi Bhaba. And I have my friend Milan Banerjee also at Cambridge and if I am not mistaken our greatest living scientist Prof. Swaminathan also is a former student of Cambridge. I had the pleasure of the company of such distinguished fellow students as Amartya Sen, Jagdish Bhagwati, Rehman Subhan, Lal Jayawardena and the late Mehboob-Ul-Haq from Pakistan. To be honoured in this manner by such a great institution is more than what I can ask for and certainly more than what I had ever dreamt of. Scholarships are an important means of making education available to all sections of society. My life is a living example of what scholarships can do for those who come from less privileged sections of society. I spent the first ten years of my life in a village without electricity, without any modern infrastructure. That a person like me, with my modest background and means, was able to study at all, not to mention at Cambridge, is testimony to the role scholarships can play in social and economic empowerment of individual and society. That is why our government has paid special attention to increasing scholarships, especially for children and youth from the less privileged sections of society. It is my sincere hope that every young person who has a burning desire to secure education is never denied the light of education for want of the means to finance it. Scholarships extended to students from different countries are also an important means of strengthening relations between people across nations and societies. Thousands of Indian students travel abroad for education. I would like to see a similar inflow of students from our region and across the world into India. We are a knowledge-based society and we should be open to the free flow of knowledge across national borders and boundaries. I hope more institutions and corporations will step forward to fund educational scholarships for our students, both at home and abroad. I once again thank St. John's College, Rolls Royce India, BP India and Tata Sons, specially my friend, Ratan, for supporting this Scholarship Programme. I hope these scholarships will reinforce the enduring bond between India and Cambridge."

4558. (27-11-2007) NEW DELHI : The foreign exchange reserves (including Gold, Special Drawing Rights and Reserve Tranche Position in the IMF) of the country, which stood at US$199.18 billion as on March 31, 2007, rose to a level of US$270.18 billion. The reserves are held in all major international currencies like US$, Euro, Pound, Yen etc. India's entire foreign exchange reserves are invested by Reserve Bank of India in multi-currency, multimarket portfolios. Since the forex reserves are invested outside the country, there is no direct impact on the prices of commodities. This information was given by Shri Pawan Kumar Bansal, Minister of State for Finance in reply to a question raised by Shri Jai Parkash Aggarwal in the Rajya Sabha today.

4559. (27-11-2007) NEW DELHI : An Exhibition of select Indian film posters was formally inaugurated by Shri Digambar Kamat, Chief Minister of Goa, at IFFI-2007 today. Titled 'A Voyage to Discover the Spirit of Freedom' the Exhibition showcases various facets of India's freedom struggle under five different categories. The categories are, Birth of Indian Cinema and the India's Freedom Struggle; Reformation-films on social reconstruction; The Dawn of Independence; Armed Aggression on India and Revisiting the Past-films made on the 1962 Indo-China war, the 1965 and 1971 wars with Pakistan and the recent Kargil war and Neo-Nationalism-depicting posters of films since 1990 showing aggressive nationalist in 'Border', 'Sarfarosh', 'Keethu Chakra' etc. and of those films which foster pride and guide the youth to take the charge of the nation as in 1942-a Love Story, Train to Pakistan, Gadar-Ek Prem Katha, Rang De Basanti, The Rising etc. Organized by National Film Archive of India (NFAI), the Exhibition brings alive the heritage of Indian cinema from its beginning to the modern days though the medium of photographs and film posters. NFAI's role involves collection of films and associated material for the purpose of preservation and permanent access in the broadest sense-research, re-use, re-release. The emphasis is on archiving for cultural purposes-to ensure the preservation and accessibility of films and related material as part of the national cultural heritage. The Documentation Section strives to trace, acquire, collect and preserve for posterity the heritage of Indian Cinema in the form of supportive documents including photographs, posters, song booklets etc. apart from the films.

4560. (27-11-2007) NEW DELHI : State-wise details of Central funds released during the years 2004-05, 2005-06, 2006-07 & 2007-08 under Sarva Shiksha Abhiyan (SSA) and unspent balance available with State/UTs as on 31.03.2007 is given at Annexure. Unspent balances remaining out of SSA grants at the end of a financial year are adjusted in grants payable in next financial year.

4561. (27-11-2007) NEW DELHI : A statement showing enrolment of Boys and Girls during 2004-05 at Primary, Upper Primary and Secondary Schools level as per Selected Educational Statistics 2004-05 is given in Annexure-I. The Government of India has launched two focused interventions-National Programme for Education of Girls at Elementary Education (NPEGEL) to reach out to never enrolled/dropout girls, working girls, older girls who have not completed elementary education and Kasturba Gandhi Balika Vidyalaya (KGBV) for girls from marginalized social groups. Under the Sarva Shiksha Abhiyan, free textbooks are provided to all girls and SC & ST children. In addition, depending on local requirements, State Governments have innovation funds under the Sarva Shiksha Abhiyan and the National Programme for Education of Girls at Elementary Level (NPEGEL) for providing uniforms to girls where necessary. Details of assistance provided to States during each of the last three years under NPEGEL and KGBV are given at Annexure-II.

4562. (27-11-2007) NEW DELHI : The Director of 'The Pool', the opening film in the Film India World Wide (FIWW) Section at the IFFI-2007, Chris Smith emphasized today that a different language did not pose any barrier to making of his film. 'The Pool' is an American film which has been shot in Hindi, a language the Director does not know. Speaking at the press conference here today, Mr. Smith highlighted that the film deals with human values which are universal in their appeal and making the film in Hindi did not pose much difficulty. Mr. Smith also informed the media persons of plans to release the 'The Pool' in USA in March 2008 and expressed optimism about the likely response from the American viewers. He also hoped that the film would be released in India in the near future though detailed plans for the same are yet to be worked out. Director Smith is known for his searching, introspective documentaries and their natural setting and universality of theme-attributes that he brings with gentle understanding to his film, The Pool.

4563. (27-11-2007) NEW DELHI : The Films Division has chalked out plans to promote documentary films by reaching out to the maximum possible viewers. The Chief Producer, Films Division, Shri Kuldeep Sinha while addressing the press conference at IFFI today, informed that the measures include holding documentary film festivals at locations all across the country, holding shows at universities, colleges and other educational institutions, partnering with NGOs etc. The Division has already held documentary festivals in the North Eastern States and Jammu & Kashmir as well as held screenings at select educational institutions. The Division aims to promote viewership of documentaries archiving the history of Indian freedom movement and has also sent a proposal to Government of India to consider a separate Documentary Film Channel to promote documentary viewership in general. The Films Division has also put on display an Exhibition

'Behind the Frames' at IFFI-2007, which exhibits antique cameras and other equipments used for making films in the olden era to the latest gadgets. Apart from these, props and rare photographs collected from different sources are also exhibited. "The rare equipments on display will give an insight into the technical nuances of film making, over the times. Films related to history of Indian cinema, film making and related subjects are also being screened at the Exhibition venue. The Exhibition is intended to take the cinema lovers to a journey down the memory lane from the magic world of film making of the yore to the digital age", Shri Sinha informed. Meanwhile, the 10th edition of the Mumbai International Film Festival (MIFF) for documentary, short and animation films will be held from February 3 to 9, 2008 at Mumbai. So far, 228 films have been received from 37 countries for the International Competition section and 543 films have been entered in the Indian Competition section. More information on MIFF can be sought from the website: www.miffindia.in.

4564. (27-11-2007) NEW DELHI : The University Grants Commission (UGC) has so far identified 21 Fake Universities/Institutions that are in existence in the country in violation of Section 22 of the UGC Act, 1956. A State-wise list of such Universities/Institutions is at Annexure. In order to curb fake educational institutes, the UGC has proposed comprehensive changes in the UGC Act, which include, inter-alia, inclusion of the expression of the word University/Vishwavidyalaya/ Vidyapeeth etc. in various regional languages and also providing for deterrent punishment including imprisonment for a period upto three years and penalty upto Rs. 10.00 lakhs, besides making the offence cognizable as well as non-bailable.

4565. (27-11-2007) NEW DELHI : The Government of India has sanctioned 2180 Kasturba Gandhi Balika Vidyalayas in the country till March, 2007. A list of the KGBVs sanctioned, operational and girls enrolled in them is annexed. A National Evaluation of the KGBV scheme was conducted through independent experts on girls education in February, 2007 covering 12 States who have found the overall working of the scheme satisfactory. The Report of the National Evaluation is available on website www.ssa.nic.in .

4566. (27-11-2007) NEW DELHI : Universities enjoy academic freedom and their academic bodies like Board of Studies, Academic Council approve the curriculum for different courses. The University Grants Commission (UGC) had prepared a Model Curriculum in 32 subjects of Sciences, Humanities and Social Sciences to provide a broad common framework for the Colleges and Universities across the Country. The Universities are free to adopt the model curriculum or to make necessary changes to suit their requirements. The Indira Gandhi National Open University (IGNOU), has developed a non-credit course on Gandhiji. According to the information furnished by IGNOU, Vardhaman Mahaveer Open University, Rajasthan is offering Certificate and Post Graduate (PG) Diploma Programmes in Gandhiji's Non-violent Conflict Resolution and P.G. Diploma

Programme in Gandhi Method for Beginners. Gujarat Vidyapeeth, Ahmedabad is offering M.Phil and Ph. D. Programmes on Gandhian Thoughts. According to information furnished by the UGC, Gandhian Studies Centres have been established in 24 Universities and 26 Colleges across the country during the Xth Plan. This information was given by Shri M.M.A Fatmi, Minister of Human Resources Development in the Lok Sabha today in a written reply to a question by Shri Raghuveer Singh Koshal.

4567. (27-11-2007) NEW DELHI : The Kapil Sibal Committee had relied on the financial estimate prepared by National University of Educational Planning and Administration (NUEPA) to put in to effect the right to free and compulsory education to all children in the age group of six to fourteen years. This financial estimate was based on four alternative scenarios, the lowest estimate being Rs.3, 21, 196 crores and the highest Rs.4, 36, 459 crores over a six year period from 2006-07 to 2011-12. The financial estimate has since been revised by NUEPA in view of (a) the decline in the child population estimates projected by the Registrar General of India, Census, and (b) the investments already made under Sarva Shiksha Abhiyan. The financial estimate now indicates a lower figure of Rs. 2, 28, 674 crores over a seven year period of 2008-09 to 2014-15. The objectives of universalization of elementary education are being addressed through the Sarva Shiksha Abhiyan programme. The Central Government has in the last three years significantly enhanced the budgetary allocations to State Governments as part of its commitment towards universalization of elementary education. This information was given by Shri M.M.A Fatmi, Minister of Human Resources Development in the Lok Sabha today in a written reply to a question by Shri Ravi Prakash Verma.

4568. (27-11-2007) NEW DELHI : A centrally sponsored scheme for universalisation of access to and improvement of quality of education at secondary stage will be implemented during the 11th Plan period. The objective of the scheme is to make secondary education of good quality available, accessible and affordable to all young persons in the age group of 15-16 years. The funding pattern of the scheme has not yet been finalized. This information was given by Shri M.M.A Fatmi, Minister of Human Resources Development in the Lok Sabha today in a written reply to a question by Smt. Susheela Bangaru Laxman.

4569. (27-11-2007) NEW DELHI : The Prime Minister in his Independence Day speech on 15.8.2007 has announced the decision of the Government to support 6, 000 high quality model schools at the rate of one in every block throughout the country to set standards of excellence for other schools in the area. Sarva Shiksha Abhiyan, which is a National programme for achieving universal elementary education by 2010, inter-alia, provides for opening of new schools, strengthening of school infrastructure, appointment of additional teachers, promotion of girls' education, supply of free text-books for girls, SC & ST students, interventions for enrollment of out of school children etc. These measures are expected to reduce the drop-out rate in elementary education. This information was given by Shri M M.A Fatmi, Minister of Human Resources Development in the Lok Sabha today in a written reply to a question by L. Rajagopal.

4570. (27-11-2007) NEW DELHI : Bharat Nirman which has been conceived as a time bound business plan by the Government for development of rural infrastructure is to be implemented over a period of 4 years *i.e.* 2005-06 to 2008-09 with the total estimated investment of Rs.1, 74, 000 crore. Bharat Nirman comprises of six components *i.e.* Irrigation, Rural Roads, Rural Housing, Rural Drinking Water Supply, Rural Electrification and Telephone Connectivity. Three components namely, Rural Roads, Rural Housing and Rural Water Supply are being implemented by the Ministry of Rural Development with the estimated investment of Rs.85, 000 crore. These components have well defined targets and the progress is closely monitored accordingly.

4571. (27-11-2007) NEW DELHI : National Rural Employment Guarantee Act (NREGA) 2005 which aims at providing enhancement of livelihood security of the households in rural areas was notified on 2nd February, 2006 in 200 identified districts in 27 States in its first phase of implementation. 130 additional districts were included in the 2nd phase of NREGA during the current financial year making a total of 330 districts. The Government has now decided to cover all the remaining rural districts of all State and Union Territories under NREGA with effect from 1.4.2008. A notification to this effect has already been issued on 28.9.2007.

4572. (27-11-2007) NEW DELHI : The Vice President of India Mohd. Hamid Ansari gave away the award for the Conservation of Nature instituted by Narayan Dharmarth Ausdhalaya Trust to Shri Ajay Rawat, a prominent and consistent activist in the conservation of nature from the Kumaon region of Uttarakhand. The first such award instituted by the Trust has been given on the occasion of Silver Anniversary of The Energy & Research Institute (TERI). Addressing on the occasion, the Vice President called upon the people to 'Protect the Earth'. He said that the natural order can be understood by the nature itself. He congratulated the award winner Shri Ajay Rawat for his distinguished work in the field of Conservation of Nature and wished that more and more people will come forward in this noble cause. He appreciated the efforts of the Narayan Dharmarth Ausdhalaya Trust for constituting such award. Smt. Kapila Vatsyayan, MP, Shri Vijay Bhushan Trustee and many distinguished persons were present on the occasion.

4573. (27-11-2007) NEW DELHI : Following is the text of the opening remarks of Shri D. Swarup, Chairman, PFRDA at a press briefing held here today. Shri C.B. Bhave, Chairman & Managing Director, National Securities Depository Ltd. also spoke on the occasion: "The Pension Fund Regulatory and Development Authority (PFRDA) and National Securities Depository Limited (NSDL) entered into a formal agreement on 26th November 2007 relating to the setting up of a Central Recordkeeping Agency (CRA) for the New Pension System (NPS). The NPS was introduced by Government of India for its new recruits (excepting the Armed Forces) w.e.f 1st January 2004.

4574. (27-11-2007) NEW DELHI : The Minister of State for Petroleum and Natural Gas Shri Dinsha Patel informed the Rajya Sabha in a written reply today that in last five years, reserve replacement ratio (RRR) in India was more than one, which means, oil companies in India have accreted more reserves than their oil and gas production. Shri Patel informed that the balance recoverable reserve position in 2002-03 was about 1485.73 million metric tones of oil and oil equivalent of gas (MMTOE), which has increased to 1843.15 MMTOE in 2006-07 achieving an increase of 24%. BP statistical review of world energy 2007 has pointed out that reserve to production (R/P) ratio for India is 19.3 years at current rate of production and assuming that no reserves are added in next 19 to 20 years.

4575. (27-11-2007) NEW DELHI : The Minister of State for Petroleum and Natural Gas Shri Dinsha Patel informed the Rajya Sabha in a written reply today that Hindustan Petroleum Corporation Limited (HPCL) has undertaken a preliminary feasibility study to set up a Petrochemicals Complex at Visakhapatnam in the State of Andhra Pradesh in consortium with a partner, after which, the capacity and costs can be firmed up. He added that HPCL plans to undertake debottlenecking of units at Visakh Refinery to augment the thruput of the Refinery to 10 MMTPA by the end of the XI Plan as well as increase the refining capacity to 16 MMTPA by the end of the XII Plan. Replying to another query, Shri Patel said that the pipeline between Vizag to Vijaywada and beyond upto Ghatkesar near Secunderabad is being utilized for evacuation of MS/HSD/SKO/Naphtha from Vizag Refinery. Further, these products are being distributed through tap-off point constructed at Rajamundhry in the Districts of East and West Godavari. He also clarified that the pipeline has been laid in private lands as per provisions of the Petroleum and Minerals Pipelines Act 1962, by acquiring the Right of Use(ROU) for the land. There is no complaint, on record, with the Company from any of the villages on the pipeline route.

4576. (27-11-2007) NEW DELHI : After obtaining Government approval on 26.10.2004, National Aluminium Company Limited (NALCO) has started implementation of second phase expansion project of its integrated aluminium complex at a revised estimated cost of Rs. 5003 crores (March, 2007 price levels) which is to be completed by December, 2008.

4577. (27-11-2007) NEW DELHI : A study has been conducted by the Indian Bureau of Mines (IBM) regarding the likely effects on the health of the labourers engaged in the mining of asbestos. The Study recommended imposition of safeguards on pollution level in work environment and other remedial measures. Recommendations of the Study have been examined in consultation with all stake holders. Some stake holders have suggested that asbestos mining can be permitted with appropriate safeguards. At present the ban on mining of asbestos has not been lifted. This information was given by Dr. T.Subbarami Reddy Minister of State for Mines in a written reply in the Lok Sabha today.

4578. (27-11-2007) NEW DELHI : Geological Survey of India (GSI) is engaged in study of landslides and is carrying out three types of landslide investigations namely landslide hazard zonation (LHZ) on different scales, landslide inventory and site-specific study of landslide. LHZ is done following Bureau of Indian Standard (BIS) or modified BIS guidelines.

4579. (27-11-2007) NEW DELHI : As per information given by Ministry of Earth Sciences, an area of 150, 000 square kilometer in the Central Indian Ocean under United Nations Convention on the Law of the Sea (UNCLOS) was allotted to India for carrying out exploration and developmental activities for polymetallic nodules programmes of which, after obligatory relinquishment of 50% of area, 75, 000 square kilometer has been retained by India. The resource potential in the retained area is of the order of 380 million tonnes of polymetallic nodules which contain minerals like copper, nickel, cobalt and manganese. Central Government has enacted the Offshore Areas Mineral (Development and Regulation) Act, 2002 and framed Offshore Areas Mineral Concession Rules, 2006, to provide for development and regulation of mineral resources in the territorial water, continental shelf, exclusive economic zone and other maritime zones of India and to provide for matters connected therewith or incidental thereto. As per information given by Ministry of Earth Sciences, as part of polymetallic nodules programme, multibeam bathymetry survey has been carried out in the 75, 000 square kilometer area in the Indian Ocean to study the topography, and sampling has been carried out at different grid intervals in selected blocks. This information was given by Dr. T.Subbarami Reddy Minister of State for Mines in a written reply in the Lok Sabha today.

4580. (27-11-2007) NEW DELHI : In order to optimize intelligence flow and coordination between multifarious agencies at the Centre and in the States in the field of counter-terrorism and counter-intelligence, a Multi-Agency Centre (MAC) and Joint Task Force on Intelligence (JTFI) have been created in the Intelligence Bureau at Delhi, supported by Subsidiary Multi-Agency Centres (SMACs) at almost all State capitals. Steps have also been taken to strengthen counter-intelligence apparatus in the Intelligence Bureau. Further, the States have been asked to revamp the Special Branches by way of filling up of vacancies; posting of competent officers in Special Branches; mandatory tenure preferably of 5 years for personnel in Special Branches and linkage of this requirement with promotion; system of incentives/disincentives; dedicated staff for intelligence work right up to the police stations level and re-activating beat constable system; making available modern equipment and gadgets for interception; special training for personnel posted in Special Branches and earmarking of up to 5% of their annual allocations under the Scheme for Modernisation of State Police Forces for strengthening of Special Branches. This was stated in a written reply to a question in the Lok Sabha today by the Minister of State in the Ministry of Home Affairs, Shri Sriprakash Jaiswal.

4581. (27-11-2007) NEW DELHI : The Government of India has sanctioned 3406 kms of fencing along the Indo-Bangladesh border. Out of this, 2529 kms of fencing has been erected. A pilot project of 277 kms of flood-lighting in the West Bengal sector was sanctioned and has since been completed. An amount of Rs.2881.58 crore has been incurred on border works which includes the expenditure incurred on the construction of 3246 kms of roads and 23051 mtrs. of bridges. The project is likely to be completed by 2008-09. This was stated in a written reply to a question in the Lok Sabha today by the Minister of State in the Ministry of Home Affairs, Smt. V. Radhika Selvi.

4582. (27-11-2007) NEW DELHI : Inaugurating the National Conference on How accessible and safe is "Safe Blood" organized by the Confederation of Indian Industry (CII) today, the Union Minister for Health & Family Welfare, Dr. Anbumani Ramadoss said that a well-organized blood transfusion service is a vital component of any healthcare system. He added that the Government is also considering a National Blood Transfusion Services Act, which is still in the draft stage and this will define the various roles and responsibilities and make it mandatory to put good laboratory practices in place and ensure high quality of services. Penalties have also been included in the Act to make the concerned personnel accountable. Besides Shri Deepender Hooda, Member of Parliament, the Director General and other senior members from CII also participated in the function.

4583. (27-11-2007) NEW DELHI : Pancheshwar Multipurpose Project, Saptakosi High dam Project, Sunkosi storage cum Diversion Scheme, Kamala Project are under investigation jointly with Nepal. Joint surveys for Pancheshwar Project have been completed except for the re-regulating dam site. For field surveys and investigation of Sapta Kosi High Dam Multipurpose Project & Sunkosi storage cum Diversion Scheme, a Joint Project Office (JPO) has been set up in Nepal which would also carry out feasibility study of Kamla and preliminary study of Bamati Multipurpose Project. The construction of these projects will depend upon the finalization of joint Detailed Project Reports (DPR) and then entering into agreements between the Governments of India and Nepal on the basis of joint DPR. This information was given by the Minister of State for Water Resources, Shri Jai Prakash Narayan Yadav in response to a question by Shri Harish Rawat in the Rajya Sabha today.

4584. (27-11-2007) NEW DELHI : The National Water Development Agency (NWDA) has prepared Feasibility Report of 16 links out of 30 identified links under the National Perspective Plan (NPP) for Water Resources Development for transfer of water from surplus basins to water deficit basins/areas. A Group head by Chairman, Central Water Commission (CWC) consisting of other officers of

CWC, NWDA and Secretaries of Irrigation/Water Resources Department from concerned states has been constituted in June, 2002 to discuss with the states the issues for arriving at a consensus regarding sharing of surplus water and preparation of Detailed Project Reports (DPRs). Five peninsular links have been identified as priority links for consensus building between the concerned states. The Group has held nine meetings on these links. The DPR for one priority link viz Ken-Betwa has been taken up by NWDA after signing of a tripartite agreement between the Government of India and concerned States of Madhya Pradesh & Uttar Pradesh on 25.08.2005. The States of MP and Rajasthan have also agreed in principle for the preparation of DPR of another priority link viz. Parbati-Kalisindh-Chambal link. The implementation of inter basin water transfer proposals depends on the consensus and cooperation of the concerned States. This information was given by the Minister of State for Water Resources, Shri Jai Prakash Narayan Yadav in response to a question by Dr. Gyan Prakash Pilania in the Rajya Sabha today.

4585. (27-11-2007) NEW DELHI : Suggestions for a National water grid for transferring water from water rich regions to water-deficit areas have been made from time to time. Two proposals, put forth earlier in the seventies which attracted considerable attention, are National Water Grid by Dr. K. L. Rao and Garland Canal by Captain Dastur. These proposals were not pursued further by the Government as they were not techno-economically feasible. The Ministry of Water Resources (erstwhile Ministry of Irrigation) and Central Water Commission formulated a National Perspective Plan (NPP) for Water Resources Development in 1980. The NPP comprises of two components viz. i) Peninsular Rivers Development and ii) Himalayan Rivers Development and envisages construction of storages on various river systems along with interlinking canal systems to transfer water from water surplus areas to water deficit regions. National Water Development Agency (NWDA) was set up in 1982 to study the feasibility of Interbasin water transfer proposals and give a concrete shape to NPP. Based on various studies NWDA has identified 30 links (16 Peninsular & 14 Himalayan) for preparation of Feasibility Reports (FRs). Out of these, FRs of 14 links under Peninsular Component & 2 links (Indian portion) under Himalayan Component have already been completed. Further, NWDA has also taken up the work of preparation of Detailed Project Report (DPR) for one priority link under Peninsular Component namely Ken-Betwa Link. The implementation of inter-linking of rivers in the country depends upon the consensus and cooperation of the concerned States and agreements with the neighbouring countries. One of the links namely, Parbati-Kalisindh-Chambal has been envisaged under NPP to provide irrigation in the water deficit/arid areas of Madhya Pradesh and Rajasthan in Chambal basin. The FR of this link had been completed in 2004. The States of Madhya Pradesh and Rajasthan have also agreed in principle for the preparation of DPR of this link. This information was given by the Minister of State for Water Resources, Shri Jai Prakash Narayan Yadav in response to a question by Shri Lalit Kishore Chaturvedi in the Rajya Sabha today.

4586. (27-11-2007) NEW DELHI : With a view to optimally utilize the available resources, several measures for development and management of water resources are undertaken by the respective State Governments which include creation of storages, restoration of water bodies, rain water harvesting, artificial recharge to ground water and adoption of better management practice etc. Storage capacity of about 225 Billion Cubic Metre (BCM) has been created so far. As per present assessment, the total estimated storage capacity of the various projects under construction is about 64 BCM. Further, the State Governments have identified various other schemes for investigation and planning and the estimated storage for such schemes is bout 108 BCM. The Ministry of Water Resources encourages conservation of water including measures such as traditional water conservation practices, rainwater harvesting and recharge to ground water and adoption of better management practices. Government of India has launched a Pilot Scheme on "National Project for Repair, Renovation & Restoration of Water Bodies directly linked to Agriculture" in January, 2005 with an estimated cost of Rs.300 crore with a view to restore and augment storage capacity of water bodies and also to recover their lost irrigation potential. The scheme has been approved for 26 district projects in 15 States, namely, Andhra Pradesh, Bihar, Chhattisgarh, Jharkhand, Karnataka, Madhya Pradesh, Orissa, Rajasthan, Tamil Nadu, West Bengal, Himachal Pradesh, Jammu & Kashmir, Gujarat, Kerala and Maharashtra at an estimated cost of Rs.299.92 crore. Central Share to tune of Rs.179.73 crore has been released to the states so far. These projects cover 1098 water bodies with total original culturable command area of 1.72 lakh hectares. No ponds/reservoirs in the NCT of Delhi are covered under the Pilot Scheme. This information was given by the Minister of State for Water Resources, Shri Jai Prakash Narayan Yadav in response to a question by Shri Pyarrelal Khandelwal in the Rajya Sabha today.

4587. (27-11-2007) NEW DELHI : The National Water Policy, 2002 (NWP) has laid due emphasis on water management. The NWP states that there should be an integrated and multi-disciplinary approach to planning, development, conservation and management of water resources. The Policy also states that adequate emphasis need to be given to physical and financial sustainability of water resources facilities and management of water resources for diverse uses should incorporate a participatory approach. Ministry of Water Resources encourages adoption of better management practices. River interlinking project has important role in equitable distribution of water resources by transferring waters from water surplus to water deficit basins/areas. The Government of India have formulated a National Perspective Plan for Water Resources Development (NPP) in August 1980. The NPP comprises of two components viz. i) Peninsular Rivers Development and ii) Himalayan Rivers Development and envisages construction of storages on various river systems along with interlinking canal systems to transfer water from water surplus areas to water deficit regions. National Water Development Agency (NWDA) under Ministry of Water Resources has been set up in 1982 to study the feasibility of inter basin water transfer proposals and give a concrete shape to NPP. NWDA after various studies identified 30 links under NPP. Out of the 30 links, five links have been prioritized for their implementation. The prioritized links are (i) Ken-Betwa link (ii) Parbati-Kalisindh-Chambal link (iii) Damanganga-Pinjal link (iv) Par-Tapi-Narmada link, and (v) Godavari (Polavaram)-Krishna (Vijayawada) link. This information was given by the Minister of State for Water Resources, Shri Jai Prakash Narayan Yadav in response to a question by Shri Raj Mohinder Singh Majitha and Shri Ram Jethmalani in the Rajya Sabha today.

4588. (27-11-2007) NEW DELHI : Corporate Identity Number (CIN) is mandatory for all types of companies registered in India. As on 21.11.2007, Corporate Identity Number has been allotted to 8, 62, 639 companies comprising of 97, 940 Public; 7, 63, 284 Private and 1, 415 Public Sector Undertakings. This was stated by the Minister of Corporate Affairs, Shri Prem Chand Gupta in written reply to a question in the Rajya Sabha today.

4589. (27-11-2007) NEW DELHI : The aim and objectives of the Indian Institute of Corporate Affairs (IICA) flow from its proposed vision which is " A holistic think tank, capacity building, service delivery institute to help corporate growth, reforms and regulation through synergized knowledge management, partnerships and problem solving in a one-stop-shop mode". The Ministry is in the process of getting a Detailed Project Report prepared for the IICA for approval of the Expenditure Finance Committee (EFC). The Ministry has identified a plot of land at IMT, Manesar, Haryana for this purpose. This was stated by the Minister of Corporate Affairs, Shri Prem Chand Gupta in written reply to a question in the Rajya Sabha today.

4590. (27-11-2007) NEW DELHI : India's share of processed food export presently in the world is only 1.5%. The Government has accorded it a high priority area, with a number of fiscal incentives to encourage and boost up the commercialization and value addition to the agricultural produce. The Ministry is assisting food processing units to improve their quality standards so that they can compete better in the international markets and exports increased. Ministry of Food Processing Industries extends financial assistance for Technology Upgradation/Modernization/Establishment of food processing units in the form of grant-in-aid @ 25% of the cost of plant and machinery and technical civil works subject to maximum of Rs. 50 lakh in general areas or 33.33% subject to a maximum of Rs. 75 lakh in difficult areas such as Jammu & Kashmir, Himachal Pradesh, Uttarakhan, Sikkim and North Eastern States, Andaman & Nicobar Island, Lakshadweep and ITDP areas. Under the Mini Mission IV of Technology Mission for Integrated Development of Horticulture in North Eastern States including Sikkim, J & K, Uttarakhand and Himachal Pradesh, assistance at still higher rates *i.e.* @ 50% upto Rs. 4 crore for promotion of new units and upto Rs. 1 crore for upgradation/modernization of existing units is available for processing of horticulture produce. This effort towards modernization would further improve their cost competitiveness and quality levels in the world markets & result in growth of exports. Government has also provided several excise/customs duty reduction and income tax exemption so as to increase cost competitiveness of food processing units. Ministry of Food Processing Industries does not set up Food Processing Industries on its own. The quantity of export can be increased by expediting research and testing work in this industry. In this regard this Ministry has been providing financial assistance to institutions for research and development work and also for setting up food testing laboratories. Ministry has provided financial assistance amounting to Rs. 16.01 crore till December 2006 for 41 R & D projects. Ministry has also provided financial assistance to the tune of Rs. 52. 83 crore to 36 food testing laboratories so far. This information was given by Shri Subodh Kant Sahai, Minister of State for Food Processing Industries in a written reply to a question by Shri Jai Parkash Aggarwal in the Rajya Sabha.

4591. (27-11-2007) NEW DELHI : The Food Processing Industries Ministry proposes to implement a revamped scheme in the 11th Plan for Infrastructure Development under which, it will give financial assistance for setting up of Mega Food Parks, cold chain infrastructure, value added centres and packaging centres. The Mega Food Park Scheme will provide backward and forward linkages as well as reliable and sustainable supply chain. The Cluster based demand driven approach will provide linkages from farm to market with linkages from local to regional level through Primary Processing Centres, Collection Centres, Strategic Distribution Centre-cum-Cold Chain at critical locations-having Controlled Atmosphere storage and distribution centres where large quantities can be stored and supplied to distribution centres for fresh sale and to processing industries for processing. The emphasis will be on building strong linkages with agriculture and horticulture, enhancing project implementation capabilities, increased involvement of private sector investments and support for creation of rural infrastructure to ensure a steady supply of good quality agri horticulture produce. The Ministry of Food Processing Industries under its Plan Scheme for Technology Upgradation/ Modernization/Establishment of Food Processing Industries, extends financial assistance in the form of grant-in-aid @ 25% of the cost of Plant & Machinery and Technical Civil works subject to a maximum of Rs. 50 lakh in general areas or 33.33% subject to a maximum of Rs. 75 lakh in difficult areas to implementing agencies/entrepreneurs for setting up/modernization/technology upgradation of food processing industries. In the 11th Plan, it has also been proposed to continue assistance in the form of grant to private sector/public sector organizations through schemes for setting up of Food Testing Labs, Implementation of Quality Systems such as HACCP, ISO 9000, GHP and GMP Practices, Promotion of Research and Development, Capacity building and Human Resources Development and other promotional activities with higher levels of assistance. The process of mergers and acquisitions of companies have to be decided by the companies themselves on the basis of the comparative strengths and complementarities of the entities. This information was given by Shri Subodh Kant Sahai, Minister of State for Food Processing Industries in a written reply to a question by Shri C. Ramachandraiah in the Rajya Sabha.

4592. (27-11-2007) NEW DELHI : The Ministry of Micro, Small and Medium Enterprises does not provide any direct financial assistance for rehabilitation of sick micro and small enterprises (MSEs). However, financial assistance, by way of debt restructuring, including fresh loans, for the rehabilitation of sick MSE is provided by the primary lending institutions (PLI), including commercial banks, which provide credit to the MSEs. For this purpose, the Reserve Bank of India (RBI) has already issued detailed guidelines to banks on detection of sickness in MSE at an early stage and taking remedial measures and for rehabilitation of sick MSEs identified as potentially viable. Further, RBI has also issued guidelines based on the "Policy Package for Stepping up Credit to Small and Medium Enterprises (SMEs)" announced by the Central Government on 10th August 2005. These guidelines relate, inter alia, to viability criteria, prudential norms for restructured accounts, provision of additional finance and time frame for working out the restructuring package and its implementation. As per the data compiled by the RBI from the scheduled commercial banks, 588 viable sick MSEs were put under nursing at the end of March 2007. This information was given by the Minister of Micro, Small & Medium Enterprises, Shri Mahabir Prasad in a written reply to a question in Lok Sabha today.

4593. (27-11-2007) NEW DELHI : Under the 'Scheme of Fund for Regeneration of Traditional Industries (SFURTI)' 122 clusters (34 khadi, 62 village industries and 26 coir) have been approved by the Scheme Steering Committee of the Scheme for their development. 19 reputed national level Institutions with expertise in cluster development methodology have been identified as Technical Agencies to provide technical support to the Nodal Agencies *i.e.* Khadi and Village Industries Commission (KVIC) and Coir Board and the Implementing Agencies of the Scheme. Further, the other formalities/activities for development of these clusters like obtaining consent of State Governments, training to staff of Nodal Agencies and Implementing Agencies, appointment of Cluster Development Executives (CDE) and their training, preparation of annual action plan, diagnostic study report, etc., have been completed in most of the clusters. SFURTI has been launched to develop around 100 clusters in khadi, village industries and coir sectors with a total plan allocation of Rs. 97.25 crore. Release of funds under this scheme is cluster specific. The Government of India releases funds to the Nodal Agencies *i.e.* KVIC and Coir Board who are responsible for holding and disbursement of funds to the approved Implementing Agencies and monitoring of the scheme. These funds are released by them to the Implementing Agencies as per their requirement. Khadi, village and coir industries including leather and pottery are covered under SFURTI. 122 traditional industry clusters from khadi, village and coir sectors covering all the States/UTs including Kerala have been approved for their development under SFURTI. The State-wise number of clusters approved is given at Annex. This information was given by the Minister of Micro, Small & Medium Enterprises, Shri Mahabir Prasad in a written reply to a question in Lok Sabha today.

4594. (27-11-2007) NEW DELHI: The Prime Minister will convene within a fortnight a meeting of Chief Ministers to tighten internal security and fight terrorism. This was stated by Home Minister Shivraj Patil in Parliament on Monday. He ruled out revival of the Prevention of Terrorism Act (POTA). Mr. Patil urged the States to strengthen policing and intelligence services to mount a joint attack on terrorism. Replying to clarifications sought in the Rajya Sabha during a discussion on the recent serial blasts in Uttar Pradesh, he turned down a BJP suggestion to bring in a new law on the lines of the POTA. He said some of the POTA provisions were included in the Unlawful Activities Act. Condemning the blasts, Mr. Patil said there was no point in the Central and State governments blaming each other after an incident occurred. There was need for "actionable intelligence" at the State level. The Intelligence Bureau, the Research and Analysis Wing and defence intelligence could give general information but to ascertain when and where an incident would occur actionable intelligence ought to be put in place. Emphasising that there was no link between acts of terror and any community or religion, Mr. Patil said: "Terrorism is a different religion in itself." Several members were, however, dissatisfied with his reply. Earlier, amid uproarious scenes, the Opposition parties demanded Mr. Patil's resignation, saying the blasts were a failure of the government. The Rajya Sabha was adjourned twice with the Opposition demanding copies of the Home Ministry's statement on the blasts.

4595. (27-11-2007) NEW DELHI : The Minister for Tourism and Culture Smt. Ambika Soni informed the Rajya Sabha today that a series of promotional activities have been undertaken by the Ministry of Tourism, through its overseas offices, for increasing the visibility of Indian tourism products and to promote India as a preferred destination in the overseas markets. These include advertising in the print and electronic media, outdoor advertising at prominent locations, on trains, buses and taxis, participation in fairs and exhibitions, organizing seminars, workshops and road shows, publication of brochures & collaterals, joint advertisement support, familiarization tours of tour operators and travel media, etc. Further, the Ministry of Tourism extends Central Financial Assistance for development of infrastructure under its Scheme of Product/Infrastructure Development for Destinations and Circuits to the State Governments/Union Territory Administrations for development and promotion of tourism. During the 10th Five Year Plan the Ministry of Tourism has sanctioned Rs. 2012.02 crore for 1160 projects to the State Governments/Union Territory Administrations for promotion and development of tourism. In the current financial year Rs. 323 crore for 128 projects has been released to the State Governments/Union Territory Administrations for upgrvadation of infrastructure at tourist destinations. In a written reply the Minister said, for the year 2007-08 the Ministry of Tourism has been allocated Rs. 953.00 crore.

4596. (27-11-2007) NEW DELHI : The Minister for Tourism and Culture Smt. Ambika Soni has said the setting up of Heritage Sites Commission Bill is under consideration of Government. In a written reply in the Rajya Sabha today she said, the proposed Heritage Sites Commission will lay down broad policy guidelines and take steps to ensure that such guidelines are observed.

4597. (27-11-2007) NEW DELHI : The Minister for Tourism and Culture Smt. Ambika Soni has said the Cave temple at Patalbhubaneshwar, situated between Ramganga and Saryu rivers about 10 km from Gangolihat in Uttarakhand is under the protection of the Archaeological Survey of India. In a written reply in the Rajya Sabha today she said, no financial aid has been provided by the Archaeological Survey of India to the State. However, Archaeological Survey of India has carried out conservation and development works including providing tourist facilities at the above Cave temple.

4598. (27-11-2007) NEW DELHI : The Minister for Tourism and Culture Smt. Ambika Soni has said, Ministry of Tourism, Government of India provides Central Financial Assistance to North Eastern States for development of infrastructure, Information Technology, Large Revenue Generating projects and for organizing fairs/festivals/events. During the Tenth Five Year Plan, Ministry of Tourism sanctioned tourism projects for Rs.392.33 crore to all States in the North Eastern Region including Rs.74.96 crore for Sikkim. During 2007-08, Rs.119.00 crore has already been sanctioned for tourism projects in North-Eastern states including Rs.54.83 crore for Sikkim. In a written reply in the Rajya Sabha today she said, the Ministry of Tourism promotes tourism to North East by launching dedicated media campaigns, website and production of publicity & collateral material. Information on North Eastern Region is disseminated through the India tourism offices in India and abroad.

4599. (27-11-2007) NEW DELHI : Shri A.Raja, Minister of Communications and Information Technology has said that postal administrations will have to assure quality services within their country and across the borders as per the needs of their customers. There is no other alternative if Post has to be competitive. The Minister was speaking at five day Executive Council Meeting of the Asian Pacific Postal Union here today. Shri Raja inaugurated the meeting. He said that we need to build a global postal network accessible to all which integrates the physical, electronic and financial dimensions of the service. Postal administrations will also need to find a mechanism which results in a win-win situation for all the participating administrations. Shri Raja said that in more than a century of its existence, the Post has stood for certain values. People still feel secure in sending their remittances and putting their savings in the Post Office and in many countries a large number of investors are with the Post. The Post Office is known for accessibility as the friendly office next door. Everybody feels comfortable to walk in to the Post Office; they may not feel as comfortable to go to any other office. The Postman is still the most popular Government representative, he added. Dr. Shakeel Ahmad, Minister of State for Communications and Information Technology, in his presidential address said that the postal network in Asia Pacific region comprises 342, 000 permanent post offices *i.e.* 51 per cent of the total number of Post Offices worldwide, manned by 17, 15, 600 postal employees *i.e.* 31 per cent of worldwide postal staff. The anomaly in the percentage of employees to the number of Post Offices needed to be changed he added. India Post is hosting the 30th Asian Pacific Postal Union, Executive Council (APPU-EC) Meeting from November 27 to December 1, 2007 here with an aim to exchange views and discuss matters of mutual interest so as to strengthen cooperation amongst postal administrations and postal service providers in the Asia-Pacific region. More than 150 foreign delegates from 29 countries are participating in the Meeting. This is the third time India Post is hosting an APPU-EC meeting. India Post earlier hosted this meeting in the years 1980 and 1992. The APPU is an inter-governmental organization of 30 postal administrations of the countries of Asian-Pacific region founded in the year 1962. India became a member in the year 1973. APPU is affiliated to the Universal Postal Union, which is a specialized agency of the United Nations. The purpose of the APPU is to extend, facilitate and improve postal relations between member countries and to promote cooperation in the field of postal services.

4600. (27-11-2007) NEW DELHI : Shri Ajay Shankar, Secretary, Department of Industrial Policy and Promotion (DIPP), Ministry of Commerce and Industry, has stated that the record of Indian cement industry in technology adoption and modernization is remarkable. Speaking at the inaugural session of the 10th NCB International Seminar on Cement and Building Materials, organized by the National Council for Cement and Building Materials (NCB), here today, Shri Ajay Shankar complimented the cement industry for making full use of the liberalized policy and observed that besides achieving an increase in the entire domestic demand, the export of 9 million tonnes of cement is an outstanding achievement. This has helped India in becoming the second largest producer of cement in the world after China, he added. “The industry needs to further concentrate on modernization and upgradation of technology, optimization of operations and increased application of automation and information technology. This will help to reduce the cost of production through saving of energy and enhancement of productivity and to create clean environment by reducing the emission levels”, the Secretary further added. Elaborating on the role of government in this regards, Shri Ajay Shankar informed that government’s efforts have been to encourage and help the industry in enhancing the level of consumption of cement by concentrating its efforts on thrust areas like faster implementation of infrastructure and irrigation projects, pushing housing development programmes, promotion of concrete highways and other roads, particularly concrete roads in rural areas. He said the potential of other emerging building materials and technologies such as high performance concrete, self compacting concrete, fibre reinforced concrete, blended cements should be fully exploited in the construction industry, particularly in view of the massive infrastructure development envisaged in the immediate future in our country. He also observed that this kind of seminar helps to take stock of technological status of plant and devise strategies for further development and for better competitiveness at national and global level. About 700 delegates from across the world are participating in the four-day (27-30 November) Seminar. On this occasion, Shri Ajay Shankar released a special publication titled "Sustainable Development of Indian Cement Industry and Infrastructure-Challenges".

4601. (27-11-2007) NEW DELHI : The Cabinet Committee on Economic Affairs today gave in principle approval to the Dedicated Multi-Modal High Axle Load Freight Corridor (DFC) Project on Eastern Corridor (Estimated Cost-Rs.11, 589 crore) and Western Corridor (Estimated Cost-Rs.16, 592 crore) at an estimated total cost of Rs.28, 181 crore. The whole corridor will be having Computerised Train Control System. On Eastern side, the Corridor will be from Ludhiana and Sonnagar and on Western side, the Corridor will connect Jawaharlal Nehru Port near Mumbai to Tughlakabad/Dadri near Delhi. The Project will immensely benefit ports, exporters, importers, shipping lines and container operators by the western corridor and coal companies, steel plants and thermal power stations by the eastern corridor. The project will provide the must needed rail infrastructure for growth of Indian economy and EXIM trade. The project will also generate indirect employment during construction phase.

4602. (27-11-2007) NEW DELHI : The Cabinet Committee on Economic Affairs today gave its approval for the Krishna Drinking Water Supply Project Phase-II for augmentation of water supply in Hyderabad city at a cost of Rs.817.62 crore. The expenditure incurred up to 31.03.2006 on the project is Rs.211.12 crore. Therefore, the cost for reimbursement under JNNURM will Rs.606.50 crore and release of Additional Central Assistance to the extent of Rs.212.275 crore being the share of the Government of India, in the manner prescribed under the guidelines. Augmentation of additional 90 Mgd (410 Mld) of treated water to the city of Hyderabad and its urban agglomeration including surrounding municipalities to bridge the gap between demand and supply. It would facilitate increase in present 80 lpcd to 150 lpcd required as the per the norms in the surrounding municipalities. It would also facilitate taking care of the water requirements of projects like Hyderabad International Airport, FAB City, Hardware sector, Textile Sector, IT and other Industrial sectors. The project is likely to be completed by November, 2007.

4603. (27-11-2007) NEW DELHI : Gen Bruno Cuche, Chief of the French Army, reached Delhi on an official visit to India. Gen Bruno Cuche started his visit by paying homage to martyrs at Amar Jawan Jyoti at India Gate and inspecting a Guard of honour. The visit will give the necessary impetus to the on-going defence relationship between India and France and broad base it further into a mutually beneficial partnership. During his visit from 26-30 Nov 2007 the French Army Chief will interact with senior military and civilian defence hierarchy, discuss defence related issues and prospects for future cooperation between the two Armies. With common concern on increased terrorism in the world, discussions on global and regional security situation including enhanced cooperation in combating terrorism are also envisaged. He will also visit Army Field Formations and training institutions in Nagrota, Rajauri, Agra and Pune. India's Army-to-Army cooperation with France is progressing very smoothly and it comprises numerous joint activities viz, visits, observers in joint exercises, training and courses, exchanges between experts and equipment procurement. The activities between the two armies in 2007 have shaped very well and the plan for 2008 will be finalized soon.

4604. (28-11-2007) NEW DELHI : The Vice-President of India, Mohd. Hamid Ansari released a book entitled 'Words Words Words : Adventures in Diplomacy' written by Shri T.P. Sreenivasan at a function here today. Addressing on the occasion the Vice-President said that the diplomats are not really adventurous and it is their vast experiences which are important. He congratulated the author Shri Sreenivasan, a former Foreign Service officer for bringing out this valuable and informative book on the diplomatic life which gives an account of various diplomatic negotiations. He wished that the author will write more such books in future to enlighten the people. The Minister for Overseas Indian Affairs, Shri Vyalar Ravi, and former Indian Ambassador in USA, Shri Naresh Chandra also addressed on the occasion. Many dignitaries were present in the function.

4605. (28-11-2007) NEW DELHI : Indian films need to recapture their earlier position in Turkey, says the noted actress from Turkey Meltem Cumbul. The Member of the Jury for the Competition Section made these remarks while addressing the media at IFFI-2007. Ms. Cumbul said that Indian films, especially those of Raj Kapoor had been very popular in her country. Of late this trend had undergone a change, she said. She herself has been a great fan of Raj Kapoor. Ms. Cumbul said that story, screenplay and presentation are the core aspects that she weighs most in evaluating a film. Ms. Cumbul has acted in over 50 films besides being involved with several radio and television shows. The film 'Lovelorn' directed by Yavuz Turgul, in which Ms Cumbul plays the lead female role is being screened in the Cinema of the World section at IFFI-07.

4606. (28-11-2007) NEW DELHI : The Tourism and Culture Minister Smt. Ambika Soni has said that we, in India, believe that tourism, because of its close links to environment, has an important role to play in the debate on climate change. Making a statement in the plenary session of the 17th General Assembly of the United Nations World Tourism Organization at Catagena de Indias, Colombia today she said, the policy responses to climate change must be balanced and comprehensive or else developing countries like India will be adversely impacted by decisions that seek to limit the industry potential. Important issues such as carbon footprints, taxes on aviation fuel, energy efficiency methods, water conservation that are being widely discussed and debated in the context of climate change should not end up being another form of non-tariff barriers for tourism against the developing countries. We need to discuss new technologies which will be good for tourism. Global action on tourism should be well informed, educated, comprehensive and balanced. I am confident that we can arrive at sound conclusions through a process of interaction that will take into consideration the concerns of the developing countries. The Minister said the UN Framework Convention on Climate Change (UNFCCC) has one of the largest numbers of State Parties of any multilateral instrument. It is, therefore, appropriate that matters relating to climate change that are discussed in this forum, are taken up by the Secretary General of the UNWTO in close consultation with the UNFCCC.

4607. (28-11-2007) NEW DELHI : The India @ 60 Section at the IFFI-2007 started today with the screening of the much acclaimed and highly popular 1965 movie 'Shaheed' (Hindi) directed by S. Ram Sharma. This Section celebrates 60 years of India's Independence and includes three prominent feature films and four documentaries. The films are, Nam Iruvar (Tamil), a landmark film by A V Meiyappan, Biyallis (Bengali), by Hemen Gupta apart from 'Shaheed', a film version of revolutionary Bhagat Singh's story. The documentaries to be screened are Films Division productions, namely, 'Then Came Gandhi' and 'India wins freedom' both by N. S. Thapa, 'Call for Swaraj and Swadeshi' by Prem Vaidya and 'Gandhi-An Emerging Reality' by D. Gautaman. The opening film of the Section 'Shaheed' starring Manoj Kumar in the title role, shows how Bhagat Singh grew up in a revolutionary household and depicts his tryst with the colonial empire of the British in India. The film shows the revolutionary activities undertaken by Bhagat Singh along with other freedom fighters such as Rajguru and Sukhdev before being hanged by the British on March 23, 1923.

4608. (28-11-2007) NEW DELHI : Lok Sabha Multi-drug resistant tuberculosis (MDR-TB) is disease by an isolate of M. tuberculosis resistant to at least isoniazid and rifampicin. Extensively-drug resistant TB (XDR-TB) is a sub-set of MDR-TB which is further resistant to at least two more drugs which are second line drugs and is thus virtually incurable. XDR TB was first described in March 2006 following a joint survey of laboratories by the WHO, IUATLD, and CDC, Atlanta. XDR-TB is a serious emerging threat to public health and TB control, raising concerns of TB epidemics with severely restricted treatment options that could jeopardize progress made in TB control. To combat this threat. WHO has recommended MDR-TB prevention through sustained high quality DOTS implementation, improvement of laboratory capacity for diagnosis of MDR and XDR TB, prevention of emergence of XDR TB through effective treatment of MDR TB, and to address indiscriminate use of second line anti-TB drugs. The Revised National TB Control Programme (RNTCP) widely known as DOTS, a

WHO recommended strategy, is being implemented in the country. The objective is to achieve cure rate of 85% of new sputum positive cases and to detect at least 70% of such cases. The country has been consistently achieving the target of 85% treatment success of new sputum positive patients put on treatment for the past several years. It is also detecting 70% of the new estimated infectious cases. It is estimated that the deaths due to TB have declined to less than 5%. The number of deaths has been brought down from 5 lakh annually in 1990 to 3, 70, 000 currently. Recent studies conducted by Tuberculosis Research Centre, Chennai suggest that there has been a 12% annual decline in the prevalence of TB. As per the latest estimates, the MDR TB incidence in new cases is less than 3%. The programme is establishing a network of quality assured accredited laboratories at least one in each large state capable of undertaking culture and drug sensitivity testing for diagnosis of MDR TB and treatment as per DOTS Plus guidelines. MDR TB treatment has been started in the states of Maharashtra and Gujarat and will be extended to entire country in a phased manner by 2010. This information was given by the Minister for Health & Family Welfare, Dr. Anbumani Ramadoss in a written reply to a question in the Lok Sabha.

4609. (28-11-2007) NEW DELHI : Voyeurism is a new type of invasion in our life and needs to be checked says noted film director Budhadeb Dasgupta. Addressing media persons at IFFI-2007 here today Shri Dasgupta said that his film 'Ami, Iyasin Ar Amar Madhubala' (Bengali), which is being screened in the Feature Film Section of Indian Panorama, is aimed to focus on this issue. Our life is under constant surveillance by the State, which goes unpunished, while at the individual level voyeurism is dealt with severely. The advancement in technology and the flood of spycams in our life has give rise to a new type of terrorism. The conflict between the State sponsored invasion on one's privacy and personal rights needs to be addressed. On his documentary on celebrated music composer Naushad 'Naushad Ali-The Melody Continues', being screened in the Non-Feature Film Section of Indian Panorama, Shri Dasgupta said that Naushad was a legend in the hard core commercial cinema of bollywood. Though commercial films are not Dasgupta's preferred choice, he ventured into making a documentary on his life as his compositions touched the core of human soul, he said.

4610. (28-11-2007) NEW DELHI : Standardization of Ayurvedic and other traditional medicine compound drugs is more complex than standardization of single or combination pharmaceutical drugs. Government of India set up the Ayurvedic Pharmacopoeia Committee for laying down pharmacopoeial standards. So far pharmaceutical standards of 418 most widely used single crude Ayurvedic drugs have been laid down. First Volume of Pharmacopoeial Standards of 50 most commonly used Ayurvedic compound drugs has also been published in October, 2007. The science of standardization of botanicals is constantly evolving and the pharmacopoeial monographs are accordingly revised from time to time. The Ayurvedic Pharmacopoeia Committee is following international norms for pharmacopoeial monographs of single and compound Ayurvedic drugs. Scientific work for laying down pharmacopoeial standards for another 200 most commonly used Ayurvedic formulations as well as the work of preparation of pharmacopoeial standards for Ayurvedic plant based extracts has also been undertaken by the Ayurvedic Pharmacopoeia Committee in collaboration with laboratories of Department of AYUSH, Council of Scientific and Industrial Research as well as other reputed laboratories. This information was given by the Minister for Health & Family Welfare, Dr. Anbumani Ramadoss in a reply to a question in the Lok Sabha.

4611. (28-11-2007) NEW DELHI : Annual average concentration of NO2 is within the permissible norms and shows uneven trend. The monitored data from 1998 onwards in various cities indicates this trend. The Central Pollution Control Board is monitoring ambient air quality including NO2 at 339 locations across the countries under the National Air Quality Monitoring Programme. Various steps taken to keep the quantity of NO2 within permissible limits include notification of general and source specific environmental standards, implementation of Bharat Stage III Emission Norms for vehicles at manufacturing stage, introduction of improved Pollution Under Control Certification System and encouraging the use of low NOx burner in Thermal Power Plants. This information was given by the Minister of State in the Ministry of Environment and Forests, Sh Namo Narain Meena. in a written reply to a question in the Lok Sabha today.

4612. (28-11-2007) NEW DELHI : 78 industrial units namely in the sectors of mining and sponge iron plants have been issued show-cause notices by the Orissa State Control Board for causing air and water pollution in Keonjhar District, Orissa. The Board also issued closure order for two units namely Tikarapada, Pyrophilite Mine, Tikarapada and Malti Minterals (P), Ltd., both in Keonjhar. This information was given by the Minister of State in the Ministry of Environment and Forests, Sh Namo Narain Meena. in a written reply to a question in the Lok Sabha today.

4613. (28-11-2007) NEW DELHI : Several Policies and Schemes of the Government seek to address the impacts of climate change on their people living in forests. Preliminary Assessments of impacts of projected climate change on forest eco-system undertaken for the preparation of India's initial national communication the United Nations Framework Convention on Climate Change during 2001-04 indicates shifts in forest boundary, changes in forest types, changes in net productivity, loss of bio-diversity and adverse socio-economic implications. This information was given by the Minister of State in the Ministry of Environment and Forests, Sh Namo Narain Meena. in a written reply to a question in the Lok Sabha today.

4614. (28-11-2007) NEW DELHI : The Central Pollution Control Board is monitoring ambient air quality at seven locations in Delhi including residential areas, industrial areas and traffic intersections. The monitored data indicates that the levels of Sulphur Dioxide concentration in ambient and are showing a decreasing trend and the Nitrogen Dioxide level increased in the year 2006 in comparison to 1996 and 2001 data. The concentration of Suspended Particulate Matter (SPM) in residential and industrial in2006 indicated that it was below the levels recorded in 1996. To mitigate pollution in Delhi, various steps have been taken which include introduction of Bharat Stage III norms at manufacturing stage for vehicles, introduction of cleaner fuel in public transport, use of beneficiated coal in Thermal Power Plants. This information was given by the Minister of State in the Ministry of Environment and Forests, Sh Namo Narain Meena. in a written reply to a question in the Lok Sabha today.

4615. (28-11-2007) NEW DELHI : Due to global warming glaciers are receding because of which there is change in water level of high altitude wetlands which ultimately effects down stream areas. Though glacial lake out burst floods (GLOF) have been reported in Nepal and Bhutan, no such incidents have been reported from India. For conservation of wetlands, Government have initiated a number of programmes, which include preparation of management action plans for survey and demarcation, catchment area treatment, desiltation, weed control, fisheries development, community participation, water management etc. This information was given by the Minister of State in the Ministry of Environment and Forests, Sh Namo Narain Meena. in a written reply to a question in the Lok Sabha today.

4616. (28-11-2007) NEW DELHI : Lok Sabha The Central government has released Rs. 175.38 crores for the implementation of National River Conservation Programme (NRCP) in the State of Andhra Pradesh. The Centre releases funds to the implementing agencies on their request on a recurring basis dependent upon the physical and financial progress achieved in implementation of NRCP as well as proportionate contribution of their share of funds by the State Government. The Central Government has released Rs.4185.00 lakh for conservation of Musi River during 2006-07. Rs.83.00 lakh were also released during 2004-05 for conservation of Banjara Lake This information was given by the Minister of State in the Ministry of Environment and Forests, Sh Namo Narain Meena. in a written reply to a question in the Lok Sabha today.

4617. (28-11-2007) NEW DELHI : The Central Pollution Control Board is monitoring ambient air quality at 339 location under the National Air Quality Monitoring Programme (MAQP). The ranking of cities is generally undertaken on the basis of levels of pollution. 67 cities in the country contains Respirable Suspended Particulate Matter (RSMP) levels very high. Haryana tops this list. A study on the 2005 Environmental Sustainability Index (ESI) which integrates various data sets including past and present pollution levels has rated India out 101 position out of 146 countries This information was given by the Minister of State in the Ministry of Environment and Forests, Sh Namo Narain Meena. in a written reply to a question in the Lok Sabha today.

4618. (28-11-2007) NEW DELHI : Eco-clubs have been set up by the Government in the Schools by the Natioal Green Corps (NGC) Programme since 2000-01. Its objective is to spread environmental awareness among school children. These clubs are set up in each District of the country with a focus on action oriented environment programme through active involvement of the students. State Governments and Union Territories are at liberty to set up any number of Eco-clubs in a District. The financial assistance under the programme is restricted to 250 Eco-clubs per district. Each Eco-club is given Rs.2500 per annum. This information was given by the Minister of State in the Ministry of Environment and Forests, Sh Namo Narain Meena. in a written reply to a question in the Lok Sabha today.

4619. (28-11-2007) NEW DELHI : An amount of Rs. 254 crores has been provided in the budget for the year 2007-08 for pollution Abatement works under the National River Conservation Plan (NRCP). It covers 164 towns in the country along with polluted stretches of 35 identified rivers spread over 20 states at a sanctioned cost of Rs. 4793 crores. Till June, 2007 Rs. 2617 crores has been incurred the pollution abatement works are implemented through Implementing Agencies nominated by the State Governments for this purpose. A study has been conducted by the Central Pollution Control Board in the year 2001. 71 polluted stretches identified across the country having the Biochemical Oxygen Demand (BOD), a key parameter indicating organic pollution, greater than 6 mg/l. This information was given by the Minister of State in the Ministry of Environment and Forests, Sh Namo Narain Meena. in a written reply to a question in the Rajya Sabha today.

4620. (28-11-2007) NEW DELHI : There is no shortage in the aggregate number of doctors and nurses in the country. As per information furnished by Medical Council of India at present there are 6, 83, 682 allopathic registered doctors in the country. Apart from this, there are 271 medical colleges with 31, 172 annual intake capacity and students passing out from these medical colleges every year are also adding to the strength of doctor in the country. In addition, there are more than 6 lakhs practitioners of Indian Systems of Medicine and Homeopathy in the country. However, there is an imbalance in the availability of doctors in the rural and urban areas of the country. As regard nurses, currently, there are 1597 Graduate Nursing Midwifery (GNM) Schools functioning in the country with an intake capacity of 80000 students (approximate) per year. At present there is no proposal to set up a task force to assess the shortage of medical professionals and healthcare workers. In order to expand the facilities of Medical Education and health related services, under Pradhan Mantri Swasthya Suraksha Yojana (PMSSY) the Government has decided to set up six AIIMS like institutions in under served-states and also to upgrade 13 existing Government Medical College / Institutions in ten States. Further, the Government encourages setting up of new college in the Government as well as private sector and also increase in intake capacity of medical students. The Government is also exploring the possibilities to allow utilization of district hospital as teaching hospital by the promoter of private medical colleges under public private partnership model in the underserved areas in the country and NRHM focus states. Under National Rural Health Mission (NRHM), all PHC's are envisaged to be strengthened by upgrading single doctor PHC to 2 doctors PHC by posting of AYUSH practitioners and skilled nurses at PHC level. The States are encouraged to appoint doctors, specialists and paramedics on contractual basis. Multi-skill training of doctors and in-service training of ANMs / Nurses is done. The States have been requested to strengthen their nursing cadre. Requirement of funds for establishment/strengthening of nursing and ANM schools, as incorporated in the PIP of some States under NRHM (2006-07) has been approved.

4621. (28-11-2007) NEW DELHI : With the view to ensure availability of doctors in the rural areas of the country, this Ministry has constituted a High Level Committee under the Chairmanship of Dr. R. Sambasiva Rao, Additional Director General of Health Services, to assess the opinion of the students community, medical faculties and other stakeholders on the proposal of the Ministry regarding one year compulsory rural posting of fresh medical graduate. The Committee will submit its report on completion of their ongoing tours to various states in the country. The terms and conditions of the compulsory rural posting have not yet been finalized. This information was given by the Minister for Health & Family Welfare, Dr. Anbumani Ramadoss in a written reply to a question in the Lok Sabha.

4622. (28-11-2007) NEW DELHI : There are some NGOs in some foreign countries engaged in activities relating to teaching of Ayurveda and running of Ayurveda & Panchkarma centres. Department of AYUSH also deputes Ayurvedic experts to conduct orientation courses in Ayurveda in medical colleges and undertakes other IEC activities for popularizing Ayurveda in other countries. An International Ayurveda Conference was held in Budapest, Hungary in collaboration with Indian Embassy and a local NGO in September, 2007. First International Conclave of Traditional Medicine was held by Department of AYUSH in November, 2006 at New Delhi and an International Meet of Traditional Medicine Regulators and Industry was held at New Delhi on the sidelines of AROGYA-2007 in October, 2007. Patents cannot be legally granted on Traditional Indian Systems of medicine, which are 'Prior Art'. Department of AYUSH in collaboration with Council for Scientific & Industrial Research have created a Traditional Knowledge Digital Library in five International languages on the basis of classical texts to prevent misappropriation of Traditional Indian Medicinal knowledge. Ayurveda is a holistic health care system comprising of preventive, promotive and curative treatment protocols, which may vary from individual based on the Prakruti of the individual. However, Government of India have established Central Council for Research in Ayurveda & Siddha for standardization and scientific validation of various Ayurvedic medicines and drugless therapies like Panchkarma and Ksharsutra. Scientific validation of 8 most widely used herbo mineral preparations and development of R&D based drugs based on classical texts has also been undertaken under the Golden Triangle Partnership initiative launched by Department of AYUSH in collaboration with Council for Scientific and Industrial Research and the Indian Council of Medical Research. In addition, Extra Mural Research projects are also given to reputed researchers and institutions for standardization and scientific validation of traditional medicines and drugless therapies. A proposal for setting up an international Institute of Ayurvedic Medical Sciences in Thiruvananthapuram, Kerala at a total cost of Rs.101.60 crores was received from the Government of Kerala in 2004. Government of Kerala was informed that the Department of AYUSH did not have any scheme under which financial support could be extended to the proposed project. However, financial assistance has been provided to Government Ayurveda College, Thiruvananthapuram under the scheme of Development of Institutions in the 10th Plan. The State Government can obtain assistance in the 11th Plan also for upgradation of this college as a Centre of Excellence in Ayurveda. This information was given by the Minister for Health & Family Welfare, Dr. Anbumani Ramadoss in a written reply to a question in the Lok Sabha.

4623. (28-11-2007) NEW DELHI : There has been some delay due to frequent design modification and the time required to procure some major assemblies. The necessary steps have been taken to ensure timely availability of all critical aggregates. Production of the MBT Arjun tank is being regularly monitored through Working Group Meeting held under the chairmanship of Director General Mechanised Forces and Steering Committee held under the Co-Chairmanship of Secretary (Defence Production) and Scientific Advisor to Raksha Mantri. This information was given by the Defence Minister Shri AK Antony in a written reply to Shri Motilal Vora and Satyavrat Chaturvedi in Rajya Sabha today.

4624. (28-11-2007) NEW DELHI : Defence Research & Development Organisation (DRDO) has evolved the preliminary report on "Soldier as a System" which would equip Soldiers with hi-tech gadgets & weapons. DRDO is in the process of discussion with the Army, as a collaborative programme. It may take about four years time after the project is sanctioned. This information was given by the Defence Minister Shri AK Antony in a written reply to Smt. Sushma Swaraj in Rajya Sabha today.

4625. (28-11-2007) NEW DELHI : Border Roads Organization (BRO) comprises of General Reserve Engineering Force (GREF) employees directly recruited, deputed from Central/State Government Department and personnel form the Armed Forces on Extra Regimental Employment (ERE) of Army Officers. The Director General Border Roads (DGBR) is the head of BRO who exercises administrative, financial and technical powers. As per existing regulations, service officers and personnel are governed by the terms and conditions of service applicable to them in Defence Services while GREF personnel are governed by Civil Service Regulations. However, some benefits as available to Defence Personnel, like Siachen Allowance, High Altitude Allowance, Ration, CSD canteen facilities, concession in air/rail fare, free uniform /uniform allowance, free accommodation etc. are also extended to GREF personnel. All matters pertaining to service conditions of GREF personnel of BRO including demands relating to service conditions, facilities and allowances are duly considered as and when any such demand is received. GREF personnel are governed by Central Civil Service Regulations and their pay and allowance are regulated according to the rules. This information was given by the Defence Minister Shri AK Antony in a written reply to Ms. Mabel Rebello and Shri Santosh Bagrodia in Rajya Sabha today.

4626. (28-11-2007) NEW DELHI : Two Indian Navy projects namely the stealth frigate project (P-17) and destroyer (P-15A) are under execution at Mazagaon Docks Ltd (MDL), Mumbai to meet the delivery dates of 2008-2009 and 2010-2012 respectively as per the delivery schedules. The construction of six Scorpene submarines at MDL slated for delivery between 2012-2017 is expected to be completed as per schedule. The construction of Indigenous Aircraft Carrier (IAC) is progressing with the scheduled "launch" of the ship in 2010 at Cochin Shipyard Ltd (CSL). However, the final delivery of the ship may be delayed from the earlier likely delivery in 2012. Adequate funds are provided to CSL for the project. The project is reviewed at various levels for early completion. The overall progress of repair and re-equipping of the ship, ex-Admiral Gorshkov, in Russia is slow. The Russian side has submitted a revised Master Schedule indicating a delay in the project. The Russian side has attributed the delays to "Growth of Work". Issues relating to the slow progress are taken up between the two countries at appropriate level. This information was given by the Defence Minister Shri AK Antony in a written reply to Shri Dharam Pal Sabharwal in Rajya Sabha today.

4627. (28-11-2007) NEW DELHI : Various monitory and non-monitory benefits are being proposed for the Scientists in addition to the recommendation of a better pay package to the 6th Central Pay Commission. However, it was considered appropriate to have an in-depth study commissioned through one of the independent professional agencies for the same. The study was assigned to the Administrative Staff College of India (ASCI), Hyderabad which has now submitted its report. The report is now under the active consideration of the Government. This information was given by the Defence Minister Shri AK Antony in a written reply to Shri Santosh Bagrodia and Shri Harish Rawat in Rajya Sabha today.

4628. (28-11-2007) NEW DELHI : Rajya Sabha, The retirement age of Regimental Commissioned Officers (RCOs) was enhanced by 2 years as in case of other regular service officers, w.e.f. 30th May 1998. The retirement age of RCOs was enhanced from 50 years or 10 years of service to 52 years or 12 years of service, whichever is earlier. A proposal to further enhance the retirement age of RCOs to 54 years of age or 14 years of service, whichever is earlier, has been referred to the VI Central pay Commission so that the RCOs become eligible for time based promotion to the rank of Lt Col after 13 years of reckonable service as recommended by the AV Singh Committee. This information was given by the Defence Minister Shri AK Antony in a written reply to Shri Gireesh Kumar Sanghi in Rajya Sabha today.

4629. (28-11-2007) NEW DELHI : A cruise shipping policy to promote tourism is on the anvil. The objectives of the proposed cruise shipping policy include making India a major cruise destination by popularizing cruise shipping, facilitating creation of requisite infrastructure and creating a conducive environment. This industry annually generates approximately US$ 14 billion worldwide and enjoys a passenger base of over 10 million, which is expected to increase two fold by 2009. India's share is only about 2%. At present, no Indian shipping line owns a luxury cruise liner.

4630. (28-11-2007) NEW DELHI : The Directorate General of Shipping does not grant approval for conducting coaching classes by private agencies and no guidelines have been issued by Directorate General of Shipping as such. However, the Directorate General of Shipping grants approval for various marine training courses. International Maritime Organisation (IMO) issues Model Courses and guidelines for various Maritime Training Courses which are generally followed by the Directorate General of Shipping. There are 23 private training institutes which are conducting Marine Engineering Courses out of about 130 training institutes conducting various types of Maritime Training Courses. No complaints have been received in the matter of conduct of coaching classes by private agencies. This information was given by the Minister of Shipping, Road Transport and Highways, Thiru T.R. Baalu in a written reply in the Lok Sabha today.

4631. (28-11-2007) NEW DELHI : There are 27 shipyards in the country out of which 3 Shipyards are under the administrative control of Ministry of Shipping, Road Transport and Highways, Department of Shipping viz. Cochin Shipyard Limited, Kochi; Hindustan Shipyard Limited, Visakhapatnam; and Hooghly Dock and Port Engineers Limited, Kolkata. Three Shipyards are under the administrative control of Ministry of Defence, viz., Mazagaon Dock Limited, Mumbai; Garden Reach Shipbuilders and Engineers Limited, Kolkata; and Goa Shipyard Limited, Goa. There are two Shipyards under the administrative control of the State Governments *i.e.* M/s Alcock Ashdown & Co. Ltd., Bhavnagar under the State Government of Gujarat; M/s Shalimar Works Ltd., Kolkata under the State Government of West Bengal. The rest are in the private sector.

4632. (28-11-2007) NEW DELHI : The Report of the Committee on Urgent Measures for Prevention of Marine Casualties and Emergency Response, headed by Director General of Shipping, Mumbai has suggested that all vessels over 25 years of age should be discouraged from plying in Indian waters during the monsoon months. There is no historical statistical record of ships wrecked or those not salvaged on the Indian coast/seabed.

4633. (28-11-2007) NEW DELHI : In the 5th meeting of the Energy Coordination Committee held on 10.02.2006, a view was taken that the Ministry of Coal would identify adequate number of coal blocks aggregating to 20 billion tonnes of reserves. Accordingly, 81 coal blocks with geological reserves of 20.02 billion tonnes were identified for allocation to public/private sector companies for specified end-uses. Out of 81 identified coal blocks, 27 blocks with 8536.38 million tonnes reserves have been allocated to Central/State Public Sector Undertakings under the Government company dispensation for power generation and other end uses. Further, 15 coal blocks with 3622.45 million tonnes reserves have been allocated to private companies (including one joint venture between a State Government enterprise and private company) under captive dispensation for power generation. 23 coal blocks offered for non-power end uses will be considered by the Screening Committee in the meeting scheduled in December 2007. Further, out of 16 coal blocks earmarked for allocation to power sector on the basis of tariff based competitive bidding, 4 blocks with 1857.24 million tonnes of reserves have been allocated to Ultra Mega Power Projects and 2 blocks have been allocated to the Rajasthan Rajya Vidyut Utpadan Nigam Ltd. This information was given by Shri Dasari Narayana Rao Minister of State for Coal in a written reply in the Lok Sabha today.

4634. (28-11-2007) NEW DELHI : The funds for Maintenance and Repair (M & R) of National Highways (NHs) are allocated for carrying out various types of M & R activities like Ordinary Repair (OR), Periodic Renewal (PR), Special Repair (SR) and Emergent Repairs due to natural calamities like flood, rain, earthquakes, tsunami etc. The funds are allocated on the basis of the prescribed norms of the Ministry and availability of the funds. The norms for allocation of funds for different types of M & R activities is based on the length, width of National Highways, terrain, climatic condition, cost of material, traffic density and also prescribes renewal cycle for periodic renewal. The funds allocated during the current year for

4635. (28-11-2007) NEW DELHI : Prof. Saifuddin Soz, the Union Minister of Water Resources has said that it is necessary to adopt immediate remedial measures to check the adverse effects of over-exploitation of water resources alongwith integrated planning and management. Delivering inaugural address at the "International Conference on Sustainable Water Management-Challenges, Technologies, Solutions", here today, he said that in certain areas ground water exploitation has resulted in lowering of the ground water table. The government of India encourages measures towards ground water recharge and we have involved experts and social workers in finding the most appropriate solutions to such problems. Another important area of concern is to improve the efficiency of the water resources facilities and to ensure optimum benefits. Prof. Soz said that the growing population, industralization and urbanization are bound to result in increased demands of water for various purposes. At the same time it remains a fact that the water resources available for meeting the demands are more or less constant. Therefore, it is important to develop the resources in a sustainable manner based on comprehensive planning to address the growing needs for various purposes. We have a few instances of development, particularly of groundwater resources, which have resulted in lowering in groundwater table in certain areas. Such lowering of ground water table has also been partly responsible for deterioration of quality of ground water. The Minister opined that for achieving the objective of integrated water management, it is necessary that the users and stakeholders are actively associated. Management of the water resources for diverse uses must incorporate a participatory approach; by involving not only the various governmental agencies but also the users and the stakeholders, in an effective and decisive manner, in various aspects of planning, design, development and management of water resources schemes. The Minister informed that the National Water Policy clearly states that adequate emphasis needs to be given to the physical and financial sustainability of existing facilities. In order to ensure sustainable development for meeting the various demands, it is necessary to adopt an integrated approach for planning and regulation of the water resources system. This is more so because industralization and urbanization are bound to change the pattern of utilization for various purposes. For India, the situation gets further complicated because of very large temporal and spatial variations in rainfall. The Minister said that the vision for integrated water resources development and management may be stated as optimal sustainable development, maintenance of quality and efficient use of the country's water resources to match the growing demands on this precious natural resource with active involvement of all stakeholders in order to achieve accelerated and equitable economic development of the country.

4636. (28-11-2007) NEW DELHI : The plantation of trees along the National Highways is being undertaken Trees are provided on either side as avenue plantation based on availability of land within Right of Way (RoW). The plantation of trees is generally taken up by the State Forest Department. In some of the projects under BOT, the tree plantation is being undertaken by the concessionaire.

4637. (28-11-2007) NEW DELHI : The Minister of External Affairs, Shri Pranab Mukherjee has denied that USA has asked India not to move forward with the planned pipeline project that would bring natural gas from Iran to India. He said this in written reply to a question in Lok Sabha today. The Minister informed the House that the Ministry of Petroleum and Natural Gas has been negotiating the pipeline project with Iran and Pakistan. The sixth meeting of the tripartite Joint Working Group was held in Delhi on 28-29 June 2007. Three meetings of the India-Pakistan Joint Working Group and five meetings of the India-Iran Special Joint Working Group have been held so far. Several key issues including pricing formula, transit fee and transportation tariff are under discussion.

4638. (28-11-2007) NEW DELHI : The country does not have any Energy Policy today. However, an Expert Committee constituted by the Planning Commission has prepared an Integrated Energy Policy Report (IEPR) covering all sources of energy including renewable energy sources. This report has highlighted the need to maximally develop domestic supply options and diversify energy sources. It has also projected that renewables may account for 5 to 6 per cent of India's energy mix by 2031-32 and has observed that the distributed nature of renewables can provide many socio-economic benefits for the country, including its rural, tribal and remote areas. The recommendations of the IEPR are yet to be accepted by the Government. Meanwhile, the Ministry has proposed an outlay of Rs.10, 460 crore for the 11th Plan period for development of new and renewable energy in the country. The renewable energy sources exploited so far in the country are solar, wind, small hydro and bio energy. Details of their estimated potential and cumulative achievements as on 30.9.2007 under different programmes are at Annexure-I.

4639. (28-11-2007) NEW DELHI : Under normal category, time target for issue of fresh passports is 30 days subject to receipt of clear Police Verification Report and completion of all formalities. In Re-issue cases, time target for issue of passports is 15 days from the date of application subject to completion of all formalities. Under the "Tatkal Scheme", passports are to be issued within 7 days or within 14 days depending upon the payment of prescribed fees and submission of documents required under the Tatkal Scheme. The re-issue of passports under the Tatkal scheme is within 3 working days on payment of prescribed fee and submission of prescribed documents. This was stated by the Minister of State in the Ministry of External Affairs Shri E. Ahamed in written reply to a question in Lok Sabha today.

4640. (28-11-2007) NEW DELHI : Branch Secretariats of the Ministry of External Affairs are functioning in Kolkata, Hyderabad and Chennai. There is a proposal to open an office in Guwahati. There is no proposal to open such offices in other parts of the country, at present. This was stated by the Minister of State in the Ministry of External Affairs Shri Anand Sharma in written reply to a question in Lok Sabha today.

4641. (28-11-2007) NEW DELHI : India Security Press Nashik had printed Jumbo passport booklets bearing numbers from Z-000001 to Z-056000 in 2006. The booklet numbers were a 'repeat' series of an earlier series issued by India Security Press, Nashik in 1995. As this resulted in problems at immigration counters for some citizens, the Government have instructed all Passport Issuing Authorities in India and abroad not to issue any of the 'repeat' series printed in 2006. The Passport Issuing Authorities were also instructed to recall the passport booklets already issued to citizens and to issue to them new passports gratis. As regards corrupt practices between the Passport issuing staff and travel agents, whenever such instances come to the notice of the Government, action against errant officials is taken immediately by sanctioning prosecution by the concerned agencies or through disciplinary proceedings, as required. The Government have also been taking a number of corrective measures to check malpractices and deficiencies in Passport Offices, such as regular and surprise inspections including vigilance inspections of Passport Offices, strengthening of vigilance mechanism in the Central Passport Organization and ensuring greater accountability in the working of Passport Offices. Whenever complaints are received by the Government regarding hardships faced by passport applicants, suitable remedial measures are taken immediately. The Government are aware that the applicants at times face some delay in issuance of passports. The reasons include delays in receipt of Police Verification Reports (PVRs) and adverse or incomplete PVRs, incomplete information and/or documents furnished by the applicants. Rapidly growing workload of the Passport Offices is also contributing to pendencies. The number of passports issued by Central Passport Organization went up by 24.4% in 2006 as compared to the corresponding figure of 2005 (from 35.7 lakhs in 2005 to 44.41 lakhs in 2006). Passport Offices have been instructed and offered assistance from time to time to clear any backlog resulting from rush of applications. The pendency figure is being closely monitored by the Ministry on a weekly basis. This was stated by the Minister of State in the Ministry of External Affairs Shri E. Ahamed in written reply to a question in Lok Sabha today.

4642. (28-11-2007) NEW DELHI : Red Fort, Delhi shall remain closed for the public and general visitors on 29.11.2007 (Thursday) from 12.30 PM to 4.15 PM. This decision has been taken by the Archaeological Survey of India under Rule 5 of the Ancient Monuments and Archaeological Sites and Remains Rules, 1959 as there is a ceremony of handing over taking over of brass plaque (World Heritage Site) of the Red Fort, Delhi on 29th November, 2007.

4643. (28-11-2007) NEW DELHI : The Government had entrusted the National Institute of Smart Government (NISG), Hyderabad, with the task of undertaking a time-bound study on the passport issuance system, including its IT aspects with the objective to deliver passport related services to the citizens in a timely, transparent, more accessible, reliable manner. NISG has submitted its report, which has been accepted by the Government, and it has been decided to launch "Passport Seva Project". The project is expected to result in the issue of passports within 3 days and in cases, which require police verification, within 3 days after the completion of the verification process. Tatkal passports are expected to be issued the same day. The proposal is to have 68 Passport Facilitation Centres all over the country where the non-sovereign functions, involved in the passport issuance process, such as initial scrutiny of the application forms, acceptance of fee, scanning of the documents, taking photos, etc. will be done by the service provider to be selected through an open bidding process. The Government staff at the Passport Facilitation Centres will verify the documents and decide on granting of passport. The other activities such as printing and dispatch will also be done by the Government staff. Police verification will be expedited through electronic linkage of the Passport Facilitation Centres with the police authorities in State Capitals. The Government have fixed a time-frame of 19 months for implementation of the 'Passport Seva Project'. This was stated by the Minister of State in the Ministry of External Affairs Shri E. Ahamed in written reply to a question in Lok Sabha today.

4644. (28-11-2007) NEW DELHI : The Union Government proposes to open new Fashion and Textile Technology Institutes during the Eleventh Plan period. New Centres of National Institute of Fashion Technology are being set up subject to the conditions that the State Government is willing to provide land and financial support and fulfilment of feasibility conditions. Decisions about the new centres are taken by NIFT Board, a Statutory body under Ministry of Textiles, as and when the proposals from State governments are received. This information was given by the Minister of State for Textiles, Shri E.V.K.S. Elangovan, in the Lok Sabha today, in a written reply to a question by Shri N.N. Krishnadas and Shri Tathagata Satpathy. The Minister further informed that proposals have been received from Government of Bihar and Government of Kerala for setting up NIFT Centre in their states. No formal proposal has been received from Government of Orissa. He further stated that proposal for setting up of NIFT Centre in Bihar has been approved by NIFT Board and the matter has been taken up with State Government for allotment of land and funding support. Proposal for setting up of NIFT Centre in Kannur, Kerala will be placed for consideration of the Board in its next meeting.

4645. (28-11-2007) NEW DELHI : The Government has chalked out a plan to promote Domestic Technical Textile Sector. This information was given by the Minister of State for Textiles, Shri E.V.K.S. Elangovan, in the Lok Sabha today, in a written reply to a question by Shri Eknath M. Gaikwad & Smt. Nivedita Mane. The Minister further informed that Based on the recommendation of an Expert Committee on Technical Textiles (ECTT), the Government has approved implementation of the "Scheme for Growth and Development of Technical Textiles" (SGDTT) with a budgetary provision of Rs.48.00 crore during the 11th Five Year Plan. The scheme consists of three components: (i) Conduct of Baseline Survey, (ii) Setting up of 4 (four) Centres of Excellence, one each for Agrotech, Buildtech, Geotech and Meditech, and (iii) Conducting Awareness Programme. Regarding the question of increase of more employment opportunities during the 11th Plan period, the Minister informed that employment generation could be assessed only after implementation of the Scheme.

4646. (28-11-2007) NEW DELHI : A separate unit, called Special Security Group, has been constituted in the Central Industrial Security Force (CISF) for protection of VIPs. As per the report received from CISF, a total of 998 security personnel out of the sanctioned strength of 1200 for this unit have been trained in VIP security duties so far. There are 23 lady personnel deployed in this unit.

These security personnel are deployed for providing security to central protectees as per requirements. This was stated in a written reply to a question in the Rajya Sabha today by the Minister of State in the Ministry of Home Affairs, Shri Sriprakash Jaiswal.

4647. (28-11-2007) NEW DELHI : Following is the statement by Shri. Kapil Sibal, Union Minister of Science and Technology and Earth Sciences representing India at the Annapolis Conference to promote Arab-Israeli peace on November 27, 2007: "India applauds the Joint Understanding reached by the President of Palestine Mr. Mahmoud Abbas and Prime Minister of Israel Mr. Ehud Olmert in Annapolis to launch vigorous, ongoing and continuing bilateral negotiations over the coming weeks and months to arrive at a negotiated solution of the core issues that will lead to the establishment of an independent, democratic and viable Palestinian State, living side by side in mutual peace and prosperity with the State of Israel. It proceeds on the assumption that violence and engagement are mutually incompatible. The President and Secretary of State of the United States have made a signal contribution to facilitate this historic agreement. We pay rich tribute to the courage, wisdom and statesmanship displayed by the Palestinian and Israeli leaderships to take risks in the cause of a just and lasting peace between two peoples who though divided by many complex and emotive issues are nevertheless joined by common geography and history. It has been repeatedly emphasized in the Joint Understanding that the negotiations will be bilateral between the parties. This is as it should be. However, at the specific request by the parties, the United States has agreed to assist them in the monitoring and judging the fulfilment of the commitments undertaken by both sides of the road map. This should reassure the parties and help in creating an atmosphere of confidence. No one realizes better than the two parties themselves how difficult the road ahead will be. Even with the best of intentions, it will require unprecedented determination, goodwill and capacity to offer and accept compromises and concessions, on both sides, if the objective enshrined in this Joint Understanding is to be achieved. In this noble endeavour the parties have declared that they need continuing encouragement and support from the international community. India is ready to play its due role in this collective endeavour to strengthen the forces of peace and stability in the region. We note with satisfaction that the Middle-East Peace Process will address the unfinished agenda on the Lebanon and Syria tracks. The Arab Peace Initiative, re-launched in Saudi Arabia in March this year, provides a constructive framework for achieving such a comprehensive peace. India's support to the Palestinian cause can be traced to the days of our freedom struggle. This support has not wavered. We recognized the PLO as the representative of the Palestinian people in 1975 and were one of the first countries to recognize the State of Palestine in 1988. India recognized the State of Israel soon after its creation. With the establishment of full diplomatic relations in 1992, we have developed close and friendly relations with Israel. Madam Chairperson, on behalf of the Government of India, I would like to convey our deep appreciation for the invitation to attend this conference.

West Asia is part of India's extended neighbourhood with which we have had a close interaction over millennia. Consequently, we have deep interest in peace and stability in the region."

4648. (28-11-2007) NEW DELHI : The Minister of State for Textiles, Shri E.V.K.S. Elangovan, informed the Rajya Sabha today, in a written reply to a question by Smt. Supriya Sule that the Government is working on a new plan to meet the demands of over 4 million skilled workers in the textile sector over the next five years. The Scheme of Neighbourhood Apparel & Textile Training Institutes for Job Assurance (NATIJA) has been formulated for establishing a network of employment-linked training facilities in basic garment manufacturing technology. The Scheme is designed to meet the projected demand of 4 million trained workers required in the garment industry over the next 5 years. This Scheme is to be operated in 400 centres at regional and sub-regional level across the country on Public Private Partnership (PPP) model-Government of India, Industry Associations and State Government agencies being the partners. The existing ITIs/ Polytechnics and other such institutes could be considered for locating such centres in the initial phase. Creation of new training centres may be considered subsequently to meet the demand, as and when required. Regarding time frame for implementation, the Minister further informed that no time frame can be indicated at this stage.

4649. (28-11-2007) NEW DELHI : Following is the full text of the Suo moto Statement made in the Parliament today by the External Affairs Minister, Shri Pranab Mukherjee on 'Stay of Ms. Taslima Nasreen in India': "I rise to inform the House of the Government of India's stand on an issue which has attracted considerable public attention in recent days. As Hon'ble members are aware, noted Bangladeshi writer Ms. Taslima Nasreen has been in India for some time. Throughout history, India has never refused shelter to those who have come and sought our protection. This civilizational heritage, which is now government policy, will continue, and India will provide shelter to Ms. Nasreen. Those who have been granted shelter here have always undertaken to eschew political activities in India or any actions which may harm India's relations with friendly countries. It is also expected that the guests will refrain from activities and expressions that may hurt the sentiments of our people. While these guests are in India, the Union and the State Governments provide them protection. This policy will also apply in Ms. Taslima Nasreen's case".

4650. (28-11-2007) NEW DELHI : For the rehabilitation of child labour, Government is implementing the National Child Labour Project (NCLP) Scheme in 250 districts in the country. Rs. 175 crores have been earmarked for implementation of child labour elimination Schemes in country during 2007-08. So far 4.57 lakh children have been mainstreamed to regular education under the NCLP Scheme. Under the Scheme, the children withdrawn from work are put in special schools where they are provided education, vocational training, nutrition, stipend and regular health check-up so as to prepare them in a maximum of three years time to join the mainstream education system. In addition, Government is also implementing the INDUS Project in 21 districts of the country. It is a joint project of Government of India and US Department of Labour. It is based on NCLP Scheme with certain additional features like Vocational Training for adolescents in the age group of 14-17 years.

4651. (28-11-2007) NEW DELHI : With a view to providing social security to unorganised sector workers, the Unorganised Sector Workers' Social Security Bill, 2007 has been introduced in Rajya Sabha on 10.09.2007. The 'Rashtriya Swasthya Bima Yojana' for BPL families in Unorganised Sector has been launched on 1st October, 2007. The unorganized sector worker and his family (unit of five) will be covered under the scheme. The total sum insured would be Rs. 30, 000/- per family per annum on a family floater basis. The benefits will start accruing from 1st April, 2008. With a view to providing death and disability cover to rural landless households, the 'Aam Aadmi Bima Yojana' has been launched on 2nd October, 2007. Under the scheme, the head of the family or one earning member in the family will be insured. The Central Government will bear 50% of the premium of Rs. 200/- per year per person and the remaining 50% of the premium will be borne by State Government. The benefits under the scheme include Rs. 30, 000/- in case of natural death; Rs. 75, 000/- in case of death due to accident. In case of partial disability to accident, the insurance cover would be Rs. 37, 500/ - . The children of beneficiaries of AABY studying in classes 9th to 12th including ITI courses are eligible to a scholarship @ Rs. 300/- per quarter per child for a maximum period of 4 years under Shiksha Sahyog Yojana. Similarly, the National Old Age Pension Scheme (Indira Gandhi National Old Age Pension Scheme) has been expanded to cover all BPL citizens above the age of 65 years with effect from 19.11.2007. This information was given by the Minister of State for Labour and Employment Shri Oscar Fernandes (Independent Charge) in a written reply in the Rajya Sabha today.

4652. (28-11-2007) NEW DELHI : There is no such proposal to pay unemployment allowance to unemployed persons according to their education. The payment of unemployment allowance to unemployed persons would divert substantial resources from development programmes to a non-development activity. The resource of such a magnitude should better be used for development activities, which would generate substantial productive employment. This information was given by the Minister of State for Labour and Employment Shri Oscar Fernandes (Independent Charge) in a written reply in the Rajya Sabha today.

4653. (28-11-2007) NEW DELHI : According to 2001 census, there were 315 million unemployed youth in the age group of 15-29 years. Number of job seekers, all of whom may not necessarily be unemployed, registered with employment exchanges in the country was 40.46 million, 39.35 million and 41.47 million respectively as on 31st December for the year 2004, 2005 and 2006. Number of persons employed in non-agricultural sector as per 1991 census was 104 million and 151 million as per 2001 census. Between 1991 and 2001, employment grew by 88.1 million and therefore, there was no loss of jobs during this period.

4654. (28-11-2007) KOLKATA: The Calcutta High Court on Tuesday issued a criminal contempt notice to three CPI(M) leaders, including Left Front Chairman Biman Bose, for their alleged comments against its order on the March 14 police firing at Nandigram.

4655. (28-11-2007) NEW DELHI : Directorate General of Employment & Training (DGE&T) under the Ministry of Labour & Employment is implementing Craftsmen Training Scheme under which children of 14 years & above including children of labourers may join training courses run in the Industrial Training Institutes / Centres spread throughout the country. Presently, training is being imparted in 110 trades in 5465 Industrial Training Institutes / Centres. Children of Labourers may also join training courses under Skill Development Initiative scheme in 211 Modular Employable Skill courses and under Apprenticeship Training Scheme in 23, 800 industrial establishments in 187 designated trades. This information was given by the Minister of State for Labour and Employment Shri Oscar Fernandes (Independent Charge) in a written reply in the Rajya Sabha today.

4656. (28-11-2007) NEW DELHI : As per Census 2001, the number of working children in the country in the age group of 9-14 years was 1.26 crores and it was 1.12 crores during 1991 Census, which shows an increase of approximately 10% between 1991 and 2001. With a view to ensure that the children withdrawn from work do not relapse to work, Government is taking various measures for the educational and vocational rehabilitation of these children under the National Child Labour Project (NCLP) Scheme and the economic rehabilitation of their families by covering them under the poverty alleviation and income generation Schemes of other Ministries so that they are not forced to send them to work. This information was given by the Minister of State for Labour and Employment Shri Oscar Fernandes (Independent Charge) in a written reply in the Rajya Sabha today.

4657. (28-11-2007) NEW DELHI : The Government has received representations from some employees unions including Indian Journalists Union for interim relief. The demand is being assessed. The issue will be referred to the Wage Boards before a final decision is taken. This information was given by the Minister of State for Labour and Employment Shri Oscar Fernandes (Independent Charge) in a written reply in the Rajya Sabha today.

4658. (29-11-2007) NEW DELHI : Shri Kamal Nath, Union Minister of Commerce and Industry, has presented his book titled, "India's Century : The Age of Entrepreneurship in the World's Biggest Democracy" to the Prime Minister Dr. Manmohan Singh, here today. Explaining the theme of his book, Shri Kamal Nath informed that the book presents an account of India's emergence, from the backwater of global economy to its frontline, generating aspirations for the future based on the recent outstanding achievements. The book explores and goes on to unwind the secret of India's present day journey of transformation in to a global economy. The book goes on to explain on how an economic engagement by the leading nations of the world with India can be profitable for everybody in the coming years. The book has gone beyond the 'flat world' view and explore his people's unique can-do attitude and the entrepreneurial spirit that, in combination with economic liberalism, has put the economy on the fast track. The book, published by McGraw-Hill of New York, is a first hand account of Shri Kamal Nath's ideas, initiatives and his successfully taking the Indian businesses on to the global platform while at the same time, laying a kind of a roadmap for the Indian entrepreneurs to benefit from emerging trade opportunities. Shri Kamal Nath is India's public face in the World Trade Organisation (WTO) and the acknowledged leader of developing nations in global trade negotiations. He held in the past responsibility of the Ministries of Textiles and Environment and Forests, and served as a General Secretary of the Congress Party.

4659. (29-11-2007) NEW DELHI : Revival and Financial Restructuring of Heavy Engineering Corporation, Ranchi was approved by the Government in December, 2005 and subsequently by High Court of Jharkhand in February, 2007. The total cost of the revival package was Rs. 2121.30 crore (excluding Government Guarantee of Rs. 150 crore) to be shared by the Government of India and the Government of Jharkhand. The Government of India has already provided financial assistance of its part for Rs. 1218 crore (conversion of Plan loan into equity Rs. 15.27 crore, waiver of Non-Plan loan and interest on Plan and Non-Plan loan of Rs. 1101.03 crore and bridge loan of Rs. 102 crore) and Government Guarantee of Rs. 150 crore has also been provided. The revival plan was discussed between the Government of India and the Government of Jharkhand on 10.5.2007. The Government of Jharkhand was requested to release its share of the package as per order of the High Court of Jharkhand. The State Government of Jharkhand is yet to provide any assistance as envisaged in the revival plan. This information was given by the Minister of State for Heavy Industries and Public Enterprises, Smt Kanti Singh in a written reply to a question in the Lok Sabha today.

4660. (29-11-2007) NEW DELHI : Mining and Allied Machinery Corporation(MAMC), Durgapur is under liquidation since 26.05.2003 as per the order of Hon'ble High Court of Calcutta. All the assets of the MAMC are under the custody of Official Liquidator appointed by the High Court of Calcutta. Coal India Ltd. and Damodar Valley Corporation(DVC) made an application before the High Court of Calcutta for taking over the company in liquidation as a going concern. High Court of Calcutta has vide order dated 5.10.2007 stayed the sale of the assets of the company for a period of 14 weeks to enable Coal India Ltd. and DVC to assess the financial position of the company in liquidation. This information was given by the Minister of Heavy Industries and Public Enterprises, Shri Sontosh Mohan Dev in a written reply to a question in the Lok Sabha today.

4661. (29-11-2007) NEW DELHI : Impressed by the landmark economic success of Indian Railways and growing worldwide interest in its spectacular performance during the past more than three years, a four member delegation led by Mr. Frank Brown, Dean, INSEAD, a leading International Business School, met the Union Minister for Railways, Shri Lalu Prasad here today. The delegation was given a detailed presentation on the historic 'turnaround story of Indian Railways' which has now become a case study for many National and International Business schools. While interacting with the delegation, the Minister told them that without imposing undue burden on the common man, the Railways have created history by generating a cash surplus before dividend of more than Rs. 20, 000/- crore during 2006-07 as against Rs. 14, 700/- in the previous year. He said that amidst the launching of more liberal schemes and new initiatives to attract a large number of clients, the credit for landmark turnaround goes to all the 14 lakh employees of Indian Railways who in the face of stiff competition conquered all odds with an indomitable spirit in displaying matchless zeal, vigour and teamwork. Mr. Frank Brown, the current Dean of INSEAD (Asia campus) is a member of the American Institute of Certified Public Accountants and the New York, New Jersey and Connecticut State Societies of Certified Public Accountants besides holding various reputed posts. The other members of the delegation are-Mr. Soumitra Dutta, Dean of External Relations INSEAD, who is actively involved in policy development at national and European levels and currently a member of the Advisory Committee for ICT for the Government of Qutar, Mr. Maziar Sabet, Director, External Relations, INSEAD is the representative of the school in the Asia Pacific Region and Mr. Nigel Yeung, Director, Partner Development has been working with corporate clients and INSEAD faculty in designing customized executive education programmes since 1999. Mr. Frank Brown has invited the Railway Minister to visit INSEAD campus and address its MBA students. It may be pertinent to add that INSEAD is also to conduct a one week training module on 'Customer Strategies' as part of Advance Management Programme for senior officers of Indian Railways. The objective of the one-week module at INSEAD is to expose Railway officers to the experience of International functional managers and provide a major shift in their perspective to a more macro plane. Based on the experience of the six pilot programmes attended by about 200 Indian Railway officers, a contract with INSEAD for conducting 30 more programmes (35 officers in each programme) during the next five years have been signed. The first programme of this series is to be held in Singapore from 10th to 14th December 2007.

4662. (29-11-2007) NEW DELHI : Two Irrigation projects have been rejected during 2006-07 and 2007-08. However, the names of 6 Irrigation projects, which were rejected during 01.08.2004 to 31.07.2006 on merits, are being ascertained from the concerned State Governments and will be placed before the House in due course of time. List of 26 Irrigation projects, which have been given Environmental clearance during 01.08.2004 to 31.07.2006 which includes 17 projects are from Andhra Pradesh, 3 each from Karnataka and Maharashtra and 1 each from Punjab, Orissa and Uttar Pradesh. The complete proposals received in the Central Government are processed on priority to ensure that there is no delay in arriving at a decision on the proposal. However, the rejected proposals are re-considered as and when the complete details as per the Forest (Conservation) Act, 1980 are received from the concerned State Governments. This information was given by the Minister of State in the Ministry of Environment and Forests, Shri R.Regupathy in a written reply to question in the Rajya Sabha today.

4663. (29-11-2007) NEW DELHI : The Government has given more than Rs. 1325.00 lakhs for conservation and management of mangroves during the last years in the country. Ten States received this assistance where the State of Gujarat tops with Rs. 300 lakh. About Rs.80 lakhs have been given for conservation and management of coral reefs during the same time. There are four states receiving this assistance namely: Andaman and Nicobar, Lakshdweep, Gulf of Mannar in Tamil Nadu and Gulf of Kutch.

4664. (29-11-2007) NEW DELHI : Kolleru Lake in Andhra Pradesh is one of the 94 identified wetlands under the National Wetland Conservation Programme, and it is also a Ramsar Site. So far, an amount of Rs. 76.05 lakhs (including Rs. 35.84 lakhs during 2006-07) has been released by the Central Government to the State of Andhra Pradesh for undertaking various conservation activities like restoration measures, protection measures and education & awareness in Kolleru Lake. As per the direction of the Hon'ble Supreme Court of India, a total of 1776 illegal fish tank bunds covering an area of about 44, 700 acres in West Godavari and Krishna District have been demolished The State Government has also engaged Wetland International South Asia (WISA) for technical assistance. This information was given by the Minister of State in the Ministry of Environment and Forests, Shri S.Regupathy in a written reply to question in the Rajya Sabha today.

4665. (29-11-2007) NEW DELHI : Only part of Kolleru Lake has been notified as Wildlife Sanctuary. There are no canals within this area, . Hence the question of preparing Action Plan for restoration of canals does not arise. However, the flood waters of the Lake are drained through Upputeru drain (which is outside the Sanctuary) into the sea. The Government of Andhra Pradesh has proposed for utilization of CAMPA funds to an extent of Rs. 40 crores (Rs. 30 crores for construction of Vents across the roads passing through the Sanctuary to facilitate the free flow of water and the balance Rs. 10 crores for developmental works in the Sanctuary This information was given by the Minister of State in the Ministry of Environment and Forests, Shri Namo Narayan Meena in a written reply to question in the Rajya Sabha today.

4666. (29-11-2007) NEW DELHI : According to a study conducted by the Central Pollution Control Board, 71 polluted stretches of rivers have been identified across the country. A statement indicating the polluted stretches with Biochemical Oxygen Demand (BOD), a key indicator for organic pollution, greater than 6 mg/l is given in Annexure-I. The sources of pollution of rivers broadly fall into two categories namely, point and non-point sources. The major pollution through point sources is of domestic and industrial origin. The non-point sources are non measurable sources of pollution such as run-off from agricultural fields, solid waste dumps and areas used for open defecation, dumping of unburnt/half burnt dead bodies and animal carcasses, dhobi ghats, cattle wallowing etc. The point sources constitute the main source of pollution of the rivers.

4667. (29-11-2007) NEW DELHI : As the date for elections in two states draws near, the Congress has geared up all its forces to ensure that in Gujarat, the absolutely undeserving government and chief minister must be thrown out by the people and in Himachal the Congress be re-voted back to power. There are several aspects of the campaign which in the next few days will be shared with you. There is a programme of addressing various gatherings and rallies by leaders which will be shared with you in the near future including visits by Smt. Sonia Gandhi, the Congress President, by Shri Rahul Gandhi and by several leading persons of the Congress Party, our top leaders to both Himachal and Gujarat. There is already a blitzkrieg in terms of dissemination of information, facts, figures, data through posters, booklets, clippings and so on in both the states which you will soon find in an exhilarated and comprehensive manner from now till mid-December. In particular already you have seen some formulations but they will be expanded and elaborated as far as charge-sheets against the Gujarat government is concerned. A coordinated action programme has not only already been made but is under implementation which will make sure that every nook and cranny of these regions is covered. We have no doubt that Gujarat will see the exit of a person who has far overstayed his welcome in that state. It will see the exit of a person and a government which has made false claims, completely misleading claims with a straight face to try to fool the people. I am not going into details. But take for example the repeated false assertion that Gujarat has been the number one FDI destination in India. Our booklet shows it, would be now known to everyone that it is not only number six but the figures are much lower than several other states including Andhra Pradesh. Nobody tells you, certainly not Mr. Modi or the BJP the figures for the number of arrests of farmers in that state for alleged electricity thefts and issues like that. Nobody tells you that the net capacity additions on electricity terms in Gujarat has been negligible and much lower than the past. There is a divided house in that state for the ruling party, there is a great amount of anger and anti-incumbency against the rulers and there is a clear feeling that those who do not deserve to be there must be thrown out at the earliest. The Congress hopes to ride back on that clear wave in support of the Congress Party. In Himanchal similarly we have to go out and show to the people the various development schemes done and that process not only is under way there is now on Monday a rally on that issue which is likely to be addressed by the Congress President. There again our several showpiece schemes, our several development programmes will be taken up especially to the remote reaches of that hilly state. All I want to say is that the Congress Party goes into the last few weeks of these elections campaigns with confidence, vigour and with absolute certainty of coming out with flying colours. To a question as to whom you would project as the Congress Party leader in Gujarat, Shri Singhvi said, I did not say that we will project anybody. As you know that the Congress system, the established practice, the established culture, not for now but for the past several decades has been for our legislators, newly elected to collectively decide on the leader, subject to approval and coordination by the high command. We are not swayed by provocative taunts because our system is different. Let the others copy our system rather than preach to us about their system. To a question on anti-incumbency, Shri Singhvi said, anti-incumbency is a reality of Indian politics but there is an equal other reality. Good governance or development-oriented governance always overcomes anti-incumbency. The best antidote to anti-incumbency, which is a natural phenomenon, a natural electoral phenomenon, is not to show and prove your good governance but to actually have done good governance. And we have no doubt that that will be proved beyond doubt in Himachal. To a question on Congress building bridges, Shri Singhvi said, we have built bridges to every citizen and every person of India by proclaiming in loud, unequivocal, unambiguous terms the merits of the deal. That process can legitimately lead to incremental changes of stand and if you have seen some changes of stand in the public interest, in the national interest it is good. But beyond that nothing else has happened. Our stand remains the same and that stand we put to everybody. To a question on Gujarat, Shri Singhvi said, the Congress Party is fortunate that it has a very strong diverse leadership headed by Smt. Sonia Gandhi including the Prime Minister, Shri Rahul Gandhi and several other leaders, all of whom have earlier contributed to such campaigns and now are bound to do so in the state of Gujarat in the forthcoming days. So let us not devalue the collective effort of the Party.

4668. (29-11-2007) NEW DELHI : As a result of various pollution abatement works carried out under the Ganga Action Plan (GAP), the water quality of river Ganga has shown an improvement over its pre-GAP quality .A total of Rs.725 crore approximately have been spent so far for the pollution abatement works in river Ganga. A statement indicating the improvement in the Bio-Chemical Oxygen Demand of the Ganga river between 1986 and 2006 is given in the Annexure-I.. Improvement has taken place at major locations in the entire stretch of 2500 km. long Ganga river.

4669. (29-11-2007) NEW DELHI : According to a study conducted by the Central Pollution Control Board, 71 polluted stretches of rivers have been identified across the country with Biochemical Oxygen Demand (BOD), a key indicator for organic pollution, greater than 6 mg/l. The First River Action Plan *i.e.* the Ganga Action Plan was taken up by the Ministry of Environment & Forests in 1985. Since then its scope has increased to cover all the major rivers of the country in stages and the programme was renamed as National River Conservation Plan (NRCP) in 1995. At present the Centrally Sponsored Scheme of NRCP covers 164 towns along polluted stretches of 35 identified rivers spread over 20 States in the country at an approved cost of Rs.4793 crore. The pollution abatement works undertaken under NRCP include interception and diversion works to capture the raw sewage flowing into the rivers for treatment, installation of Sewage Treatment Plants, creation of low cost sanitation facilities, Electric/improved wood crematoria, River Front Development etc.

4670. (29-11-2007) NEW DELHI : The First River Action Plan *i.e.* the Ganga Action Plan was taken up by the Ministry of Environment & Forests in 1985. Since then its scope has increased to cover all the major rivers of the country in stages and the programme was renamed as National River Conservation Plan (NRCP) in 1995. At present the Centrally Sponsored Scheme of NRCP covers 164 towns along polluted stretches of 35 identified rivers spread over 20 States in the country at an approved cost of Rs.4793 crore. The pollution abatement works undertaken under NRCP include interception and diversion works to capture the raw sewage flowing into the rivers for treatment, installation of Sewage Treatment Plants, creation of low cost sanitation facilities, Electric/improved wood crematoria, River Front Development etc. Conservation of rivers through pollution abatement works is a continuous activity under the NRCP and aimed at ameliorating the water quality in rivers. Due to continuous increase in the population of the towns located along the banks of the rivers resulting in increased pollution load, and gap in the availability of financial resources to take up works commensurate with the requirements, there is likely to be persistent divergence between the tackled pollution load and the actual pollution load. The details of river-wise expenditure are given in Annexure-II.

4671. (29-11-2007) NEW DELHI : A meeting of the Consultative Committee of the Ministry of Home Affairs was held here this morning to discuss the subject of "Central Law Enforcement Agency/Federal Investigation Agency". The Union Home Minister, Shri Shivraj Patil who chaired the meeting pointed out that the matter has been discussed in several committees and fora. Whenever some incident takes place in a State, the Government of India is expected to take action, but Police and Public Order being state subjects, the Centre has its own limitations. It has, therefore, become necessary to discuss the need for a Central agency to investigate certain types of crimes and the manner in which it should be done. Taking part in the meeting, members generally stressed the need for a central agency to investigate cases of terrorism and other related crimes that have inter-State and international ramifications. They were of the view that such crimes should be clearly defined and a proper law framed for a central agency to investigate such cases. The final decision in this regard should be taken after consultations with the State Governments. The members who attended today's meeting included S/Shri Lalhmingliana, D. Raja and Dr. K. Malaisamy of the Rajya Sabha and S/Shri Manoranjan Bhakta, Sarbananda Sonowal and Mohan Singh of the Lok Sabha. The Ministers of State for Home, Shri Manikrao H. Gavit and Smt. V. Radhika Selvi and the Union Home Secretary, Shri Madhukar Gupta were among those present at the meeting. The process of consultation on the subject will continue. The next meeting of the Consultative Committee will also discuss the same subject.

4672. (29-11-2007) NEW DELHI : The Government has made it mandatory for manufacture, sale and distribution of 17 steel products to carry the standard mark of the Bureau of Indian Standards. A gazette notification to this effect has been issued by the Department of Consumer Affairs. The order covers semis for re-rolling, Long products used in infrastructure/construction, Steel Plates for pressure vessels and Boilers, Electrical Steel Sheets for electrical machines and Tinplates for packaging food products. However, it excludes Bars and Rods of diameter and thickness less than 6mm and structural (angles) below 50mmX50mmX6mm, which are normally made from re-rollable scrap by small re-rollers and used for non-critical and non-load bearing applications like grills, window frames, etc. As per this order, no person shall manufacture or store for sale, sell or distribute in the domestic market any of these steel products which do not conform to the specified standards and do not bear the Standard ISI Mark of the Bureau of Indian Standards on obtaining Certification Marks Licence. The sub-standard or defective steel product not conforming to the specified standards shall be deformed by the manufacturer by cutting into lengths less than 1.5 mtrs. and disposed off as scrap within three months. Before issue of this Order consultations were held by the Ministry of Steel with the major steel producers and associations representing the medium and small steel producers and processors wherein it was decided to go in for the Mandatory Quality Certification Marks Scheme for the 17 steel products with exemption to be given to the aforesaid non-critical products. Accordingly, Ministry of Steel had recommended the matter to Department of Consumers Affairs. The Order shall come into force after a period of six months from the date of its publication in the Official Gazette. This gestation period has been consciously allowed so that within this period, the producers of these steel products can equip themselves with in-house testing facilities or arrange outsource facilities so that they can get the ISI Certification Marks on their product as per the Scheme. All manufacturers of the aforesaid steel products shall make an application to the Bureau of Indian Standards for obtaining licence for use of the Standard ISI mark within 45 days of the issue of this Order, if not already obtained. Any contravention of the provisions of this Order shall be dealt with in terms of the BIS Act which interalia provides imprisonment for a term which may extend to one year or with fine which extend to 50, 000 rupees or with both. The aforesaid Quality Control Order would go a long way in making available steel of certified quality to the consumers. The Order will give right to the consumers to insist for quality steel for such critical applications and also take legal course against supply of sub-standard products.

4673. (29-11-2007) NEW DELHI : Indian Oil Corporation Limited (IOC) has reported that during the first six months of the current financial year 2007-08, *i.e.* April-September, 2007, Lanka IOC Private Limited Company, a subsidiary of IOC in Sri Lanka has earned profits amounting to US$11.67 million. The cumulative profit reported by Lanka IOC upto 30.9.2007 is US$1246 million.

4674. (29-11-2007) NEW DELHI : The Minister for Petroleum & Natural Gas, Shri Murli Deora informed the Lok Sabha in a written reply today that ONGC has approved to invest Rs. 2230.15 crore in Assam Renewal Prosject (ARP) to upgrade/modernize surface facilities and pipeline network, improve efficiency and reliability. In addition, ONGC is implementing Improved Oil Recovery (IOR) schemes in three major fields of Assam namely, Rudrasagar, Geleky and Lakwa at an investment of Rs. 1483.54 crore to improve production. He further said that ONGC Board in its meeting held on 3.10.07 has approved the investment of Rs. 2230.15 crore. The Board has also decided to take up these jobs in three groups to invite competitive bidding.

4675. (29-11-2007) NEW DELHI : The Minister of Petroleum and Natural Gas, Shri Murli Deora informed the Lok Sabha in a written reply today that in an effort to supplement the consumption of petroleum products particularly for vehicular applications and also to curb emissions, research has been carried out by the Ministry of New & Renewable Energy (MNRE) to explore the possibility of utilizing alternatives for supplementing petrol and diesel. He added that bio-fuels namely, bio-ethanol and bio-diesel, hydrogen energy and battery operated vehicles have been identified as potential future alternatives to supplement petrol and diesel. Shri Deora also informed the House that the efforts of these R&D projects on bio-fuels have resulted in development of optimized process conditions for production of bio-diesel from non-edible oils such as Jatropha curcas, Pongamia pinneta etc., design, fabrication and development of 200 litre capacity bio-reactor for production of bio-diesel and isolation of efficient strains of micro-organisms for production of alcohol from waste materials. Performance of diesel car engine using bio-diesel under actual field conditions has been tested. The Minister further told the House that the efforts of R&D carried out on hydrogen including fuel cells have led to development of hydrogen based motor cycles, three wheelers, small capacity engine gen-sets and also fuel cell based power packs, uninterrupted power supply systems and hybrid van. The MNRE has supported research for development of advanced batteries, super capacitors, and components of electric vehicles for reducing the cost and improving the performance of the electric vehicles for wider acceptability and use to leading R&D institutions. "Field trials of an electric hybrid van rickshaw for rural transportation has been completed "he said.

4676. (29-11-2007) NEW DELHI : Red Fort, Delhi has formally received the status of World Heritage Site. At a ceremony inside the Red Fort on the lawns in front of Diwan-I-Khas here today Mr. Koïchiro Matsuura, Director-General of UNESCO handed over the certificate to Secretary (Culture) Shri Abhijit Sengupta in the presence of Secretary (Tourism) Shri S. Banerjee and unveiled the plaque inscribing Red Fort Complex on the World Heritage List. The inscription of the Red Fort Complex is also significant for the country since it was from the ramparts of the Red Fort that the country's Independence was declared .The Independence Day Celebrations, every year, are organized at the ramparts of the Red Fort and the Prime Minister unfurls the National Flag. The monument was first referred for inscription on World Heritage List in the year 1992 but was deferred due to multi-administrative control of the Red Fort. The nomination was re-submitted by the Archaeological Survey of India to UNESCO in 2006. The World Heritage Committee in its meeting held on 23rd to 27th June, 2007 at Christchurch, New Zealand accepted the nomination of the Red Fort Complex, Delhi for inscription on the World Heritage List.

4677. (29-11-2007) NEW DELHI : Shri Kamal Nath, Union Minister of Commerce and Industry, has stated that the agriculture sector needs diversification, modern marketing, cold chain management and private sector linkages. Speaking at the inaugural session of the 8th India-EU Summit: Technology and Innovation for Sustainable Development, organised by the Confederation of Indian Industry (CII), he informed that India is the world's second largest producer of fruits and vegetables and has a huge opportunity to become global food supplier if only it has the right marketing strategies with efficient supply chain. The Minister said: "I believe India's farm sector can be lifted up just like the manufacturing sector and the country has the potential to become an international powerhouse. I am also confident that with some inclusive planning and smart innovation, Indian agriculture can lift its growth rates above the last ten years average of 2.5% to around 4-5%. The Farm Policy recently presented in the Parliament is the beginning of new Green Revolution-green linked to agriculture, environment and dollars. The Summit was attended by Mr. Peter Mandelson, European Union (EU) Trade Commissioner; Dr. Basilio Horta, President of the Portuguese Development Agency; Shri Ajay Shankar, Secretary, Department of Industrial Policy & Promotion; Shri G.K. Pillai, Commerce Secretary; senior officials and representatives of business communities from both India and EU. Highlighting the relevance of the Indo-EU Summit, Shri Kamal Nath informed that the focus of the summit on innovation and its linkage with sustainable development is timely. India is primarily a services economy and that is where it holds the greatest promise for innovation-not just in terms of creation, discovery or invention but in creating processes, business models, cultural and societal value adds. It is a country well positioned to ride the innovation wave with its clever and innovative workforce. He was quoting the latest study, "Booz and Hamilton" annual study on innovation and R&D on the subject. Speaking at the concluding session, Shri Kamal Nath said: "As an innovating nation, India has come a long way. Global products and services are increasingly bearing "Made in India" or "Served from India" stamp. For this to happen on a sustained basis, we need to encourage more public-private partnerships between government research bodies and private companies. There is also a need to create a more collaborative environment within industries, and I am glad to report that this has started happening in the biotech and auto sector, he added. The Minister said that India and EU have a lot to discover together. The EU is in a strong position to drive sustainable innovation; currently 8 of the world's top 20 R&D spenders are of European origin. Many of these companies run very successful businesses in India. "I would call on them to look at the grassroots sector more carefully and search for sources of sustainable innovation-they hold potential for generating the growth markets of the future. India-EU Business Summits have established themselves as important and effective multiparty platform for not only exchange of information on opportunities but also feedback on improving business climate. Efforts of industry apex organisations of both the sides are appreciated in this context. The cumulative FDI inflows from EU is US $ 11.8 billion (23.77%), excluding amount of acquisition of existing shares (upto 1999), RBI's-NRI schemes, stock swapped and advance pending for issue of shares. Top sectors attracting FDI inflows (from January 2000 to June 2007) from EU are services sector (financial and non-financial)-36%; computer software and hardware-5.49%; automobile industry-5.33%; chemicals (other than fertilisers)-4.93%; and electronics-3.83%.

4678. (29-11-2007) NEW DELHI : The conversion of Delhi-Gurgaon section of NH-8 from km 14.300 to km 36.630 to 8-lane and from km 36.630 to km 42.000 to 6-lane is in progress. The work is under implementation on Build, Operate and Transfer (BOT) (Toll) basis and targeted for completion by 31.12.2007. National Highways Authority of India (NHAI) has also prepared feasibility report for six laning of Gurgaon-Kotputli-Jaipur section of NH-8 under National Highways Development Project (NHDP) Phase-V to be taken up on Build, Operate and Transfer (BOT) following Design, Build, Finance and Operate (DBFO) pattern. The project is scheduled for completion by December, 2012. The estimated basic construction cost for Gurgaon-Kotputli-Jaipur section is Rs. 1517 crore. This information was given by the Minister of State for Shipping, Road Transport and Highways, Shri K.H. Muniyappa in a written reply in the Rajya Sabha today.

4679. (29-11-2007) NEW DELHI : Development and improvement of National Highways is a continuous process and the works are undertaken depending upon availability of funds and their inter-se priority on all India basis. North Eastern Region is served by 28 National Highways aggregating to 6880 km length. All the state capitals of the region are connected by a network of National Highways. However, special programmes have been envisaged by the Ministry for upgradation of road connectivity of the region. To connect the region with rest of the country, East-West corridor is being constructed to 4-lane standards, 678 km length of which is located in North East from Silchar to Srirampur, the border of Assam and West Bengal. All State capital towns of the region are proposed to be connected by 4-lane and all the district headquarters are proposed to be connected by at least 2-lane roads under National Highways Development Programme-III (NHDP-III) and the Special Accelerated Road Development Programme for North Eastern Region (SARDP-NE), covering improvement / upgradation of 9788 km roads of various categories, viz. National Highways, State roads, Strategic roads and GS roads. The Special Accelerated Road Development Programme is divided in 2 phases. Only Phase 'A' comprising 2304 km roads has been approved by the Government for implementation. 678 km portion of East West corridor under National Highways Development Programme-II is targeted for completion by 2010. NHDP-III covering widening to 4-lane of 1051 km National Highways and Phase 'A' of SARDP-NE are targeted for completion by 2013. Regarding Phase 'B' covering improvement of 6433 km roads, it is too early to indicate the target for its completion, as implementation decision is yet to be taken by the Government .This information was given by the Minister of State for Shipping, Road Transport and Highways, Shri K.H. Muniyappa in a written reply in the Rajya Sabha today.

4680. (29-11-2007) NEW DELHI : The main problems affecting the progress have been the delay in disbursement of compensation for land acquisition in Assam, Bihar, Madhya Pradesh and Uttar Pradesh. There has also been some delay in Uttar Pradesh due to the condition stipulated by the State Government for providing 10 m strip of land for afforestation before allowing tree cutting. Law and Order in Assam has also to some extent affected the work in that State. However, all these issues are being pursued with the respective State Governments and efforts are being made to speed up the work. In view of the provision of cost escalation clause in the contracts, the cost of construction may increase and final cost of construction can be assessed only after completion of the project. This information was given by the Minister of State for Shipping, Road Transport and Highways, Shri K.H. Muniyappa in a written reply in the Rajya Sabha today

4681. (29-11-2007) NEW DELHI : The Union Minister of Social Justice and Empowerment Smt. Meira Kumar has said that the State Channelising Agencies responsible for disbursing loans to persons with disabilities (PWDs) should become pro-active and ensure that their services reached the unreached. Emphasizing that since the agencies implementing the schemes and programmes of the Social Justice Ministry cater to the needs of the marginalized sections of the society, these will have to make extra efforts to reach the beneficiaries as they are not in a position to come forward on their own to take advantages of the schemes meant for them. Smt. Kumar was speaking at the National Conference of the State Channelising Agencies (SCAs) of the National Handicapped Finance and Development Corporation (NHFDC) here today. Speaking on the occasion Smt. Kumar said that SCAs should explore new areas of intervention through which they can make the life better for the persons with disabilities. The Minister said that we must multiply our activities to ensure that the benefits of our schemes and programmes reach the marginalized people living in the remotest and most inaccessible areas of the country. Smt. Kumar said that the ultimate aim of all strategies and programmes for the rehabilitation of the persons with disabilities is their fullest inclusiveness and integration into the main stream of the society. The disabled persons would not become fully integrated in the society, unless they earn for themselves and become productive, the Minister said. Lauding the NHFDC's efforts that it has provided financial assistance to the tune of Rs. 151.20 crore and also the fact that thousands of beneficiaries have been productively rehabilitated, the Minister said that much more requires to be done to match the aspirations of a large number of PWDs. Speaking on the occasion, the Secretary, Ministry of Social Justice & Empowerment Smt. Veena Chhotray said that SCAs are not only financial agencies which extend monitory assistance but they are also promotional agencies and therefore are expected to actively reach the potential beneficiaries in their respective areas. Shri M. Ravi Kanth, Chairman and Managing Director, NHFDC also spoke on the occasion. NHFDC is responsible for promoting economic development activities and self-employment ventures for the benefit of persons with disabilities. The State Channelising agencies from all the states are participating in the Conference.

4682. (29-11-2007) NEW DELHI : Smt. Renuka Chowdhury, Minister for Women and Child Development has said that nutritionally rich coarse cereals and organic cultivation should be promoted to ensure better health of children and women. Addressing the farmers and participants at India Organic trade fair today, she said that the disruption of traditional modes of agriculture has resulted in change in nutritional patterns of the population which lead to 'lifestyle diseases', while organic diet stresses on traditional food and improves the immune system of the body. Organic cultivation is a holistic system of agriculture with sustainability as its watchword, she added. Appreciating the initiative taken by the panchvati foundation to promote organic food, Smt. Chowdhury said that the Ministry of Women and Child Development would take up sensitization and training of women agriculture labours and farmers for adopting organic food cultivation. She also said that school should allow only fibre rich and organic cultivated food in their canteen for better health of our children. Four days' Indian Organic trade fair has been organized by International Competence Centre for Organic Agriculture (ICCOA) in association with Agricultural and Processed Food Products Export Development Authority (APEDA).

4683. (29-11-2007) NEW DELHI : The Defence Minister Shri AK Antony will go on a two-day visit to Sikkim beginning Saturday. He will be accompanied by the Army Chief Gen Deepak Kapoor and other Senior Officials of the Ministry of Defence. During his stay, Shri Antony will be visiting forward areas in the State including Nathu La. He will be briefed by the Army Commanders. The Defence Minister will also interact with the troops and review the security situation besides meeting State Government Officials. This is going to be the first visit of the Defence Minister to the State after he took charge of the Ministry in October last year.

4684. (29-11-2007) NEW DELHI : The Scientists of the Atomic Minerals Directorate for Exploration and Research (AMD), a constituent unit of the Department of Atomic Energy, have participated for 3 years during 1973-75 in Puga-Chumathang multi-purpose multi-disciplinary project of the Geological Survey of India (GSI), Ladakh area. Detailed investigations have been carried out near Chumathang area. AMD has reported low grade uranium mineralization in association with fluorite mineralization in a shear zone from Chumathang area. Grab samples (whole rock) have been analyzed and found to contain up to 0.021% U3O8. This information was given by the Minister of State in the Prime Minister's Office, Shri Prithviraj Chavan in the Rajya Sabha today.

4685. (29-11-2007) NEW DELHI : The Minister of State for Housing & Urban Poverty Alleviation, Kumari Selja informed the Rajya Sabha today, in a written reply to a question by Smt. Surpiya Sule that a provision of Rs. 30 crores has been made in the Budget for the year 2007-08 of this Ministry for Interest Subsidy Scheme for Housing the Urban Poor. The Minister further informed that a National Conference on "Affordable Housing for All" was organized in Mumbai on 1st & 2nd June, 2007 by the Government in collaboration with Confederation of India Industry (CII) to address the issues & problems relating to Housing Sector of the country. The inputs received in the Conference have been incorporated in the draft National Urban Housing & Habitat Policy, 2007.

4686. (29-11-2007) NEW DELHI : The Minister of State for Housing & Urban Poverty Alleviation, Kumari Selja informed the Rajya Sabha today, in a written reply to a question by Dr. (Smt.) Najma A Heptulla & Shri Mahendra Mohan that the Technical Group (11th Five Year Plan: 2007-2012) on estimation of urban housing shortage has estimated urban housing shortage as 2.89 million dwelling units for the Lower Income Groups (LIG) out of total urban housing shortage of 24.71 million dwelling units as on 2007. In percentage terms the housing shortage for LIG in urban areas is 11.70% of total urban housing shortage as on 2007. Housing being a State subject, it is primarily the responsibility of the State governments. However, the Central Government has been taking several initiatives for addressing the issue of housing shortage time to time. Under the Jawaharlal Nehru National Urban Renewal Mission (JNNURM) structured for a seven year period (2005-06 to 2011-12), the Basic Services to the Urban Poor (BSUP) programme seeks to provide housing and basic services to the urban poor in 63 selected Mission Cities and the Integrated Housing and Slum Development Programme (IHSDP) makes a similar provision for non-mission cities. Houses at affordable cost for Lower Income Groups (LIG) is an identified component under both these Schemes. Further, the government with a view to provide interest rate subsidy for housing loan availed by urban poor categorized as Economically weaker Sections (EWS) and Lower Income Groups (LIG) has made a budget provision of Rs. 30 crore for the financial year 2007-08. The Minister further informed that the Technical Group has estimated the shortfall in urban area for the Middle Income Group (MIG) along with Higher Income Group (HIG) as 0.04 million dwelling units in the country as on 2007. Keeping in view the changing socio-economic parameters of the urban areas and growing requirement of shelter and related infrastructure, it has been decided to have a new National Urban Housing and Habitat Policy in place of the existing National Housing Policy 1998. The draft national urban Housing and Habitat Policy 2007 inter-alia provides for strong partnership among private, public and cooperative sectors and facilitates to bridge the gap between demand and supply of housing and infrastructure.

4687. (29-11-2007) NEW DELHI : With a view to improve Tatkal utilization in those trains in which the utilization of Tatkal accommodation is less than 50% in sleeper class and to save the botheration of general wait listed passengers to go to reservation counter again to book berths under Tatkal scheme, instructions have been issued to Zonal Railways that wait listed passengers of such trains should be given an opportunity to opt for booking under Tatkal Quota (upto 50% of total Tatkal quota) at the time of buying their waitlist ticket itself even before start of the advance reservation period of Tatkal booking for that train. It is not feasible to quantify the additional revenue likely to be generated on this account. Reservation under Tatkal Scheme is available only upto the time of preparation of chart and the unutilized Tatkal accommodation is released to general waitlist passengers at that point of time This information was given by the Minister of State for Railways Shri R.Velu in written reply to a question in the Lok Sabha today.

4688. (29-11-2007) NEW DELHI : The total approximate earnings of Indian Railways on originating basis during the period 11th November-20th November 2007 were Rs. 1990.29 crore compared to Rs. 1734.63 crore during the same period last year, registering an increase of 14.74 per cent. The total goods earnings have gone up from Rs. 1180.72 crore during 11th November-20th November 2006 to Rs. 1333.00 crore during 11th November-20th November 2007, showing an increase of 12.90 per cent. The total passenger revenue earnings during the period 11-20 November 2007 were Rs. 591.58 crore compared to Rs. 493.67 crore during the same period last year, reflecting an increase of 19.83 per cent. The revenue earnings from other coaching amounted to Rs. 49.69 crore during this period compared to Rs. 42.43 crore during the same period last year, showing an increase of 17.11 per cent. The total approximate number of passengers booked during the period 11-20 November 2007 were 198.83 million compared to 180.98 million during the same period last year, showing an increase of 9.86 per cent. In the suburban and non-suburban sectors, the number of passengers booked during 11-20 November 2007 were 111.60 million and 87.23 million compared to 103.87

million and 77.11 million during the same period last year, registering an increase of 7.44 per cent and 13.12 per cent respectively.

4689. (29-11-2007) NEW DELHI : Ministry of Railways submitted an application to UNESCO (United Nations Educational Scientific and Cultural Organization) in January' 2005, for the inscription of the Kilka-Shimla Railway (KSR), as a World Heritage Site, serial to "Mountain Railways of India" that includes Darjeeling Himalayan Railway and Nilgiri Mountain Railway. Since UNESCO considered only one site per country per year, in 2006, KSR was not presented and India's other nomination was not successful. Similarly, KSR was not presented on 2007 and India's other nomination, the Red Fort was inscribed as a World Heritage Site. A revised application in a new format applicable from 2007 was submitted to UNESCO in January' 2007. This is being considered by UNESCO and a team from International Council on Monuments and Sites (ICOMOS) an organ of UNESCO for cultural heritage sites, inspected the KSR in September, 2007. Based on their report and recommendations, further examination of the application will be done internally by ICOMOS & UNESCO and KSR may come come up for consideration to be listed as a World Heritage Site in the next session of the UNESCO World Heritage Committee in Canada in July'2008. Technical problems faced in the operation and maintenance of the KSR are being attended regularly. The inspection of track, bridges and tunnels are being done as per schedule laid down and necessary maintenance works/renewal are being done regularly. Moreover, as a direct result of widening and repairs of road formation located just above the rail alignment, the train services affected from time to time. This information was given by the Minister of State for Railways Shri R.Velu in written reply to a question in the Lok Sabha today.

4690. (29-11-2007) NEW DELHI : With a view to maximize the utilization of Brakevans and thereby increase earnings, Railways had launched a scheme for leasing of parcel space in Brakevans (Second class, Luggage cum brake van) of passenger carrying trains. At present it is proposed to take up bar-coding of parcels on a n experimental basis on one pair of trains running between Delhi-Howrah on an experimental basis to assess the efficacy of the system in tracking and tracing of parcels using the parcel Management System which also has been taken up as pilot project on the Delhi-Howerah Corridor. Based on the outcome of the trials a final decision would be taken on introduction barcoding of parcels.

4691. (29-11-2007) NEW DELHI : In order to carry additional freight and passenger traffic in future, Railways have on hand 272 track capacity works, which on completion would add 20, 852 kilometres to the Broad Gauge system. The estimated throwforward cost of these works is approximately Rs. 55, 000 crore. A substantial amount of traffic moves on the High density routes viz. the ones which connect the four metropolitan cities of Delhi, Mumbai, Chennai, Kolkatta, and the Delhi-Gaulhati route. Railways have already announced construction of two Dedicated Freight Corridors between JNPT-Tughlakabad (1483 kms) and Sonenagar-Ludhiana, (to be later extended to the deep sea port of Kolkatta) (1279 kms) at a cost of more than Rs. 28, 000 crores to give relief to two of the densely saturated routes viz. Delhi-Mumbai and Delhi-Kolkata routes. In addition, feasibility studies have been ordered on four other corridors-(i) North-South (Delhi-Chennai); (ii) East-West (Mumbair-Kolkotta); (iii) South-East (Vijayawada-Kharagpur) and (iv) South-South (Chennai-Goa). In addition, Railway proposes to augment its track capacity in XI Plan by 15, 500 kilometres, including 2000 kilometer of new lines, 3500 kilometres of doubling and 10, 000 kilometres of gauge conversion. The revenue earning freight traffic in the XI Five Year Plan period is expected to increase from 728 million tonnes in 2006-07 to 1100 million tonnes in 2011-12. The corresponding freight output is expected to increase from 475 billion ton kilometres in 2006-07 (prov.) to 707 billion ton kilometres in 2011-12. In order to cater to the projected freight traffic, it is expected that 62000 wagons would be required during the XI Plan. Railways will also require to induct 1800 electric and 1800 diesel locomotives for carrying the projected traffic in the XI plan. In addition to enhance the capacity of the existing diesel and electric locomotive manufacturing units, Railways are also going in for setting up a diesel locomotive factory at Marhowra and electric loco factory at Madhepura which will produce 150 and 120 locos per year respectively. Since capacity augmentation takes time, Railways have taken immediate steps to enhance the throughput by increasing the carrying capacity of wagons by 6 tonnes on most of the routes and by 8 tonnes on selected routes and also strengthen the track, bridges and allied structures. In addition, 28 heavy mineral routes with over 6900 route kilometres have been further identified for implementation of 25 tonne Axle load. Also on selected routes, double stack containers trains have been permitted to further enhance the throughput per train. Railways also plan to induct wagons of better design, higher capacity, longer life and low on maintenance. The passenger traffic in the XI Five Year Plan is expected to increase from 6242 million passengers in 2006-07 (RE) to 8400 million in 2011-12. The correspondence passenger output is expected to increase from 700 billion passenger kilometres to 880 billion passenger kilometres. In order to cater to this increase in traffic, it is expected that 22500 coaches would be required during the XI Five Year Plan, implying a yearly requirement of 4500 coaches. In order to meet this requirement, the production capacities of the existing units-integral Coach Factory, Prembur and Rail Coach Factory, Kapurthanla-are being enhanced to 1500 and 1400 coaches per annum respectively from the present capacity of 1000 coaches per annum each. Further, a new coach factory is also being planned to be set up at Rai Bareily to bridge the shortfall in requirement and production capacities.

4692. (29-11-2007) NEW DELHI : Ministry of Steel has received a representation from Confederation of Indian Industry (CII), an industry association, on 26.4.2007 requesting for according infrastructure status to the steel sector. This has been examined in consultation with Ministry of Finance, Department of Revenue (Central

Board of Direct Taxes) and it has been replied that, since in case of steel plant there is no positive externality and all the benefits are internalized, there is no case for granting any tax holiday to the steel industry. There is no proposal with Government to set up a Steel Financial Corporation for easy availability of credit to steel purchase since the existing arrangement of Financial Institutions is serving the needs. This information was given by the Minister of State for Steel Dr. Akhilesh Das in a written reply in the Lok Sabha today.-Hide quoted text.

4693. (29-11-2007) NEW DELHI : There is shortage of skilled staff in domestic shipping lines. As per estimates received from the Indian National Shipowners' Association (INSA), there is a shortfall of about 834 officers in Indian flag vessels, as of June, 2007. Government has taken note of the shortage of manpower and has taken various steps for increasing the availability of trained manpower, which include: Expanding the facilities for marine education & training by allowing private colleges to be opened. (i) Ensuring quality training at the maritime institutes as per international standards and introducing several new courses for pre and post sea training. (ii) Action has been initiated for facilitating induction of retired naval officers into the merchant navy. (iii) Introduction of tonnage tax obligation on shipping companies to give onboard training to cadets. (iv) Permitting two years age relaxation and fee concession to encourage girl candidates to join maritime sector. (v) The training and examination systems have been reviewed to minimize the avoidable delays for obtaining certificate of competency. (vi) This information was given by the Minister of Shipping, Road Transport and Highways, Thiru T.R. Baalu in a written reply in the Rajya Sabha today.

4694. (29-11-2007) NEW DELHI : Central Inland Water Transport Corporation (CIWTC) is operating its vessels between Kolkata and North-East (Guwahati, Karimganj, Badarpur etc.) through riverine route via Bangladesh. Kolkata is a riverine port on the tip of Bay of Bengal. This information was given by the Minister of Shipping, Road Transport and Highways, Thiru T.R. Baalu in a written reply in the Rajya Sabha today.

4695. (29-11-2007) NEW DELHI : There has been no instance of any ship from developed countries unloading hazardous waste products, including medical, municipal, surgical, bio-medical and e-wastes, in any of the major ports of the country. A High Powered Committee on Management of Hazardous Wastes was constituted on 17.12.1997 in accordance with the Supreme Court Order dated 13.10.1997 to report the quantum and nature of Hazardous Waste lying at the Docks/Ports/ICDs and recommend a mechanism for its safe disposal or re-export to the original exporter. Its report submitted inter-alia contained the following recommendations:-On the basis of the reports of the analysis, zinc ash, waste oil and batteries held in/by the ports/customs/ICDs are recommended for sale to actual users who fulfil the following conditions: Valid authorization from the State Pollution Control Boards for handling of hazardous wastes under the hazardous Wastes Management and Handling Rules, 1989; (a) Valid Consent letters from the State Pollution Control Boards under Air and Water Act; (b) (c) Environmentally accepted technology for recycling with proof of the existence/operation of proper wastes disposal facilities. (d) The Central Pollution Control Board (CPCB) will oversee and report on compliance of the conditions prescribed". This information was given by the Minister of Shipping, Road Transport and Highways, Thiru T.R. Baalu in a written reply in the Rajya Sabha today.

4696. (29-11-2007) NEW DELHI : The Minister of State for Housing & Urban Poverty Alleviation, Kumari Selja informed the Rajya Sabha today, in a written reply to a question by Smt. Surpiya Sule that a provision of Rs. 30 crores has been made in the Budget for the year 2007-08 of this Ministry for Interest Subsidy Scheme for Housing the Urban Poor. The Minister further informed that a National Conference on "Affordable Housing for All" was organized in Mumbai on 1st & 2nd June, 2007 by the Government in collaboration with Confederation of India Industry (CII) to address the issues & problems relating to Housing Sector of the country. The inputs received in the Conference have been incorporated in the draft National Urban Housing & Habitat Policy, 2007.

4697. (29-11-2007) NEW DELHI: The much-awaited debate on the India-United States civilian nuclear deal took place on Wednesday in the Lok Sabha but it failed to produce a "broad national consensus" despite a spirited defence of the accord by External Affairs Minister Pranab Mukherjee. The entire Opposition staged a walkout, but not before Leader of the Opposition L.K. Advani declared that if the BJP-led National Democratic Alliance came to power, it would renegotiate the nuclear deal. The walkout, ahead of Mr. Mukherjee's reply, was to protest against the government's refusal to concede the NDA demand for a reply from Prime Minister Manmohan Singh. The Left, which lends crucial support to the United Progressive Alliance government, also remained unconvinced and the Communist Party of India (Marxist) described the nuclear deal as "surrender" to Washington. At the end of the seven-hour debate, it managed to extract an assurance from Mr. Mukherjee that the government would come back to Parliament at every stage of the process of negotiations on the deal. However, he refused to accept the Left demand that the government accept the absence of consensus on the issue as "sense of the House" and not to proceed any further. "Unless the process is complete, where is the question of taking the sense of the House," he responded. In his brief intervention midway through the discussion, Dr. Singh said there was nothing in the 123 Agreement that prevented India from conducting further nuclear tests, if necessary. Criticising the deal, Mr. Advani said "the 123 Agreement, as it stands, is unacceptable to the nation because it is deeply detrimental to India's vital and long-term interests." During his hour-long response, Mr. Mukherjee said the India-specific safeguards agreement with the International Atomic Energy Agency was aimed at ensuring fuel supply and the country's right to create strategic reserves to meet any interruption in fuel supply, besides securing recognition for India's strategic programme by accepting the separation plan. As for the Left's specific concern whether India's fast breeder reactors would be put under safeguards, the Minister's response was a categorical 'no.' The deal, according to him, would provide India a passport to enter into nuclear trade with a host of countries as well as facilitate access to technology.

4698. (29-11-2007) NEW DELHI : While inaugurating the UNESCO Regional Conference UPA Chairperson Smt Sonia Gandhi said that Millennium Development Goals (MDGs) 2015 must be achieved. Recalling the vision of late Shri Rajiv Gandhi she said that with the effort of the National Literacy Mission the literacy has jumped from 44% to 52% during 81-91 and it further climbed up from 52% to 65% during 91-2001. But regional variations exist. The National Literacy Mission is now being given a new direction. The objectives are to bring a sharper emphasis on female literacy in poorer areas and amongst disadvantaged communities, to effect convergence of existing schemes and programmes, to link literacy to improved livelihood and career opportunities, particularly in the knowledge economy. The Mission will be implemented by institutions of local self governments, to ensure greater accountability and responsiveness. Smt. Sonia Gandhi reiterated India's commitment to universalize elementary education by 2010. She said our challenge is to ensure full enrollment, reduction in the drop out rates and to impart quality education. 'A cooked mid day meal programme is an integral part of this strategy. Today, some 120 million children are being fed daily in schools', she said. She also said that India, Bangla Desh and Pakistan should redouble their efforts to eradicate illiteracy. This will include greater focus on Information and Communication Technologies and linking education with job opportunities (vocational education). We are at a moment of convergence between technological development and educational need, as well as between educational need and political will. Lt us grasp this moment. While speaking in the conference, Human Resource Development Minister Shri Arjun Singh said that in a rapidly globalizing age, nothing is immune to change. It has been our experience that large numbers of our people have been able to take advantage of these changes. Indian professionals, whether in software, IT, medicine or management, are leading the movement for change around the world. This is true of other countries in Asia. We are proud of their achievements and wish them well. However, as responsible governments our attention needs to focus on the larger numbers who have not been able to ride the crest of the wave; the people who, if I may extend the metaphor, run the risk of being swept away. It is here that we need to concentrate, and here that there is most at risk. The Minister also said that the challenge of literacy is not just of finding the means. It is one of commitment and perseverance. Literacy has to be brought to the centre stage not just in our respective countries but also amongst the comity of nations. This needs community mobilization, societal awareness, national commitment and international understanding. 'Our goal is that every child at primary level is enrolled and retained in school. Taken along with our efforts under the National Literacy Mission, we hope to achieve 85% literacy by the end of this Plan period', he said. Director General UNESCO, Mr. Koichiro

Matsuura said that India is among the countries that have made remarkable strides since 2000 towards EFA, with a range of targeted initiatives that reach disadvantaged children, youth and adults across the country. But in South, South-west and Central Asia, despite such progress the gender disparity remains a problem. Girls account for 66 per cent of out-of-school children in the sub-region, the highest share worldwide. This threatens to perpetuate inequalities in access to learning opportunities throughout life. 'Quality is also a concern. Rates of grade repetition and drop-out are high across South and West Asia and learning assessments systematically show that too many children leave school without acquiring basic literacy and numeracy skills. Dr. Shantha Sinha delivered the keynote address. In her address she said that India has been witness to some of the large-scale movements for literacy involving millions of volunteers-the kala jatha cultural campaigns being important testaments to their role in fostering social mobilization of peace, solidarity and active citizenship. Volunteers are at the core of such endeavours to reach out to the illiterate, which recognise the potential of literacy for individuals as well as for societal transformation. Within their enthusiastic struggle to empower their learners are also the heart rendering stories about the emergence of the poorest, and women as campaigners in the movement for literacy. She also said we are together today in this Conference, transcending boundaries of language, culture, nation to meet, empathize with and act in solidarity for all those who have been left behind. During the Conference an exhibition on the theme of creating literate environments has also been displayed at Vigyan Bhawan. Part of the exhibition will focus on how ICTs can be utilized in literacy and non-formal education: increasing access, localizing content and creating an environment conducive to literacy. Literacy materials are also on display in the "Fair of Best Practices". The welcome address was given by Mr.M.A.A. Fatmi, Minister of State for HRD. Video message from Mrs. Laura Bush, First lady of the United States of America, Honorary Ambassador for the United Nations Literacy Decade was shown to the audience. The first lady of Sri Lanka, Madam Shiranthi Rajapakse, was guest of honour in the function. Shri Arun Kumar Rath, Secretary School Education and Literacy proposed a vote of thanks.

4699. (29-11-2007) NEW DELHI : The Minister of Tourism and Culture Smt. Ambika Soni has said that construction of hotels is primarily a private sector activity and the Ministry of Tourism extends facilitation. However, Ministry of Tourism has been in regular touch with the various land owning agencies like Ministry of Civil Aviation, DDA, Ministry of Urban Development and State Land Owning Agencies etc. for identifying hotel sites in view of the forthcoming Commonwealth Games 2010. Ministry of Tourism has also floated schemes like the approval of Guest Houses and Incredible India Bed and Breakfast establishments for increasing the room inventory in Delhi and the NCR especially in the budget category. In a written reply in the Lok Sabha today she said, DDA has identified 34 hotel sites. They will provide 6600 hotel rooms. To ensure that hotels are constructed before Commonwealth Games, it has been provided that construction will have to be completed within particular period and to ensure compliance of this obligation, performance security to the tune of 5% of the bid amount has been obtained in the shape of bank guarantee. In case of delay in completion of hotel, it will be encashed as per schedule mentioned in the disposal conditions. The review of progress is done regularly. Smt. Soni said, in the budget proposal 2007-08, the Ministry of Finance has granted a 5 year Tax Holiday to hotels of 2, 3, and 4 star categories set up between 1.4.2007 to 31.3.2010 in the National Capital Territory of Delhi and the districts of Faridabad, Gurgaon, Gautam Budh Nagar and Ghaziabad.

4700. (29-11-2007) NEW DELHI : The Minister for Tourism and Culture Smt. Ambika Soni has said under the Incredible India Bed and Breakfast Scheme, 97 units with 280 rooms have been approved upto September, 2007. In a written reply in the Lok Sabha today, she said, the Incredible India Bed and Breakfast Scheme was launched all over the country. All the twenty Indiatourism Offices located at various centres in India are authorized to accept applications and facilitate the house owners.

4701. (29-11-2007) NEW DELHI : Following steps to further improve availability of urea in all part of the country have been taken: Each State is now required to prepare a monthly supply plan for ensuring availability of fertilizers on a month-wise, company wise and district-wise format. Since the district and not the State is the basis of planning for fertilizers availability, the subsidy is now being paid to fertilizer companies only on reaching fertilizers to each district in conformity with the agreed Supply Plan. To ensure that fertilizer companies supplying urea are able to reach it to each district, the urea manufacturers are compensated for freight based on actual rail and road leads. The monthly supply plans are being drawn up with minimum pre-positioning of stock for the succeeding month. The supply of fertilizers by manufacturers/suppliers in according with the agreed Supply Plan is being monitored through a Web-based Fertilizer Monitoring System, which is able to track production, imports, dispatch, arrival and sales upto the district-level. The State Government have been advised to (a) strengthen the State institutional agencies which will coordinate with manufactures and importers of fertilizers for streamlining the supplies (b) undertake assessment of demand at the block level and ensure availability upto the block level (c) review the dealer network in their respective States to ensure sufficient availability of dealers upto the block level. They have also been requested to review the railway infrastructure in their States and suggest improvements required to ensure availability of fertilizers in all parts of their States. This information was given by the Minister of State for Chemicals & Fertilizers Shri B.K. Handique in a written reply in the Lok Sabha today.

4702. (29-11-2007) NEW DELHI : The demand for Rabi 2007-08 has been assessed at 140.02 lakh metric tonnes (LMT) for Urea, 49.13 LMT for DAP and

19.61 LMT for MOP. The indigenous production of urea and DAP during the season has been estimated to be about 106.88 LMT and 26.13 LMT and the requirement of MOP is totally met from imports as there are no indigenous sources for its production. The gap between the assessed requirement and indigenous availability are being filled through imports. Sufficient availability of fertilizers to sustain sales has been ensured for Rabi 2007-08 at the State level. This information was given by the Minister of State for Chemicals & Fertilizers Shri B.K. Handique in a written reply in the Lok Sabha today.

4703. (29-11-2007) NEW DELHI : As part of backward integration, Steel Authority of India Limited (SAIL) is installing new steel melting facilities of 180, 000 tonnes per annum at Salem Steel Plant to make it an integrated plant. Initially scrap will be used as input material for steel making. However in future Direct Reducing Iron (DRI) is also being considered as a substitute for it. For this, SAIL has already applied for lease of Kanjamalai iron ore reserve to the Government of Tamil Nadu. The expansion plan envisages a production of 0.34 Million Tonne (MT) per annum of saleable steel from the current level of 0.18 Million Tonne (MT) per annum. Additional facilities proposed to be installed under expansion plan of Salem Steel Plant will provide direct and indirect employment opportunities though their exact numbers have not been quantified at this stage. This information was given by the Minister of State for Steel Dr. Akhilesh Das in a written reply in the Lok Sabha today. First-time producer Shri Avinash Onkar plans to remake his Marathi film 'Kaalchakra' screened as part of the Indian Panorama Section at IFFI-2007 in Hindi. While speaking to media persons here today, Shri Onkar informed that he was inspired to make Kaalchakra, a film that deals with the life situation of HIV + persons and how the society excludes them at large, after having personally witnessed the plight of some of the HIV + persons known to him in real life. The Hindi version would allow spreading the message of the film to a much wider audience, the producer commented. The film's director, Shri Vishal Bhandari stressed that great amount of research had gone in finalizing the film's story such as acquiring authentic information on AIDS and HIV + cases from the National AIDS Research Institute, Pune and interaction with real life HIV + people. Meanwhile, commenting on his decision to play the main protagonist of the film *i.e.* Shekhar, Sachin Khedekar said "It was a rare opportunity to work in a film that provided me an opportunity to give back to the society which has given so much to me". The film revolves around the life of Shekhar whose dreams come crashing down, when he discovers that he is HIV +. He loses his family, job and self-respect. The film deals with the problems that Shekhar faces in terms of social exclusion and how he gradually acquires the will and determination to give himself a better future. Finally Shekhar succeeds.

4704. (29-11-2007) NEW DELHI : The revised guidelines for regularization of unauthorized colonies in Delhi have been finalized by the Government. A copy of the revised guidelines has been sent to Government of NCT of Delhi (GNCTD) and Delhi Development Authority (DDA) for taking necessary preparatory steps. GNCTD has informed that it has issued public notice in leading newspapers inviting lay-out plan and other information from resident associations/resident societies. However, guidelines and modalities have to be brought before the Hon'ble Supreme Court & High Court. This information was given in the Rajya Sabha today by Shri Ajay Maken, Minister of State in the Ministry of Urban Development in a written reply to a question by Shri Keshubhai S. Patel.

4705. (29-11-2007) NEW DELHI : The Government of India is providing support to metro rail projects in the form of equity, subordinate debt and Pass Through Assistance (PTA) (for the loan of Japan Bank of International Cooperation (JBIC)). For those metro projects executed in the Public Private Partnership model, 'grant' in the form of Viability Gap Funding upto 20% of the project cost is provided under the "scheme of financial support to Public Private Partnership (PPP) in infrastructure" by Ministry of Finance. This information was given in the Rajya Sabha today by Shri Ajay Maken, Minister of State in the Ministry of Urban Development in a written reply to a question by Smt. Kanimozhi.

4706. (29-11-2007) NEW DELHI : The Central Ground Water Board has, however, reported that exploratory drillings are carried out by the Board with the objective of delineating aquifers worthy of ground water development and ascertaining their yield characteristics. So far, the total of 334 exploratory boreholes have been drilled by the Board in National Capital Territory of Delhi. The maximum depth explored by the Board is 308 meters below ground level at Rajouri Garden in the South West District of Delhi. This information was given in the Rajya Sabha today by Shri Ajay Maken, Minister of State in the Ministry of Urban Development in a written reply to a question by Smt. Jaya Bachchan.

4707. (29-11-2007) NEW DELHI : Shri Kamal Nath, Minister of Commerce & Industry, presented his book "India's Century : The Age of Entrepreneurship in the World's biggest Democracy" to the Prime Minister Dr. Manmohan Singh. Following is the text of the remarks of the Prime Minister on the occasion: "There is an old English saying 'those who can do, those who can't teach'. Kamal Nath has been an active participant in political processes. He has been a very successful businessman. Now this third role I did not imagine that he would perform and perform so admirably. I congratulate him for the vision, for the dedication and commitment that he has shown to our country's future. He has been enormous support to me as Sharad Pawar has been. They are the modern faces of our government and I feel very proud of both of them. When I was a student at Cambridge some 50 years ago I had a great teacher Lord Nicholas Kaldor and in a lecture that he delivered after having visited China, the capitalist evolution in the light of Tenzian economics, the conclusion of that lecture was that there is no technical necessity for any system to do better than the other. There is no technical necessity for socialism to do better than capitalism or vice-versa. It all depended on the mindset of the people who made the key decisions of nations, the mindset of its politicians, the mindset of its businessmen, the mindset of the media baron, the mindset of the trade unions. I think we have crossed many hurdles. But we have still many hurdles to cross. India is a country of enormous possibilities. We have only scratched the surface. But I draw comfort for the fact that if you look at our top ten/fifteen business houses/firms I think many of them didn't exist in 1991. Narayana Murthy is the product of the reform era that began in 1991. That task is still not complete. India has to be a big industrializing nation. India has to be a big trading nation. People do not recognize that on a per capita basis India is not well endowed with many natural resources. If we have to overcome this scarcity of natural resource base, we have to be a major trading nation of the world. If we have to be a major trading nation of the world, we have to be a major manufacturing nation of the world. I was just now five minutes ago talking to a group of distinguished businessman from various parts of Asia. The industrial revolution in England transformed England. It took away surplus population from agriculture to manufacturing. The same process has been underway in East Asia, in South-East Asia and in China. In our country the manufacturing has moved forward but it has not performed that historic task of taking lot of surplus population from agriculture into industry. I think governmental regulations, a mindset where government knew better than anybody else what is good for the country and excessively capital intensive design of development process plus also I think the rigidities of the labour legislation have created a situation that we have industry but it does not grow at a fast enough pace to create lot more jobs for our young population. Therefore, problems of labour rigidity, labour flexibility, these are still I think hurdles in India realizing it chosen destiny.

4708. (29-11-2007) NEW DELHI : The Kerala Legislative Assembly has passed the Kerala Sports Act 2000, which was brought in force with effect from December 2003. The Act envisages the formation of Sports Councils at State, District, Municipal-corporation, Municipalities, block and village levels. The sports councils are expected to function in partnership with local self Governments for the promotion of sports. In order to enable the effective functioning of these institutions (Sports Councils) at the grassroots level, Central assistance to local self governments such as Panchayats/Nagarpalikas for creation of infrastructure facilities and conducting training programmes has been sought. A new scheme named the Panchayat Krida Aur Khel Abhiyan (PYKKA) has been proposed by the Ministry to provide basic sports infrastructure and equipment at the Panchayat level and to encourage sports and games in rural areas through annual competitions at the block and district levels. PYKKA will help States in promoting sport at the grassroots level, which they have not been able to achieve on their own so far due to severe resource constraints. The Planning Commission has conveyed in-principle approval for PYKKA and has also indicated a tentative allocation of Rs.1500 crore during the Eleventh Five-Year Plan period. All the Panchyayats/ equivalent units are proposed to be covered under PYKKA in a phased manner over a period of 10 years. This information was given by Shri Mani Shankar Aiyar,

Minister of Panchayati Raj, Youth Affairs & Sports and DoNER in the Rajya Sabha today in a written reply to a question by ShriVijayaraghvan.

4709. (29-11-2007) NEW DELHI : The Minister of State for Coal Dr. Dasari Narayana Rao informed the Rajya Sabha in a written reply today that out of 172 coal blocks allocated so far, 77 coal blocks with reserves of about 11.68 billion tonnes have been allocated to private sector companies. He added that the Coal Controller under the Ministry of Coal has been mandated to monitor the development of mines and associated end-use projects. Dr. Dasari Narayana Rao emphasized that mining of coal from captive coal blocks allocated to private companies would also be subject to the same legal and regulatory framework as is applicable in the case of public sector coal mining companies. Coal mining would be subject to, inter alia, the provisions of the Coal Mines (Nationalisation) Act, the Mines and Minerals (Development and Regulation) Act, the Mines Act, the Coal Mines (Conservation and Development) Act, the Coal Mines Regulations, and the Mineral Concession Rules, and all other mineral, forest, environment, and labour laws governing the mining activity.

4710. (30-11-2007) NEW DELHI : Smt.D.Purandeswari, Minister of State for HRD has said that the 11th Plan has given due emphasis on literacy. It has fixed the target of achieving 85% of literacy by the end of the Plan. Another critical area for the XI plan is the introduction of vocational education in literacy programme which should motivate the neo literates to sustain their interest in literacy programme. Minister of State was making a Valedictory speech at the regional conference on Global Literacy here today. Following is the full text of the speech: This conference comes at an opportune moment, just when the mid decade assessment of the goals of Education for All is on the anvil. It focuses attention on an issue which has been neglected over the past few years and brings it back centre stage. Literacy is indeed crucial to this region, three of the nine E-9 countries fall in this region, who are together home to nearly 50% of the world's illiterates. The range of countries present here present a rich confluence in terms of cultures, ethnicities and religion. The thread which binds them together is the thread of illiteracy. Even from a limited perspective, this Regional Conference on Literacy is taking place at an appropriate time in the midst of some national challenges and opportunities. At the national level we are in the process of finalization of the 11th Five Year Plan where under our national goal is to achieve at 85% literacy by 2012 which is a formidable goal. Even more formidable is the challenge that the gender gap be bridged to 10% or less, given the fact that the gender gap in literacy is still 21% as per 2001 census. We can learn from the best experiences and practices of other nations in order to achieve our targets.

4711. (30-11-2007) NEW DELHI : Lieutenant General Mohan Pande, relinquishes the appointment of Director General of Military Operation on 30 November 2007. During his illustrious career, the General Officer has held varied command, staff and instructional assignments to include Brigade Major of a Brigade, Colonel General Staff of a Mountain Division and Additional Director General Operational Logistics at Army Headquarters. He has had instructional tenures at the National Defence Academy, Pune, Officers Training Academy, Chennai and Defence Services Staff College, Wellington. First as Brigadier General Staff and later as Director General of Military Operations, the General Officer has been closely associated with the conceptualisation and development of various doctrinal issues. He was Chief of Staff, Headquarters Army Training Command before taking over the present appointment. Lieutenant General Amarjeet Singh Sekhon was commissioned into Infantry in June 1970. The General Officer has attended all prestigious courses like Defence Services Staff College, Higher Command and National Defence College and has seen active service in all theatres, in both regimental and staff appointments, including the Indo-Pak conflict 1971. Having commanded his unit in North East and Punjab, the General Officer went on to command an Infantry Brigade along the sensitive Line of Control in the State of Jammu and Kashmir, where he was decorated with 'YSM' for his distinguished service during Operation VIJAY in 1999. In addition to command, the General Officer has held a number of important staff and instructional appointments including instructional tenures at National Defence Academy and Army War College. The General Officer has been Brigade Major of an Infantry Brigade in High Altitude Area, Deputy Military Secretary and Brigadier General Staff (Operations) in Command Headquarters. After the National Defence College course, the General Officer went on to hold the appointment of Deputy Director General at the Directorate General of Military Operations. The General has had the distinction of commanding Infantry Division in J&K and was awarded the AVSM for his distinguished service along the Line of Control. He has also held the appointment of Additional Director General of Perspective Planning. He has been posted as Director General of Military Operation after completion of a successful command of 15 Corps in the North Sector. During his command at 15 Corps, the violence levels in the Kashmir valley have dropped significantly during the current year. Considerable attrition on the terrorist cadres was ensured by the Army with 337 terrorists killed in action in 2006 and 324 during the current year. Besides, 566 terrorists were apprehended during 2006 and 2007. At the same time the local terrorists were motivated to surrender to own forces and 195 terrorists have surrendered to own troops since January 2006. The Amarnath Yatra was conducted without any major incidents and the flow of tourists to the valley has been very encouraging. Today, the Political leaders are freely coming out to address the public and garner support of the people, without the fear of terrorists.

4712. (30-11-2007) NEW DELHI : Vice Admiral Birinder Singh Randhawa, AVSM VSM has assumed the appointment of Chief of Material in Integrated Headquarters, Ministry of Defence (Navy) on 01 Dec 07. The post fell vacant on supernnuation of Vice Admiral DSP Verma. Vice Admiral Randhawa is an alumni of the National Defence Academy. He was commissioned on 01 Jan. 1969.

He graduated in Marine Engineering from the Naval Collage of Engineering and completed post-graduation from the Royal Naval Engineering College, UK, in the same discipline. The admiral is the senior most technical officer of the Indian Navy and held a number of important assignments both at sea and ashore. He was Controller Warship Production & Acquisition, prior to taking up the present assignment.

4713. (30-11-2007) NEW DELHI : The Committee, constituted by the Government to recommend revised subscriber based Spectrum allocation criterion for allocation of spectrum in a scientific and practical manner, met for whole day on 30.11.2007 for the third meeting under the chairmanship of Shri R. Bandhopadhyay, Additional Secretary (Telecom), Department of Telecommunications. All the members of the Committee namely, Dr. Bhaskar Ramamurti, IIT Chennai; Dr. Ajit Kumar Chaturvedi, IIT Kanpur; Shri P.K. Garg, Wireless Advisor; Shri Vijay Madan, ED, C-DOT; Shri Dilip Sahay, AUSPI; Shri T.V. Ramachandran, COAI; Shri A.K. Srivastava, DDG(AS), DOT were present in the meeting. Presentations were made by the representatives of the following companies/groups on their views before the committee on the issue of allocation of spectrum.

4714. (30-11-2007) NEW DELHI : Suspension of Operations arrangements with the National Democratic Front of Bodoland (NDFB) have been extended for a period of 6 months up to 31.5.2008. The arrangements have been in operation since 01.06.2005. It was mutually agreed to extend the arrangements after discussions at a tripartite meeting held in New Delhi yesterday. Representatives of the Government of India, Government of Assam and NDFB took part in the meeting. Issues relating to extension of Suspension of Operations arrangements beyond 30th November, 2007, movement of cadres into the designated camps and adherence to the Agreed Ground Rules by the NDFB were discussed at the meeting.

4715. (30-11-2007) NEW DELHI : An Agreement on S & T Cooperation between India and Austria has been signed by the Austrian Minister of Science & Technology Dr. Johannes Hahn and Shri Kapil Sibal, Minister for Science & Technology and Earth Sciences here today. The Agreement provides for exchange of scientific and technological information, documentation and publications, exchange of scientists and experts and implementation of bilateral-projects of mutual interest. The Agreement also provides for exchange of scientists and experts for consultations, symposia and special studies, support to joint scientific-telelogical events and other scientific programmes such as joint workshops, seminars. The Indo-Austrian Joint Committee shall be set up for scientific and technological cooperation. The joint committee would finalise areas of cooperation and periodic working programme of cooperation specifying collaborative activities for the future. Under this Agreement both sides will encourage and support the development of direct scientific-technological cooperation between national institutions, Academies of

Sciences, schools of higher education, research centres for science and technology and other institutions.

4716. (30-11-2007) NEW DELHI : Vice Admiral Dilip Deshpande, AVSM, VSM has assumed the appointment of Controller of Warship Production and Acquisition(CWPA) in the Integrated Headquarters, Ministry of Defence (Navy) on 01 Dec 07. Vice Admiral Dilip Deshpande was commissioned in the Indian Navy on 19 Sep 1969. He underwent Marine Engineering conversion course at INS Shivaji, Lonavla and the Air Engineering conversion course at Air Force Technical Collage, Bangalore. The admiral was awarded Gold medal for best thesis on the subject of Management of Technologies while undergoing Naval Higher Command Course at National Defence Collage. The admiral has had number of important assignment as Air Engineering and Marine Engineer which included the appointment of Admiral Superintendent of the Naval Dockyard at Visakhapatnam. He was Assistant Chief of Material (Dockyard & Refits) prior to taking up the present appointment.

4717. (30-11-2007) CHANDIGARH: Following is the text of the address of Vice President of India Mohd. Hamid Ansari at 'Haksar Memorial Lecture' at Centre for Research in Rural and Industrial Development, Chandigarh today : " The task is daunting, the capability questionable. To be called upon to deliver the P.N. Haksar Memorial Lecture would be a great honour at any time; it is to me particularly because I belong to a generation of Indians who witnessed Haksar saheb's work in two phases of his life-of action and of introspection. Neither of these, let me add, was totally exclusive. By the time of his death in 1998, some of the major premises of his belief system-democracy, secularism, socialism, nonalignment-had come under pressure and were the cause of disillusionment. In an editorial in Man and Development many years back, Haksar spoke of the need 'to hold aloft the banner of the moral universe' and opined that 'human passions' and 'permanent values' play a role in history. Elsewhere, he expressed surprise over the 'symptoms of of utter confusion in its value system' displayed by the Indian society in a period of change. 'Preserving the moral health of body politic and maintaining the ecological balance', he wrote, 'are conditions precedent to survival and growth not only of India, but of this entire earth'.

4718. (30-11-2007) NEW DELHI : All India Consumer Price Index Number for Industrial Workers (CPI-IW) on base 2001=100 for the month of October, 2007 remained stationary at 134 (one hundred and thirty four). During October, 2007, the index recorded an increase of 4 points in Jalpaiguri, Mariani-Johar, Lucknow and Rangapara-Tezpur Centres, 3 points in 3 centres, 2 points in 14 centres and 1 point in 30 centres. The index decreased by 1 point each in Sholapur, Chhindwara, Delhi and Quilon centres while in the remaining 23 centres the index remained. 24 centres the index remained stationary. The increase of 4 points in Jabalpur centre is mainly on account of increase in the prices of wheat Atta, Rice, Onion,

Vegetable & Fruit items etc. The increase of 4 points in Mariani-Johar centre is mainly due to increase in the prices of Vegetable & Fruit items, Wheat Atta and Onion etc. In Lucknow centre this increase of 4 points is due to increase in Primarch School Fee charges. While in case of Rangapara-Tezpur centre the increase of 4 points is due to increase in the prices of Vegetable & Fruit items, Rice, Wheat Atta, Masur Dal, Pork, Chillies Green, Toilet Soap etc. The decrease of 1 point each in Sholapur, Chhindwara, Delhi and Quilon centres is mainly due to decrease in the prices of Rice, Wheat, Fish Fresh, Chillies Green, Onion, Garlic, Vegetable & Fruit items etc.

4719. (30-11-2007) NEW DELHI : The Ministry of Social Justice and Empowerment, and the Army Wives Welfare Association (AWWA) in association with the Artificial Limb Manufacturing Corporation of India (ALIMCO) organized an assistive devices camp for the persons with disability in the TAWANG region of Arunachal Pradesh. The seven day camp was held between November 15, 2007 to November 21, 2007. The inauguration ceremony was held in the presence of Dr. Sundeep Khanna, Additional Secretary, Ministry of Social Justice and Empowerment, Ms Ritu Jaswal, President, AWWA, HQ 4 Corp, Tezpur, Brigadier Sanjay Kulkarni, Commander Tawang Army Brigade and Colonel TK Chatterjee, Nodal Officer Mission Ability Beyond Disability and representative President of AWWA, Indian Army. The Camp was held on successive days at different areas of the Tawang district beginning from Tawang (Nov 15), Lumla (Nov 16), Jang (Nov 17). Later the campaign was extended to Lower Dahung(Nov 20) and Tenga (Nov 21) of West Kameng District. The services were also extended to the beneficiaries of border villages of the district including Shergaon, Seppa and Bomidila. Villagers of the remote areas were transported to the camps by the Army Vehicles. All the necessary administrative support was provided by the Indian Army. Through the camp more than 750 persons with disabilities were extended free rehabilitation services. The disability of the people were assessed by the specialists at the camp and assistive devises provided immediately.

4720. (30-11-2007) NEW DELHI : December 1st is celebrated as World AIDS Day. HIV/AIDS is one of the fourteen major communicable diseases that affect the population in India. The government has formulated the National AIDS prevention and control policy with the objectives and goals: to prevent the spread of HIV infection and reduce any adverse economic and social impact, to generate a feeling of ownership among all the participants at government and non-government levels to make it a national effort, to create an enabling socio-economic environment for prevention of HIV/AIDS. The policy also aims at providing care and support to people living with HIV/AIDS and to ensure protection/promotion of their human rights. The annual UNDP report on the international health scenario has clearly pointed out that a large percentage of HIV infected persons belong to the 15 to 24 age group and has emphasized that awareness programmes on HIV infection and training in AIDS prevention should concentrate on teenagers-especially students from rural areas. The aspect of peer pressure affecting the attitudes and habits of this age group and the fact that the best way to counter the spread of such attitudes and habits is through positive peer pressure has also been pointed out in the report. Efforts are being made by conducting a series of programmes on AIDS Awareness, collectively called Teenagers Awareness, Counselling and Training (TACT) Against AIDS. The programmes were organized in cooperation with various colleges, schools and NGOs. The programme basically aims at creating a large peer group to which teenage students-both college and school-can turn for free counselling and heart to heart talks. TACT also underlines the importance of tactful approach towards teenagers while making them aware of the AIDS epidemic and the steps they should take to avoid risky situations. Counselling and training are the two major components of the programme. Realizing that youth and women are the two major groups that are most vulnerable to this epidemic, TACT Against AIDS programme focuses its attention on school children, especially girls.

4721. (30-11-2007) NEW DELHI : A National Biotechnology Development Strategy has been approved by the Government of India. The strategy is an outcome of a two-year long nationwide consultation process with multiple stakeholders including concerned ministries, universities, research institutes, private sector, civil society, consumer groups, non-government and voluntary organizations and international bodies. The strategy, while enabling the full utilization of currently available opportunities in manufacturing and services, lays a strong foundation for discovery and innovation, effectively utilizing novel technology platforms with potential to contribute to long term benefits in agriculture, animal productivity, human health, environmental security and sustainable industrial growth. The cornerstone of the strategy is the focus on building coherence and connectivity between disciplines and to bring together variegated skills across sectors to enhance synergy. The strategy seeks to address a number of challenges relating to the biotech sector in terms of R&D, creation of investment capital, technology transfer, absorption and diffusion, IPR, regulatory issues, building public confidence, and tailor made human capital for all these aspects. The stated vision of the strategy is responsible use lf life sciences and biotechnology to promote balanced growth of all sections of the society. The strategy has been released by the Government on 13th November, 2007. This information was given by the Union Minister of Science & Technology and Earth Sciences, Shri Kapil Sibal in the Lok Sabha today.

4722. (30-11-2007) NEW DELHI : The number of colleges in the country state-wise can be seen at Annexure. The main institutions under the Ministry including medical education are: All India Institute of Medical Sciences, New Delhi, Post Graduate Institute of Medical Education & Research, Chandigarh, Jawaharlal Institute of Post Graduate Medical Education & Research, Puducherry, Lady Hardinge Medical College, New Delhi, Safdarjung Hospital & UMMC, New

Delhi, Ram Manohar Lohia Hospital, New Delhi, National Institute of Mental Health & Neuro Sciences, Bangalore, Central Institute of Psychiatry, Ranchi, All India Institute of Speech & Hearing, Mysore, All India Institute of Physical Medicine and Rehabilitation, Mumbai and All India Institute of Hygiene & Public Health, Kolkata. The reservation policy for SC and ST is being implemented in the medical institutions managed by the Central Government as per provisions of the Constitution. There was a complaint regarding the policy not being implemented properly by AIIMS. The matter is being looked into by the Government. This information was given by the Minister for Health & Family Welfare, Dr. Anbumani Ramadoss in a written reply to a question in the Rajya Sabha.

4723. (30-11-2007) NEW DELHI : The State Medical Councils who grant registration to practitioners take action where called for against Quacks. The provisions exist in the Indian Medical Council Act, 1956 and Indian Medicine Central Council Act, 1970 and Homoeopathy Central Council Act, 1973 to take action against unqualified/unregistered practitioners of medicine. Any person who acts in contravention of the provision can be punished with imprisonment and fine under respective Acts. The responsibility of enforcement of the statutory provisions is that of various State Governments. This information was given by the Minister for Health & Family Welfare, Dr. Anbumani Ramadoss in a written reply to a question in the Rajya Sabha.

4724. (30-11-2007) NEW DELHI : Health is a State subject. It is, therefore, the responsibility of the State Government to provide tertiary health care services in the States. Government of India augments the effort of the State Governments. Under the Pradhan Mantri Swasthya Suraksha Yojana (PMSSY), it is proposed to address imbalance in the availability of affordable/reliable tertiary healthcare services and also to augment facilities for quality medical education in the country, by establishing AIIMS-like institutions in six States, i.e in Bihar (Patna), Chhattisgarh (Raipur), Madhya Pradesh (Bhopal), Orissa (Bhubaneshwar) Rajasthan (Jodhpur) and Uttaranchal (Rishikesh). In addition upgradation of 13 existing Government Medical College institutions in the States of Maharashtra, Gujarat, Uttar Pradesh, Jammu & Kashmir, West Bengal, Jharkhand, Andhra Pradesh, Karnataka, Kerala and Tamil Nadu has also been taken up under PMSSY. The institutions which has been taken up under upgradation has been decided by the respective State Governments. There is presently no proposal for opening super-speciality hospital in Nagpur under PMSSY. However, the State Government could send the proposal for upgradation of its existing institution, in the XIth Five Year Plan, with the objective of increasing availability of trained Medical/Dental manpower. This information was given by the Minister for Health & Family Welfare, Dr. Anbumani Ramadoss in a written reply to a question in the Rajya Sabha.

4725. (30-11-2007) NEW DELHI : During 2006-07 the Government of Assam proposed three new district hospitals at Bangaigaon, Baksha Hospital (Mushalpur), and Amingaon (Kamrup Rural). These proposals were approved and an amount of Rs 6 Crore @ Rs 2 crore per hospital for construction has been released as first instalment. The Government of Assam has intimated that the work of these hospitals will be completed by August 2009. This information was given by the Minister for Health & Family Welfare, Dr. Anbumani Ramadoss in a written reply to a question in the Rajya Sabha.

4726. (30-11-2007) NEW DELHI : The Rajya Sabha today passed the Rajiv Gandhi Institute of Petroleum Technology (RGIPT) Bill 2007 moved by Shri Murli Deora, Minister of Petroleum and Natural Gas. Shri Deora had introduced the bill in the Rajya Sabha on 7th September, 2007. Speaking while moving the Bill for consideration of the House, Shri Deora emphasized that the Institute has been designed to serve as a fountain head for nurturing world class human resources capable of serving as leaders and innovators of tomorrow in the field of petroleum technology. He informed that the academic operations will commence by admitting students in basic undergraduate courses from the next academic year *i.e.* 2008-09. Elaborating the need of such an Institute as an Institute of the national importance, Shri Deora pointed to the fact of increasing E&P activities ever since launch of New Exploration Licensing Policy in 1999. NELP has evoked great enthusiasm among Indian and foreign companies. He also informed the House that Government has planned to increase exploration coverage to 100% by year 2015 from about 30% of Indian sedimentary basins as on date. As per a study, the gap between the availability and requirement of trained manpower in the field of petroleum technology in India would be about 36, 000 by the year 2019. Referring to the need of RGIPT enjoying support of the Ministry of Petroleum & Natural Gas, Government of India, Shri Deora said "It is in the interest of the nation that the Government nurture the Institute in its nascent and crucial stage of development to enable the Institute to launch and run its programmes without compromise and set up world-class infrastructure while offering courses of a high standard". He added, "In the absence of the status of the "Institute of National Importance", it would not be possible to attract eminent faculty members and meritorious students".

4727. (30-11-2007) NEW DELHI : Based on the fluorine content of the drinking water in the country, fluorosis is a problem in 19 States, which are Andhra Pradesh, Gujarat, Rajasthan, Karnataka, Orissa, Punjab, Maharashtra, Madhya Pradesh, Haryana, Bihar, Tamil Nadu, Uttar Pradesh, West Bengal, Kerala, Assam, Delhi, Jammu & Kashmir, Jharkhand & Chhattisgarh. Accordingly to the WHO sponsored project carried out by Regional Occupational Health Centre (ICMR), Kolkata, 6 million people across 9 districts of West Bengal are exposed to arsenic contaminated water. Fluorosis is combated by provision of safe drinking water. Provision of safe drinking water is a State subject. However, Government of India supplements the efforts of the State Governments/Union Territories by providing funds under the Accelerated Rural Water Supply Programme (ARWSP) and Prime Minister's Gramoddya Yojana (PMGY)-Rural Drinking Water for tackling quality related problems and sustainability issues in respect of rural drinking water supply. A new Centrally Sponsored Scheme entitled 'National Programme for Prevention and Control of Fluorosis' has been prepared for the 11th Five Year Plan with a budget provision of Rs. 68 crores. Planning Commission has approved the scheme in principle and a token provision of Rs. 1 crore has been made for the year 2007-08 in order to prevent and control fluorosis. This information was given by the Minister for Health & Family Welfare, Dr. Anbumani Ramadoss in a written reply to a question in the Rajya Sabha.

4728. (30-11-2007) NEW DELHI : As per data collected through National Cancer Registry Programme (NCRP) by Indian Council of Medical Research (ICMR), an estimated 4.4 lakhs people die of cancer every year and about 7-9 lakh new cancer cases are detected every year. At any given point of time there are 2.5 million cancer patients in the country. Common cancers among men in India include that of mouth, lung, stomach, oesophagus and prostate. Common cancers among women in India include that of cervix, breast, ovary, oesophagus, mouth, stomach etc. Each site of cancer has a different aetiology, which often is multi-factorial in nature. Cancer of several sites like lung, oral cavity, oesophagus etc. is predominantly caused by tobacco use. Risk factors for cervical cancer include HPV infection, multiple sexual partners sexual hygiene, multiple pregnancies etc. Diet especially high fat & devoid of fruits and vegetables is important in causation of cancer of breast, colon etc. Health being a State Subject, it is for the State Governments to ensure that adequate facilities for early detection, diagnosis and treatment of cancer are made available. Central Government under the schemes of National Cancer Control Programme lays special emphasis on early detection of Cancer through screening, promoting health education, creating awareness etc. under District Cancer Control Programme. There are 25 Regional Cancer Centres in the country providing comprehensive cancer care treatment. This information was given by the Minister for Health & Family Welfare, Dr. Anbumani Ramadoss in a written reply to a question in the Rajya Sabha.

4729. (30-11-2007) NEW DELHI : The Ministry of New and Renewable Energy had been implementing the centrally sponsored scheme Modified Integrated Rural Energy Programme (IREP) on 50:50 cost sharing basis with the States from 2003-04 to 2006-07. The programme aimed at development of planning and institutional capabilities of the States to prepare and implement rural energy projects in the selected clusters of villages. Renewable Energy and energy conservation devices were installed in the projects taken up under the programme to meet energy needs in identified village clusters. Five IREP Training Centres were also set up in Bakoli (Delhi), Lucknow (Uttar Pradesh), Anand (Gujarat), Bangalore (Karnataka) and Shillong (Meghalaya) with support from the programme. Under the IREP Programme, there was a provision for preparing the micro-level energy plans for selected clusters of villages. The Programme was implemented upto Tenth Five Year Plan *i.e.* upto 2006-07 only. The modified IREP scheme was implemented in 21 States / UTs covering 323 districts in the country. The State-wise details of villages taken up under the programme as on 31.03.2007 are given in the Annexure. A budget provision of Rs.10 crores has been made in the current financial year for meeting the 10th Plan spillover liabilities of the programme. Further, a provision for one time grant to States for the five training Centres in the current financial year has also been proposed.

4730. (30-11-2007) NEW DELHI : No import of rice, pulses and other cereals was done by Government during the last three years *i.e.* 2004-05, 2005-06 and 2006-07. During 2004-05, 2005-06 no wheat was imported by the Government. However, during 2006-07, 54.54 lakh MT of wheat were imported on Government account. During 2004-05, 7.45 lakh MT of wheat and 0.90 lakh MT of rice were exported from the Central Pool maintained by the Government. No export of wheat and rice was done during 2005-06 and 2006-07. Also no export of pulses and other cereals was done by the Government during the last three years. The Government maintains stocks of wheat in Central Pool for meeting the requirements of Targeted Public Distribution System (TPDS), various welfare schemes, Open Market Sales (OMS) to control market prices as and when necessary and relief for calamities besides maintaining the required buffer stocks. Since the total available stock of wheat from domestic procurement was not adequate to meet these requirements, Government had to import wheat for the Central Pool during 2006-07. Some complaints were received from Maharashtra about quality of imported wheat allocated for Open Market Sale in March, 2007. However, samples jointly drawn by FCI and State Government representatives on testing were found conforming to quality norms. Subsequently, Government of Maharashtra has been directed not to distribute the wheat if found not meeting quality standards on testing. Further, the Government have also advised all State Governments to ensure that during transportation and storage all precautions are taken to ensure that there is no deterioration in the quality of foodgrains till they are distributed to the ration card holders. State Governments have also been advised that stocks available with State Government Agencies and Fair Price Shops should be regularly inspected to ensure that only foodgrains conforming to the quality specifications are distributed to ration card holders. The Government imported 54.54 lakh MT of wheat during 2006-07 through State Trading Corporation of India (STC). The wheat was imported from Australia, Russia, Canada, Argentina, France, Ukraine, Bulgaria, Romania, Hungry and Czech Republic of Slovakia.

4731. (30-11-2007) NEW DELHI : The Government has approved the National Urban Transport Policy in April, 2006. As such, there is no proposal for reviewing the policy for the present. This information was given in the Lok Sabha today by Shri Ajay Maken, Minister of State in the Ministry of Urban Development in a written reply to a question by Shri Mahavir Bhagora.

4732. (30-11-2007) NEW DELHI : The Government has allocated substantial budget for subsidizing Targeted Public Distribution System to ensure food security for the poor/deprived. Funds for release of subsidy to FCI and De-centralized Procurement States are provided in the budget as consolidated amount. From this, payment is made to FCI and De-centralized Procurement States depending upon the release of foodgrains made from the stocks with FCI and decentralized procurement States. During 2007-08, the budget allocated for payment of subsidy to FCI, others and decentralized procurement states is of Rs. 25425 crore. For making TPDS tidy and corruption-free, the Government has taken a number of steps to curb leakages and diversion of foodgrains. A 9-Point Action Plan has been evolved and is under implementation by State/UT Governments since July, 2006. Its implementation is monitored by Department of Food & Public Distribution. To make functioning of TPDS transparent and amenable to public security, a revised Citizens' Charter has been issued in July, 2007 to facilitate use of provisions of Right to Information Act in relation to functioning of TPDS. It is also proposed to computerize operations of TPDS. This information was given in the Rajya Sabha today by the Minister of State for Consumer Affairs, Food and Public Distribution, Dr. Akhilesh Prasad Singh in a written reply.

4733. (30-11-2007) NEW DELHI : Primarily, there are three Government agencies *i.e.* Central Warehousing Corporation, Food Corporation of India and State Warehousing Corporations which are engaged in building storage/warehousing capacities for foodgrains which provides scientific storage facilities to avoid post harvest losses of the produce. The Central Warehousing Corporation (CWC) is having adequate warehousing facilities throughout the country for storage of foodgrains to avoid the post harvest losses of the produces of the farmers. As on 01.10.2007, it had 498 Nos. of General Warehouses having total average capacity of 100.50 lakh MT and the average utilization of 77.70 lakh MT. The total foodgrains stored in the warehouses of CWC were 25.68 lakh MT. CWC offers a rebate of 30% in storage charges to the bona-fied farmers. It has launched Farmers Extension Service Scheme (FESS) since 1978-79 to educate farmer about the benefit of Scientific storage and use of public warehouses and is also imparting training to the farmers on the techniques of scientific storage and preservation of foodgrains so that storage losses at their level are minimized and demonstrates the spraying and fumigations methods to farmers to control insects and rodents. Although the FCI does not provide warehousing facilities directly to the farmers yet, it constructs storage capacity at nodal points to manage the procured foodgrains stocks on central pool account. Concerned State Governments also construct godowns to provide warehousing facilities to the farmers at village, block, district and taluq level. The FCI holds adequate storage capacity all over the country. As on 1.11.2007, total capacity held by the FCI is 239.67 lakh MT (151.47 lakh tonnes owned and 88.20 lakh tonnes hired from various agencies) which is sufficient at macro level. For micro level, space requirement, FCI has proposed to the Govt. of India for construction of about 4.00 lakh tonnes capacity in various states including the newly declared procurement States during the 11th Five Year

Plan to successfully manage the procurements/maintenance of adequate stocks for supplies in the Public Distribution system and other schemes.

4734. (30-11-2007) NEW DELHI : There are more than 500 Energy Parks in the country, out of which 26 are State Level Energy Parks and 484 are District Level Energy Parks. They are in various States and UTs.The Ministry of New and Renewable Energy under it's Energy Parks Programme, has supported this project. The Ministry has so far sanctioned an amount of Rs.40.57 crores and has released an amount of Rs. 27.21 crores for the Energy Parks to the States/UTs. The State-wise details are given at Annexure I.

4735. (30-11-2007) NEW DELHI : A total of 52 projects with an aggregate capacity of about 95 MW on energy recovery from Urban and Industrial Wastes have so far been taken up in ten States. There are seven projects with 19.50 MWeq have been completed in five States namely Andhra Pradesh, Gujarat, Punjab, Tamil Nadu and Uttar Pradesh where as one project with 3 MWeq is under installation in Gujarat. These projects are based on urban waste like Municipal solid waste, vegetable market waste, bio-gas at sewage treatment plants and cattle dung. Ten States in the country have projects based on industrial waste with a total capacity of 72.19 MWeq. This project use waste from distillery, abattoir, slaughterhouses, food processing and paper units, tannery etc. The cost of each project varies depending upon its location, capacity, waste characteristics, technology deployed and the nature of the project, whether demonstration or commercial. Ministry of New and Renewable Energy is promoting Energy Recovery from Wastes through separate Programmes for Urban and Industrial Wastes. The programmes also provide for capacity buildings, dissemination of information and creation of awareness through training programmes, workshops, seminars, etc. The projects can be taken up by urban local bodies and other Government organizations or through public private partnership. Private developers and industries having adequate technical financial and managerial capabilities are also eligible to undertake the projects. This information was given by the Minister of State in the Ministry of New and Renewable Energy Shri Vilas Muttemwar in a written reply to question in the Lok Sabha today.

4736. (30-11-2007) NEW DELHI : Private sector participation is encouraged in developing agricultural marketing infrastructure and in providing alternate marketing channels for agri-produce in order to facilitate establishment of private markets, allow direct marketing and contract farming to improve post-harvest management. As per the data compiled by Central Statistical Organization, the private sector investment measured in terms of Gross Capital Formation (GCF) (at constant 1999-2000 prices) in the Agriculture and allied sectors has increased from Rs.43, 035 crore in 2003-04 to Rs.46, 215 crore in 2004-05 and further to Rs.49, 987 crore in 2005-06. Under the Central Sector Scheme "Development and Strengthening of Infrastructure Facilities for Production and Distribution of Quality Seeds", assistance is provided for boosting seed production in the private sector. Under the Scheme, back-ended capital subsidy is provided to private companies, individual entrepreneurs, self-help groups and seed co-operatives at the rate of 25 per cent of the project cost subject to a maximum limit of Rs.10.00 lakh per unit on seed infrastructure development. This information was given in the Rajya Sabha today by the Minister of State for Agriculture, Shri Kanti Lal Bhuria in a written reply.

4737. (30-11-2007) NEW DELHI : The expansion of Rourkela Steel Plant (RSP) has been approved "in-principle" by SAIL Board in May'07. The proposed expansion plan of RSP envisages increase of hot metal production from 2.12 million tonnes per annum (2006-07) to 4.5 million tonnes per annum at an indicative cost of Rs.7, 668 crore. Employment opportunities for qualified personnel will get a boost as recruitment of technical personnel, Diploma Holders and ITI certificate holders would continue to be carried out for meeting skilled manpower recruitment in view of the modernization/expansion of RSP. Retraining, Redeployment and Multi-skill training will also help in meeting skilled/semi-skilled manpower requirement from the existing employees. In addition to direct employment generation, expansion is likely to create employment opportunity for the ancillary and other support industries in the region. It may be relevant to mention that while Corporate Plan envisages enhanced production level by expansion/modernization of steel plant, it simultaneously lays emphasis upon achieving higher labour productivity, manpower rightsizing through natural separations and VR and selective recruitments. As such the total manpower strength of SAIL after capacity expansion is likely to be less than the present manpower strength of 130419 as on 1.11.2007. While rationalization would continue further to increase competitiveness, simultaneously selective recruitments shall be undertaken to meet skilled manpower requirement for new projects/ modernization. Accordingly, for meeting manpower requirement for new projects/ modernization and existing facilities, provision is made in the recruitment plan under the Annual Human Resource Planning (HRP). Under the Human Resource Plan for 2007-08, the recruitment plan of SAIL is 3260 out of which 250 recruitments are allocated for RSP. This information was given by the Minister of State for Steel Dr. Akhilesh Das in a written reply in the Rajya Sabha today.

4738. (30-11-2007) NEW DELHI : To meet the increasing demand of power as projected by 17th Electric Power Survey, a capacity addition of over 78, 000 MW has been envisaged during the 11th Plan. Given the fact that this envisaged capacity is much more than the actual achievements in the last three Five Year Plans, capacity for manufacturing power equipment also needs to be increased substantially. Ministry of Power and Central Electricity Authority have taken up with all the stakeholders both in public and private sector to enhance/establish manufacturing capacities in the country. The Department of Heavy Industry has informed that Bharat Heavy Electricals Limited (which is the leading manufacturer of power equipments) is augmenting its capacity to deliver 10, 000 MW per annum by December, 2007 and 15, 000 MW per annum by December, 2009. No new policy in this regard, at present, is being contemplated. This information was given by the Power Minister Shri Sushilkumar Shinde in the Lok Sabha today.

4739. (30-11-2007) NEW DELHI : The Power Grid Corporation of India Ltd. (PGCIL) has been notified as the Central Transmission Utility (CTU) of India, under the Electricity Act, 2003. It undertakes the development of inter-State transmission systems at Extra High Voltage (EHV) level. Besides its core business of power transmission, PGCIL has also diversified into the Telecom business, leveraging its country wide power transmission infrastructure. The Government of India has approved an investment of about Rs.934 crore for this activity. Most of the telecom network has already been installed and connectivity has been provided to all metros and major cities. During the Xth Plan, out of a total investment of about Rs.18, 919 crore, by PGCIL, the investment in the telecom business was 3.5% (about Rs.663 crore) and in the current year *i.e.* 2007-08, investment in the telecom business is envisaged to be only Rs.11 crore (0.17% of the total budgetary outlay of Rs.6504 crore). The PGCIL has secured consultancy in the area of power transmission in Bhutan, Nepal, Afghanistan, Sri Lanka, Bangladesh and Dubai. This information was given by the Power Minister Shri Sushilkumar Shinde in the Lok Sabha today.

4740. (30-11-2007) NEW DELHI : The investment approval to the Kameng Hydro Electric Project (600 MW) in Arunachal Pradesh was accorded on 2.12.2004 by the Cabinet Committee on Economic Affairs (CCEA). The cost of the project as per CCEA clearance is Rs.2496.90 crore at March, 2004 price level. The total power generation capacity of project is expected to be 600 MW with 4 units of 150 MW each. The project is currently under construction and an expenditure of Rs.606.26 crore (provisional) has been incurred so far upto 31.10.2007. The project is now scheduled for commissioning by March, 2011. This information was given by the Power Minister Shri Sushilkumar Shinde in the Lok Sabha today.

4741. (30-11-2007) NEW DELHI : An MoU was signed among NTPC Ltd., Gujarat Power Corporation Ltd. (GPCL) and Gujarat Electricity Board on 20.02.2004 for development of a 1000 MW thermal power project at Pipavav in Joint Venture with GPCL. Basic inputs for the project were tied-up and most of site specific studies were completed. However, in September 2006, Government of Gujarat conveyed its decision that the project would be developed based on imported coal or any other suitable fuel in collaboration with a strategic partner. Accordingly, NTPC Ltd. has been allowed by the Government to dissociate from the project. This information was given by the Power Minister Shri Sushilkumar Shinde in the Lok Sabha today.

4742. (30-11-2007) NEW DELHI : The Reserve Bank of India has constituted a Technical Advisory Group (TAG) for developing methodology for evolving Housing Startup Index (HSUI). National Building Organization, an attached office under the Ministry of Housing & Urban Poverty Alleviation is a member of TAG. So far two meetings of the Group have taken place. This was stated by the Minister of State for Housing & Urban Poverty Alleviation, Kumari Selja in the Lok Sabha today, in a written reply to a question by Shri Anandrao V. Adsul and Shri Ravi Prakash Verma.

4743. (30-11-2007) NEW DELHI : The Minister of State for Housing & Urban Poverty Alleviation, Kumari Selja informed the Lok Sabha today, in a written reply to a question by Shri Haribhau Rathod that the Planning Commission releases estimates of urban poor form time to time based on the national sample surveys conducted by the National Sample Survey Organisation (NSSO). Recently, Planning Commission has released State-wise estimates of urban poor for the year 2004-2005 on the basis of 61st Round of NSSO survey. At present, there is no proposal to conduct any new all India survey of the urban poor. The Minister further informed that in the urban areas, in order to improve the living conditions of the urban poor, an employment-oriented urban poverty alleviation programme named Swarna Jayanti Shahari Rozgar Yojana (SJSRY) is being implemented on all India basis since 1.12.1997. Under SJSRY, the urban poor are assisted to set up individual/ group micro enterprises for self-employment and also provided wage employment by utilizing their labour in the construction of socially and economically useful public assets. Also, the shelter and basic amenities requirements of urban poor are addressed through the newly launched Sub-Mission of Basic Services for Urban Poor (BSUP) of the Jawaharlal Nehru National Urban Renewal Mission (JNNURM) for 63 identified Cities and through the Integrated Housing and Slum Development Programme (IHSDP), for cities/towns other than the 63 identified cities. Under Jawaharlal Nehru National Urban Renewal Mission (JNNURM), the facility of medical and health are secured through convergence of all relevant programmes of the Central and State Governments at the urban local body level.

4744. (30-11-2007) NEW DELHI : Air Marshal KM Sundara AVSM VSM will take over as Air Officer-in-charge Maintenance at Air Headquarters, New Delhi, responsible for Maintenance Management of all Weapon Systems and Equipment of IAF, on 01 Dec 07. Air Marshal Rama Sundara is an Electrical Engineering graduate from MC Hassan, Karnataka. He holds a Masters Degree in Defence Studies from the prestigious "Defence Services Staff College". Wellington. He has undergone the Senior International Defence Management Course at the Naval Post Graduate School, Monterery, USA besides being trained abroad on the MiG-23 & Mig-29 fighter aircraft systems. He is a fellow of Institution of Engineers and Institution of Electrical & Tele Communication Engineers and active member of the Aeronautical Society of India. The Air Marshal has a rich and varied experience in various facets of the maintenance organization in the IAF ranging from fighter aircraft to the ground based communication systems. He was involved in induction of MiG-23 and MiG-29 aircraft into Indian Air Force and setting up of the MiG-29 overhaul facilities. He has worked as the Chief Engineering Officer at Air Force

Station Kalaikonda besides commanding Air Force Station Sulur. As the Assistant Chief of Air Staff (Systems), he was responsible for the maintenance of a varied range of Radars, Communications, Armament, Guided weapons, Avionics Modification and System development in his previous appointment as Senior Maintenance Staff Officer at Headquarters Maintenance Command, the Air Marshal was overseeing the indigenisation and modernization of all assets of IAF. He took keen interest in undertaking the extension of Airframe/Aeroengine which were otherwise meant to be disposed off without any effective utilization. He was actively involved with PSUs, DRDO Academic Institutions and Civil Agencies for industry-service interaction and evolving better maintenance service support. For his distinguished service, Air Marshal Rama Sundara was conferred the Vishisht Seva Medal in 1994 and Ati Vishisht Seva Medal in year 2006 by the President of India. The Air Marshal is an avid sportsman, his speciality being the Adventure sports. He has undergone a Skydiving course and likes to relax with a sedate game of gold. Born in year 1950, Air Marshal Rama Sundara is married to Nalini, who hold Masters Degree in Physics and trained Teacher.

4745. (30-11-2007) NEW DELHI : Steel Authority of India Limited (SAIL) Board has accorded in-principle approval for starting production facilities at Kulti; viz. Non-Ferrous Foundry, Steel Foundry and required supporting shops like Pattern Shop and Machine Shop. The future products of this plant would be Steel castings, Non-Ferrous castings and engineering spares. The capital cost has been estimated as at around Rs.8.88 crore. SAIL proposes to engage Centre for Engineering & Technology (CET), in-house consultants of SAIL, to prepare Comprehensive Feasibility Report which includes technology upgradation/ diversification for the products envisaged. This information was given by the Minister of State for Steel Dr. Akhilesh Das in a written reply in the Rajya Sabha today.

4746. (30-11-2007) NEW DELHI : Following a severe cyclone in Bangladesh on November 15, 2007, resulting in heavy loss of life and widespread destruction in coastal areas, India has pledged assistance to Bangladesh with a sense of urgency. To convey solidarity of the people of India, the External Affairs Minister Shri Pranab Mukherjee will be visiting Bangladesh tomorrow. During his visit, Shri Mukherjee will be meeting Bangladesh Chief Advisor. Dr. Fakhruddin Ahmed and Foreign Advisor. Dr. Iftekhar Ahmed Chowdhury. Shri Mukherjee will also be surveying some cyclone affected areas and meet the victims. Over the last few days Indian Air Force aircraft have been expeditiously delivering relief materials consisting of medicines, tents, blankets, ready-to-eat meals and portable water-purifiers to Bangladesh. An IL-76 aircraft left New Delhi this afternoon for Dhaka carrying the last consignment of relief supplies. Shri Mukherjee is expected to formally hand over this consignment to the Bangladesh authorities tomorrow. As announced by the External Affairs Minister earlier, India is also sending essential food items such as food aid including rice, wheat and milk powder worth nearly

100 crores to Bangladesh. Delivery of these items is being expedited. One such consignment consisting of more than 9, 000 metric tonnes of rice reached Chittagong (Bangladesh) during the Ramadan. Earlier, following torrential rains which caused mudslides in Chittagong in June 2007, India had also extended US $10 million cash assistance to Bangladesh. In a gesture, India has also lifted the current ban on export of rice with respect to Bangladesh allowing it to import 50, 000 metric tonnes from India.

4747. (30-11-2007) NEW DELHI : The National Minerals Development Corporation (NMDC) will invest Rs. 18000 crore in the next five years to increase its capacity to 50 million tonnes. Talking to newsmen after handing over an interim dividend cheque to the Minister for Steel, Chemicals and Fertilisers Shri Ram Vilas Paswan here today the Chairman and Managing Director of NMDC Shri Rana Som said, the company will focus on investigation and exploration and will apply for prospective license for increasing its capacity. He said, NMDC would like to diversify and increase its capacity in minerals other than iron ore while retaining its leadership in iron ore mining as well. Receiving the dividend cheque the Minister said, MNDC should immerge as a global mining company with a futuristic vision. Shri Paswan said, the company should adopt the latest technology with a new vision. He said, 80 percent of the iron ore available in the country is low grade and the challenge for the industry is to convert this low grade ore into high grade by inducting new technology. The Minister lauded the performance of the company saying MNDC spends 5 per cent of its net profit on various corporate social responsibility activities. NMDC earned a net profit of Rs.2300 crore last year and targets Rs.3005 crore in the current year. It has paid 100 per cent interim dividend amounting to over Rs.130 crore to the government.

4748. (30-11-2007) NEW DELHI : The cement industry should explore alternate/ non-conventional sources of energy. With the ever-growing thrust on conservation of fossil fuel resources, Shri N.N. Prasad, Joint Secretary, Department of Industrial Policy & Promotion (DIPP), Ministry of Commerce and Industry has emphasised that there is a need for integrating the alternate and renewable energy into the system. "I understand that the cement industry has already made a beginning in this direction. Some of the cement plants have tried waste derived fuels in the recent past. Government on its part, is giving special emphasis to generation of grid quality power from non-conventional and renewable energy sources, like hydropower, wind power, solar energy etc.", he further stated while delivering the valedictory address at the Concluding Session of the 10th NCB International Seminar on Cement and Building Materials, here today, organised by the National Council for Cement and Building Materials (NCB). Senior officials from DIPP, representatives from the cement & building materials industry and officials from the NCB were present on the occasion. While presenting the National Awards for Energy Efficiency, Environmental Excellence and Quality Excellence in Indian Cement Industry for the years 2005-06 and 2006-07, Shri Prasad congratulated all the award winners and underlined the role of NCB in motivating the cement industry for competitive improvement. He further said, these success stories of such plants will generate larger interest amongst the industry and more and more number of plants would join the bandwagon of energy savers. Giving an overview of the Seminar, Shri M. Vasudeva, Director General of NCB said that the quality of cement and building materials produced in India meets international standards and benchmarks and can compete in international markets. He said the Seminar provided a comprehensive update on cement and construction technologies including related plant and machinery. More than 100 technical papers were presented under seventeen technical sessions including five special lectures during the past four days. While keeping in mind the missions of earlier nine NCB International Seminars, the organizing body and the authors have given emphasis to issues related to all areas of cement manufacture & utilisation, use of alternate fuels and wastes, blended and special cements, performance and durability as well as emerging trends in building materials and construction. In the special publication brought out on the occasion of the seminar, experts have drawn attention to various issues to achieve higher energy efficiency, environmental standards & productivity in cement manufacture, efficient transport of cement, design of energy efficient and disaster resistant buildings/structures and quality construction through advanced technologies as well as human resource development in the rapidly changing scenario. Utilisation of low-grade raw materials, optimization of mining operations using computer modeling are some of the areas discussed in the seminar. New techniques and strategies for conservation of natural resources have been highlighted in the discussions. There is greater emphasis on the need to modernize construction methods leading to faster implementation and improved durability. Performance and durability constitute the backbone of any sustainable construction. The papers presented highlighted measures to ensure durability in different service conditions. The deliberations in the seminar over the four days have given an exhaustive coverage on the issues relating to the cement, building materials and construction industries. We hope that the cement and construction industry professionals will benefit from the intense interactions which took place.

4749. (30-11-2007) NEW DELHI : Twelve State Governments were approached by Ministry of Railways to find out their willingness for participating in pre-feasibility studies. Out of twelve, nine State Governments namely Andhra Pradesh, Maharashtra, Gujarat, Haryana, Punjab, Kerala, Karnataka, Tamil Nadu and West Bengal have agreed 'in principle' to participate in any pre-feasibility studies and for possible support in form of land, right of way to build elevated tracks and equity for proposed project. This proposal is in its initial stages. Pre-feasibility studies are to be conducted. These studies will take about two years. On the basis of recommendations of these studies, decision to start the work will be taken. This information was given by the Minister of State for Railways Shri R.Velu in written reply to a question in the Rajya Sabha today.

4750. (30-11-2007) NEW DELHI : All possible steps are undertaken on a continuing basis to prevent accidents. These measures include timely replacement of over-aged assets, adoption of suitable technologies for up-gradation and maintenance of track, rolling stock, signalling and interlocking systems, safety drives and inspections at regular intervals to monitor and educate staff for observance of safe practices and provision of appropriate gradient and surface at level crossings, warning signs and public awareness campaigns for observing safe practices while negotiating the level crossings. As a result, there has been a declining trend in the number of accidents from 351 in 2002-03 to 195 in 2006-07 as mentioned above.

4751. (30-11-2007) NEW DELHI : The Cabinet Committee on Economic Affairs today gave its approval to the Shipping Corporation of India (SCI) to acquire six (6) Nos. of Handymax Bulk Carriers of about 57, 000 Dead Weight Tonnage (DWT) each at price of US $44.90 million per vessel (Rs.179.60 crore per vessel). The total investment for the six vessels would be US $269.40 million (Rs.1077.60 crore). SCI would be availing of External Borrowing up to 80% of the Contract price of each vessel from Banks/financial Institutions either from the international market or the domestic market and the balance from its internal resources.

4752. (30-11-2007) NEW DELHI : The Cabinet Committee on Economic Affairs today gave its approval for implementation of the revised Centrally Sponsored Scheme Drugs Quality Control with 11th Plan provision of Rs.225.00 crore. The implementation of Centrally Sponsored Scheme of Quality Control of ASU&H drugs will definitely improve upgradation of infrastructure of Drug Testing Laboratories and State Pharmacies and Enforcement Mechanism of ASU drugs at State level. This will prove helpful for capacity building of State ASU&H Drug testing Laboratories, ASU manufacturing units to establish in-house quality control laboratories for batch to batch testing of raw materials and finished products for ensuring Quality Control of ASU&H medicines. This will also improve ASU&H units and their infrastructure to acquire WHO Good Manufacturing Practices/ USFDA / EU Good Manufacturing Practices required for export purposes.

4753. (30-11-2007) NEW DELHI : The Cabinet Committee on Economic Affairs today gave its approval for implementation of the Scheme of "Development of the AYUSH Institutions" with a Plan Outlay of Rs.550 crore in the 11th Plan. The financial assistance under various components for Government and Government-aided Ayush colleges will be scaled up from Rs.62 lakh to Rs.2 crore for Under Graduate colleges; from Rs. 2 crore to 3 crore for Post Graduate colleges and from Rs.3 crore to Rs.5 crore for Model Colleges and shall be based on college-specific upgradation plans. It will benefit in upgrading the infrastructure of AYUSH teaching institutions for ensuring minimum standards laid down by statutory councils and raising the quality of AYUSH education in the country.

4754. (30-11-2007) NEW DELHI : The Cabinet Committee on Economic Affairs today approved 'Revised Cost Estimates for the Common Effluent Treatment Plant (CETP) project at Calcutta Leather Complex, Kolkata at an estimate cost of Rs.135.44 crore under Ganga Action Plan Phase-II as part of the ongoing umbrella scheme of the National River Conservation Plan (NRCP) of the Ministry of Environment & Forests. The project is being implemented on cost sharing basis in the ratio of 50:50 between the Government of India and Government of West Bengal. The CCEA had earlier approved the CETP project at CLC at an indicative cost of Rs.65 crore in 1995 for treating the waste of about 30 million liters per day (mld) of trade effluents from more than 500 tanneries relocated from three clusters namely Tangra, Tiljala and Topsia in Kolkata city with an installed capacity to process about 850 tonnes of hides/skins per day. The project not only envisages reuse of chromium and safe disposal of hazardous solid wastes generated at CLC essential to met the current environmental norms. Proper operation & maintenance of the assets created under the project as well as relocation of industries to the new modern site at CLC in time bound manner is the responsibility of the State Government. The project will not only result in minimizing the pollution of river Ganga but also lead to improvement of the general environment in the city and prevent danger of groundwater pollution caused by the tanneries. Setting up of modern and environment friendly complex is expected to help operation of tanners, traders and buyers of leather goods under a single roof resulting in integrated growth of the leather industry and the export of the products to international markets. The works under the project are scheduled to be completed by March, 2010.

4755. (30-11-2007) NEW DELHI : The Cabinet Committee on Economic Affairs today gave its approval to the revised proposal from Central Board of Excise & Customs(CBEC) for providing quality services to Tax-payers and other stakeholders by consolidating its information technology infrastructure. These services include implementation of the Customs EDI system to a total of 162 locations and introduction of an electronic workflow based system in Central Excise and Service Tax covering all Central Excise and Service Tax Offices. The approval entails an outlay of Rs.598.97 crore over a period of five year period, includes creation of data centre facilities, wide area network connecting 582 buildings and computing facilities at 1200 offices.

4756. (30-11-2007) NEW DELHI : The Cabinet Committee on Economic Affairs today gave its approval for a 100% Centrally sponsored Scheme of Post-matric scholarship for students belonging to the minority communities in the following manner: (i) The scheme will be launched during the financial year 2007-08 targeting 15 lakh scholarships for the XIth Five Year Plan (2007-2012) period. The scholarships will be awarded to students from the minority communicates, fulfilling the merit-cum-means criteria, studying in India in Government or private higher secondary schools/colleges/universities, including residential Government institutes, eligible private institutes elected and notified in a transparent manner by the State Government / Union Territory Administration concerned and technical & vocational courses in Industrial Trade Institutes (ITIs)/Industrial Trade Centres (ITCs) affiliated with the National Council for Vocational Training. (ii) Incurring recurring expenditure of Rs.1530 crore during the XIth Five Year Plan. (iii) The Scheme will be implemented by the Ministry of Minority Affairs. The approval will result in giving away 15 lakh scholarships to the meritorious students belonging to the notified minority communities during XIth Five Year Plan (2007-2012) period to enable them to pursue higher education and technical & vocational courses. By pursuing these courses, the students will become employable. The scheme has the potential to lift the economic condition of minority communities, which in turn, will contribute to the economic development of the country.

4757. (30-11-2007) NEW DELHI : Shri P. Chidambaram, the Union Finance Minister and Mr. Peter Mandelson, Trade Commissioner, the European Commission have signed a Memorandum of Understanding (MOU) on the first Multi-annual Indicative Programme (MIP) for 2007-2010. The MOU was signed during the India-European Union (EU) Summit held, here today. The European Commission conceptualizes multi-annual economic and development cooperation programmes to be implemented in partner countries through their country strategy papers (CSP). The CSP generally covers two consecutive MIPs of 3-4 years and the MIP, in turn, defines priorities for spending an indicative budgetary break down for the programme period. The current CSP is for the period 2007-2013 and the indicative budgetary allocation by the EC is of € 460 million divided into two MIPs of € 260 million and € 200 million for 2007-2010 and 2011-2013 respectively.

4758. (30-11-2007) NEW DELHI : 'The Last Lear' an English film by director Rituparno Ghosh will premiere here today at IFFI-2007. Starring Amitabh Bachchan and Preity Zinta in the lead, the film is a story of Harry-65 year old recluse, eccentric and a passionate man. Besides being a Shakespearean stage actor and an ardent fan of The Master, his life seems like a play after he meets Siddharth. A play replete with action, drama, love, emotions, tension-and an expected friendship. Siddharth is a new-age film director-his cool clothes and casual persona well disguise his eccentricities. He is a visionary, a visionary who would stop at nothing to get what he wants. As opposites attract, may be life-minded people get along well too. How else would one explain the fast blossoming friendship between these two eccentrically creative minds? When the cinema-ignorant Harry is offered a magnificent role in Siddharths' next film, he is apprehensive at first, reluctant later and finally acceptable to the idea. As the shoot takes them to the sprawling mountainous landscapes of India, new relationships bloom. Upcoming actor Shabnam, who is struggling hard to cope with her messy personal life, finds an unexpected mentor in Harry. He teaches her more than merely the nuances of acting. From being a complete outsider to the world of commercial cinema, Harry soon becomes one of them-open to learning new methods of working, chatting with the unit members and sipping tea from a fancy thermos he never knew was invented, he is enjoying ! Little does he know that as the film rolls and he gets into the skin of the character of the Joker that he is playing, he may be taking his role a bit too seriously. Is he that good an actor, or is fate really making him out to be a Joker on the set? As the intense moments unfold, which are even more engaging that the film itself, masks would be taken off a few faces. Towards the sunset of his life, long after the last shot is taken, as his memory fades, all that Harry can remember are his Masters words. Rituparno Ghosh has 14 films to his credit most of which have won national level awards. His cinema is cause-driven, modern, witty and more often an astute commentary of the time we live in, at the same time.

4759. (30-11-2007) NEW DELHI : Rajkamal Bhuyan, the producer of the Assamese film 'Jaatingaa Ityaadi' screened at IFFI-2007 said that he was motivated by the urge to call a spade a spade to make the film. Jaatingaa Ityaadi shows how militancy in Assam has created a deep fear psychosis among people and how militants lure innocent young men and women into their fold. "This film is an attempt to showcase the real face of militancy which has destroyed the social fabric of Assam", he said. Shri Bhuyan told the press persons that it was difficult to screen the film across theatres in Assam and other North Eastern States as most of the theatres were either in poor shape or were not receiving enough viewers due to the fear of militant attacks. Therefore, the effort was being made to reach maximum viewers through release of VCDs/DVDs. "A good response has been received from overseas markets, especially Australia and USA for the film's VCDs/DVDs", he informed. The film was shot in a period of three weeks at a cost of Rs. 40 lakhs.

4760. (30-11-2007) NEW DELHI : Survey of India, the National Mapping Agency and Government of Delhi today joined their hands to make Delhi a world-class city by empowering the people of Delhi through geo-spatial data by launching Delhi State Spatial Data Infrastructure (DSSDI) project. The project is an outcome of a pilot project by Department of science and technology, government of India on 3D GIS in Chandani Chowk area. As part of the project, a monitoring room was established to receive images from 10 cameras placed at vantage points to do the change detection on real time as occurring on ground. Government of Delhi felt that the 3D database is immensely useful for various applications and it should immediately be created for entire NCT of Delhi and should be completed well before Common Wealth games-2010. The project will cover a total area of NCT Delhi of approx 1500 Sq. km Development of a 3D-GIS database for NCT of Delhi will be carried out by Survey of India in respect of all lands and buildings and all under ground utilities within the NCTD. The project will facilitate detection of illegal constructions by the government of Delhi and enable monitoring of any changes being made in respect of land and building in GNCTD on real time basis. The project comprises two major components, Land Information System (LIS) of NCT of Delhi and Urban Spatial Information System (USIS). The LIS will have up to date cadastral information. The USIS will meet the spatial data/information requirements of urban planning for routine functions of the line departments of Delhi. The innovative technologies developed for the project will be used for disaster management, traffic management, security of important building and other valuable infrastructural assets in Delhi. The Survey of India and government of Delhi will also be launching special purpose vehicles (SPV) Geo-spatial Delhi, which will be authorized to keep the records of the land-holdings ownership, land use etc. The project is going to be harbinger of many such SDI projects within the country, which will give a very sound foundation for e-governance and knowledge based informed society in Indian urban areas.

4761. (30-11-2007) NEW DELHI : The Ministry of Tribal Affairs implements various Central Sector/ Centrally Sponsored Schemes/ Programmes for the welfare and development of tribal people/ areas in the country, including the State of Uttarakhand. The schemes/ programmes of this Ministry are not Tribal area specific, as the funds are released to the Departments in charge of Tribal Welfare in the State/ Union Territory Governments who have to ensure that the benefits of these schemes/ programmes reach the target groups/ areas.

4762. (30-11-2007) NEW DELHI : The Ministry has so far released an amount of Rs.307.45 Crore to 24 States for setting up of 100 Eklavya Model Residential Schools (EMRS) meant for Scheduled Tribe boys and girls in the Country. This was stated by Shri P.R. Kyndiah, Minister for Tribal Affairs in a reply to a question by Shri Sugrib Singh in Lok Sabha today. He said that the Ministry has already enhanced recurring expenditure from a maximum of Rs. 30 lakh to Rs. 72.50 lakh per Eklavya Model Residential School from the current financial year *i.e.* 2007-08.

4763. (30-11-2007) NEW DELHI : Under Special Central Assistance to Tribal Sub-Plan (SCA to TSP), the Ministry of Tribal Affairs has released annual grant of Rs. 74 crore to the State of Orissa during 2007-08. The allocation of annual grant under SCA to TSP is based on the population and the area of Scheduled Tribes in the States concerned in accordance with guidelines laid down for the purpose. This was stated by the Minister for Tribal Affairs, Shri P.R. Kyndiah in a reply to a question by Shri Sugrib Singh in Lok Sabha today. He added that the proposals are received from various States including Orissa for increase in grants under SCA to TSP from time to time. However the allocation of funds to the States is done based on the criteria laid down under the guidelines.

4764. (30-11-2007) NEW DELHI : The Ministry has been implementing a Central Sector Scheme of Exchange of visits by Tribal" which aims at organizing exposure visits of tribal delegates to enable them to get a wider perspective of culture; traditions and economic development/practices of other States/UTs. The States Governments are encouraged to organize such visits for duration of 10 days excluding journey time, comprising a group of 10 tribals in a manner that include a minimum of 3 women and minimum of 3 elected members of the local body or Panchayats.

4765. (30-11-2007) NEW DELHI : Under the Scheme of Post Matric Scholarship to students belonging to the Scheduled Tribes, scholarships are to be given to all ST students studying at post matriculation or post secondary stage to enable them to complete their education, provided the income of parents/guardians from all sources does not exceed Rs. 1, 08, 000/- per annum. Further, in case of professional courses, the Post Matric Scholarship is available only to those students who are admitted against "free seats" (also known as Government seats or aided seats), whether in Government or private institutions; and in case of private institutions, where admission is on the basis of 12th standard examination marks, there is a bench mark of 60% for availing of the Post Matric Scholarship in case of professional courses. This was stated by the Minister for Tribal Affairs, Shri P.R. Kyndiah in a reply to a question by Shri Mahavir Bhagora in Lok Sabha today. He further added that the conditions relating to "free seats" and bench mark of 60% have been included in the Post Matric Scheme for Scholarships for STs following a decision of the Government to include these changes in a similar scheme of Post Matric Scholarships for SCs being implemented by Ministry of Social Justice & Empowerment.

4766. (30-11-2007) NEW DELHI : The Rural Employment Generation Programme (REGP), is implemented through the Khadi and Village Industries Commission (KVIC), to help eligible entrepreneurs to set up village industry units and thus create employment opportunities in villages including small towns with population upto 20, 000. Under this programme, entrepreneurs can establish village industries by availing of margin money assistance from KVIC and loans from public sector scheduled commercial banks, selected regional rural banks, cooperative banks, etc., for projects with a maximum cost of Rs. 25 lakh. Under REGP, banks appraise the projects as per the scheme and take credit decision.

4767. (30-11-2007) NEW DELHI : The National Institute for Entrepreneurship and Small Business Development (NIESBUD), under the Ministry of Micro, Small & Medium Enterprises mulls taking help of business partners for entrepreneurship training. NIESBUD has prepared a new scheme under which Entrepreneurship Development Programmes will be organised throughout the country in association with Partner Institutions. This was stated by the Union Minister for Micro, Small & Medium Enterprises, Shri Mahabir Prasad while chairing the Governing Council Meeting of NIESBUD here today. The Minister said under this programme, the people residing in remote areas of the country will be able to derive the benefit of expertise from NIESBUD through Video Conferencing. Shri Mahabir Prasad said, in 2006-07 NIESBUD arranged 90 Training Programmes and imparted training to 2178 persons. Besides, the 'cost recovery' rate has also been enhanced from 67% to 90% which is a step forward towards self-reliance. Keeping in view the ever-increasing requirements of the country in this field, the Minister urged NIESBUD to take its Training Programmes to remote and underdeveloped village areas of the country in collaboration with other organisations. The Minister informed that considering the immense potential of readymade garments and textile industry in the National Capital Region, a Textile incubator has been established in the premises of NIESBUD at NOIDA.

4768. (30-11-2007) NEW DELHI : The Scheme of Conditional Cash Transfer for girl child with insurance cover has been included in the Annual Plan 2007-08 and includes cash transfers to the family of the girl child based on the fulfilment of four important conditionalities viz. birth and registration of the girl child, immunization, retention in school and delaying marriage beyond 18 years of age. The procedural formalities for approval of the above scheme are under process. This was stated by Smt. Renuka Chowdhury, Minister for Women and Child Development in a reply to a question by Shri S.K. Kharventhan in Lok Sabha today.

4769. (30-11-2007) NEW DELHI : India played a significant role on the debate on Tourism & Climate change in the 17th Session of the General Assembly of the United Nations World Tourism Organisation (UNWTO) concluded at Cartegena de Indias, Colombia this morning. The Indian delegation led by Union Minister of Tourism and Culture Smt. Ambika Soni presented a draft text of the resolution to the UNWTO Secretariat which received wide acceptance from all the countries. .In the ensuing debate on climate change in the General Assembly Brazil, Peru, China, Cuba, Chile, Mexico and Argentina expressed fears that Davos Declaration in the present form would adversely impact the scope of tourism. Smt. Ambika Soni commended UNWTO's efforts in sensitizing member states on the challenges of climate change through expert studies and research. She urged Secretary General to take up at the forthcoming Bali meeting of UNFCCC next month in December the most important issue of transfer of advanced clean technologies and financial assistance to developing countries so to adapt to the challenges of climate change. UNWTO emphasized that it should not discriminate against developing countries by creating obstacles and in particular of those developing countries located in long distances from tourist generating markets. The resolution reiterates that mitigation of green house gases should be in accordance with the principle of common and differentiated responsibilities as per UNFCCC. Further, UNWTO has been urged to work within the framework of UNFCCC in this regard. Developing countries expressed appreciation of India's leadership role on the debate on Tourism and climate change within the UNWTO.